**Butterworths
Family Law Guide**

Butterworths
Family Law Guide

General editor
David Burrows BA
Solicitor

Contributors
Simon Bruce MA (Oxon)
Solicitor, partner in Farrer & Co, London

Judith Hughes LLB (Hons), QC
Bencher, of the Middle Temple

Robert Purdie LLB (Wales)
Barrister, of the Middle Temple

Stephen Wildblood LLB (Hons)
Barrister, of Albion Chambers, Bristol

Butterworths
London, Edinburgh, Dublin
1997

United Kingdom	Butterworths, a Division of Reed Elsevier (UK) Ltd, Halsbury House, 35 Chancery Lane, London WC2A 1EL and 4 Hill Street, EDINBURGH EH2 3JZ
Australia	Butterworths, SYDNEY, MELBOURNE, BRISBANE, ADELAIDE, PERTH, CANBERRA and HOBART
Canada	Butterworths Canada Ltd, TORONTO and VANCOUVER
Ireland	Butterworth (Ireland) Ltd, DUBLIN
Malaysia	Malayan Law Journal Sdn Bhd, KUALA LUMPUR
New Zealand	Butterworths of New Zealand Ltd, WELLINGTON and AUCKLAND
Singapore	Reed Elsevier (Singapore) Pte Ltd, SINGAPORE
South Africa	Butterworths Publishers (Pty) Ltd, DURBAN
USA	Michie, CHARLOTTESVILLE, Virginia

All rights reserved. No part of this publication may be reproduced in any material form (including photocopying or storing it in any medium by electronic means and whether or not transiently or incidentally to some other use of this publication) without the written permission of the copyright owner except in accordance with the provisions of the Copyright, Designs and Patents Act 1988 or under the terms of a licence issued by the Copyright Licensing Agency Ltd, 90 Tottenham Court Road, London, England W1P 9HE. Applications for the copyright owner's written permission to reproduce any part of this publication should be addressed to the publisher.

Warning: The doing of an unauthorised act in relation to a copyright work may result in both a civil claim for damages and criminal prosecution.

Any Crown copyright material is reproduced with the permission of the Controller of Her Majesty's Stationery Office.

© Reed Elsevier (UK) Ltd 1996

A CIP Catalogue record for this book is available from the British Library.

ISBN 0 406 081417

Printed by Redwood Books, Trowbridge, Wiltshire

Preface

As we were writing what follows, one of the most uneven pieces of legislation imaginable, certainly in the field of family and child law, reached the statute book — just. I speak, of course, of the Family Law Act 1996. On the one hand, Part IV of the Act (occupation orders and domestic violence) provides a piece of competent law reform (its treatment of non-owning cohabitants apart), which will be generally welcomed. Meanwhile Part II saddles this country with one of the most needlessly complicated divorce laws in the Western world; and the limited nature of the provisions on mediation in Part III are a profound disappointment. Part IV is likely to be in operation by October 1997 and has been considered in some detail in Appendix 1. The rest of the Act has been dealt with more superficially for, if it ever comes into force, it is unlikely to be so during the early to middle life of this book.

Writing any book on family law is always akin to trying to hit a moving target. To write a book on the entire subject with five authors at a time when a piece of reforming legislation is being fought clause by clause through Parliament makes the task only the more challenging still. And then — as was inevitable — on the point of going to press the income support rates changed, necessitating recalculation of all the child support figures.

Family and child law is not an easy subject to define; still less is there a straightforward statutory definition of the term 'family proceedings'. A considerable array of statutory material — both primary and delegated — confronts the practitioner. We have endeavoured to cover the vast majority of this, as well as to take in such matters as enforcement, judicial review and legal aid. Meanwhile we have borne in mind current case management concerns as Lord Woolf's *Access to Justice* (civil justice review) looks down at all practitioners in the civil courts (which we must take to include family practitioners).

With all that, I am grateful to each of my four co-authors (with Jeremy Gordon who drafted the section on bankruptcy) for all the work they have done. More especially I am grateful to them for their willingness to make this what we believe to be a consistent treatment of a wide subject within a relatively concise framework. All of us are grateful to the publishers for promoting this project and for the patience they have shown as it has developed and now reached fruition.

The law is stated as we understand it to be at 18 November 1996.

David Burrows   November 1996
Bristol

Contents

Preface v
Abbreviation of Statutes and Statutory Instruments xiii
Table of Statutes xvii
Table of Statutory Instruments xxxi
Table of Cases xli

PART I INTRODUCTION 1

Chapter One   Introduction by David Burrows 3
Family law at a threshold 3
'Family law' – towards a definition 5
Aim of this book 5
The court process 5
'Non-adversarial' procedures 6
Full relevant disclosure 6
Legal aid 6
Family Law Act 1996 7

Chapter Two   Procedure by David Burrows 9
Introduction 9
Pleadings 12
Procedure 14
Evidence 19
Disclosure and discovery 24
Expert evidence 31
Appeals 35

PART II MARRIAGE BREAKDOWN 41

Chapter Three   Matrimonial Causes by David Burrows 43
Introduction 43
Matrimonial causes 45
The new law: a summary 50

vii

viii   *Contents*

PART III   FINANCIAL PROVISION   59

Chapter Four   Maintenance and Property Distribution by Simon Bruce   61
Introduction   61
Overview of the available orders for income, capital and property adjustment   62
Section 25 factors   66
Periodical payments and the clean break   76
Lump sum orders   83
Property adjustment orders   87
Order for the sale of property   96
Pensions   100
Maintenance pending suit   109
Variations   112
Consent orders and agreements   115
Injunctions and financial relief   127
Financial provision in the case of neglect to maintain   137
Matrimonial and Family Proceedings Act 1984, Part III   139
Family Law Act 1996   142
Tax considerations   149
Bankruptcy and family breakdown   152

Chapter Five   Financial Provision outside the Matrimonial Causes Act by Stephen Wildblood   163
Introduction   163
Relationships defined   163
Parental responsibility for children   164
Financial disputes in general   165
The law of trusts   168
Personal property   180
Procedure   182
Financial provision for children   186

Chapter Six   Inheritance by Robert Purdie   195
Succession   195
Family provision   202

PART IV   CHILDREN   217

Chapter Seven   Children by Stephen Wildblood   219
Introduction   219
Parental responsibility   219
Guardians   223
Child defined   227
Wardship and the High Court's inherent jurisdiction   231
Surrogacy and embryology   237
Legitimacy   241
Blood tests   243

Adoption 245
Who may apply to adopt? 250
Who may be adopted? 253
Parental agreement to adoption 255
Freeing for adoption 259
Adoption procedure 261

Chapter Eight   Children Proceedings by Stephen Wildblood 265
Introduction 265
The welfare of the child 266
Welfare and social work reports 270
Section 8 orders 273
Statutory restriction on making section 8 orders 283
Applicants for section 8 orders 285
Section 8 orders with conditions 292
Family assistance orders 293
The threshold criteria 293
Evidence and procedure 299
Disposal of applications 302
Supervision orders 304
Contact with children in care 305
Section 37 reports 311
Discharge and variation of care and supervision orders 312
Guardians ad litem 312
Protection of children 314
Child assessment orders 315
Child assessment orders/emergency protection orders 315
Emergency protection orders 316
Prohibition against further applications without leave 321
Appeals 322
Practice and procedure 324

Chapter Nine   Children and Judicial Review by Judith Hughes 331
Duties of the local authority to children in their area 331
Judicial review 341

Chapter Ten   Child Support by Judith Hughes 351
The law before the Child Support Act 1991 351
The child support legislation 352
The Child Support Agency 355
Reviews and appeals 379
Collection and enforcement 385

PART V   DOMESTIC VIOLENCE 391

Chapter Eleven   Domestic Violence by Robert Purdie 393
Introduction 393
Procedure 402

x *Contents*

Restraint of molestation 417
Exclusion injunctions 420
Re-entry to the matrimonial home 431
Power of arrest 433

PART VI ENFORCEMENT 439

Chapter Twelve Financial Orders by Robert Purdie 441
Introduction 441
Orders to be enforced 441
Methods of enforcement 442

Chapter Thirteen Children by Judith Hughes 465
Residence orders 465
Contact orders 467
Prohibited steps order 468
Specific issue order 469
Family assistance order 470
Emergency protection orders 471
Care orders 473
Orders in wardship 475

Chapter Fourteen Injunctions by Robert Purdie 477
Committal to prison 477
The application to commit 479
The affidavit in support 481
Service of the application and affidavit in support 481
The affidavit in answer 482
The hearing of the application to commit 483
Court orders upon proof of breach 484
Orders for committal 485
Suspended committal orders 487
Applications to commit non-parties 488
Discharge from prison of person committed for contempt 489

PART VII LEGAL AID AND COSTS 491

Chapter Fifteen Legal Aid and Costs by David Burrows 493
The legal aid scheme 493
Conduct of proceedings 498
Costs 500
Costs in legal aid cases 502
The legal aid statutory charge 505

APPENDIX 1　DOMESTIC VIOLENCE – THE NEW LAW　511

Domestic Violence – the New Law by Robert Purdie　513
Introduction　513
Definitions　513
Parties to applications　514
Occupation orders　523
Non-molestation orders　541
Undertakings　543
Third party applications　544
Ex parte orders　544
Power of arrest　546

APPENDIX 2　INTESTACY　551
Table 1　Table of distribution on intestacy　553
Table 2　Intestate succession　556
Table 3　Interest on the fixed net sum　557

APPENDIX 3　OCCUPATION ORDERS　559

Table 1　Entitlement to apply　561
Table 2　Range of orders available　562
Table 3　Criteria for exercise of powers　564
Table 4　Duration　567

Index　569

Abbreviation of Statutes and Statutory Instruments

Administration of Justice Act 1985	AJA 1985
Adoption Act 1958	AA 1958
Adoption Act 1976	AA 1976
Adoption of Children Act 1949	ACA 1949
Affiliation Proceedings Act 1957	APA 1957
Affiliation Proceedings (Amendment) Act 1972	AP (Amendment) A 1972
Attachment of Earnings Act 1971	AEA 1971
Bankruptcy Act 1914	BA 1914
Births and Deaths Registration Act 1953	BDRA 1953
Capital Gains Tax Act 1979	CGTA 1979
Child Abduction Act 1984	CAA 1984
Child Abduction and Custody Act 1985	CACA 1985
Child Benefit Act 1975	CBA 1975
Child Care Act 1980	CCA 1980
Child Support Act 1991	CSA 1991
Children Act 1972	CA 1972
Children Act 1975	CA 1975
Children Act 1989	CA 1989
Children and Young Persons Act 1933	CYPA 1933
Children and Young Persons Act 1969	CYPA 1969
Civil Evidence Act 1968	CEA 1968
Courts and Legal Services Act 1990	CLSA 1990
Civil Jurisdiction and Judgments Act 1982	CJJA 1982
Civil Jurisdiction and Judgments Act 1991	CJJA 1991
Domicile and Matrimonial Proceedings Act 1973	DMPA 1973
Domestic Proceedings and Magistrates Courts Act 1978	DPMCA 1978
Domestic Violence and Matrimonial Proceedings Act 1976	DVMPA 1976
Education Act 1944	EA 1944
Family Income Supplement Act 1970	FISA 1970
Family Income Supplement Payments Act 1972	FISPA 1972
Family Law Act 1986	FLA 1986
Family Law Act 1996	FLA 1996
Family Law Reform Act 1969	FLRA 1969
Family Law Reform Act 1987	FLRA 1987

xiv *Abbreviation of Statutes and Statutory Instruments*

Family Proceedings Courts (Children Act 1989) Rules 1991 (SI 1991/1395)	FPC(CA)R 1991
Family Proceedings Courts (Matrimonial Proceedings etc) Rules 1991 (SI 1991/1991)	FPC(MP etc)R 1991
Family Proceedings Rules 1991 (SI 1991/1247)	FPR 1991
Finance Act 1971	FA 1971
Finance Act 1972	FA 1972
Finance Act 1974	FA 1974
Finance Act 1981	FA 1981
Finance Act 1982	FA 1982
Finance Act 1983	FA 1983
Finance Act 1984	FA 1984
Finance Act (No 2) Act 1983	FA (No 2) 1983
Foster Children Act 1980	FCA 1980
Guardianship Act 1973	GA 1973
Guardianship of Minors Act 1971	GMA 1971
Health and Social Services and Social Security Adjudications Act 1983	HSSSSAA 1983
Human Fertilisation and Embryology Act 1990	HFEA 1990
Income and Corporation Taxes Act 1970	ICTA 1970
Inheritance (Provision for Family and Dependants) Act 1975	I(PFD)A 1975
Law of Property Act 1925	LPA 1925
Law Reform (Miscellaneous Provisions) Act 1970	LR(MP)A 1970
Legal Aid Act 1974	LAA 1974
Legal Aid Act 1979	LAA 1979
Legal Aid Act 1982	LAA 1982
Legal Aid Act 1988	LAA 1988
Legitimacy Act 1976	LA 1976
Maintenance Enforcement Act 1991	MEA 1991
Maintenance Orders Act 1950	MOA 1950
Maintenance Orders Act 1958	MOA 1958
Maintenance Orders Act 1968	MOA 1968
Maintenance Orders (Reciprocal Enforcement) Act 1972	MOA 1972
Marriage Act 1949	MA 1949
Marriage Act 1983	MA 1983
Marriage (Prohibited Degrees of Relationship) Act 1986	M(PDR)A 1986
Married Women's Property Act 1882	MWPA 1882
Married Women's Property Act 1893	MWPA 1893
Married Women's Property Act 1964	MWPA 1964
Matrimonial Causes Act 1967	MCA 1967
Matrimonial Causes Act 1973	MCA 1973
Matrimonial Causes (Property and Maintenance) Act 1958	MC(PM)A 1958
Matrimonial and Family Proceedings Act 1984	MFPA 1984
Matrimonial Homes Act 1983	MHA 1983
Matrimonial Homes and Property Act 1981	MHPA 1981

Matrimonial Proceedings Act 1983	MPA 1973
Matrimonial Proceedings (Polygamous Marriages) Act 1972	MP(PM)A 1972
Matrimonial Proceedings and Property Act 1970	MPPA 1970
National Health Service Act 1977	NHSA 1977
National Insurance (Old Persons' and Widows' Pensions and Attendance Allowance) Act 1970	NI(OPWPAA)A 1970
National Insurance Surcharge Act 1976	NISA 1976
Recognition of Divorces and Legal Separations Act 1971	RDLSA 1971
Social Security Administration Act 1992	SSAA 1992
Social Security Act 1973	SSA 1973
Social Security Act 1974	SSA 1974
Social Security Act 1975	SSA 1975
Social Security Act 1979	SSA 1979
Social Security Act 1980	SSA 1980
Social Security Act 1986	SSA 1986
Social Security (No 2) Act 1980	SS(No 2)A 1980
Social Security (Consequential Provisions) Act 1975	SS(CP)A 1975
Social Security (Consequential Provisions) Act 1992	SS(CP)A 1992
Social Security (Contributions) Act 1981	SS(C)A 1981
Social Security (Contributions) Act 1982	SS(C)A 1982
Social Security and Housing Benefit Act 1982	SSHBA 1982
Social Security (Miscellaneous Provisions) Act 1977	SS(MP)A 1977
Social Security Pensions Act 1975	SSPA 1975
Supplementary Benefits Act 1976	SBA 1976
Surrogacy Arrangements Act 1985	SAA 1985

Table of Statutes

References in **bold** type in this Table indicate where a section of an Act is set out in full or in part. References in this Table to *Statutes* are to Halsbury's Statutes of England (4th edition) showing the volume and page at which the annotated text will be found. References in *italics* are to pages of the Appendices.

	PARA
Administration of Estates Act 1925 (17 *Statutes* 302)	
s 1(1)	6.8
3(4)	6.8
33(1), (2)	6.6
43(2A)	6.7
46	6.6, *556*
(1)(i)	6.8, *557*
Table para 1	*555*
2(a), (b)	*555*
3(a)	*555*
(b)(ii)	*555*
(ii)–(vi)	*555*
(3)	6.7
47(2)(a)	*555*
47A(5)	6.8
55(1)(x)	6.8, *555*
Sch 2 para 5(2)	6.8
Administration of Justice Act 1960 (11 *Statutes* 178)	
s 12	11.29
13(3)	14.11
Administration of Justice Act 1970 (4 *Statutes* 691)	
s 49(1)	12.15
Sch 8	12.14, 12.28, 12.47
para 2A, 3, 4	12.10
Administration of Justice Act 1977 (11 *Statutes* 898)	
s 28	*557*
Administration of Justice Act 1982 (13 *Statutes* 586)	6.4
Administration of Justice (Appeals) Act 1934 (11 *Statutes* 788)	
s 1	2.2
Affiliation Proceedings Act 1957	5.44, 5.59, 7.55, 10.2

	PARA
Adoption Act 1950	7.98
Adoption Act 1958	7.98
Adoption Act 1976 (6 *Statutes* 220)	2.4, 7.44, 7.56, 7.85, 8.45, A.28
s 1(1)–(4)	7.59
6	**8.134**
7	8.134
11	7.62
(3)	7.61
12	7.3, A.24, A.27
(1)	4.4, 7.57
(2)–(4)	7.57
(5), (7)	7.71
13 (3)	7.68
14	7.66, 8.57
(2)	7.4
15	7.65
(3)	7.67
16	A.27
(1)	7.76, 7.77
(2)	7.76, 7.87
(a)	7.79
(b)	7.78, 7.80
(3), (4)	7.77
(5)	7.84
17	7.65, 7.66, 7.95, 7.99
18	7.91, A.27
(1)–(3)	7.87
(5)	7.86, A.25
(6)	7.87, 7.89
(7)	7.87
19 (2)–(4)	7.89
20	7.90
21	7.91
22	7.91
(1), (1A), (2)–(4)	7.64
24 (1)	7.69
(2)	7.70
25 (1)	A.24

xviii *Table of Statutes*

	PARA
Adoption Act 1976—*contd*	
s 38	7.98
39	7.50, A.27
(1)(a)	6.9, 6.17, 7.57
(b)	6.9, 7.57
(2)	6.17, 7.57, A.23
(3)	7.57
(4)	6.17, 7.57
(6)	6.17
42	6.9, 7.58
43–46	7.58
47, 50	7.58
55	8.63
(1)	A.24
57	7.70
61	7.77
72	7.19, 7.61, 7.68
(1)	7.71, 7.77
(2)	7.99
Sch 1	7.58
Adoption of Children Act 1926	7.56
Adoption (Scotland) Act	
s 18	A.27
Air Force Act 1955 (3 *Statutes* 247)	
s 150, 151A	12.17
Army Act 1955 (3 *Statutes* 49)	
s 150, 151A	12.17
Attachment of Earnings Act 1971 (22 *Statutes* 466)	12.4
s 1(1)	12.17
(2)(a)	12.17
(3)(a)	12.17
2(a)	12.17
3(1)(d)	12.18
(3), (3A)	12.18
(4)(a)	12.11
6(1)(a), (b)	12.23
(5)(a), (b)	12.23
(6)(a)	12.23
(b)(i), (ii)	12.23
(7), (8)	12.23
9(1), (4)	12.23
11(1)(a)	12.48
14(1)	12.21
(a)(i)–(iii)	12.22
(b)	12.22
(3)	12.21
(4)	12.19
19(1)	12.21
23(1), (1A), (11)	12.20
24(1)(a)–(c)	12.17
(2)(a)–(d), (f)	12.17
Sch 1	12.17
Sch 3	
Pt I	12.23
British Nationality Act 1981 (31 *Statutes* 127)	
s 1(5)	7.58

	PARA
Charging Orders Act 1979 (22 *Statutes* 502)	12.4
s 1(2)(a)–(c)	12.30
2	15.30
(2)(a)–(c)	12.30
Child Abduction and Custody Act 1985 (6 *Statutes* 294)	2.4, 2.28, 3.14, 13.25
Child Support Act 1991 (6 *Statutes* 638)	2.4, 5.58, 10.2, 10.3, 10.26, 10.29, 10.34, 10.42, 10.52, 10.67, 10.75, 10.83, 10.85, 10.89, A.67
s 1	3.3
(1)–(3)	10.4
2	10.8
3(2)	10.76
(4), (6)	10.7
4	3.3, 10.43, 10.44, 10.86
(1)	10.9, 10.99
(2)–(4)	10.99
(9)	10.41
6	10.7, 10.41, 10.44, 10.63, 10.99
(1)	10.43, 10.86
(2), (9)	10.43
7(3)	10.99
8	10.40
(3)	4.197, 5.14, 5.46, 10.5
(3A)	10.5
(4)	10.75
(5)	10.5
(6)–(8)	5.46, 10.5, 10.88
9(5)	10.5
11	10.4
(1)	10.44
(2)	10.11
12(4)	10.48
16	10.53, 10.63, 10.67
(3)	10.69
(5)(a)	10.70
17	10.53, 10.54, 10.63, 10.67, 10.70
(1)	10.61
(5)	10.69, 10.71
(6)	10.61
18	10.53, 10.54, 10.63, 10.67, 10.74
(5), (6)	10.73
(9)	10.69
(10A)	10.63
(12)	10.73
19	10.53, 10.63
(1)	10.67
(2), (3)	10.69
20	10.74, 15.7
(3), (4)	10.77
24	10.80
(1)	10.78

Table of Statutes xix

	PARA
Child Support Act 1991—*contd*	
s 24(2), (3)	10.81
(6)	10.78
25	10.81
(4)	10.82
26	2.33, 10.65
(2)	10.64
27	10.65, 10.66, 15.7
(3)	10.64
28B	10.54
28F	10.53
29(1)(a)	10.86
(b)	10.50
(2)	10.74
30	10.88
31(2), (4)	10.90
(5)	10.90, 10.91
(6), (7)	10.90
32(2)(a)	10.90
(3)(a)	10.90
(8), (10), (11)	10.92
33	10.93
35(1)	10.95, 10.97
(2), (3), (5), (6), (8)	10.95
36	10.96, 10.97
40(1)	10.97
(2)(b)	10.97
(3)(b)	10.97
(5)	10.97
41(5)	10.98
43	10.22
44	10.5
(3)	10.62
45	10.84
46(7)	10.74
54	10.4, 10.64
55(2)	10.7
Sch 1	10.14
Pt I	10.11
para 2	10.20
5(1)	10.12
(3)	10.22
7	10.22
15	10.61
16(1)(a), (c), (d)	10.62
(4), (6)	10.63
Child Support Act 1995	4.42, 10.3
s 1	10.52, 10.53
2	10.52, 10.53, 10.54
3	10.52
(5)	10.55
4	10.52, 10.56
5	10.52
6	10.52, 10.57
7	10.52, 10.58
8, 9	10.52
10	10.59
11	10.48
12(4), (5), (7), (8)	10.61

	PARA
Child Support Act 1995—*contd*	
s 14	10.61
15(4)(a)	10.60
(6), (7)	10.60
Children Act 1975	7.98
Children Act 1989 (6 *Statutes* 387)	1.1, 1.3, 2.4, 2.16, 2.22, 2.23, 2.46, 2.50, 2.61, 2.63, 3.11, 3.29, 4.30, 7.1, 7.27, 7.33, 7.44, 7.55, 7.57, 7.77, 7.85, 8.1, 8.18, 8.22, 8.25, 8.38, 8.69, 8.71, 8.72, 8.107, 8.129, 8.130, 8.131, 8.132, 9.14, 9.35, 9.38, 10.64, 11.18, 11.32, 11.40, 11.42, 15.1, 15.7, 15.8, A.2, A.28
Pt I (ss 1–7)	8.45, 11.13, 11.17
s 1	7.18, 8.61, 8.88, 8.94, 8.100
(1)	**8.2**, 8.78, 11.6
(2)	**8.3**
(3)	2.73, 7.17, 7.22, 8.4, 8.5, 8.78
(a), (b), (e)	8.34
(4)	8.4
(5)	2.17, 8.12, 8.61
2	A.23
(1)	5.6, 7.3, 7.45
(2), (3), (6)–(10)	7.3
(11)	5.6, 7.3
3	A.23
(1), (5)	7.2
(6)(a)	7.3
4	5.6, 7.45, 7.87, 13.12
(1)(a)	7.4, 7.6
(b)	7.4
(2)	7.5
(3), (4)	7.7
5	7.2, 7.4
(1)	7.8, 7.9, A.24
(2)	7.9
(3)	7.8, 7.11, 7.15
(4)	7.8, 7.15
(5)	7.11, 7.12
(6)	7.13
(7)	7.14
(a), (b)	7.14, A.24
(9)	7.9, 7.14
(11), (12)	7.10, 8.1
(13)	7.8
6(1)	7.15
(3)	7.15, 8.83
(4)	7.15
(5), (6)	7.16
(7)	7.17
7	8.14
(1)	2.65, 8.13

Table of Statutes

Children Act 1989—*contd*

	PARA
s 7 (3)	8.13
(4)	2.65, 8.13
(5)	8.13
Pt II (ss 8–16)	2.8, 2.65, 8.1, 8.45, 11.13, 11.17
s 8	2.3, 2.17, 3.11, 7.21, 7.23, 7.34, 7.85, 8.4, 8.36, 8.39, 8.42, 8.46, 8.47, 8.48, 8.50, 8.58, 8.127, 9.9, 9.13, 10.7, 13.7, 13.13
(1)	7.31, 8.19, 13.1, 13.10, A.24
(2)	8.19
(3)	2.4, 8.45
(4)	8.45, A.26
9	8.36
(1)	8.43, 13.10
(2)	8.43
(3)	8.42, 8.48
(a), (c)	9.9
(5)	8.41, 8.43, 13.11, 13.13
(b)	13.10
(6)	8.42
(7)	7.21, 7.23, 8.42
10	7.87, 9.9
(1)	8.45
(b)	13.10, 13.13
(4)–(6)	8.46
(8)	8.50
(9)	8.50, 8.91
(c)	8.47
11(1)	2.17, 8.3
(2)	2.17
(b)	13.15
(4)	8.57
(5)	8.20
(6)	8.24
(7)	8.58, 13.1
(d)	8.59
12(1)	8.20
(2)	5.6, 7.3, 7.4, 8.20, A.24
(3)	7.2, 8.20
13(1)	8.20
(a)	7.2, 8.40
(b)	7.2
(2)	8.20
14(2)	13.6
15	3.3, 5.44, 10.2, 10.6
16	3.11
(1)–(3), (5)	8.59
(6)	13.14
(7)	8.59, 13.14
Pt III (ss 17–30)	7.63, 8.1, 9.15, 15.10
s 17	7.31, 9.32
(1), (6)–(8)	9.1
(10), (11)	9.2
18(5)	9.4

Children Act 1989—*contd*

	PARA
s 19(5)	9.4
20	7.21, 9.32
(1)(a)–(c)	9.6
(5)	9.7
(8)	9.6
21	9.7
22	9.6, 9.32
(1)	8.79
(3)(a)	9.7
(b)	9.4
23(2)(a)	9.7, 9.8
(b)	9.10
(3), (4)	9.8
(5)	10.39
(6)	9.8
(7)(a)	9.8
24(8), (9)	9.7
25	15.9
(1)(a), (b)	9.12
(2)(a)	9.12
(3), (4), (6)	9.12
26(3), (4), (7)	9.15
27(1)–(3)	9.4
28H	10.75
Pt IV (ss 31–42)	2.8, 7.17, 7.31, 8.4, 8.44, 8.45, 8.73
s 31	4.146, 8.61, 8.67, 8.70, 8.74, 8.89, 8.93, 15.9
(1)	8.61, 8.62
(a)	8.79
(2)	2.26, 2.73, 8.61, 8.66, 8.94, A.47
(3)	7.23, 8.62
(4)	8.62
(5)	8.65
(7)	8.62
(9)	8.9, **8.61**, 8.104, 8.110, A.55
(10)	8.61, A.55, A.56
(11)	8.79
32	8.64
(1)(a)	A.56
33(1)	8.63, 13.21
(3)	8.63, 13.21, A.25
(a)	7.3
(4)	8.63, 13.21
(5)–(8)	8.63
34	7.31, 8.31, 8.51, 8.89, 8.91, 8.113, 13.16, 13.21
(1)	8.85, 8.86
(2)	8.86
(3)	8.87, 8.90
(4)	8.86
(5)	8.90
(6)	8.86
(7)	8.87
(9)	8.92
(11)	8.61, 8.90
35	8.82

Children Act 1989—contd

	PARA
s 36	8.93
37	8.35, 8.98, 8.127, 13.15
(1)	3.11, 8.51, 8.94, 8.99
(2)–(6)	8.99
38	8.79
(1)	8.94, 8.124
(2)	8.73, 8.94
(4), (5)	8.95
(6)–(8)	8.96
39(1), (2)	8.100
(4)	8.51
41	8.52
(4)	8.101
(6)	2.64, 8.51, 8.93, 8.101
(10)(a)	2.64
(11)	2.64
42(1)	8.101
(2)	2.28, 2.64, 8.101
(3)	2.64
Pt V (ss 43–52)	2.8, 8.51, 8.73
s 43	15.9
(1)	8.104
(3), (4)	8.105
(5)	8.104
(6)–(8)	8.106
(9), (10)	8.104
44	15.9, A.69
(1)(a)	8.108
(b)	8.109
(c)	8.110
(2)(b)	8.110
(3)	8.110
(4)(a)	8.111, 13.16
(b)(i), (ii)	8.111
(c)	8.111, 13.16, A.24
(5)	13.16
(a), (b)	8.111
(6)	8.112
(7)	13.17
(8)	8.113
(9)(b)	13.17
(10)–(12)	8.114, 13.16
(13)	8.113, 13.16
(15), (16)	13.18
44A(3)	A.69
45	15.9
(1)–(4), (6)	8.115
(8), (9)	8.117, 13.17
(10)	8.118, 13.17
(12)	13.17
46	13.22, 13.23
(1), (2)	13.20
(3)(d)	13.20
(5)	13.20
(6)	8.120, 13.20
(8)	13.20
47(1)	8.102
(b)	8.109

Children Act 1989—contd

	PARA
s 48(3)(a), (b)	8.103
(4)–(8)	8.103
(1), (3)	8.119
(4)	13.20
(9)	13.20
(b)	13.19
49(3)	13.22
50(1)	8.120
(3)–(7)	13.23
(8)(b)	13.23
(9), (11)	13.24
(12)	13.23
51	13.20
53(4)	9.10
61(1)	9.10
71	9.4
76	7.62
91(14)	8.10, **8.121**
94	2.75, 5.61, 8.124
(1), (4), (5)	8.122
98	2.47
100(1)	7.30
(2)	7.30, 7.31, 8.43
(c)	9.36
(3)	7.30, 7.35
(4)(a)	7.31
105	5.52, 7.19, 8.42, 8.46
(1)	5.50, 5.51, 8.9, 8.79, A.55
Sch 1	2.50, 3.3, 5.14, 5.44, 5.45, 5.56, 5.59, 5.61, 10.2, 10.5, 10.6, 12.10, 15.17, 15.31, 15.33, A.63
para 1	2.24, 5.47
(1)(b)	5.49
(2)(a)–(c)	12.2
(d), (e)	12.2, A.49, A.51, *565*
2	5.48, 5.50, 5.51
(1), (2)	5.57
(3)	5.57, 5.59
(4)	5.57, 5.58
4	5.55
(1)	5.53
(2), (3)	5.54
5	5.55
(2)	2.24, 5.49
6	5.47, 5.51
(4)	5.58
7	5.47
15	5.50, 9.8, 9.9
16	5.51, 7.19
(2)	5.50
Sch 2	
Pt I (paras 1–11)	
para 2, 3	9.3
5	9.7
(a), (c)	9.13
8, 9	9.4

Table of Statutes

Children Act 1989—contd
  Sch 2—contd
    Pt I—contd
      para 11 .... 8.79
      Pt II (paras 12–20) 9.9
      para 17(2), (5) 9.11
        19 .... 8.63
          (1) 8.79, 8.80
          (2) 8.79, 8.81
          (3)–(5), (8) 8.80
  Sch 3 .... 8.77
    para 1(2) 8.84
      3 .... 8.84
      6(1), (4) 8.83
  Sch 14 .... 8.1
    para 7 .... A.24
Civil Evidence Act 1968 (17 *Statutes* 168)
  s 11(1) 2.33
    12(1), (2) 2.33
    14 .... 2.47
Civil Evidence Act 1972 (17 *Statutes* 199)
  s 5 .... 2.60
Civil Evidence Act 1995
  s 1(1) 2.29
    11 .... 2.29
Common Law Procedure Act 1854 (5 *Statutes* 340)
  s 79 .... 11.1
Contempt of Court Act 1981 (11 *Statutes* 185)
  s 14 .... 14.11
    (1), (4A) 14.10
County Courts Act 1984 (11 *Statutes* 603)
  s 6 .... 8.14
    14(1), (4A) A.85
    23 .... 2.15
      (b)(ii) 2.4, 5.41
      (c) 12.33
    24 .... 2.15, 5.41
    25 .... 6.29
    38 .... 11.1, 11.4, 11.36,
                     11.38, 11.41, 12.34,
                     12.37, 12.46
    39 .... 11.1
    76 .... 12.37
    107 .... 12.46
    108, 109 .... 12.24
County Courts (Penalties for Contempt) Act 1983 (11 *Statutes* 206) 14.10
Courts and Legal Services Act 1990 (11 *Statutes* 720) 11.3
  s 9 .... 2.23
    58 .... A.26
    71 .... 10.79

Criminal Justice Act 1982 (27 *Statutes* 326)
  s 37(1) 13.24
    (2) 13.18
Criminal Justice and Public Order Act 1994 (32 *Statutes* 654)
  s 54 .... 11.33
Debtors Act 1869 (4 *Statutes* 660) 12.13
  s 4 .... 14.1
    5 .... 12.4, 12.11
    6 .... 12.49
Divorce Reform Act 1969 .... 1.2, 3.4
  s 2(5) 11.8, A.5
    3(6) 11.8, A.5
Domestic Proceedings and Magistrates' Courts Act 1978 (27 *Statutes* 816) 2.21, 2.75, 3.2,
                     4.8, 5.7, 5.44, 8.45,
                     10.2, 11.38, 15.7, A.1
  Pt I (ss 1–35) 12.10
  s 2(1) 2.24
    (a)–(d) 12.2
    (3) 2.24
    16 .... A.29
    18(2) A.76, A.79
    32(4) 12.9
    88(1) A.29
  Sch 2 .... 14.12
Domestic Violence and Matrimonial Proceedings Act 1976 (27 *Statutes* 812) 2.4, 5.5, 8.45, 11.5,
                     11.7, 11.9, 11.14,
                     11.20, 11.24, 11.42,
                     14.4, A.1, A.34, A.37
  s 1(1) 11.3
    (a) 11.2, 11.32
    (b) 11.2, 11.32, A.29
    (c) 11.2, 11.40, 11.44
    (d) 11.44, 11.46
    (2) 11.8, 11.10, 11.23,
                     11.26, 11.40, 11.44
    2 .... A.71
    (1) **11.47**, A.76
    (c) 11.44
    (2) 11.40, 11.44, A.4, A.5
    (3) 11.48, 14.12, A.76, A.79
    (4) 11.49
    3(1) 3.13
    4(2) 3.13
Domicile and Matrimonial Proceedings Act 1973 (27 *Statutes* 802):3.14, 3.20
  s 5(2)(a)–(c) 3.12
Education Act 1944 (15 *Statutes* 120)
  s 1 .... 9.16
    9(2) 9.17
    15 .... 9.17
    76 .... 9.16

Table of Statutes xxiii

	PARA
Education Act 1980 (15 *Statutes* 264)	
s 7(4)	9.17, 9.21
Sch 2	
Pt I	9.17, 9.21
Education Act 1981 (15 *Statutes* 300):	9.17
s 1(1), (2)	9.18
5(1), (3), (4)	9.18
(6)–(8)	9.19
6(1)	9.18
7(6)	9.20
8(2)	9.21
(4)(a), (b)	9.21
(5)–(7)	9.21
20(1)	9.16
Education Act 1996	9.16
Education (No 2) Act 1986 (15 *Statutes* 335)	
s 26(5)	9.17
Sch 3	9.17
Education Reform Act 1988	9.16
Family Law Act 1986 (6 *Statutes* 324)	2.4
s 34	13.9
(1), (2)	13.4, 13.8
Pt II (ss 44–54)	6.4
s 56	10.65
(1A), (1B)	7.51
(2)(b)	7.51
(2A), (3)	7.51
63	7.51
Family Law Act 1996	2.19, 3.4, 4.59, 4.108, 4.111, 4.136, 4.209, 4.210, 5.2, 5.4, 5.5, A.60
Pt I (s 1)	4.215
s 1(c)(iii)	4.215
Pt II (ss 2–25)	1.1, 1.3, 1.10, 3.18, 3.33, 4.215, A.26
s 2(1)(a)	3.19
(b)	3.1, 3.19
3(1)	3.19
(a)	3.31
(c)	3.27, 3.31
(d)	3.31
(2)	3.31
4(1)–(5)	3.32
5(1)	3.33
(c)	3.1
(2)	3.32
(3)	3.34
6(3), (4)	3.24
7	3.1
(1)	**3.25**
(3)–(5)	3.26
(6)	3.24
(10)–(12), (14)	3.26
8(2)	3.22, 3.24
(6)(a), (b)	3.22
(7)(b)	3.22

	PARA
Family Law Act 1996—*contd*	
s 8(9)(b)	3.22
9(2)(a)	3.27
(d)	3.27, 4.223
(5)	3.29
(7)	3.27
10	3.17, 3.31, 3.32
(2)–(5), (6)	3.30
11(1)	3.29
(2)	3.23, 3.29
(3)–(5)	3.29
13	3.35
14(1)(a), (b)	3.35
(2)–(4)	3.35
15	4.216
16	3.30, 4.231
19	3.19
(2)	3.20
20(2)	A.16
22A	4.54
Pt III (ss 26–29)	1.3, 1.10, 3.18, 4.215
Pt IV (ss 30–63)	1.1, 1.3, 1.10, A.1, A.2, A.19, A.26, A.30, A.55, A.59, A.65, A.69, A.73, A.76
s 30	A.31, A.37
32	A.32, A.50, A.64
33	A.52, A.64, A.67
(1)(a)(i)	A.31, A.38, *563*
(ii)	A.31
(b)(i), (ii)	A.31
(2)	A.22, A.31
(3)	A.31, A.48, *564, 565*
(a)–(c)	A.38, *562*
(d)–(g)	A.38, *563*
(4)	A.31, A.38, *563*
(5)	A.31, A.32, A.38, *563*
(6)(a)–(d)	A.48, A.53, *564*
(7)	A.56, A.57
(a)	A.48, A.53, *565*
(b)	A.48, A.53, *566*
(9)(b)	*567*
(10)	A.61, A.75, *567*
34	A.62
35	3.3, A.52, A.67
(1)(a)–(c)	A.32
(2)	A.32
(3)	A.49, *564*
(a), (b)	A.40, *562*
(4)	A.49, *564*
(a), (b)	A.40, *562*
(5)	A.50, *565*
(a)	A.41, *562*
(b)–(d)	A.41, *563*
(6)	A.75
(a)–(e)	A.49, A.50, *564, 565*

xxiv *Table of Statutes*

	PARA
Family Law Act 1996—*contd*	
s 35(6)(f)	A.49, 564
(g)(i)	A.49, A.62, 565
(ii), (iii)	A.49, 565
(7)	A.50, 565
(8)	A.56, A.57, 565
(a), (b)	A.50, 566
(9)(b)	567
(10)	A.62, A.75, 567
36	3.3, A.67
(1)(a)–(c)	A.33
(2)	A.33
(3)	A.51, 564
(a), (b)	A.43, 562
(4)	A.51, 564
(a), (b)	A.43, 562
(5)	A.52, 565
(a)	A.44, 562
(b)–(d)	A.44, 563
(6)(a)–(d)	A.51, A.52, 564, 565
(e)	A.51, A.52, 564
(f), (g)	A.51, 564
(h)	A.51, 565
(j)(i), (ii)	A.51, 565
(7)(a), (b)	A.52, 565
(8)	A.56
(a), (b)	A.52, 565
(9)(b)	567
(10)	A.63, A.75, 567
37	A.34, A.66, A.67
(1)(a)	A.35
(b)(i), (ii)	A.35
(2)	A.35
(3)	A.53, 564
(a), (b)	A.45, 562
(c) (d)	A.45, 563
(4)	A.53, A.56, A.57
(5)	A.53, A.62, A.75, 567
38	A.34, A.66, A.67
(1)(a)	A.36
(b)(i), (ii)	A.36
(2)	3.3, A.36
(3)	A.54, 564
(a), (b)	A.46, 562
(c), (d)	A.46, 563
(4)(a)–(e)	A.54, 564
(5)	A.56
(a), (b)	A.54, 565
(6)	A.63, A.75, 567
39(1)	A.67
(2)	A.59
(a)	A.69
(3), (4)	A.59
40	A.64
(1)(a)	A.67)
(i), (ii)	A.65
(b)	A.65, A.67
(c)–(e)	A.65

	PARA
Family Law Act 1996—*contd*	
s 40(2)	A.67
(3)	A.65, A.67
41	A.51, A.52
(1), (2)	566
42(1)	A.2
(a), (b)	A.69
(2)(a)	A.69
(b)	A.69, A.70
(3)	A.69
(4)	A.22, A.69
(5)	A.75
(a), (b)	A.69
(6)	A.69
(7), (8)	A.70
44	A.18
(1)	A.20
(2)	A.77
(a), (b)	A.21
45(1)	A.74, A.77
(2)(a), (b)	A.74
(c)(i), (ii)	A.74
(4)(a), (b)	A.75
(5)	A.75
46	A.67
(1)	A.71, A.81
(2), (3)	A.71
(4)	A.71, A.72
47(1)	A.72, A.76, A.81
(2)	A.72, A.77
(3)(a), (b)	A.77
(4)	A.77, A.81
(5)	A.77
(6)	A.79
(7)(a), (b)	A.82
(8)	A.72, A.81
(9)(a), (b)	A.81
(10)	A.82
48(2)–(4)	A.83
49(1)(a), (b)	A.64, A.70, 567
(2)	A.70
(3)	A.64, 567
50(1)	A.85
57	A.59, A.69
58(1)(a)	A.3
(3)	A.26
(g)	A.16
(4)	A.23
60	A.59
(1), (2)	A.73
(3)(a), (b)	A.73
62(1)(b)	A.3, A.8
(2)(a)–(c)	A.28
(3)(a)	A.10
(b)	A.9
(c)	A.13, A.14
(d)	A.15
(e)	A.18, A.31, A.69

Table of Statutes xxv

	PARA
Family Law Act 1996—*contd*	
s 62(3)(f)	A.23, A.25
(g)	A.25, A.26
(5)(a)	A.27
(b)(i), (ii)	A.27
(6)	A.25
63(1)	A.15, A.17, A.23, A.26, A.50, A.51, A.52, A.53, A.54, A.55, A.59, A.65, A.69, A.72, A.82
(2)	A.26, A.59, A.69
(a)	A.16
(3)	A.56
Sch 1	3.27
Sch 2	1.1, 3.27, 4.216
para 6	4.225
7	4.229
Sch 5	
para 2(1)(a), (b)	A.82
(2), (3)	A.82
Sch 7	A.49, A.51
Sch 8	4.232
Sch 10	4.219
Family Law Reform Act 1969 (6 *Statutes* 128)	6.9
s 1	7.18, 7.29
(1)	11.6
2	7.53
7	7.30
8	7.2, 7.21, 7.24
(1)	**7.22**
(2)	7.22
20	7.53, 7.55, 10.64
(1)	7.52, 10.66
(1A), (2)	7.52
21	10.64
(1)–(3)	7.53
23	10.64
(1)	7.55
26	2.35, 7.46
Family Law Reform Act 1987 (6 *Statutes* 363)	5.44, 6.9, 10.2, 10.64
s 1	5.6
(1)	**7.45**, A.23
(2), (4)	7.45
27(2)	7.47
Family Provision Act 1966 (17 *Statutes* 373)	
s 1	*556*
Finance Act 1973 (42 *Statutes* 315)	
s 15	4.101
Finance Act 1985 (41 *Statutes* 369)	
s 83(1)	4.248
Finance Act 1988 (42 *Statutes* 923)	4.246, 12.23
s 36	4.238, 4.242
(4)	4.237

	PARA
Finance Act 1988—*contd*	
s 37	4.242
38	4.242
(3)	4.238
39	4.242
Finance Act 1994 (48 *Statutes* 665)	
s 79(2)	4.238
Guardianship Act 1973	10.2
Guardianship of Minors Act 1971	10.2
s 1	11.38, 11.42
Housing Act 1985 (21 *Statutes* 35)	4.66
Pt III (ss 58–78)	11.39
Pt IV (ss 79–117)	11.45
s 91(3)(b)	11.4, 11.45
Housing Act 1988 (23 *Statutes* 735)	
Pt I (ss 1–45)	4.66
Human Fertilisation and Embryology Act 1990 (28 *Statutes* 316)	2.35
s 27	6.9
28	7.67
(2)–(4)	6.9, 7.41
(5)	7.41
(6)(b)	6.9
30	6.17, 7.43, 10.65, A.26
(1)(a), (b)	7.42
(2)–(5)	7.42
(6)	7.42, 7.43
(7)	7.42
Income and Corporation Taxes Act 1988 (44 *Statutes* 1)	12.23
s 226	4.101
347B	4.238
Pt XIV, Ch III (ss 618–629)	4.101
Pt XIV, Ch IV (ss 630–655)	4.101
s 633	4.108
Inheritance (Family Provision) Act 1938	6.28
Inheritance (Provision for Family and Dependents) Act 1975 (17 *Statutes* 388)	2.4, 2.5, 2.10, 2.15, 2.20, 4.48, 4.135, 6.7, 6.12, 6.13, 6.34, 11.1, 11.2, 15.31, 15.33, A.11
s 1	6.30
(1)	6.12, 6.20
(a)	6.14, 6.16
(b)	6.16
(ba)	6.16
(c)	6.17
(d)	6.18
(e)	6.14, 6.16, 6.19, 6.24
(1A)	6.16
(2)(a)	6.20, 6.22
(b)	6.20
(3)	6.19
2	6.21
(1)(a)–(f)	6.37

xxvi Table of Statutes

	PARA
Inheritance (Provision for Family and Dependents) Act 1975—contd	
s 2(4)	6.37
3	2.73, 6.21, 6.31, 6.37
(1)(a)–(c)	6.21
(d)	6.21, 6.22, 6.25
(e), (f)	6.21
(g)	6.21, 6.25
(2)	6.23
(a), (b)	6.22
(2A)(a), (b)	6.24
(3)	6.25
(a)–(c)	6.26
(4)	6.27
4	6.28
8(1), (2)	6.32
9(1)	6.33
10(1), (2)	6.35
11(2)(a)–(d)	6.36
(i), (ii)	6.36
14(1)	6.22
(a), (b)	6.23
(2)	6.22
15	4.110, 6.12, 6.14
15A	6.12
19(3)	6.30, 6.31
25(1)	6.17, 6.19, 6.32
(4)	6.14
(5)	6.15
Insolvency Act 1986 (4 Statutes 717)	4.249
s 283(2)(b)	4.271
284	4.278, 4.279
285	4.275
306	4.250, 4.251, 4.277
307	4.273
308	4.272
310	4.274, 4.275
336	4.252, 4.256
(4), (5)	4.253, 4.258, 4.261
337	4.252, 4.253
339	4.263, 4.264, 4.268, 4.269
340	4.263
(6)	4.269
382	4.280, 4.281
385	4.250, 4.274
425	4.265, 4.266
435, 440	4.266
443	4.268
Intestates' Estates Act 1952 (17 Statutes 359)	
s 1	556, 557
5	6.8
Sch 2	
para 1(1)	6.8
3(1)(a)	6.8
Judgments Act 1838 (22 Statutes 436)	4.59

	PARA
Land Registration Act 1925 (37 Statutes 516)	4.178
s 54(1), (2)	4.62
57(1)	4.62
Law of Property Act 1925 (37 Statutes 72)	2.15
s 30	2.4, 2.5, 2.20, 2.68, 4.37, 4.258, 4.261, 5.14, 5.29, 5.40, 11.40, 12.33, 15.10, 15.31, 15.33
35, 36	5.13
53	**5.16**
177	6.3
184	6.7
188	4.37, 5.14, 5.31
Law Reform (Miscellaneous Provisions) Act 1970 (27 Statutes 573)	
s 1	A.19
2	5.4, **5.8**, 5.12, 5.30, 5.41, A.19, A.22
(2)	5.10
5	11.43
Law Reform (Succession) Act 1995	6.4, 6.7, 6.12, 6.16, 6.24
Legal Aid Act 1988 (24 Statutes 9)	3.1, 3.18
s 2(2), (4)	15.4
(11)	15.22
Pt II (ss 3–7)	15.2
s 9(1)	15.5
14(1)	15.4
15(1)	15.6
(2)	15.8
(3)(a)	15.8
(3B)–(3E)	15.9
16(6)	15.29, 15.30, 15.36
(7)	15.29, 15.30, 15.31
17	15.20, 15.22, 15.25
(1), (3)	15.21
18	15.13, 15.18, 15.22
(1)	15.23
(4)(a)	15.24
(b)	15.26, 15.27
(c)	15.28
(7)	15.23
31(1)(b)	15.20
Sch 2	
Pt I	15.4, 15.7
Pt II	15.7
para 5	12.12
5A	15.7
Legitimacy Act 1926	
s 3–5	6.9
Legitimacy Act 1976 (6 Statutes 212)	
s 1	6.9
(1), (2), (4)	7.49
2, 3	6.9, 7.48

Table of Statutes xxvii

	PARA
Legitimacy Act 1976—*contd*	
s 5	6.9
14(2)	6.9
18(2)	6.9
Local Authority Social Services Act 1970 (25 *Statutes* 148)	8.101
Magistrates' Courts Act 1980 (27 *Statutes* 143)	9.34
s 53	12.21
55(1)–(4)	12.21
59(3)(a)–(d)	12.16
63(3)	13.6, 13.9
(a), (b)	A.85
76	12.15
(1), (3)	12.14
79(1)	12.16
92(1)(a)	12.14
93	12.4
(5)	12.15
(6)(a)	12.15
(7)	12.14
(8)	12.16
94	12.16
95	12.9
(1), (2)	12.16
96(1)	12.14
111(6)	9.30
128, 129	A.82
150(1)	12.14
Sch 4	
para 3	12.14
Maintenance Enforcement Act 1991 (27 *Statutes* 887)	12.15, 12.47
s 1(1)	4.145, 12.18, 12.28
(2)	12.28
(3)	12.18, 12.28
(4)	12.28
(a)	4.145, 12.29
(b)	12.29
(5)(a)	4.38, 12.29
(b)	12.29
(6)	12.29
(7)(a), (b)	12.29
(8)	12.29
(10)	12.28
27	12.4
Maintenance Orders Act 1958 (27 *Statutes* 662)	12.4
s 1(1)	12.47
2(2)	12.47
(5)	12.48
(6ZA)(b)	12.48
(6ZB)	12.47
3, 4	12.48
Malicious Communications Act 1988 (12 *Statutes* 1189)	11.33
Marriage Act 1949 (27 *Statutes* 500)	A.21
s 3	7.21

	PARA
Married Women's Property Act 1882 (27 *Statutes* 595)	2.4, 2.10, 4.149, 5.29, 5.41, 15.33, A.22
s 1	**5.30**
17	2.20, 3.2, 4.37, 5.8, **5.10**, 5.11, 5.14, 5.33, 5.34, 5.35, 5.38, 5.39
Matrimonial and Family Proceedings Act 1984 (27 *Statutes* 857)	6.22
Pt III (ss 12–27)	2.4, 4.10, 4.201, 4.202, 4.203, 4.204, 4.205, 4.206, 8.45, 15.33
s 14(1)	4.205
16(2)	4.205
17	4.207
(1)(a), (b)	12.2
20	4.208
23	4.207, 4.208
32	11.43
33(3)	11.4, 11.15
40(1)	11.3
42	5.39
Matrimonial Causes Act 1973 (27 *Statutes* 734)	1.2, 2.4, 2.51, 3.4, 3.5, 4.19, 4.100, 4.206, 4.232, 5.7, 5.44, 5.50, 8.45, 10.6, 15.31, 15.33, A.49
s 1(1)	3.1, 3.6, 3.33
(2)	3.1, 3.6, 3.7
(a), (b)	2.9
(c)–(e)	2.9, 3.16
(3)	3.10
(4)	3.6
(5)	3.10
2(1), (3)	3.15
(5)	3.16
(6)	11.8, A.5
3(1)	3.15, 3.24
(2)	3.15
5	3.6
(1), (2)	3.17
(3)	3.17, 3.30
6(1)	3.23
10	4.106
(2)–(4)	3.17
11	3.8, 3.18, 5.3, 6.2
(a)(i)–(iii)	A.21
(b)–(d)	A.21
12	3.8, 3.18, 5.3, 6.2
13	3.18
(2), (4)	3.8
16	3.8, 7.49
17(1)	3.7
(2)	3.10
18(1)	3.7, 11.2, 11.4
(2)	6.5

xxviii *Table of Statutes*

PARA

Matrimonial Causes Act 1973—*contd*
s 19 .... 3.18
   (1), (3) 3.9
  Pt II (ss 21–40) 1.1, 1.10,
                   2.18, 3.1, 3.3, 12.10
  s 21 .... 4.3, 4.218
   (2) 4.226
  22 .... 2.8, 4.5, 4.9, 4.129,
                 4.150, 4.176, 4.219,
                 12.2
  22A 4.217
   (2) 4.218
   (3) 4.221
   (4) 4.219
   (5)(a), (b) 4.222
   (7), (8) 4.222
  22B 3.17, 4.217, 4.218
   (1) 4.220
   (4) 4.223
  22C, 22D 3.17
  23 .... 2.8, 3.27, 4.13, 4.54,
               4.87, 4.117, 4.143,
               4.150, 4.155, 4.176,
               4.216, 4.217, 4.224,
               10.5, 10.88
   (1)(a) 4.3, 4.14, 4.32,
                 4.44, 4.125, 12.2
   (b) 4.3, 4.14, 4.32,
                 4.44, 4.46, 12.2
   (c) 4.3, 4.9, 4.14, 4.32,
                4.53, 4.135, 12.2, 12.49
   (d)–(f) 4.3, 10.1, 12.2
   (3) 4.197
   (c) 4.135
   (5) 4.52
   (6) 4.59
  23A 4.226, 4.227, 10.88, 565
   (3) 4.226
  23B 4.226, 10.88
   (1), (4) 4.227
  24 .... 2.8, 3.27, 4.3, 4.13,
               4.14, 4.32, 4.61, 4.67,
               4.78, 4.79, 4.80, 4.81,
               4.86, 4.87, 4.143,
               4.150, 4.155, 4.176,
               4.216, 4.225, 5.8,
               10.88, *565*
   (1) 4.63
   (a) 4.9, 4.64, 4.65,
                11.41, 11.45, 12.2
   (b) 4.9, 4.64, 4.68,
                4.135, 12.2
   (c), (d) 4.9, 4.64, 4.77,
                4.135, 12.2
   (2) 4.225
  24A 2.8, 3.27, 4.4, 4.13,
               4.14, 4.32, 4.39, 4.89,
               4.99, 4.143, 4.150,
               4.155, 4.207, 12.4,
               12.36, 12.41

PARA

Matrimonial Causes Act 1973—*contd*
s 24A(1) 4.9, 4.87, 4.95, 4.135
   (2) 4.95
   (3) 4.9, 4.88
   (5) 4.98
   (6) 4.96, 4.97
  24B 1.1
  24C 1.1
   (2) 4.50
  24D 1.1
  25 .... 2.48, 2.73, 4.15,
               4.20, 4.39, 4.41,
               4.143, 4.166
   (1) 3.28, 4.12, 4.13,
                4.25, 4.27, 4.96,
                4.139, 4.158, 4.196
   (d), (f) 6.22
   (2) 3.28, 4.12, 4.14, 4.112,
                4.139, 4.166, 4.169,
                4.170, 4.196, 6.23
   (a) 4.16, 4.29, 4.30,
                4.101, 4.159
   (b) 4.20, 4.30
   (c) 4.23, 4.30
   (d) 4.24
   (e) 4.26, 4.30
   (f) 4.27
   (g) 4.28, 4.168, 6.21
   (h) 4.29
   (3) 4.31
   (a)–(e) 4.30
   (4)(a)–(c) 4.31
  25A 4.1, 4.32, 4.143
   (1) 4.39
   (2) 4.40
   (3) 4.44, 4.45
  25B 3.30, 4.112, 4.117,
               4.119, 4.160,
               4.163, 4.231
   (1) 4.16, 4.29
   (4) 4.117, 4.124, 4.135
   (5)–(7) 4.117
  25C 3.30, 4.118, 4.119,
               4.135, 4.160, 4.163
   (2) 4.109, 4.118
   (a), (b) 4.124
  25D 3.30, 4.231
   (3)(a) 4.123
   (4) 4.115, 4.123
  27 .... 2.20, 3.2, 4.9, 4.143,
               4.150, 4.176, 4.198
   (1) 4.194
   (a), (b) 4.6
   (2) 4.195
   (3), (3A) 4.196
   (5) 4.197
   (6)(a)–(c) 4.197, 12.2
   (d)–(f) 12.2
   (7)(a) 4.197
   (b) 4.135

Matrimonial Causes Act 1973—contd

Section	PARA
s 28	4.36
(1)	4.40
(a)(i)	4.228
(ii), (iii)	4.229
(1A)	4.35, 4.40, 4.45, 4.170
(2)	4.37
(3)	4.33, 4.37, 5.7
29	4.229
(1), (3)	4.197
30	12.4
(a)	4.51, 12.45
(b)	4.51
31	4.11, 4.35, 4.45, 4.48, 4.136, 4.149, 4.176, 4.233
(1)	4.134
(2)	4.135
(a)	4.9
(d)	4.57
(dd)–(f)	4.9
(2A)	4.57
(4)	4.135
(5)	4.136
(6)	4.138, 4.176
(7)	4.139
(a)	4.134
(8)	4.138
(10)	4.137
31A(6)	4.229
(7)(a), (b)	4.230
32(1)	12.9
33A(1)	4.154
(2), (3)	4.143
34(1)	4.170
35	4.176
(1)	4.9
37	4.173, 4.175, 4.176, 4.180, 4.181, 4.182, 4.183, 4.184, 4.185, 4.208, 11.4, 11.41
(1)	4.176
(2)(a)–(c)	4.177, 4.178
(3)	4.177
(4), (5)	4.178
(6)	4.179
39	4.263
41	3.29, 11.4
(1), (2)	3.11
50	2.4
52(1)	10.1, 11.32, A.29

Matrimonial Causes (Property and Maintenance) Act 1958 (27 Statutes 605)

Section	PARA
s 7	5.8, 5.10, 5.11, 5.29
(4)	5.11
(7)	5.11, 5.14

Matrimonial Homes Act 1967 .... 11.38

Matrimonial Homes Act 1983 (27 Statutes 614)

Section	PARA
	2.4, 2.10, 4.145, 4.253, 11.12, 11.16, 11.20, 11.36, 11.42, 14.4, A.37
s 1	4.62, 4.252, 4.258, 8.45, 11.25, 11.37, 11.39, 11.41
(1)(a), (b)	11.5, 11.37
(2)	11.37
(a)	11.5, 11.25, 11.28
(b)	11.5
(c)	11.5, 11.46
(3)	4.255, 11.38, 11.40, 11.41, 11.42, 11.46, A.29, A.47, A.65
(a)	11.39
(b), (c)	11.45
(4)	11.39, 11.45
(a), (b)	11.5
(5), (7)	11.45
(9)	11.5
(10)	11.5, 11.37, 11.44
2(4)	11.41
(a), (b)	11.39
(8)(a)	4.62
3	11.7
7	11.45
8	11.7
9	8.45, 11.5, 11.25
(1), (3)	11.37
10(1)	11.5, 11.37
(2)	11.5
Sch 1	4.66, 11.45

Matrimonial Proceedings and Property Act 1970 (27 Statutes 684) 1.2

Section	PARA
s 37	5.8, **5.12**, 5.24, 6.8
39	5.10

Mental Health Act 1983 (28 Statutes 846) 8.53, A.1

Section	PARA
s 35	A.83

Naval Discipline Act 1957 (3 Statutes 442)

Section	PARA
s 128E	12.17

Naval Forces (Enforcement of Maintenance Liabilities) Act 1947 (3 Statutes 1072) 12.17

Offences against the Person Act 1861 (12 Statutes 87)

Section	PARA
s 47	A.76

Pensions Act 1995 .... 4.112

Section	PARA
s 1	4.123
166	4.16, 4.100, 4.101, 4.109, 4.111, 4.116, 4.121, 4.122
(2)	4.29
(3)	4.135
167	4.116

xxx Table of Statutes

	PARA
Police Act 1964 (33 *Statutes* 672)	9.24
s 18, 19	A.79
Sch 2	A.79
Rent Act 1977 (23 *Statutes* 514)	4.66, 11.37, 11.45
Rent (Agriculture) Act 1976 (1 *Statutes* 664)	4.66, 11.45
Sexual Offences Act 1956 (12 *Statutes* 239)	
s 10, 11	7.58
Social Security Act 1986 (40 *Statutes* 367)	
s 24	10.3
Social Security Administration Act 1992 (40 *Statutes* 786)	10.3
Social Security Contributions and Benefits Act 1992 (40 *Statutes* 492)	
s 141, 143	10.28
Solicitors Act 1974 (41 *Statutes* 19)	
s 73	15.29
Supreme Court Act 1981 (11 *Statutes* 966)	2.4
s 18(1)	2.2
29(3)	9.30
31	9.22
(3)	9.24
(5)	9.30
(6)	9.31
37	2.4, 4.173, 11.4, 11.36, 11.38, 11.41
(1)	4.186, 11.1, 11.4

	PARA
Supreme Court Act 1981—*contd*	
s 37(2), (3)	4.186
38	12.4
39	12.4, 12.34
(1)	12.46
40, 40A	12.24
41	11.29
51	15.15
(6), (13)	15.19
Supreme Court of Judicature Act 1873	11.1
Surrogacy Arrangements Act 1985 (12 *Statutes* 980)	7.38
s 1(2), (6)	7.39
1A	7.40
2(1), (2)	7.40
3, 4	7.40
Taxation of Chargeable Gains Act 1992 (43 *Statutes* 1439)	
s 58(1)	4.244
222(1)	4.246
223(1)	4.245
Telecommunications Act 1984 (45 *Statutes* 134)	
s 43	11.33
Trusts of Land and Appointment of Trustees Act 1996	4.74, 5.30
Wills Act 1837 (50 *Statutes* 150)	7.11
s 18(1), (2)	6.2
(3)	6.3
(4)(b)	6.3
18A(1)(a), (b)	6.4

Table of Statutory Instruments

	PARA
Administration of Justice Act 1977 (Commencement No 2) Order 1977, SI 1977/1490	557
Adoption Agencies Regulations 1983, SI 1983/1964	7.56
reg 2, 3, 5, 6	7.60
7	7.60
(2)(c)	7.72
(3)	7.72
8	7.60, 7.73
9	7.60, 7.74
10	7.74
11	7.75
14, 15	7.60
Adoption (Designation of Overseas Adoptions) Order 1973, SI 1973/19	
art 4	7.94
Adoption (Northern Ireland) Order 1987, SI 1987/2203	
art 17, 18	A.27
Adoption Rules 1984, SI 1984/265	2.5, 2.16, 7.56
r 3(2)	2.6
4–7	7.92
8	7.92, 7.97
9–13	7.92
14	7.91
15	7.85, 7.91
16–19	7.91
20	7.77, 7.91
21–25	7.91
27–36	7.95
53(2)	8.17
Sch 1	
Form 6	7.91
7, 15	7.58
Arrangements for Placement of Children (General) Regulations 1991, SI 1991/890	9.8
Attachment of Debts (Expenses) Order 1983, SI 1983/1621	12.24
Child Maintenance (Written Agreements) Order 1993, SI 1993/620	5.46, 110.5

	PARA
Child Support Appeal Tribunals (Procedure) Regulations 1992, SI 1992/2641	
reg 11, 13, 15	10.76
Child Support (Arrears, Interest and Adjustment of Maintenance Assessments) Regulations 1992, SI 1992/1816	
reg 2	10.99
3	10.99
(2), (6)	10.100
4(1)(a), (b)	10.100
5(1), (2)	10.98
(3), (4)	10.100
(7)	10.98
Child Support (Collection and Enforcement of Other Forms of Maintenance) Regulations 1992, SI 1992/2643	
reg 2	10.88
Child Support (Collection and Enforcement) Regulations 1992, SI 1992/1989	10.88
Pt II (regs 2–7)	10.87
Pt IV (regs 8–25)	10.94
reg 16	10.90
22(1)	10.91
(2)(a)	2.21
(3)	10.91
27	10.94
33, 34	10.97
Child Support Commissioners (Procedure) Regulations 1992, SI 1992/2640	10.78, 10.80
reg 25	10.82
Child Support Departure Direction (Anticipatory Application) Regulations 1996, SI 1996/635	10.52
Child Support Fees Regulations 1992, SI 1992/3094	
reg 3(5)	10.45
4	10.45

xxxii *Table of Statutory Instruments*

PARA

Child Support (Information, Evidence and Disclosure) Regulations 1992, SI 1992/1812
reg 7 .... 10.60

Child Support (Maintenance Arrangements and Jurisdiction) Regulations 1992, SI 1992/2645
reg 2(5) 10.7
3(5) 10.43
4(2) 10.7

Child Support (Maintenance Assessment Procedure) Regulations 1992, SI 1992/1813
reg 1(2) 10.7, 10.29
2 .... 10.5, 10.44
(a), (b) 10.27
5–7 .... 10.46
8(1) 10.48
(2)(e) 10.48
(6) 10.49
17(5) 10.69
19 .... 10.71
(2) 10.69
20 .... 10.29
24 .... 10.73
30 .... 10.7
31 .... 10.72
(2) 10.70
33(2), (4) 10.47
34 .... 10.43
36(4) 10.51
41 .... 10.73
51 .... 10.7
(1) 10.41

Child Support (Maintenance Assessments and Special Cases) Regulations 1992, SI 1992/1815
reg 1(2) 10.7
Pt II (regs 2–18) 10.12
reg 5(b) 10.20
7(3) 10.14
8(3)–(5) 10.90
9(1), (2) 10.14
13 .... 10.22, 10.25, 10.33
14 .... 10.14
15 .... 10.14, 10.15
16 .... 10.14
17 .... 10.14, 10.28
18 .... 10.14
(2) 10.16
(a)(ii) 10.7
19(3) 10.27
20(4) 10.31
(6) 10.30
21 .... 10.31
23 .... 10.34
24(1) 10.35
(2)(a)–(c) 10.35
25 .... 10.36

PARA

Child Support (Maintenance Assessments and Special Cases) Regulations 1992—*contd*
reg 26 .... 10.33, 10.37
27 .... 10.38
27A 10.39
28 .... 10.22, 10.33
Sch 1
Pt I (paras 1–5)
para 1(2) 10.14
2 .... 10.14
Pt II (paras 6–7) 10.14
Pt III (paras 8–16) 10.14
Pt IV (paras 17–24) 10.14
Pt V (paras 25–32)
para 25 .... 10.14
Sch 2
para 1–48 .... 10.14
Sch 3
para 2, 6 .... 10.15
Sch 4 .... 10.33

Child Support (Miscellaneous Amendments and Transitional Provisions) Regulations 1994, SI 1994/227 .... 10.3

Child Support (Miscellaneous Amendments) Regulations 1995, SI 1995/123 .... 10.3
Sch 3 .... 10.17
Sch 3A 10.18

Children Act 1989 (Amendment and Transitional Provisions) (No 2) Order 1991, SI 1991/1990 .... 8.1

Children (Admissibility of Hearsay Evidence) Order 1993, SI 1993/621 .... 2.29

Children (Allocation of Proceedings) Order 1991, SI 1991/1677 .... 8.116, 8.129, 10.64, A.59
art 1(1), (3) 3.2
3 .... 2.15
(1) 2.3
(3) 2.24
4 .... 2.24, 13.17
5 .... 2.3
6 .... 2.3, 2.24
7 .... 2.3, 2.24, 7.43
8–13 .... 2.3, 2.24

Children (Secure Accommodation) (No 2) Regulations 1991, SI 1991/2034
reg 2 .... 9.12

Children (Secure Accommodation) Regulations 1991, SI 1991/1505
reg 7(3)(a), (b) 9.12
10–12 .... 9.12
15 .... 9.14
16(1) 9.14
17 .... 9.14

Table of Statutory Instruments xxxiii

PARA

Civil Legal Aid (Assessment of
  Resources) Regulations 1989,
  SI 1989/338 .... 15.3
  reg 4(a), (b) 15.6
  Sch 2 .... 15.6
  Sch 3 .... 15.6
Civil Legal Aid (General) Regulations
  1989, SI 1989/339 .... 15.3
  reg 3(1) 15.9, 15.33
    67(1)(a), (b) 15.12
    70(1)(a) 15.13, 15.18
    (2) 15.13
  71 .... 15.12
  Pt X (regs 74–86) 15.12
  reg 85 .... 15.32
  Pt XI (regs 87–99) 15.32
  reg 90(2) 15.32
    94 .... 15.29, 15.31
    95(1), (2) 15.32
    96(1) 15.33
    (2)(b) 15.33
    (3)(b) 15.33
    (7) 15.33
    97(1), (3), (4) 15.33
    98 .... 15.33
    99(4) 15.33
    100(6) 15.14
    101(1)(a) 15.14
    102 .... 15.13
  Pt XIII (regs 123–133) 15.21
  Pt XIV (regs 134–147) 15.22
Contact with Children Regulations
  1991, SI 1991/891 .... 8.86
County Court (Forms) Rules 1982,
  SI 1982/586
  Form 79 .... 14.11
County Court Rules 1981, SI
  1981/1687 ...... 2.1, 2.4, 2.5, 2.6, 2.16
  Ord 1
    r 3 .... 2.63, 11.23, 11.24
  Ord 2
    r 6 .... 8.14
  Ord 3
    r 4(3) 2.20
    (4)(a) 11.25
  Ord 4
    r 8 .... 2.10, 5.39
    (a)(ii) 11.12
  Ord 6
    r 8 .... 2.17
  Ord 7
    r 1 .... 12.7
    2 .... 14.2
    6(1)(b) 11.23, 11.24, 11.25
    10 .... 12.19
  Ord 10
    r 1 .... 2.63
  Ord 11
    r 10 .... 15.18

PARA

County Court Rules 1981—*contd*
  Ord 13
    r 1(2) 11.23, 11.24, 11.25
    (3) 11.23, 11.24
    (4A) 13.3
    (5) 11.25
    3 .... 11.31
    6(2) 4.186, 4.190
    (3) 11.10, 11.11, 11.12,
                                        11.13, 11.23
    (3A) 11.10, 11.11, 11.12, 11.13
    (4) 11.11, 11.12
    (4A) 11.12
    (6), (7) 11.23, 11.24, 11.25
    8(1) 2.49
  Ord 14 .... 2.40
    r 2(1) 2.49
    10(3) 14.7
    11 .... 2.50
  Ord 20
    r 12(8) 2.52
    27 .... 2.56
  Ord 21
    r 5(1)(d) 5.42
    (2B) 4.186, 4.190
  Ord 22
    r 12 .... 12.4, 12.36, 12.41, 12.43
  Ord 24
    r 5 .... 2.44
  Ord 25
    r 3 .... 12.6, 12.37
    (1), (3) 12.7
    (4) 12.7, 12.8
    (5) 12.8
    (5A) 12.7
    5A 12.7, 12.19, 12.31, 12.46
  Ord 26
    r 1 .... 12.38
    5 .... 12.37
    17 .... 12.4
    (4), (5) 12.38
  Ord 27 .... 12.4
    r 5(1), (2) 12.19
    7(1) 12.20
    17(2) 12.19
    (3) 12.9
    (3A) 12.19
    (4) 12.18
    (5) 12.20
    (7) 12.23
  Ord 28 .... 12.4
    r 3 .... 12.11
    10(1) 12.12
    (2)(b) 12.12
  Ord 29 .... 13.3
    r 1 .... 4.146, 13.12
    (2), (3) 11.23, 11.24,
                                      11.25, 11.47, 14.2
    (4) 11.49, 14.4, 14.5, 14.7

Table of Statutory Instruments

	PARA
County Court Rules 1981—*contd*	
Ord 29—*contd*	
r 1(6)	14.2
(7)	14.2, 14.5, 14.7, 14.11
1A	4.146, 14.3
3	4.174
(1)	14.11, 14.14
Ord 30	12.4
r 1(1)	12.24
(2)	12.25
2(a)–(e)	12.24
3(1)	12.25
(2)(a), (b)	12.25
5	12.26, 12.27
7(1), (2)	12.27
8	12.26
9, 11	12.27
Ord 31	12.4
r 1(1)(b), (c)	12.30
(2), (4), (6), (9)	12.31
2	12.32
4	12.33
Ord 37	
r 1	2.69
2(1)	2.69
6	2.68
8	2.74
Ord 38	
r 1	15.19
(3)	15.15
Ord 47	
r 8(7)	11.49, 14.2
(8)	11.49
Ord 48	2.20
r 2	6.30
(a)–(c) (e)–(i)	6.31
3(1)(b), (c)	6.31
(2), (3)	6.31
4(1)(a)	6.31
5(a)–(d)	6.31
7–9	6.31
County Courts (Interest on Judgment Debts) Order 1991, SI 1991/1184	4.59
County Courts Jurisdiction Order 1981, SI 1981/1123	2.15, 5.41
Divorce etc (Pensions) Regulations 1996, SI 1996/1676	
reg 3	4.120
6–10	4.121
Education (Special Educational Needs) Regulations 1994, SI 1994/1047	
reg 6–9	9.18
10	9.20
Family Proceedings (Amendment) (No 2) Rules 1996, SI 1996/1674	
r 4(1)	4.160
Family Proceedings (Costs) Rules 1991, SI 1991/1832	2.4

	PARA
Family Proceedings Courts (Children Act 1989) Rules 1991, SI 1991/1395	2.1, 2.5, 2.16, 7.6, 7.43, 8.53, 8.126, 8.128
r 3	2.17
4	2.17, 5.60
(4)	8.23
(5)	8.116
5	7.10, 8.71
10	2.64, 8.52
(7)	8.101
11(4)	2.64
(9)(c)	2.64
12	8.52, 8.101
13(3)	8.16
14	5.60
(2)(a)	2.17
17	8.97
(1), (5)	2.17
18	2.17
(1)	2.61
21	8.97, 8.128
(8)	8.116
21A–21J	7.43
23	2.45, 2.61, 8.73
(1)	2.17
27	8.99
Sch 1	
Form C1, C11	8.116
Sch 2	7.10
Family Proceedings Courts (Matrimonial Proceedings etc) Rules 1991, SI 1991/1991	2.5, 2.16, 2.21, 4.8
Family Proceedings Fees Order 1991, SI 1991/2114	
Sch 1	
Pt I	
para 5	13.5
Family Proceedings Rules 1991, SI 1991/1247	2.5, 2.16, 7.6, 8.125, 8.126
r 1.1(2)	3.2, 11.16
1.2	11.26
(1)	2.4, 12.42
(2)	2.15, 2.24, 3.20
1.3(1)	2.1, 2.6, 2.16, 8.14
1.4(1)	5.39
(2)	2.15
Pt II (rr 2.1–2.68)	2.16
r 2.1	3.10
2.2	2.36, 3.10
(1)	3.10
(2)	3.11
2.3	2.9, 2.36, 3.10
2.4, 2.5	2.36, 3.10
2.6	2.36, 3.10
(1)	2.15, 11.11

Family Proceedings Rules 1991—*contd*
r 2.6(2), (3) 11.11
    (5) 11.4, 11.11
  2.7–2.10 .... 2.36, 3.10
  2.11 .... 2.36
    (8) 3.10
  2.12–2.19 .... 2.19, 2.36, 3.10
  2.20–2.23 .... 2.9, 2.19, 2.36, 3.10
  2.24 .... 2.9, 2.19, 2.36
    (3)(a) 3.10
  2.25–2.27 .... 2.9, 2.19, 2.36, 3.10
  2.28 .... 2.9, 2.19, 2.36, 3.10
    (1) 2.19
  2.29–2.31 .... 2.9, 2.19, 2.36, 3.10
  2.32–2.35 .... 2.19, 2.36, 3.10
  2.36 .... 2.19, 2.36, 3.10
    (1)(a) 3.10
    (2) 3.10
  2.37 .... 2.36, 3.10
  2.38 .... 2.36, 3.10, 3.11
  2.39 .... 2.36, 3.10
    (1) 3.11
    (2)(b) 3.11
    (3) 3.11
  2.40 .... 2.36, 3.10
    (1) 2.15, 11.13, 11.17
  2.41, 2.42 .... 2.36, 3.10
  2.43 .... 3.10
    (1)(a), (b) 12.25
  2.44–2.50 .... 3.10
  2.51 .... 3.10, 6.7
  2.53 .... 2.8
    (2) 4.9
    (3) 4.140
  2.58 .... 1.8, 4.130
    (1) 4.9
    (2) 2.10, 4.131, 4.140
    (3) 4.132, 4.185
  2.59 .... 4.9, 4.82, 4.180, 4.182
    (1)(a), (b) 4.83
      (c) 4.181
    (2) 4.181
    (3) 4.85, 4.86, 4.181
      (a) 4.85
    (4) 4.85, 4.86, 4.161
    (5) 4.86, 4.181
  2.60(1) 4.86
  2.61 .... 4.127, 4.143, 4.150,
                          4.153, 4.154, 4.200
    (1) 4.151, 4.163
      (a) 4.155, 4.156
      (b) 4.155, 4.157
      (c) 4.155, 4.158
      (d) 4.155, 4.159
      (dd) 4.160, 4.163
      (e) 4.155, 4.161
      (f) 4.155, 4.162
    (2) 4.163

Family Proceedings Rules 1991—*contd*
r 2.62(4) 2.28, 5.38
    (5) 4.97, 5.38, 11.28
    (6) 5.38
    (7) 2.18, 2.53, 4.107
    (8) 2.18, 2.53
    (9) 2.18
  2.63 .... 1.8, 2.18, 2.43, 2.50,
                        2.51, 2.53, 4.27, 4.101,
                        4.200, 4.206, 5.38
  2.64 .... 5.38
    (3) 4.99, 12.36, 12.41
    (4) 2.52
  2.65 .... 4.180, 5.38
  2.66 .... 5.38
  2.67 .... 4.125, 4.133
    (2) 4.133
  2.68 .... 4.180
  2.69 .... 15.18
Pt III (rr 3.1–3.20) 2.20, 11.26
r 3.1 .... 2.20
    (1) 4.9, 4.198
    (2), (3) 4.198
    (4) 4.9
    (5) 4.9, 4.199
    (8), (9) 4.199
    (10) 4.200
  3.6 .... 2.10, 2.20, 5.10, 5.33, 5.38
    (1) 5.34, 5.35, 11.16, 11.28
    (b) 11.25
    (2) 5.35
    (3) 5.34, 5.39, 11.25
    (4) 5.36
    (5) 5.37, 11.28
    (6) 5.36
    (7), (8) 5.37, 11.28
    (9) 5.38
    (10) 11.28
    (11) 5.38
  3.7 .... 5.10, 5.39
    (1) 5.39
  3.8 .... 2.10
    (2) 11.16, 11.25, 11.28
    (3) 11.12, 11.16, 11.25,
                              11.27, 11.28
    (4) 11.19, 11.24, 11.25, 11.28
    (5) 11.25, 11.28
  3.9 .... 11.3
  3.9(2) 11.3, 11.10, 11.14,
                        11.19, 11.23, 11.26
    (3) 11.26
    (5) 11.23
    (6) A.78
    (b) 11.47
    (7) 11.47, A.78
    (8) 11.49
    (10) 11.19, 11.23, 11.24, 11.27
  3.10 .... A.78

Table of Statutory Instruments

Family Proceedings Rules 1991—*contd*

	PARA
r 3.12	2.20
3.13, 3.14	2.20, 7.51
3.15	2.20
3.17(2)	4.205
(e)	4.206
3.18	4.208
(1), (3)	4.206
3.21	10.64
Pt IV (rr 4.1–4.28)	8.127, 11.13, 11.17
4.3	2.17
(2)–(4)	7.35
4.4	2.8, 2.17, 5.60, 13.5
(4)	8.23, 11.13, 11.17
4.5	7.10, 8.71
4.9	2.8
4.10	2.64
(7)	8.101
4.11	13.17
(4)	2.64
(9)(c)	2.64
4.12	8.52, 8.101
4.12A	13.12
4.13(3)	8.16
4.14	5.60
(2)(a)	2.17
(d)	8.55
4.17	1.8
(1), (5)	2.17
4.18	2.17, 2.56
(1)	2.61
4.21(a)	8.127
4.21A	13.2, 13.7
4.22	2.75
(2)	8.122, 8.125
(3)	8.124
(7)	8.125
4.23	2.45, 8.73
(1)	2.17, 2.61
4.24	8.80
4.26	8.99
4.31A	13.13
Pt IVA	7.43
Pt V (rr 5.1–5.4)	2.10, 7.19
r 5.1	11.6, 11.18
(1)	7.35, 11.29
(3)–(9)	7.35
5.2	13.26
5.3(1)	11.29
Pt VI (rr 6.1–6.16)	7.19
Pt VII (rr 7.1–7.38)	7.19
r 7.1	12.31, 12.46
(1)	12.10, 12.19, 12.24
(5)(a), (b)	12.7
7.2(1)	14.4
(2)	14.14
7.4	12.4
(2)(a), (b)	12.11

Family Proceedings Rules 1991—*contd*

	PARA
r 7.4(4)–(6), (8)	12.11
(9)(a), (b)	12.11
(10)	12.11
7.5	12.4
(3), (6)	12.12
7.6	12.4
7.23(1)	12.48
Pt VIII (rr 8.1–8.2)	2.68, 7.19
r 8.1	2.67, 5.61
(3)	2.74
8.2	2.75
Pt IX (rr 9.1–9.5)	7.19
r 9.1	8.53
(1)	2.63
9.2	2.63, 8.53
(a)(i)	8.54
(ii), (iv), (vi), (viii)	8.55
9.2A	2.63, 8.53, 8.54, 15.10
9.3	8.53
9.5	2.63
(1)	8.55
10.2	11.27
10.8(2)(b)	11.28
10.9	11.24, 11.29, 12.9, 12.42, 12.44, 12.46
(a), (b)	11.27
10.10	5.38
10.17	11.24
Appendix 1	2.8
Form M7(a)–(e)	3.10
Form M10	11.26
Form M11	4.9, 4.37, 4.82, 4.84, 4.85, 4.140, 4.150, 4.152, 4.161
Form M13	4.9, 4.37, 4.82, 4.84, 4.85, 4.150, 4.152, 4.161
Form M15	111
Form M16, M20	4.199
Form M19	4.9
Appendix 2	3.10
para 1(m)	2.9, 2.36
Appendix 3	7.10, 8.127
Family Provision (Intestate Succession) Order 1993, SI 1993/2906	6.8, *555*, *556*
Foster Placement (Children) Regulations 1991, SI 1991/910	9.8
Guardians Ad Litem and Reporting Officers (Panels) Regulations 1991, SI 1991/2051	8.101
High Court and County Courts Jurisdiction Order 1991, SI 1991/724	
art 2	5.40
(1)(a)	12.33
(3)	5.31
7(5)	6.29
9(1)(b)(i)	6.29
Insolvency Rules 1986, SI 1986/1925	
r 6.200	4.273

	PARA
Insolvency Rules 1986—contd	
r 12(3)	4.276, 4.280, 4.281
12.3(2)(a)	12.11
Intestate Succession (Interest and Capitalisation) Order 1977 (Amendment) Order 1983, SI 1983/1374	557
art 3	6.8
Schedule	
Table	6.8
Intestate Succession (Interest and Capitalisation) Order 1977, SI 1977/1491	557
art 3	6.8
Land Registration (Matrimonial Homes) Rules 1990, SI 1990/1360	
r 3	4.61
Land Registration Rules 1925, SI 1925/1093	
r 66	4.62
215(1), (4)	4.62
230(1)	4.62
Legal Advice and Assistance Regulations 1989, SI 1989/340	15.3
reg 9(4)(a)–(c)	15.5
11(1)	15.5
13(2)	15.5
14(1)	15.8
21(1)	15.8
22(5), (6)	15.8
30A(1)	15.14
Legal Advice and Assistance (Scope) Regulations 1989, SI 1989/550	15.3
reg 9	15.7
Schedule	15.7
Legal Aid in Civil Proceedings (Remuneration) Regulations 1994, SI 1994/228	15.3
Legal Aid in Family Proceedings (Remuneration) Regulations 1991, SI 1991/2038	15.3
Magistrates' Courts (Adoption) Rules 1984, SI 1984/611	7.56, 7.93
r 13	7.85
20	7.77
Sch 1	
Form 6, 13	7.58
Magistrates' Courts (Attachment of Earnings) Rules 1971, SI 1971/809	12.4
r 4	12.21
Magistrates' Courts Rules 1981, SI 1981/552	
r 14	12.21
55	12.16
59(1)	12.14
Matrimonial Causes (Costs) Rules 1988, SI 1988/1328	
r 15	15.19

	PARA
Parental Responsibility Agreement Regulations 1991, SI 1991/1478	7.5
Pensions Act 1995 (Commencement) (No 5) Order 1996, SI 1996/1675	
art 4	4.122
(2)	4.16, 4.29
5	4.122
Placement of Children with Parents etc Regulations 1991, SI 1991/893	8.77
Representations Procedure (Children) Regulations 1991, SI 1991/894	
reg 8	9.15
Review of Children's Cases Regulations 1991, SI 1991/895	
reg 4(1)	9.13
5, 7	9.13
Sch 2	9.13
Rules of the Supreme Court 1965, SI 1965/1776	2.1, 2.5, 2.6, 2.16
Ord 1	
r 4(1)	2.7
Ord 6	
r 2(2)	11.26
Ord 7	
r 2(2)	11.29
3	2.10
(1)	11.26
Ord 10	
r 1(2)	11.26
5	11.26
Ord 15	
r 13	6.30
Ord 18	
r 2	2.8
7	2.36
(1)	2.9
Ord 22	
r 14(1), (2)	15.18
Ord 24	2.18, 2.40
r 5(2)	2.44
7(1)	2.49
8	2.43, 2.49
16(3)	14.7
Ord 26	2.18
r 1(1)	2.43, 2.50
2(2)	2.50
3(1)	2.50
4, 6	2.50
Ord 27	
r 1, 2, 5	2.34
Ord 28	2.18, 2.20
r 1A(1)	2.10
2(2)	11.26
3(2), (3)	11.26
Ord 29	
r 1(1)	11.29
(2)	11.14, 11.15, 11.16, 11.17, 11.18, 11.27

xxxviii *Table of Statutory Instruments*

	PARA
Rules of the Supreme Court 1965—*contd*	
Ord 29—*contd*	
r 1(3)	11.14, 11.16, 11.18
Ord 30	
r 1	12.46
Ord 31	2.4
r 1	4.99, 5.38, 12.4, 12.36
Ord 32	
r 1	12.41
2(1)	12.43
(2)(a)–(h)	12.43
3	11.27, 11.29
4	11.31
6	2.69
7	2.52
11(1)(d)	11.29
(2)	11.29
Ord 35	
r 2(1)	2.69
Ord 38	
r 2(3)	2.28
13	2.18, 2.53
(2)	2.53
14	2.18
36	2.29, 2.56, 2.61
38	2.57
Ord 40	2.61, 2.62, 8.14
Ord 41	
r 5(2)	2.28
Ord 45	
r 3	12.4
(2)	12.37
5(1)(i)	12.40
6	12.40
7(2)	11.26, 11.27, 11.28, 11.29, 11.49, 14.2
(4)	11.26, 11.27, 11.28, 11.29, 11.47, 14.2
(6), (7)	14.2, 14.11
11	12.37
Ord 46	
r 2	12.37
3	12.38
4	12.37
5	12.4
6	12.38
Ord 48	12.6
r 1(1), (2)	12.7
3	12.8
Ord 49	12.4
r 1(1)	12.24
(2)	12.25
2(a)–(d)	12.24
3(1)(a), (b)	12.25
(2)	12.25
4(1), (2)	12.27
5	12.27
Ord 50	12.4

	PARA
Rules of the Supreme Court 1965—*contd*	
Ord 450—*contd*	
r 1(2), (3)	12.31
2	12.31
3	12.32
9A	12.33
Ord 51	12.4
r 2	12.46
Ord 52	
r 4(2)	14.5, 14.7
(3)	14.5, 14.7, 14.11
6(1)	14.4
(a)	14.9
(3)	14.5
(4)	14.8, 14.9
(5)	14.9
7	14.12
8	14.14
(1)	14.11
Ord 53	2.4, 2.11, 7.33, 9.22, 9.30
r 3(2)	2.7
(4), (6)	9.23
(7)	9.24
(10)(a), (b)	9.28
4	11.49
(1)	9.31
5	2.7
(3), (5)	9.27
6(4)	9.27, 9.29
7	9.23
8	9.28
13	9.23
14(1)	9.26
(12)	9.27
(42)	9.29
Ord 55	8.122
Ord 58	
r 1	2.68, 2.74
Ord 59	2.75, 5.61, 10.83
r 1B	2.2
3(1)	2.68
10(2), (3)	2.68
11(2)	2.69
Ord 62	
Pt II	15.15
r 3	15.20
(3)	15.15, 15.17
(5)	15.15
9(1)(d)	15.18
10(1)	15.16
11	15.19
14	15.18
5	11.29
8	11.26, 14.2
Ord 80	
r 1, 2	2.63
Ord 90	7.19

	PARA
Rules of the Supreme Court 1965—*contd*	
Ord 99	2.20
r 2	6.29
3(1)–(3)	6.30
r 4	6.31
(2)	6.30
5	6.31
(1)	6.30
(2)(a)–(d)	6.30

	PARA
Rules of the Supreme Court 1965—*contd*	
Ord 99—*contd*	
r 7, 8	6.30
Appendix A	
Form 85	14.11
Stamp Duty (Exempt Instruments) Regulations 1987, SI 1987/516	
para H	4.248

Table of Cases

PARA

A

A (a minor), Re (1979) 2 FLR 173, 10 Fam Law 49, CA 7.83
A (a minor), Re [1991] FCR 569, [1991] 2 FLR 394, [1992] Fam Law 64,
 CA 8.8, 8.21
A, Re [1991] FCR 844, [1991] 2 FLR 473, [1991] Fam Law 476 .... 8.72
A (a minor), Re [1993] 2 FLR 645, sub nom R (a minor), Re [1994] 1 FCR 104,
 [1993] 31 LS Gaz R 38, 137 Sol Jo LB 180, CA 7.88, 8.31
A (a minor: paternity refusal of blood tests), Re [1994] 2 FLR 463, [1994]
 Fam Law 622, sub nom Re GW [1994] 2 FCR 908, CA 7.55, 10.66
A (a minor), Re [1995] 3 All ER 401, [1995] 1 WLR 482, [1995] 2 FCR
 114, [1995] 1 FLR 335, 138 Sol Jo LB 228, CA 8.83
A (section 8 order: grandparents' application), Re [1996] 1 FCR 467,
 [1995] 2 FLR 153, [1995] Fam Law 540, CA 8.30, 8.48
A (minors), Re. See JR v Merton London Borough
A v A [1974] Fam 6, [1974] 1 All ER 755, [1974] 2 WLR 106, 118 Sol Jo 77 .... 6.18
A v A (1979) 1 FLR 380, 10 Fam Law 116, CA 8.38
A v A (minors) [1995] 1 FCR 91, [1994] 1 FLR 669, [1994] Fam Law 431, CA 8.57
A v A (a minor) [1995] 1 FCR 309, [1994] 1 FLR 657, [1994] Fam Law 368 .... 5.56
A v A [1995] 2 FCR 137, [1995] 1 FLR 345, [1995] Fam Law 242 .... 4.28, 4.60
A v A (costs: appeal) [1996] 1 FCR 186, [1996] 1 FLR 14, [1996] Fam
 Law 79 .... 4.27, 15.18
A v A and Newham London Borough Council [1993] 1 FCR 870 .... 8.47
A v Berkshire County Council [1989] FCR 180, [1989] 1 FLR 273, [1988]
 Fam Law 385; affd [1989] FCR 184, [1989] 1 FLR 273, [1989] Fam
 Law 184, CA 7.36
A v Liverpool City Council [1982] AC 363, [1981] 2 All ER 385, [1981]
 2 WLR 948, 79 LGR 621, 2 FLR 222, 145 JP 318, 125 Sol Jo 396,
 HL 7.33, 11.6
A v M and Walsall Metropolitan Borough Council [1994] 1 FCR 606, [1993]
 2 FLR 244, [1993] Fam Law 619 .... 8.89
A and B (minors) (No 2), Re [1995] 3 FCR 449, [1995] 1 FLR 351 .... 8.3, 8.14
AB (a minor), Re [1995] 1 FCR 280, [1995] 1 FLR 181, [1995] Fam Law 62 .... 2.59,
 8.132
AB (adoption: shared residence order), Re [1996] 1 FCR 633, [1996] 1 FLR 27,
 [1995] Fam Law 663 .... 8.57
Abbott (a bankrupt), Re, ex p Trustee of the Property of the Bankrupt v
 Abbott [1983] Ch 45, [1982] 3 All ER 181, [1982] 3 WLR 86, 126 Sol
 Jo 345 .... 4.265
Abdi v Jama (contempt: committal) [1996] 2 FCR 658, [1996] 1 FLR 407,
 [1996] Fam Law 276, CA 14.11
Abram, Re [1996] 2 FLR 379, [1996] Fam Law 666 .... 6.37
Adams v Adams (1965) 109 Sol Jo 899 .... 11.43, A.16
Adams v Riley [1988] QB 372, [1988] 1 All ER 89, [1988] 2 WLR 127,
 131 Sol Jo 1514, [1987] LS Gaz R 3341, [1987] NLJ Rep 1086 .... 15.27

xlii *Table of Cases*

PARA

Adeoso (otherwise Ametepe) v Adeoso [1981] 1 All ER 107, [1980] 1 WLR
 1535, 124 Sol Jo 847, CA 11.9, A.5
Administrative Directive [1992] 2 FCR 601, [1992] 2 FLR 503 .... 8.122
Ainsbury v Millington [1986] 1 All ER 73, [1986] 1 FLR 331, CA; affd
 [1987] 1 All ER 929, [1987] 1 WLR 379n, 131 Sol Jo 361, [1987]
 LS Gaz R 1241, HL 11.7, 11.32, 11.42
Al Nahkel for Contracting and Trading Ltd v Lowe [1986] QB 235, [1986]
 1 All ER 729, [1986] 2 WLR 317, 130 Sol Jo 130, [1986] NLJ Rep 164 .... 12.49
Allington v Allington [1985] FLR 586, [1985] Fam Law 157, CA 8.7, 8.21
Alston v Alston [1946] P 203, [1946] 2 All ER 62, 115 LJP 70, 90 Sol Jo
 530, 175 LT 107, 62 TLR 450 .... 11.4
Ancliffe v Ancliffe [1980] CA Transcript 520 .... 11.34
Anderson v Anderson [1984] FLR 566, [1984] Fam Law 183, 14 HLR 141, CA .. 11.38
Andrew v Andrew [1990] 2 FLR 376, [1991] Fam Law 146 .... 11.1
Angelic Wings, The. See Third Chandris Shipping Corpn v Unimarine SA
Ansah v Ansah [1977] Fam 138, [1977] 2 All ER 638, [1977] 2 WLR 760,
 121 Sol Jo 118, CA 11.19, 11.20, 11.21,
 14.10, 14.12, A.74, A.75, A.84
Arif (Mohamed) (an infant), Re [1968] Ch 643, [1968] 2 WLR 1290, sub nom
 Re A (an infant), Hanif v Secretary of State for Home Affairs [1968] 2 All
 ER 145, 112 Sol Jo 295, CA 11.6
Ashley v Blackman [1988] Fam 85, [1988] 3 WLR 222, [1988] FCR 699,
 [1988] 2 FLR 278, [1988] Fam Law 430, 132 Sol Jo 897, [1988] 38 LS
 Gaz R 52 .... 4.20
Aslam v Singh [1987] 1 FLR 122, [1986] Fam Law 362, CA 14.11
Associated Provincial Picture Houses Ltd v Wednesbury Corpn [1948] 1 KB 223,
 [1947] 2 All ER 680, 45 LGR 635, 112 JP 55, [1948] LJR 190, 92 Sol
 Jo 26, 177 LT 641, 63 TLR 623, CA 9.30, 10.85
Atkinson v Atkinson [1995] 2 FLR 356, [1995] Fam Law 604, sub nom A v A
 [1995] 2 FCR 353; affd [1995] 3 FCR 788, [1996] 1 FLR 51, [1996] Fam
 Law 18, CA 4.19, 4.40, 4.73, 4.104
Attar v Attar [1985] FLR 649, [1985] Fam Law 252 .... 2.43
Attar v Attar (No 2) [1985] FLR 653, [1985] Fam Law 252 .... 4.25

B

B (a minor), Re (1983) 4 FLR 683, 13 Fam Law 176, CA 11.38
B, Re [1989] FCR 191, [1988] 1 FLR 484 .... 9.35
B (a minor), Re [1991] FCR 414, [1991] 2 FLR 405, [1991] Fam Law 305, CA 8.21
B (minors), Re [1991] FCR 976, [1992] 1 FLR 140, [1992] Fam Law 148, CA 8.27
B (minors), Re [1992] Fam 162, [1992] 3 All ER 867, [1992] 3 WLR 113,
 [1992] 1 FCR 555, [1992] 2 FLR 1, [1992] Fam Law 384, CA 8.41,
 11.13, 11.17, 13.1
B (a minor), Re [1993] Fam 142, [1993] 1 All ER 931, [1993] 2 WLR 20,
 [1992] 2 FCR 617, [1993] 1 FLR 191, [1993] Fam Law 26, CA 8.17
B (minors) (termination of contract: paramount consideration), Re [1993]
 Fam 301, [1993] 3 All ER 524, [1993] 3 WLR 63, 91 LGR 311, [1993]
 1 FCR 363, [1993] 1 FLR 543, [1993] Fam Law 291, [1993] 5 LS Gaz R
 42, 137 Sol Jo LB 13, CA 8.89
B (a minor), Re [1993] 1 FCR 565, [1993] 1 FLR 815, [1993] Fam Law 335 .... 8.94
B (minors), Re [1993] 2 FCR 24, sub nom Barking and Dagenham London
 Borough Council v O [1993] Fam 295, [1993] 4 All ER 59, [1993] 3
 WLR 493, [1993] 2 FLR 651, [1993] Fam Law 670 .... 8.72
B (a minor), Re [1993] 1 FLR 421, [1993] Fam Law 128 .... 8.68
B (a minor), Re [1994] 1 FCR 905, [1994] 2 FLR 269, [1994] Fam Law 614 .... 8.32
B (minors), Re [1994] 2 FCR 812, [1994] 2 FLR 1, [1994] Fam Law 491,
 CA 8.22, 8.33
B (a minor), Re [1995] 1 WLR 232, [1995] 1 FCR 142, [1994] 2 FLR 707, CA 9.12

Table of Cases xliii

PARA

B (T) (a minor), Re [1995] 2 FCR 240, CA 8.21
B (a minor) (contempt: evidence), Re [1996] 1 WLR 627, [1996] 1 FCR 158,
  [1996] 1 FLR 239, [1996] Fam Law 147, [1995] 44 LS Gaz R 30, 140 Sol
  Jo LB 12 .... 14.8, 14.9
B (a minor) (supervision order: parental undertaking), Re [1996] 1 WLR 716,
  [1996] 3 FCR 446, [1996] 1 FLR 676, [1996] Fam Law 267, CA 4.146, 8.84
B (minors) (change of surname), Re [1996] 2 FCR 304, [1996] 1 FLR 791,
  [1996] Fam Law 346, 140 Sol Jo LB 28, CA 8.40
B (care: expert witness), Re [1996] 1 FLR 667, [1996] Fam Law 347, CA .. 2.55, 8.132
B (parentage), Re [1996] 2 FLR 15, [1996] Fam Law 536 .... 7.42
B v B [1978] Fam 26, [1978] 1 All ER 821, [1978] 2 WLR 160, 121 Sol Jo 759,
  CA 11.8, 11.40
B v B [1978] Fam 181, [1979] 1 All ER 801, [1978] 3 WLR 624, 122 Sol Jo
  643 .... 2.40
B v B [1988] 2 FLR 490, [1988] Fam Law 435 .... 5.7
B v B (financial provision) [1989] FCR 146, [1989] 1 FLR 119, [1989] Fam
  Law 105, [1989] NLJR 186 .... 2.39, 2.43
B v B [1991] FCR 1, [1991] 1 FLR 402, [1991] Fam Law 174 .... 8.21
B v B [1991] FCR 386, [1991] 2 FLR 588, [1992] Fam Law 58, CA 14.10
B v B (grandparent: residence order) [1993] 1 FCR 211, [1992] 2 FLR 327,
  [1992] Fam Law 490 .... 8.12
B v B [1994] 1 FCR 805, [1994] 1 FLR 323n, [1994] Fam Law 377 .... 2.22
B v B [1994] 1 FCR 885, [1994] 1 FLR 219 .... 4.72
B v B (minors) [1994] 2 FCR 667, [1994] 2 FLR 489, [1994] Fam Law 613,
  [1994] 21 LS Gaz R 40, CA 8.3, 8.5, 8.21
B v B [1995] 1 FLR 9, [1995] Fam Law 70, sub nom SB v PB [1995] 2 FCR 62 ..... 4.34
B v B (P Ltd intervening) (No 2) [1995] 2 FCR 670, [1995] 1 FLR 374,
  [1995] Fam Law 244, CA 4.178
B v B (No 2) [1995] 2 FCR 827, [1995] 1 FLR 913, [1995] Fam Law 408 .... 2.53
B v Derbyshire County Council [1992] 2 FCR 14, [1992] 1 FLR 538, [1992]
  Fam Law 287 .... 2.32
B v Miller & Co [1996] 3 FCR 435, [1996] 2 FLR 23, [1996] Fam Law 466 .... 4.143
B and G (minors), Re [1985] FLR 134, [1985] Fam Law 58; affd [1985] FLR
  493, [1985] Fam Law 127, CA 8.21
BA, Re [1985] FLR 1008, [1985] Fam Law 306 .... 7.80
B-T v B-T [1990] FCR 654, [1990] 2 FLR 1, [1990] Fam Law 294 .... 2.72
Baggott v Baggott [1986] 1 FLR 377, [1986] Fam Law 129, CA 11.38, 11.39
Baker v Baker [1996] 1 FCR 567, [1995] 2 FLR 829, [1996] Fam Law 80, CA 4.28
Balfour v Balfour [1919] 2 KB 571, 88 LJKB 1054, [1918-19] All ER Rep
  860, 63 Sol Jo 661, 121 LT 346, 35 TLR 609, CA 4.165
Bamgbose v Daniel [1955] AC 107, [1954] 3 All ER 263, [1954] 3 WLR 561,
  98 Sol Jo 732, PC 6.9
Barclays Bank plc v O'Brien [1994] 1 AC 180, [1993] 4 All ER 417, [1993]
  3 WLR 786, [1994] 1 FCR 357, [1994] 1 FLR 1, [1994] Fam Law 78,
  26 HLR 75, [1993] 46 LS Gaz R 37, [1993] NLJR 1511, 137 Sol Jo LB
  240, HL 2.35
Barder v Caluori [1988] AC 20, [1987] 2 All ER 440, [1987] 2 WLR 1350,
  [1987] 2 FLR 480, [1988] Fam Law 18, 131 Sol Jo 776, [1987] LS Gaz
  R 2046, [1987] NLJ Rep 497, HL 2.66, 2.70
Barrett v Barrett [1988] FCR 707, [1988] 2 FLR 516, [1988] Fam Law 475,
  CA 4.23
Barrister, a (No 1 of 1991), Re [1993] QB 293, [1992] 3 All ER 429, [1992]
  3 WLR 662, 95 Cr App Rep 288, [1992] 24 LS Gaz R 31, [1992] NLJR
  636, 136 Sol Jo LB 147, CA 15.19
Barry v Barry [1992] Fam 140, [1992] 3 All ER 405, [1992] 2 WLR 799,
  [1992] 2 FLR 233, [1992] Fam Law 485 .... 1.2, 4.7, 4.55, 4.99
Basham, Re [1987] 1 All ER 405, [1986] 1 WLR 1498, [1987] 2 FLR 264,
  [1987] Fam Law 310, 130 Sol Jo 986, [1987] LS Gaz R 112 .... 5.25, 6.8

PARA

Bassett v Bassett [1975] Fam 76, [1975] 1 All ER 513, [1975] 2 WLR 270,
119 Sol Jo 30, CA 11.35, 11.38, A.58
Bawden v Bawden [1979] QB 419n, [1978] 3 All ER 1216, [1978] 3 WLR 798n,
74 LGR 347, 143 JP 114, CA 14.13, A.15
Bayer AG v Winter [1986] 1 All ER 733, [1986] 1 WLR 497, [1986] FSR 323,
130 Sol Jo 246, [1986] LS Gaz R 974, [1986] NLJ Rep 187, CA 4.173, 12.49
Baynham v Baynham [1969] 1 All ER 305, [1968] 1 WLR 1890, 112 Sol Jo 839,
209 Estates Gazette 379, CA 11.45
Beach v Beach [1995] 2 FCR 526, [1995] 2 FLR 160, [1995] Fam Law 545 .... 3.28,
4.28, 4.166
Beard v Beard [1981] 1 All ER 783, [1981] 1 WLR 369, 11 Fam Law 84,
CA 11.1, 11.4, 11.41
Beaumont, Re, Martin v Midland Bank Trust Co Ltd [1980] Ch 444, [1980]
1 All ER 266, [1979] 3 WLR 818, 123 Sol Jo 803 .... 6.19, 6.27
Beese (Managers of Kimpton Church of England Primary School) v Woodhouse
[1970] 1 All ER 769, [1970] 1 WLR 586, 114 Sol Jo 132, CA 11.20
Belcher v Belcher [1995] 2 FCR 143, [1995] 1 FLR 916, [1995] Fam Law 408,
CA 4.65
Belton v Belton [1987] 2 FLR 343, [1987] Fam Law 344, 151 JP 679, CA 8.38
Benson v Benson [1996] 1 FLR 692, [1996] Fam Law 351 .... 2.72
Berkshire County Council v C [1993] Fam 205, [1993] 2 WLR 475, [1993]
1 FCR 608, [1993] 1 FLR 569 .... 8.96
Berkshire County Council v Y [1994] 2 FCR 367, [1994] 2 FLR 699, [1994]
Fam Law 615 .... 8.121
Bernard v Josephs [1982] Ch 391, [1982] 3 All ER 162, [1982] 2 WLR 1052,
4 FLR 178, 126 Sol Jo 361, CA 5.16, 5.19
Besterman, Re, Besterman v Grusin [1984] Ch 458, [1984] 2 All ER 656,
[1984] 3 WLR 280, [1984] FLR 503, [1984] Fam Law 203, 128 Sol Jo 515,
CA 6.22
Birch v Birch (1883) 8 PD 163, 52 LJP 88, 32 WR 96 .... 12.39
Birmingham City Council v D [1994] 2 FCR 245, [1994] 2 FLR 502, [1994]
Fam Law 610 .... 8.74
Birmingham City Council v H [1993] 1 FCR 247, [1992] 2 FLR 323 .... 8.58
Birmingham City Council v H (a minor) [1994] 2 AC 212, [1994] 1 All ER 12,
[1994] 2 WLR 31, 92 LGR 349, [1994] 1 FCR 896, [1994] 1 FLR 224,
[1994] 6 LS Gaz R 36, [1994] NLJR 17, 138 Sol Jo LB 13, HL 8.2
Birmingham City Council v M [1994] 2 FCR 245, [1994] 2 FLR 502, [1994]
Fam Law 610 .... 8.74
Bishop v Plumley [1991] 1 All ER 236, [1991] 1 WLR 582, [1991] 1 FLR 121,
[1991] Fam Law 61, [1990] NLJR 1153, CA 6.19
Bluffield v Curtis [1988] 1 FLR 170, [1988] Fam Law 20, CA 14.12
Bowen-Buscarlet's Will Trusts, Re, Nathan v Bowen-Buscarlet [1972] Ch 463,
[1971] 3 All ER 636, [1971] 3 WLR 742, 115 Sol Jo 872 .... 6.6
Boylan v Boylan (1980) 11 Fam Law 76, CA 11.49, 14.10, A.84
Bradshaw v Bradshaw [1897] P 24, 61 JP 8, 66 LJP 31, 45 WR 142, [1895-9]
All ER Rep 1155, 75 LT 391, 13 TLR 82 .... A.7
Bramblevale Ltd, Re [1970] Ch 128, [1969] 3 All ER 1062, [1969] 3 WLR 699,
[1971] 3 WLR 821n, 113 Sol Jo 775, CA 12.11, 14.9
Brent v Brent [1975] Fam 1, [1974] 2 All ER 1211, [1974] 3 WLR 296,
118 Sol Jo 442 .... 11.4, 11.41
Brent v Brent (1978) 9 Fam Law 59, CA 4.94
Brill v Proud [1984] Fam Law 59, CA 6.23
Brooks v Brooks [1996] AC 375, [1995] 3 All ER 257, [1995] 3 WLR 141,
[1995] 3 FCR 214, [1995] 2 FLR 13, [1995] Fam Law 545, [1995] 31
LS Gaz R 34, [1995] NLJR 995, 139 Sol Jo LB 165, HL 4.79, 4.108
Brown v Brown [1959] P 86, [1959] 2 All ER 266, [1959] 2 WLR 776, 103
Sol Jo 414, CA 6.37
Browne v Browne [1989] 1 FLR 291, [1989] Fam Law 147, CA 4.19, 4.80

PARA

Buckinghamshire County Council v M [1994] 1 FCR 859, [1994] 2 FLR 506, CA ... 8.3
Buckley v Crawford [1893] 1 QB 105, 57 JP 89, 62 LJQB 87, 5 R 125, 41 WR
    239, 37 Sol Jo 67, 67 LT 681, 9 TLR 85.. 12.11
Bunning, Re, Bunning v Salmon [1984] Ch 480, [1984] 3 All ER 1, [1984] 3 WLR
    265, [1985] FLR 1, [1985] Fam Law 21, 128 Sol Jo 516..................................... 6.22
Burgess v Burgess [1996] 2 FLR 34, [1996] Fam Law 465, CA................................ 4.188
Burke v Burke [1987] 2 FLR 71, [1987] Fam Law 201, 151 JP 404, CA............... 11.38,
    11.39, A.58
Burnett v Burnett [1936] P 1, 105 LJP 1, [1935] All ER Rep 490, 79 Sol Jo
    642, 153 LT 318, 51 TLR 574.. 4.78
Burnett v George [1993] 1 FCR 1012, [1992] 1 FLR 525, [1992] Fam Law
    156, CA... 11.33
Burns v Burns [1984] Ch 317, [1984] 1 All ER 244, [1984] 2 WLR 582,
    [1984] FLR 216, [1984] Fam Law 24, 128 Sol Jo 173, [1984] LS Gaz R
    893, CA... 5.23
Burris v Azadani [1995] 4 All ER 802, [1995] 1 WLR 1372, [1996] 1 FCR
    618, [1996] 1 FLR 266, [1996] Fam Law 145, [1995] NLJR 1330,
    CA... 11.33, A.16, A.68
Burrows v Iqbal (No 2) [1985] Fam Law 188, CA 14.11
Burton v Burton [1986] 2 FLR 419, [1986] Fam Law 330.. 4.278
Butler v Butler [1993] Fam 167, [1992] 4 All ER 833, [1992] 3 WLR 813,
    [1993] 1 FCR 405, [1993] 1 FLR 773, [1993] Fam Law 467, [1992] NLJR
    1339, CA 14.1
Butt v Butt [1987] 3 All ER 657, [1987] 1 WLR 1351, 131 Sol Jo 1286,
    [1987] LS Gaz R 2194, CA 11.34

C

C (an infant), Re [1959] Ch 363, [1958] 2 All ER 656, [1958] 3 WLR 309,
    102 Sol Jo 582.. 11.6
C (a minor), Re [1985] FLR 846, [1985] Fam Law 191, [1985] NLJ Rep 106 .... 7.38
C (a minor), Re [1986] 1 FLR 578, [1986] Fam Law 187, CA 14.10, 14.11
C (a minor) (adoption: conditions), Re [1989] AC 1, [1988] 1 All ER 705,
    [1988] 2 WLR 474, [1988] FCR 484, [1988] 2 FLR 159, [1988] Fam
    Law 428, 132 Sol Jo 334, [1988] 15 LS Gaz R 35, [1988] NLJR 64, HL 7.85
C (a minor), Re [1991] FCR 308, [1991] 2 FLR 438, [1992] Fam Law 14, CA 8.17
C, Re [1992] 1 FCR 169, [1992] 1 FLR 628, [1992] Fam Law 201, CA..................... 8.1
C (a minor) (care proceedings), Re [1992] 2 FCR 341, sub nom C v Solihull
    Metropolitan Borough Council [1993] 1 FLR 290, [1993] Fam Law
    189 .... 8.3, 8.58, 8.94
C (child cases: evidence and disclosure), Re (1994) 159 LG Rev 849, [1995]
    2 FCR 97, [1995] 1 FLR 204 .... 2.46, 2.57, 2.61, 8.132
C (a minor), Re [1994] 1 FCR 447 .... 8.94
C (a minor), Re [1994] 1 FCR 837, [1994] 1 FLR 26 .... 8.50
C (a minor), Re [1994] 2 FCR 1122 .... 5.60
C (a minor), Re [1995] 2 FCR 276, sub nom Re C (section 8 order: court welfare
    officer) [1995] 1 FLR 617, CA... 8.16
C (minors) (guardian ad litem:disclosure of report), Re [1995] 2 FCR 837,
    [1996] 1 FLR 61, [1996] Fam Law 78 .... 8.73
C (residence:child's application for leave), Re [1996] 1 FCR 461, [1995] 1
    FLR 927, [1995] Fam Law 472 .... 8.50
C (family assistance order), Re [1996] 1 FLR 424, [1996] Fam Law 202 .... 13.15
C (disclosure), Re [1996] 1 FLR 797, [1996] Fam Law 462 .... 8.101
C (care proceedings: disclosure), Re (1996) Times, 22 October, CA........................ 2.47
C v C (financial provision: personal damages) [1996] 1 FCR 283, [1995]
    2 FLR 171, [1995] Fam Law 605 .... 4.19, 4.20, 4.48
C v C [1988] FCR 411, [1988] 2 FLR 291, [1988] Fam Law 338, [1988] 10
    LS Gaz R 44, CA 8.21

xlvi *Table of Cases*

	PARA
C v C [1989] FCR 558, [1989] 1 FLR 11	4.40
C v C [1990] FCR 682, [1990] 1 FLR 462, [1990] Fam Law 220, CA	13.8
C v C [1991] FCR 254, [1991] 1 FLR 223, [1991] Fam Law 175, CA	8.21

C v Hackney London Borough Council [1995] 2 FCR 306, [1995] 2 FLR 681, [1996] Fam Law 23, CA 14.11
C v K (inherent powers: exclusion order) [1996] 3 FCR 488, [1996] 2 FLR 506 ... 11.7, 11.42, 11.43
C v S [1988] QB 135, [1987] 1 All ER 1230, [1987] 2 WLR 1108, [1987] 2 FLR 505, [1987] Fam Law 269; affd [1988] QB 135, [1987] 1 All ER 1230, [1987] 2 WLR 1108, [1987] 2 FLR 505, [1987] Fam Law 269, 131 Sol Jo 624, [1987] LS Gaz R 1410, CA 7.20
C v Salford City Council [1994] 2 FLR 926, [1995] Fam Law 65, sub nom Re P (a minor [1994] 2 FCR 1093 .... 8.48
CB (a minor), Re [1981] 1 All ER 16, [1981] 1 WLR 379, 79 LGR 153, 145 JP 90, 125 Sol Jo 219, CA 7.28
CB (a minor), Re [1992] 1 FCR 320, CA 8.16
CB (a minor), Re [1993] 1 FCR 440, [1993] 1 FLR 920, [1993] Fam Law 462 .... 7.6
CE (a minor), Re [1995] 1 FCR 387, [1995] 1 FLR 26, [1995] Fam Law 67 .... 8.99
CH (contact: parentage), Re [1996] 1 FCR 768, [1996] 1 FLR 569, [1996] Fam Law 274 .... 8.27
CN (a minor), Re [1992] 2 FCR 401, sub nom Kent County Council v C [1993] Fam 57, [1993] 1 All ER 719, [1992] 3 WLR 808, [1993] 1 FLR 308, [1993] Fam Law 133 .... 8.3, 8.68, 8.94
CS (expert witnesses), Re [1996] 2 FLR 115, [1996] Fam Law 538 .... 8.132
CT (a minor), Re [1992] 2 FCR 92 .... 8.55
Cairnes, Re, Howard v Cairnes (1982) 4 FLR 225, 12 Fam Law 177 .... 6.32
Calderbank v Calderbank [1976] Fam 93, [1975] 3 All ER 333, [1975] 3 WLR 586, 119 Sol Jo 490, CA 15.18
Callaghan, Re [1985] Fam 1, [1984] 3 All ER 790, [1984] 3 WLR 1076, [1985] FLR 116, [1985] Fam Law 28, 128 Sol Jo 705 .... 6.26
Camm v Camm (1982) 4 FLR 577, 13 Fam Law 112, CA 3.28, 4.166
Cantliff v Jenkins [1978] Fam 47n, [1978] 1 All ER 836, [1978] 2 WLR 177n, 121 Sol Jo 849, CA 11.8, 11.40
Caprice v Boswell [1986] Fam Law 52, 149 JP 703, CA 14.9
Capron v Capron [1927] P 243, 96 LJP 151, 71 Sol Jo 711, 137 LT 568, 43 TLR 667 .... 12.39
Carpenter v Carpenter [1987] CA Transcript G25, CA 11.47
Carpenter v Carpenter [1988] 1 FLR 121, [1988] Fam Law 56, CA 11.34, 11.47, A.71
Chadda v Chadda (1980) 11 Fam Law 142, CA 11.39
Chaggar v Chaggar [1995] 4 All ER 795, [1996] 1 FLR 450, [1996] Fam Law 281 .... 15.21
Chakravorty v Braganza (1983) Times, 12 October 14.5
Chamberlain v Chamberlain [1974] 1 All ER 33, [1973] 1 WLR 1557, 4 Fam Law 46, 117 Sol Jo 893, CA 5.56
Chamberlain v de la Mare (1982) 4 FLR 434; revsd 4 FLR 434, 13 Fam Law 15, CA 8.38
Chanel v FGM Cosmetics Ltd [1981] FSR 471 .... 14.5
Chanel Ltd v F W Woolworth & Co Ltd [1981] 1 All ER 745, [1981] 1 WLR 485, 125 Sol Jo 202, CA 11.34
Chaudhry v Chaudhry [1987] 1 FLR 347, [1987] Fam Law 122, CA 11.37, 11.44
Cherrington, Re [1984] 2 All ER 285, [1984] 1 WLR 772, [1984] FLR 559, [1984] Fam Law 181, 128 Sol Jo 302, [1984] CLY 3660 .... 6.4
Cheshire County Council v M [1992] 2 FCR 817, [1993] 1 FLR 463, [1993] Fam Law 207 .... 8.22
Cheshire County Council v P [1993] 2 FCR 397, sub nom sub nom Re P (minors) [1993] 2 FLR 742, CA 8.3, 8.94
Chief Constable of the North Wales Police v Evans [1982] 3 All ER 141, [1982] 1 WLR 1155, 147 JP 6, 126 Sol Jo 549, [1982] LS Gaz R 1257, HL: 9.22

PARA

Chiltern District Council v Keane [1985] 2 All ER 118, [1985] 1 WLR 619,
83 LGR 573, 129 Sol Jo 206, CA 14.5, 14.7, 14.11
Chocoladefabriken Lindt and Sprungli AG v Nestlé Co Ltd [1978] RPC 287 .... 2.46
Church's Trustee v Hibbard [1902] 2 Ch 784, 72 LJ Ch 46, 51 WR 293, 87
LT 412, CA 14.11
Churchard v Churchard [1984] FLR 635, CA 13.2
Churchman v Joint Shop Stewards' Committee of Workers of Port of London
[1972] 3 All ER 603, [1972] 1 WLR 1094, [1972] ICR 222, 116 Sol Jo
617, CA 14.14
Cinderby v Cinderby (1978) 8 Fam Law 244, 122 Sol Jo 436, CA 14.11
Citro (a bankrupt), Re [1991] Ch 142, [1990] 3 All ER 952, [1990] 3 WLR
880, [1991] 1 FLR 71, [1990] Fam Law 428, 134 Sol Jo 806, [1990] 28
LS Gaz R 43, [1990] NLJR 1073, CA 4.254
Clark v Clark [1989] FCR 101, [1989] 1 FLR 174, [1989] Fam Law 111,
[1988] NLJR 101 .... 12.39, 15.35
Clark v Clark (No 2) [1991] 1 FLR 179, [1991] Fam Law 58, [1990] NLJR
206 .... 12.39, 15.12
Clarke v Clarke [1990] FCR 641, [1990] 2 FLR 115, [1990] Fam Law 331, CA ... 14.11
Cleveland County Council v F [1995] 2 All ER 236, [1995] 1 WLR 785,
[1995] 3 FCR 174, [1995] 1 FLR 797, [1995] Fam Law 473 .... 8.73
Clutton v Clutton [1991] 1 All ER 340, [1991] 1 WLR 359, [1991] FCR 265,
[1991] 1 FLR 242, [1991] Fam Law 304, [1990] NLJR 1682,
CA 4.39, 4.70, 4.73
Coleman, Re, Coleman v Coleman [1976] Ch 1, [1975] 1 All ER 675,
[1975] 2 WLR 213, 119 Sol Jo 86 .... 6.3
Collins, Re [1990] Fam 56, [1990] 2 All ER 47, [1990] 2 WLR 161, [1990]
FCR 433, [1990] 2 FLR 72, [1990] Fam Law 337, 134 Sol Jo 262 .... 6.16, 6.25
Columbia Picture Industries Inc v Robinson [1987] Ch 38, [1986] 3 All ER
338, [1986] 3 WLR 542, [1986] FSR 367, 130 Sol Jo 766 .... 4.189
Colverson v Bloomfield (1885) 29 Ch D 341, 54 LJ Ch 817, 33 WR 889, 52
LT 478, CA 12.49
Comet Products UK Ltd v Hawkex Plastics Ltd [1971] 2 QB 67, [1971] 1 All
ER 1141, [1971] 2 WLR 361, 114 Sol Jo 975, CA 14.8
Coombes v Smith [1986] 1 WLR 808, [1987] 1 FLR 352, [1987] Fam Law
123, 130 Sol Jo 482, [1986] LS Gaz R 2238 .... 5.25
Corbett v Corbett (otherwise Ashley) [1971] P 83, [1970] 2 All ER 33,
[1970] 2 WLR 1306, 114 Sol Jo 131 .... A.21
Cornick v Cornick (No 2) [1996] 1 FCR 179, [1995] 2 FLR 490, [1996]
Fam Law 19, CA 4.20, 4.139
Council of Civil Service Unions v Minister for the Civil Service [1985] AC
374, [1984] 3 All ER 935, [1984] 3 WLR 1174, [1985] ICR 14, 128 Sol
Jo 837, [1985] LS Gaz R 437, sub nom R v Secretary of State for Foreign
and Commonwealth Affairs, ex p Council of Civil Service Unions [1985]
IRLR 28, HL 9.30
Coventry, Re, Coventry v Coventry [1980] Ch 461, [1979] 3 All ER 815,
[1979] 3 WLR 802, 123 Sol Jo 606, CA 6.20, 6.25
Cowcher v Cowcher [1972] 1 All ER 943, [1972] 1 WLR 425, 116 Sol Jo
142 .... 4.257, 5.16
Crabb v Arun District Council [1976] Ch 179, [1975] 3 All ER 865, [1975]
3 WLR 847, 119 Sol Jo 711, CA 5.25
Cramer v Cramer [1987] 1 FLR 116, [1986] Fam Law 333, [1986] LS Gaz R
1996, CA 3.13
Crawford, Re (1982) 4 FLR 273 .... 6.23, 6.34
Crisp v Mullings (1975) 239 Estates Gazette 119, CA 5.19
Crispin's Will Trusts, Re, Arkwright v Thurley [1975] Ch 245, [1974] 3 All
ER 772, [1974] 3 WLR 657, 118 Sol Jo 739, CA 6.8
Crittenden v Crittenden [1991] FCR 70, [1990] 2 FLR 361, [1990] Fam Law
432, CA 4.67

xlviii *Table of Cases*

PARA

Crosthwaite v Crosthwaite [1989] 2 FLR 86, [1989] Fam Law 315, CA 4.99, 12.36
Croydon London Borough Council v A [1992] Fam 169, [1992] 3 All ER
788, [1992] 3 WLR 267, [1992] 1 FCR 522, [1992] 2 FLR 341, [1992]
Fam Law 441, [1992] 16 LS Gaz R 28, 136 Sol Jo LB 69 .... 2.75,
8.36, 8.84, 13.11
Croydon London Borough v A (No 3) [1992] 2 FCR 481, [1992] 2 FLR 350,
[1993] Fam Law 70 .... 8.23
Crutcher v Crutcher (1978) Times, 18 July, 128 NLJ 981 .... 11.3
Cutts v Head [1984] Ch 290, [1984] 1 All ER 597, [1984] 2 WLR 349, 128
Sol Jo 117, [1984] LS Gaz R 509, CA 2.46

D

D (minors), Re [1973] Fam 209, [1973] 3 All ER 1001, [1973] 3 WLR 595,
138 JP 18, 117 Sol Jo 696 .... 7.81
D (a minor) (wardship: sterilisation), Re [1976] Fam 185, [1976] 1 All ER
326, [1976] 2 WLR 279, 119 Sol Jo 696 .... 11.6
D (a minor), Re [1987] 3 All ER 717, [1987] 1 WLR 1400, 86 LGR 442,
[1988] 1 FLR 131, [1988] Fam Law 89, 131 Sol Jo 1485, [1987] LS Gaz
R 3415, CA 9.18
D (a minor), Re [1992] 1 All ER 892, [1992] 1 WLR 315, [1992] 1 FLR 637,
CA 8.41
D (a minor), Re [1992] 1 FCR 461, CA 7.85
D (minors), Re [1993] Fam 231, [1993] 2 All ER 693, [1993] 2 WLR 721,
[1993] 1 FCR 877, [1993] 1 FLR 932, [1993] Fam Law 410, [1993]
NLJR 438, CA 8.18
D (a minor), Re [1993] 1 FCR 964, [1993] 2 FLR 1, [1993] Fam Law 465,
CA 8.25, 8.26
D, Re [1993] 2 FCR 88, [1993] 2 FLR 423, [1993] Fam Law 518 .... 8.77
D (minors) (adoption reports: confidentiality), Re [1996] AC 593, [1995]
4 All ER 385, [1995] 3 WLR 483, [1996] 1 FCR 205, [1995] 2 FLR
687, [1996] Fam Law 8, [1995] NLJR 1612, HL 7.91, 8.17
D (prohibited steps order), Re [1996] 2 FLR 273, [1996] Fam Law 605, CA 11.7
D v D (child of the family) (1981) 2 FLR 93, CA 6.18
D v D (1982) 4 FLR 82, 12 Fam Law 150, CA 11.38
D v D [1991] FCR 323, [1991] 2 FLR 34, [1991] Fam Law 365, CA 13.7
D v D (county court jurisdiction: injunction) [1993] 2 FLR 802, [1993] 37
LS Gaz R 49, 137 Sol Jo LB 199, CA 8.36
D v D [1994] 1 FCR 694 .... 8.26
D v D [1995] 3 FCR 183, [1995] 2 FLR 497, [1995] Fam Law 670 .... 2.53
D v Hereford and Worcester County Council [1991] Fam 14, [1991] 2 All
ER 177, [1991] 2 WLR 753, 89 LGR 524, [1991] FCR 56, [1991] 1 FLR
205, [1991] Fam Law 272 .... 7.6
D v M [1983] Fam 33, [1982] 3 All ER 897, [1982] 3 WLR 891, 126 Sol Jo
562, sub nom Dicocco v Milne 4 FLR 247, 12 Fam Law 210, CA 8.7, 8.21
D v Q [1990] Fam Law 302 .... 11.7
D v R [1995] 1 FCR 501, sub nom D, Re [1995] 1 FLR 495, [1995] Fam Law
239 .... 8.4, 8.32
DB and CB (minors), Re [1993] 2 FCR 607, [1993] 2 FLR 559, CA 7.31, 8.71
DH (a minor), Re [1994] 2 FCR 3, [1994] 1 FLR 679, [1994] Fam Law 433,
22 BMLR 146 .... 8.59, 8.69, 8.72, 8.132
DSV Silo-und Verwaltungsgesellschaft mbH v Sennar (Owners), The Sennar
[1985] 2 All ER 104, [1985] 1 WLR 490, [1985] 1 Lloyd's Rep 521, 129
Sol Jo 248, [1985] LS Gaz R 1863, [1985] NLJ Rep 316, HL 2.32
Danchevsky v Danchevsky [1975] Fam 17, [1974] 3 All ER 934, [1974] 3
WLR 709, 118 Sol Jo 701, CA 5.29, 14.10, 14.11
Dart v Dart [1996] 2 FLR 286, [1996] Fam Law 607, CA 1.2, 4.13,
4.15, 4.20, 4.27, 6.22

PARA

Daubney v Daubney [1976] Fam 267, [1976] 2 All ER 453, [1976] 2 WLR 959,
120 Sol Jo 330, CA 4.19
Davis v Davis [1993] 1 FCR 1002, [1993] 1 FLR 54, [1993] Fam Law 59, CA 6.22
Davis v Johnson [1979] AC 264, [1978] 1 All ER 1132, [1978] 2 WLR 553,
122 Sol Jo 178, HL 11.3, 11.8,
11.33, 11.40, 11.46, A.68
Davy-Chiesman v Davy-Chiesman [1984] Fam 48, [1984] 1 All ER 321,
[1984] 2 WLR 291, 127 Sol Jo 805, [1984] LS Gaz R 44, CA 15.12
Dawkins, Re, Dawkins v Judd [1986] 2 FLR 360, [1986] Fam Law 295 .... 6.35, 6.36
Day v Day [1980] Fam 29, [1979] 2 All ER 187, [1979] 2 WLR 681, 9 Fam
Law 54, 123 Sol Jo 251, CA 2.19
Dean v Dean [1987] FCR 96, [1987] 1 FLR 517, [1987] Fam Law 200,
CA 12.11, 14.9
Debenham, Re [1986] 1 FLR 404, [1986] Fam Law 101 .... 6.18
Delaney v Delaney [1991] FCR 161, [1990] 2 FLR 457, [1991] Fam Law 22,
CA 4.20
Delaney v Delaney [1996] QB 387, [1996] 1 All ER 367, [1996] 2 WLR 74,
[1996] 2 FCR 13, [1996] 1 FLR 458, [1996] Fam Law 207, CA 11.49, A.82
Delorey v Delorey (1967) 111 Sol Jo 757 .... 11.41
Dennis, Re, Dennis v Lloyds Bank Ltd [1981] 2 All ER 140, 124 Sol Jo 885,
131 NLJ 210 .... 6.20, 6.25, 6.28
Dennis v McDonald [1982] Fam 63, [1982] 1 All ER 590, [1982] 2 WLR
275, 3 FLR 409, 12 Fam Law 84, 126 Sol Jo 16, CA 11.46
Deraux v Deraux (1959) Times, 4 September 14.7
Derby & Co Ltd v Weldon (No 6) [1990] 3 All ER 263, [1990] 1 WLR 1139,
134 Sol Jo 1041, [1990] 28 LS Gaz R 45, [1990] NLJR 1001, CA 4.185
de Reneville (otherwise Sheridan) v de Reneville [1948] P 100, [1948] 1 All
ER 56, [1948] LJR 1761, 92 Sol Jo 83, 64 TLR 82, CA 6.2, 6.7,
A.3, A.11, A.12
Des Salles d'Epinoix v Des Salles d'Epinoix [1967] 2 All ER 539, [1967] 1
WLR 553, 111 Sol Jo 94, CA 11.1
Devon County Council v George [1989] AC 573, sub nom R v Devon County
Council, ex p G [1988] 3 WLR 49, 86 LGR 647, [1988] 2 FLR 411,
[1988] Fam Law 478, 152 JP 586, 132 Sol Jo 851, CA; revsd sub nom
Devon County Council v George [1989] AC 573, [1988] 3 WLR 1386,
87 LGR 413, [1989] 1 FLR 146, [1989] Fam Law 149, 153 JP 375,
[1989] 4 LS Gaz R 41, sub nom George v Devon County Council
[1988] 3 All ER 1002, HL 9.30
Devon County Council v S [1992] Fam 176, [1992] 3 All ER 793, [1992]
3 WLR 273, [1992] 1 FCR 550, [1992] 2 FLR 244, [1993] Fam Law 190 ...... 8.70
Devon County Council v S [1993] 2 FCR 36, [1993] 1 FLR 842, [1993] Fam
Law 620 .... 8.101
Devon County Council v S [1994] Fam 169, [1995] 1 All ER 243, [1994]
3 WLR 183, [1994] 2 FCR 409, [1994] 1 FLR 355, [1994] Fam Law
371 .... 7.31, 8.44
Dickens v Pattison [1985] FLR 610, [1985] Fam Law 163, 149 JP 271, 129
Sol Jo 31, [1985] LS Gaz R 438 .... 12.9
Dinch v Dinch [1987] 1 All ER 818, [1987] 1 WLR 252, [1987] 2 FLR 162,
[1987] Fam Law 267, 131 Sol Jo 296, [1987] LS Gaz R 1142, HL 4.142
Douglas's Will Trusts, Re, Lloyds Bank Ltd v Nelson [1959] 2 All ER 620,
[1959] 1 WLR 744, 103 Sol Jo 657; affd [1959] 3 All ER 785, [1959]
1 WLR 1212, 104 Sol Jo 126, CA 6.6
Drake v Whipp [1996] 2 FCR 296, [1996] 1 FLR 826, [1996] Fam Law 472,
28 HLR 531, CA 5.15, 5.27
Draskovic v Draskovic (1980) 11 Fam Law 87, 125 Sol Jo 306 .... 15.36
Dunning v United Liverpool Hospital's Board of Governors [1973] 2 All ER
454, 117 Sol Jo 167, sub nom Dunning v United Liverpool Hospitals'
Board of Governors [1973] 1 WLR 586, CA A.56

Table of Cases

PARA

Duo v Duo [1992] 3 All ER 121, sub nom Duo v Osborne (formerly Duo) [1992] 1 WLR 611, [1992] 2 FCR 583, [1992] 2 FLR 425, [1993] Fam Law 193, CA 11.47
Duxbury v Duxbury [1992] Fam 62n, [1990] 2 All ER 77, [1991] 3 WLR 639n, [1987] 1 FLR 7, [1987] Fam Law 13, CA 4.41
Dyer v Dyer (1788) 2 RR 14, 2 Cox Eq Cas 92, [1775-1802] All ER Rep 205 ...... 4.257

E

E (a minor), Re [1989] FCR 118, [1989] 1 FLR 126, [1989] Fam Law 108, CA 7.80
E (minors), Re [1990] FCR 921, [1990] 2 FLR 397, [1990] Fam Law 343, CA 7.80, 7.88
E, Re [1994] 1 FCR 584, [1994] 1 FLR 146, CA 8.89
E (a minor), Re [1994] 2 FCR 709, [1995] 1 FLR 392, [1995] Fam Law 121, CA 7.6, 13.10
E (a minor), Re [1995] 1 FCR 245, [1994] 2 FLR 548, [1995] Fam Law 9 .... 10.66
E v C (child maintenance) [1996] 1 FCR 612, [1996] 1 FLR 472, [1996] Fam Law 205 .... 4.20, 4.22
E v E [1989] FCR 591, [1990] 2 FLR 233, [1990] Fam Law 297 .... 4.85
E v E [1994] 2 FCR 773, [1995] 1 FLR 224, CA 11.38
EC (disclosure of material), Re [1996] 2 FLR 123, [1996] Fam Law 603 .... 1.7, 8.73
Edgar v Edgar [1980] 3 All ER 887, [1980] 1 WLR 1410, 2 FLR 19, 124 Sol Jo 809, CA 3.28, 4.28, 4.166, 4.168
Edgcome, Re, ex p Edgcome [1902] 2 KB 403, 71 LJKB 722, 9 Mans 227, 50 WR 678, [1900-3] All ER Rep 862, 46 Sol Jo 649, 87 LT 108, 18 TLR 734, CA 12.13
Edmonds v Edmonds [1965] 1 All ER 379n, [1965] 1 WLR 58, 108 Sol Jo 1047 .... 12.17
Egan v Egan (1971) 115 Sol Jo 673 .... 14.11
Elder v Elder [1986] 1 FLR 610, [1986] Fam Law 190, CA 11.38
El-G (minors), Re (1987) 4 FLR 589, CA 7.80
Elgindata Ltd (No 2), Re [1993] 1 All ER 232, [1992] 1 WLR 1207, [1993] BCLC 119, [1992] 27 LS Gaz R 33, 136 Sol Jo LB 190, CA 15.16, 15.17
Elsworth v Elsworth (1978) 1 FLR 245, CA 11.35
Emanuel v Emanuel [1982] 2 All ER 342, [1982] 1 WLR 669, 3 FLR 319, 12 Fam Law 62, 126 Sol Jo 276 .... 4.188
Escritt v Escritt (1981) 3 FLR 280; affd (1981) 3 FLR 280, CA 6.28
Essex County Council v B [1993] 1 FCR 145, [1993] 1 FLR 866, [1993] Fam Law 457 .... 8.93, 8.125
Essex County Council v F [1993] 2 FCR 289, [1993] 1 FLR 847, [1993] Fam Law 337 .... 8.118, 13.17
Essex County Council v R [1994] Fam 167n, [1994] 2 WLR 407n, [1993] 2 FLR 826, [1993] Fam Law 670, sub nom Re R (a minor) [1993] 4 All ER 702, [1994] 1 FCR 225 .... 8.72
Evans v Bartlam [1937] AC 473, [1937] 2 All ER 646, 106 LJKB 568, 81 Sol Jo 549, 53 TLR 689, sub nom Bartlam v Evans 157 LT 311, HL 2.68, 2.74
Evans v Evans [1989] FCR 133, [1989] 1 FLR 351, [1989] Fam Law 193, CA 4.28
Evans v Evans [1990] 2 All ER 147, [1990] FCR 498, [1990] 1 FLR 319, [1990] Fam Law 215, 134 Sol Jo 785, [1990] 12 LS Gaz R 40, [1990] NLJR 291, sub nom Practice Note [1990] 1 WLR 575n 2.43, 2.51, 2.57
Evers's Trust, Re, Papps v Evers [1980] 3 All ER 399, [1980] 1 WLR 1327, 10 Fam Law 245, 124 Sol Jo 562, CA 5.29
Eves v Eves [1975] 3 All ER 768, [1975] 1 WLR 1338, 119 Sol Jo 394, CA 4.257, 5.17, 5.23, 5.27

F

F (R) (an infant), Re [1970] 1 QB 385, [1969] 3 All ER 1101, [1969] 3 WLR 853, 133 JP 743, 113 Sol Jo 835, CA 7.79

PARA

F (a minor), Re [1982] 1 All ER 321, [1982] 1 WLR 102, 3 FLR 101, 12
 Fam Law 58, 125 Sol Jo 861, CA 7.80
F (wardship: adoption), Re [1984] FLR 60, 13 Fam Law 259, CA 7.63
F, Re (1984) Times, 25 August 11.19
F, Re [1988] Fam 122, [1988] 2 WLR 1288, [1988] 2 FLR 307, [1988]
 Fam Law 337; affd [1988] Fam 122, [1988] 2 All ER 193, [1988]
 2 WLR 1288, [1988] FCR 529, [1988] 2 FLR 307, [1988] Fam Law
 337, 132 Sol Jo 820, [1988] NLJR 37, CA 7.29
F (a ward), Re [1988] 2 FLR 116, [1988] Fam Law 295, CA 8.38
F (a minor), Re [1990] Fam 125, [1989] 1 All ER 1155, [1989] 3 WLR 691,
 [1989] FCR 165, [1989] 1 FLR 233, [1988] Fam Law 474, CA 7.32
F, Re [1990] 2 AC 1, [1989] 2 WLR 1025, [1989] 2 FLR 376, 133 Sol Jo
 265, [1989] 10 LS Gaz R 42, [1989] NLJR 183, CA; affd [1990] 2 AC 1,
 [1989] 2 WLR 1025, [1989] 2 FLR 376, [1989] Fam Law 390, 133 Sol
 Jo 785, [1989] NLJR 789, sub nom F v West Berkshire Health Authority
 (Mental Health Act Commission intervening) [1989] 2 All ER 545,
 4 BMLR 1, HL 7.37
F, Re [1992] 2 FCR 433, sub nom F v Kent County Council [1993] 1 FLR
 432, [1993] Fam Law 132, [1992] 34 LS Gaz R 39, 136 Sol Jo LB 258 .... 8.121
F (a minor), Re [1993] Fam 314, [1993] 3 All ER 596, [1993] 3 WLR 369,
 [1993] 1 FCR 932, [1993] 1 FLR 598, [1993] Fam Law 407, [1993]
 NLJR 472, CA 7.54
F (a minor), Re [1993] 1 FCR 389, [1993] 2 FLR 9, [1993] Fam Law 517 .... 8.71
F (minors), Re [1993] 1 FCR 945, [1993] 2 FLR 677, [1993] Fam Law 673,
 CA 8.27
F (child: surname), Re [1994] 1 FCR 110, [1993] 2 FLR 837n, CA 8.40
F (a minor), Re [1994] 1 FCR 729, [1994] 1 FLR 240, [1994] Fam Law 424 .... 8.97
F (a minor), Re [1994] 2 FCR 1354, [1995] 1 FLR 510, [1995] Fam Law 231 .... 8.89
F (minors), Re [1995] 2 FCR 200, [1995] 1 FLR 819, CA 8.40
F (minors) (contact: restraint on applications), Re [1996] 1 FCR 81, [1995]
 1 FLR 956, [1995] 11 LS Gaz R 37, CA 8.121
F v Cambridgeshire County Council [1995] 2 FCR 804, [1995] 1 FLR 516,
 [1995] Fam Law 240 .... 8.35
F v F (Exclusion Order) (1980) 3 FLR 202 .... 11.1
F v F [1989] 2 FLR 451, [1990] Fam Law 224 .... 11.32
F v F (Duxbury calculation: rate of return) [1996] 1 FLR 833, [1996] Fam
 Law 467 .... 4.28, 4.41
F v F (ancillary relief: substantial assets) [1996] 2 FCR 397, [1995] 2 FLR
 45, [1995] Fam Law 546 .... 2.40, 4.7,
 4.20, 4.41, 4.55, 4.127
F v Leeds City Council [1994] 2 FCR 428, [1994] 2 FLR 60, [1994] Fam Law
 610, CA 8.2
F v S (adoption: ward) [1973] Fam 203, [1973] 1 All ER 722, [1973] 2 WLR
 178, 137 JP 301, 117 Sol Jo 109, CA 7.63
F and R (section 8 order: grandparents application), Re [1995] 1 FLR 524,
 [1995] Fam Law 235, sub nom Re R (minors) [1995] 1 FCR 563 .... 8.48
Farrow, Re [1987] 1 FLR 205, [1987] Fam Law 14 .... 6.23
Felton v Callis [1969] 1 QB 200, [1968] 3 All ER 673, [1968] 3 WLR 951,
 112 Sol Jo 672 .... 12.4, 12.49
Fender v St John-Mildmay [1938] AC 1, 81 Sol Jo 549, 53 TLR 885, sub nom
 Fender v Mildmay [1937] 3 All ER 402, 106 LJKB 641, 157 LT 340, HL A.19
Fisher v Fisher [1989] FCR 309, [1989] 1 FLR 423, [1989] Fam Law 269, CA 4.22
Flint (a bankrupt), Re [1993] Ch 319, [1993] 2 WLR 537, [1993] 1 FCR 518,
 [1993] 1 FLR 763, [1993] Fam Law 210, [1993] 5 LS Gaz R 40, 136 Sol
 Jo LB 221 .... 4.269
Fowler v Fowler (1979) 2 FLR 141, 10 Fam Law 119 .... 12.9
Frary v Frary [1994] 1 FCR 595, [1993] 2 FLR 696, [1993] Fam Law 628, CA 2.53
Freedman v Freedman [1967] 2 All ER 680n, [1967] 1 WLR 1102, 111 Sol
 Jo 518 .... 11.34, 11.40

lii *Table of Cases*

PARA

Freeman, Re [1984] 3 All ER 906, [1984] 1 WLR 1419, [1985] FLR 543,
   [1985] Fam Law 256, 128 Sol Jo 769, [1984] LS Gaz R 3254 .... 6.28
Freeman v Swatridge and Swatridge [1984] FLR 762, [1984] Fam Law 215,
   148 JP 619, CA 4.40
Frost v Frost [1968] 1 WLR 1221, 112 Sol Jo 462, sub nom F v F [1968] 2 All
   ER 946, CA 2.32
Fullard, Re, Fullard v King [1982] Fam 42, [1981] 2 All ER 796, [1981] 3 WLR
   743, 11 Fam Law 116, 125 Sol Jo 747, CA 6.23
Fuller (otherwise Penfold) v Fuller [1973] 2 All ER 650, [1973] 1 WLR 730,
   117 Sol Jo 224, CA A.7

G

G (wardship), Re (1982) 4 FLR 538, 13 Fam Law 50, 126 Sol Jo 746, 133
   NLJ 1101, CA 7.32, 11.47, 13.26
G (minors), Re [1992] 2 FCR 720, [1993] 1 FLR 910, [1993] Fam Law 460,
   CA 8.23
G (minors), Re [1994] 1 FCR 37, [1993] 2 FLR 293, [1993] Fam Law 570,
   CA 8.17
G, Re [1994] 2 FCR 106, [1994] 2 FLR 291, [1994] Fam Law 428, 20 BMLR
   10 .... 2.61, 8.132
G, Re [1994] 2 FCR 359, [1994] 2 FLR 301, [1994] Fam Law 568 .... 8.38, 8.80
G (a minor) (parental responsibility order), Re [1994] 2 FCR 1037, [1994]
   1 FLR 504, [1994] Fam Law 372, CA 7.6
G (a minor: blood test), Re [1994] 1 FLR 495, [1994] Fam Law 310, sub nom
   Re CG (a minor) [1994] 2 FCR 889, ... 7.55
G (a minor), Re [1995] Fam 16, [1994] 3 WLR 1211, [1994] 2 FLR 69,
   [1994] Fam Law 485, sub nom sub nom Hackney London Borough
   Council v G [1994] 2 FCR 216 .... 8.70
G (a minor), Re [1995] 2 FCR 53, [1994] 2 FLR 964, [1994] Fam Law 492, CA ... 8.36
G, Re [1995] 3 FCR 26, [1995] 1 FLR 403, [1995] Fam Law 230, CA 7.61
G (a minor) (social worker: disclosure), Re [1996] 2 All ER 65, [1996] 1 FLR
   276, [1996] Fam Law 143, [1995] 44 LS Gaz R 30, [1996] NLJR 85,
   [1995] TLR 588, 140 Sol Jo LB 10, sub nom G (a minor) (care proceedings:
   disclosure), Re [1996] 3 FCR 77, CA 8.73
G (child case: parental involvement), Re [1996] 2 FCR 1, [1996] 1 FLR 857,
   [1996] Fam Law 459, CA 7.6, 8.121
G v G [1985] 2 All ER 225, [1985] 1 WLR 647, [1985] FLR 894, [1985]
   Fam Law 321, 129 Sol Jo 315, HL 2.68, 2.75, 8.123
G v G [1990] FCR 572, [1990] 1 FLR 395, [1990] Fam Law 254, CA 11.20
G v G [1993] Fam 253, [1993] 2 WLR 837, [1993] 2 FCR 27, [1993] 2 FLR
   306, [1993] Fam Law 613 .... 8.31
G v G (periodical payments: jurisdiction) (30 July 1996, unreported), CA 4.33
G v J [1993] 1 FLR 1008, [1993] Fam Law 341, CA 11.39
G v Kirklees Metropolitan Borough Council [1993] 1 FCR 357, [1993] 1 FLR
   805, [1993] Fam Law 278 .... 8.48
G v L [1891] 3 Ch 126, 60 LJ Ch 705, 40 WR 10, sub nom Re Infant, G v L
   64 LT 732, 7 TLR 589 .... 13.26
G and M (minors), Re [1995] 3 FCR 514, [1995] 2 FLR 416, [1995] Fam
   Law 669 .... 8.121
Gandolfo v Gandolfo [1981] QB 359, [1980] 1 All ER 833, [1980] 2 WLR
   680, 10 Fam Law 152, 124 Sol Jo 239, CA 12.17
Garner v Garner [1992] 1 FCR 529, [1992] 1 FLR 573, [1992] Fam Law 331,
   CA 4.139
Gatehouse v Robinson [1986] 1 WLR 18, [1986] 1 FLR 504, [1986] Fam Law
   158, 130 Sol Jo 13, [1986] LS Gaz R 118 .... 7.61
Gateshead Metropolitan Borough Council v N [1993] 1 FCR 400, [1993] 1 FLR
   811, [1993] Fam Law 456 .... 8.95

Table of Cases liii

PARA

Gayway Linings Ltd v Law Society [1982] AC 81, [1981] 1 All ER 641, [1981]
2 WLR 335, 125 Sol Jo 167, HL 15.26
Genie, The. See Third Chandris Shipping Corpn v Unimarine SA
George v George [1986] 2 FLR 347, [1986] Fam Law 294, CA 14.10
Ghoth v Ghoth [1992] 2 All ER 920, [1993] 1 FCR 177, [1992] 2 FLR 300,
[1992] Fam Law 531, [1992] NLJR 673, CA 4.185
Gibson v Austin [1993] 1 FCR 638, [1992] 2 FLR 437, [1993] Fam Law 20,
CA 8.2, 11.40
Gilbert v Gilbert (1961) 105 Sol Jo 807, (1961) Times, 15 September 14.7
Gillick v West Norfolk and Wisbech Area Health Authority [1986] AC 112,
[1985] 3 All ER 402, [1985] 3 WLR 830, [1986] 1 FLR 224, [1986]
Crim LR 113, 129 Sol Jo 738, 2 BMLR 11, [1985] LS Gaz R 3551,
[1985] NLJ Rep 1055, HL 7.2, 7.24
Gissing v Gissing [1971] AC 886, [1970] 2 All ER 780, [1970] 3 WLR 255,
21 P & CR 702, 114 Sol Jo 550, 216 Estates Gazette 1257, HL 4.257,
5.18, 5.22, 6.8
Gojkovic v Gojkovic [1992] Fam 40, [1990] 2 All ER 84, [1991] 3 WLR 621,
[1990] FCR 119, [1990] 1 FLR 140, [1990] Fam Law 100, CA 4.41
Gojkovic v Gojkovic (No 2) [1992] Fam 40, [1992] 1 All ER 267, [1991]
3 WLR 621, [1991] FCR 913, [1991] 2 FLR 233, [1991] Fam Law 378,
CA 15.13, 15.15
Goodman v Gallant [1986] Fam 106, [1986] 1 All ER 311, [1986] 2 WLR
236, 52 P & CR 180, [1986] 1 FLR 513, [1986] Fam Law 159, 129 Sol
Jo 891, CA 5.16, 5.27
Gordon v Douce [1983] 2 All ER 228, [1983] 1 WLR 563, 4 FLR 508,
13 Fam Law 149, 127 Sol Jo 324, CA 5.28
Gordon v Gordon [1946] P 99, [1946] 1 All ER 247, 115 JP 39, 174 LT 172,
62 TLR 217, CA 14.1
Gorman (a bankrupt), Re, ex p Trustee of the bankrupt v Bankrupt [1990]
1 All ER 717, [1990] 1 WLR 616, [1990] 2 FLR 284, [1990] Fam Law
430, [1990] 19 LS Gaz R 41 .... 5.16
Gould v Gould [1970] 1 QB 275, [1969] 3 All ER 728, [1969] 3 WLR 490,
113 Sol Jo 508, CA 4.165
Grace v Grace [1980] CA Transcript 418 .... 11.4, 11.41
Grant v Edwards [1986] Ch 638, [1986] 2 All ER 426, [1986] 3 WLR 114,
[1987] 1 FLR 87, [1986] Fam Law 300, 130 Sol Jo 408, [1986] LS
Gaz R 1996, [1986] NLJ Rep 439, CA 5.17, 5.18, 5.23, 5.25, 5.27
Graves v Graves (1973) 4 Fam Law 124, 117 Sol Jo 679 .... 4.25
Greasley v Cooke [1980] 3 All ER 710, [1980] 1 WLR 1306, 124 Sol Jo 629,
CA 5.25
Green v Green [1993] 1 FLR 326, [1993] Fam Law 119 .... 4.67, 4.99
Gregory, Re, Gregory v Goodenough [1971] 1 All ER 497, [1970] 1 WLR
1455, 114 Sol Jo 532, CA 6.21
Griffiths v Dawson & Co [1993] 2 FCR 515, [1993] 2 FLR 315, [1993] Fam
Law 476 .... 4.106
Griffiths v Griffiths [1974] 1 All ER 932, [1974] 1 WLR 1350, 5 Fam Law
59, 118 Sol Jo 810, CA 5.7
Gupta v Comer [1991] 1 QB 629, [1991] 1 All ER 289, [1991] 2 WLR 494,
[1990] NLJR 1606, CA 15.19
Gurasz v Gurasz [1970] P 11, [1969] 3 All ER 822, [1969] 3 WLR 482,
113 Sol Jo 565, 211 Estates Gazette 727, CA 11.37, 11.43, 11.44

H

H (infants), Re [1977] 2 All ER 339n, [1977] 1 WLR 471n, 7 Fam Law 138,
121 Sol Jo 303, CA 7.77, 7.80
H (a minor), Re (1980) 2 FLR 253, 10 Fam Law 248 .... 8.21
H (adoption: parental agreement), Re (1983) 4 FLR 614, 13 Fam Law 144,
127 Sol Jo 86, CA 7.80

liv Table of Cases

PARA

H, Re (1985) Times, 7 November, CA 14.10
H, Re [1991] FCR 896, CA 8.121
H (a minor), Re [1991] FCR 985, [1991] 2 FLR 109, [1991] Fam Law 370, CA 8.21
H (minors) (access), Re [1992] 1 FCR 70, [1992] 1 FLR 148, [1992] Fam Law
  152, CA 8.25
H, Re [1992] 1 FCR 449, [1992] Fam Law 383, CA 8.1
H (a minor), Re [1992] 2 FCR 330, [1993] 1 FLR 440, [1993] Fam Law 200 .... 8.4
H (a minor), Re [1993] 1 FCR 85, [1993] 1 FLR 484, [1993] Fam Law 273,
  CA 7.6, 8.27
H (a minor) (residence order), Re [1993] 1 FCR 671, sub nom Re H (a minor)
  (shared residence) [1994] 1 FLR 717, [1993] Fam Law 463, CA 8.57
H, Re [1993] 2 FCR 277 .... 8.99
H (a minor), Re [1994] Fam 11, [1994] 4 All ER 762, [1993] 3 WLR 1109,
  [1993] 2 FCR 437, [1993] 2 FLR 552, [1993] Fam Law 614 .... 8.55
H (a minor), Re [1994] 1 FCR 673, [1994] 2 FLR 981, [1994] Fam Law 422,
  CA 8.23
H (minors), Re [1994] 2 FCR 1, [1994] 2 FLR 979, [1994] Fam Law 486 .... 8.84
H (a minor), Re [1994] 2 FCR 249, [1994] 2 FLR 969, [1993] Fam Law 673,
  CA 8.16
H (a minor), Re [1994] 2 FCR 419, [1994] 2 FLR 776, [1995] Fam Law 13,
  CA 8.26, 8.30
H (a minor), Re [1994] 3 FCR 183, [1994] 2 FLR 80, [1994] Fam Law 556 .... 8.78
H (minors), Re [1995] 4 All ER 110, [1995] 1 WLR 667, [1995] 2 FCR 547,
  [1995] 1 FLR 638, [1995] Fam Law 293, CA 8.39, 13.11
H (shared residence: parental responsibility), Re [1995] 2 FLR 883, [1996]
  Fam Law 140, CA 8.57
H (a minor) (blood tests: parental rights), Re [1996] 4 All ER 28, [1996]
  3 WLR 506, [1996] 3 FCR 201, [1996] 2 FLR 65, [1996] Fam Law 461,
  [1996] NLJR 406, CA 7.55, 8.28
H (contact: enforcement), Re [1996] 2 FCR 784, [1996] 1 FLR 614, [1996]
  Fam Law 348 .... 13.3, 13.8
H (a minor) (parental responsibility order), Re [1996] 3 FCR 49, [1996]
  1 FLR 867, [1996] Fam Law 402, CA 7.6
H v C [1993] 1 FCR 1, [1993] 1 FLR 787, [1993] Fam Law 394, CA 14.9
H v H (1989) 87 LGR 166, [1989] FCR 257, [1989] 1 FLR 212, [1989] Fam
  Law 148, CA 8.27
H v H (financial provision: capital allowance) [1993] 2 FCR 308, [1993]
  2 FLR 335, [1993] Fam Law 520 .... 4.101, 4.103, 4.112, 6.22
H v H [1994] 2 FCR 1031, [1994] 2 FLR 801 .... 4.28
H v H [1995] 2 FCR 469, [1995] Fam Law 238, [1995] 1 FLR 529n, CA 8.4
H v O [1992] 1 FCR 125, [1992] 1 FLR 282, [1992] Fam Law 105, 135
  Sol Jo LB 76, sub nom Hager v Osborne [1992] Fam 94, [1992] 2 All
  ER 494, [1992] 2 WLR 610 .... 5.59
H and R (minors) (sexual abuse: standard of proof), Re [1996] AC 563,
  [1996] 1 All ER 1, [1996] 2 WLR 8, [1996] 1 FCR 509, [1996] 1
  FLR 80, [1996] Fam Law 74, 140 Sol Jo LB 24, HL 2.26, 2.73,
                                                                                   8.66, 8.67, 8.108, A.56
HIV Tests, Re [1994] 2 FLR 116, [1994] Fam Law 559, sub nom Re X (a minor)
  [1994] 2 FCR 1110 .... 8.40
HG, Re [1993] 1 FCR 553, [1993] 1 FLR 587, [1993] Fam Law 403 .... 8.40
Haig, Re, Powers v Haig [1979] LS Gaz R 476, 129 NLJ 420 .... 6.27
Hale v Hale [1975] 2 All ER 1090, [1975] 1 WLR 931, 30 P & CR 98, 119
  Sol Jo 256, CA 4.66, 11.45
Halifax Building Society v Brown [1995] 3 FCR 110, [1996] 1 FLR 103,
  [1996] Fam Law 85, 27 HLR 511, CA 5.19
Hall v Hall [1971] 1 All ER 762, [1971] 1 WLR 404, 115 Sol Jo 94, CA 11.35
Hall v King (1988) 55 P & CR 307, [1988] 1 FLR 376, [1988] Fam Law 88,
  19 HLR 440, 131 Sol Jo 1186, [1987] 2 EGLR 121, [1987] LS Gaz R 2273,
  [1987] NLJ Rep 616, 283 Estates Gazette 1400, CA 11.45

PARA

Hall v Selvaco (1996) Times, 27 March, CA 2.43
Hamlin v Hamlin [1986] Fam 11, [1985] 2 All ER 1037, [1985] 3 WLR 629,
   [1986] 1 FLR 61, [1985] Fam Law 323, 129 Sol Jo 700, CA 4.177, 5.10
Hammond v Mitchell [1992] 2 All ER 109, [1991] 1 WLR 1127, sub nom
   H v M [1991] FCR 938, [1992] 1 FLR 229, [1991] Fam
   Law 473 .... 5.14, 5.17, 5.45
Hands v Hands (1881) 43 LT 750 .... 12.49
Hanlon v Law Society [1981] AC 124, [1980] 2 All ER 199, [1980] 2 WLR
   756, 124 Sol Jo 360, HL 15.31
Hanning v Maitland (No 2) [1970] 1 QB 580, [1970] 1 All ER 812,
   [1970] 2 WLR 151, 114 Sol Jo 14, CA 15.27, 15.28
Harben v Harben [1957] 1 All ER 379, [1957] 1 WLR 261, 101 Sol Jo
   150 .... 7.29, 14.7
Harman v Glencross [1986] Fam 81, [1986] 1 All ER 545, [1986] 2 WLR
   637, [1986] 2 FLR 241, [1986] Fam Law 215, 130 Sol Jo 224, CA 12.32
Harmsworth v Harmsworth [1987] 3 All ER 816, [1987] 1 WLR 1676,
   [1988] 1 FLR 349, [1988] Fam Law 169, 131 Sol Jo 1625, [1988] 1
   LS Gaz R 36, CA 14.5
Harnett v Harnett [1973] Fam 156, [1973] 2 All ER 593, [1973] 3 WLR 1,
   117 Sol Jo 447; affd [1974] 1 All ER 764, [1974] 1 WLR 219, 118 Sol
   Jo 34, CA 5.12
Harrington v Gill (1983) 4 FLR 265, CA 6.19, 6.21, 6.27
Harris v Harris [1986] 1 FLR 12, [1986] Fam Law 16, CA 11.39
Harwood v Harwood [1992] 1 FCR 1, [1991] 2 FLR 274, [1991] Fam Law
   418, CA 4.65, 5.16
Hashmi v Hashmi [1972] Fam 36, [1971] 3 All ER 1253, [1971] 3 WLR
   918, 115 Sol Jo 929 .... 6.9
Heard v Heard [1996] 1 FCR 33, [1995] 1 FLR 970, [1995] Fam Law 477,
   CA 2.70, 4.72
Hegarty v O'Sullivan [1985] NLJ Rep 557, Times, 8 May, CA 14.11
Hennie v Hennie [1993] 1 FCR 886, [1993] 2 FLR 351, [1993] Fam Law
   472, CA 11.41
Hense v Hense and Churchill [1976] CA Transcript 403, CA 11.43, A.16
Hereford and Worcester County Council v R and G [1994] 2 FCR 981 .... 8.84
Hertfordshire County Council v W [1992] 2 FCR 885, [1992] 39 LS Gaz R 33,
   136 Sol Jo LB 259, sub nom W v Hertfordshire County Council [1993]
   1 FLR 118, [1993] Fam Law 75 .... 8.133
Hewitson v Hewitson [1995] Fam 100, [1995] 1 All ER 472, [1995] 2
   WLR 287, [1995] 2 FCR 588, [1995] 1 FLR 241, [1995] Fam Law
   129, [1994] 41 LS Gaz R 41, [1994] NLJR 1478, 138 Sol Jo LB 211,
   CA 4.201, 4.204
Hildebrand v Hildebrand [1992] 1 FLR 244, [1992] Fam Law 235 .... 2.43, 2.50, 2.51
Hill Samuel & Co Ltd v Littaur (No 2) (1985) 129 Sol Jo 433, [1985] LS Gaz
   R 2248, [1985] NLJ Rep 556, CA 14.2
Hills v Bushby [1977] CA Transcript 398b 11.8, 11.9, 11.40
Hipgrave v Hipgrave [1962] P 91, [1962] 1 All ER 75, [1962] 2 WLR 1,
   105 Sol Jo 991 .... 11.34, 14.1,
                                                                                                      14.3, 14.7, 14.10, A.71
Hipkin v Hipkin [1962] 2 All ER 155, [1962] 1 WLR 491, 106 Sol Jo 246 .... 12.39
Hollens v Hollens (1971) 115 Sol Jo 327 .... 11.8, A.5
Holmes v Holmes [1989] Fam 47, [1989] 3 All ER 786, [1989] 3 WLR 302,
   [1990] FCR 157, [1989] 2 FLR 364, [1989] Fam Law 470, CA 4.201
Holtom v Holtom (1981) 11 Fam Law 249, 125 Sol Jo 724, CA 11.43
Hope-Smith v Hope-Smith [1989] FCR 785, [1989] 2 FLR 56, [1989] Fam
   Law 268, [1989] NLJR 111, CA 2.70, 4.72
Hopper v Hopper [1979] 1 All ER 181, [1978] 1 WLR 1342n, 122 Sol Jo
   610, CA 11.39, 11.40, A.60
Horner v Horner [1982] Fam 90, [1982] 2 All ER 495, [1982] 2 WLR 914,
   4 FLR 50, 12 Fam Law 144, 126 Sol Jo 243, CA 11.33, A.68

Table of Cases

PARA

Hounslow London Borough Council v A [1993] 1 WLR 291, [1993] 1 FCR
  164, [1993] 1 FLR 702, [1993] Fam Law 397 .... 8.3, 8.94
Humberside County Council v B [1993] 1 FCR 613, [1993] 1 FLR 257,
  [1993] Fam Law 61 .... 8.94
Hunt v Severs [1993] QB 815, [1993] 4 All ER 180, [1993] 3 WLR 558,
  [1993] NLJR 1225, [1994] PIQR Q6, CA; revsd [1994] 2 All ER 385,
  [1994] 2 WLR 602, [1994] 2 Lloyd's Rep 129, [1994] 32 LS Gaz R 41,
  [1994] NLJR 603, 138 Sol Jo LB 104, HL 7.20
Huntingford v Hobbs [1993] 1 FCR 45, [1993] 1 FLR 736, [1992] Fam Law
  437, 24 HLR 652, [1992] NPC 39, CA 5.16, 5.21
Hurwitt v Hurwitt (1979) 3 FLR 194, 10 Fam Law 183, CA 8.38
Hussain v Hussain [1983] Fam 26, [1982] 3 All ER 369, [1982] 3 WLR 679,
  4 FLR 339, 126 Sol Jo 624, CA 11.2
Hussain v Hussain [1986] Fam 134, [1986] 1 All ER 961, [1986] 2 WLR 801,
  [1986] 2 FLR 271, [1986] Fam Law 269, 130 Sol Jo 341, [1986] NLJ
  Rep 358, CA 4.146, 11.34, 14.1, 14.3, A.71
Husseyin v Husseyin (1982) 12 Fam Law 154, CA 14.1
Husson v Husson [1962] 3 All ER 1056, [1962] 1 WLR 1434, 106 Sol Jo 737 .... 14.2
Hutchings v Hutchings (1975) 237 Estates Gazette 571, CA 4.66
Hutchinson v Hutchinson [1947] 2 All ER 792, 92 Sol Jo 55, 63 TLR 645 .... 11.2
Hyde v Hyde and Woodmansee (1866) LR 1 P & D 130, 35 LJP & M 57, 12
  Jur NS 414, 14 WR 517, [1861-73] All ER Rep 175, 14 LT 188 .... 5.3
Hyman v Hyman [1929] AC 601, 27 LGR 379, 93 JP 209, 98 LJP 81, [1929]
  All ER Rep 245, 73 Sol Jo 317, 141 LT 329, 45 TLR 444, HL 3.28, 4.166

I

I (a minor), Re (1987) Times, 22 May 12.49

J

J (a minor), Re [1984] FLR 535, [1984] Fam Law 308, 128 Sol Jo 280 .... 11.6
J (a minor), Re [1990] 2 AC 562, [1990] 3 WLR 492, [1991] FCR 129,
  134 Sol Jo 1039, sub nom C v S (minor) [1990] 2 All ER 961, [1990]
  2 FLR 442, [1991] Fam Law 57, [1990] NLJR 1191, HL 3.14
J (a minor), Re [1990] FCR 135, [1989] 2 FLR 304, [1989] Fam Law 394,
  CA 8.21, 13.1
J (a minor), Re [1991] Fam 33, [1990] 3 All ER 930, [1991] 2 WLR 140,
  [1991] FCR 370, [1991] 1 FLR 366, [1990] 2 Med LR 67, 6 BMLR 25,
  [1990] NLJR 1533, CA 7.34
J (a minor), Re [1993] 1 FCR 74, [1993] 1 FLR 699, [1992] Fam Law 399 .... 8.40
J (specific issue order: leave to apply), Re [1995] 3 FCR 799, [1995] 1 FLR
  669, [1995] Fam Law 403 .... 8.41
J, Re [1995] 1 FLR 660, [1995] Fam Law 300 .... 11.9
J (minors: care plan), Re. See R (minors), Re
J v C [1970] AC 668, [1969] 1 All ER 788, [1969] 2 WLR 540, sub nom Re
  C (an infant) 113 Sol Jo 164, HL 11.42
J v J (a minor: property transfer) [1993] 1 FCR 471, [1993] 2 FLR 56,
  [1993] Fam Law 461 .... 5.50
JC (care proceedings: procedure), Re (1995) 160 LG Rev 346, [1996] 1 FCR
  434, [1995] 2 FLR 77, [1995] Fam Law 543 .... 2.40, 2.44, 2.48, 8.131
JR v Merton London Borough [1992] 2 FCR 174; revsd sub nom A (minors),
  Re [1992] Fam 182, [1992] 3 All ER 872, [1992] 3 WLR 422, 91 LGR 401,
  [1992] 2 FCR 174, [1992] 2 FLR 154, [1992] Fam Law 439, CA 8.47, 8.48
JS (a minor), Re [1981] Fam 22, [1980] 1 All ER 1061, [1980] 3 WLR 984,
  2 FLR 146, 10 Fam Law 121, 124 Sol Jo 881, CA 11.6
James v James [1964] P 303, [1963] 2 All ER 465, [1963] 3 WLR 331, 127
  JP 352, 107 Sol Jo 116 .... 12.15

	PARA
Jedfield v Jedfield (1960) Times, 10 November	11.41
Jefferson Ltd v Bhetcha [1979] 2 All ER 1108, [1979] 1 WLR 898, 144 JP 125, 123 Sol Jo 389, CA	14.9
Jelley v Iliffe [1981] Fam 128, [1981] 2 All ER 29, [1981] 2 WLR 801, 125 Sol Jo 355, CA	6.19
Jelson (Estates) Ltd v Harvey [1984] 1 All ER 12, [1983] 1 WLR 1401, 127 Sol Jo 697, CA	14.5
Jennings, Re [1994] Ch 286, [1994] 3 All ER 27, [1994] 3 WLR 67, [1995] 1 FCR 257, sub nom Re Jennings, Harlow v National Westminster Bank plc [1994] 1 FLR 536, [1994] Fam Law 439, CA	6.25
Jessop v Jessop [1992] 1 FCR 253, [1992] 1 FLR 591, [1992] Fam Law 328, CA	6.22, 6.33
John's Assignment Trusts, Re, Niven v Niven [1970] 2 All ER 210n, [1970] 1 WLR 955, 114 Sol Jo 396	5.29
Jones v Jones [1971] 2 All ER 737, [1971] 1 WLR 396, 115 Sol Jo 76, CA	11.43, A.16
Jones v Jones [1993] 2 FCR 82, [1993] 2 FLR 377, [1993] Fam Law 519, CA	A.84
Joyce v King (1987) Times, 13 July, CA	11.31

K

K (a minor), Re [1990] 3 All ER 795, [1990] 1 WLR 431, [1990] FCR 553, [1990] 2 FLR 64, [1990] Fam Law 256, 134 Sol Jo 49, CA	8.21
K (a minor), Re [1995] Fam 38, [1994] 3 All ER 553, [1994] 3 WLR 572, [1994] 2 FCR 617, [1994] 2 FLR 557, [1994] Fam Law 554, CA	7.71
K (contact: psychiatric report), Re [1996] 1 FCR 474, [1995] 2 FLR 432, [1995] Fam Law 597, CA	2.61, 8.14
K v H [1993] 1 FCR 683, [1993] 2 FLR 61, [1993] Fam Law 464	5.60, 8.12
K v K [1992] 2 All ER 727, [1992] 1 WLR 530, [1992] 2 FCR 253, [1992] 2 FLR 220, [1992] Fam Law 336, [1992] 16 LS Gaz R 31, 136 Sol Jo LB 69, CA	5.56
K v K [1992] 2 FCR 161, [1992] 2 FLR 98, sub nom Re K (a minor) [1992] Fam Law 240	8.38
K v P [1995] 2 FCR 457, [1995] 1 FLR 248, [1995] Fam Law 178	2.32
KD (a minor) (ward: termination of access), Re [1988] AC 806, [1988] 1 All ER 577, [1988] 2 WLR 398, [1988] FCR 657, [1988] 2 FLR 139, [1988] Fam Law 288, 132 Sol Jo 301, HL	8.21
KDT (a minor), Re [1994] 2 FCR 721, sub nom Re T (a minor) [1994] 2 FLR 423, [1994] Fam Law 558, [1994] 21 LS Gaz R 40, CA	8.68
Kavanagh v Kavanagh (1978) 128 NLJ 1007, CA	14.11
Keller v Keller and Legal Aid Board [1995] 2 FCR 189, [1995] 1 FLR 259, [1995] Fam Law 128, [1994] 42 LS Gaz R 37, 138 Sol Jo LB 223, CA	15.24
Kelly v London Transport Executive [1982] 2 All ER 842, [1982] 1 WLR 1055, 126 Sol Jo 262, CA	15.23
Kemmis v Kemmis (Welland Intervening) [1988] 1 WLR 1307, [1988] 2 FLR 223, [1989] 3 LS Gaz R 43, CA	4.176
Kendrick v Kendrick [1990] FCR 780, [1990] 2 FLR 107, [1990] Fam Law 301, CA	11.47
Kepa v Kepa (1982) 4 FLR 515	4.188
Kerr v Kerr [1897] 2 QB 439, 66 LJQB 828, 4 Mans 207, 46 WR 46, [1895-9] All ER Rep 865, 41 Sol Jo 679, 77 LT 29, 13 TLR 534	12.9
Khanna v Lovell White Durrant (a firm) [1994] 4 All ER 267, [1995] 1 WLR 121, [1994] 45 LS Gaz R 37	2.53
Khorasandjian v Bush [1993] QB 727, [1993] 3 All ER 669, [1993] 3 WLR 476, [1993] 2 FCR 257, [1993] 2 FLR 66, [1993] Fam Law 679, 25 HLR 392, [1993] 15 LS Gaz R 40, [1993] NLJR 329, 137 Sol Jo LB 88, CA	11.33, A.68
Kiely v Kiely [1988] 1 FLR 248, [1988] Fam Law 51, CA	5.56

Table of Cases

PARA

Kinzler v Kinzler [1985] Fam Law 26, CA 11.37
Kowalczuk v Kowalczuk [1973] 2 All ER 1042, [1973] 1 WLR 930, 117 Sol
 Jo 372, CA 5.7
Krubert, Re [1996] 3 WLR 959, [1996] 27 LS Gaz R 28, 140 Sol Jo LB 167,
 CA 6.22
Kumar (a bankrupt), Re, ex p Lewis v Kumar [1993] 2 All ER 700, [1993] 1
 WLR 224, [1994] 2 FCR 373, [1993] 2 FLR 382, [1993] Fam Law 470,
 [1993] BCLC 458 .... 4.265
Kumari v Jalal [1996] 4 All ER 65, [1996] 2 FLR 588, [1996] NLJR 1349, CA ... 14.10
Kusminow v Barclays Bank Trust Co Ltd and Sokolow and Sitnikova [1989]
 Fam Law 66 .... 6.21

L

L (a minor), Re [1988] 1 All ER 418, [1988] 1 FLR 255, [1987] NLJ Rep
 760 .... 11.29, 14.13
L (a minor) (removal from jurisdiction), Re [1993] 1 FCR 325, [1993] Fam
 Law 280 .... 8.37
L (minors) (police investigation: privilege), Re [1995] 2 FCR 12, [1995] 1
 FLR 999, [1995] Fam Law 474; on appeal [1996] 1 FCR 419, [1995]
 1 FLR 999, [1995] Fam Law 474, 24 BMLR 69, CA; affd [1996] 2 All
 ER 78, [1996] 2 WLR 395, 160 LG Rev 417, [1996] 2 FCR 145, [1996]
 1 FLR 731, [1996] Fam Law 400, [1996] 15 LS Gaz R 30, [1996] NLJR
 441, 140 Sol Jo LB 116, HL 1.7, 2.17, 2.45,
 2.47, 2.61, 8.72, 8.73
L (a minor), Re [1995] 3 FCR 684, [1995] 2 FLR 445, [1995] Fam Law 598 .... 8.15
L (care proceedings: appeal), Re [1996] 2 FCR 352, [1996] 1 FLR 116, [1996]
 Fam Law 73, CA 8.3, 8.94
L v C [1995] 3 FCR 125, sub nom Re L [1995] 2 FLR 438, [1995] Fam
 Law 599 .... 8.27
L v L (minors) (separate representation) [1994] 1 FCR 890, [1994] 1 FLR
 156, [1994] Fam Law 432, CA 2.63, 8.55
L v L (lump sum: interest) [1995] 1 FCR 60, [1994] 2 FLR 324, [1994] Fam
 Law 620 .... 4.59, 4.222
LW (a minor), Re [1991] FCR 867, CA 7.77
Lacey v W Silk & Son Ltd [1951] 2 All ER 128, 95 Sol Jo 516 .... 15.11
Ladd v Marshall [1954] 3 All ER 745, [1954] 1 WLR 1489, 98 Sol Jo 870, CA 2.68
Lamagni v Lamagni [1996] 1 FCR 408, [1995] 2 FLR 452, [1995] Fam Law
 607, CA 4.203
Lamb v Lamb [1984] FLR 278, [1984] Fam Law 60, CA 14.7, 14.11
Langley v Langley [1994] 2 FCR 294, [1994] 1 FLR 383, [1994] Fam Law
 564, CA 14.11
Latkin v Latkin [1984] CA Transcript 488 .... 14.5
Leach, Re, Leach v Lindeman [1986] Ch 226, [1985] 2 All ER 754, [1985]
 3 WLR 413, [1985] FLR 1120, [1985] Fam Law 319, 129 Sol Jo 318,
 CA 6.18, 6.26
Lee v Lee [1984] FLR 243, [1984] Fam Law 243, 12 HLR 114, 127 Sol Jo
 696, [1983] LS Gaz R 2678, CA 11.38, 11.40
Lee v Walker [1985] QB 1191, [1985] 1 All ER 781, [1985] 3 WLR 170,
 [1985] FLR 701, [1985] Fam Law 164, 129 Sol Jo 484, [1985] LS Gaz
 R 2996, CA 14.10, 14.12, A.85
Leeds City Council v C [1993] 1 FCR 585, [1993] 1 FLR 269, [1993] Fam
 Law 73 .... 8.59
Lehmann, Re, ex p Hasluck (1890) 7 Morr 181, 39 WR 16, 62 LT 941,
 6 TLR 376, DC 12.49
Le Marchant v Le Marchant [1977] 3 All ER 610, [1977] 1 WLR 559,
 7 Fam Law 241, 121 Sol Jo 334, CA 3.30
Levermore v Levermore [1980] 1 All ER 1, [1979] 1 WLR 1277, 1 FLR 87,
 10 Fam Law 87, 123 Sol Jo 689 .... 12.46

Table of Cases lix

PARA

Lewis v Averay (No 2) [1973] 2 All ER 229, [1973] 1 WLR 510, 117 Sol Jo 188, CA 15.28
Lewis v Lewis [1978] Fam 60, [1978] 1 All ER 729, [1978] 2 WLR 644, 122 Sol Jo 161, CA 11.22, 11.47, 14.12, A.76
Linnett v Coles [1987] QB 555, [1986] 3 All ER 652, [1986] 3 WLR 843, 84 Cr App Rep 227, 130 Sol Jo 841, [1986] NLJ Rep 1016, CA 14.11
Littaur v Steggles Palmer [1986] 1 All ER 780, [1986] 1 WLR 287, 130 Sol Jo 225, [1985] LS Gaz R 1138, CA 15.11
Livesey (formerly Jenkins) v Jenkins [1985] AC 424, [1985] 1 All ER 106, [1985] 2 WLR 47, [1985] FLR 813, [1985] Fam Law 310, 129 Sol Jo 17, [1985] NLJ Rep 55, HL 1.8, 2.40, 2.42, 2.48, 2.66, 2.69, 3.28, 4.42, 4.146, 4.166
Lloyds Bank plc v Rosset [1991] 1 AC 107, [1990] 1 All ER 1111, [1990] 2 WLR 867, 60 P & CR 311, [1990] 2 FLR 155, [1990] Fam Law 395, 22 HLR 349, [1990] 16 LS Gaz R 41, [1990] NLJR 478, HL 4.257, 5.17, 5.18, 5.23, 5.25, 6.8
Lonslow v Hennig (formerly Lonslow) [1986] 2 FLR 378, [1986] Fam Law 303, [1986] LS Gaz R 1554, CA 8.38
Loseby v Newman [1996] 1 FCR 647, [1995] 2 FLR 754, [1996] Fam Law 24, CA 11.19, 14.11
Lucas v Lucas [1991] FCR 901, [1992] 2 FLR 53, [1992] Fam Law 100, CA 11.41

M

M (minors), Re [1985] FLR 921, CA 7.80
M (minors), Re [1991] FCR 272, [1991] 1 FLR 355, [1991] Fam Law 265, CA ... 14.11
M (a minor), Re [1992] 1 FCR 313, CA 8.125
M (minors), Re [1992] 1 FCR 422, sub nom M v M (minors) [1992] 2 FLR 303, [1992] Fam Law 291, CA 8.38
M, Re [1993] 1 FCR 78, [1993] 1 FLR 275, [1993] Fam Law 76 .... 8.101
M (child), Re [1993] 2 FCR 721, [1993] 2 FLR 706, [1993] Fam Law 616 .... 8.5
M (a minor) (care order: threshold conditions), Re [1994] 2 AC 424, [1994] 3 All ER 298, [1994] 3 WLR 558, 92 LGR 701, [1994] 2 FCR 871, [1994] 2 FLR 577, [1994] Fam Law 501, [1994] 37 LS Gaz R 50, 138 Sol Jo LB 168, HL 8.66, A.56
M (a minor), Re [1994] 1 FCR 678, [1994] 1 FLR 272, [1994] Fam Law 252 .... 8.29
M (minors), Re [1994] 1 FCR 866, [1994] 1 FLR 749, [1994] Fam Law 430 .... 8.132
M (minors), Re (children's welfare: contact) [1995] 1 FCR 753, [1995] 1 FLR 274, [1995] Fam Law 174, CA 8.25, 8.27, 8.34
M (minors), Re [1995] 2 FCR 1, [1994] 1 FLR 760, [1994] Fam Law 312, CA 8.17
M (a minor), Re [1995] 2 FCR 435, [1995] 1 FLR 546, [1995] Fam Law 236, CA 8.123
M (minors), Re [1995] 2 FCR 643, [1995] 1 FLR 825, [1995] Fam Law 404 .... 8.40
M, Re [1995] 3 FCR 550, [1995] 2 FLR 86, [1995] Fam Law 540, CA 8.48, 8.91
M, Re [1995] 1 FLR 1029, [1995] Fam Law 476 .... 8.33
M v A [1994] 2 FCR 57, [1993] 2 FLR 715, [1993] Fam Law 625 .... 8.38
M v C [1993] 1 FCR 264, [1993] 2 FLR 584, [1993] Fam Law 616 ..... 8.15, 8.23, 8.41
M v C and Calderdale Metropolitan Borough Council [1993] 1 FCR 431, [1993] 1 FLR 505, [1993] Fam Law 401, sub nom Re C (minors [1994] Fam 1, [1993] 3 All ER 313, [1993] 3 WLR 249, 91 LGR 192, CA 8.48
M v Hampshire County Council [1993] 1 FCR 23, sub nom Hampshire County Council v S [1993] Fam 158, [1993] 1 All ER 944, [1993] 2 WLR 216, [1993] 1 FLR 559, [1993] Fam Law 284 .... 8.97
M v M (1980) 2 FLR 39, CA 6.18
M v M [1993] 1 FCR 5, [1993] Fam Law 396, CA 8.5
M v M [1994] Fam Law 440 .... 8.36, 11.7, 11.32, 11.42, 11.43
M v M (property adjustment: impaired life expectancy) [1994] 2 FCR 174, [1993] 2 FLR 723, [1993] Fam Law 521, CA 4.26

	PARA
M v M [1994] 2 FCR 448, [1994] 1 FLR 399	4.201
M v P [1993] Fam 167, [1992] 4 All ER 833, [1992] 3 WLR 813, [1993] 1 FCR 405, [1993] 1 FLR 773, [1993] Fam Law 467, [1992] NLJR 1339, CA	14.1
M v Warwickshire County Council [1994] 2 FCR 121, [1994] 2 FLR 593, [1994] Fam Law 611	8.70, 8.83
M and R (minors) (expert opinion: evidence), Re [1996] 2 FCR 617, sub nom Re M and R (child abuse: evidence) [1996] 2 FLR 195, [1996] Fam Law 541, CA	2.55, 2.59, 2.60, 2.64, 2.65, 8.9, 8.132
MD and TD, Re [1994] 2 FCR 94, sub nom Re D (minors) [1994] 2 FLR 336, [1994] Fam Law 228	2.22, 8.131
MH v GP [1995] 2 FLR 106, [1995] Fam Law 542, sub nom Harris v Pinnington [1995] 3 FCR 35	8.37, 8.38
MT v MT [1991] FCR 649, [1992] 1 FLR 362, [1992] Fam Law 99	4.19, 4.104
McBroom, Re [1992] 2 FLR 49, [1992] Fam Law 376	6.28
McGibbon v McGibbon [1973] Fam 170, [1973] 2 All ER 836, [1973] 2 WLR 1013, 117 Sol Jo 356	11.1
McHardy and Sons (a firm) v Warren [1994] 2 FLR 338, [1994] Fam Law 567, CA	5.19
McIlraith v Grady [1968] 1 QB 468, [1967] 3 All ER 625, [1967] 3 WLR 1331, 111 Sol Jo 583, 203 Estates Gazette 687, CA	14.11
McIvor v Southern Health and Social Services Board [1978] NI 1, [1978] 2 All ER 625, [1978] 1 WLR 757, 122 Sol Jo 368, HL	A.56
McKee, Re, Public Trustee v McKee [1931] 2 Ch 145, 100 LJ Ch 325, 75 Sol Jo 442, 145 LT 605, 47 TLR 424, CA	6.6
Mackintosh v Mackintosh [1986] CA Transcript 262	11.37
McLean v Burke (1980) 3 FLR 70, CA	11.8, A.4
McLean v Nugent (1980) 1 FLR 26, 123 Sol Jo 521, CA	11.8, 11.20, 11.47, 11.49, 14.10, 14.13, A.76
McNare, Re, McNare v McNare [1964] 3 All ER 373, [1964] 1 WLR 1255, 108 Sol Jo 839	6.28
McTaggart v McTaggart [1949] P 94, [1948] 2 All ER 754, 46 LGR 527, [1949] LJR 82, 92 Sol Jo 617, 64 TLR 558, CA	2.46
Malone v Harrison [1979] 1 WLR 1353, 123 Sol Jo 804	6.19, 6.27
Manchester City Council v F [1993] 1 FCR 1000, [1993] 1 FLR 419n, [1993] Fam Law 29	8.69
Manchester City Council v T [1994] Fam 181, [1994] 2 All ER 526, [1994] 2 WLR 594, [1994] 3 FCR 81, CA	8.101
Manley v Law Society [1981] 1 All ER 401, [1981] 1 WLR 335, 125 Sol Jo 81, CA	15.35
Mareva Cia Naviera SA v International Bulkcarriers SA, The Mareva [1980] 1 All ER 213n, [1975] 2 Lloyd's Rep 509, 119 Sol Jo 660, CA	4.173
Marsh v Marsh [1993] 2 All ER 794, [1993] 1 WLR 744, [1993] 1 FLR 467, [1993] Fam Law 346, [1993] NLJR 364, CA	2.74
Marsh v Von Sternberg [1986] 1 FLR 526, [1986] Fam Law 160	5.20, 5.21, 5.22
Marshall v Marshall (1966) 110 Sol Jo 112, CA	14.10
Martin v Martin [1978] Fam 12, [1977] 3 All ER 762, [1977] 3 WLR 101, 121 Sol Jo 335, CA	4.70
Masefield v Alexander [1995] 1 FLR 100, [1995] Fam Law 130, 159 JP 663, CA	4.88
Masich v Masich (1977) 7 Fam Law 245, 121 Sol Jo 645, CA	11.20, 11.46, A.74
Mesher v Mesher and Hall [1980] 1 All ER 126n, CA	4.25, 4.70
Mette v Mette (1859) 28 LJP & M 117, 1 Sw & Tr 416, 7 WR 543, 33 LTOS 139	6.2
Michael v Michael [1986] 2 FLR 389, [1986] Fam Law 334, 130 Sol Jo 713, [1986] LS Gaz R 2488, CA	4.19
Midland Bank plc v Cooke [1995] 4 All ER 562, [1996] 1 FCR 442, [1995] 2 FLR 915, [1995] Fam Law 675, 27 HLR 733, [1995] 30 LS Gaz R 34, [1995] NLJR 1543, 139 Sol Jo LB 194, CA	1.2, 4.257, 5.18, 5.22, 5.23, 5.27

PARA

Miles v Miles [1979] 1 All ER 865, [1979] 1 WLR 371, 9 Fam Law 53, 123
Sol Jo 232, CA 12.17
Miller v Miller (1983) 4 FLR 115, 12 Fam Law 150, CA 11.43
Mitchell v Mitchell [1979] CA Transcript 221 .... 11.38
Montgomery v Montgomery [1965] P 46, [1964] 2 All ER 22, [1964] 2 WLR
1036, 108 Sol Jo 260 .... 11.1, 11.4, 11.43
Moody v Stevenson [1992] Ch 486, [1992] 2 WLR 640, [1992] 1 FCR 107,
[1992] 1 FLR 494, [1992] Fam Law 284, 135 Sol Jo LB 84, sub nom Re
Moody, Moody v Stevenson [1992] 2 All ER 524, CA 6.21, 6.22, 6.37
Moran v Moran [1959] CLY 1471, (1959) Times, 25 September 14.7
Mordant, Re, Mordant v Halls [1996] 1 FLR 334, [1996] Fam Law 211, [1995]
BCC 209 .... 4.279
Morgan v Morgan [1977] Fam 122, [1977] 2 All ER 515, [1977] 2 WLR 712,
121 Sol Jo 157 .... 2.52
Morgan v Morgan (1978) 9 Fam Law 87, [1978] CA Transcript 423,
CA 11.19, 11.21, 11.22
Mossop v Mossop [1989] Fam 77, [1988] 2 All ER 202, [1988] 2 WLR 1255,
[1988] 2 FLR 173, [1988] Fam Law 334, 132 Sol Jo 1033, [1988] NLJR
86, CA 5.8
Mouncer v Mouncer [1972] 1 All ER 289, [1972] 1 WLR 321, 116 Sol Jo 78 .... 11.9
Myers v Myers [1982] 1 All ER 776, [1982] 1 WLR 247, 3 FLR 173, 12 Fam
Law 117, 126 Sol Jo 48, CA 11.35

N

N (infants), Re [1967] Ch 512, [1967] 1 All ER 161, [1967] 2 WLR 691,
110 Sol Jo 924 .... 11.29
N (residence: hopeless appeals), Re [1996] 1 FCR 244, [1995] 2 FLR 230,
[1995] Fam Law 600, CA 2.75, 8.123
N (a minor) (child abuse: evidence), Re [1996] 2 FCR 572, [1996] 2 FLR 214,
[1996] Fam Law 460, [1996] NLJR 715, CA 2.37, 2.59, 8.101
N v B [1993] 1 FCR 231 .... 8.133
N v N (consent order: variation) [1994] 2 FCR 275, [1993] 2 FLR 868, [1993]
Fam Law 676, CA 4.13, 4.40, 4.149, 4.170
N v N (valuation: charge-back order) [1996] 1 FLR 361, [1996] Fam Law 81 .... 4.94
NW (a minor), Re [1994] 1 FCR 121, [1993] 2 FLR 591, [1993] Fam Law 617 ..... 8.32
Newham London Borough v AG [1992] 2 FCR 119, [1993] 1 FLR 281, [1993]
Fam Law 122, CA 8.66
Nguyen v Phung [1984] FLR 773, [1985] Fam Law 54, CA 14.11
Nicholas v Nicholas [1984] FLR 285, [1984] Fam Law 118, CA 4.67
Nicholson, Re, Nicholson v Perks [1974] 2 All ER 386, [1974] 1 WLR 476,
118 Sol Jo 133 .... 5.12
Niven v Niven. See John's Assignment Trusts, Re, Niven v Niven
North London Rly Co v Great Northern Rly Co (1883) 11 QBD 30, 52 LJQB
380, 31 WR 490, 48 LT 695, CA 11.41
North Yorkshire County Council v G [1994] 1 FCR 737, [1993] 2 FLR 732,
[1993] Fam Law 623 .... 8.48
Nottinghamshire County Council v H [1995] 2 FCR 365, [1995] 1 FLR 115,
[1995] Fam Law 63 .... 2.54, 8.73
Nottinghamshire County Council v P [1993] 2 WLR 406, [1993] 1 FCR 180,
[1993] 1 FLR 514, [1993] Fam Law 222; on appeal sub nom Nottingham
County Council v P [1994] Fam 18, [1993] 3 All ER 815, [1993] 3 WLR
637, 92 LGR 72, [1994] 1 FCR 624, [1993] 2 FLR 134, [1993] 26 LS Gaz
R 37, 137 Sol Jo LB 147, CA 8.36, 8.44, 8.84, 13.10

O

O (minors) (medical examination), Re [1992] 2 FCR 394, [1993] 1 FLR 860,
[1993] Fam Law 473, [1993] NLJR 814 .... 8.96

lxii Table of Cases

PARA

O (a minor) (medical treatment), Re [1993] 1 FCR 925, [1993] 2 FLR 149,
  [1993] Fam Law 454, [1993] 4 Med LR 272, 19 BMLR 148, 137 Sol Jo
  LB 107 .... 7.31
O, Re [1993] 2 FCR 482, [1993] 1 FLR 172, [1994] Fam Law 127 .... 8.23
O (a minor) (contact: imposition of conditions), Re [1996] 1 FCR 317,
  [1995] 2 FLR 124, [1995] Fam Law 541, CA 8.29
O v Berkshire County Council [1992] 4 All ER 905, [1992] 1 WLR 912,
  [1992] 1 FCR 489, [1992] 2 FLR 7, [1992] Fam Law 487, [1992] 21 LS
  Gaz R 26 .... 8.93
O'Brien v O'Brien [1985] FLR 801, [1985] Fam Law 191, CA 11.38
O'Connor v A and B [1971] 2 All ER 1230, [1971] 1 WLR 1227, 135 JP 492,
  115 Sol Jo 586, HL 7.80
O'D v O'D unreported 4.20
Official Solicitor to the Supreme Court v K [1965] AC 201, [1963] 3 All ER
  191, [1963] 3 WLR 408, 107 Sol Jo 616, HL 8.17
O'Malley v O'Malley [1982] 2 All ER 112, [1982] 1 WLR 244, 3 FLR 418,
  12 Fam Law 87, 126 Sol Jo 154, CA 11.4, 11.41
Omielan v Omielan [1996] 3 FCR 329, [1996] 2 FLR 306, [1996] Fam Law
  608, CA 4.135
Osborne v Osborne [1982] CA Transcript 420 .... 11.38
Overbury, Re, Sheppard v Matthews [1955] Ch 122, [1954] 3 All ER 308,
  [1954] 3 WLR 644, 98 Sol Jo 768 .... 7.46
Oxfordshire County Council v M [1994] Fam 151, [1994] 2 All ER 269, [1994]
  2 WLR 393, [1994] 1 FCR 753, [1994] 1 FLR 175, CA 2.45, 8.72, 8.132
Oxfordshire County Council v P [1995] Fam 161, [1995] 2 All ER 225,
  [1995] 2 WLR 543, [1995] 2 FCR 212, [1995] 1 FLR 552, [1995] Fam
  Law 294 .... 8.73, 8.101

P

P (infants), Re [1962] 3 All ER 789, [1962] 1 WLR 1296, 60 LGR 532, 127
  JP 18, 106 Sol Jo 630 .... 7.82
P (GE) (an infant), Re [1965] Ch 568, [1964] 3 All ER 977, [1965] 2 WLR
  1, 108 Sol Jo 916, CA 7.29, 11.6
P (minors), Re [1988] FCR 428, [1988] 2 FLR 209, [1988] Fam Law 333, CA 8.27
P (a minor), Re [1989] FCR 689, [1989] 2 FLR 43, [1989] Fam Law 312, CA 2.56
P (a minor), Re [1992] 1 FCR 91, CA 8.29
P (a minor), Re [1993] 2 FCR 417, [1993] 1 FLR 915, [1993] Fam Law 462,
  CA 8.23
P (minors), Re [1993] 2 FLR 156, [1993] Fam Law 394 .... 8.85
P (minors), Re [1994] 2 FCR 1306, [1994] 2 FLR 1000, [1995] Fam Law 61,
  CA 7.80, 7.88
P (a minor) (parental responsibility order), Re [1994] 1 FLR 578, [1994] Fam
  Law 378 .... 7.6
P, Re [1994] 1 FLR 771, [1994] Fam Law 310 .... 7.91
P (a minor), Re [1995] 1 FCR 583, [1994] 2 FLR 751 .... 8.67
P (terminating parental responsibility), Re [1995] 3 FCR 753, [1995] 1 FLR
  1048, [1995] Fam Law 471 .... 7.7
P (sexual abuse: standard of proof), Re [1996] 2 FLR 333, [1996] Fam Law
  531, CA 8.9
P v P [1993] Fam Law 283 .... 11.38
P v W [1984] Fam 32, [1984] 1 All ER 866, [1984] 2 WLR 439, 128 Sol Jo
  171, sub nom Patterson v Walcott [1984] FLR 408, [1984] Fam Law 209,
  148 JP 161 .... 13.9
PB (a minor), Re [1985] FLR 394, [1985] Fam Law 198 .... 7.84
Palmer v Townsend (1979) 123 Sol Jo 570, 129 NLJ 1028, CA 14.11
Parker v Parker [1972] Fam 116, [1972] 1 All ER 410, [1972] 2 WLR 21,
  115 Sol Jo 949 .... 3.30

Table of Cases lxiii

PARA

Pascoe v Turner [1979] 2 All ER 945, [1979] 1 WLR 431, 123 Sol Jo 164,
  CA 5.25
Passee v Passee [1988] 1 FLR 263, [1988] Fam Law 132, CA 5.22, 5.28
Paton v British Pregnancy Advisory Service Trustees [1979] QB 276, [1978]
  2 All ER 987, [1978] 3 WLR 687, 142 JP 497, 122 Sol Jo 744 .... 7.20, 11.33,
    11.34, A.68
Paul v Constance [1977] 1 All ER 195, [1977] 1 WLR 527, 7 Fam Law 18, 121
  Sol Jo 320, CA 5.32
Pavlou (a bankrupt), Re [1993] 3 All ER 955, [1993] 1 WLR 1046, [1993]
  2 FLR 751, [1993] Fam Law 629, [1993] 11 LS Gaz R 43 .... 5.27
Peacock v Peacock [1984] 1 All ER 1069, [1984] 1 WLR 532, [1984] FLR
  263, [1984] Fam Law 112, 148 JP 444, 128 Sol Jo 116, 134 NLJ 126 .... 4.17
Pearce v Pearce [1959] CLY 1451, (1959) Times, 30 January 14.7
Pearson v Franklin [1994] 2 All ER 137, [1994] 1 WLR 370, [1994] 2 FCR
  545, [1994] 1 FLR 246, [1994] Fam Law 379, CA 11.7, 13.13
Pearson v Pearson (1981) 3 FLR 137 .... 11.31, 11.41
Peart v Stewart [1983] 2 AC 109, [1983] 1 All ER 859, [1983] 2 WLR 451,
  4 FLR 723, [1984] Fam Law 54, 127 Sol Jo 206, HL 14.10
Peek v Peek [1948] P 46, [1948] 2 All ER 297, 92 Sol Jo 454, 64 TLR 429,
  66 (pt 2) TLR 503, CA 2.66
Pekesin v Pekesin (1978) 8 Fam Law 244, 122 Sol Jo 436, CA 14.11
Penrose v Penrose [1994] 2 FCR 1167, [1994] 2 FLR 621, [1994] Fam Law
  618, CA 4.57
Pettitt v Pettitt [1970] AC 777, [1969] 2 All ER 385, [1969] 2 WLR 966,
  20 P & CR 991, 113 Sol Jo 344, 211 Estates Gazette 829, HL 4.257,
    5.10, 5.16, 5.24, 6.8
Phelps, Re, Wells v Phelps [1980] Ch 275, [1979] 3 All ER 373, [1980] 2 WLR
  277, 124 Sol Jo 85, CA 6.8
Phillips v Pearce [1996] 2 FCR 237, sub nom Phillips v Peace [1996] 2 FLR
  230, [1996] Fam Law 603 .... 15.17
Phillips v Phillips (1905) 49 Sol Jo 724, Times, 19 December 11.33, A.68
Phillips v Phillips [1973] 2 All ER 423, [1973] 1 WLR 615, 117 Sol Jo 323,
  CA 11.1, 11.4
Phonographic Performance Ltd v Amusement Caterers (Peckham) Ltd [1964]
  Ch 195, [1963] 3 All ER 493, [1963] 3 WLR 898, 107 Sol Jo 853 .... A.85
Phonographic Performance Ltd v Tsang [1985] LS Gaz R 2331, (1985) Times,
  17 May, CA 14.7
Pickering v Pickering [1980] CA Transcript 193, CA 14.10, A.84
Pidduck v Molloy [1992] 1 FCR 418, [1992] 2 FLR 202, [1992] Fam Law
  529, CA 14.12
Piller (Anton) KG v Manufacturing Processes Ltd [1976] Ch 55, [1976] 1 All
  ER 779, [1976] 2 WLR 162, [1976] RPC 719, 120 Sol Jo 63, CA 4.173
Pinckney v Pinckney [1966] 1 All ER 121n, 110 Sol Jo 33 .... 11.43
Pittortou (a bankrupt), Re, ex p Trustee of the Property of the Bankrupt v
  Bankrupt [1985] 1 All ER 285, [1985] 1 WLR 58, 129 Sol Jo 47,
  [1985] LS Gaz R 680 .... 4.262, 5.26
Poel v Poel [1970] 1 WLR 1469, 114 Sol Jo 720, sub nom P (LM) (otherwise E)
  v P (GE) [1970] 3 All ER 659, CA 8.38
Poon v Poon [1994] 2 FCR 777, [1994] 2 FLR 857 .... 4.23
Potter v Potter [1990] FCR 704, [1990] 2 FLR 27, [1990] Fam Law 59, CA 12.34
Pounds v Pounds [1994] 4 All ER 777, [1994] 1 WLR 1535, [1994] 2 FCR
  1055, [1994] 1 FLR 775, [1994] Fam Law 436, [1994] NLJR 459,
  CA 3.28, 4.166
Powell v Osbourne [1993] 1 FCR 797, [1993] 1 FLR 1001, [1993] Fam Law
  287, CA 6.33
Practice Direction (injunctions: husband and wife) [1972] 2 All ER 1360,
  [1972] 1 WLR 1047, 116 Sol Jo 572 .... 11.20, 11.30
Practice Direction [1974] 2 All ER 400, [1974] 1 WLR 576 .... 11.19

Table of Cases

PARA

Practice Direction [1974] 2 All ER 1119, [1974] 1 WLR 936 .... 11.19, 11.24, 11.26, 11.27
Practice Direction (22 May 1975, unreported) 12.48
Practice Direction [1975] 2 All ER 384, [1975] 1 WLR 787, 119 Sol Jo 344 .... 11.11
Practice Direction [1976] 2 All ER 447, sub nom Practice Note [1976] 1 WLR 418 .... 6.30
Practice Direction [1977] 2 All ER 714, [1977] 1 WLR 759 .... 3.10
Practice Direction (23 January 1980, unreported) 11.49
Practice Direction [1980] 1 All ER 1007, [1980] 1 WLR 354 .... 12.47
Practice Direction [1981] 2 All ER 642, [1981] 1 WLR 1010 .... 2.51
Practice Direction [1983] 2 All ER 672, [1983] 1 WLR 790, 4 FLR 640, 13 Fam Law 216, 127 Sol Jo 448 .... 7.36
Practice Direction [1984] 1 All ER 684, [1984] 1 WLR 306, [1984] FLR 356, [1984] Fam Law 82, 128 Sol Jo 120 .... 11.29
Practice Direction [1989] 1 All ER 765, [1989] 1 WLR 219, [1989] 1 FLR 307, [1989] Fam Law 166, [1989] NLJR 296 .... 12.9
Practice Direction (statutory charge: form of order of court) [1991] 3 All ER 896, [1991] 1 WLR 955, [1991] 2 FLR 384, 135 Sol Jo LB 117 .... 15.33
Practice Direction [1992] 1 All ER 864, [1992] 1 WLR 261, [1992] 1 FLR 463, [1992] Fam Law 121 .... 8.122
Practice Direction [1992] 3 All ER 151, [1992] 1 WLR 586, [1992] 2 FLR 87, [1992] Fam Law 276, 136 Sol Jo LB 176 .... 4.180, 4.190
Practice Direction [1993] 1 All ER 820, [1993] 1 WLR 313, [1993] 1 FCR 584, [1993] 1 FLR 668, [1993] 13 LS Gaz R 38, 137 Sol Jo LB 95 .... 2.3, 8.50
Practice Direction [1994] 1 All ER 155, [1994] 1 WLR 16, [1994] 1 FCR 419, [1994] 1 FLR 108 .... 8.131
Practice Direction [1994] 4 All ER 52, [1994] 1 WLR 1233, [1995] 1 FCR 347, [1994] 2 FLR 704, [1994] RPC 617, [1994] NLJR 1134 .... 4.187, 4.191
Practice Direction [1996] 2 FLR 368 .... 4.2, 4.27, 4.83
Practice Direction (1996) Times, 31 October 4.187
Practice Note (matrimonial cause: injunction) [1978] 2 All ER 919, sub nom Practice Direction [1978] 1 WLR 925, 122 Sol Jo 460 .... 11.20, A.74
Practice Note [1978] 2 All ER 1056, sub nom Practice Direction (injunction: domestic violence) [1978] 1 WLR 1123, 122 Sol Jo 528 .... 11.39, 11.40, A.60
Practice Note [1981] 1 All ER 224, [1981] 1 WLR 27 .... 11.47
Practice Note [1993] 3 All ER 222, [1993] 2 FCR 657, [1993] 2 FLR 222, [1993] 4 Med LR 302, [1993] 35 LS Gaz R 35, [1993] NLJR 1067, 137 Sol Jo LB 154 .... 8.40
Practice Note [1995] 1 All ER 586, sub nom Practice Direction [1995] 1 WLR 332, [1995] 2 FCR 340, [1995] 1 FLR 456 .... 2.1, 2.22, 2.28, 2.37, 2.39, 2.40, 8.130
Practice Note [1996] 1 FCR 78, [1995] 2 FLR 479 .... 2.63, 8.56
Practice Note (Official Solicitor: sterilisation) [1996] 3 FCR 95, [1996] 2 FLR 111, [1996] Fam Law 439 .... 7.31, 8.41
Pratt v Inman (1889) 43 Ch D 175, 59 LJ Ch 274, 38 WR 200, [1886-90] All ER Rep 1030, 61 LT 760, 6 TLR 91 .... 12.39
Preston v Preston [1982] Fam 17, [1982] 1 All ER 41, [1981] 3 WLR 619, 2 FLR 331, 12 Fam Law 57, 125 Sol Jo 496, CA 4.20
Protector Endowment Co v Whitlam (1877) 36 LT 467 .... 12.7
Pythia, The. See Third Chandris Shipping Corpn v Unimarine SA

Q

Quinn v Quinn (1983) 4 FLR 394, 126 Sol Jo 481, 133 NLJ 615, CA 11.1, 11.4, 11.41

R

R (adoption), Re [1966] 3 All ER 613, [1967] 1 WLR 34, 65 LGR 65, 131 JP 1, 110 Sol Jo 652 .... 7.79

PARA

R (MJ) (a minor), Re [1975] Fam 89, [1975] 2 All ER 749, [1975] 2 WLR 978,
5 Fam Law 154, 119 Sol Jo 338 .... 11.6
R (a minor), Re [1988] FCR 497, [1988] 1 FLR 206, [1988] Fam Law 129, CA 8.27
R (a minor), Re [1991] 1 FLR 291n, [1991] Fam Law 303, sub nom Re J [1991]
FCR 193 .... 2.58, 2.59
R (a minor), Re [1992] Fam 11, [1991] 4 All ER 177, [1991] 3 WLR 592,
[1992] 2 FCR 229, [1992] 1 FLR 190, [1992] Fam Law 67, [1992] 3
Med LR 342, 7 BMLR 147, [1991] NLJR 1297, CA 7.26
R (a minor), Re [1993] 1 FCR 954, [1993] 2 FLR 762, [1993] Fam Law 570,
CA 8.28
R (a minor), Re [1993] 2 FCR 525, [1993] 2 FLR 163, [1993] Fam Law 460,
CA 8.5, 8.21
R (a minor), Re [1993] 2 FCR 544, [1993] 2 FLR 757, [1993] Fam Law 577 .... 7.31
R (minors), Re [1994] 2 FCR 136, sub nom Re J (minors) [1994] 1 FLR 253,
[1994] Fam Law 248 .... 8.3, 8.69, 8.94
R, Re [1995] 2 FCR 573, [1995] 1 FLR 451, [1995] Fam Law 237 .... 2.54
R (a minor), Re [1995] 3 FCR 334, [1995] 2 FLR 612, [1995] Fam Law 601,
CA 8.57
R and G (minors), Re [1994] 1 FLR 793, [1994] Fam Law 314 .... 8.77
R v Ashford (Kent) Justices, ex p Richley [1955] 2 All ER 327n, [1955]
1 WLR 562, 99 Sol Jo 338, DC 9.31
R v Avon County Council, ex p K [1986] 1 FLR 443 .... 9.33
R v B County Council, ex p P [1991] 2 All ER 65, [1991] 1 WLR 221, [1991]
1 FLR 470, [1991] Fam Law 313, sub nom Re P [1991] FCR 337, [1991]
NLJR 163, CA 2.65
R v Bedfordshire County Council, ex p C (1986) 85 LGR 218, [1987] 1 FLR 239,
[1987] Fam Law 55, 151 JP 202 .... 9.33
R v Chan-Fook [1994] 2 All ER 552, [1994] 1 WLR 689, 99 Cr App Rep 147,
[1994] Crim LR 432, CA 11.47, A.76
R v Chief Constable of Merseyside Police, ex p Calveley [1986] QB 424,
[1986] 1 All ER 257, [1986] 2 WLR 144, 130 Sol Jo 53, [1986] LS Gaz
R 124, CA 9.24
R v Cornwall County Council, ex p Cornwall and Isles of Scilly Guardians ad
Litem and Reporting Officers Panel [1992] 2 All ER 471, [1992] 1 WLR
427, 90 LGR 159, [1992] 1 FCR 511, [1992] 4 LS Gaz R 33, 135 Sol Jo
LB 204, sub nom R v Cornwall County Council, ex p G [1992] 1 FLR 270,
[1992] Fam Law 110 .... 8.101, 9.38
R v Derby Magistrates' Court, ex p B [1996] AC 487, [1995] 4 All ER 526,
[1995] 3 WLR 681, [1996] 1 Cr App Rep 385, [1996] 1 FLR 513,
[1996] Fam Law 210, 159 JP 785, [1996] Crim LR 190, [1995] NLJR
1575, 139 Sol Jo LB 219, HL 2.45, 8.72
R v Derbyshire County Council, ex p T [1990] Fam 164, [1990] 1 All ER
792, [1990] 2 WLR 101, 88 LGR 245, [1989] FCR 713, [1990] 1 FLR 237,
[1990] Fam Law 141, 133 Sol Jo 1626, [1990] 1 LS Gaz R 31, CA 9.33
R v Disciplinary Committee of the Jockey Club, ex p Aga Khan [1993] 2 All
ER 853, [1993] 1 WLR 909, CA 9.25
R v Dover Magistrates' Court, ex p Kidner [1983] 1 All ER 475, 13 Fam Law
208, 147 JP 254, 127 Sol Jo 105 .... 9.33
R v East Sussex County Council, ex p R [1990] FCR 873, [1991] 2 FLR 358,
[1991] Fam Law 359 .... 9.37
R v Essex County Council, ex p Washington (1986) 85 LGR 210, [1987] 1
FLR 148, [1987] Fam Law 18, 151 JP 258 .... 9.30
R v Green (1992) Times, 14 July, CA 14.9
R v Hampshire County Council, ex p K [1990] 2 QB 71, [1990] 2 All ER 129,
[1990] 2 WLR 649, 88 LGR 618, [1990] FCR 545, [1990] 1 FLR 330,
[1990] Fam Law 253 .... 2.40, 2.41, 2.48, 9.33
R v Harrow London Borough Council, ex p D [1990] Fam 133, [1990] 3 All
ER 12, [1989] 3 WLR 1239, 88 LGR 41, [1989] FCR 729, [1990] 1 FLR 79,
[1990] Fam Law 18, 133 Sol Jo 1513, [1989] NLJR 1153, CA 9.37

Table of Cases

	PARA
R v Hereford and Worcester County Council, ex p D [1992] 1 FCR 497, [1992] 1 FLR 448, [1992] Fam Law 238	8.101, 9.33
R v Hertfordshire County Council, ex p B (1986) 85 LGR 218, [1987] 1 FLR 239, [1987] Fam Law 55, 151 JP 202	9.33
R v Ireland [1996] 3 WLR 650, [1996] 2 Cr App Rep 426, 160 JP 597, [1996] 23 LS Gaz R 35, 140 Sol Jo LB 148, CA	11.33, 11.47, A.68, A.76
R v Jackson [1891] 1 QB 671, 55 JP 246, 60 LJQB 346, 39 WR 407, [1891-4] All ER Rep 61, 64 LT 679, 7 TLR 382, CA	11.32
R v Johnson (1996) 160 JP 605, [1996] 22 LS Gaz R 26, 140 Sol Jo LB 183, CA	11.33
R v Kensington Income Tax General Comrs, ex p Princess de Polignac [1917] 1 KB 486, 86 LJKB 257, 61 Sol Jo 182, 116 LT 136, 33 TLR 113, CA	4.187, 11.10
R v Lancashire County Council, ex p M [1992] 1 FCR 283, [1992] 1 FLR 109, [1992] Fam Law 146, CA	9.37
R v Leeds County Court, ex p Morris [1990] 1 QB 523, [1990] 1 All ER 550, [1990] 2 WLR 175, 154 JP 385, 134 Sol Jo 285, [1990] 4 LS Gaz R 41	15.26
R v London Borough of Greenwich, ex p Patterson [1994] 2 FCR 323, [1993] 2 FLR 886, [1993] Fam Law 678, CA	9.31
R v London Borough of Wandsworth, ex p P (1989) 87 LGR 370, [1989] 1 FLR 387, [1989] Fam Law 185	9.33
R v Luton Magistrates' Court, ex p Sullivan [1992] 1 FCR 475, [1992] 2 FLR 196, [1992] Fam Law 380	9.34, 12.15
R v Miller [1954] 2 QB 282, [1954] 2 All ER 529, [1954] 2 WLR 138, 38 Cr App Rep 1, 118 JP 340, 98 Sol Jo 62	11.47, A.76
R v Norfolk County Council, ex p X [1989] 2 FLR 120, sub nom R v Norfolk County Council Social Services Department, ex p M [1989] QB 619, [1989] 2 All ER 359, [1989] 3 WLR 502, 87 LGR 598, [1989] FCR 667, [1989] Fam Law 310, [1989] NLJR 293	9.33
R v North Yorkshire County Council, ex p M [1989] QB 411, [1989] 1 All ER 143, [1988] 3 WLR 1344, 87 LGR 186, [1989] FCR 128, [1989] 1 FLR 203, [1989] Fam Law 102, [1989] 5 LS Gaz R 42	9.33
R v North Yorkshire County Council, ex p M (No 2) [1989] FCR 394, [1989] 2 FLR 79, [1989] Fam Law 350	9.37
R v North Yorkshire County Council, ex p M (No 3) [1989] FCR 403, [1989] 2 FLR 82, [1989] Fam Law 350	9.35
R v Nottingham County Court, ex p Byers [1985] 1 All ER 735, [1985] 1 WLR 403, [1985] FLR 695, 128 Sol Jo 873	3.10
R v Oxfordshire County Council [1992] Fam 150, [1992] 3 All ER 660, [1992] 3 WLR 88, sub nom Oxfordshire County Council v R [1992] 1 FLR 648, [1992] Fam Law 338	8.125, 8.133
R v R (1979) 10 Fam Law 56, CA	14.10
R v R [1992] 1 AC 599, [1991] 4 All ER 481, [1991] 3 WLR 767, 94 Cr App Rep 216, [1992] 1 FLR 217, [1992] Fam Law 108, 155 JP 989, [1992] Crim LR 207, 135 Sol Jo LB 181, HL	11.33
R v Reigate Justices, ex p Counsell (1983) 148 JP 193	11.47
R v Savage [1992] 1 AC 699, [1991] 4 All ER 698, [1991] 3 WLR 914, 94 Cr App Rep 193, 155 JP 935, HL	A.68
R v Secretary of State for Education and Science, ex p Lashford (1988) 86 LGR 13, [1988] 1 FLR 72, [1988] Fam Law 59, CA	9.20
R v Secretary of State for Foreign and Commonwealth Affairs, ex p Everett [1989] QB 811, [1989] 1 All ER 655, [1989] 2 WLR 224, [1989] Imm AR 155, 133 Sol Jo 151, [1989] 8 LS Gaz R 43, CA	9.25
R v Secretary of State for Social Security, ex p Biggin [1995] 2 FCR 595, [1995] 1 FLR 851	10.91
R v Secretary of State for the Home Department, ex p Brassey and Brassey [1989] FCR 423, [1989] 2 FLR 486, [1989] Fam Law 356, [1989] Imm AR 258, 133 Sol Jo 388, [1989] 15 LS Gaz R 36	9.33

                                                              PARA
R v Secretary of State for the Home Department, ex p Rukshanda Begum
  [1990] Imm AR 1, [1990] COD 107, CA 9.24
R v Sheppard [1981] AC 394, [1980] 3 All ER 899, [1980] 3 WLR 960, 72
  Cr App Rep 82, 145 JP 65, [1981] Crim LR 171, 124 Sol Jo 864, HL A.56
R v Slough Justices, ex p Lindsay (1996) Times, 14 November 9.34, 10.97, 12.15
R v Solihull Metropolitan Borough Council, ex p C [1984] FLR 363, [1984]
  Fam Law 175 .... 9.33
R v South East Hampshire Family Proceedings Court, ex p D [1994] 2 All
  ER 445, [1994] 1 WLR 611, [1994] 1 FCR 620, [1994] 2 FLR 190,
  [1994] Fam Law 560 .... 9.34
R v Stratford-on-Avon District Council, ex p Jackson [1985] 3 All ER 769,
  [1985] 1 WLR 1319, 84 LGR 287, 51 P & CR 76, 129 Sol Jo 854, [1985]
  LS Gaz R 3533, CA 9.31
R v Thornley (1980) 72 Cr App Rep 302, [1981] Crim LR 637, CA 11.48, A.80
R v Wareham Magistrates' Court, ex p Seldon [1988] 1 All ER 746, [1988]
  1 WLR 825, [1988] FCR 273, [1988] 2 FLR 269, [1988] Fam Law 390,
  132 Sol Jo 994, [1988] 27 LS Gaz R 39 .... 9.33
R v West Malling Juvenile Court, ex p K [1986] 2 FLR 405, [1986] Fam Law
  328, 150 JP 367, 130 Sol Jo 650, [1986] LS Gaz R 1804 .... 9.33
R v Willesden Justices, ex p London Borough of Brent (1989) 86 LGR 197,
  [1989] FCR 2, [1988] 2 FLR 95, [1988] Fam Law 341 .... 9.33
R v Worcester City Juvenile Court, ex p F [1989] 1 All ER 500, [1989] FCR 110,
  [1989] 1 FLR 230, [1989] Fam Law 143, 132 Sol Jo 1526 .... 9.33
Rashid v Rashid (1978) 9 Fam Law 118, CA 8.27
Raymond v Honey [1983] 1 AC 1, [1982] 1 All ER 756, [1982] 2 WLR 465,
  75 Cr App Rep 16, 126 Sol Jo 188, HL 14.14
Razelos v Razelos [1969] 3 All ER 929, 114 Sol Jo 167, sub nom Razelos v
  Razelos (No 2) [1970] 1 WLR 390 .... 5.10
Refson (PS) & Co Ltd v Saggers [1984] 3 All ER 111, [1984] 1 WLR 1025,
  128 Sol Jo 152 .... 11.19
Regan v Regan [1977] 1 All ER 428, [1977] 1 WLR 84, 75 LGR 257, 7 Fam
  Law 17, 121 Sol Jo 84 .... 4.66, 11.45
Reid v Reid (1984) Times, 30 July, CA 11.38, 11.39
Reiterbund v Reiterbund [1975] Fam 99, [1975] 1 All ER 280, [1975] 2 WLR
  375, 118 Sol Jo 831, CA 3.30
Rendell v Grundy [1895] 1 QB 16, 64 LJQB 135, 14 R 19, 43 WR 50, 39 Sol
  Jo 26, 71 LT 564, [1891-4] All ER Rep Ext 1341, CA 12.8
Rennick v Rennick [1978] 1 All ER 817, [1977] 1 WLR 1455, 121 Sol Jo
  792, CA 11.19, 11.20, 11.35, A.74
Richards v Richards [1984] AC 174, [1983] 2 All ER 807, [1983] 3 WLR
  173, [1984] FLR 11, 13 Fam Law 256, 147 JP 481, 12 HLR 73, 127 Sol
  Jo 476, [1983] LS Gaz R 2134, 133 NLJ 725, HL 8.2, 11.35, 11.38,
                                                                          11.41, 11.42, A.1, A.48,
                                                                          A.50, A.52, A.53, A.54
Richardson v Richardson [1993] 4 All ER 673, [1994] 1 WLR 186, [1994]
  1 FCR 53, [1994] 1 FLR 286 .... 4.45, 4.170
Richardson v Richardson (No 2) [1994] 2 FCR 826, [1994] 2 FLR 1051,
  [1995] Fam Law 14 .... 4.35
Ridehalgh v Horsefield [1994] Ch 205, [1994] 3 All ER 848, [1994] 3 WLR
  462, [1994] 2 FLR 194, [1994] Fam Law 560, [1994] BCC 390, CA 15.19
Roberts, Re, Roberts v Roberts [1978] 3 All ER 225, [1978] 1 WLR 653,
  122 Sol Jo 264, CA 6.2
Roberts v Roberts [1986] 2 All ER 483, [1986] 1 WLR 437, [1986] 2 FLR
  152, 130 Sol Jo 315, [1986] LS Gaz R 1554 .... 4.104
Roberts v Roberts [1990] FCR 837, [1990] 2 FLR 111, [1990] Fam Law
  330, CA 4.146
Roberts v Roberts [1991] FCR 590, [1991] 1 FLR 294, [1991] Fam Law
  65, CA 11.49, A.82

Table of Cases

	PARA
Robin v Robin (1983) 4 FLR 632, 13 Fam Law 147, CA	5.7
Robinson v Collins [1975] 1 All ER 321, sub nom Re Collins, Robinson v Collins [1975] 1 WLR 309, 119 Sol Jo 66	6.8
Robinson v Robinson [1965] P 39, [1963] 3 All ER 813, [1964] 2 WLR 138, 107 Sol Jo 620	11.1, 11.4
Robinson v Smith [1915] 1 KB 711, 84 LJKB 783, 59 Sol Jo 269, 112 LT 929, 31 TLR 191, CA	A.19
Rochdale Borough Council v BW [1991] FCR 705, sub nom Rochdale Borough Council v A [1991] 2 FLR 192, [1991] Fam Law 374	2.30, 2.48, 2.59
Romilly v Romilly [1964] P 22, [1963] 3 All ER 607, [1963] 3 WLR 732, 106 Sol Jo 1034	12.39
Ross v Pearson [1976] 1 All ER 790, [1976] 1 WLR 224, 140 JP 282, 119 Sol Jo 864	12.9
Ruddell v Ruddell (1967) 111 Sol Jo 497	11.4
Russell v Russell [1986] 1 FLR 465, [1986] Fam Law 156, 129 Sol Jo 684, [1985] LS Gaz R 3084, [1985] NLJ Rep 829, CA	12.9

S

S (minors), Re (1980) 11 Fam Law 55, CA	11.6
S (a minor), Re [1985] FLR 579, [1985] Fam Law 132, [1985] LS Gaz R 278, CA	7.61
S (a minor), Re [1991] FCR 155, [1991] 2 FLR 388, [1991] Fam Law 302, CA	8.8, 8.21
S (minors), Re [1992] 1 FCR 158, [1992] Fam Law 148, CA	8.21
S (a minor), Re [1992] 2 FCR 554, [1993] 1 FLR 110, [1993] Fam Law 129, [1992] 31 LS Gaz R 35, 136 Sol Jo LB 206, CA	8.101
S (a minor) (independent representation), Re [1993] Fam 263, [1993] 3 All ER 36, [1993] 2 WLR 801, [1993] 2 FLR 437, [1993] Fam Law 465, [1993] NLJR 435, CA	8.55
S (J) (a minor), Re [1993] 2 FCR 193, [1993] 2 FLR 919, [1993] Fam Law 621	8.48, 8.77
S (a minor), Re [1994] 1 FCR 604, [1994] 2 FLR 1065, [1995] Fam Law 20	7.18, 7.26
S, Re [1994] 2 FCR 414, [1994] 2 FLR 222, [1994] Fam Law 425, CA	8.89
S (minors), Re [1994] 2 FCR 986, [1994] 1 FLR 623, [1994] Fam Law 426	7.31, 7.34, 8.44, 13.12
S, Re [1995] 1 FCR 617, [1994] 2 FLR 1057, [1995] Fam Law 12, CA	8.121
S, Re [1995] 2 FCR 697, [1995] 1 FLR 151, [1995] Fam Law 64, CA	8.75
S (a minor), Re [1995] 3 FCR 225, [1995] 2 FLR 648, [1995] Fam Law 596, CA	7.6
S (minors), Re [1995] 2 FLR 639, [1995] Fam Law 667, [1995] 31 LS Gaz R 33, CA	8.76, 8.100
S (financial provision: non-resident), Re [1996] 1 FCR 148, CA	4.173
S (care or supervision order), Re [1996] 2 FCR 719, [1996] 1 FLR 753, [1996] Fam Law 268, CA	8.77
S (contact: grandparents), Re [1996] 3 FCR 30, [1996] 1 FLR 158, [1996] Fam Law 76, CA	8.12, 8.101
S v E [1993] 1 FCR 729, [1993] Fam Law 407	8.70
S v R (parental responsibility) [1993] 1 FCR 331, [1993] Fam Law 339	7.6, 8.12, 8.18
S v S (1980) 10 Fam Law 153, 124 Sol Jo 219	11.44
S v S [1986] Fam 189, [1986] 3 All ER 566, [1986] 3 WLR 518, [1987] 1 FLR 71, [1986] Fam Law 364, 150 JP 561, 130 Sol Jo 573, [1986] LS Gaz R 2488; on appeal [1987] 2 All ER 312, [1987] 1 WLR 382n, [1987] 2 FLR 342n, [1987] Fam Law 312, CA	4.136
S v S [1988] FCR 219, [1988] 1 FLR 213, [1988] Fam Law 128, CA	8.27
S v S [1993] Fam 200, [1993] 2 WLR 401, [1993] 1 FLR 606, [1993] Fam Law 224	5.61

  PARA

S v S and P [1962] 2 All ER 1, 106 Sol Jo 152, sub nom S v S [1962] 1 WLR
    445, CA 8.25
S v W (1980) 11 Fam Law 81, CA 8.7
SC (a minor) (leave to seek residence order), Re [1994] 1 FCR 837, [1994] 1
    FLR 96, [1993] Fam Law 618 .... 8.50
SH (care order: orphan), Re [1996] 1 FCR 1, [1995] 1 FLR 746, [1995] Fam
    Law 354 .... 8.74
SM (a minor), Re [1991] FCR 492, [1991] 2 FLR 333, [1991] Fam Law 308 .... 8.27
S, S and A (care proceedings:issue estoppel), Re [1995] 2 FLR 244, [1995] Fam
    Law 601, sub nom L (minors) (care proceedings: issue estoppel), Re [1996]
    1 FCR 221 .... 2.32
SW (a minor), Re [1993] 1 FCR 896, [1993] 2 FLR 609, [1993] Fam Law 409 ...... 8.45
Salmon, Re, Coard v National Westminster Bank Ltd [1981] Ch 167, [1980] 3
    All ER 532, [1980] 3 WLR 748, 124 Sol Jo 813 .... 6.28
Samson v Samson [1960] 1 All ER 653, [1960] 1 WLR 190, 104 Sol Jo 208, CA .. 5.19
Samson v Samson [1982] 1 All ER 780, [1982] 1 WLR 252, 3 FLR 178, 12
    Fam Law 118, 126 Sol Jo 155, 133 NLJ 233, CA 11.35
Sansom v Sansom (1879) 4 PD 69, 48 LJP 25, 27 WR 692, 39 LT 642 .... 12.39
Santos v Santos [1972] Fam 247, [1972] 2 All ER 246, [1972] 2 WLR 889,
    116 Sol Jo 196, CA 6.16, 11.8, A.5, A.7, A.13
Saunders, Re, Public Trustee v Saunders [1929] 1 Ch 674, 98 LJ Ch 303, 141
    LT 27, 45 TLR 283 .... 6.8
Savage v Norton [1908] 1 Ch 290, 77 LJ Ch 198, 98 LT 382 .... 12.34
Savage v Savage [1979] CA Transcript 537 .... 11.23, 11.24, 11.27, 14.7
Savill v Goodall [1994] 1 FCR 325, [1993] 1 FLR 755, [1993] Fam Law 289,
    CA 5.18, 5.27
Scott, Re, Widdows v Friends of the Clergy Corpn [1975] 2 All ER 1033,
    [1975] 1 WLR 1260, 119 Sol Jo 508 .... 6.11
Seaford, Re, Seaford v Seifert [1968] P 53, [1968] 1 All ER 482, [1968] 2 WLR
    155, 111 Sol Jo 981, CA 6.7
Searle, Re, Searle v Siems [1949] Ch 73, [1948] 2 All ER 426, [1948] LJR
    1843, 92 Sol Jo 456, 64 TLR 397 .... 6.28
Seaward v Paterson [1897] 1 Ch 545, 66 LJ Ch 267, 45 WR 610, [1895-9] All
    ER Rep 1127, 76 LT 215, 13 TLR 211, CA 14.13, A.15
Sehota, Re, Surjit Kaur v Gian Kaur [1978] 3 All ER 385, [1978] 1 WLR
    1506, 122 Sol Jo 844 .... 6.7, 6.14, 11.2, A.11
Sennar, The. See DSV Silo-und Verwaltungsgesellschaft mbH v Sennar (Owners),
    The Sennar
Seray-Wurie v Seray-Wurie [1987] Fam Law 124, CA 11.3, 11.5, A.11
Shaw v Fitzgerald [1992] 1 FCR 162, [1992] 1 FLR 357, sub nom S v F
    [1992] Fam Law 107, 135 Sol Jo 127 .... 5.4, A.19, A.21
Shipman v Shipman [1991] FCR 628, [1991] 1 FLR 250, [1991] Fam Law
    145 .... 4.176, 4.186
Shipp v Shipp [1988] 1 FLR 345, [1988] Fam Law 168, CA 11.39
Silverstone v Silverstone [1953] P 174, [1953] 1 All ER 556, [1953] 2 WLR
    513, 97 Sol Jo 156 .... 11.43
Sinclair, Re, Lloyds Bank plc v Imperial Cancer Research Fund [1985] Ch
    446, [1985] 1 All ER 1066, [1985] 2 WLR 795, [1985] FLR 965, [1985]
    Fam Law 227, 129 Sol Jo 206, [1985] LS Gaz R 1567, CA 6.4
Sinclair-Jones v Kay [1988] 2 All ER 611, [1989] 1 WLR 114, 133 Sol Jo
    220, [1989] 10 LS Gaz R 42, [1988] NLJR 99, CA 15.19
Siskina (Cargo Owners) v Distos Cia Naviera SA, The Siskina [1979] AC
    210, [1977] 3 All ER 803, [1977] 3 WLR 818, [1978] 1 CMLR 190,
    [1978] 1 Lloyd's Rep 1, 121 Sol Jo 744, HL 11.1
Smith v Smith (1979) 10 Fam Law 50, CA 11.38
Smith v Smith [1988] FCR 225, [1988] 1 FLR 179, [1988] Fam Law 21,
    CA 11.49, 14.10, A.84
Smith v Smith [1991] FCR 233, [1991] 2 FLR 55, [1991] Fam Law 413, CA 14.9

PARA

Smith v Smith (Smith intervening) [1992] Fam 69, [1991] 2 All ER 306, [1991] 3 WLR 646, [1991] FCR 791, [1991] 2 FLR 432, [1991] Fam Law 412, CA 2.70
Smith v Smith [1992] 2 FCR 33, [1992] 2 FLR 40, CA 14.11
Smollen v Smollen [1979] CA Transcript 794 .... 11.20
Snoek, Re (1983) 13 Fam Law 18 .... 6.21
South Glamorgan County Council v W and B [1993] 1 FCR 626, [1993] 1 FLR 574, [1993] Fam Law 398, 11 BMLR 162 .... 7.31
Spence, Re, Spence v Dennis [1990] Ch 652, [1990] 2 All ER 827, [1990] 2 WLR 1430, [1990] FCR 983, [1990] 2 FLR 278, [1990] Fam Law 475, CA 6.9
Spencer v Camacho (1983) 4 FLR 662, 13 Fam Law 114, 12 HLR 130, 127 Sol Jo 155, CA 11.40, A.61
Spindlow v Spindlow [1979] Fam 52, [1979] 1 All ER 169, [1978] 3 WLR 777, 1 FLR 133, 9 Fam Law 22, 122 Sol Jo 556, CA 11.34, 11.35
Spooner v Spooner (1962) 106 Sol Jo 1034, (1962) Times, 4 December................... 14.7
Springette v Defoe (1992) 65 P & CR 1, [1992] 2 FCR 561, [1992] 2 FLR 388, [1992] Fam Law 489, 24 HLR 552, CA 5.17, 5.19
Spurling's Will Trusts, Re, Philpot v Philpot [1966] 1 All ER 745, [1966] 1 WLR 920, 110 Sol Jo 408 .... 15.18, 15.28
Stewart v Stewart [1973] Fam 21, [1973] 1 All ER 31, [1972] 3 WLR 907, 116 Sol Jo 920 .... 11.1, 11.4, 14.10
Stock v Brown [1994] 2 FCR 1125, [1994] 1 FLR 840, [1994] Fam Law 254 .... 6.28
Stockport Metropolitan Borough Council v D [1995] 1 FLR 873, [1995] Fam Law 405, sub nom D (a minor), Re [1995] 2 FCR 681 .... 8.70
Summers v Summers [1986] 1 FLR 343, [1986] Fam Law 56, CA 11.38, 11.39
Summers v Summers (1987) Times, 19 May, CA 11.38, 11.39
Suttill v Graham [1977] 3 All ER 1117, [1977] 1 WLR 819, 7 Fam Law 211, 121 Sol Jo 408, CA 5.7
Symmons v Symmons [1993] 1 FLR 317, [1993] Fam Law 135 .... 12.10, 12.17
Szczepanski v Szczepanski [1985] FLR 468, [1985] Fam Law 120, 134 NLJ 944, CA 14.9

T

T (a minor), Re [1986] Fam 160, [1986] 1 All ER 817, [1986] 2 WLR 538, [1986] 2 FLR 31, [1986] Fam Law 184, 130 Sol Jo 88, [1986] LS Gaz R 520, CA 7.77
T (a minor), Re, T v T [1987] 1 FLR 181, [1986] Fam Law 298, CA 11.38, 11.42
T (a minor), Re [1993] 1 FCR 973, [1993] 2 FLR 450, [1993] Fam Law 572, CA 7.6, 8.27
T (a minor), Re [1994] 1 FCR 663, [1994] 1 FLR 103, [1994] Fam Law 75, CA ... 8.77
T (a minor), Re [1994] 1 FLR 632; revsd [1994] 1 FLR 632, [1994] NLJR 123, CA 8.101
T, Re [1995] 1 FCR 517, [1995] 1 FLR 159, [1995] Fam Law 125 .... 9.32, 9.33
T, Re [1995] 2 FCR 537, [1995] 2 FLR 251, [1995] Fam Law 536, CA 7.85, 8.31
T (disclosure), Re [1995] Fam Law 603 .... 8.73
T v S [1994] 1 FCR 743, [1994] 2 FLR 883, [1995] Fam Law 11 .... 5.56
T and E, Re [1995] 3 FCR 260, [1995] 1 FLR 581, [1995] Fam Law 232 ..... 8.2, 8.131
TB (care proceedings:criminal trial), Re [1996] 1 FCR 101, [1995] 2 FLR 801, [1996] Fam Law 13, CA 8.75
Thaha v Thaha [1987] 2 FLR 142, [1987] Fam Law 234, [1987] NLJ Rep 904 .... 12.4, 12.49
Third Chandris Shipping Corpn v Unimarine SA [1979] QB 645, [1979] 3 WLR 122, 123 Sol Jo 389, sub nom Third Chandris Shipping Corpn v Unimarine SA, The Pythia, The Angelic Wings, The Genie [1979] 2 All ER 972, [1979] 2 Lloyd's Rep 184, CA 4.187
Thomas v Fuller-Brown [1988] 1 FLR 237, [1988] Fam Law 53, CA 5.24
Thomas v Thomas [1996] 2 FCR 544, [1995] 2 FLR 668, [1995] Fam Law 672, CA 1.2, 4.19

Table of Cases lxxi

PARA

Thompson v Thompson [1976] Fam 25, [1975] 2 All ER 208, [1975] 2 WLR
 868, 73 LGR 488, 30 P & CR 91, 119 Sol Jo 255, CA 4.66, 11.45
Thompson v Thompson [1994] 1 FCR 97, [1993] 2 FLR 464, [1993] Fam Law
 626, CA 15.15
Thorne RDC v Bunting (No 2) [1972] 3 All ER 1084, 71 LGR 111, 137 JP
 40, CA 14.13, A.15
Thurley v Smith [1984] FLR 875, [1985] Fam Law 31, CA 11.39
Tribe v Tribe [1996] Ch 107, [1995] 4 All ER 236, [1995] 3 WLR 913, 71
 P & CR 503, [1996] 1 FCR 338, [1995] 2 FLR 966, [1996] Fam Law
 29, [1995] 32 LS Gaz R 30, [1995] NLJR 1445, 139 Sol Jo LB 203, CA 2.35
Trott, Re, Trott v Miles [1958] 2 All ER 296, [1958] 1 WLR 604, 102 Sol
 Jo 401 .... 6.28
Tuck v Nicholls [1989] FCR 300, [1989] 1 FLR 283, [1989] Fam Law 103,
 CA 11.39
Turton v Turton [1988] Ch 542, [1987] 2 All ER 641, [1987] 3 WLR 622,
 55 P & CR 88, [1988] 1 FLR 23, [1987] Fam Law 383, 131 Sol Jo 540,
 [1987] LS Gaz R 1492, CA 5.28
Tyler v Tyler [1990] FCR 22, [1989] 2 FLR 158, [1989] Fam Law 316, CA 8.38

U

U (T) (a minor), Re [1993] 2 FCR 565, [1994] Fam Law 316 .... 8.125
Underwood, Re, Re Bowles, U v W (1903) 51 WR 335, CA 12.49
Universal Thermosensors Ltd v Hibben [1992] 3 All ER 257, [1992] 1 WLR
 840, [1992] FSR 361, [1992] 26 LS Gaz R 31, [1992] NLJR 195 .... 4.191

V

V (a minor), Re (1979) 123 Sol Jo 201 .... 11.32, 11.42
V (care or supervision order), Re [1996] 2 FCR 555, [1996] 1 FLR 776,
 [1996] Fam Law 269, CA 8.77
V (residence order), Re [1996] 3 FCR 101, sub nom V (residence: review), Re
 [1995] 2 FLR 1010, [1996] Fam Law 78, CA 8.15
Van Hoorn v Law Society [1985] QB 106, [1984] 3 All ER 136, [1984] 3
 WLR 199, [1984] FLR 203, 13 Fam Law 261, 128 Sol Jo 483, [1984]
 LS Gaz R 2623 .... 15.29, 15.30
Vaughan v Vaughan [1973] 3 All ER 449, [1973] 1 WLR 1159, 117 Sol Jo
 583, CA 11.33, 11.46, 14.12, A.68
Vernon v Bosley (No 2) [1995] 2 FCR 78 .... 8.131

W

W (an infant), Re [1971] AC 682, [1971] 2 All ER 49, [1971] 2 WLR 1011,
 135 JP 259, 115 Sol Jo 286, HL 7.80
W (a minor), Re [1981] 3 All ER 401, 11 Fam Law 207, CA 11.7, 11.32, 11.42
W (a minor), Re [1985] AC 791, [1985] 2 WLR 892, 83 LGR 669, [1985]
 FLR 879, [1985] Fam Law 326, 149 JP 593, 129 Sol Jo 347, [1985]
 LS Gaz R 2087, [1985] NLJ Rep 483, sub nom W v Hertfordshire County
 Council [1985] 2 All ER 301, HL 7.33
W (a minor), Re [1986] Fam 54, [1985] 3 All ER 449, [1985] 3 WLR 945,
 [1986] 1 FLR 179, [1986] Fam Law 57, 129 Sol Jo 794, [1985] NLJ Rep
 964, CA 7.71
W (minors) (residence order), Re [1992] 2 FCR 461, CA 8.5, 8.20
W (a minor) (residence order: baby), Re [1992] 2 FCR 603, [1992] 2 FLR 332,
 [1992] Fam Law 493, CA 8.8, 8.21
W (a minor) (medical treatment), Re [1993] Fam 64, [1992] 4 All ER 627,
 [1992] 3 WLR 758, [1992] 2 FCR 785, [1993] 1 FLR 1, [1992] Fam
 Law 541, 9 BMLR 22, [1992] NLJR 1124, CA 7.22, 7.26,
 7.27, 7.31, 7.34, 8.5

lxxii Table of Cases

	PARA
W, Re [1993] 2 FCR 427, CA | 7.6
W (child), Re [1993] 2 FCR 731, [1994] 1 FLR 843, [1994] Fam Law 376 | 8.133
W (a minor), Re [1993] 2 FLR 625, CA | 8.21
W (a minor), Re [1994] 2 FCR 1216, [1994] 2 FLR 441, [1994] Fam Law 614, CA | 8.25, 8.26
W, Re [1994] 3 FCR 242, [1994] 2 FLR 1087, [1995] Fam Law 119 | 8.80
W, Re [1994] 2 FLR 1092, [1995] Fam Law 19 | 9.12
W (a minor), Re [1995] 2 FCR 184 | 8.6
W (welfare reports), Re [1995] 3 FCR 793, [1995] 2 FLR 142, [1995] Fam Law 544, CA | 8.14
W v A (child: surname) [1981] Fam 14, [1981] 1 All ER 100, [1981] 2 WLR 124, 11 Fam Law 22, 124 Sol Jo 726, CA | 8.40
W v Ealing London Borough Council [1994] 1 FCR 436, [1993] 2 FLR 788, [1993] Fam Law 575, CA | 7.6, 8.22
W v Nottinghamshire County Council [1986] 1 FLR 565, [1986] Fam Law 185, CA | 7.33
W v Official Solicitor (or W) [1972] AC 24, [1970] 3 All ER 107, [1970] 3 WLR 366, 114 Sol Jo 635, HL | 7.54, 7.55
W v W [1961] P 113, [1961] 1 All ER 751, [1961] 2 WLR 878; affd [1961] P 113, [1961] 2 All ER 56, [1961] 2 WLR 878, 105 Sol Jo 403, CA | 12.25
W v W (1981) 2 FLR 291, 11 Fam Law 247 | 2.52
W v W [1988] FCR 640, [1988] 2 FLR 505, [1989] Fam Law 63, [1988] 85 LS Gaz R 38, CA | 2.55
W v W [1995] 2 FLR 259, [1995] Fam Law 548 | 4.24, 4.25, 4.27
W v Wakefield City Council [1994] 2 FCR 564, [1995] 1 FLR 170, [1995] Fam Law 68 | 8.78
W and S (minors), Re [1992] 2 FCR 665 | 8.125
WB (minors) (residence orders), Re [1995] 2 FLR 1023, [1993] Fam Law 395 | 8.37, 8.57, 8.133
Wachtel v Wachtel [1973] Fam 72, [1973] 1 All ER 113, [1973] 2 WLR 84, 116 Sol Jo 762; varied [1973] Fam 72, [1973] 1 All ER 829, [1973] 2 WLR 366, 117 Sol Jo 124, CA | 4.20
Walker v Hall [1984] FLR 126, [1984] Fam Law 21, 127 Sol Jo 550, [1983] LS Gaz R 2139, CA | 5.28
Walker v Walker [1978] 3 All ER 141, [1978] 1 WLR 533, 122 Sol Jo 94, CA | 11.35
Ward v Ward and Greene [1980] 1 All ER 176n, [1980] 1 WLR 4, 10 Fam Law 22, 123 Sol Jo 838, CA | 12.41
Warwick v Warwick (1981) 3 FLR 393, CA | 11.39
Waterman v Waterman [1989] FCR 267, [1989] 1 FLR 380, [1989] Fam Law 227, CA | 4.40
Watson v Nikolaisen [1955] 2 QB 286, [1955] 2 All ER 427, [1955] 2 WLR 1187, 119 JP 419, 99 Sol Jo 370 | 7.82
Waugh v Waugh (1981) 3 FLR 375 | 11.4, 11.41
Wayling v Jones (1993) 69 P & CR 170, [1996] 2 FCR 41, [1995] 2 FLR 1029, [1996] Fam Law 88, [1995] Conv 409, CA | 5.25
Webb v Webb [1986] 1 FLR 541, [1986] NLJ Rep 843, CA | 11.4, 11.41
West Oxfordshire District Council v Beratec Ltd (1986) Times, 30 October | 14.9
Westcott v Westcott [1985] FLR 616, [1985] Fam Law 278, CA | 14.10, 14.11
Whiston v Whiston [1995] Fam 198, [1995] 3 WLR 405, [1995] 2 FCR 496, [1995] 2 FLR 268, [1995] Fam Law 549, CA | 6.14
White v White [1983] Fam 54, [1983] 2 All ER 51, [1983] 2 WLR 872, 4 FLR 696, 13 Fam Law 149, 127 Sol Jo 224, CA | 11.47
Whiting v Whiting [1988] 2 All ER 275, [1988] 1 WLR 565, [1988] FCR 569, [1988] 2 FLR 189, [1988] Fam Law 429, 132 Sol Jo 658, [1988] NLJR 39, CA | 4.40, 6.12
Whitter v Peters [1982] 2 All ER 369, [1982] 1 WLR 389, 4 FLR 8, 12 Fam Law 84, 126 Sol Jo 100, CA | 14.10

Table of Cases lxxiii

PARA

Whytte (or Whyte) v Ticehurst [1986] Fam 64, [1986] 2 All ER 158, [1986] 2 WLR 700, [1986] 2 FLR 83, [1986] Fam Law 192, 130 Sol Jo 185, [1986] LS Gaz R 875 .... 6.12
Wilkinson, Re, Neale v Newell [1978] Fam 22, [1978] 1 All ER 221, [1977] 3 WLR 514, 7 Fam Law 176, 121 Sol Jo 375 .... 6.19, 6.27
Williams v Fawcett [1986] QB 604, [1985] 1 All ER 787, [1985] 1 WLR 501, [1985] FLR 935, [1986] Fam Law 51, 129 Sol Jo 224, [1985] NLJ Rep 227, CA 14.4, 14.5, 14.11
Williams v Johns [1988] 2 FLR 475, [1988] Fam Law 257 .... 6.19, 6.25
Willmott v Willmott [1921] P 143, 90 LJP 206, [1921] All ER Rep 747, 65 Sol Jo 358, 125 LT 27, 37 TLR 429 .... 11.41
Wilson v Carnley [1908] 1 KB 729, 77 LJKB 594, [1908-10] All ER Rep 120, 52 Sol Jo 239, 98 LT 265, 24 TLR 277, CA A.19
Windeler v Whitehall [1990] FCR 268, [1990] 2 FLR 505, [1990] Fam Law 424 .... 3.3
Winstone v Winstone [1960] P 28, [1959] 3 All ER 580, [1959] 3 WLR 660, 103 Sol Jo 875 .... 11.1
Witten (an infant), Re (1887) 57 LT 336, 3 TLR 811 .... 13.26
Wood v Wood (1978) 9 Fam Law 254, [1978] CA Transcript 766, CA 11.38
Woodley v Woodley [1993] 1 FCR 701, [1992] 2 FLR 417, [1993] Fam Law 24, CA 4.280, 12.11
Woodley v Woodley (No 2) [1993] 4 All ER 1010, [1994] 1 WLR 1167, [1993] 2 FCR 661, [1993] 2 FLR 477, [1993] Fam Law 471, [1993] NLJR 475n, CA 12.11
Woolley v Woolley (1974) 124 NLJ 768 .... 14.5, 14.6
Wooton v Wooton [1984] FLR 871, [1985] Fam Law 31, [1983] LS Gaz R 1662, CA 11.38, 11.40
Wright v Jess [1987] 2 All ER 1067, [1987] 1 WLR 1076, [1987] 2 FLR 373, [1987] Fam Law 380, 131 Sol Jo 942, [1987] LS Gaz R 1241, [1987] NLJ Rep 245, CA 14.7
Wright v Wright [1970] 3 All ER 209, [1970] 1 WLR 1219, 114 Sol Jo 619, CA 4.166

X

X (a minor), Re [1975] Fam 54, [1975] 1 All ER 702, 119 Sol Jo 12, CA 11.6
X County Council v A [1985] 1 All ER 53, 128 Sol Jo 873, [1984] LS Gaz R 3259, sub nom Re X (a minor) [1984] 1 WLR 1422, sub nom Re AB [1985] FLR 470, [1985] Fam Law 59 .... 11.32

Y

Y (a minor), Re [1993] 2 FCR 422, [1994] Fam Law 127 .... 8.23
Yager v Musa [1961] 2 QB 214, [1961] 2 All ER 561, [1961] 3 WLR 170, 105 Sol Jo 568, CA 14.14

Z

Z v Z [1992] 2 FCR 152, [1992] 2 FLR 291 .... 4.204

Part I

Introduction

Chapter One

Introduction

David Burrows

Family Law at a Threshold   3
'Family Law' – Towards a Definition   5
Aim of this Book   5
The Court Process   5
'Non-Adversarial' Procedures   6
Full Relevant Disclosure   6
Legal Aid   6
Family Law Act 1996   7

FAMILY LAW AT A THRESHOLD

1.1 Family law approaches a threshold: the Family Law Act 1996 is now on the statute book; legal aid again is proposed for radical reform[1]; the Lord Chancellor's Advisory Group on Ancillary Relief, under Thorpe LJ, has set up a pilot scheme which starts in a variety of courts for ancillary relief proceedings started after 1 October 1996[2]; and watching over all this is Lord Woolf's report on civil justice[3] which will inevitably have a profound effect on the way in which family procedure develops. The Children Act 1989 is, generally speaking, working well[4] both in practice and in application of the law; though court delays and issues over case management remain a real concern[5]. Now it is the turn for radical reform of the substantive law relating to divorce and domestic violence[6]. Reform of statutory provision for matrimonial financial relief may ultimately follow; though with pension provision reform very much in the air[7] and the extensive reframing of the financial provisions of the Matrimonial Causes Act 1973, Part II in the Family Law Act 1996[8] a considerable adjustment of this area of family law is already under way. The area which remains unreconstructed, save in connection with children and their financial support, is cohabitation law[9].

---

1 In May 1995 the Government published a consultation paper, *Legal Aid – Targeting Need* which was followed by a White Paper, *Striking the Balance: The future of legal aid in England and Wales* (June 1966, Cm 3305).

2 See eg *Ancillary Relief Pilot Scheme: Practitioner's Guide* (August 1996, Lord Chancellor's Department SFLA, FLBA) which contains a new Practice Direction, draft rule and new and amended court forms.
3 *Access to Justice: Final Report* (July 1996, HMSO).
4 For commentary on the working of the CA 1989 see, eg Children Act Advisory Committee Annual Reports 1991/2, 1992/3, 1993/4, 1994/5.
5 Dame Margaret Booth, DBE, *Avoiding Delay in Children Act Cases* (July 1996).
6 FLA 1996, Parts II and IV; and see chapter 3 and Appendix 1.
7 MCA 1973, s 24B–D and FLA 1996, s 16; and see para 4.100 et seq.
8 FLA 1996, s 15 and Sch 2.
9 The Law Commission is looking at reform in this area; and eg SFLA have set up a working party to consider proposals to be put to the Government.

1.2 This summarises the position in 1996; but family law has already seen dramatic changes in emphasis and structure over the past 25 years, that is, since the coming into operation on 1 January 1971 of the Divorce Reform Act 1969 and the Matrimonial Proceedings and Property Act 1970 (amalgamated into the Matrimonial Causes Act 1973). This was followed by the extensive development of the law in the field of financial provision and matrimonial property adjustment pioneered by Ormrod LJ[1] and now sustained by Waite LJ[2], who brings to his task the added dimension of looking at family law through the prism of equitable principles.

1 See Thorpe LJ's analysis of these developments in *Dart v Dart* [1996] 2 FLR 286, CA.
2 See eg such cases as *Barry v Barry* [1992] Fam 140, [1992] 2 FLR 233, Waite J; *Midland Bank v Cooke* [1995] 2 FLR 915, CA; *Thomas v Thomas* [1995] 2 FLR 668,CA.

1.3 In the late 1990s there are many more marriages dissolved than there were in the early 1970s; and the extension of property holding over the same period has led to the need for more sophisticated property adjustment on marriage breakdown. Developments in matrimonial property law have been broadened still further by the change to private pension provision. Broadly welcomed by public and practitioners alike, the Children Act 1989 has been assimilated more or less seamlessly into the legal system. Whether the same will be the case with the Family Law Act 1996 remains to be seen: the occupation order and domestic violence provisions[1] seem likely to be acceptable, in many cases most welcome (especially the new children provisions); but whether the same can be said of the divorce provisions[2] and the inadequate (because not properly funded[3]) mediation services[4] must be much more questionable. It is certain that the new law will for a long time be difficult for the average lay person to understand: it only remains to be seen whether practitioners can remain ahead of their clients in comprehension of the artificialities of the Family Law Act 1996, Part II.

1 FLA 1996, Part IV; and see Appendix 1.
2 FLA 1996, Part II; and see para 3.18 et seq.
3 The Government was alerted to this and to the lack of satisfactory regulation of services even before the passing of the Act by Dr Stephen Cretney at the Joseph Jackson Memorial Lecture on 11 January 1996: published as, 'A bit of a racket' in [1996] NLJ 91.
4 FLA 1996, Part III.

'FAMILY LAW' – TOWARDS A DEFINITION

1.4 For most practitioners, family law involves dissolution of marriage, resolution of financial issues between the spouses (whether by agreement or by contested court application); and, sometimes, it involves dealing with a disputed issue concerning a child of the family. However, as we understand the term, 'family law' comprises a wider subject area than this. As will be seen[1], to define 'family proceedings' by reference to the existing law is not an easy task. But what do we mean by the term 'family law' itself? Essentially family law represents the incidence of the law and court process upon families and their children where this is necessitated by relationship breakdown, by domestic violence, by death of a member of the family; or by the failure of the family or the state properly or adequately to provide for children. According to this definition, a little wider, perhaps, than some might accept, we have dealt with a broad spectrum of family topics, including such slightly more recondite aspects of the subject as judicial review, child support, enforcement of orders and so on.

1 Para 2.4.

AIM OF THIS BOOK

1.5 With the above definition in mind we have devised a book whose aim is to provide a guide to enable the practitioner to identify the relevant statutory provisions, both in primary and in delegated legislation, and to apply them to the particular case. Thus the provisions of all primary legislation with which the family and child lawyer will be confronted are commented upon; and, within the context of the primary legislation, the relevant rules and regulations are then considered. Where appropriate and within the statutory framework relevant procedural aspects of a given court process are looked at in outline and the reader referred to the appropriate court rules.

THE COURT PROCESS

1.6 If one or both spouses want their marriage dissolved or a couple wish to adopt a child, application to the court is essential; and then the court is vested with an administrative power to grant what amounts to declaratory relief: a decree of divorce[1], an adoption order and so on. So too it may be necessary where a family issue cannot be resolved, where the local authority seek to assume parental responsibility for a child, by seeking a care order, or where the subject (here normally on behalf of a child) wishes to challenge a local authority decision (judicial review). In all other respects resort to court process must be the last resort[2], where private or formally mediated negotiation has failed. Where it becomes necessary court process will be the means whereby the family dispute, whether concerning a child or family property, comes before the judge. We therefore consider, albeit briefly, questions of procedure and evidence before the courts.

1 A 'divorce order' under the new legislation: see para 3.31.
2 See eg *Solicitors Family Law Association Code* (SFLA).

'NON-ADVERSARIAL' PROCEDURES

1.7 Despite recent pronouncements of some judges in the Family Division[1], family proceedings cannot technically be non-adversarial in the present English and Welsh legal system; for our court processes are not designed in that way. So long as an individual has the right to bring a matter before the court for adjudication on one or more issues, to which reply is made in the manner of a debate by one or more other parties then there is an adversarial process. What need not happen is for the lawyers to make the process more adversarial, in the conventional sense of the word[2]; but until court processes are reformed the lawyer has a duty to the client and, within the best of his or her ability and according to his or her conception of human decency, the lawyer must assist the client within the legal system available.

1 For a recent example see Wall J in *Re EC (Disclosure of Material)* [1996] 2 FLR 123 at 146C–147H; and see *Re L (Police Investigation: Privilege)* [1996] 1 FLR 731 at 743C–H, HL per Lord Nicholls for an explanation of the term 'adversarial' in children proceedings.
2 Hence the development of such groups as the Solicitors Family Law Association and the Family Law Bar Association.

FULL RELEVANT DISCLOSURE

1.8 Essential to the proper working of a system of family justice is the concept of 'full relevant disclosure'[1] (generally termed 'full and frank disclosure'[2]). This is entirely a judge-made development[3]; and it relies to a large measure upon the more or less co-operative approach of practitioners if it is truly to work[4]. When all is said and done, courts cannot compel disclosure of that of which they are ignorant; and however skilful the cross-examination or testing the interrogatory or rule 2.63 question[5], a party determined not to disclose may largely succeed in so doing. Co-operation in a system which remains essentially adversarial, in the technical sense, must be the essence of an effective family and child law process.

1 *Livesey (formerly Jenkins) v Jenkins* [1985] AC 424, [1985] FLR 813, HL; and see further para 2.42.
2 For reasons for our preference for the term 'full relevant disclosure' see para 2.42.
3 See eg the FPR 1991, r 2.58 (applications for matrimonial financial relief) and r 4.17 (statements in children proceedings) which are totally silent on the subject.
4 In contrast with the FPR 1991, r 2.58 ff, the bedrock of the Ancillary Relief Pilot Scheme (see para 1.1) is disclosure of matrimonial assets.
5 FPR 1991, r 2.63; and see para 2.51.

LEGAL AID

1.9 Pervasive to family law for the majority of practitioners and, sadly, for a declining number of their clients, is legal aid. We deal with this subject briefly and in the knowledge that substantive law reform and extensive adjustment of the legal aid scheme are high on the political agenda of the main political parties.

FAMILY LAW ACT 1996

1.10 During the course of preparation of this book the Family Law Act 1996 finally received Royal Assent after a stormy legislative passage. By the Autumn of 1997 it is likely that the provisions of Part IV of the Act (occupation of the family home and domestic violence) will have been brought into operation. We have therefore included reference to the new statutory provisions as appropriate. It is likely to be much longer before the remaining provisions of the Act come into operation; and we have only therefore referred to the remaining provisions of the Act[1] in outline in those parts of the text where the existing law is considered.

1 Part II (divorce and marital orders, including amendments to MCA 1973, Part II (financial provision)) and Part III (mediation).

Chapter Two

Procedure

David Burrows

Introduction 9
Pleadings 12
Procedure 14
Evidence 19
Disclosure and Discovery 24
Expert Evidence 31
Appeals 35

INTRODUCTION

2.1 Procedure is the means by which a particular form of application comes for hearing before the court[1]. The function of pleadings is to define the issues for trial by the court; and evidence is the means whereby facts in issue in the proceedings are considered by the court. In family courts procedure is, for the most part, defined as clearly as in any other division[2]; whilst rules of pleading, by contrast, are almost non-existent. Rules of evidence apply, theoretically, as much in family courts as in any other; though it remains the case that there is much more latitude allowed by courts, largely because of the wide discretion vested in the family judiciary.

---

1 Pressure is mounting for reform to family procedure, as in other divisions. Lord Woolf's report on procedural reforms is likely to propose wide-ranging changes. In January 1995 Practice Directions were published in all Divisions including *Practice Direction (Family Proceedings: Case Management)* [1995] 1 WLR 332, [1995] 1 FLR 456 covering proceedings in family courts; for case management see para 2.22.
2 Most family process is defined by the FPR 1991, in the High Court and county courts and the Family Proceedings Courts (Children Act 1989) Rules 1991 in the magistrates' courts; as well as by the RSC 1965 and the CCR 1981 where these are applicable or are not inconsistent with FPR 1991 (see FPR 1991, r 1.3(1)).

The family courts

2.2 At first instance family process is commenced in the family proceedings (magistrates') courts, in the county courts and in the High Court. Appeals[1] from the magistrates are to the High Court, from district judges in the county court to a judge, from judges whether in the High Court or in the county court to the Court of Appeal and from there to the House of Lords. From district judge and magistrates' courts appeals are as of right; whereas from judges they are, for the most part, with leave of the judge or, failing that, with leave of the Court of Appeal[2]. Appeals to the House of Lords are only with leave of the Court of Appeal or the House of Lords[3].

1 For appeals generally see para 2.66 et seq.
2 Supreme Court Act 1981, s 18(1); and see RSC Ord 59, r 1B which sets out the list of judgments or orders in respect of which leave to appeal is needed.
3 Administration of Justice (Appeals) Act 1934, s 1.

2.3 Certain types of process will dictate where they are to be issued; whereas in others the application can be made in any court of first instance. For instance, care proceedings and a number of other public law children applications can only be commenced in a magistrates' court[1]; whereas all applications by children for leave to seek a section 8 order must be commenced in the High Court[2]. In theory all other CA 1989 applications can be dealt with in any court; but if issued at an inappropriate level they are likely to be transferred[3].

1 Children (Allocation of Proceedings) Order 1991, art 3(1).
2 *Practice Direction of 22 February 1993* [1993] 1 FLR 668, [1993] 1 WLR 313.
3 Children (Allocation of Proceedings) Order 1991, arts 5–13; and see para 2.23.

Family proceedings – an attempt at definition

2.4 The definitions of the term 'family proceedings' are many and comprise a wide variety of court processes and rules[1]. A narrow definition[2] of the term can be found in FPR 1991, r 1.2(1)[3] which has the effect of excluding, for example, proceedings under the Married Women's Property Act 1882, the Inheritance (Provision for Family and Dependants) Act 1975 and the Matrimonial Homes Act 1983; but which, surprisingly, includes non-contentious probate business. A wider definition can be found by reference to the Family Proceedings (Costs) Rules 1991. This, by reference to a repealed section of the MCA 1973[4] leads to a definition which includes the statutes mentioned above save for the Inheritance (Provision for Family and Dependants) Act 1975[5]. A definition of the term, which is wider still, might include proceedings under the following statutes and other forms of jurisdiction which, for the purposes of what follows, will be treated as family proceedings:

Adoption Act 1976

Child Abduction and Custody Act 1985

Child Support Act 1991

Children Act 1989

Domestic Violence and Matrimonial Proceedings Act 1976

Family Law Act 1986

Inheritance (Provision for Family and Dependants) Act 1975

Judicial review: Supreme Court Act 1981, RSC Ord 31, RSC Ord 53

Law of Property Act 1925, s 30

Married Women's Property Act 1882

Matrimonial Causes Act 1973

Matrimonial and Family Proceedings Act 1984, Part III

Matrimonial Homes Act 1983

Proceedings for declarations as to trusts[6]

Supreme Court Act 1981, s 37: *Mareva* and other such injunctions

Wardship and the inherent jurisdiction

1 For example, those practising civil litigation will find the vast majority of the procedural rules which concern them in RSC 1965 (set out and annotated in *Supreme Court Practice* ('the White Book')) or CCR 1981 (*County Court Practice* ('the Green Book')), whereas the equivalent book for the family lawyer, *Family Court Practice* ('the Red Book') contains over 50 sets of rules and other forms of delegated legislation which define court procedure.
2 For the purposes only of CA 1989 a still narrower definition is to be found in s 8(3) of that Act.
3 The definition is found by referring to the Matrimonial and Family Proceedings Act 1984, s 32 which refers on to the Supreme Court Act 1981, Sch 1, para 3. This is also the route to a definition taken by the Courts and Legal Services Act 1990, s 9.
4 MCA 1973, s 50.
5 Whether proceedings under this Act are regarded as 'family proceedings' by most practitioners remains a moot point. The view is taken in this work is that they are family proceedings: procedurally and in terms of disposal they bear many similarities with proceedings for matrimonial financial relief; and see chapter 6.
6 See, eg County Courts Act 1984, s 23(b)(ii).

Rules for family process

2.5 Most of the rules which cover the above forms of process are to be found in FPR 1991; or, where proceedings are in the magistrates' courts, in the Family Proceedings Courts (Children Act 1989) Rules 1991 (for children proceedings) and the Family Proceedings Courts (Matrimonial Proceedings etc) Rules 1991 for matrimonial proceedings. Adoption proceedings has its own set of rules: Adoption Rules 1984; whilst proceedings under the Inheritance (Provision for Family and Dependants) Act 1975, the Law of Property Act 1925, s 30, for declarations and injunctions (where not interlocutory to other forms of court process) will be covered by the relevant civil proceedings rules[1].

1 RSC 1965 or CCR 1981 depending on the court in which proceedings are continuing.

12 *Procedure*

2.6 Above all it must not be forgotten that RSC 1965 and CCR 1981 (depending on the forum) apply, with 'necessary modifications' in all family proceedings[1]. The competent family practitioner is therefore familiar not only with rules directly relevant to family processes, but also with the civil courts rules as well.

1 Adoption Rules 1984, r 3(2); FPR 1991, r 1.3(1).

PLEADINGS

2.7 Pleadings perform the task of defining issues for trial by the court; but, defined in this way, pleadings in the family jurisdiction are almost unknown. The nearest the family lawyer, in the ordinary course of practice, comes to a pleading answering this definition is in the divorce petition; yet as defined by RSC 1965 the petition is specifically defined as not a pleading[1]. That said, the Form 86A and notice of motion in judicial review process[2] and the notice of application to commit are pleadings and procedures attached to these processes have more akin to the conventionally pleaded case than many family proceedings.

1 RSC Ord 1, r 4(1).
2 RSC Ord 53, rr 3(2) and 5.

Pleadings contrasted with applications in family proceedings

2.8 The two most common forms of process in family courts (apart from the more or less formulaic divorce petition) is the financial relief application under the MCA 1973, ss 22–24A and applications concerning children under the CA 1989, Parts II, IV and V. Financial relief applications contain only sufficient information to identify the sections under the MCA 1973 under which application is to made[1]. Children applications are on standard forms and contain a variety of information which may be of assistance to the court[2]; but the forms require relatively little by way of information which will define the issues. Further, the rules do not require a response to the notice (other than by way of acknowledgement in children applications[3]); whereas in civil proceedings, if an application is to be opposed, a fully pleaded defence must be served[4]. This requirement enables the parties to see what the issues are between them; and should enable the court to be reasonably clear, in a properly pleaded case, as to what issues are to be tried.

1 FPR 1991, r 2.53 ff. Appendix 1 to these rules contains the forms.
2 FPR 1991, r 4.4 and Appendix 1.
3 FPR 1991, r 4.9.
4 See eg RSC Ord 18, r 2.

2.9 The exception to the generality of impressionistic pleading in family proceedings is the divorce petition. This has all the hallmarks of civil pleading. It is a requirement of pleadings in the civil courts that they consist of a statement of the 'material facts on which [a party] relies ... not the evidence by which those facts are to be proved'[1]. The particulars to be included in a divorce petition are precisely defined[2]; and this definition includes the requirement that the petition include 'brief particulars of the individual facts relied on but not the evidence by which they are to be proved'[3]: that is particulars must be pleaded of the fact or facts alleged to prove irretrievable breakdown[4]. If a petition is defended the rules provide for the case to be prepared for trial with all appropriate procedural provisions in almost exactly the same way as defended proceedings begun by writ[5].

1 RSC Ord 18, r 7(1).
2 FPR 1991, r 2.3 and Appendix 2.
3 FPR 1991, Appendix 2 para 1(m).
4 MCA 1973, s 1(2)(a)–(e).
5 FPR 1991, rr 2.20–2.31.

Originating summons procedure

2.10 Other forms of family process, such as wardship, declarations as to land-holding, claims under the Inheritance (Provision for Family and Dependants) Act 1975, the Matrimonial Homes Act 1983 and the Married Women's Property Act 1882 are to be based on the originating summons procedure[1]; though procedure in wardship and under the last two statutes is formally governed by FPR 1991[2]. The originating summons procedure, then, forms the procedural basis also for financial relief applications. All applications of this type rely on posing a question to the court or seeking from it a remedy or some other form of relief[3]. The application or summons is then supported by affidavit evidence[4]. Affidavits are evidence, not forms of pleading; and this contrast must now be considered further.

1 RSC Ord 28; or the originating application in the county courts: CCR Ord 4, r 8.
2 See Part V and rr 3.6 and 3.8 respectively.
3 And see RSC Ord 7, r 3 for a full definition of the content of an originating summons.
4 For example, RSC Ord 28, r 1A(1) requires a plaintiff to file 'the affidavit evidence on which he intends to rely'. Echoing this terminology FPR 1991, r 2.58(2) requires an applicant to file 'an affidavit ... stating the facts relied on in support of the application'.

Pleadings contrasted with affidavits and statements

2.11 In most forms of family proceedings[1] the application will be supported, either at the time of filing, or in due course thereafter, by affidavit evidence, or by one or more statements. These documents, though not pleadings, will be the nearest the court is likely to have as a means of defining the issues at a pre-trial stage[2]. However these documents will be a mixture of fact and of evidence in support of an application. They do not have the merit, which competent pleading has, of defining the cause of action, setting out the facts in support and enumerating the relief sought from the court.

1 Divorce is the obvious exception; but judicial review also has its own separate form of process: see RSC Ord 53.

14 *Procedure*

2 Increasingly in all Divisions the courts are ordering or expecting to have filed skeleton arguments. These quasi-pleadings will, or certainly should, define the issues between the parties from each individual advocate's standpoint.

Evolving issues

2.12 One of the reasons why it would often be difficult accurately to plead an application in many types of family case is that the facts of the case are essentially dynamic; that is to say, the facts which are brought before the court are evolving as the application proceeds[1]. This can be particularly so in children cases where family arrangements shift during the course of preparation for a case; but it can also happen, for example, in financial relief cases where at the outset the applicant spouse will not know what are the means of the other spouse: full disclosure such as to make a proper assessment of the case may only emerge long after the application was issued. At the outset of the case it will, therefore, often be impossible precisely to plead the case; and consequently it will often not be possible to define the issues till relatively late in the proceedings.

1 By contrast, in most civil, and in all criminal, proceedings the issues are static at the time of issue of court process. The facts giving rise to the case are all in the past. For example, in a running down action liability will be argued on the basis of facts which have already happened and must now be proved to the court. Only quantum of general damages may be effected by a dynamic issue where the plaintiff has not recovered fully from his injuries.

Crystallisation of issues

2.13 At some point it is necessary to define the issues, so far as possible. This should be possible once disclosure is complete in financial cases (unless a trial is needed to elicit all financial information from a reluctant spouse); but in some of the more complicated public law children cases the issues may not all crystallise finally till a day or so before the hearing. However, from the point of view of preparation of the case it is essential to take a view on the issues at a given time:

(a) so as to be clear as to what evidence needs to be called; for only evidence which is relevant to the issues before the court is admissible[1]; and

(b) so that the advocate can be clear as to the basis for his/her submissions to the court.

1 And see para 2.36 for relevance and cogency.

PROCEDURE

2.14 It is beyond the scope of this work to consider procedure in any detail; but a brief consideration of the framework of the main family applications and of the procedure by which they come to a hearing follows, after a preliminary consideration of the courts in which process may be started.

The family courts

2.15 Family proceedings may be commenced in the High Court, the county courts or the magistrates' courts (family proceedings courts). The court in which proceedings are commenced will depend:

(a) on the type of process: divorce proceedings can only be started in a county court or the Principal Registry[1], whereas care proceedings can only be started in the family proceedings courts[2];

(b) on whether other family proceedings are pending[3];

(c) sometimes, on the requirements of the Legal Aid Board: often free-standing children applications will be required to be started in the family proceedings court[4], and claims under, for example the Inheritance (Provision for Family and Dependants) Act 1975 will be limited to the county courts; and

(d) occasionally, on the quantum of the claim: for example under the LPA 1925 or for a declaration as to how land is held under an implied trust[5].

1 FPR 1991, rr 2.6(1) and 1.4(2).
2 Children (Allocation of Proceedings) Order 1991, art 3.
3 FPR 1991, r 2.40(1); and see r 1.2(2).
4 Notes for Guidance 7–22 (see *Legal Aid Hand Book*).
5 The county courts have power to hear cases in equity (County Courts Act 1984, s 23) subject to an upper limit on the value of the land of £30,000 (County Courts Jurisdiction Order 1981) and subject to the parties agreeing to the county courts assuming a higher jurisdiction (County Courts Act 1984, s 24).

Procedural rules

2.16 The sets of rules with which the family lawyer will be primarily concerned are as follows:

Rules of the Supreme Court 1965

County Court Rules 1981

Family Proceedings Rules 1991

Family Proceedings Courts (Children Act 1989) Rules 1991

Family Proceedings Courts (Matrimonial Proceedings etc) Rules 1991

Adoption Rules 1984

Of these, quite the most important are FPR 1991. Allied to those rules are the rules of the two systems of civil courts; for it must always be recalled that RSC 1965 and CCR 1981 apply in the family courts to the extent that they are not inconsistent with FPR 1991[1]. RSC 1965 and CCR 1981 are in many respects

16 *Procedure*

complimentary; and certain parts of FPR 1991 clearly echo provisions in the civil proceedings rules[2]. However the rules relating to children proceedings have been developed solely for proceedings under the CA 1989 and they contain a number of novel features.

1 FPR 1991, r 1.3(1).
2 See eg FPR 1991, Parts II and III.

Children Act 1989 proceedings

2.17 Children proceedings under the CA 1989 are commenced by a prescribed form of application[1] which can then be supplemented by other forms according to the type of application being made: for example leave to commence proceedings[2] or for a care or supervision order and so on. These type of forms are a novel departure: for example, it is not known whether the applicant or his/her solicitor who is going on the record signs the form[3]. In due course this application will be supported by a statements from the parties[4]. No child can be examined for the purposes of a report without leave of the court[5]; and if leave to disclose documents to an expert is given[6] legal professional privilege does not apply to any report thus obtained and it must be filed at court[7]. At present the progress of children proceedings is unique in that the court is required, consistent with the CA 1989, s 1(5) (avoidance of delay), to set a timetable leading up to the hearing of the application[8].

1 FPR 1991, r 4.4; FPC(CA)R 1991, r 4.
2 FPR 1991, r 4.3; FPC(CA)R 1991, r 3.
3 Though applicants generally seem to sign, this is probably wrong (and can delay issue): CCR Ord 6, r 8 (an example of where it is necessary to turn to the civil proceedings rules where FPR 1991 are silent).
4 FPR 1991, r 4.17(1); FPC(CA)R, r 17(1); and note that in s 8 proceedings no statement may be filed without leave of the court: ibid rr 4.17(5) and 17(5).
5 FPR 1991, r 4.18; FPC(CA)R, r 18.
6 FPR 1991, r 4.23(1); FPC(CA)R, r 23(1).
7 *Re L (Police Investigation: Privilege)* [1996] 2 All ER 78, [1996] 1 FLR 731, HL.
8 CA 1989, s 11(1) and (2); FPR 1991, r 4.14(2)(a); FPC(CA)R, r 14(2)(a).

Financial relief proceedings

2.18 Proceedings for financial relief under the MCA 1973, Part II can be said to follow, broadly, the originating summons procedure[1]: originating application, affidavit, timetable for reply and minimal oral evidence. However FPR 1991 has developed its own variation on discovery and interrogatories[2] and on subpoenas duces tecum and the production appointment[3].

1 RSC Ord 28.
2 FPR 1991, r 2.63: cf RSC Ords 24 and 26; and see para 2.49.
3 FPR 1991, r 2.62(7)–(9): cf RSC Ord 38, rr 14 and 13; and see para 2.52.

Matrimonial causes

2.19 Almost uniquely amongst court process the matrimonial cause is begun by petition and, where contested, proceeds much like a writ action[1] save that there is no provision for service of statements or other summaries of oral evidence. Where causes are not defended the court is in the position which, in family proceedings, is only shared by an uncontested adoption, of giving a declaration on a state of affairs, rather than of resolving an issue between parties. Disposal of the modern matrimonial cause has all the sense of a process which has long lost most of its logic[2]: petitions are dealt with under the 'special procedure'[3] which is anything but special, since all but a handful of causes are disposed of in this way; the real decision as to disposal of the cause is dealt with then[4], though a judge or district judge must still robe fully to sit alone with his clerk in open[5] (though a more or less empty) court to declare decrees nisi for a list of absent petitioners; and six weeks later application can be made for the decree nisi to be made absolute. The marriage has been dissolved by an administrative process, and yet in a forum, and by means of a system, pre-eminently designed for the hearing, and evaluation, of oral evidence.

1 FPR 1991, rr 2.12 – 2.35.
2 All this will soon change when the procedure under the Family Law Act 1996 is published and comes into effect.
3 FPR 1991, r 2.36.
4 *Day v Day* [1980] Fam 29, [1979] 2 All ER 187, CA.
5 FPR 1991, rr 2.28(1) and 2.32.

Other forms of process: originating summons

2.20 A variety of family processes are dealt with by a procedure which, as with financial relief proceedings, is dealt with by a process akin to the originating summons procedure. Many of these are provided for in FPR 1991, Part III: for example proceedings under the MCA 1973, s 27 (neglect to maintain)[1]; applications under Married Women's Property Act 1882, s 17[2]; applications for various declarations[3]. Proceedings for a declaration as to beneficial entitlement or under the LPA 1925, s 30 are by originating summons or application[4]; whilst applications under the Inheritance (Provision for Family and Dependants) Act 1975 are also commenced by originating summons or application, but with their own specific rules[5].

1 FPR 1991, r 3.1.
2 FPR 1991, r 3.6.
3 FPR 1991, rr 3.12 – 3.15.
4 RSC Ord 28; CCR Ord 3, r 4(3).
5 RSC Ord 99 (High Court: either Chancery or Family Division); CCR Ord 48.

Magistrates' court process

2.21 In the magistrates' courts (other than for children proceedings[1]) process is by application to the court[2] or by complaint and summons issued by the court[3]. Evidence is almost invariably entirely oral; but magistrates have considerable latitude to decide their own proceedings.

1 See para 2.17.
2 See eg proceedings under the Domestic Proceedings and Magistrates' Courts Act 1978; the Family Proceedings Courts (Matrimonial Proceedings etc) Rules 1991.
3 See eg appeals against deductions from earnings orders: Child Support (Collection and Enforcement) Regulations 1992, reg 22(2)(a).

Procedure

Case management

2.22 The government and, to an extent, the judiciary have become increasingly concerned over recent years at the delays and mounting cost of litigation. To an extent this is the fault of the sometimes cumbersome procedures and of the lack of sufficient judges; but it is also the fault of the lawyers and their clients. Lord Woolf has proposed extensive reforms to civil procedures[1] which are bound to have an extensive influence on family cases. In the meantime *Practice Direction of 31 January 1995 (Case Management)*[2] was issued with the intention that judges should, under the present rules, exercise more control over court processes, such as by limiting discovery, insisting that all evidence-in-chief be contained in statements and that issues be defined clearly[3]. A series of quasi-practice directions have also issued from the judges, particularly Wall J[4]; and the Children Act Advisory Committee in its recent annual reports has helpfully put forward suggestions for ways of better managing proceedings[5].

1 *Access to Justice* (HMSO, 1996).
2 [1995] 1 FLR 456, [1995] 1 WLR 332.
3 Ibid paras 2(a), 3 and 4.
4 See eg *B v B (Court Bundles: Video Evidence)* [1994] 1 FLR 323n; *MD and TD (minors) (Time Estimates)* [1994] 2 FLR 336.
5 See eg joint letter of instruction to expert instructed in children cases: *Children Act Advisory Committee Annual Report 1994/5* reproduced as *Best Practice Note January 1996* in *Family Court Practice*.

Allocation and transfer

2.23 The Lord Chancellor's Department has devised directions of labyrinthine complexity to define before whom family proceedings should be tried[1]. These directions are intended to enable the court administration to define what type of judge[2] (that is to say, 'allocation to the judiciary') should try a particular type of case by referring to a table which consists of columns indicating the type of process, before whom it can be tried and in what circumstances the allocation direction applies.

1 Family Proceedings (Allocation to the Judiciary) Directions 1993 in which 'family proceedings' is accorded the same meaning as in the Courts and Legal Services Act 1990, s 9 (and see para 2.4).
2 As defined by the Courts and Legal Services Act 1990, s 9: ie judges and district judges.

2.24 Allocation of proceedings, that is to say in what court proceedings must, or may, be issued, depends on the type of process[1]. Thus all proceedings for financial relief, save for maintenance and lump sum applications up to £1,000[2] (where any marriage is not to be dissolved), are commenced in the High Court or county courts (almost invariably the county court). Meanwhile children proceedings (mostly, though not exclusively, under the CA 1989) are allocated to courts according to the type of application[3] or to whether there are proceedings pending in another court concerning the child[4]. The Children (Allocation of Proceedings) Order 1991[5] also deals with transfer of a case from one court to another, whether parallel or vertically – the object being that children cases are dealt with as quickly as possible and in the court with the expertise appropriate to the issues for trial.

1 And see para 2.15.
2 Domestic Proceedings and Magistrates' Courts Act 1978, s 2(1) and (3); CA 1989, Sch 1, paras 1 and 5(2).
3 Children (Allocation of Proceedings) Order 1991. For example, art 3 states that proceedings must be started in the family proceedings court unless there are proceedings concerning the child pending in another court: art 3(3).
4 Ibid arts 3(3) and 4; and see FPR 1991, r 1.2(2) (pending matrimonial proceedings despite grant of a final decree).
5 Arts 6 – 13.

EVIDENCE

2.25 Rules of evidence exist to assist in the court's aim of finding out the truth, so far as possible and where a fact is in issue, and to do so as fairly as possible between the parties. In family proceedings there is a particular additional dimension to evidence. In almost all other forms of process, whether crime or civil litigation, the court is dealing with static past evidence: did some thing happen and if so how? In family cases the court is frequently dealing with dynamic states of affairs, so that the evidence is constantly changing, especially in children proceedings. Further the court is concerned, often, to make predictions whether dealing with a child's welfare or with a spouse's future needs. Thus evidence will be called, often opinion evidence[1], to assist the court in the speculative task of predicting the outcome for children or the spouses.

1 See para 2.55 et seq.

Burden and standard of proof

2.26 The burden of proving a fact is upon the person who asserts it. The standard of proof in all family cases is upon the balance of probabilities, otherwise described as the 'preponderance of probability'[1]; for as Lord Nicholls said in *Re H and R*: 'Built into the preponderance of probability standard is a generous degree of flexibility in respect of the seriousness of the allegation'[2], that is to say, the more serious the allegation the greater is the degree of cogency needed to prove the allegation. For example, in care proceedings, the probability must be sufficient to justify the court in crossing the line between the interests of parents to be left to care for their children and the interests of children in having their care entrusted to others[3].

1 *Re H and R (Sexual Abuse: Standard of Proof)* [1996] AC 563, [1996] 1 FLR 80, HL.
2 *Re H and R (Sexual Abuse: Standard of Proof)* [1996] 2 WLR 8 at 23H, [1996] 1 FLR 80 at 96, HL.
3 *Re H and R (Sexual Abuse: Standard of Proof)* (above) where the House of Lords on the evidence before them followed the judge and the Court of Appeal and refused to find that they were satisfied for the purposes of the CA 1989, s 31(2) that the 'threshold' for a finding of significant harm had been achieved.

20 *Procedure*

Means of proof

2.27 Proof of any case depends on evidence which must be proved and certain facts which do not require proof. In all cases the probative value of the evidence will depend on its weight, or cogency and its admissability will dictate whether or not a party is entitled to rely upon it. Each of the factors arising from this short introduction will now be examined in turn.

Forms of evidence

PRIMARY EVIDENCE

2.28 Primary evidence is the direct evidence which is before the court. First there is what is conventionally known as 'real evidence': oral evidence, exhibits (rarely in family proceedings) and demeanor (the appearance or facial expressions of a witness, which at times can be an important, if unwitting, aspect of their evidence). Documents as primary evidence can only be evidence of the existence of the document itself (as distinct from its contents[1]) unless it is agreed or formally proved to the court. Failing this the content of the document is only hearsay and therefore, though it may be technically admissible, its weight may only be limited.

In certain types of application an affidavit may be treated as primary evidence, notably interlocutory applications and those commenced by originating summons[2]. In many such applications it is open to a party or the court to require attendance of the deponent to give evidence[3]. Statements of information or belief may be included provided that sources and grounds are set out[4]; and if hearsay evidence is included the source of the hearsay must be included or good reason given for not including it[5]. Statements are not evidence, but only a summary of evidence; though if proved at the hearing they may be treated as part or all of a party's evidence-in-chief[6].

1 An exception to this rule exists where a guardian ad litem produces copy documents from local authority files when the contents of the document can be treated as evidence: CA 1989 s 42(2); and see further para 2.64.
2 For example it will be very rare for the court to hear oral evidence in applications for judicial review or under the Child Abduction and Custody Act 1985.
3 For example, RSC Ord 38, r 2(3) enables the court to order the attendance for cross-examination of a deponent in proceedings begun by motion (eg judicial review) or originationg application (eg wardship or under the Child Abduction and Custody Act 1985); and FPR 1991, r 2.62(4) enables a district judge to 'order the attendance of any person for the purpose of being examined or cross-examined'.
4 RSC Ord 41, r 5(2).
5 *Practice Direction of 31 January 1995 (Case Management)* [1995] 1 WLR 332, [1995] 1 FLR 456, para 3.
6 Ibid para 3; though it is doubted whether it is intra vires for the court to restrict totally the oral evidence which a party seeks to adduce.

SECONDARY EVIDENCE

2.29 Secondary evidence consists of opinion and hearsay evidence. The evidence of an expert may be primary insofar as he or she saw the evidence of abuse of a child, or saw the property being valued; but where it is based on opinion derived from primary evidence or from someone else's evidence it is secondary. As opinion evidence it may, as a rule, only be adduced by agreement of the parties or order of the court[1] and where it has been disclosed to all parties. The otherwise complicated rules against hearsay are excluded from most children proceedings[2]. In practice they have rarely applied in other family proceedings; and once the Civil Evidence Act 1995 comes into effect they will be excluded altogether from all civil proceedings[3], which includes family proceedings[4].

1 RSC Ord 38, r 36; and see para 2.56.
2 Children (Admissibility of Hearsay Evidence) Order 1993.
3 Civil Evidence Act 1995, s 1(1).
4 As with earlier Civil Evidence Acts, the Civil Evidence Act 1995, s 11 defines 'civil proceedings' in terms of applying to those courts or tribunals 'to which the strict rules of evidence apply'.

TERTIARY EVIDENCE

2.30 Tertiary evidence may be said to be text books and other sources upon which expert evidence is based; provided that it has been read by the witness who relies upon it[1].

1 See eg comments by Douglas Brown J in *Rochdale Borough Council v A* [1991] 2 FLR 192; and see further para 2.59.

Facts not needing proof

JUDICIAL NOTICE

2.31 Certain facts or assumptions are judicially taken for granted and need not therefore be proved. For example, should the date of Christmas be in issue, it can be assumed that the judge will take it for granted that it is 25 December. More difficult in the realm of children work is to know how much the judge will know of a particular aspect of child development or personality disorder or illness. Normally it would be best to assume limited knowledge and to have expert evidence available if need be. In the field of matrimonial finance it is probably reasonable to assume judicial knowledge of an assumption that building societies will normally lend two-and-a-half to three times a person's income; whereas it would be unwise to assume that judicial notice will be taken of values of property in a particular area of the country.

ISSUE ESTOPPEL — RES JUDICATA

2.32 One of the principles underlying issue estoppel is that there is a public interest in there being an end to litigation; and that no-one should be sued twice on the same ground. Thus where there has already been a court decision on one set of facts it is not open to a party to re-open those facts in another action or application: the route for re-opening a case is by means of appeal or application to set aside the original order[1]. The conditions which must be satisfied for operation of issue estoppel are: first, that there is a decision by a court of competent jurisdiction, that is to say a court acting in an adjudicative capacity; secondly, the parties in the earlier and the later action are the same; and finally the issues in the earlier and later case are the same[2]. There is no rule that issue estoppel does not apply in children proceedings[3]; but in cases where circumstances may alter the case so much (as with many children cases) it will be rare for it to apply[4]. In deciding whether to apply the rule in children proceedings the court needs to balance the two questions of public policy: the principle of certainty of decision and of protection of a litigant from being vexed twice by the same complaint; against the need for protection of children[5].

1 See para 2.66.
2 *DSV Silo-und Verwaltungsgesellschaft mbH v Owners of The Sennar* [1985] 2 All ER 104, [1985] 1 WLR 490, HL.
3 *K v P (Children Act Proceedings: Estoppel)* [1995] 1 FLR 248, Ward J; *Re S, S and A (Care Proceedings: Issue Estoppel)* [1995] 2 FLR 244, Wilson J (estoppel held to apply in care proceedings).
4 *Frost v Frost* [1968] 1 WLR 1221, CA; *B v Derbyshire County Council* [1992] 1 FLR 538.
5 *K v P (Children Act Proceedings: Estoppel)* (above): 'The overwhelming justification for setting aside the rule must be to do justice' (per Ward J at 257H).

JUDICIAL FINDINGS

2.33 A similar principle to issue estoppel operates to prevent a person from denying certain facts where they have already been proved. A finding of sexual abuse will be evidence in later proceedings between the same parties. Conviction of a relevant offence in a criminal court is admissable in family proceedngs as evidence of proving the offence[1]. Adultery, once proved, avoids proof in subsequent proceedings[2]; and if paternity is in issue, proof of adultery avoids the need for further proof, and vice versa[3]. For the purposes of the Child Support Agency certain findings and court orders are sufficient to prove paternity[4].

1 Civil Evidence Act 1968, s 11(1).
2 Ibid s 12(1).
3 Ibid s 12(2).
4 Child Support Act 1991, s 26.

ADMISSIONS

2.34 Where a party admits a fact on the pleadings or otherwise, for example in solicitor's correspondence, statement or affidavit, this need not be proved[1].

1 RSC Ord 27, r 1; and, in an endeavour to save costs and court time, a party may be given notice to admit facts (RSC Ord 27, rr 2 and 5).

Presumptions

2.35 Presumptions enable the court to pronounce on a fact even though there is no evidence in support of it. This may have the effect of shifting the burden of proof to the respondent where a presumption operates in favour of an applicant. Most presumptions are rebuttable by proof which tends to the opposite assumption. For example, it is a rebuttable presumption that a child born in wedlock is legitimate[1]. In equity there are the important presumptions of advancement and of undue influence applicable to certain family relationships².

1 See now the Family Law Reform Act 1969, s 26; but see also the Human Fertilisation and Embryology Act 1990.
2 See eg *Barclays Bank v O'Brien* [1994] 1 FLR 1, HL for an example of the presumption of undue influence as between husband and wife; or *Tribe v Tribe* [1995] 2 FLR 966, CA where the presumption of advancement was rebutted.

Issues in the case: relevance and cogency

Issues

2.36 The pleadings in an action should state 'the material facts on which the party pleading relies for his claim ... but not the evidence by which those facts are to be proved'¹. In proceedings which are fully pleaded it should be possible from them to deduce the issues to be decided by the court. Because pleadings (as distinct from affidavits and statements, which are not pleadings but a means of adducing evidence or summarising evidence²) in family cases are so impressionistic³ and because the parties' circumstances often change as a hearing approaches, it is not always easy to define issues from the documents filed at court: (in most cases) originating or other application, statements or affidavits, reports required to be filed. However it is essential in terms of evidence to be able to define the issues: for determination of the issues determines relevance and therefore what is admissable as evidence before the court.

1 RSC Ord 18, r 7; and see eg FPR 1991, Appendix 2, para 1(m) for similar requirements for the particulars of a divorce petition.
2 See para 2.11.
3 Save in the case of matrimonial causes where cases must be precisely pleaded: see FPR 1991, rr 2.1 – 2.42; and see para 2.9.

Relevance to the issues

2.37 Central to the rules of evidence in that it determines what evidence may be heard by the court is the rule that all evidence which is relevant to the issue or issues before the court is admissible; and that all evidence which is not relevant, or which is insufficiently relevant, is inadmissible. From the policy point of view establishing issues and therefore excluding irrelevant evidence can do much to shorten trials¹; and there may therefore be increasing pressure on litigants to exclude evidence of doubtful relevance. It is for the judge to hear the evidence and to decide, first what is admissible and, consistent with that, what the cogency is of the admissible evidence².

1 Hence the concern of the president that parties define issues: *Practice Direction (Family Proceedings: Case Management)* [1995] 1 WLR 332, [1995] 1 FLR 456, para 4(c).
2 See eg *Re N (Child Abuse: Evidence)* [1996] 2 FLR 572, CA.

Cogency

2.38 Admissibility of evidence must then be distinguished from cogency, or the weight of the evidence. This determines the extent to which particular evidence weighs with a judge in reaching his decison. Thus hearsay evidence may be admissable; but if that evidence is contradicted by a credible witness who gives first-hand evidence, the latter's evidence is likely to be preferred as being the more cogent.

DISCLOSURE AND DISCOVERY[1]

Introduction

2.39 Without full disclosure of information and documents as between the parties, any litigation may fail to do justice as between the parties. In the family jurisdiction this is especially so. Rules have been developed to ensure that disclosure is as full as it can be; though there is a countervailing concern that lawyers are being too purist in seeking full disclosure, whilst losing sight of the expense and the possible relevance of some of the information they seek[2].

1 Properly disclosure and discovery are a branch of the rules of evidence; but because of the importance of the subject in family proceedings they are given separate treatment here.
1 *Practice Direction of 31 January 1995 (Case Management)* [1995] 1 WLR 332, [1995] 1 FLR 456 in the context of cost-saving stresses that the courts may exercise its discretion to limit discovery (para 2(a)). Lord Woolf's enquiry (*Access to Justice*) focuses on discovery and disclosure. And, although not directly on the point, Anthony Lincoln J's comments on the multiplicity of valuation evidence in *B v B (Financial Provision)* [1989] 1 FLR 119 are characteristic of occasional judicial comment on excessive attempts to ensure full disclosure.

Discovery and disclosure defined

2.40 All parties to family proceedings have a duty to disclose relevant evidence[1], insofar as this evidence is not privileged[2]. Discovery is the formal process whereby the parties give disclosure of documents or are required by the court to do so[3]. Dunn J defined the duty of disclosure and the court's powers to order discovery, in the context of matrimonial proceedings, thus:

'A party to a suit must disclose all the documents in his possession, custody or power which are relevant to the matters in issue. The court has a discretion whether or not to order him to make disclosure ... The discretion is a judicial discretion, and in exercising it the court will have regard to all the circumstances.'[4]

This definition is equally applicable to all family proceedings; and it stresses two fundamental components of discovery: first, the fact the discovery is only appropriate in respect of matters which are relevant to the court; and secondly, that it is a matter for the court's discretion as to whether disclosure is ordered. Dunn J mentioned that disclosure would not be ordered where an order would cause undue hardship when balanced against the need to do justice; and that it would only be ordered where disclosure was 'necessary for disposing fairly of the issues between the parties.'[5] However discovery will not be ordered where a document is covered by privilege or is protected on grounds that its disclosure would be against the public interest (public interest immunity and 'without prejudice' correspondence).

1 See eg *Livesey (formerly Jenkins) v Jenkins* [1985] AC 424, [1985] 1 All ER 106, HL; *R v Hampshire County Council* [1990] 1 FLR 330, QB Div Ct; *Re JC (Care Proceedings: Procedure)* [1995] 2 FLR 77, Wall J and *F v F (Ancillary Relief: Substantial Assets)* [1995] 2 FLR 45, Thorpe J; and see *Practice Direction of 31 January 1995 (Case Management)* [1995] 1 WLR 332, [1995] 1 FLR 456 at para 4.
2 See para 2.44 et seq.
3 RSC Ord 24; CCR Ord 14.
4 *B v B (Matrimonial Proceedings: Discovery)* [1978] Fam 181, [1979] 1 All ER 801.
5 See further consideration of the term 'necessary' in this context at para 2.43.

2.41 As will be seen, the duty to disclose is absolute (subject to a document being privileged from disclosure); but its incidence varies slightly according to the proceedings involved. For example, as between parties to a matrimonial financial relief application the duties are equal and complementary; whereas in children proceedings involving the local authority judges have imposed on them a very high duty of disclosure and consequent impartiality[1].

1 See eg *R v Hampshire County Council, ex p K* [1990] 2 QB 71, [1990] 1 FLR 330, Div Ct; and see para 2.48.

Relevant disclosure

2.42 The catch-phrase applied to disclosure is 'full and frank disclosure'[1]; but in the context of rules of evidence Lord Hailsham of St Marylebone LC preferred the term 'full relevant disclosure'[2]. Given the judiciary's concern at excessive disclosure being sought in some cases and the important rule of evidence that only material relevant to the issues before the court is admissable[3] Lord Hailsham's terminology might perhaps be preferred today. Frankness remains as important as ever; but over-emphasis on 'full' disclosure can lead to excesses in litigation which do little to resolve the case.

1 This term was most prominently used by Lord Brandon of Oakbrook in *Livesey v Jenkins* [1985] AC 424, [1885] FLR 813 eg at 823C: 'Each party concerned in claims for financial provision and property adjustment (or other forms of ancillary relief ...) owes a duty to the court to make full and frank disclosure of all material facts to the other party and to the court.'
2 *Livesey v Jenkins* (above) at FLR 815F.
3 See para 2.36 for consideration of admissability and relevance of evidence.

Discretion to order disclosure

2.43 In whatever context disclosure is sought (whether from a party to the proceedings or from a third party) and in whatever form that disclosure is sought (whether by affidavit, by questionnaire under FPR 1991, r 2.63, by subpoena or prodution appointment) it is a feature of the rules which permit the ordering of disclosure that such orders are entirely a matter for the court's discretion. In making any order for disclosure or discovery the court is likely to have regard to whether or not the order is 'necessary either for disposing fairly of the cause or matter or for saving costs'[1]; and to be alert to the frequent judicial criticism of over-enquiry[2]. Where a third party is concerned, in particular, the court will further be concerned that no order should be oppressive[3].

> 1 This form of words is used in both RSC Ord 24, r 8 (discovery) and Ord 26, r 1(1) (interrogatories); and see *Hall v Selvaco Ltd* (1996) Times, 27 March for an explanation of the term 'necessary'.
> 2 See eg *Attar v Attar* [1985] FLR 649, Booth J: in the case of a very wealthy husband with complicated financial affairs the court is not likely to be assisted by full and exact disclosure of his means; *B v B (Financial Provision)* [1989] 1 FLR 119, Anthony Lincoln J; and *Evans v Evans* [1990] 1 FLR 319, Booth J.
> 3 See eg *Hildebrand v Hildebrand* [1992] 1 FLR 244; and cf requirements of RSC Ord 26, r 1 concerning interrogatories, below at para 2.50.

Immunity from disclosure

2.44 In certain limited circumstances disclosure will be permitted; but then, where formal discovery is given in a case by list[1] the documents exempted from disclosure must be referred to and the reasons given why they are exempt[2]. Privilege from disclosure arises in the following three areas.

> 1 Though in practice discovery by list is rare in family proceedings, practitioners need to be aware of the rules as to privilege; and Wall J has expressed the view that conventional discovery should be the rule in children proceedings: *Re JC (Care Proceedings: Procedure)* [1995] 2 FLR 77.
> 2 RSC Ord 24, r 5(2); though a matter of law also applicable in the county courts there is no provision equivalent to Ord 24, r 5 in CCR 1981.

Legal professional privilege

2.45 Legal professional privilege is conventionally divided between solicitor and client communications (whether or not litigation is pending) and solicitor communications with third parties where litigation is pending. Communications between a solicitor and client are absolutely privileged[1]. Generally speaking communications in the second category are also privileged. This is subject to the important exception of communications and reports which come into existence following the grant of leave by the court[2] in children proceedings for release of confidential court documents to an expert instructed on behalf of the party given leave: any report filed after that must be filed at court and served on all parties. Normal 'litigation privilege'[3] does not apply to such reports[4].

> 1 *R v Derby Magistrates' Court, ex p B* [1996] AC 487, [1996] 1 FLR 513, HL in which Lord Taylor of Gosforth CJ reviews earlier authorities on this question and in a magisterial exposition of the law reaches an unequivocal conclusion on this question: 'No exception should be allowed to the absolute nature of legal professional privilege, once established' (at FLR 528F).
> 2 Under FPR 1991, r 4.23 and FPC(CA1989)R, r 23.
> 3 A term coined by Lord Jauncey of Tullichettle in *Re L (Police Investigation: Privilege)* [1996] 2 All ER 78, [1996] 1 FLR 731, HL.
> 4 *Re L (Police Investigation: Privilege)* (above) affirming *Oxfordshire County Council v M* [1994] Fam 151, [1994] 1 FLR 175, CA. This area of law remains unsettled. For example the question of whether any communication between a client and solicitor which affects the welfare of a child will remain privileged is very much at large.

Privilege on grounds that disclosure would injure the public interest

2.46 This area of privilege consists of two principal categories of document:

(a) *'Without prejudice' correspondence.* It is public policy to encourage litigants to settle cases rather than litigate them to a finish[1]. Thus it is public policy to exempt from disclosure any letter or other document, whether or not marked 'without prejudice'[2], which is an attempt to settle a case. This principle probably[3] applies also to any discussions with a welfare officer and mediator concerning settlement of issues before the court, subject to the important qualification that for a welfare officer confidentiality will be overriden where to withhold information, for example from the police or social services department, might effect the welfare of a child[4].

(b) *Public interest immunity.* This area of immunity is based on the question of whether the public interest in the withholding of confidential documents is greater than the public interest that the administration of justice should be able to function by means of there being full relevant disclosure between parties[5]. In all cases it is a matter for the judge's discretion as to whether a document is held to be privileged from disclosure; and where necessary the judge will have to read the documents before deciding.

1 *Cutts v Head* [1984] Ch 290, [1984] 1 All ER 597, CA.
2 *Chocoladefabriken Lindt and Springli AG v Nestle Co Ltd* [1978] RPC 287.
3 See *McTaggart v McTaggart* [1949] P 94, [1948] 2 All ER 754, CA, though this case applies only to negotiations concerning reconciliation.
4 See eg *Working Together Under the Children Act 1989: a guide to arrangements for inter-agency co-operation for the protection of children from abuse* (HMSO, 1991) para 3.15.
5 Where the local authority wish to invoke public interest immunity to protect documents procedure is governed by *Re C (Expert Evidence: Disclosure: Practice)* [1995] 1 FLR 204, Cazalet J.

Documents tending to criminate

2.47 Discovery need not be given of any document which will tend to expose the party to a criminal penalty[1]; though in children proceedings this principle has been diluted considerably[2].

1 Civil Evidence Act 1968, s 14.
2 See eg *Re L (Police Investigation: Privilege)* [1996] 2 All ER 78, [1996] 1 FLR 731, HL; and even more so where the party is giving evidence where he is intended to be immune from prosecution in respect of evidence given in court and therefore unable to refuse to give answers which might otherwise incriminate him: Children Act 1989, s 98. Now see also *Re C (Care Proceedings: Disclosure)* (1996) Times, 22 October, CA (police entitled to see documents in children proceedings as part of their criminal investigation).

Disclosure by parties

2.48 All parties to proceedings have a duty of disclosure of documents relevant to the issues before the court (subject to privilege[1]). In the field of financial relief and to enable the court to perform its duties under the MCA 1973, s 25 the parties have a duty to disclose all material information[2]. In children proceedings involving the local authority the authority, especially as applicant, has

> 'a high duty in law, not only on grounds of general fairness but also in the direct interests of a child whose welfare they served, to be open in the disclosure of all relevant material affecting that child in their possession or power (excluding documents protected on established grounds of public immunity) which might be of assistance to the natural parent or parents in rebutting charges against one or both of them in any way ill-treating the child.'[3]

Social workers must disclose all information upon which they base their case, both negative and positive[4]: their judgment must be based on objectively reviewed and disclosed material[5].

1 Privilege from disclosure: see para 2.46.
2 *Livesey v Jenkins* [1985] AC 424, [1985] FLR 813: 'unless the parties [to a financial relief application] make full and frank disclosure of all material matters, the court cannot lawfully or properly exercise' its discretion under s 25, per Lord Brandon Oakbrook at FLR 822.
3 *R v Hampshire County Council, ex p K* [1990] 2 QB 71, [1990] 1 FLR 330, Div Ct.
4 *Rochdale Borough Council v A* [1991] 2 FLR 192, Douglas Brown J.
5 *Re JC (Care Proceedings: Procedure)* [1995] 2 FLR 77, Wall J.

Compelling discovery as between parties

Discovery of particular documents

2.49 Whilst application may be made to the court for an order for discovery of particular documents[1], the wording of the rules makes it clear that the ordering of disclosure is a matter for the court's discretion. Further if the court finds that disclosure is 'not necessary' the application is to be dismissed or adjourned; and the court must refuse an order if it is of the 'opinion that discovery is not necessary either for disposing fairly of the cause or matter or for saving costs'[2].

1 RSC Ord 24, r 7(1); CCR Ord 14, r 2(1): the wording of both rules is in identical terms.
2 RSC Ord 24, r 8; CCR Ord 13, r 8(1).

Interrogatories

2.50 Interrogatories[1] may be served on other parties to the proceedings without leave[2]; or leave of the court to serve may be applied for[3]. Failure to comply with any court order for the answering of interrogatories renders a party liable to committal[4]. Unless otherwise ordered replies must be on oath[5] (an advantage over replies to a questionnaire under FPR 1991, r 2.63) and they would then appear to have a status equivalent to other affidavits in the application. The purpose of interrogatories is to elucidate matters 'which are necessary either (a) for disposing fairly of the cause or matter, or (b) for saving costs'[6]. Whether or not they are ordered is a matter for the court's discretion[7].

The court has power to order interrogatories in family proceedings[8]; though they are likley to be rarely used. In financial relief proceedings a rule 2.63 questionnaire[9] has a broadly similar effect to interrogatories[10]; and it is difficult to imagine circumstances where a court would order interrogatories in most proceedings under the CA 1989. An exception is proceedings for financial provision for children under the CA 1989, Sch 1 where further information about a parent's financial circumstances is requested: in these proceedings there is no equivalent to FPR 1991, r 2.63 (which applies only to ancillary relief proceedings) so it is difficult to see what alternative to interrogatories there is.

1 RSC Ord 26; CCR Ord 14, r 11 (which applies RSC Ord 26 in the county courts).
2 RSC Ord 26, r 3(1).
3 RSC Ord 26, r 4.
4 RSC Ord 26, r 6.
5 RSC Ord 26, r 2(2).
6 RSC Ord 26, r 1(1); and see *Hall v Selvaco Ltd* (para 2.43) for a consideration of the term 'necessary'.
7 See further para 2.49.
8 *Hildebrand v Hildebrand* [1992] 1 FLR 244, Waite J; and see FPR 1991, r 1.3(1).
9 See para 2.51.
10 The main differences are that replies to a rule 2.63 questionnaire are not normally on oath; the answers are not filed at court; and the consequences of failure to reply are not so drastic as where the court has ordered interrogatories.

Questionnaire under Family Proceedings Rules 1991, r 2.63

2.51 Questionnaires under FPR 1991, r 2.63 can be used to seek discovery in the MCA 1973 ancillary relief proceedings, that is information further to that in an affidavit by either of the parties, information on any other relevant matter and a list of documents or inspection of documents. Though the rule provides for enquiries to be raised by letter, practice tends to be to raise the questions in the form of a pleading[1]. If replies are not given voluntarily, the questioner may 'apply to the district judge for directions'[2]; and if directions are to be given (that is to say, that the court is to order replies, lists of documents and so on) then such an order is a matter for the court's discretion[3]. If one party presses for information the court can order that, if the replies prove to be irrelevant, the cost of providing such replies should fall on that party[4].

1 Neither the questionnaire nor the replies are pleadings and should not be filed at court. If they are to be brought to the court's attention they should be included in a court bundle or otherwise brought to the court's attention at the hearing of the application.
2 FPR 1991, r 2.63.
3 See eg *Evans v Evans* [1990] 1 FLR 319, Booth J; *Hildebrand v Hildebrand* [1992] 1 FLR 244, Waite J; and see para 2.49.
4 *Practice Direction* [1981] 2 All ER 642, [1981] 1 WLR 1010.

Evidence from third parties

Subpoena/witness summons

2.52 In practice it is likely to be rare that third parties will need to be summoned to attend court. Where this is needed for proceedings in the High Court leave for issue of a subpoena is required[1]. Leave may not be given if it is thought that to do so would be oppressive for the witness[2]. In county courts leave is only needed for a witness summons for a directions hearing[3]. The witness is that of the party who issued the subpoena and thus cannot be cross-examined by him; for a person who is neither a party nor has filed an affidavit cannot be ordered to attend a hearing solely to be cross-examined under FPR, r 2.64(4)[4].

1 RSC Ord 32, r 7 (because the proceedings are in chambers).
2 *Morgan v Morgan* [1977] Fam 122.
3 CCR Ord 20, r 12(8): to require a witness at a directions hearing is likely to be very rare.
4 *W v W* (1981) 2 FLR 291, Balcombe J; though the district judge if willing to do so has powers to question a witness: FPR 1991, 2.64(4).

Production appointment

2.53 A party to proceedings can seek discovery from a third party prior to trial either at a pre-trial hearing[1]; or by issue of a subpoena duces tecum (or witness summons in the county court) for attendance of the witness at a pre-trial hearing[2]. In applications for ancillary relief a specific procedure (akin to RSC Ord 38, r 13) is provided for[3]; but this does no more than provide a procedural basis for bringing forward to a pre-hearing stage the time when a witness can be required to produce documents[4]. A witness can only be required to produce documents which he/she could be compelled to produce at the hearing[5]. As always in this jurisdiction the remedy is discretionary and is likely to be exercised by the court on similar bases to the making of an order for replies under FPR 1991, r 2.63 or to interrogatories[6]. Application for an appointment should be made inter partes and supported by affidavit[7]; though an application could be made ex parte if it was feared that documentary evidence might be destroyed. Where there is evidence of avoidance of disclosure the court is entitled to set the production net wide[8].

1 RSC Ord 38, r 13.
2 *Khanna v Lovell White Durrant (a firm)* [1994] 4 All ER 267, Sir Donald Nicholls V-C.
3 FPR 1991, r 2.62(7).
4 *Frary v Frary* [1993] 2 FLR 696, CA.
5 RSC Ord 38, r 13(2); FPR 1991, r 2.62(8).
6 See paras 2.50 and 2.51.
7 Procedure on a production appointment was considered in *B v B (No 2) (Production Appointment: Procedure)* [1995] 1 FLR 913, Thorpe J.
8 *D v D (Production Appointment)* [1995] 2 FLR 497, Thorpe J (order for production in circumstances even if this might breach the professional confidentiality of clients of an accountant acting in the estate of the wife's late father).

Specific discovery by third parties

2.54 Where the local authority sought disclosure from the Crown Prosecution Service of documents relating to forthcoming criminal proceedings, disclosure might be ordered, for example, where it was sought to enable the local authority to make a more informed decision about the future of the children in their interim care[1]. Disclosure to all parties in the case would not necessarily be ordered. Further, hospitals and police have been urged to release video evidence to solicitors, on undertakings not to copy (save to expert witnesses)[2].

1 *Nottinghamshire County Council v H* [1995] 1 FLR 115, Johnson J.
2 *Re R (Child Abuse: Video Evidence)* [1995] 1 FLR 451, Johnson J.

EXPERT EVIDENCE

2.55 The general rules concerning opinion evidence apply whether the proceedings concern children or are other family proceedings. The object of expert evidence is that the expert should assist the court impartially in areas where the judge is not expected to be knowledgeable[1]. Where there are issues before the court which require special knowledge or skill, a witness is entitled to draw inferences from the facts, that is express an opinion, provided that the question is within his/her expertise[2]. The judge is entitled to adopt a course other than that recommended by the expert; but if doing so the judge must give reasons[3].

1 See eg *Re B (Care: Expert Witness)* [1996] 1 FLR 667, CA: 'The court has no expertise of its own, other than legal expertise ... The expert advises, but the judge decides.', per Ward LJ at 670C–D.
2 *Re M and R (Child Abuse: Evidence)* [1996] 2 FLR 195, CA.
3 See eg *W v W (A Minor: Custody Appeal)* [1988] 2 FLR 505, CA; and *Re B (Care: Expert Witness)* (above).

Mutuality of evidence

2.56 Because the expert has evidence which will go into areas which are not familiar to the courts and to the parties, court rules are framed so as to ensure mutuality (or fairness) between the parties and that all parties have advance notice of any expert evidence to be called[1]. This general statement of principle can be eroded in children cases: for example, where it may be necessary to protect children from excessive assessment or examination[2]; and where it is more or less impossible for a parent to call evidence from an independent welfare officer to counter an adverse welfare officer's or guardian ad litem's report[3]. The rules reflect the requirement for mutuality by providing that expert evidence can only be adduced by leave of the court or by agreement of the parties[4]. A party who fails to comply with these rules should be prevented from relying upon his expert evidence; save, perhaps, where the welfare of a child might be affected by keeping out the evidence (here public policy in ensuring mutuality might have to be balanced against the needs of the child).

1 RSC Ord 38, r 36.
2 See eg FPR 1991, r 4.18.
3 See eg *Re P (A Minor) (Independent Welfare Officer)* [1989] 2 FLR 43.
4 RSC Ord 38, r 36; CCR Ord 20, r 27.

Meeting of experts

2.57 An important feature of RSC Ord 38 is that it enables application to be made to the court for a direction that experts meet, on a 'without prejudice' basis, 'for the purpose of identifying the parts of their evidence which are in issue'[1]. They may then produce a joint statement identifying points agreed and points remaining in issue. The aim of this is to clarify areas of agreement and identify areas of disagreement which will have to be resolved at the hearing, which should reduce expense and shorten the length of the hearing[2].

1 RSC Ord 38, r 38.
2 See eg comments on this practice of Booth J in *Evans v Evans* [1990] 1 FLR 319, [1990] 2 All ER 147 (property valuation); and see *Re C (Expert Evidence: Disclosure: Practice)* [1995] 1 FLR 204, Cazalet J.

Characteristics of expert evidence

Impartiality

2.58 The essence of the evidence of the expert must be its impartiality; and this should be so, whoever he may be instructed by[1]. In *Note: Re R (A Minor) (Experts' Evidence)* [1991] 1 FLR 291n, Cazalet J stated the position (at 292 C):

> 'Expert witnesses are in a privileged position; indeed, only experts are entitled to give an *opinion* in evidence. Outside the legal field the court itself has no expertise and for that reason frequently has to rely on the evidence of experts. Such experts must express only opinions which they genuinely hold and which are not biased in favour of one particular party.'

1 See eg *Evans v Evans* (above): 'All professional witnesses should be careful to avoid a partisan approach and should maintain proper professional standards'.

Credibility

2.59 Any evidence must be credible. The more essential to the case the evidence, the more important that it be credible[1]. The following principles can be enunciated to deal with the question of credibility of an expert. In part they are derived from *Rochdale Borough Council v A* [1991] 2 FLR 192 and *Note: Re R (A Minor) (Experts' Evidence)* [1991] 1 FLR 291; and, although these cases are children cases, the observations of the judges in both are applicable to expert evidence generally:

(a) *The expert should speak from expertise based on an acknowledged qualification.* An expert should not give evidence beyond or outside his/her expertise; and the court or the parties are entitled to test that expertise[2]. By extension, an expert should not be tempted to give an opinion on facts or hypotheses for which he is not properly prepared. If he does so, he should stress to the court his awareness of the limits of his expertise.

(b) *The expert should express opinions only from known sources.* In *Rochdale* Douglas Brown J was highly critical of the relatively inexperienced doctor who gave evidence by means of 'vague citation'. She spoke of source books indicating certain factors; but at best she was referring to secondary sources and had not read the primary literature to which she was referring. Where an expert relies on sources he should be specific in his citation and be sure that he has considered the sources in the original or from reliable summaries.

(c) *Avoidance of partiality*. One of the easiest ways for an expert to taint his evidence will be for him to show partiality to one or other party. The temptation to call the witness recommended by the client (his accountant, for example or the local authority's preferred child psychiatrist) should therefore be avoided wherever possible.

(d) *Avoidance of personal prejudices and obsessions*. Experts must avoid personal prejudices; and if an expert advances an hypothesis which is controversial he must tell the court[3].

1 See eg criticism of GAL's evidence in *Re N (Child Abuse: Evidence)* [1996] 2 FLR 572, CA.
2 *Re M and R (Child Abuse: Evidence)* [1996] 2 FLR 195, CA.
3 *Re AB (Child Abuse: Expert Witnesses)* [1995] 1 FLR 181, Wall J.

Evidence on the issue: cogency

2.60 An expert is entitled to give an opinion on the issue before the court[1]; but the real question for the court, in relation to any expert evidence, will be the cogency of the evidence and the relevance to the issue of the expertise of the witness[2].

1 Civil Evidence Act 1972, s 5; *Re M and R (Child Abuse: Evidence)* [1996] 2 FLR 195, CA.
2 *Re M and R (Child Abuse: Evidence)* [1996] 2 FLR 195, CA.

Expert evidence before the court

2.61 Subject to questions of leave and mutuality[1] it is a matter for the parties (or, conceivably, the courts[2]) to arrange and to call their expert evidence[3]. Where expert evidence is to be called in children proceedings the court must exercise control over the directing of such evidence[4]; and the general rules relating to opinion evidence are subject to two very important reservations:

(a) *Examination of children*. A child involved in court proceedings may not be medically or physically examined for the preparation of a court report, without leave of the court[5].

(b) *Confidential documents*. If a party seeks to disclose confidential court documents the leave of the court must first be obtained[6]. If such leave is obtained by a party for the purposes of obtaining an expert's report then it will be a condition of such leave that the report be disclosed to all parties and filed at court[7]. Normal legal professional privilege does not then apply[8].

1 RSC Ord 38, r 36; and see para 2.56.
2 RSC Ord 40; and see *Re K (Contact: Psychiatric Report)* [1995] 2 FLR 432, CA.
3 See *Children Act Advisory Committee Annual Report 1994/1995* (Lord Chancellor's Department, 1995) p 24 ff with letter of instruction to expert at p 28.
4 *Re G (Minors) (Expert Witnesses)* [1994] 2 FLR 291, Wall J in which guidelines are given as to the grant of leave to examine children and as to directions thereafter.

5 FPR 1991, r 4.18(1); FPC(CA1989)R 1991, r 18(1); and see *Re C (Expert Evidence: Disclosure: Practice)* [1995] 1 FLR 204, Cazalet J as to the steps to be taken prior to seeking leave and concerning disclosure following the obtaining of expert evidence.
6 FPR 1991, r 4.23(1); FPC(CA1989)R 1991, r 23.
7 *Re L (Police Investigation: Privilege)* [1996] 2 All ER 78, [1996] 1 FLR 731, HL; and see para 2.45.
8 For legal professional privilege see para 2.45.

The Official Solicitor, guardians ad litem, court welfare officers

2.62 In children proceedings the court can call upon its own opinion evidence (apart from its limited powers under RSC Ord 40) by referring a case to the Official Solicitor, a court welfare officer or guardian ad litem. Each of these has slightly different though often largely overlapping roles.

The Official Solicitor

2.63 A person under a disability[1] may only sue by his/her next friend or be sued by his/her guardian ad litem[2]. Where the court thinks that a child in children proceedings should be separately represented then the Official Solicitor or 'some other proper person'[3] may be appointed to represent the child[4]. Once appointed, the position of the Official Solicitor is a hybrid between an ordinary solicitor representing the child and a court welfare officer. In practice a member of his staff interviews the child and other interested parties and, almost invariably, commissions a report from a medical expert, often a child psychiatrist. Strictly speaking the member of the Official Solicitor's staff has no expertise; but his opinion, nevertheless, is normally given weight by the court.

1 Which includes a child, or, as the rules provide at this point, a 'minor', which comes to exactly the same thing: RSC Ord 80, r 1; CCR Ord 1, r 3; FPR 1991, r 9.1(1).
2 RSC Ord 80, r 2; CCR Ord 10, r 1; FPR 1991, r 9.2; and see further para 8.51 et seq. FPR 1991, r 9.2 is subject to the provisions of r 9.2A which enables a mature child to take or defend proceedings under CA 1989 or the inherent jurisdiction of the High Court: see further para 8.54.
3 See eg *L v L (Minors) (Separate Representation)* [1994] 1 FLR 156, CA where the Court of Appeal appointed a solicitor to be the child's representative.
4 FPR 1991, r 9.5; and see *Practice Note: The Official Solicitor: Appointment in Family Proceedings (8 September 1995)* [1995] 2 FLR 479 which sets out the circumstances in which the Official Solicitor will accept instructions.

Guardians ad litem

2.64 By contrast with the Official Solicitor, guardians ad litem do have expertise, given their background and training; but also, by virtue of their role and appointment in proceedings, they are accorded the right to express an opinion. They are appointed in 'specified proceedings'[1] (almost entirely public law proceedings) to represent the child[2]. Amongst the duties of the guardian are to 'advise' the court on such matters as the child's understanding, the options available to the court in terms of disposal of the proceedings[3]; and the court can direct him or her as to the obtaining of 'professional assistance'[4]. The contents of a guardian's report are exempt from any exclusionary rules of evidence[5]; and any copy documents taken from local authority records by the guardian are admissable as evidence of the contents of that document[6]. Whilst the document are admissable, it will still be a matter for the court to consider the cogency and reliability of the document[7].

1 CA 1989, s 41(6).
2 CA 1989, s 41; FPR 1991, r 4.10; FPC(CA1989)R 1991, r 10; and see para 8.51.
3 FPR 1991, r 4.11(4); FPC(CA1989)R 1991, r 11(4).
4 CA 1989, s 41(10)(a); FPR 1991, r 4.11(9)(c); FPC(CA1989)R 1991, r 11(9)(c).
5 CA 1989, s 41(11). With the hearsay rule more or less at an end this provision is of minimal significance.
6 CA 1989, s 42(2) and (3).
7 See eg *Re M and R (Child Abuse: Evidence)* [1996] 2 FLR 195, CA; and see para 2.36.

Court welfare officers

2.65 The court may appoint a court welfare officer when considering any question under the CA 1989[1], though in practice this will mostly be questions under Part II of the Act. The role of the welfare officer is not as central to the proceedings as that of the guardian ad litem though the welfare officer may be asked to report on particular matters. He may be expected to make a recommendation; and, by virtue of his position, he is entitled to express an opinion on matters before the court. Any exclusionary rules of evidence do not apply to his report[2]; but whilst these rules may not apply, it will still be a matter for the court to consider the cogency and reliability of the evidence[3].

1 CA 1989, s 7(1); and see further para 8.13 et seq.
2 CA 1989, s 7(4).
3 *R v B County Council, ex p P* [1991] 1 FLR 470; *Re M and R (Child Abuse: Evidence)* [1996] 2 FLR 195, CA.

APPEALS

Introduction

2.66 A person appeals where he/she alleges that the court erred on the basis of the evidence before it; whereas if a person alleges that the court erred because information was kept from it and therefore a trial of the real issues between the parties was not possible, then the application is to set aside[1]. Where factors occur after the making of the order which fundamentally alter the basis on which the order was made then application may be made for leave to appeal out of time[2]. Application to set aside is to the court which made the order; whereas appeals follow the routes described below.

1 *Peek v Peek* [1948] P 46, [1948] 2 All ER 297, CA; and see *Livesey v Jenkins* [1985] AC 424, [1985] FLR 813, HL for an example of an application to set aside where a spouse failed to reveal her intention to remarry.
2 *Barder v Barder (Caluori Intervening)* [1988] AC 20, [1987] 2 FLR 480, HL: spouse killed herself soon after the financial relief hearing; and see further para 2.68.

Routes to appeal

2.67 RSC Ord 59 deals with appeals from courts of first instance to the appellate courts whether as of right, with leave of the court below or of the appellate court. FPR 1991, r 8.1 deals with appeals (as of right) from district judges to a judge. Time for appeal is limited; but the period varies according to the forum from which appeal is made.

Basis for allowing appeals

2.68 An appeal is an application by the appellant to show that the decision of the court below was wrongly made on the basis of the evidence available. In most instances the appellate court will deal with the appeal on the basis of the evidence before the court below[1]. Though described as a 'rehearing'[2], this does not mean rehearing evidence but only that the court considers the evidence below and has the power to make further or other orders on the appeal[3]. Further, the court has a discretion to admit further evidence[4] which will normally be exercised subject to the *Ladd v Marshall*[5] conditions, namely:

(a) that, with reasonable diligence the evidence could not have been obtained for use at the trial;

(b) that the evidence if given would have had an important influence on the outcome, though it need not be determinative of the case; and

(c) that the evidence is apparently credible.

In addition, in appeals involving children, the court will admit further evidence which may not satisfy the *Ladd v Marshall* test if the welfare of the minor requires it, and especially where it relates to events which have occurred since the hearing below[6].

1 The exception to this is that appeals from a district judge to a circuit judge from interlocutory decisions in proceedings not covered by FPR 1991 (these are covered by FPR 1991, Part VIII: see para 2.74) the hearing is de novo: ie the judge can rehear the application admitting fresh evidence: *Evans v Bartlam* [1937] AC 473; and see RSC Ord 58, r 1 and CCR Ord 37, r 6. In proceedings covered by this work such appeals will be very rare since most orders under, eg the Law of Property Act 1925, s 30 or on an originating application will be final orders.
2 RSC Ord 59, r 3(1).
3 RSC Ord 59, r 10(3).
4 RSC Ord 59, r 10(2).
5 [1954] 3 All ER 745, [1954] 1 WLR 1489, CA per Lord Denning MR.
6 *G v G (Minors: Custody Appeal)* [1985] FLR 894, HL.

Application to set aside orders and for a rehearing

2.69 The court has power in a number of circumstances to set aside its own order: for example, where an order was made in the absence of a party[1] or where the order has been made ex parte[2]. Application may also be made to set aside an order on the grounds that information material to its decision was withheld from the court[3]; though not every failure to disclose will give rise to an order to set aside; the criterion is whether the failure to disclose has led the court to make 'an order which is substantially different from the order' sought to be set aside[4]. In the county courts application can be made for 'a rehearing'[5] which effectively means that the order is set aside.

The Court of Appeal has power to order a rehearing, for example on the ground of 'improper admission or rejection of evidence'[6].

The consequence of an order being set aside is that a rehearing[7] of the application, or such part of it as remains in issue, will result. This will be a fresh hearing, either before the same judge (if available) unless the setting aside results from misconduct of the proceedings by the judge.

1 RSC Ord 35, r 2(1); CCR Ord 37, r 2(1).
2 RSC Ord 32, r 6.
3 See eg *Livesey v Jenkins* [1985] AC 424, [1985] FLR 813, HL.
4 *Livesey v Jenkins* [1985] AC 424, [1985] FLR 813 per Lord Brandon at FLR 830E.
5 CCR Ord 37, r 1.
6 RSC Ord 59, r 11(2).
7 The term 'rehearing' can here be distinguished from use of the same term in hearings in the Court of Appeal.

Leave to appeal out of time: *Barder*

2.70 Any appeal which is out of time may attract an application for leave to appeal. However the question addressed here is what happens where events subsequent to the order have nullified its effect or otherwise rendered it unfair to one or other of the parties: the classic example is where one spouse dies soon after the making of the order[1]. The circumstances did not exist at the time of the hearing, so there is no question of failure to disclose, and therefore no possibility of an application to set aside. In such circumstances it is open to a party to apply for leave to appeal; but such applications are subject to conditions in *Barder v Barder (Caluori Intervening)*[2], as follows:

(a) the new events have invalidated a fundamental assumption on which the order was made so that, if leave were given, the appeal would be certain or very likely to succeed;

(b) the events had occurred within a relatively short time (probably less than a year[3]) after the order;

(c) the application had been made promptly; and

(d) the grant of leave does not prejudice third parties who had acquired interests in the property the subject of the order.

1 *Smith v Smith (Smith intervening)* [1992] Fam 69, [1991] 2 FLR 432, CA.
2 [1988] AC 20, [1987] 2 FLR 480, HL.
3 But cf *Hope-Smith v Hope-Smith* [1989] 2 FLR 56, CA and *Heard v Heard* [1995] 1 FLR 970, CA where appeals out of time were allowed relating to events over two years after the order.

Procedure

Appeals

2.71 The procedure for appealing (with references to the relevant rules) and for seeking leave, where this is needed, is referred to at para 2.67. Where leave is sought out of time, application for leave will be included in the notice.

Applications to set aside

2.72 The procedure to be followed where application is made to set aside is comprehensively considered by Ward J in *B-T v B-T (Divorce: Procedure)*[1] in which the learned judge also summarises in tabular form the routes by which such applications proceed, according to whether the order is made by consent or following a contested hearing, to whether the hearing was before a judge or district judge, and to whether the application leading to the order had been in the High Court or the county courts. More recently procedure has been further considered and practitioners urged to issue their application in the family courts, rather than by separate writ in the Queen's Bench Division[2].

1 [1990] 2 FLR 1.
2 *Benson v Benson* [1996] 1 FLR 692, Bracewell J.

Disposal of appeals

2.73 The vast majority of decisions appealed from in family proceedings depend on the judge at first instance exercising his or her discretion[1]; though there are also instances where facts must first be found proved before the court can be satisfied that an order should be made[2]. Where the decision at first instance is one for the court's discretion then as a rule appellate courts will be reluctant to interfere, unless the judge below can be shown to have been wholly wrong; whereas if the question is one of law then the appellate court will only interfere if the judge below is shown to have erred in law. The approach of the appellate court in the extent to which it will exercise its own discretion varies according to whether the appeal is from a district judge or from other courts.

1 See eg MCA 1973, s 25; CA 1989, s 1(3), I(PFD)A 1975, s 3.
2 See eg CA 1989, s 31(2) (threshold conditions for making a care or supervision order) and the dicta of Lord Nicholls on this question in *Re H and R (Sexual Abuse: Standard of Proof)* [1996] AC 563, [1996] 1 FLR 80, HL.

Appeals from district judge

2.74 Where an appeal is heard by a judge (whether of the High Court or a circuit judge) the judge is free to exercise his or her discretion in substitution for that of the district judge[1]; though the judge will pay due regard to the way in which the district judge exercised his or her discretion[2]. This is in marked distinction to most other appeals, as will be seen from the following paragraph.

1 FPR 1991, r 8.1(3) (and see *Marsh v Marsh* [1993] 1 FLR 467, CA), family proceedings in the county courts; CCR Ord 37, r 8, all other county court proceedings; *Evans v Bartlam* [1937] AC 473, HL and RSC Ord 58, r 1, High Court proceedings.
2 *Evans v Bartlam* [1937] AC 473, HL.

Other appeals

2.75 On appeals from the family proceedings courts to the High Court[1] and from all judges to the Court of Appeal[2] the appellate may only interfere with a judge's, or the magistrates', exercise of their discretion if it was plainly wrong[3]. It is by no means sufficient that the appellate court would have dealt with the case differently; and the Court of Appeal has been highly critical of practitioners who have pursued appeals where a judge's discretion, perhaps on a finely balanced point, is in issue[4].

1 CA 1989, s 94 and FPR 1991, r 4.22 (CA 1989 appeals) and FPR 1991, r 8.2 (DPMCA 1978 appeals).
2 RSC 1965, Ord 59.
3 *G v G (Minors: Custody Appeal)* [1985] FLR 894, HL ; *Croydon London Borough Council v A* [1992] 2 FLR 341 (in respect of appeals from magistrates).
4 See eg *Re N (Residence: Hopeless Appeals)* [1995] 2 FLR 230, CA.

Part II

Marriage Breakdown

Chapter Three

Matrimonial Causes

David Burrows

Introduction 43
Matrimonial Causes 45
The New Law: a Summary 50

INTRODUCTION

Divorce law: the new and the old

3.1 With the passing of the Family Law Act 1996 the law relating to marriage breakdown will be radically changed. Irretrievable breakdown remains the sole basis for dissolution of marriage[1]; but the proof of irretrievable breakdown is now to be based on time[2] rather that proof of one or more of the five facts set out in the MCA 1973[3]. Completely new procedures will be involved with the new law; and mediation at last finds statutory recognition in the new Act, albeit as an amendment to the Legal Aid Act 1988. However the new provisions only affect divorce and judicial separation[4]. Nullity remains unaffected by the new Act and will be governed still entirely by the MCA 1973; and, though the substantive law relating to financial provision was not intended to be affected, there are amendments to the MCA 1973, Part II which will have a substantial effect on practice[5].

1 MCA 1973, s 1(1); FLA 1996, s 5(1).
2 The 'period for reflection and consideration': FLA 1996, ss 5(1)(c) and 7; and see para 3.33.
3 Section 1(2); and see para 3.4.
4 To be known as 'separation': FLA 1996, s 2(1)(b).
5 See para 4.210 et seq.

Framework of the existing law

3.2 In the breakdown of any marriage where there are dependant children the adviser is confronted by three principal problems: the children, finance and the marriage itself. If there has been domestic violence then a fourth area for advice arises. Proceedings relating to children and for domestic violence can be free-standing; but if there are existing matrimonial proceedings then such proceedings will generally be commenced alongside the matrimonial suit[1]. However financial relief can only be obtained ancillary to a matrimonial suit save in the limited circumstances of the MCA 1973, s 27 (neglect to maintain)[2], the Married Women's Property Act 1882, s 17 and the Domestic Proceedings and Magistrates Courts Act 1978 (maintenance and minimal lump sums in magistrates' courts).

1 For example, care proceedings must normally be commenced in a family proceedings court (Children (Allocation of Proceedings) Order 1991, art 1(1)); but if there are pending proceedings already in another court then proceedings are commenced there (art 1(3)). Matrimonial causes remain 'pending' even though a final decree or order has been made (FPR 1991, r 1.1(2)).
2 See para 4.194 et seq.

Cohabitants

3.3 The cohabitant has the same rights to protection as a married person where domestic violence is concerned (subject to the Family Law Act 1996, s 38(2) and to minor aspects of ss 35 and 36[1]); and the children of a married couple, so far as financial support for themselves is concerned, are in the same position as those of an unmarried couple[2]. Rules on parental responsibility differ according to whether a couple are or are not married[3]. However in the field of financial support for themselves cohabitants find that there is no provision for them which is even remotely similar to the MCA 1973, Part II[4]. As Millett J has chillingly observed (of a cohabitant's claim to a share in property):

'If this were California, this would be a claim for palimony, but it is England and it is not. English law recognises neither the term nor the obligation to which it gives effect. In this country a husband has a legal obligation to support his wife even if they are living apart. A man has no legal obligation to support his mistress even if they are living together.'[5]

Cohabitants must therefore rely upon property law where the legal title to property is vested in their names jointly; upon contract law if they have a cohabitation agreement which regulates their arrangements; or, failing either of these and where they have no legal title to shared property, they must rely upon equity[6].

1 See paras A.30 et seq.
2 Child Support Act 1991, s 1; CA 1989, s 15 and Sch 1; and see chapter 10 and para 5.44 et seq.
3 CSA 1991, s 4; and see para 10.9.
4 The Law Commission is now looking at the law relating to cohabitation.
5 *Windeler v Whitehall* [1990] 2 FLR 505 at 506C.
6 See para 5.13 et seq.

Irretrievable breakdown

3.4 The aim of the Divorce Reform Act 1969, replaced by the MCA 1973, Part I, was to make irretrievable breakdown the basis of divorce in place of the matrimonial offence[1]. Unfortunately to prove irretrievable breakdown the (then) new law made it necessary to prove one or more of five facts, three of which (adultery, unreasonable behaviour and desertion) bore all the hallmarks of the old matrimonial offences. This remains the position until the coming into operation of the Family Law Act 1996.

1 Based upon the report of the Archbishop of Canterbury's Committee on divorce reform: 'Putting Asunder' (1966).

MATRIMONIAL CAUSES

Introduction

3.5 Matrimonial causes under the MCA 1973 comprise divorce, nullity, judicial separation and petitions for presumption of death and dissolution. Save where there are contested proceedings, the court adopts in a declaratory function: it is required to check that a state of affairs exists and, if it so finds, then to grant the appropriate decree. In view of the procedure now adopted this is rarely more than a paperwork exercise performed by district judges in the county courts[1].

1 See further para 2.19.

Divorce

3.6 The sole ground for divorce is 'that the marriage has broken down irretrievably'[1]. A marriage will not be held to have broken down irretrievably unless the court is satisfied that one or more of the five facts set out in the MCA 1973, s 1(2) apply in respect of the marriage namely: (a) adultery and petitioner finds living with the respondent intolerable; (b) unreasonable behaviour; (c) desertion for two years; (d) living apart for two years with the respondent; (e) living apart for five years. As can be seen, two of these, adultery and unreasonable behaviour, enable the petitioning spouse to apply immediately to the court; whilst the remaining three involve a wait of at least two or five years. The first three facts are fault based, such that they frequently attract an order for costs against the respondent.

If satisfied as to one or more of the five facts, the court shall grant a decree (subject to the hardship bars in s 5[2]) unless satisfied that the marriage has not broken down[3]. Given the rudimentary procedure for establishing breakdown on an undefended basis, it is difficult to imagine this provision operating in practice.

1 MCA 1973, s 1(1).
2 See para 3.17.
3 MCA 1973, s 1(4).

Judicial separation

3.7 A petitioner obtains a decree of judicial separation on proof of one or more of the five facts set out in the MCA 1973, s 1(2)[1] but without the need to prove irretrievable breakdown. The effect of a decree of judicial separation is that the spouses are no longer bound to cohabit[2]; but the marriage is not dissolved – the essential difference from divorce.

1 MCA 1973, s 17(1): see para 3.6.
2 Ibid, s 18(1).

Nullity

3.8 A marriage is annulled because it is void from the outset or because it is voidable. A void marriage is deemed never to have existed and is established on one of the following grounds: (a) invalidity within the terms of the Marriage Acts (eg prohibited degrees of relationship); (b) bigamy; (c) parties of the same sex – even after a sex change; or (d) polygamous marriage where one party was domiciled in England and Wales[1].

A voidable marriage subsists till a decree absolute avoiding the marriage is granted[2] and such decree is petitioned for on one of the following six grounds: (a) inability to consummate; (b) wilful refusal to consummate; (c) lack of valid consent; (d) unfitness of one party due to mental health; (e) respondent suffering from a communicable venereal disease; and (f) pregnancy *per alium*[3]. Detailed bars to applications for decrees of nullity in respect of voidable marriages are set out in MCA 1973, s 13, such as that, in the case of applications under (c), (d), (e) or (f), no application can be made after three years save with leave of the court[4].

1 MCA 1973, s 11.
2 Ibid, s 16.
3 Ibid, s 12.
4 Ibid, s 13(2) and (4).

Presumption of death and dissolution

3.9 A petition for presumption of death and dissolution can be presented to the court where a party to the marriage alleges that the other spouse has been continually absent for seven years or more and the petitioner has no reason to believe that the absent spouse is alive[1]. There is then a rebuttable presumption that the absent spouse is dead[2].

1 MCA 1973, s 19(1) and (3).
2 Ibid, s 19(3).

Procedure

3.10 Procedure relating to matrimonial causes is set out in the FPR 1991, rr 2.01 – 2.51[1]. The cause is pleaded by petition praying for dissolution of the marriage, judicial separation and so on[2] and must contain the information prescribed by the rules[3]. If opposed by the respondent spouse he or she files an answer and then, if no compromise can be achieved the matter proceeds as a defended suit, with many similarities to defended civil suits[4]. If undefended and the petitioner can prove service of the petition (normally by reference to the acknowledgment of service by the respondent[5]). Most divorces proceed under the 'special procedure'[6] by which a petitioner (or respondent if the cause is proceeding on a respondent's answer) files a prescribed affidavit[7], a district judge checks the paperwork filed and if satisfied that the grounds are made out and service has been effected the district judge so certifies[8]. It remains the case that the district judge has a duty, in cases of petitions for divorce and judicial separation 'to enquire so far as it reasonably can, into the facts alleged' by either party[9]; but it has been held that the special procedure leaves no room for an overly technical approach by district judges[10]. The signing of the district judge's certificate leads to a brief formal decree nisi hearing[11] and then to the grant of a decree absolute, not earlier than six weeks later[12], save with leave[13].

1 And see a brief consideration of procedure at para 2.19.
2 FPR 1991, r 2.2(1).
3 Ibid, r 2.3 and Appendix 2.
4 See eg FPR 1991, rr 2.20 (discovery), 2.21 (interrogatories), 2.24 (directions for trial) and 2.28 ff (evidence).
5 For service of the petition generally, and of other pleadings, see FPR 1991, rr 2.9 and 2.11(8).
6 FPR 1991, rr 2.24(3) and 2.36.
7 Ibid, r 2.24(3)(a) and Form M7(a)–(e) (as appropriate).
8 Ibid, r 2.36(1)(a).
9 MCA 1973, ss 1(3) and 17(2).
10 *R v Nottingham County Court, ex p Byers* [1985] FLR 695, Latey J.
11 FPR 1991, r 2.36(2).
12 MCA 1973, s 1(5) as amended by the Matrimonial Causes (Decrees Absolute) Order 1972 (as amended).
13 *Practice Direction of 15 June 1977 (Expedition of Decree Absolute: Special Procedure Cases)* [1977] 2 All ER 714, [1977] 1 WLR 759.

3.11 In parallel with this procedure the district judge considers the arrangements for the children by reference to the statement of arrangements for the children filed with the petition[1] and to the provisions of the MCA 1973, s 41(1)[2]. If there are children of the family the district judge either so certifies and that the court need not exercise any of its powers under the CA 1989[3]. If the court is not satisfied about the arrangements for the children further evidence may be requested[4]; and grant of a decree absolute in the cause may then be delayed[5].

1 FPR 1991, rr 2.2(2) and 2.38.
2 Ibid, r 2.39(1).
3 Ibid, r 2.39(2)(b): eg to make orders under ss 8, 16 (family assistance orders) or 37(1) (local authority to investigate).
4 FPR 1991, r 2.39(3).
5 MCA 1973, s 41(2).

Jurisdiction

3.12 A spouse may file a petition in the courts of England and Wales where either of the parties are domiciled in England and Wales on the date when the petition is filed[1] or they have been habitually resident in England and Wales for a year prior to the filing of the petition[2]. Additionally, in the case of nullity, jurisdiction may be assumed if the respondent is dead and at the date of death he or she was domiciled or resident for a year before death in England and Wales[3].

1 Domicile and Matrimonial Proceedings Act 1973, s 5(2)(a).
2 Ibid, s 5(2)(b).
3 Ibid, s 5(3)(c).

Domicile

3.13 Domicile may be 'of origin', 'of choice' or 'of dependence'. Domicile of origin is acquired at birth and from a child's parents. Domicile of dependence, where a child's parents are not living together, is with a child's mother if his or her home is with the mother and the child has 'no home with his or her father'[1]. a person can seek to change domicile (domicile of choice) on attaining sixteen or earlier marriage[2]; but it has been stressed that 'the burden of establishing a change of domicile (from a domicile of origin to a domicile of choice) is.... a heavy one'[3].

1 Domestic Violence and Matrimonial Proceedings Act 1976, s 4(2).
2 Ibid, s 3(1).
3 *Cramer v Cramer* [1987] 1 FLR 116, CA per Stephen Brown LJ at 120.

Habitual residence

3.14 'Habitual residence' is not defined in the Domicile and Matrimonial Proceedings Act 1973. However, in the context of the Child Abduction and Custody Act 1985, the term has been considered by the House of Lords[1] where it was held that the term should be 'understood according to the ordinary and natural meaning of the two words which it contains'. It is 'a question of fact to be decided by reference to all the circumstances of any particular case'.

1 *Re J (a Minor) (Abduction: Custody Rights)* [1990] 2 AC 562, sub nom *C v S (a Minor) (Abduction)* [1990] 2 FLR 442, HL per Lord Brandon of Oakbrook at AC 578 and FLR 454.

Time bars

3.15 No petition for divorce can be presented within one year of the marriage[1]; though a petition presented after that time limit may, nevertheless, contain particulars which relate to the first year of the marriage[2]. These provisions do not prevent presentation of a judicial separation petition; nor, of course, a petition for nullity. Where couples have lived together for more than six months after the last allegation of adultery or of unreasonable behaviour a petitioner cannot rely on those allegations to found a petition on either of those two facts[3].

1 MCA 1973, s 3(1).
2 Ibid, s 3(2).
3 Ibid, s 2(1) and (3).

Assistance to attempting reconciliation

3.16 Section 2(5) of the MCA 1973 contains a provision which may be regarded as, in part, designed to assist couples in attempting reconciliation: that is to say, it provides that in calculating time-based petitions[1] no account is to be taken of a period, or periods totalling, six months in breaking the time; but the period is added to the period required for the relevant fact. Thus if after 18 months living apart a couple resume cohabitation for five months and then separate, if one consents the other can file a petition based on two years living apart; but the total period from initial separation before a petition can be filed is then not less than two years and five months.

1 Desertion and living apart for two or five years: MCA 1973, s 1(2)(c)–(e).

Financial hardship bars

3.17 Two provisions in the Act enable a respondent spouse, normally the wife, to delay grant of a decree of divorce.

(a) *Consideration of financial position of respondent.* A respondent to a petition based on living apart for two or five years (only) can apply to the court to delay making the decree nisi absolute till it is satisfied, upon consideration of all the circumstances, that the petitioner should not be required to make provision for the respondent or that the provision made is reasonable[1]. The court can proceed to decree absolute if satisfied either that there are circumstances making it desirable so to do or the petitioner has given a suitable undertaking to provide for the respondent[2].

(b) *Refusal of decree on grounds of grave financial hardship*[3]. In respect of a petition based on five years living apart the respondent can ask the court to refuse to grant any decree on the ground that dissolution of the marriage would result in grave financial hardship to the respondent[4]. If upon consideration of all the circumstances the court finds that dissolution will result in 'grave financial or other hardship'[5] and that it would be wrong to dissolve the marriage it 'shall dismiss the petition'[6].

The main ill to which these sections are addressed is the loss of pension rights; but with the coming into operation of the MCA 1973, ss 22B – 22D[7] with provisions for pension ear-marking it becomes increasingly difficult to see how use of either of these sections can be justified.

1 MCA 1973, s 10(2) and (3).
2 Ibid, s 10(4).
3 A ground similar to this has been preserved in the FLA 1996, s 10: see para 3.30.
4 MCA 1973, s 5(1).
5 Hardship includes the loss of a benefit, eg pension, which the respondent might acquire if the marriage subsisted: MCA 1973, s 5(3).

50 *Matrimonial Causes*

6 MCA 1973, s 5(2).
7 See para 4.100 et seq.

THE NEW LAW: A SUMMARY

3.18 The Family Law Act 1996 received Royal Assent on 4 July 1996. Part II of the Act completely recasts the divorce laws; though it is unlikely to come into operation for at least two years. Part III, by amendment to the Legal Aid Act 1988, provides for mediation for those eligible for legal aid. What follows is a summary of the new law. Much of the law is procedural; but detail will have to await the making of rules under the Act. The law of nullity and of presumption of death and dissolution continues to be governed by the MCA 1973[1] and is not affected by Part II of the Act.

1 MCA 1973, ss 11–13 and 19; and see paras 3.8 and 3.9.

The marital orders

3.19 In marital proceedings[1] the court can make the following orders on application of one or both spouses[2]:

(a) a divorce order, that is an order which dissolves a marriage[3]; or

(b) a separation order – that is an order for 'separation of the parties to a marriage'[4].

1 As defined by the FLA 1996, s 19, ie from the filing of the statement: see para 3.24.
2 FLA 1996, s 3(1).
3 Ibid, s 2(1)(a).
4 Ibid, s 2(1)(b).

Jurisdiction

3.20 The court has jurisdiction in marital proceedings and any other jurisdiction arising from the filing of a statement in circumstances almost identical to the Domicile and Matrimonial Proceedings Act 1973[1]:

(a) one of the parties is domiciled in England and Wales;

(b) one of the parties was habitually resident in England and Wales for at least one year ending with the filing of the statement; or

(c) nullity proceedings are pending[2] when the marital proceedings commence.

1 FLA 1996, s 19(2). For consideration of the Domicile and Matrimonial Proceedings Act 1973, 'domicile' and 'residence' see para 3.14.
2 For the purposes of the rules, a cause remains pending even though a final decree is granted: FPR 1991, r 1.2(2). Whether this is the sense in which 'pending' is used here may have to await publication of rules under FLA 1996.

Outline of steps to the obtaining of a marital order

3.21 The following is an outline of the steps which must be taken by one or both spouses to lead to the obtaining of a marital order.

(a) An information meeting must be attended by a spouse who is contemplating filing a statement.

(b) A statement of marital breakdown is filed at court.

(c) A period for reflection and consideration of varying lengths follows the filing of the statement.

(d) Arrangements for the future (essentially concerning finance) must be made before application can be made for an order.

(e) The welfare of any child of the family is considered by the court and, in exceptional circumstances, the court may delay an order because of unsatisfactory arrangements for the children.

(f) If the court considers it appropriate it may make an order preventing divorce – essentially because of financial loss to a spouse or having regard to the welfare of a child of the family.

(g) Application for an order, divorce or separation, is made.

(h) An order for divorce or separation is made if the above has been done; the marriage is taken irretrievably to have broken down.

Each of these aspects of the leading up to the order will now be considered in turn.

The information meeting

3.22 The first formal step in taking marital proceedings is for a spouse to file a 'statement' (see below). Not less than three months before a spouse can file the statement he or she must attend[1] an 'information' meeting[2]. This is intended to provide 'relevant information' in connection with the divorce process and to encourage referral for counselling[3]. The person who conducts the meeting must have 'no financial or other interest in any marital proceedings between the parties'[4]; so that if, for example, solicitors have a licence to provide information meetings neither they nor their staff can then go on to act for any spouse who came to a session given by them. Statutory requirements of the meetings[5] include information about:

(a) children's welfare: 'the importance to be attached to [their] welfare, wishes and feelings'[6] and how the parties can be helped to help them cope with the relationship breakdown;

(b) the nature of financial questions which may arise on divorce;

(c) services available for mediation and counselling;

(d) availability of independent legal advice and legal aid.

1 Certain categories of spouse may be exempt from attendance, for example 'the elderly, the disabled or those in prison': White Paper, para 7.18 (see n 1 to para 3.23).
2 FLA 1996, s 8(2).
3 Ibid, s 8(6)(a) and (b).
4 Ibid, s 8(7)(b).
5 Ibid, s 8(9).
6 Ibid, s 8(9)(b).

LEGAL ADVICE

3.23 The White Paper[1] explains the Government's view of the distinction between information in this context and legal advice:

> 'Legal information ... is an abstract statement of legal principles and procedures relating to divorce and its consequences ... Legal advice involves an explanation of how the law applies to the facts of a particular case and the recommendation of a course of action. This latter would be outside the scope of the information session.'

For their part legal advisers will be required to provide clients with information as to marriage counselling and mediation services and concerning their children's welfare, wishes and feelings and to certify that they have done so[2].

1 *Looking to the Future: Mediation and the Ground for Divorce*, 1995, Cm 2799, para 7.9.
2 FLA 1996, s 11(2); and cf MCA 1973, s 6(1).

Statement of marital breakdown

3.24 The first formal step in the process towards divorce or separation is the filing of a statement at court[1]: marital proceedings have then started; though the statement cannot be filed until three months after attendance at the information meeting[2]. The object of the statement is to enable either or both parties to the marriage to express the belief that their marriage has broken down. Both parties to the marriage are likely to be able to file a joint statement[3]. Section 7(6) preserves the one year bar to divorce (though not for a separation order) by making a statement filed before the first anniversary of the marriage ineffective for the obtaining of a divorce order[4].

1 FLA 1996, s 6(4).
2 Ibid, s 8(2).
3 See *Looking to the Future: Mediation and the Ground for Divorce*, 1993, Cm 2424 Appendix D, para D4; and FLA 1996, s 6(3) clearly contemplates this.
4 And cf MCA 1973, s 3(1) (bar on petition for divorce within one year of marriage).

Period for reflection and consideration

3.25 The filing of the statement must be followed by a period for reflection and consideration at the end of which a party to the marriage can apply for a marital order. The object of this period is to enable the parties[1]:

> '(a) to reflect on whether the marriage can be saved and to have an opportunity to effect a reconciliation, and
>
> (b) to consider what arrangements should be made for the future.'

1 FLA 1996, s 7(1); the Lord Chancellor described this as 'a period with a purpose – namely to reflect on whether the difficulties in the marriage could be resolved so that the relationship could continue': Foreword to Cm 2424 referred to at n 3 to para 3.24.

3.26 The period for reflection and consideration runs as follows:

(a) *Basic period.* Nine months from two weeks after the date on which the statement is received at court[1].

(b) *Six month extension: children.* Where there are one or more children of the family under the age of 16 at the time of the application for divorce the period for reflection and consideration is automatically extended by six months[2]. This extra period comes to an end if during its currency 'on there ceasing to be any children of the family to whom' this provision applies[3].

(c) *Six month extension: request for further time for reflection.* If one spouse applies for a divorce order the other may apply for an extension of six months for further reflection[4].

(d) *Delay in service of statement.* Where there is a delay in service because of 'failure to comply with the rules' then, on application to the court by the spouse to be served the period may be extended; but for no longer than the period of delay in service[5].

Neither six month extension applies where[6]:

(i) there is an occupation or non-molestation order in existence in 'favour of' the applicant for divorce, or of a child of the family and the order is against the other party to the marriage; or

(ii) the court is satisfied that to delay the making of a divorce order 'would be significantly detrimental to the welfare of any child of the family'.

1 FLA 1996, s 7(3).
2 Ibid, s 7(11).
3 Ibid, s 7(14).
4 Ibid, s 7(10).
5 Ibid, s 7(4) and (5).
6 Ibid, s 7(12).

Arrangements for the future

3.27 Upon filing an application for a marital order the applicant (or both spouses in the case of a joint application) must show that the Act's requirements as to their arrangements for the future are satisfied[1]. Arrangements for children of the family are considered below[2]. Financial arrangements are proved by production to the court of one of the following:

(a) *A court order.* Under the Act orders of financial relief will be obtainable before marital orders; and the MCA 1973, ss 23 – 24A has been amended accordingly[3]. Application can be made once the statement has been filed and the parties can then comply with the requirement that there be 'a court order (made by consent or otherwise) dealing with their financial arrangements'[4].

(b) *A negotiated agreement*[5].

(c) *A declaration as to financial arrangements.* Whilst an aim of the Act is to promote opportunities for mediation some of the less guarded comments in the White Paper concern agreements[6].

(d) *Declaration of no significant assets.* One spouse can make a declaration, to which the other does not object, that no financial arrangements are to be made because he or she has no significant assets; he or she does not intend to apply to the court for financial provision; and he or she believes the other spouse has no significant assets and that he or she does not intend to apply for financial provision[7].

(e) *Exemption from financial arrangements.* In certain circumstances it is possible to obtain a marital order even though the requirements as to arrangements set out in s 9(2) have not been complied with[8]. Each depend on the requirements of the Act as to the welfare of the child having been complied with and are concerned with circumstances where parties have failed, for the reasons set out in Sch 1, to reach agreement.

1 FLA 1996, s 3(1)(c).
2 See para 3.29.
3 FLA 1996, Sch 2; and see para 4.216 et seq.
4 Ibid, s 9(2)(a).
5 The Act does not distinguish between a 'negotiated agreement' and 'financial arrangements': perhaps a distinction is to be drawn between the former as intended to cover a 'separation agreement' arrived at between the parties (and legal advisers) and the latter being arrangements set up as a consequence of mediation.
6 For example, it is suggested that one solicitor might give 'advice' to both parties on drafting of agreements or on the incidence of tax or state benefits (paras 6.22 and 6.23); and, it is suggested that 'There would ... be no requirement that parties ask for their agreement to be approved as a court order unless they wished to do so.' Most family lawyers would regard that as very poor advice.
7 FLA 1996, s 9(2)(d).
8 Ibid, s 9(7) and Sch 1.

3.28 It must be observed that the Act seems to overlook two fundamental components of matrimonial law:

(a) The court's duty to consider financial circumstances under the MCA 1973, s 25, which plainly remains on the statute book. If the court is to make an order, s 25(1) requires that it must consider 'all the circumstances of the case' with first consideration being given to the welfare of children of the family under 18 and in particular to the factors set out in the MCA 1973, s 25(2). If agreement is reached then authority for that arrangement does not derive from the agreement but only from a court order recording it[1]. To fail to obtain an order only risks the possibility that one spouse will seek to upset the arrangements later[2].

(b) It follows from this that for the court to exercise its powers under the MCA 1973, s 25 the parties must give 'full relevant disclosure' of all matters material to the court's consideration of their financial circumstances[3]. There is no clear requirement in the Act that such approval be sought from the court, beyond that clearly implied by the MCA 1973, s 25. Agreements or declarations, thus, would seem to be of even more limited value.

1 *Hyman v Hyman* [1929] AC 601, HL; *Edgar v Edgar* (1981) FLR 19, [1981] 1 WLR 1410, CA.
2 *Edgar v Edgar* (1981) 2 FLR 19, [1981] 1 WLR 1410, CA; *Pounds v Pounds* [1994] 1 FLR 775, [1994] 1 WLR 1535, CA; but see also *Camm v Camm* (1982) 4 FLR 577, CA and *Beach v Beach* [1995] 2 FLR 160, Thorpe J where agreements were set aside, albeit both in unusual circumstances.
3 *Livesey (formerly Jenkins) v Jenkins* [1985] AC 424, [1985] FLR 813, HL.

Children of the family

3.29 Included in the parties arrangements for the future is the provision that the Act's requirements concerning the welfare of any children of the family must have been satisfied[1]. Section 11 deals with arrangements for children of the family, and in part repeats exactly the MCA 1973, s 41:

(a) s 11 applies to children of the family not yet 16 or any older child to whom the court directs the section to apply[2];

(b) the court must decide whether there are such children of the family and if so whether it should exercise any powers under the CA 1989 in respect of them[3];

(c) if the exercise of powers under the CA 1989 is needed, or this seems likely (and in deciding the question the court treats the welfare of the child as paramount[4]) but the court is not yet in a position to determine the point, the court may direct a stay on the making of any marital order[5]. In 'making that decision' the court must have regard to the wishes and feelings of the child, to the conduct of the parties in the child's upbringing, to a form of presumption of contact (barring evidence to the contrary) and any risk to the child[6].

1 FLA 1996, s 9(5).
2 Ibid, s 11(5).
3 Ibid, s 11(1).
4 Ibid, s 11(3).
5 Ibid, s 11(2).
6 Ibid, s 11(4).

Orders preventing divorce

3.30 Where a divorce order (ie not a separation order) has been applied for by one spouse, the other can apply for an 'order preventing divorce', otherwise known a 'section 10 order', in circumstances where the court is satisfied[1]:

(a) that the divorce 'would result in substantial financial or other hardship to [the spouse applying for the order] or to a child of the family; and

(b) that 'it would be wrong in all the circumstances (including the conduct of the parties and the interests of any child of the family) for the marriage to be dissolved'.

An order may be made that the other spouse is directed to comply with (for example as to setting up an annuity or life policy for the applicant spouse, or as to the purchase of property or the provision of a fund from which periodical payments can be paid to her) before application can be made for cancellation of the order[2]. 'Hardship' includes the loss of a chance to obtain a future benefit as well as of an existing benefit[3]. The case law is meagre and mostly dates from the 1970s[4] and before. With the advent of provision for pension ear-marking[5] and plans for consideration of pension-splitting[6] it is difficult to see how a spouse could set up a claim to suffer substantial financial hardship, certainly as regards future benefit[7]. 'Other hardship' is likely to be even more difficult to prove if it is born in mind that the spouse alleging it must also show that it is such that it would be 'wrong ... for the marriage to be dissolved'. If an order preventing divorce is cancelled a fresh application for a divorce order has to be made[8]. If application is made to cancel the order it shall be granted unless the conditions pertaining to the original order continue[9].

1 FLA 1996, s 10(2).
2 Ibid, s 10(5).
3 Ibid, s 10(6); and cf MCA 1973, s 5(3).
4 See eg *Le Marchant v Le Marchant* [1977] 3 All ER 610, [1977] 1 WLR 559, CA; *Reiterbund v Reiterbund* [1975] Fam 99, [1975] 1 All ER 280, CA affirming Finer J.
5 MCA 1973, ss 25B–25D; and see para 4.111 et seq.
6 FLA 1996, s 16.
7 See eg *Parker v Parker* [1972] Fam 116: where it was pointed out (in 1972 be it noted) that loss of a police pension could be made up by a deferred annuity or life policy.
8 FLA 1996, s 10(4).
9 Ibid, s 10(3).

Application for a matrimonial order

3.31 Either a divorce or separation order can be applied for by one spouse, or both spouses, if the following conditions apply:

(a) the marriage has broken down irretrievably[1];

(b) the requirements about attending an information meeting have been complied with[2];

(c) the requirements about future arrangements are satisfied[3]; and

(d) there is no section 10 order preventing divorce in effect[4].

1 FLA 1996, s 3(1)(a).
2 Ibid, s 3(1)(d); and see para 3.22.
3 Ibid, s 3(1)(c); and see para 3.27.
4 Ibid, s 3(2); and see para 3.30.

3.32 The application need not be made by the spouse who made the statement[1]. A separation order can be converted to a divorce order on application by either spouse[2] and provided arrangements for the children are satisfactory, unless[3]:

(a) the separation order was made before two years from the date of the marriage, in which case it cannot be made into a divorce order till after two years;

(b) there is a section 10 order preventing divorce;

(c) there are children of the family under 16 and the non-applicant spouse applies for further time for reflection and consideration; unless there is in existence an occupation or non-molestation order; or to delay would be 'significantly detrimental' to the welfare of a child of the family or six months has already passed since the end of the original period for reflection and consideration.

1 FLA 1996, s 5(2).
2 Ibid, s 4(3).
3 Ibid, s 4(1),(2),(4) and (5).

Irretrievable breakdown

3.33 Irretrievable breakdown remains the sole ground for divorce[1]; but proof of irretrievable breakdown is derived from the following[2]:

(a) that one or both spouses have made a statement that the maker of the statement believes, or both of them believes, that the marriage has broken down;

(b) that the period for reflection and consideration as defined by s 7 of the Act[3] has ended; and

(c) the application made in accordance with s 3 is accompanied by a declaration by the spouse making the application. The declaration must state that the applicant has 'reflected on the breakdown' and has considered the requirements of Part II 'as to the parties' arrangements for the future'; and that, with these two considerations in mind, the applicant states that the marriage cannot be saved.

1 Cf MCA 1973, s 1(1).
2 FLA 1996, s 5(1).
3 See para 3.25.

3.34 No application can be made for a marital order where the parties have jointly given notice of their intention to withdraw the statement; or where more than a year has passed since the end of the period for reflection and consideration which is applicable to the couple's circumstances[1].

1 FLA 1996, s 5(3).

3.35 Once it has received a statement, the court may by direction require the parties to attend a meeting to be informed of the availability of mediation and to provide them with an opportunity to attend for mediation[1]. The direction may be made on application of either of the parties or on the court's initiative. The court may also order adjournment of any proceedings for the parties to comply with a direction under s 13. The court may adjourn[2], not only for mediation to be considered, but also 'for the purpose of enabling disputes to be resolved amicably'[3]. In adjourning the court is required to have regard to the needs of 'any child of the family'[4]. An adjournment can only be for such maximum period as is specified by the rules[5]; and the parties 'shall' be ordered to prepare a report for the court save where the adjournment was to enable them to consider mediation under s 13[6].

1 FLA 1996, ss 13 and 14(1)(a).
2 Ibid, s 14.
3 Ibid, s 14(1)(b).
4 Ibid, s 14(2).
5 Ibid, s 14(3): this may prove unfortunate unless the court has power to extend the period.
6 Ibid, s 14(4).

Part III

Financial Provision

Chapter Four

Maintenance and Property Distribution

Simon Bruce

Introduction 61
Overview of the Available Orders for Income, Capital and Property
    Adjustment 62
Section 25 Factors 66
Periodical Payments and the Clean Break 76
Lump Sum Orders 83
Property Adjustment Orders 87
Order for the Sale of Property 96
Pensions 100
Maintenance Pending Suit 109
Variations 112
Consent Orders and Agreements 115
Injunctions and Financial Relief 127
Financial Provision in the Case of Neglect to Maintain 137
Matrimonial and Family Proceedings Act 1984, Part III 139
Family Law Act 1996 142
Tax Considerations 149
Bankruptcy and Family Breakdown (author: Jeremy Gordon) 152

INTRODUCTION

4.1 Marriage breakdown is the passport to a variety of financial relief orders. They are for income and capital. Even short marriages can result in maintenance orders being made for an indefinite period, and can result in lump sum and property adjustment orders being awarded. If the marriage ends in divorce or nullity, the statutory aim is to bring about a clean break[1], the purest form of clean break being dismissal of all conceivable claims that could be made by the parties for both capital and income. Any practitioner will give early consideration to advising a client to make an application for financial relief in the course of proceedings[2], subject to mediation or any realistic prospects of successful negotiations[3]. Similarly, a solicitor acting for the respondent to an application or potential application will be seeking to get the applicant's claims resolved so as to prevent a sword of Damocles over-hanging him or her in the future.

1 MCA 1973, s 25A.
2 For present purposes 'proceedings' means divorce, judicial separation and nullity.
3 Albeit that a party may be advised to adjourn any application for a lump sum.

4.2 Table 1 (pp 64–65) shows the kind of relief for which an application can be made during the marriage, the time for such application, an explanation of when the relief is effective, and the statutory authority. References are made also to the ancillary relief pilot scheme which came into force in certain courts on 1 October 1996[1].

1 *Practice Direction* [1996] 2 FLR 368.

OVERVIEW OF THE AVAILABLE ORDERS FOR INCOME, CAPITAL AND PROPERTY ADJUSTMENT

Financial provision orders in connection with proceedings for divorce, nullity or judicial separation

4.3 On or after the decree nisi, or the making of the decree of judicial separation, the court may make any one or more of the following orders (which are themselves defined in the MCA 1973, s 21):

(a) A periodical payments order for the benefit of a spouse or for the benefit of a child of the family, for such term as may be specified in the order[1].

(b) An order for secured periodical payments for the benefit of a spouse or for a child of the family, again for a specified term[2].

(c) An order that a party to the marriage shall pay to the other such lump sum or sums as may be so specified[3]. Similarly, a lump sum order may be made for the benefit of a child of the family[4].

(d) Under the MCA 1973, s 24 the court may make an order for property adjustment[5] on or after the decree nisi.

1 MCA 1973, s 23(1)(a) and (d).
2 Ibid, s 23(1)(b) and (e).
3 Ibid, s 23(1)(c).
4 Ibid, s 23(1)(f).
5 For a description and explanation of each type of property adjustment order, see paras 4.61 ff.

Orders for sale of property

4.4 The court has the power, under the MCA 1973, s 24A, to make an order for the sale of property in specific circumstances when an order for secured periodical payments, lump sum or property adjustment order has been made.

Maintenance pending suit

4.5 On the filing of a petition for divorce, nullity or judicial separation, the court may make an order for maintenance pending suit[1] under the MCA 1973, s 22. This will require a party to the marriage to make maintenance payments for the benefit of the other party. This provides only temporary relief and lasts until replaced by a periodical payments order.

1 See paras 4.125 ff.

Financial provision orders in the cases of neglect by a party to marriage to maintain the other party or a child of the family

4.6 Either party to a marriage can apply to the court for financial relief under the MCA 1973, s 27[1] if the other party has failed to provide reasonable maintenance for the applicant[2] or any child of the family[3].

1 See paras 4.194 ff.
2 MCA 1973, s 27(1)(a).
3 Ibid, s 27(1)(b).

Barry directions[1]

4.7 Under a line of case law developing from *Barry*[2], the court has been prepared to make interim capital orders in the course of proceedings[3]. Their authority derives not from statute, but from the inherent jurisdiction of the court. By such means the court is enabled to re-order the capital of the parties in a practical fashion and before the final hearing.

1 See para 4.55.
2 *Barry v Barry* [1992] 2 FLR 233.
3 In *F v F (Ancillary Relief: Substantial Assets)* [1995] 2 FLR 45 the court held that there was no such order as an 'interim lump sum order'.

Domestic Proceedings and Magistrates' Courts Act 1978

4.8 This statute enables a party to a marriage to apply inter alia for maintenance (and lump sum payments limited to £1,000). Application is made in the magistrates' courts under the Family Proceedings Courts (Matrimonial Proceedings etc) Rules 1991.

Alteration of agreements by the court during the lives of the parties

4.9 Where a maintenance agreement is subsisting[1], either party may apply to the court for alteration of the agreement under the MCA 1973, s 35. The section is little used because parties to a marriage will normally instead either apply to

TABLE 1

Financial Relief for parties to marriage under the MCA	Earliest possible date when payments/transfers will be made pursuant to the Order	When can the Order be made?
1 Financial provision on neglect to maintain (S 27 MCA)	Date of application	Any time after application subject to FPR r 3.1(4) and (5)
2 Maintenance pending suit (S 22 MCA)	Date of petition if relief applied for in the petition: otherwise date of Form M13 or M11 (or Form A)	Any time after application made and until date of Decree Absolute
3 Periodical payments (S 23(1) MCA)	Date of petition if relief applied for in the petition: otherwise date of Form M13 or M11 (or Form A)	Any time after Decree Nisi
4 Lump sum orders (S 23(1)(c) MCA)	Decree Absolute	Any time after Decree Nisi
5 Property adjustment orders (S 24(1)(a)–(d))	Decree Absolute	Any time after Decree Nisi
6 Orders for sale (S 24A(1) MCA)		Any time after Decree Nisi (S 24A(1) MCA)
7 Avoidance of disposition		Any time after proceedings for financial relief have commenced

Overview of the Available Orders

When is the Order effective?	Mode of application	Is Order variable?
Date of Order	Originating application in Form M19 (FPR r 3.1(1))	Yes (unless it is a lump sum not payable by instalments)
Date of Order	Form M13 (if relief applied for in petition/answer or Form M11 (or Form A) (FPR rr 2.58(1) and 2.53(2))	Yes (S 31(2)(a) MCA)
Decree Absolute	Form M13 (if relief applied for in petition/answer or Form M11 (or Form A) (FPR rr 2.58(1) and 2.53(2))	Yes
Decree Absolute	Form M13 (if relief applied for in petition/answer or Form M11 (or Form A) (FPR rr 2.58(1) and 2.53(2))	No (unless payable in instalments (S 31(2)(d)) or unless a deferred order relating to pension rights (see s 31(2)(dd))
Decree Absolute	Form M13 (if relief applied for in petition/answer or Form M11 (or Form A) (FPR rr 2.58(1) and 2.53(2)) (for service on third party refer to FPR r 2.59)	No, subject to variation of settlement order on JS (S 31(2)(e) MCA)
Decree Absolute (S 24A(3))	Form M13/Form M11 (or Form A)	Yes (S 31(2)(f) MCA)
Date of Order	CCN 16A (for service on third party refer to FPR r 2.59)	Yes

the court for a periodical payments order (assuming that there is no substantive order in existence) or apply for a variation, under the MCA 1973, s 31, of any order that may be in existence.

1 Each of the parties to the agreement must be either domiciled or resident in England and Wales: MCA 1973, s 35(1).

Financial relief in England and Wales after overseas divorce

4.10 Part III of the Matrimonial and Family Proceedings Act 1984[1] enables the court to make provision for financial relief to be available where a marriage has been dissolved or annulled, or the parties to a marriage have been legally separated, in a country overseas.

1 See paras 4.201 ff.

Variations and discharge of certain orders for financial relief

4.11 The court has power under the MCA 1973, s 31 to vary or discharge a wide range of orders made under the MCA 1973 for the benefit of a party to a marriage or children of the family[1].

1 See paras 4.134 ff.

SECTION 25 FACTORS

4.12 Having briefly considered the orders for financial relief which a court can make, it is necessary to consider the factors which the court considers when determining what kind of order should be made. The factors are listed in the MCA 1973, s 25. Judges frequently use each of the section 25 factors in their judgments (not least to demonstrate to the parties that the exercise has been fulfilled and to minimise the possibility of an appeal); but it must not be forgotten that the list is not conclusive: 'all the circumstances of the case'[1] must be considered, and in particular the factors in s 25(2).

1 MCA 1973, s 25(1).

Children of the family

4.13 Under the MCA 1973, s 25(1), it shall be the duty of the court in deciding whether to exercise its powers under ss 23, 24 or 24A and if so in what manner, to have regard to all the circumstances of the case, first consideration being given to the welfare while a minor of any child of the family who has not attained the age of 18. This does not mean that the welfare of the child is paramount. It means simply that the judge will first consider, before any other relevant matter, the welfare of a child. The welfare of the child will be the most important consideration[1]. It follows that the court will not normally impose a term on the periodical payments made by a husband to a wife who is at home looking after young children. The welfare of the children in that kind of case is generally best served by a periodical payments order in favour of a wife on which no term is placed. The principle also emerges very obviously in cases where capital falls to be distributed. The court will be looking to see how the children are going to be housed. If there is any capital in the case, the court will normally want that to be used towards the housing of the children[2]. This principle will often also dictate whether or not the former matrimonial home will be retained or sold.

1 See, eg *N v N (Consent order: Variation)* [1993] 2 FLR 868, and in particular, per Roch LJ at 881E–F.
2 So, eg, per Butler-Sloss LJ in *Dart v Dart* [1996] 2 FLR 286 at 303 G–H: 'in the low income cases the assessment of the needs of the parties will lean heavily in favour of the children and the parent with whom they live. If, therefore, the only asset is the house, and the mother is caring for the children, she will get the house and probably outright, even though the effect of that order is to deprive the husband of the whole of the capital accrued during the marriage and directly financed from his resources'.

The section 25 exercise

4.14 Under the MCA 1973, s 25(2), as regards the exercise of the powers of the court under ss 23(1)(a), (b) or (c), 24 or 24A in relation to a party to the marriage, the court shall in particular have regard to eight matters, which are considered one by one. Note again that the court is simply enjoined to have regard to these matters in particular; it will also have regard to any other matter which does not fall into the eight sub-headings.

Needs and resources

4.15 The most obvious balancing act to be performed is that between needs on the one hand, and resources on the other hand. The needs of the parties, and the resources available to meet those needs, are likely to be the most significant of the eight listed factors[1].

1 Thorpe LJ has recently described the 'needs' factor and its relationship with the other factors in the following way: 'there must be an objective appraisal of what the applicant subjectively requires to ensure that it is not unreasonable. But the objective appraisal must have regard to the other criteria of the section [viz MCA 1973, s 25], obviously including what is available, the standard of living to which the parties are accustomed, their age and state of health and, perhaps less obviously, the duration of the marriage, contributions, and pension rights both as affected by the marriage and accrued or likely to accrue. Used thus the consideration of needs ceases to be paramount or determinative but an elastic consideration that does not exclude the influence of any of the others' (from the judgment in the Court of Appeal in *Dart v Dart* [1996] 2 FLR 286 at 296 F–H).

68 Maintenance and Property Distribution

The income, earning capacity, property and other financial resources which each of the parties to the marriage has or is likely to have in the foreseeable future, including in the case of earning capacity any increase in that capacity which it would in the opinion of the court be reasonable to expect a party to the marriage to take steps to acquire (s 25(2)(a))

4.16 The Pensions Act 1995, s 166 introduced s 25B(1) into the MCA 1973 on 1 July 1996. This provides, inter alia, that in relation to benefits under a pension scheme, s 25(2)(a) shall have effect as if 'in the foreseeable future' were omitted, but this only applies to petitions for divorce, nullity or judicial separation presented on or after 1 July 1996 (Pensions Act 1995 (Commencement) (No 5) Order 1996, art 4(2)). See further paras 4.112 ff.

INCOME

4.17 This means income from all sources, both earned and unearned. It is necessary to consider gross income and income net of any kind of tax[1]. The benefits in kind received by a spouse by virtue of any employment (for instance car and petrol allowance, payment of domestic bills and health insurance) will also be taken into account.

1 The net income figure will be most relevant: see, eg *Peacock v Peacock* [1984] 1 All ER 1069, [1984] 1 WLR 532.

EARNING CAPACITY

4.18 A court looks at the realities of a situation. The court therefore may criticise or penalise a party who gives up a well-paying job in the hope or expectation that it will reduce his maintenance obligations; it may not do so. The debate about earning capacity is most obviously encountered when considering the level of maintenance that should be paid to a spouse. Again the court will look at the reality of the situation and may take judicial notice of unemployment figures. A point considered in para 4.40 is the extent to which the mother of a young child would be expected to earn an income. It is necessary to consider the qualifications of each of the parties and the extent to which a party might need training or rehabilitation before an earning capacity can be exercised.

PROPERTY AND OTHER FINANCIAL RESOURCES

4.19 This description is to be construed in its widest possible terms[1]. The court will look at the reality of the position and may infer the existence of relevant 'financial resources' from the evidence presented at any hearing. There is no definition of 'property' in the MCA 1973, but the term is to be construed as comprising both real and personal property; indeed any asset which could be of financial benefit to a party will be taken into account. Purely by way of example, matrimonial property will include:

(a) real property;

(b) chattels[2];

(c) insurance policies (which may have a surrender value);

(d) trust interests (both absolute and in reversion, and including an interest under a discretionary trust[3]);

(e) shares/interests in companies, including small family companies[4];

(f) damages[5];

(g) inheritances[6];

(h) the means of a co-habitee/new spouse[7].

1 In *Thomas v Thomas* [1995] 2 FLR 668, the court held that it was not limited to making orders relating simply to resources of capital or income which were shown to exist. When a party enjoys access to wealth, but no absolute entitlement to it, the availability of unidentified resources might be inferred. The court accepted that it should not apply undue pressure to a third party to ameliorate the financial position of a party, but it could frame its order so as to provide judicious encouragement to the third party to provide the spouse with the means to satisfy its orders.
2 Taking sale rather than insurance values.
3 In *Browne v Browne* [1989] 1 FLR 291, the court had regard to the fact that trustees had in the past met every reasonable request from the beneficiary who, in the event, could only satisfy the order by accessing funds held under a discretionary trust. In this case the court concluded that the sum could be raised without any problem, and that it was likely that the money would be forthcoming.
4 In *Thomas v Thomas* [1995] 2 FLR 668, the court made a clean break order which was based, in part, of an assessment of the value of the interest in a small family company. An analogy was drawn by the court between this kind of case and a case involving the accessing of funds held in a discretionary trust: see *Browne v Browne* [1989] 1 FLR 291.
5 In *Daubney v Daubney* [1976] 2 All ER 453, CA, it was held that damages for pain and suffering and loss of amenity are resources to be taken into account. In *C v C (Financial Provision; Personal Damages)* [1995] 2 FLR 171, the wife applied for financial relief and in particular for lump sum provision to be provided out of the husband's damages in respect of the husband's personal injury action. It was the first reported lump sum application against damages paid by way of structured settlement. The total of the sums due to the husband stood to exceed £5m. On an analysis of the parties' position however the court held that there was in reality virtually no readily available capital which might be transferred from the husband to the wife, and so no lump sum was ordered.
6 Not only inheritances which have already been received will be taken into account; so will inheritances which are likely to fall in the reasonably near future: *Michael v Michael* [1986] 2 FLR 389, and see *MT v MT* [1992] 1 FLR 362 for a case in which the lump sum application was adjourned until receipt of the prospective inheritance.
7 See *Atkinson v Atkinson* [1995] 2 FLR 356.

The financial needs, obligations and responsibilities which each of the parties to the marriage has or is likely to have in the foreseeable future (s 25(2)(b))

INCOME

4.20 The financial needs of both parties have to be calculated in a case almost as a matter of routine, even in the biggest of 'big money'[1] cases. That is not to say that the maintenance figure will be restricted by the pure 'needs' calculation; in a big money case, a wife may get even more maintenance than she needs if the husband's income and other resources are so great that he may be expected to pay more than may be strictly required by a mathematical calculation of her expenditure[2]. Some practitioners have a precedent for a budget form which they will assist their clients in completing. The budget is likely to find its way into the solicitors' correspondence and then into an affidavit of means, or will be produced in answer to a questionnaire. It will be an important document in any court bundle at any hearing where a spouse is seeking to establish needs. It has been held that needs equate to 'reasonable requirements' of a spouse[3]. The needs of the bread-winner must be balanced against those of the dependent party[4]. A husband will often do a precise budget of his financial requirements when, for instance, making an application for a downwards variation in the periodical payments he makes to his former wife and children. Such an approach may be an important feature at the first application for periodical payments.

1 This epithet was used in *F v F (Ancillary Relief: Substantial Assets)* [1995] 2 FLR 45 and throughout the judgment of the Court of Appeal judges in *Dart v Dart* [1996] 2 FLR 286.

2 In *Cornick v Cornick (No 2)* [1995] 2 FLR 490 the appellant's counsel argued that the calculation of periodical payments was an arithmetical exercise based on need alone, and that the court should be constrained by the wife's budget. The appellant's counsel went on to submit that if the court supported an approach which differed from what he termed 'the budgetary approach', it would have a serious effect upon the administration of the practice and settlement of financial relief applications throughout the country. The Court of Appeal rejected the proposition, and instead left undisturbed a level of periodical payments which was fixed at least in part by reference to the appellant's broad financial circumstances.

3 In the Court of Appeal decision in *Dart v Dart* (see above) the court held that in a line of cases including *O'D v O'D* (unreported) and *Preston v Preston* [1981] 2 FLR 331, Ormrod LJ, the great interpreter of s 25, held that 'needs' are equivalent to 'reasonable requirements' and so operates to 'cap' a party's financial relief. In *Dart* Thorpe LJ relied on a line of cases determined by Ormrod LJ in repelling the argument of the appellant's counsel that 'the entire corpus of ... decisions [subsequent to *Wachtel v Wachtel* [1973] 1 All ER 113] in this court on the application of the s 25 criteria to what are known as big money cases is wrongly decided'. And see *F v F (Ancillary Relief: Substantial Assets)* [1995] 2 FLR 45, Thorpe J (as he then was) applied a sharp pen to the budget of a former wife of a multi-millionaire.

4 In cases such as *Ashley v Blackman* [1988] 2 FLR 278, *Delaney v Delaney* [1990] 2 FLR 457 and *C v C* [1995] 2 FLR 171, the court dismissed the applicant's claims for periodical payments as a result of the impecuniosity of the respondent. One of the reasons for refusal of a periodical payments order in *C v C* was that it would remove the wife from the 'passport' benefits (such as payments of council tax) which she received as a result of being in receipt of DSS benefits. The case of *E v C (Child Maintenance)* [1996] 1 FLR 472 draws from *Delaney* in emphasising the principle that the income of a party on benefit is intended to provide basic subsistence only and does not therefore provide enough income to fund periodical payments orders.

CAPITAL

4.21 The needs of the parties which the court will be taking into account are also those of a capital nature. Conventionally, therefore, the wife may be asking for such capital as will enable her to have a home in her own right. If the former matrimonial home is likely to be sold, she will be producing estate agents' particulars showing the kind of properties which she would like to purchase. The husband will be doing exactly the same thing relating to his own needs. He may also need to show that he needs to put capital into a business and that a specific portion of the pot should be ear-marked for that purpose[1].

1 This was argued on behalf of appellant in *Thomas v Thomas* [1995] 2 FLR 668, the appellant husband appealing partly on the basis that the judge at first instance had not taken into account that he required capital against which he could secure his Lloyds liability.

THE FINANCIAL OBLIGATIONS AND RESPONSIBILITIES

4.22 It may be that a party has dependants by a prior marriage or relationship. Those will be disclosed and may be taken into account by the court[1].

1 See *E v C (Child Maintenance)* [1996] 1 FLR 472, and particular paragraph E at 476. Contrast *Fisher v Fisher* [1989] 1 FLR 423 where the existence of dependants from a husband's second marriage did not assist the husband's application for a downwards variation of the periodical payments made to his former wife.

The standard of living enjoyed by the family before the breakdown of the marriage (s 25(2)(c))

4.23 Broadly speaking the court will try to keep the status quo[1], although inevitably in some cases the standard of living of both parties declines as the available income has to be divided between two households. In a 'needs' case therefore it may be impossible to retain the status quo. The standard of living of the parties is often a good gauge of their resources. It can be a pointer to undisclosed wealth, undeclared income, and cash dealings. A wife may refer to the standard of living that she enjoyed during the marriage, backing it up (in appropriate cases) with proof of holidays that the parties have taken and the frequency of expensive entertainment.

1 This broad principle was applied, to provide a remedy before the final hearing, in *Poon v Poon* [1994] 2 FLR 857.

The age of each party to the marriage and the duration of the marriage (s 25(2)(d))

THE AGE OF EACH PARTY

4.24 The age of each party is going to be relevant because it will impact upon the earning capacity of each party, and the proximity to retirement. Therefore, for example, a middle-aged wife without any pension provision and with children to look after will be protected by the court as the resources of the husband allow. It may be difficult for the husband in that kind of case to achieve a 'clean break'[1]. Conversely, a young spouse is both statistically and as a matter of experience likely to have a relationship with someone else or to remarry, and this will be a background factor which the court will have in mind when considering financial relief[2]. If a party is just about to retire, the level of maintenance may be fixed with reference to his existing income, with a defined decrease when the husband receives his pension. Case law suggests that a very old applicant who has been married for a substantial period will have reasonable needs which are less than those of a younger applicant, and therefore paradoxically an old applicant in these circumstances may not achieve financial relief as substantial as that of a younger applicant[3].

1 So, eg *Barrett v Barrett* [1988] 2 FLR 516.

2 And case law experience shows that a young wife's maintenance claims will be calculated on an appropriately discounted *Duxbury* basis.
3 In *W v W (Judicial Separation: Ancillary Relief)* [1995] 2 FLR 259, it was held that the 78 year old wife of an 87 year old husband (the two of them having had a relationship lasting 55 years) was not entitled to a half and half share of the assets, but should have enough to cater for her reasonable needs (and she received about 20% of the joint assets).

THE DURATION OF THE MARRIAGE

4.25 The shorter the marriage, the less are a spouse's chances of obtaining substantial financial relief. Short marriages often produce only short-term relief[1]. Where there are children, even in a short marriage of two or three years, a wife will have a strong claim for a substantial proportion of the capital in the case, to facilitate the purchase of accommodation for herself and the children[2]. Any co-habitation by the parties prior to the marriage[3] may also be put into the equation and may strengthen a party's claims to financial relief. So if, for example, parties have lived together for a period of five years before the marriage, and divorce proceedings are brought two years after the marriage, the wife may be able to show that she has had seven years of dependence on her husband. This may influence the kind of order that the court will make[4].

1 In *Graves v Graves* (1973) 4 Fam Law 124, Ormrod J (as he then was) held that where a marriage was of short duration and the parties were young, a nominal order was the appropriate order unless there were children or the wife was handicapped in some way which prevented her from working. In *Attar v Attar (No 2)* [1985] FLR 653, the applicant, who was young and who had an earning capacity, was allowed a re-adjustment period of two years to enable her to find employment to become self-sufficient and to re-establish herself, and received financial support over those two years. The case is authority, at the very least, for what financial order may be made in favour of a young wife of limited means against a husband of very great wealth at the end of a very short marriage.
2 Albeit that the capital may be tied up in trust with a direction that a proportion of the capital is released to the husband on a determining event, for instance the youngest child attaining the age of 18: see, eg *Mesher v Mesher and Hall* [1980] 1 All ER 126n.
3 The co-habitation does not fall within the ambit of s 25 and therefore is taken into account as one of the circumstances of the case, pursuant to the MCA 1973, s 25(1).
4 The husband and wife in *W v W (Judicial Separation: Ancillary Relief)* [1995] 2 FLR 259 co-habitated for 39 years before their marriage.

Any physical or mental disability of either of the parties to the marriage (s 25(2)(e))

4.26 Any disability will impinge on the financial needs of the parties. A disability may inhibit earning capacity and the time over which property is required[1]. The disability will have to be proved by reference to medical evidence, which may be tested by the other spouse.

1 See *M v M (Property Adjustment: Impaired Life Expectancy)* [1993] 2 FLR 723, CA.

The contributions which each of the parties has made or is likely in the foreseeable future to make to the welfare of the family, including any contribution by looking after the home or caring for the family (s 25(2)(f))

4.27 The contributions by the parties are therefore financial and otherwise. The financial contributions will be relevant, and are often recited in the affidavit evidence. A spouse may therefore try to trace the way in which he or she has contributed to the purchase of successive family homes. A substantial imbalance in the way in which the financial contributions have been made may tip the balance on the division of capital one way or the other. That said, the court is unlikely to be impressed by too slavish an approach to who, or whose family, contributed what to the marriage[1]. A wife who has made a contribution to a husband's business will also wish to spell that out in any affidavit evidence: it may bolster the wife's claims[2]. Against that, as the statute spells out, the contribution of a wife in looking after the home and children of the family are to be considered[3]. The court is of course more likely to be impressed by a wife's care of her family than of her home. However in those cases where a wife has overseen the refurbishment or redecoration of a property and thereby enhanced its value, she will wish to explain this in her affidavit. If a case is being presented as a contributions case alone, and other aspects (such as reasonable requirements) are not really relevant, that should simplify the ancillary relief procedures and may just amount to an exercise of totting-up the contributions made[4].

1 The pilot scheme of the proposed new procedure for ancillary relief cases, which came into force on 1 October 1996, provides for new standard forms to replace affidavit of means. It is illustrative of the lack of importance attached by the court to the contribution by either party, within the whole s 25 exercise (at least in the view of the Lord Chancellor's Working Party), that only one inch of space is given over to the explanation that a spouse can provide, in his or her standard form, of a contribution which is considered to be relevant. See *Practice Direction* [1996] 2 FLR 368.
2 It was held to be significant in the case of *W v W (Judicial Separation: Ancillary Relief)* [1995] 2 FLR 259 that the wife had not contributed to the husband's business assets. And it is clear from the Court of Appeal judgment in *Dart v Dart* [1996] 2 FLR 286, that the wife would have received a much higher proportion of the overall assets in the case if she had helped to generate the husband's wealth.
3 So a wife who is likely in the foreseeable future to be the carer of minor children will need her accommodation requirements to be provided by the husband in suitable circumstances. This is an example of how one of the s 25 factors gels with another (needs) and with the overriding factor in s 25 (1), viz the first consideration being given to the welfare of a minor child of the family.
4 As in *A v A (Costs Appeal)* [1996] 1 FLR 14, in which Singer J, criticising the conduct of solicitors who had been over-zealous in the questions contained in r 2.63 questionnaires, commented 'it does seem to me that the scope of the husband's enquiries and the extent to which they sought to delve back into history indicated that on his side at that stage sight had been lost of the fact that this was a contributions case and not primarily, if at all, a needs case. It was, moreover, a case where the precise extent of the wife's capital and income were more or less irrelevant...'.

The conduct of each of the parties, if that conduct is such that it would in the opinion of the court be inequitable to disregard it (s 25(2)(g))

4.28 Conduct, or behaviour, will only very rarely be relevant in any financial application. Having said that, the way in which the parties behave in the marriage may be a factor which the court takes into account in a very general way and may influence slightly the outcome of the application. The subsection covers blatant conduct such as has featured in reported cases to date, for example:–

(a) Attempted murder, or inciting a third party to murder a spouse[1].

74 *Maintenance and Property Distribution*

(b) Reckless gambling.

(c) Behaving in such an unreasonable way in the proceedings themselves that the court will wish to penalise a party, for instance:

  (i) a party lying on oath about his financial disclosure[2]. A court may in these circumstances make an inference that a party has other assets which are not disclosed, and may either increase the lump sum payment and other financial provision for the wife or make a punitive costs order accordingly (perhaps ordering the costs to be paid by the husband on an indemnity rather than on a standard basis);

  (ii) seeking to unsettle a previously made agreement[3]. The fact that the parties may have compromised matters in a deed of separation will, notwithstanding that it is impossible to oust the jurisdiction of the court to make orders in matrimonial proceedings, be of special importance in a financial relief application;

  (iii) if a party has behaved in an obstructive, oppressive or needlessly aggressive manner in the litigation itself (for instance by continual disobedience to disclosure orders or making a series of ill-founded applications), the conduct may be classified as so inequitable as to be taken into account by the court, but the court normally deals with such conduct by making appropriately oppressive costs orders[4].

(d) Financial mismanagement[5].

(e) Assault[6].

1 *Evans v Evans* [1989] 1 FLR 351.
2 See *Baker v Baker* [1995] 2 FLR 829, where the Court of Appeal upheld the judge at first instance who had come to the view that there had been substantial non-disclosure, and who had therefore made orders which, although they could not be paid from the disclosed assets, could in the court's view be financed out of undisclosed assets.
3 The locus classicus on the upholding of agreements between parties is *Edgar v Edgar* [1980] 1 WLR 1410. For a helpful review of 'agreement' cases, reference should be made to an article by D Burrows in the *Solicitors' Journal*, 31 March 1995, pp 294 and 295; and see *Beach v Beach* [1995] 2 FLR 160.
4 See *F v F (Duxbury Calculation: Rate of Return)* [1996] 1 FLR 833.
5 See *Beach v Beach* [1995] 2 FLR 160 (which was also, coincidentally, an *Edgar* type case involving a previous made agreement, see further para 4.166). The court held in this case the husband's financial mismanagement was a significant factor, which was taken into the equation.
6 Compare *H v H (Financial Provision: Conduct)* [1994] 2 FLR 801 where a husband's assault affected the wife's material security to a significant degree (and so where conduct was a predominant factor); and *A v A (Financial Provision: Conduct)* [1995] 1 FLR 345, in which the judge held that although the husband's assault of the wife constituted conduct which it would be inequitable to disregard, it was only one of the factors to be reflected in the s 25 exercise. Note, however, how in the latter case the conduct did affect the way in which the order was made; rather than applying a deferred charge on the former matrimonial home in favour of the husband, because of the violent conduct the judge imposed a lump sum order, to be paid on sale of the former matrimonial home: 'in the light of the history of violence ... it would be unwise to

perpetuate a financial relationship between the husband and wife over the course of years to come'.

In the case of proceedings for divorce or nullity of marriage, the value to each of the parties to the marriage of any benefit (for example, a pension) which, by reason of the dissolution or annulment of the marriage, that party will lose the chance of acquiring s 25(2)(h)[1]

4.29 Pensions and financial relief are considered separately[2]. The extent to which a pension is going to be considered to be relevant depends on the ages of the parties and all the other circumstances described above. For instance, the pension may be a long way off and may be only a small percentage of the overall assets. It becomes more of a factor if the parties are nearing pensionable age and the pension constitutes a large percentage of the overall pot.

1 Under the MCA 1973, s 25B(1), it is directed that the court is to have regard, in the case of paragraph (a), to any benefit under a pension scheme which a party to the marriage will lose the chance of acquiring. The words '(for example, a pension)', which are included in the text of s 25(2)(h) after the words 'benefit' were deleted from the section by the Pensions Act 1995, s 166(2), in respect of petitions for divorce, nullity or judicial separation filed after 1 July 1996 (The Pensions Act 1995 (Commencement) (No 5) Order 1996, art 4(2)).
2 See paras 4.100 ff.

The section 25 considerations applicable to orders made in relation to children of the family

4.30 The matters which the court considers are set out in the MCA 1973, s 25(3)(a) to (e), and include the financial needs of the child, his income, earning capacity, property and other financial resources; any physical or mental disability of the child; the manner in which he was being and the parties to the marriage expected him to be educated or trained; and the s 25(2) factors set out at s 25(2)(a), (b), (c) and (e). These matters are rarely encountered in practice, for the following reasons:

(a) There is only limited jurisdiction now to make periodical payments orders in favour of children[1].

(b) Lump sum payments and property adjustment orders in favour of children or for their benefit are extremely rare[2].

(c) The CA 1989 sets out a separate (but analogous) regime for orders for the benefit of children.

1 See para 10.5.
2 See paras 5.56 ff.

Child of the family

4.31 A party's liability for a child of the family who is not a child of that party will depend on the factors set out in the MCA 1973, s 25(4). The court will have regard not only to the s 25(3) factors but also to whether that party assumed any responsibility for the child's maintenance, and, if so, the extent to which, and the basis upon which, that party assumed such responsibility and to the length of time for which that party discharged such responsibility (s 25(4)(a)); to whether in assuming and discharging such responsibility that party did so knowing that the child was not his or her own (s 25(4)(b)); and to the liability of any other person to maintain the child (s 25(4)(c)).

Terminating each party's financial obligations

4.32 The court is obliged to consider whether it would be appropriate, when making periodical payments, lump sum and property adjustment orders for the benefit of a party under the MCA 1973, s 23(1)(a), (b) or (c), and s 24, and orders under s 24A on or after the grant of a decree of divorce or nullity, to terminate the financial obligations of each party towards the other as soon after the grant of the decree as the court considers just and reasonable[1].

1 MCA 1973, s 25A and see para 4.39.

PERIODICAL PAYMENTS AND THE CLEAN BREAK

Types of orders for periodical payments

4.33 The kinds of periodical payments orders which a court can make are as follows:

(a) *Orders without a term.* Periodical payments may be expressed to last without any kind of limitation. A periodical payments order for a spouse comes to an end on:

   (i) the remarriage of the payee[1];

   (ii) the death of the payer (unless it is a secured order);

   (iii) the death of the payee.

(b) *Term orders.* Periodical payments may be expressed to last for a specific term, say five years. If nothing else about the term is expressed in the order, the periodical payments will be paid for five years and the entitlement to periodical payments will come to an end on the expiration of that five year period[2].

1 MCA 1973, s 28(3).
2 *G v G (Periodical Payments: Jurisdiction)* [1996] Fam Law, November, 704–705, CA.

Term orders and dismissals

4.34 The periodical payments may be expressed to last for a defined term, whereupon they will come to an end, and the original claim will be dismissed. The payee may still apply to the court for an extension of the term of the maintenance within the specified period during which maintenance is payable[1].

If, however, the payee does not make an application for an extension before the termination of the periodical payments, the periodical payments will come to an end at the conclusion of the term.

1 See, eg *B v B (Consent order: Variation)* [1995] 1 FLR 9 and *G v G* (para 4.33, n 2).

Non-extendable term orders and dismissals

4.35 The periodical payments can be expressed to last for a specific term, with an additional direction being made by the court pursuant to the MCA 1973, s 28(1A) directing that the payee shall not be entitled to apply under the MCA 1973, s 31 for an extension of the term specified in the order. The direction which is made by the court under s 28(1A) must, to be immediately effective, be an immediate direction[1]. If the operation of the direction is postponed until a certain event (for instance until the payment of a lump sum) it will be possible for the payee to apply for a variation of the term, as the s 28(1A) direction will not by then have come into effect.

1 See, eg *Richardson v Richardson (No 2)* [1994] 2 FLR 1051.

Duration of the periodical payments order

4.36 The law is set out in the MCA 1973, s 28. The term cannot begin earlier than the date when the application for the order is made (which, for a petitioner, will be the date of the petition so long as the relevant applications have been made in the petition). For a respondent, the date will be the date of the answer, if the relevant applications were made in the answer, failing which it will be the date of the Form M11 which initiated his application.

Effect of remarriage

4.37 If a party to the marriage has not applied for a financial provision order, or for a property adjustment order, whether in the petition, answer, Form M13 or Form M11, an application for them cannot be made by him or her after that spouse's remarriage (MCA 1973, s 28(3))[1]. A lawyer's failure to advise a client of this is prima facie evidence of negligence. In these unhappy circumstances a party who has remarried, not having made the relevant applications, will have to have recourse to one or more of the following options:

(a) An application to the court for determination of any application for financial relief by the other spouse (in the course of which the court will declare the interest of the remarried party in the matrimonial assets).

(b) An application under the Married Women's Property Act 1882, s 17[2]. This has to be made within three years of decree absolute. It serves to obtain a declaration from the court as to the legal interest of the parties in any matrimonial assets.

(c) An application under the LPA 1925, s 188, relating to chattels.

78 *Maintenance and Property Distribution*

(d) An application under the Law of Property Act 1925 s 30, relating to the ownership and realisation of assets held on trust for sale.

1 That will not however prejudice the ability of a payee to sue for maintenance arrears following her remarriage (MCA 1973, s 28(2)).
2 See para 5.11.

Payment of periodical payments

4.38 The periodical payments will, unless otherwise ordered, be payable in arrears. They may be ordered to be paid in any currency and may be ordered to be paid by standing order to the payee's bank account if she has one[1].

1 See the Maintenance Enforcement Act 1991, s 1(5)(a).

Towards a clean break: section 25A factors

4.39 It is important to bear in mind that the section 25A factors are only part of the equation. They do not predominate. The section 25 considerations, which include the needs of the parties, will also come into play. In other words, there is not a bias towards judges imposing a clean break in cases. There is simply a statutory duty imposed on judges to consider whether a clean break is reasonable in all the circumstances of a case. Where the court decides to exercise its powers to make periodical payments, secured periodical payments, lump sum and property adjustment orders, or orders for the sale of the property under s 24A, it shall be the duty of the court to consider whether it would be appropriate so as to exercise those powers that the financial obligations of each party towards the other will be terminated as soon after the grant of the decree as the court considers just and reasonable (MCA 1973, s 25A(1))[1].

1 For an example of the clean break in action, see *Clutton v Clutton* [1991] 1 WLR 359, and for a survey of clean break cases see the articles by S J Bruce, in Solicitors' Journal, 4 and 11 September 1992.

Further duty of the court

4.40 The court shall in particular consider whether it would be appropriate to require those payments to be made or secured only for such term as would in the opinion of the court be sufficient to enable the party in whose favour the order is made to adjust without undue hardship to the termination of his or her financial dependence on the other party (MCA 1973, s 25A(2)). The obligation rests with the court properly to consider whether such an order would be appropriate[1]. The case law which has arisen since s 25A(2) was incorporated in the MCA 1973 in 1984 shows that, although the consideration must be real and substantial, the court will take a lot of convincing before dismissing periodical payments orders for a dependent wife. A wife looking after young children will not normally have her periodical payments claims dismissed[2], unless she happens to be wealthy in her own right[3], or unless she has a relationship with someone who is, or may be expected to be, supporting her[4]. Where, however, there is an equality of poverty, the court will tend not to impose any periodical payments orders. Therefore if both spouses are on income support, the likelihood is that there will be a clean break between them[5].

1 As emphasised by Slade LJ in *Whiting v Whiting* [1988] 2 All ER 275. In this case the husband failed, on appeal, to obtain the dismissal of his former wife's nominal periodical payments order. The dissenting judgment of Balcombe LJ, which has in fact set the tone of case law since then, argues against preserving maintenance orders as 'last back stops' for former wives who are now financially independent.
2 See *N v N* [1993] 2 FLR 868, and, per Roch LJ at 883B and C: 'it can be anticipated that it will be an exceptional case that an order for periodical payments will be limited to a term under s 28(1) where there is a child of the family who remains in the care and control of the party in whose favour the order for periodical payments is being made and who has yet to attain the age of 18 years, and that it would only be in the most exceptional and unusual case for a direction under s 28(1A) to be made in such circumstances, cf the decision in *Waterman v Waterman* [1989]1 FLR 380, and especially the remarks of Sir Stephen Brown at 386E'.
3 See *C v C (Financial Provision)* [1989] 1 FLR 11, per Ewbank J at 20A: 'I have to say in my judgment that for a young or middle-aged wife in possession of substantial capital the idea of periodical payments for life is largely obsolescent'.
4 See *Atkinson v Atkinson* [1995] 2 FLR 356. In this case Thorpe J held that although co-habitation was not to be equated with marriage, it was a factor which the court should take into account since it had a bearing upon the parties' financial circumstances, and, in particular, the assessment of the reasonable needs of the co-habiting spouse. In this case the judge reduced the former wife's periodical payments in proportion to the financial contribution to her living costs which he judged was being, or could be, made by her co-habitee.
5 But see the judgment in the Court of Appeal case of *Freeman v Swatridge* [1984] FLR 762: 'there was no general principle or rule of law that a man in receipt of supplementary benefit should not be able to pay maintenance'.

Duxbury sums[1]

4.41 Where there is sufficient capital, it is possible for the court to bring about a clean break to pay off a wife's maintenance entitlement by payment of a lump sum[2]. As a payment to buy-off maintenance, the *Duxbury* sum is additional to any other capital for which the applicant may be applying. The Duxbury sum is made by carrying out an actuarial calculation to show what lump sum would be required to equate to annual maintenance payments for an applicant over the period of years which she should be expected to survive. A certain rate of return on the capital would be built into the equation (normally 4.25%)[3]. The expectation is that the recipient will draw on both the capital and the income derived from it over the term of years which she is expected to live, and that there will be 'enough money to pay for the funeral' (but no more) on the date that she is expected to die. Most firms of accountants, barristers and solicitors who specialise in this kind of work have computer systems which enable *Duxbury* calculations to be done[4]; and the calculations can be made more specific and suited to a particular case by factoring in the possibility of remarriage or co-habitation within a certain term, and discounting the overall sum[5]. However, *Duxbury* calculations are only a tool[6]. They cannot, and do not, impose an obligation on courts to follow exactly the guidelines which are suggested by the information in the tables, principally because they derive their force and meaning from only one of the s 25 criteria, namely needs[7].

1 After the case of *Duxbury v Duxbury* [1987] 1 FLR 7, CA.
2 Not all courts in other jurisdictions offer the facility of such payments, and their existence in this jurisdiction can often sway an applicant to opt to proceed in this jurisdiction in preference to another.
3 After *F v F (Duxbury Calculation: Rate of Return)* [1996] 1 FLR 833.
4 However the most convenient and perhaps best used *Duxbury* guidance is contained in *At a Glance* (published annually by the FLBA).
5 See, for instance, the Tables in Volume 2 of *Duckworth's Matrimonial Property and Finance*, 5th edn.
6 So, eg in *Gojkovic v Gojkovic* [1990] 1 FLR 140, CA.
7 Other s 25 factors such as the age of the parties will come into play. For example, see *F v F (Ancillary Relief)* [1995] 2 FLR 45, and in particular at 67E: 'This is not a capitalisation to be achieved by straightforward application of the *Duxbury* formula. Any just conclusion has to recognise the extent to which the wife's claim is founded on her status as mother of ... three children. It has to reflect her comparative use and the comparative brevity of the union'.

Factors for consideration by the parties

4.42 It can be seen that there is an element of risk for both parties when accepting a *Duxbury* payment.

(a) For the paying party, there is the risk that the payee may remarry (or even cohabit) in the future[1]. A husband will often offer a *Duxbury* sum at a discount to take into account a wife's chances of remarriage. That presents even more of a risk for the receiving party, but the fact is that the courts will not apply conventional *Duxbury* calculations to divorces involving young recipients (the FLBA tables do not even show the entitlement of spouses aged under 42).

(b) In cases where a clean break has been imposed and a wife's maintenance entitlement has come to an end, the court has been willing to increase the children's periodical payments to deal with the needs of mother and children[2]. For example, where the mother and children are in mortgaged accommodation, the wife's periodical payments have been discharged, and the court agrees that it is in the children's best interests to stay in that mortgaged accommodation, the court may be prepared (subject to the operation of the Child Support Act 1995) to increase the children's periodical payments to cover payments.

1 Inadequate disclosure on this point could enable an application to be made for the order to be set aside: *Livesey v Jenkins* [1985] AC 424.
2 For the principle, refer to Butler-Sloss L J at 876H and 877A of *N v N* [1993] 2 FLR 868.

Occasions for payment of Duxbury sums

4.43 *Duxbury* payments may be encountered in the following categories of cases:

(a) Most obviously, in big money cases in which a Duxbury sum can be funded without difficulty.

(b) In cases where young wives are prepared to take a risk and accept a dismissal of their periodical payments claims in exchange for a sizeable capital payment.

(c) In cases where there may be no current maintenance entitlement, but where the wife has no, or only a restricted, pension in her own right (and would therefore be entitled to ask for a nominal periodical payments order which she could apply to be varied upwards on her retirement). She may be prepared to accept a capital sum, calculated on *Duxbury* principles, in lieu of the maintenance order.

Dismissal of the periodical payments order – MCA, s 25A(3)

4.44 If the court considers that no continuing obligation should be imposed on either party to make or secure periodical payments in favour of the other, the court may dismiss the application with a direction that the applicant should not be entitled to make any future application in relation to that marriage for an order under s 23(1)(a) or (b) s 25A(3), MCA 1973. The effect of this subsection is that a court can direct that there will be no future application for maintenance.

The interrelation of s 25A(3) and s 28(1A)

4.45 The question that then arises, and has in the past arisen, is the co-relation between that subsection and s 28(1A)[1], which enables the court to direct that a party shall not be entitled to apply under s 31 for the extension of a maintenance term. The position can be analysed as follows:

(a) Where the s 25A direction is made without a s 28(1A) direction, the applicant will not be entitled to make any further application and the lack of a s 28(1A) direction will not be relevant.

(b) Where there is no s 25A(3) direction, but an immediate direction under s 28(1A), then the parties could apply for a variation of the periodical payments order, but they could not apply for an extension of the term of maintenance payments.

(c) If neither a s 25A(3) nor a s 28(1A) direction is made, there is no fetter on the powers of the court to vary the periodical payments order.

1 See *Richardson v Richardson (No 1)* [1994] 1 FLR 286.

Secured orders

4.46 Under s 23(1)(b) the court may make an order that either party shall secure to the other to the satisfaction of the court such periodical payments, and for such term, as may be so specified.

When a secured order may be appropriate

4.47 An applicant will generally only seek an order for secured periodical payments in clearly defined circumstances.

(a) The applicant may be concerned that the periodical payments order may not be paid, and there may be a capital asset which could conveniently be charged with its payment. Thus if a periodical payment is not made, the applicant can ask that the security should be realised to make up for the deficiency in the periodical payments.

(b) Where the payer lives outside the jurisdiction and it may be difficult to enforce payment of any arrears of periodical payments.

4.48 A secured periodical payment order may be varied under the MCA 1973, s 31 after the payer's death. In those circumstances the payee may have a choice of remedy, between applying for a variation of the periodical payments under s 31 or making an application under the Inheritance (Provision for Family and Dependants) Act 1975 (the latter remedy being available if the deceased died domiciled in England and Wales)[1].

1 A secured periodical payments order (for the benefit of a child whose father was domiciled outside England and Wales) was made in *C v C* [1995] 2 FLR 171.

The security itself

4.49 A variety of assets may be used as security for a secured periodical payments order. Those most commonly used are:

(a) *Real property.* If real property is going to be security, it will be necessary to draw up an appropriate mortgage deed and have it properly registered. Ideally the practitioner would negotiate the terms of the charge, in any matter decided by consent application, before the filing of the draft order so as to be able to exhibit the charge to the draft order when it is sent to the court for approval.

(b) *Bank accounts.* In these circumstances it will be necessary to protect the payee by getting the payer to provide suitable undertakings in the court order to maintain a certain balance in the specified account, and perhaps to give irrevocable instructions to the bank:

   (i) not to allow the balance in the specified account to go below a specified amount;

   (ii) to pay out to the applicant any amount of periodical payments as may be proved by her to be due under the court order.

(c) *Endowment policies.*

(d) *Share certificates/securities.*

(e) *Jewellery/other chattels.*

Security after payer's death

4.50 Part of the process of negotiating maintenance payments to be made to a wife will be consideration of her position after the death of the payer. That is why the payee will often ask that the application for secured periodical payments should not be dismissed, even if there is no immediate intention to ask for a secured periodical payments order to be made. The point is that the payee will then be able to ask for a substantive secured periodical payments order to be made at an appropriate date in the future[1]. In these circumstances the payee may wish to reserve the right to trigger an application for secured periodical payments which can be varied after the payer's death as an added option to an Inheritance Act claim.

1 This aspect is often tied up with the pension provision which a husband may or may not be able to make for a wife. Pension scheme trustees generally have an overall discretion as to the payments which they make out of the scheme, so even if a payer requested pension scheme trustees to make specific benefit out of the pension for the benefit of the wife, they may not actually do so. Since 1 July 1996, however, the court can, under s 25C(2), require trustees to exercise their discretion in a certain way in relation to petitions for divorce, judicial separation and nullity filed on or after 1 July 1996.

The drafting of the security documentation

4.51 There is a specific power for the court to refer the drafting of the security documentation to one of the conveyancing counsel of the court, when the court has decided to make a financial provision order whereby any payments are to be secured, or a property adjustment order[1]. Where such an order is to be made in proceedings for divorce, nullity or judicial separation, the court may also defer the grant of the decree until the instrument has been duly executed[2]. However, reference to conveyancing counsel of the court it is hardly ever met in practice. It is far preferable for the parties to settle the terms of the document in advance of filing the draft order at the court, not least to sift out any important points of principle which could emerge in the drafting.

1 MCA 1973, s 30(a).
2 Ibid, s 30(b).

The date when the secured periodical payments order takes effect

4.52 As noted in Table 1 above, neither the periodical payments nor any settlement made in pursuance of the order shall take effect unless the decree has been made absolute[1].

1 MCA 1973, s 23(5).

LUMP SUM ORDERS

4.53 The MCA 1973, s 23(1)(c) provides that on the granting of the decree of divorce, a decree of nullity or a decree of judicial separation or at any time thereafter the court may make an order that either party to the marriage shall pay to the other such lump sum or sums as may be specified.

One lump sum order

4.54 The court can only make *one* lump sum order, albeit that the order itself can provide for the payment of a lump sum made up of a number of constituents. There have been a number of attempts to persuade judges to make interim lump sum orders, but there has been no reported decision where an applicant has met with success. It has been unsuccessfully argued, for example, that the court can make a lump sum order at an interim stage after the decree nisi has been pronounced which consists of:

(a) a specified lump sum (an amount, required, for example, to purchase accommodation before the substantive hearing); and

(b) an unspecified further amount, the precise amount to be decided at the final hearing.

It must therefore be right for practitioners to take the cautious view that the court has jurisdiction to make only one lump sum order[1]. However, the court can make what amounts to lump sum orders pending conclusion of the proceedings to cover particular expenses[2].

1 The Family Law Act 1996, s 22A, will enable the court to make interim lump sum orders: see paras 4.219 ff.
2 MCA 1973, s 23(3)(a).

Appropriation directions[1]

4.55 Notwithstanding that the court will not make an interim lump sum order, courts have shown imagination in the way they have dealt with an applicant's request for capital before the final hearing, by means of appropriation of an asset or fund to a particular party[2]. There is a large number of situations where it would be desirable to have, for the benefit of a spouse, a capital payment before a final hearing. Examples may include:

(a) a situation where either spouse wants to have capital in order to purchase a house before the final hearing;

(b) a situation where a wife needs a payment of capital to discharge a debt before the final hearing, and cannot persuade either her husband or a third party such as a bank to lend her the money, etc.

In these circumstances the court has been willing to appropriate the assets of the parties in such a way as to enable a need to be met. The court will in suitable circumstances facilitate the re-ordering of the finances of the parties. So if, for example, a wife was living in rented accommodation and a husband unreasonably refused to allow her to use a proportion of family assets to purchase a house for herself before the final hearing, she could apply to the court for an order requiring him to make funds available for that purpose. There would have to be proceedings in existence, but there does not have to be a decree nisi in place at the time of the application and order.

1 For a helpful article on this subject see David Burrows' article in Solicitors' Journal, 26 May 1995, page 496.
2 As in the case of *Barry v Barry* [1992] 2 FLR 233, and as discussed in the judgment of Thorpe J in *F v F (Ancillary Relief: Substantial Assets)* [1995] 2 FLR 45. In the latter case, the judge accepted the principle that the court had an inherent jurisdiction to re-order the capital of the parties prior to the final hearing; the jurisdiction was not founded upon statute.

4.56 In acting for an applicant for an appropriation order, it will be necessary to provide suitable assurances and undertakings. For example, the wife should at the very least facilitate the registration of a caution against dealings in favour of the husband in relation to the property which she proposes to purchase. Alternatively the property would be purchased in the joint names of the spouses, or in the name of one spouse on trusts reflecting the parties' beneficial interest in the purchase monies. There may be capital gains tax considerations which would militate in favour of the property being conveyed into the name of one party[1]. The order may also in suitable cases recite that the amount used by the wife in the purchase of a property is without prejudice to any contention the husband might make in the future that she is over-housed.

1 If, for instance, the other party already owned another property which he had selected to be his principal private residence; there may be little point in inviting a capital gains tax problem for the husband arising out of any subsequent transfer of the property bought for the wife into her name. See paras 4.244 ff.

Payment of lump sum by instalments

4.57 The lump sum order can be expressed to be payable by instalments. It may be that a lump sum payment for a wife will be financed out of the lump sum payment commuted from a husband's pension scheme on his normal retirement date, or the lump sum will be financed out of the sale proceeds of a property which is to be sold at some stage in the future. In that case an instalment payment could be expressed to be payable on the decree absolute with a further instalment due at some specified time thereafter. There is a risk to both the payee and the payer inherent in any lump sum instalment order, because it is possible for either party to make an application to the court for a variation of the order[1]. On the other hand, the payer may need to ask for the instalment payment to be waived, and the court has the power to do this[2]. The prospective payee may therefore find herself in a position where the payer has suffered a financial catastrophe and wishes to be released from the obligation to pay the instalment which was going to be payable at some date in the future[3]. Any instalment payment remains payable notwithstanding the applicant's remarriage after the lump sum order (though in such circumstances it may be variable on application by the payer).

1 MCA 1973, s 31(2)(d).
2 Ibid, s 31(1).
3 A prospect referred to by the Court of Appeal judges who gave judgment against the appellant husband in *Penrose v Penrose* [1994] 2 FLR 621. In this case Balcombe LJ stated at 634D: 'Clearly it is a jurisdiction to be exercised with caution'. The existence of that remedy served to bolster the decision of the court in that case to refuse the husband leave to appeal against an order out of time.

Securing a lump sum order

4.58 A lump sum payable in instalments can be secured by taking security as with secured periodical payments[1].

1 See paras 4.49 ff.

Interest on lump sums

4.59 Any lump sum order over £5,000 carries interest from the date when it is payable, whether made in the High Court or the county court. The rate of interest is judgment rate (currently 8% per annum), and is payable as soon as there is default in payment. It is good practice to provide that any lump sum payment of under £5,000 per annum made in a county court should carry interest automatically[1]. Where the court makes a lump sum order and either directs that payment of that sum or any part of it should be deferred, or that the lump sum or any part of it should be paid in instalments, the court may order that the amount deferred or the instalments shall carry interest at such rate as may be specified by the order from such date, not earlier than the date of the order, as may be so specified, until the date when payment of it is due[2]. Provision should be made in any order, whether by consent or after a contested hearing for the interest (if any) that should be paid on a deferred lump sum payment[3]. A lawyer who fails to deal with this may be held negligent if there is no such provision.

1 A High Court lump sum order automatically carries interest from the date of the order under the Judgments Act 1838; a county court lump sum order will only automatically carry interest from the date of the order where the order is for £5,000 or more (County Courts (Interest on Judgment Debts) Order 1991).
2 MCA 1973, s 23(6).
3 Refer, for instance, to the interest provision at Precedent 37 of the *Precedents for Consent Orders* (4th edn) published by the Solicitors' Family Law Association in July 1995. For a case where no interest was provided, and where the court was not able, subsequent to the final order, to insert provision for interest (a final order having been made) see *L v L (Lump Sum: Interest)* [1994] 2 FLR 324. Note however that under the amending provisions of the Family Law Act, the court will have power to order interest to be paid (see paras 4.222 ff).

Time for payment of the lump sum

4.60 The order should specify the time when the lump sum should be paid. There are, however, occasions where the timing of the payment will be left vague, with liberty to apply given to the parties to fix a specific date in the case of a dispute about the appropriate timing. The parties may wish the lump sum only to be payable out of the sale proceeds of a property that has to be retained until the youngest child of the family is independent. Since the date of independence may be some time off, the precise time depending upon whether the child attends further education or training, the parties may wish to give themselves some flexibility on the precise timing of the payment[1].

1 Precisely this scenario was provided for by Thorpe J in *A v A (Financial Provision: Conduct)* [1995] 1 FLR 345. Practitioners are however recommended to avoid such elasticity, to prevent scope for future litigation.

PROPERTY ADJUSTMENT ORDERS

Types of order

4.61 There are four types of property adjustment orders provided for by the MCA 1973, s 24: first, orders which deal with the transfer of property; second, orders dealing with settlement of property; and third and fourth, orders dealing with the variation and reduction of ante-nuptial and post-nuptial settlements.

Precautionary measures

4.62 Whenever it is likely that an application for ancillary relief will relate to real property, the lawyer will consider what precautionary measures could be taken, for example:

(a) where one spouse only owns the former matrimonial home, protecting the occupying spouse's rights of occupation of the property by registering a Class F[1] (and desisting from applying for the decree nisi to be made absolute when this is all that protects your client's occupation of the property)[2]. There are registration complications if the property is registered not in a spouse's name but in the name of an alter ego such as a service company[3];

(b) filing a caution against dealings against the property[4] (in which case the statutory declaration in support[5] must recite the application for financial relief that has been made and the interest in the land asserted by the applicant; the title holder of the property in question will receive notice of the caution);

(c) registering an inhibition in circumstances where an order has been made by the court preventing any disposition of the property[6];

(d) in appropriate circumstances, severing any joint tenancy.

1 See MHA 1983, s 2(8)(a) and Land Registration (Matrimonial Homes) Rules 1990, r 3 (Form 99).
2 In suitable circumstances the lawyer will advise the spouse in occupation to apply for an order continuing his or her rights of occupation of the property beyond decree absolute (such orders will often be made by consent): see the Matrimonial Homes Act 1983, s 1.
3 The applicant's lawyers will have to demonstrate to the staff of HM Land Registry, to the best of their ability, that the other spouse stands behind the company in whose name the property is registered.
4 See the Land Registration Act 1925, s 54(1) and Land Registration Rules 1925, r 215(1) (Form 63).
5 See ibid, s 54(2) and ibid, rr 66 and 215(4) (Form 14).
6 See ibid, s 57(1) and ibid, r 230(1).

Timing of the property adjustment order

4.63 The court may make one or more of the orders available under s 24 on the granting of a decree of divorce, a decree of nullity, or a decree of judicial separation or at any time thereafter (MCA 1973, s 24(1)). The order can be made before or after the decree is made absolute, albeit that it is not effective until the decree absolute.

The jurisdiction of the court to make one or more orders under s 24

4.64 Under s 24(1), the court may make any one or more of the orders set out in s 24(1)(a) to (d). It is therefore possible for the court to make an order in favour of a party under s 24(1)(a) on one occasion; and on subsequent occasions to make orders under any of s 24(1) (b), (c) and (d). In the vast majority of cases, therefore, the lawyers acting for a respondent to an application will try to ensure finality by providing that on the making of any one of the orders available under s 24(1), the applicant's claims for property adjustment generally are dismissed.

Transfer of property

4.65 Under the MCA 1973, s 24(1)(a), the court has power to order that a party to the marriage shall transfer to the other party, to any child of the family or to such person as may be specified in the order for the benefit of such a child such property as may be so specified, being property to which the first-mentioned party is entitled, either in possession or in reversion. There is no definition in the MCA 1973 of 'property'. It comprises, for example: real property; personal property (such as chattels, cars, jewellery etc); the benefit of any insurance policies; and an interest in a partnership[1].

1 Authority for the proposition that the court has power to order a party to assign his share of partnership assets to the other party may be found in *Harwood v Harwood* [1991] 2 FLR 274. Per Slade LJ at 295F: 'this court ... would have power to order the husband, inter alia, to assign to the wife all or part of his interest in the dissolved partnership; and if such assignment were executed, she would be entitled to receive the

share of the partnership assets to which the husband was entitled...'. For further authority, see *Belcher v Belcher* [1995] 1 FLR 916, where it was likewise held that the court had power to order the husband to assign his share of the assets of a partnership to the wife.

Practicality of transfer

4.66 It does not follow that if a party has an interest in property the court will be prepared to transfer that property to the other party, because the court will need to look at the practical effect and the mechanics of any transfer. So, if the husband has a lease or tenancy of a property and there is a covenant against assignment, the court will not make an order for transfer of that property to the wife without the consent of the landlord[1]. The position is different if the tenancy is within the ambit of Sch 1 of the Matrimonial Homes Act 1983[2].

1 See *Jackson's Matrimonial Finance and Taxation* (6th edn, Butterworths) 233, and the cases quoted including *Thompson v Thompson* [1975] 2 All ER 208, CA; *Hale v Hale* [1975] 2 All ER 1090; *Hutchings v Hutchings* (1975) 237 Estates Gazette 571, CA; *Regan v Regan* [1977] 1 All ER 428, Sir George Baker.
2 See the detailed commentary in *Jackson's Matrimonial Finance and Taxation* (6th edn, Butterworths) 240. The Schedule gives the courts specific powers to order the transfer of a protected tenancy under the Rent Act 1977; a secure tenancy under the Housing Act 1985; a statutory tenancy under the Rent Act 1977; a statutory tenancy under the Rent (Agriculture) Act 1976; or an assured tenancy or assured agricultural occupancy under Part I of the Housing Act 1988.

Property held in the name of a third party on behalf of one of the parties to the marriage

4.67 An asset of this type falls within the scope of s 24, for, in appropriate circumstances, the court has power to pierce the corporate veil. If a party to divorce proceedings is the alter ego of a one-man company over which he had control, there is jurisdiction and power to order a sale or transfer of part of the land belonging to the company in which that party was the effective sole shareholder[1].

1 See *Green v Green* [1993] 1 FLR 326 where Connell J made an order for sale of land belonging to such a company. The judge favoured the authority of *Nicholas v Nicholas* [1984] FLR 285, in which the Court of Appeal pierced the corporate veil, disregarding the corporate ownership and making an order which, in effect, was an order against the husband; this Court of Appeal authority was not apparently cited to the Court of Appeal which determined the case of *Crittenden v Crittenden* [1990] 2 FLR 361, in which by contrast it was held that 'property' should extend to the shares of a company in which half of the shares were owned by the husband and half by the wife, but could not apply to the assets.

Settlement of property

4.68 Under s 24(1)(b), the court may order that a settlement of such property as may be so specified, being property to which a party to the marriage is so entitled, be made to the satisfaction of the court for the benefit of the other party to the marriage and to the children of the family or either or any of them. This provision gives the court the flexibility of putting property into trust for the benefit of a party or a child of the family. So by way of example, the court could give a wife a life interest in a specified fund, leaving either the husband or the children as the reversionary beneficiaries.

Settlements and the former matrimonial home

4.69 A settlement of this kind is perhaps most commonly found in dealings relating to the former matrimonial home. The court can make the property subject to a settlement which may cater for any of the following situations.

Martin and *Mesher* orders

4.70 A property held in the husband's name may be made the subject of a trust for sale. The terms of the trust may be that the wife should be allowed to occupy the property until a determining event (for instance her death, remarriage, or co-habitation with another man for a period exceeding a certain number of months[1], or the youngest child of the family attaining the age of 18 or 21 or ceasing his full-time education or training[2]; the precise determining events are matters for negotiation) whereupon the trust for sale will be exercised and the sale proceeds will be distributed as between the parties in the proportions defined in the trust deed or court order. Practitioners must exercise care in drafting the conditions on which operation of the order occurs, and be wary of the consequences for the wife of a *Mesher* order where she may be left with insufficient capital to rehouse herself[3].

1 See *Martin v Martin* [1977] 3 All ER 762.
2 As in *Mesher v Mesher and Hall*, a 1973 case not reported until [1980] 1 All ER 126n.
3 See *Clutton v Clutton* [1991] 1 All ER 340: 'There are still cases where, if only by way of exception, the *Mesher* order provides the best solution. Such a case may be where the family assets are amply sufficient to provide ... a roof over their heads if the matrimonial home were sold, but nevertheless the interests of the children require that they remain in the matrimonial home. In such a case it may be just and sensible to postpone the sale until the children have left home, since, ex hypothesi, the proceeds of sale will then be sufficient to enable the wife to rehouse herself ... but where there is doubt as to the wife's ability to rehouse herself, on the charge taking effect, then a *Mesher* order should not be made' per Lloyd LJ, imposing a *Martin* order on appeal against a *Mesher* order.

Charges in favour of a party

4.71 Another way of dealing with the husband's share in a property which the wife and children will occupy would be for a charge to be created for the benefit of the husband, with the property transferred into the name of the wife. In this situation a property would be held by the wife in her name, and the husband's share in the property would be protected by way of a charge either for a fixed amount of money, or for a proportion of the sale proceeds. The charge can be expressed to enure for a fixed term of years, or until one of the determining events described above. The terms of the charge will be a matter for negotiation. There will be tax implications for the party who leaves the property and therefore will not have the benefit of the principal private residence exemption relating to CGT; and to a party receiving the benefit of an income arising out of a charge on the property in his favour[1].

1 See *Butterworths Family Law Service*, Section D.

Charges: fixed sum or proportion of equity/sale proceeds?

4.72 The wife may be financially better off if the husband's share in the property is defined in such a way as will ensure that he receives a fixed amount (with accruing interest), rather than a share of the sale proceeds. The reason for this is that property prices may increase and the wife's interest may therefore be proportionally greater than her interest in the property calculated at the date of the agreement/court order[1]. Experience since the recession in property prices from 1988 onwards has however shown that in a declining housing market[2], the husband may actually be better off with the certainty of a fixed sum to be paid to him out of the sale proceeds; the wife will in those circumstances see her equitable interest in the property decline between the date of agreement/order and the date when the property is sold and the husband's interest is paid out.

1 In *Hope-Smith v Hope-Smith* [1989] 2 FLR 56, the husband delayed and/or frustrated the implementation of an order for a lump sum charged against the matrimonial home, with a result that by the time the property came to be sold it had increased substantially in value and the original order for the wife was too small; she was given leave to appeal out of time.
2 In *Heard v Heard* [1995] 1 FLR 970, a successful application for leave to appeal out of time (on appeal against refusal at first instance) the best offer which a husband could obtain for a property was £33,000, against an estimated sale price (on which the original order had been postulated) of £67,000. Compare the husband's unsuccessful attempt in *B v B (Financial Provision: Leave to Appeal)* [1994] 1 FLR 219 where the judge declined to set aside an order where the estimated value of the property in dispute had fallen from £340,000 to less than £250,000. The moral of these cases is surely to be as certain as possible of the value of the principal asset in a case before agreeing terms, and to have in mind the various possible permutations in value.

The terms of any trust/charge[1]

4.73 It cannot be over-emphasised that the terms of any trust/charge created over the former matrimonial home should be the subject of careful drafting as part of the negotiation process leading up to the resolution of the parties' claims for financial relief. The practitioner will need to consider, inter alia:

(a) whether a settlement giving the husband a share is appropriate: the wife will be better off owning a property outright without the fetter of the various terms of the settlement[2];

(b) how long the wife will need the benefit of the occupation of the property. For example, the wife may well wish the property to be retained for at least as long as the children are undergoing undergraduate education.

The wife should not be pressed into necessarily accepting co-habitation as a determining event which will bring the trust for sale into operation. The practitioner will have to bear in mind the general law relating to co-habitation and its effect upon the maintenance of the wife: co-habitation does not necessarily bring the wife's maintenance to an end[3].

1 Refer, for instance, to the precedents numbered 44 and 45 in the *Precedents for Consent Orders* (4th edn) published by the SFLA. Note that the Trusts of Land and Appointment of Trustees Act 1996 makes any trust for sale a 'trust of land' (with effect from 1 January 1997).
2 But note a transfer with a charge back has been held to amount to a clean break: *Clutton v Clutton* [1991] 1 FLR 242.
3 See, eg *Atkinson v Atkinson* [1995] 2 FLR 356.

Purchase of substitute property

4.74 The practitioner will also want to consider whether, for instance, the wife will wish to buy a substitute property or properties, during the subsistence of the trust. On the face of it there is no reason why she should not be given the opportunity of doing so, and for appropriate provision to be made in the settlement deed, but then thought will have to be given to who should bear the costs of sale and purchase on each relevant occasion. It may be appropriate in a case, by way of example, to make provision for the costs of only one sale and purchase to be borne by the parties equally, following which the wife would pay any future purchase and sale costs.

Responsibility for outgoings

4.75 Careful thought must be given to the responsibility for the outgoings relating to the property in the trust. The parties' respective liabilities for items such as buildings insurance and council tax will be the subject of negotiation. The occupying spouse in these situations has a valid argument that the other party should bear at least a proportion of the buildings insurance if he is going to benefit from a share in the trust property at some stage in the future, and therefore has an interest in ensuring that the property remains a saleable asset. For the same reason the spouse who is not in occupation may wish to spell out the repairing obligations and to reserve his right of re-entry on the premises if the occupier fails to repair defects within a specified time.

Redemption of the charge before the determining event

4.76 The wife can redeem the husband's charge on the property before any of the 'determining events' set out in the settlement; her ability to do so should, for the avoidance of doubt, be recited in the settlement deed.

Variation of ante-nuptial and post-nuptial settlements – MCA 1973, s 24(1)(c) and (d)

4.77 Under the MCA 1973, s 24(1)(c) the court may make an order varying for the benefit of the parties to the marriage and of the children of the family or either or any of them any ante-nuptial or post-nuptial settlement (including such a settlement made by will or codicil) made on the parties to the marriage. Further, under s 24(1)(d), the court may make an order extinguishing or reducing the interest of either of the parties to the marriage under any such settlement.

Definition of ante-nuptial or post-nuptial settlement

4.78 A nuptial settlement is one made by reference to a marriage. It is clear from the decided cases that the marriage by reference to which a settlement is made must be a specific marriage, it having been held[1] that 'the particular marriage must be a fact of which the settlor takes account in framing the settlement'. If the particular marriage is recited or referred to, it is patently a factor. Hence a settlement made before marriage, 'is within it if from its recitals or substance it is apparent that it is related to a particular marriage'. Accordingly, a nuptial settlement for the purposes of s 24 is not simply restricted to a marriage settlement, but has a much wider net. For instance, a discretionary settlement which included as its object a primary beneficiary and his spouse and children, and which is made with the intention of providing for the parties and the children of a specific marriage, would come within s 24. A particular question which may arise is whether, if a person has a power in a settlement to appoint property to a spouse, this will bring it within the terms of s 24. If the settlement as a whole is made with the intention of providing for the parties to a specific marriage or their children then it will be a nuptial settlement (regardless of whether there is a power to appoint property to a spouse or not), but the presence of a power to appoint property to a spouse in a settlement made at a time when the primary beneficiary is neither married nor engaged to be married cannot make that a nuptial settlement. In short the intention of the settlor when the settlement is made is the important factor.

1 *Burnett v Burnett* [1936] P1.

4.79 A recent leading case on nuptial settlements is *Brooks*[1]. This case related to a marriage where the husband had his own firm and had established a pension fund for his benefit, the terms of which allowed provision to be made on the husband's nomination for a spouse and/or other financial dependants. The court's view was that the characteristics of the scheme which would allow not only Mr Brooks but also his spouse gave the scheme the character of a settlement, and the inclusion of a spouse within its objects gave the settlement its nuptial element. Where a settlement does come within the s 24 description the court is able to make an order varying that settlement as it thinks fit, for instance by providing a fund from which a spouse will receive the income for his or her life.

1 *Brooks v Brooks* [1995] 2 FLR 13. Per the leading judgment of Lord Nicholls, 'in the Matrimonial Causes Act "settlement" is not defined, but the context of s 24 affords some clues. Certain indicia of the type of disposition with which this section is concerned can be identified reasonably easily. The section is concerned with a settlement "made on the parties to the marriage". So, broadly stated, the disposition must be one which makes some form of continuing provision for both or either of the parties to a marriage, with or without provision for their children. Conversely, a disposition which confers an immediate, absolute interest in an item of property does not constitute a settlement of that' at 19A to C; and, further, 'in order to promote the best interests of the parties and their children in the fundamentally changed situation, it is desirable that the court should have power to alter the terms of the settlement. The purpose of the section is to give the court this power. This object does not dictate that "settlement" should be given a narrow meaning. On the contrary, the purpose of this section would be impeded, rather than advanced, by confining its scope. The continuing use of the archaic expressions "ante-nuptial" and "post-nuptial" does not point in the opposite direction.' (at 19D to F).

Settlements which are neither ante-nuptial nor post-nuptial

4.80 The question arises as to what effect the settlements which do not come within s 24 will have on the financial provision to be made on a divorce. Although the court has no direct powers to vary settlements unless they come within the s 24 definition, it will nevertheless take account of the settlement as a resource in making the final order[1]. The extent to which the court takes account of the spouse's interest under a settlement varies according to the nature of that interest. Where a spouse is entitled to the income from a settlement for life, he or she has a clear-cut benefit which the court will take into account. However, if the spouse is a beneficiary under a discretionary settlement the extent to which this should be taken into account is more problematical, as the court may feel that it cannot make an order against a party who would have no chance of paying unless he or she was able to call upon money held by trustees at the trustees' discretion.

1 See para 4.19, and in particular *Browne v Browne* [1989] 1 FLR 291.

4.81 The court will look at the reality of the situation rather than the form. For example, if the court considers that property held on discretionary trust is, as a matter of practice, within the control of the spouse, the court will make a presumption based on that underlying reality; and, for example, it may be important to trace the distributions out of the trust made in the past, and the extent to which the spouse has benefited from them, or made requests for financial assistance from the trustees which have been met by them. In summary, therefore, the court will take into account any settlement in which the spouse had an interest, in any application for financial relief within the proceedings. If the settlement comes within the s 24 definition the court may make an order varying the settlement, and if the settlement is outside that definition the court will nevertheless take account of that resource in making an order for financial relief.

Procedure on applications for property adjustment order

4.82 The relevant provisions are set out in the FPR 1991, r 2.59. As to the contents of the affidavit in support, the notice in Form M11 or M13, and the service of the documentation on parties (including third parties) the position is as follows.

The affidavit

4.83 The affidavit in support should contain the full particulars known by the applicant of the property/settlement in question and of the involvement/ownership rights of the other party in the property/settlement[1].

1 FPR 1991, r 2.59(1)(a) and (b). In pilot scheme cases refer to the procedure set out in the *Practice Direction* [1996] 2 FLR 368.

Form M11/M13

4.84 Where an application for a property adjustment order relates to land, the notice in Form M11 or M13 should identify the land, state whether it is registered (in which case the Land Registry title number will be supplied) or unregistered, and give such particulars as are known by the applicant of any mortgage on the land or any interest therein.

Service on third parties

4.85 If the applicant has applied for an order for variation of a settlement, the trustees of the settlement and the settlor if living should be served with a copy of Form M11 or M13, together with a copy of the supporting affidavit[1]. In the case of an application for a property adjustment order relating to land, the mortgagees must be served, but only with a copy of the application. The mortgagees may then apply to the court, in writing, within 14 days after service, for a copy of the applicant's affidavit[2]; or they may ask the applicant's solicitors direct to let them have a copy of the affidavit.

1 FPR 1991, r 2.59(3); and see *E v E* [1990] 2 FLR 233.
2 FPR 1991, r 2.59(4).

Affidavit in answer by third party

4.86 Any person who is served with an affidavit pursuant to the FPR 1991, r 2.59(3), or who receives an affidavit following an application made in accordance with the FPR 1991, r 2.59(4) may, within 14 days after service or receipt, as the case may be, file an affidavit in answer[1]. That affidavit should be served on the opposite party[2]. The third party may wish to oppose the application for a transfer/settlement of an asset in which the third party has a beneficial interest. The third party may alternatively wish to put forward a case that the asset in question does not fall within the scope of s 24[3].

1 FPR 1991, r 2.59(5).
2 Ibid, r 2.60(1).

3 So in the case of a discretionary trust, the trustees may assert on affidavit that the court should not draw inferences that the trust fund will be an available resource for the discretionary beneficiary.

ORDER FOR THE SALE OF PROPERTY

4.87 The MCA 1973, s 24A provides the formal means of getting capital into the hands of a spouse to facilitate the effecting of orders that have been made for secured periodical payments, lump sum or property adjustment orders. Specifically, s 24A(1) provides that in these circumstances the court may, on making an order under ss 23 or 24 for secured periodical payments, lump sum or property adjustment, or at any time thereafter, make a further order for the sale of such property as may be specified in the order, being the property in which or in the proceeds of sale of which either or both parties to the marriage has or have a beneficial interest, either in possession or in reversion.

Examples of s 24A orders

4.88 Occasions when s 24A may be useful are, inter alia, as follows:

(a) where the husband is ordered to pay a lump sum to his wife out of the sale proceeds of a property;

(b) where the husband is ordered to pay a lump sum without any reference to the sale of any particular property, but should he fail to make the lump sum payment within the specified time, the property should be put on the market for sale and the lump sum paid out of the sale proceeds[1]. Unless the time by which the lump sum is due to be paid is made of the essence in the order (and it may not be easy to construe whether time has been made of the essence) the parties will be able to apply to the court for the time period to be varied[2].

The order for sale may be made either at the same time as the substantive final order, or at any time thereafter. It will therefore be possible for a party to go back to the court (for instance when the other party has failed to make a lump sum payment) to make a further order that the other party should sell a property in which he had a beneficial interest. The order does not take effect unless the decree has been made absolute[3].

1 See paras 4.89 ff for directions on sale.
2 See *Masefield v Alexander (Lump Sum: Extension of Time)* [1995] 1 FLR 100.
3 MCA 1973, s 24A(3); and see Table 1.

The terms of the section 24A order

4.89 It is vital for practitioners to consider what directions the court should make when ordering the sale of property. The more that is agreed and embodied into any order, the less scope there is for the parties to have to take the matter back to the court for directions. Therefore an order for sale may typically contain the following elements.

The timing of the sale

4.90 It may be that the parties will want the sale to take place forthwith; or that it should be postponed for a particular period. If the sale is dependent on a party buying another house it will be desirable for the party who remains in occupation of the property to specify that the property should be sold 'as soon as practicable'; the term 'practicable' gives some scope to that party to delay the sale: he or she may be unable to find a substitute property at the right price; or may reasonably hold out for a higher sale price for the property being sold. Alternatively the parties may agree that the property shall be sold 'as soon as possible', a formula which gives less scope for procrastination than if a sale 'as soon as practicable' had been ordered.

The sale price

4.91 Every effort should be made to agree the market price of the property and even the price which the parties expect to obtain on the sale of the property. There may be a conflict of interests between the parties on this subject[1]. If the parties do agree, and perhaps even record in the recitals to the order, the price they expect the property to achieve it will be clear what offers should be deemed acceptable, and will minimise the possibilities of future litigation on the subject of the sale price.

1 A husband may have agreed to pay a certain and fixed lump sum which will be partly financed by the sale proceeds: in that kind of case circumstances the wife will not mind what the property fetches, as she is due to receive a certain lump sum whatever price is obtained for the property. It may be alternatively that the wife is due to receive only the net sale proceeds of the property. In those circumstances she will wish to maximise the sale proceeds and may therefore unreasonably (at least in the respondent's view) refuse offers for the property in the hope of maximising her return from it. The parties' attitudes are often also going to depend on what maintenance provision has been negotiated up to completion of sale. The husband may be desperate to clear a large mortgage on the property for which he is liable under the terms of the agreement between the parties – he may be wanting to sell the property to clear the debt and may have negotiated a lesser level of maintenance following completion of sale. Alternatively the wife's maintenance may be due to increase following the sale and she may therefore wish to shift the property as soon as possible.

Estate agents

4.92 The order should recite which estate agent or agents should act in the sale; or the parties can agree to appoint such estate agents as may be agreed between them[1].

1 A party may object to the appointments of agents chosen by the other party for reasons including lack of expertise, or level of fees (especially if there is to be a multiple agency sale).

Conduct of sale

4.93 The order should state which party should have conduct of sale, or whether there is to be joint conduct of sale between husband and wife. It is generally desirable for each client to be able to have a say about how the property should be marketed, for what price, and how the marketing conditions should be varied[1].

> 1 In which case there would be joint conduct of sale. There may of course be reasons in a particular case why only one party should have conduct of sale.

Arbitration clauses

4.94 It is common for consent orders to provide a means whereby a third party will arbitrate between the parties if they fail to agree the sale terms. Therefore the terms of the order may oblige the parties to appoint the President of the Royal Institute of Chartered Surveyors, or one of his agents, to determine the market price and/or agents to be instructed in a sale, if there is stalemate between the parties themselves in deciding these issues. The court will be concerned to ensure that any arbitration clause has been complied with by the parties if an order provides for its use, rather than allowing a party to bypass the arbitrator and go straight to the court for a decision[1].

> 1 See *N v N (Valuation: Charge-back order)* [1996] 1 FLR 361. In this case the judge held that the parties were stuck with the valuation arrived at by the valuer allotted in accordance with the terms of the order; Singer J distinguished the Court of Appeal case of *Brent v Brent* (1978) 9 Fam Law 59, in which it was held that in the absence of the parties' agreement, the court would not order them to be bound by an expert opinion; the parties, could, therefore adduce further evidence as to the correct valuation of their property. In *N v N* Singer J referred to the way in which the Family Division is now more directive of cases, playing a more pro-active role than when *Brent* was decided, and there is therefore some question as to whether *Brent* would be resolved in the same way now. The lesson is clear: take care to specify in the order exactly what valuation mechanisms are to be employed.

Supplemental provisions

4.95 Any order made under s 24A(1) may contain such consequential or supplementary provisions as a court thinks fit and may include:

(a) provision requiring a making of a payment out of the proceeds of sale of property to which the order relates; and

(b) provision requiring any such property to be offered for sale to a person, or class of persons, specified in the order[1].

> 1 MCA 1973, s 24A(2).

Orders for sale involving third parties

4.96 The MCA 1973, s 24A(6) provides that where a party to a marriage has a beneficial interest in any property, or any proceeds of sale thereof, and some other person who is not a party to the marriage also has a beneficial interest in that property or in the proceeds of sale thereof then, before deciding to make an order under this section in relation to that property, it shall be the duty of the court to give that other person an opportunity to make representations with respect to the order; and any representations made by that other person shall be included among the circumstances to which the court is required to have regard under the MCA 1973, s 25(1). A person who, or entity which, has a beneficial interest in real property will fall within this subsection, as will any party who has an interest in property which could be protected by way of caution[1].

1 See para 4.62 as to the authority enabling a party to register a caution.

Procedure

4.97 Despite s 24A(6), there is no procedural step for the service of the application and affidavit in support on the third party who has a beneficial interest in a property along with the respondent's spouse. Because no specific provision is made, the procedural directions will be dealt with by the district judge at a directions appointment (under the jurisdiction at any stage of the proceedings to give directions as to the filing of service and pleadings and as to the further conduct of pleadings[1]).

1 FPR 1991, r 2.62(5).

Termination of order

4.98 A s 24(A) order used to secure periodical payments ceases to have effect on the death or remarriage of the payee[1].

1 MCA 1973, s 24A(5).

Orders for the sale of property

4.99 The facility to obtain an order for the sale of the property before the substantive lump sum or property adjustment orders have been made is available to applicants for financial relief[1]. RSC Ord 31, r 1 (power to order sale of land) shall apply to applications for ancillary relief as it applies to causes and matters in the Chancery Division. In turn RSC Ord 31, r 1 provides that where, in any cause in the Chancery Division relating to land, it appears necessary or expedient for the purposes of the cause that the land be sold, the court may order that land to be sold and any party bound by the order and in possession may be compelled to deliver up such possession. It has been held in *Green v Green*[2] that there is therefore jurisdiction, deriving from the FPR 1991, r 2.64(3), to enable sales of property at an interim stage in the proceedings. A party therefore may wish to use the sale mechanism of Ord 31 coupled with an application for an appropriation direction[3]. A question which is left open by *Green* and r 2.64(3) is whether the court has jurisdiction to make such an order even before decree nisi. On the authorities it would appear that in the absence of any requirement that r 2.64(3) should apply only following pronouncement of the decree, the relief is available before decree nisi.

1 FPR 1991, r 2.64(3). This rule was introduced to rectify a lacuna exposed by *Crosthwaite v Crosthwaite* [1989] 2 FLR 86, where the court held that there was no power under the MCA 1973, s 24A to grant an order for possession against the wife in the face of her equity interest as joint tenant in possession.
2 [1993] 1 FLR 326.
3 *Barry v Barry* [1992] 2 FLR 233, and see para 4.55.

PENSIONS

Introduction

4.100 There are 170,000 divorces in England and Wales each year, involving some 350,000 spouses and perhaps half a million children[1]. For many of these couples the pension may be a major asset or a major proportion of the overall assets. It is perhaps inevitable that, as the spotlight has moved onto pensions generally over the last decade or so, not only informed pension commentators but also public opinion have demanded that pensions should be available for distribution in matrimonial cases. The law is set out as it stands, amendments to the MCA 1973 made by the Pensions Act 1995, s 166[2] are explained, and the way in which the law is likely to develop is discussed.

[1] See, for example, Judicial Statistics 1990, chapter 5.
[2] The Pensions Act 1995, s 166 was inserted into that Act because of the head of steam which built up following the report of the working group set up by the Pensions Management Institute in conjunction with the Law Society ("Pensions and Divorce") published in May 1993; and the Pension Law Review Committee's report ("Pensions and Law Reform") under the chairmanship of Professor Roy Goode QC of September 1993.

Disclosure of pension

4.101 In the course of the proceedings for financial relief, the parties will in the usual way make a disclosure of their financial resources[1]. Pension interests form part of the assets of the parties which must be disclosed[2]. These will include:

(a) the state pension[3];

(b) self-employed retirement annuity contracts[4];

(c) their interest under any personal pension policies[5];

(d) occupational pension schemes;

(e) any interest which a party may have under a self-administered pension scheme[6];

(f) unapproved schemes and arrangements[7].

1 MCA 1973, s 25(2)(a): a financial resource which a party has or is likely to have – note that the court is not now restricted in cases where the petition for divorce, nullity or judicial separation is filed on or after 1 July 1996, following the Pensions Act 1995, s 166, to considering the pension benefit that would be acquired in the foreseeable future. Compare H v H [1993] 2 FLR 335, where Thorpe J considered that it was more important to look at the value of what was earned during the period of co-habitation than to look at the prospective value of what would be earned.
2 If not voluntarily, then pursuant to the FPR 1991, r 2.63: see para 2.51.
3 Any person who wishes to obtain information about state benefits should send Form PR19 to the DSS, RPFA Unit, Room 37T, Central Office, Newcastle-upon-Tyne NE96 17X.
4 These contracts are now regulated by Income and Corporation Taxes Act 1988, ss 618–629, and were only available until 1 July 1988. They are still commonly referred to as 'section 226 policies'. They were available to the self-employed and those in non-pensionable employment.
5 These are governed by the Income and Corporation Taxes Act 1988, ss 630–655, and became available after 1 July 1988 as a successor to the self-employed retirement annuity contract. They are designed for employees as well as for the self-employed.
6 These schemes are aimed at controlling directors with a 20% or greater interest in their companies and were introduced by the Finance Act 1973, s 15 (they will generally have fewer than 12 members, who may be members of the same family).
7 These schemes, which may be either funded or unfunded, are frequently established by employers who wish to provide retirement benefits for employees in excess of benefits allowed under approved schemes.

Application of the law

4.102 The court will look at the totality of the assets and will bear in mind the fact that one or both of the parties may in the future have the benefit of a pension.

Pension as the source of periodical payments

4.103 On the one hand the court will consider that the pension will be the source of any periodical payments which the person with pension rights may be making in the future. Therefore it is not correct, in law, to equate the transfer value of a pension that may be paid in the future with realisable capital which is available at present. There would be an element of double accounting if a wife was to receive *both* a slice of capital equating to a certain percentage of the pension scheme at the time of the divorce, *and* expect to receive maintenance payments out of the other party's pension scheme in the future. The position would be entirely different in a case in which there was going to be a clean break. In such a case there is no possibility of the wife needing to be maintained in the future, and therefore the transfer value may have to be brought into account as part of the assets[1].

1 See H v H [1993] 2 FLR 335; but Thorpe J gives no assistance as to how the transfer value should be dealt with.

The capital locked up in pension schemes

4.104 On the other hand, most pension schemes allow for a proportion (up to 25%) of the capital value of the pension as at the normal date of retirement (defined in a party's pension documentation) to be commuted by the pensioner at retirement date. There is therefore likely to be a capital sum available for distribution at that stage. The court is ready, willing and able to make a lump sum order for the wife which will 'attack' that element of the husband's pension. In this kind of case, the options would be as follows:

(a) to make a lump sum in favour of a wife, payable by instalments, the second instalment being the normal retirement age of the husband and consisting of a certain amount referable to the expected commutable lump sum; the husband may be subjected to obligations in the court order to use his best endeavours to make pension contributions at their current rate (or for so long as he is employed/has an income) until then;

(b) to make a certain lump sum order at the time of the divorce, taking into account the capital which would be available to the husband if he elected to commute part of his pension on normal retirement date;

(c) to order the payment of a lump sum to a wife (on an immediate or deferred basis) enabling her to purchase an annuity which will provide an income for her on retirement;

(d) to adjourn the wife's lump sum (and perhaps also property adjustment) claims until the pension can be 'attacked'. This may be appropriate in a case where the pension is the only asset of the parties, substantial pension contributions have been made and there are no other assets against which an order can be made[1].

The court is reluctant to adjourn a party's claims[2] and will only do so if it is clear that justice to the wife can only be done if her claims are adjourned to be dealt with at a later date. The court will far prefer to get the parties' claims dealt with at the time of the proceedings, but there may be occasions such as where a party is shortly going to come into substantial money, when it will be sensible for the parties' (or at least one of the parties') claims to be adjourned[3]. The court is accustomed to dealing with divorces involving high-spending spouses, and husbands who have been able to put a lot of money away into a pension scheme at an early age and may not have any savings. The court will be keen to enable a wife in these circumstances to obtain a share of the capital invested by the husband in a pension if that is really the only capital in the case, if necessary by adjourning her lump sum claims.

---

1 This may be coupled with a direction by the court that the amount of the lump sum is to be limited to a proportion of the commutable pension; otherwise the wife may later wish to extend her lump sum claim to include assets acquired by the husband after the divorce. In *Atkinson v Atkinson* [1995] 2 FLR 356 the court at first instance had directed that the wife's lump sum claim should be limited to the acquisition of a car and an amount equivalent to debts against which the husband was to indemnify her. Thorpe J commented obiter that such a direction or record of the court's intention may not be effective in restricting the scope of any subsequent lump sum application.
2 *MT v MT* [1992] 1 FLR 362.
3 *Roberts v Roberts* [1986] 2 FLR 152.

Loss of pension rights

Opting for judicial separation rather than for divorce

4.105 The loss of pension rights is often an incentive for a wife to want a judicial separation rather than a divorce. She will then retain her married status and is likely to benefit from the husband's pension on his death[1].

1 Close attention will have to be paid to the terms of the pension for the definition of a financial dependant.

MCA 1973, s 10 and decree absolute

4.106 Loss of pension rights may also class as such extreme hardship as to enable a wife to defend the husband's divorce petition, under the MCA 1973, s 10[1]. Loss of pension rights may also be an incentive for a petitioner for divorce to hold back the application for decree absolute until resolution of the financial matters[2]. This may also be a good defence to a respondent's application (on notice) for a decree absolute.

1 See para 3.17.
2 See *Griffiths v Dawson & Co* [1993] 2 FLR 315 for the practitioners' duties in pension cases, and aspects of negligence arising out of conduct of a divorce case.

Dealing with pensions

4.107 When putting together the financial disclosure of a party, his or her interest under a pension should be documented and explained. The Law Society's Family Law Committee has devised a useful letter of instruction to be sent to an actuary requesting a value of occupational pension rights and quantifying the spouse's loss arising out of any divorce. The Family Law Committee have also devised a specimen questionnaire which can be sent to the person with pension rights in suitable cases[1]. If the person with pension rights fails to provide the information requested, it may be possible to obtain information from the relevant pension manager/insurance company direct under the production appointment procedure set out in the FPR 1991, r 2.62(7)[2]. In any case where pensions are a factor, the practitioner will refer to the rules of the pension scheme and the pension deed itself; and will consider, in cases where the wife is dependent on the husband, what kind of nomination the husband can make for the wife's benefit so as to enable her to benefit from his pension, as a dependant, after his death.

1 See *Law Society Gazette* of 13 January 1993, p 34 ff.
2 See para 2.53.

Orders and undertakings relating to pension

Variation of settlement[1]

4.108 The ambit of this avenue is narrow. The wife will have to show that an interest in the fund has been settled for her benefit, and she will have to argue successfully that the fund constitutes an ante-nuptial or post-nuptial settlement. The House of Lords[2] has also made it clear that the court will not want to interfere with a pension in these circumstances where the interests of third parties are going to be affected. This means that the ability to make property adjustment orders relating to pension funds is in practice going to be restricted to small schemes in which third parties do not have an interest and where Inland Revenue approval (when it is required)[3] may easily be obtained[4].

1 And see para 4.77.
2 Per Lord Nicholls in *Brooks v Brooks* [1995] 2 FLR 13 at 23D and E: 'Even when a scheme does fall within the court's jurisdiction to vary a marriage settlement, it would not be right for the court to vary one scheme member's right to the prejudice of other scheme members. Directing a variation which does not meet with Inland Revenue approval would normally be prejudicial to the rights of the other scheme members. A feature of the instant cases is that there is only one scheme member and, moreover, the wife has earnings of her own from the same employer which will sustain provision of an immediate pension for her. If the court is to be able to split pension rights on divorce in the more usual case of a multi-member scheme where the wife has no earnings of her own from the same employer, or to direct the taking out of life insurance, legislation will still be needed'.
3 As in the case of personal pensions under the Income and Corporation Taxes Act 1988, s 633: the provision of benefits for a wife does not fall within the scope of benefits capable of receiving Inland Revenue approval. A similar doubt exists in relation to self-employed retirement annuity contracts.
4 *Brooks* does not leave the law relating to variations of settlement and their application to pensions in a certain state. Commentators on *Brooks* have on the one hand argued that the case establishes that property adjustment orders are only going to be made in these circumstances in relation to small self-administered schemes the only members of which are the husband and/or the wife (see, eg the article by Andrew White, *Law Society Gazette*, 19 July 1995, pp 18 and 19); on the other hand, it has been argued, eg by district judge Plumstead and David Salter at [1995] Fam Law 490 and following that arguably *Brooks* could be applied to almost the whole range of pension schemes. It is perhaps as well that the Family Law Act 1996 promises pension-splitting, which is likely to consign *Brooks* to a footnote of legal history. See further para 4.231.

Undertaking to make nomination

4.109 Often the husband will undertake in the recitals to a financial order that the wife should receive all or a certain proportion of the death-in-service benefit and/or dependant's pension payable by the trustees after his death. The terms of nomination itself should be agreed if filing a consent application: for example by reference to an annex to an order[1]. To preserve a wife's opportunities to obtain financial advantage from her husband's pension, it may also be advisable for the husband to be asked to undertake not to draw down on, commute any part of, or otherwise deal with his pension policies in any way without the consent of the wife. Invariably the trustees of the pension scheme have a discretion whether or not to make payments, and therefore it is impossible for a husband to make such a nomination in favour of his wife as will with certainty lead to her receiving those pension payments[2].

1 In relation to any petition filed on or after 1 July 1996, the courts are able to impose an order in relation to nomination of the lump sum payable out of the pension scheme: see paras 4.111ff. If, however, it proves impossible to obtain a satisfactory undertaking from a husband who refuses to volunteer to provide one, a wife must consider taking out life insurance on the husband (and this can be done without his consent).

2 Unless, in the case of a petition filed on or after 1 July 1996, an order is made under s 25C(2) (inserted by the Pensions Act 1995, s 166) directing the making of a nomination in relation to benefits arising out of the pension.

Inheritance Act claims

4.110 For this and other reasons, it may be vital for the wife to preserve her ability to make an application against the husband's estate under the Inheritance (Provision for Family and Dependants) Act 1975 so that, if the pension is not actually received by her, she can attempt to get maintenance out of the deceased's estate. Any practitioner acting for a wife in these circumstances should therefore be extremely careful about accepting that the wife's claims under the Inheritance Act should be barred[1] when the husband has complied with an undertaking to nominate the wife as beneficiary of the pension. It is one thing for the husband to make that undertaking; it is a totally different thing for the trustees to accept the nomination and then actually to make the payments after the payer's death. Even a conditional disentitling order (for example that a wife's Inheritance Act claims be dismissed upon the very first payment to her of the dependant's pension) presents an element of risk to the wife. She would be better off giving an undertaking not to make a claim under the Inheritance Act unless she did not receive all the payments due to her. She could then apply to be released from the undertaking if necessary.

1 Inheritance (Provision for Family and Dependants) Act 1975, s 15; see para 6.22.

Pensions Act 1995, s 166

4.111 In response to the demand for reform of the pension law insofar as it applies to divorce[1], the Government introduced pension ear-marking (rather than pension-splitting). The point was to enable a spouse's pension to be ear-marked for the benefit of the other spouse at the time that the benefits under the pension become payable[2]. The Family Law Act does however provide for pension-splitting to be brought into effect following a Green Paper (which was published in the summer of 1996) and subsequent consultation. There follows a summary of the substantive changes in the law brought in under s 166.

1 See para 4.100 above.
2 Rather than splitting the pension at the time of the order.

Amendments to the MCA 1973, s 25

4.112 First, the Pensions Act incorporates s 25B into the MCA 1973, to amend slightly the s 25(2) considerations insofar as they relate to pensions[1]. The effect of this is that the duty of the court to consider only such pension benefit as would be payable in the foreseeable future is so amended as to require the court simply to take into consideration any benefit which is likely to be payable under the pension scheme (ie whether in the foreseeable future or not). The intention behind this amendment is to endeavour to ensure there would be no rule whereby pension benefits which did not come into payment beyond a fixed period of years would not be taken into account[2]. The court does, therefore, have a wider explicit discretion with regard to pension benefits in this respect than it has with regard to other assets[3].

1 In relation to petitions filed on or after 1 July 1996.
2 See *H v H* [1993] 2 FLR 335 for the way in which the court dealt with this subject for pre-1 July 1996 petitions.
3 Such as inheritances, for example.

Attachment of pension orders

4.113 Secondly, the court has the power to order that a payment referable to the pension should be made by the trustees direct to the wife (therefore by-passing the person with pension rights altogether). The power to make directions relating to pension schemes therefore takes on the character of attachment of earnings. The payment would be made on behalf of the scheme member and would fulfil part or all of the scheme member's obligation to make payments to the former spouse under the financial provision order.

Commutation of benefit

4.114 The court also has power to order a scheme member to commute all or part of the benefit which he or she has or is likely to have under the pension scheme so long as this is permitted by the scheme and Inland Revenue rules.

Lump sum orders

4.115 A further amendment extends the power of the court to make lump sum and deferred lump sum orders to include orders relating to a lump sum payable on death under a pension scheme[1]. The orders which the court may make regarding a lump sum payable on death include an order requiring the scheme member to nominate the former spouse to receive all or part of the lump sum payable on death. Such an order can only be made where the scheme member is able to nominate the person who should receive the lump sum. The court also has power to override the discretion of the trustees or managers and order them to pay all or part of a lump sum payable on death to the former spouse when it becomes due.

1 The court has no power to make orders in relation to the death-in-service benefit which derives from insurance, rather than a pension policy. See the definition of pension schemes in MCA 1973, s 25D(4).

Duty to consider making an order relating to the pension

4.116 It is a duty of the court, in any proceedings for a financial provision order, to consider whether a financial provision order should be made which relates to a party's pension. It is therefore to be expected that orders will commonly provide for periodical payments and lump sums to be made out of the pension scheme direct to a payee (the Government expects that there will be 19,600 orders requiring payments to be made by schemes during the first full year after implementation and a similar number in subsequent years)[1].

1 *Compliance Cost Assessment – Regulations under sections 166 and 167 of the Pensions Act 1995*, Consultation Document (March 1996).

Orders directed at trustees

4.117 In any case in which the court determines to make an order under the MCA 1973, s 23 in which the court has had regard to any benefits under a pension scheme, s 25B empowers the court, and restricts its jurisdiction, in the following way:

(a) The order *may* require the trustees of the pension scheme to make a payment for the benefit of the other party, if at any time any payments in respect of any benefits under the scheme becomes due to the party with pension rights (s 25B(4)). The direction that the person with pension rights should be by-passed is therefore not mandatory. The court may continue to make orders in the same kind of way, simply requiring the person with the pension rights to make the lump sum payment when he retires. It is far preferable, however, for the prospective payee to obtain a court order requiring payment direct to her out of the scheme, that is from the trustees to the prospective payee.

(b) Section 25B does not allow or enable payments to be made out of a pension in excess of the amount that is due to the party with pension rights. It is provided[1] that the amount of any payment which the trustees are required to make under the order at any time shall not exceed the amount of the payment which is due at that time to the party with pension rights.

(c) Any payment made by the trustees will both discharge so much of the trustees' liabilities to the party with pension rights as corresponds to the amount of the payment, and shall be treated for all purposes as a payment made by the party with pension rights in or towards the discharge of his liability under the order[2].

(d) The order may require a party with pension rights to commute any benefits which he could himself require to be commuted (s 25B(7)).

1 MCA 1973, s 25B(5).
2 Ibid, s 25B(6), which does prompt an interesting point relating to the incidence and payment of tax: presumably the payment will be made by the trustees net of tax at the marginal rate of the payee entitled to receive the periodical payment.

Determining the discretion of the trustees

4.118 The MCA 1973, s 25C provides that where a lump sum is payable out of a pension scheme on death, the court can in effect determine how the trustees' discretion to apply that payment is applied. This overcomes the uncertainty inherent under the law applicable to petitions filed prior to 1 July 1996, whereby a payee of maintenance cannot be sure that a nomination by the payer will be acted upon by the trustees. In any case in which either the whole or part of the death benefit is going to be nominated in favour of a spouse, the provision is going to be made the subject of a court order with a direction made, often by consent, under s 25C(2). This power only applies to the death-in-service provision which is part and parcel of a party's pension; it does not apply to death-in-service benefits generally, which are commonly provided without any reference to pension.

4.119 If the party with pension rights is able to shift his benefits from a scheme which has been subjected to a s 25B or s 25C order into another scheme, then so long as the trustees of the new scheme have been given notice in accordance with the regulations, the order shall have effect as if it had been made instead in respect of the new scheme. There is nothing to prevent the party with pension rights being made to undertake in the recitals to the order (very much in accordance with the pre-1 July 1996 law and practice) that he will not deal with his pension without the other party's consent. This is however not a realistic option in respect of a person with pension rights under an administered scheme, who may have no say in the way that his pension is dealt with.

Regulations under the Pensions Act 1995, s 166

4.120 The regulations deal with matters such as the value of benefits to be calculated in a prescribed manner for the purpose of divorce proceedings. This is intended to encourage uniformity of approach to the valuation of pensions. Indeed the court will not be empowered to consider any other method[1]. The basic state pension will not be subject to valuation. Legislation already provides for its treatment in the event of divorce.

1 The Divorce etc (Pensions) Regulations 1996, reg 3.

The provision of information by and to pension schemes

4.121 The regulations provide for the form of notices to be given to the trustees in relation to change of circumstances[1] (for instance the prospective payee's change of address). The regulations will also prescribe what charges can be made by the trustees for complying with the new form of order the person with pension rights will have to pay for the compliance costs of the trustees[2].

1 The Divorce etc (Pensions) Regulations 1996, regs 6 – 9.
2 Ibid, regs 9 and 10.

Commencement of the new pension provisions

4.122 The court has the new powers under s 166 when it is considering applications for financial provision where the petition for divorce, judicial separation or nullity has been filed with the court on or after 1 July 1996[1]. Since it was anticipated that pension schemes will require time to adjust their administrative systems to be able to accommodate court orders which directly affect them, however, those provisions which directly affect pension schemes to the extent of their having to make payments will not come into effect until 6 April 1997[2].

1 The Pensions Act 1995 (Commencement) (No 5) Order 1996, art 4.
2 Ibid, art 5.

Definition of pension scheme

4.123 A pension scheme is defined as an occupational pension scheme or a personal pension scheme[1]. Further, references to a pension scheme include a retirement annuity contract; or an annuity, or insurance policy, purchased or transferred for the purpose of giving effect to rights under a pension scheme (s 25D(3)(a)).

1 Applying the definitions in the Pensions Act 1993, s 1 but as if the reference to employed earners in the definition of 'personal pension scheme' were to any earners (s 25D(4)).

Variation of pension orders

4.124 Under the MCA 1973, s 31(2)(dd) a party may apply to the court to vary any deferred lump sum order, including provision made by virtue of s 25B(4) or s 25C. A deferred lump sum order aimed at a pension may therefore be varied, like any other deferred lump sum order[1]. The powers of the court to vary a s 25C order will therefore encompass the following:

(a) The requirement imposed on trustees of pension schemes requiring benefit to be paid to the spouse of the person with pension rights. The person with pension rights may instead wish a further dependant to benefit from the part of the pension nominated under s 25C(2)(a).

(b) A party may wish to vary or discharge the nomination imposed under s 25C(2)(b).

1 So would a wife's remarriage prior to receipt of the deferred lump sum (on death in service or on commutation on retirement) be ground for variation? It seems as if it would be.

MAINTENANCE PENDING SUIT

4.125 As soon as a petition is filed, either spouse can apply to the court for maintenance pending suit: that is for a periodical payments order which lasts until decree nisi[1], following which maintenance becomes periodical payments under the MCA 1973, s 23(1)(a).

1 FPR 1991, r 2.67.

Retention of status quo

4.126 The conventional advice to give to spouses is that the status quo on maintenance should be retained if possible, with the same measure of financial support being given to a spouse as subsisted immediately before the separation or commencement of proceedings.

When there is no existing regime of maintenance

4.127 The question that then arises is what level of financial relief is appropriate when there is no existing maintenance arrangement. In these cases, when acting for the dependent party, a practitioner may draw up a budget showing a party's reasonable expenditure, which will be sent for consideration by the other spouse's solicitors. There may then follow the normal routine of negotiation on the figures leading to an agreement which (if an application for maintenance pending suit has already been issued) could conveniently be made into a consent order[1]. The practitioner will in these situations be balancing on the one hand the costs and the risks of taking a maintenance pending suit application to the court against, on the other hand, the desirability of leaving the quantum of periodical payments to be determined with all the other matters at a final hearing. However, the message from the judges nowadays is loudly and clearly that the quantum of maintenance pending suit orders should not be seen as a precedent for the amount of an eventual periodical payments order, and that it will be easy to make corrections at a final hearing; not least because during the period between the order for maintenance pending suit and the final hearing it will be possible to check the needs and spending of a spouse, and make a more mature judgment based on a broader knowledge of the financial circumstances of the parties when all the financial disclosure has been made[2].

1 Following the procedure under FPR 1991, r 2.61 (see para 10.10 et seq).
2 See *F v F (Ancillary Relief: Substantial Assets)* [1995] 2 FLR 45.

Child Support Act implications

4.128 One of the functions of the application for maintenance pending suit will be to assist in cases where no assessment is yet available from the Child Support Agency. In those circumstances the court may be prepared to make such an order for maintenance pending suit (dealing with the totality of needs of the caring spouse and dependent children) as may be appropriately reduced in due course by receipt of the child support payments[1].

1 See para 10.10 et seq.

Time for making the application

4.129 An order for maintenance pending suit may be made under the MCA 1973, s 22 following the filing of a petition for divorce, judicial separation or nullity. The order can be back-dated to the date of the petition.

Procedure for the making of the application

4.130 The provisions as to the evidence to be supplied on the application for maintenance pending suit, and the way in which the application is pursued, are contained, inter alia, in the FPR 1991, r 2.58. Maintenance pending suit classes as a type of 'ancillary relief', and the procedures are explained in full at para 4.3 et seq.

Contents of the affidavit in support of the application

4.131 The affidavit in support of the application must contain full particulars of the applicant's property and income, and must state the facts relied on in support of the application. If the affidavit in support of the application is going to be the first affidavit filed by the applicant in the action, it must comply with the FPR 1991, r 2.58(2) by setting out the full particulars of property and income required by the rule. The application may however be prompted by a development in the parties' financial position *following* the filing of a full affidavit earlier in the action. In that case the applicant will want to file a brief affidavit updating his or her financial position and stating the facts on which he or she is relying in making the application for maintenance pending suit. Commonly in these circumstances the respondent may have changed the maintenance arrangements and the applicant will be explaining the change and its effect on her financial position in the affidavit in support.

Affidavit in reply

4.132 The respondent is required to file an affidavit in answer to the applicant's affidavit, containing full particulars of his property and income. That has to be done by the respondent within 28 days after service of the affidavit[1]. Sometimes however the hearing date is fixed by the court providing less than 28 days' notice, in which case the respondent should file his affidavit as soon as practicable, but in any case before the hearing. He may alternatively wish to apply for an adjournment of the hearing and may be unsuccessful in doing so if the applicant resists a change in the date on the basis that there is a pressing requirement for the applicant to receive urgent financial relief.

1 FPR 1991, r 2.58(3).

Corresponding orders

4.133 Under the FPR 1991, r 2.67, where, at or after the date of a decree nisi of divorce or nullity an order for maintenance pending suit is in force, the party in whose favour the order was made may (provided that an application for periodical payments for himself was made in the petition or answer) request the district judge in writing to make a corresponding order providing for payment at the same rate as that provided for by the order for maintenance pending suit. The procedure for obtaining a corresponding order is as follows. When the applicant has made the request to the district judge, the other spouse will be served with a notice in Form M15 requiring him to give notice of any objection to the making of a corresponding order within 14 days after service of Form M15[1]. If the other spouse does not object within that time, the district judge may make the corresponding order without further ado. Most frequently however the court will have pre-empted the need to obtain corresponding orders by making an order at the maintenance pending suit hearing along these lines: 'the respondent to pay maintenance pending suit until decree absolute and then periodical payments at the rate of £x per annum ... etc'.

1 FPR 1991, r 2.67(2).

VARIATIONS

Powers of the court

4.134 The court has power under the MCA 1973, s 31(1) in respect of the orders referred to below to vary or discharge the order or to suspend any provision of the order temporarily and to revive the operation of any provision so suspended. An application by a party to vary an order may be met by a cross-application by the other party to vary or discharge that order. Alternatively, having regard to all the circumstances of the case, the court may itself determine (without any cross-application being filed) that a continuing order should be discharged[1].

1 Section 31(7)(a) obliges the court to consider, in the case of a periodical payments or secured periodical payments order, whether in all the circumstances it will be appropriate to vary the order in such a way that the payments are required to be made or secured only for such further period as will be sufficient to enable the party to adjust without undue hardship to the termination of those payments.

The orders that can be varied

4.135 Orders which can be varied consist of the following:

(a) Any order for maintenance pending suit and any interim order for maintenance. It will be rare that a party will apply for a variation of a maintenance pending suit order. Normally the final hearing will have taken place within a reasonable time of the maintenance pending suit order and therefore the order for maintenance pending suit would have been substituted by a periodical payments order.

(b) Any periodical payments order.

(c) Any secured periodical payments order. An applicant may wish to vary the secured periodical payments order because (for instance) the rate of periodical payments has increased and as the applicant wishes the security backing the maintenance payments to be increased beyond the amount negotiated and incorporated in the original order. Alternatively, the payer of maintenance may wish to 'free up' the security, to which, after years of payment of the maintenance in question the court may be prepared to accede. It will be a serious step for a court to discharge any secured periodical payments order, because an order for secured periodical payments survives the payer's death and is therefore an invaluable weapon in the armoury of anyone receiving periodical payments. There may be jurisdictional aspects of significance, for instance the payer may be domiciled outside England and Wales and therefore it may not be possible for the payee to make any application against the payer's estate under the Inheritance (Provision for Family and Dependants) Act 1975.

(d) Any order made by virtue of the MCA 1973, s 23(3)(c) or s 27(7)(b) (provision for payment of a lump sum by instalments)[2].

(e) Any deferred order made by virtue of the MCA 1973, s 23(1)(c). This includes provisions made by virtue of s 25B(4), or s 25C[3], relating to pension rights.

(f) Any order for a settlement of property under the MCA 1973, s 24(1)(b) or for a variation of settlement under s 24(1)(c) or (d), being an order made on or after the grant of a decree of judicial separation. In this sense, it is accurate to say that it is impossible to achieve a 'clean break' in judicial separation proceedings[4]. A party who has obtained the benefit of a property adjustment order in the judicial separation proceedings may therefore come back for a second bite of the cherry and obtain an order for settlement under s 24(1)(b) or for a variation of the settlement under s 24(1)(c) or (d) in the divorce proceedings themselves[5].

(g) Any order made under the MCA 1973, s 24A(1) for the sale of property[6]. It may be that the court had ordered that a party should sell a property to raise a lump sum. If this party has managed to raise the lump sum without needing to sell the property, it would be possible for that party to vary the order for sale.

1 MCA 1973, s 31(2).
2 See para 4.57 for the risks in accepting a lump sum payable by instalments, namely the prospective payer being able to apply to the court to have the 'arrears' of any lump sum payment due in instalments either varied downwards or discharged.
3 Inserted by the Pensions Act 1995, s 166(3).
4 By contrast only one lump sum order can be made, whether in judicial separation or divorce proceedings.
5 MCA 1973, s 31(4).
6 See para 4.87 and refer to *Omillan v Omillan* [1996] 2 FLR 306.

Limitation on the orders that may be made in any variation application

4.136 It is specifically provided by the MCA 1973, s 31(5) that no property adjustment order or lump sum order shall be made in favour of a party to a marriage on an application for the variation of a periodical payment or secured periodical payments order. This does not, however, prevent the capitalisation of a party's maintenance payments on a s 31 application. The way in which a respondent may capitalise the applicant's periodical payments on a variation is by undertaking to make a certain payment to the applicant, and the order itself will recite that on the making of that payment the periodical payments claims of the applicant will be dismissed. However there is no power to require a respondent to make a lump sum payment to capitalise the maintenance payments in these circumstances[1].

1 See eg *S v S* [1986] 3 All ER 566. The law is reversed in the Family Law Act, see para 4.233.

4.137 The court may direct that the variation or discharge will not take effect until the expiration of such period as may be specified in the order[1].

1 MCA 1973, s 31(10).

Variation of a secured periodical payments order

4.138 If it is proposed to make an application to vary the secured periodical payments order payable by someone who has died, the application should be made either by the person entitled to the payments under the order or by the personal representativies of the deceased person, but no application shall be made without leave after the end of the period of six months from the date on which representation in regard to the estate of that person is first taken out[1]. There is a consequential saving provision for personal representativies who are not liable for having distributed any part of the estate of the deceased after the expiration of the period of six months and are not at risk in relation to any secured periodical payments variation order if they distribute the estate after the six months referred to in s 31(6)[2].

1 MCA 1973, s 31(6).
2 See Ibid, s 31(8).

The factors to be taken into account on a variation application

4.139 Section 31(7) states that the court shall have regard to all the circumstances of the case. This includes all the relevant circumstances, which themselves include all the matters particularised in the MCA 1973, s 25(2)[1]. First consideration is given to the welfare while a minor of any child of the family who has not attained the age of 18[2]. Section 31(7) goes on to state that the circumstances of the case which the court will be considering shall include any change in any of the matters to which the court was required to have regard when making the order to which the application relates. However, this does not imply that the change in circumstances predominates over the other circumstances in the case. So, if the payer of periodical payments experiences a drop in his income from the date of the periodical payments order to the date when he makes an application for a variation in the periodical payments, the drop in his income is only one of the circumstances which the court will be bearing in mind along with the rest of the circumstances of the case, which may include his overall capital position (which may or may not have changed since the date of the first order). It is therefore a mistake to suppose that the court will just look at the extent to which matters have changed since the order. The court takes a fresh and broad look at the new set of circumstances, and may make a variation order accordingly[3].

1 See paras 4.14 ff.
2 A mirror image of the MCA 1973, s 25(1).
3 See, eg *Garner v Garner* [1992] 1 FLR 573. Quoting the head-note, 'there were wide judicial powers to step outside any actual changes which might have occurred since the

making of the original order and to look at the totality of all the circumstances afresh, without being confined solely or essentially to matters of change.' And see para 4.20 in relation to the submissions in *Cornick v Cornick (No 2)* [1995] 2 FLR 490.

Procedure for making the variation application

4.140 The application is initiated by Form M11[1]. This must be supported by an affidavit by the applicant containing full particulars of his property and income, and stating the facts relied on in support of the application[2]. Within 28 days after the service of the affidavit of the applicant, or within such other time as the court may fix, the respondent to the application shall file an affidavit in answer containing full particulars of his property and income.

1 FPR 1991, r 2.53(3) (or by Form A in the pilot scheme).
2 Ibid, r 2.58(2).

CONSENT ORDERS AND AGREEMENTS

Introduction

4.141 In this chapter we look at the manner in which financial relief applications are compromised both in consent orders and in agreements between the parties. Private agreements between the parties cannot oust the jurisdiction of the court to make orders for financial relief in proceedings for divorce, judicial separation or nullity. Therefore it is appropriate first to consider the making of consent orders and then, later in the chapter, to deal with private agreements.

Consent orders

4.142 It is therefore essential for any family law practitioner to be able to draft a consent order in an efficient manner[1]. The practitioner can often do no better than follow the model of the *Precedents for Consent Orders* (4th edn) produced by the Solicitors' Family Law Association in July 1995[2]. This document is broadly accepted by judges to be the most useful book of precedents, and it provides examples of how to draft the clauses that will be required in most cases.

1 *Dinch v Dinch* [1987] 2 FLR 162, and per Oliver of Aylmerton LJ at 164: 'It is in all cases the imperative professional duty of those invested with the task of advising the parties to these unfortunate disputes to consider with due care the impact which any terms which they agree on behalf of their clients has, and is intended to have, upon any outstanding application for ancillary relief, and to ensure that such appropriate provision is inserted in any consent order made as will leave no room for any future doubt or misunderstanding, or saddle the parties with the wasteful burden of wholly unnecessary costs. It is, of course, also the duty of any court called upon to make such a consent order to consider for itself, before the order is drawn up and entered, the

jurisdiction which it is being called upon to exercise and to make clear what claims for ancillary relief are being finally disposed of. I would, however, like to emphasise that the primary duty in this regard must lie upon those concerned with the negotiation and drafting of the terms of the order and that any failure to fulfil such duty occurring hereafter cannot be excused simply by reference to some inadvertent lack of vigilance on the part of the court or its officers in passing the order in a form which the parties have approved'.

2 And see 16 *Forms and Precedents* (5th edn) Form 2.

Statutory authority for the making of consent orders

4.143 A consent order for financial relief may be made by the court on the basis only of the prescribed information furnished with the application[1]. The MCA 1973, s 33A actually says that the consent order may be made 'notwithstanding anything in the preceding provisions of this part of this Act'. The question has therefore arisen as to whether the court in making a consent order for financial relief[2] may make a consent order without having any regard at all to the MCA 1973, s 25 and s 25A factors[3].

1 That is, the statement filed pursuant to FPR 1991, r 2.61 (see para 4.153).
2 An 'order for financial relief' is defined in s 33A(3) as an order under the MCA 1973, ss 23, 24, 24A or 27. Further, a consent order may be made which varies or discharges an order for financial relief (s 33A(2)).
3 For a detailed consideration of this aspect, and matrimonial orders and agreements generally, see David Salter and Simon Bruce, *Matrimonial Consent Orders and Agreements* Encyclopaedia of Forms and Precedents (Butterworths, 5th edn) vol 16(2) Family. The best view is that the court may only make the consent order if it considers that in view of the information on the FPR 1991, r 2.61 statement (which is meant to distil the relevant s 25 circumstances) the order should properly be made, and the court will therefore go through the s 25 exercise in approving the draft consent order. See also *B v Miller & Co* [1996] 2 FLR 23.

The contents of the draft order

The recitals to the order

4.144 The draft order will contain a preamble, or recitals, which will generally consist of what has been agreed between the parties, or what the parties have undertaken to do; followed by the body of the order itself, which contains such matters as the court has jurisdiction to order.

The subject matter of the orders themselves

4.145 It is generally desirable to incorporate as orders such matters as the court has jurisdiction to order. The reason for this is that a party can more effectively attempt to enforce an order, rather than an agreement or an undertaking. Additionally, the respondent in the application may wish to have the protection of having had the court dealing with an applicant's lump sum and property adjustment claims (by way of order property adjustment and lump sum orders, as if the court makes those orders in divorce and nullity proceedings, it will not have jurisdiction to make any orders in favour of the applicant for that relief in the future). As well as making orders for financial relief[1] the court may also make substantive orders under the Matrimonial Homes Act 1983[2] (and the other legislation relating to property and tenancy transfers), the Maintenance Enforcement Act 1991[3], etc.

1 As summarised in para 4.3 et seq.
2 For example, continuing the Class F protection beyond decree absolute.
3 Under s 1(4)(a), to the effect that periodical payments are made by standing order, for example.

Undertakings[1]

4.146 As to what cannot as a matter of jurisdiction be ordered by the court, the parties' legal advisers will want to consider how they wish the agreed obligations to be performed by the parties. If a party will be taking on an obligation to do something which he cannot be ordered to do, then it will conventionally be put into the undertakings section of the order, the party undertaking to the court that he will perform the variety of matters which he has consented to do. A party may, for example, undertake to take out a policy on his life for the benefit of his wife; or to indemnify her relating to outgoings on a jointly owned property[2]. An undertaking will often be enforceable by the other party by an application for the committal to prison of the giver of the undertaking if he does not perform the undertaking[3]. Therefore the parties have to be very carefully advised, before entering into undertakings, on the sanctions available to the other party on any breach of the undertaking[4]. One of the reasons why it is good practice for both parties to sign the minutes of consent order, as well as the parties' solicitors, is that if it is desired to enforce the obedience of the person who has supplied the undertaking, by issuing proceedings for his committal[5], it is necessary to show that he was aware of the undertaking, and his signature will be good evidence of that.

1 Some controversy arose following the publication of the report of the Court of Appeal decision in *In re B (a minor) Supervision Order: Parental Undertaking* [1996] 1 FLR 676. The case concerned the local authority's application for a care order in respect of a child pursuant to the CA 1989, s 31, and the court held that as a county court had no inherent jurisdiction to grant injunctions, it could have no inherent jurisdiction to accept undertakings in care proceedings. Some commentators went on to speculate that this judgment was authority for the novel proposition in relation to consent orders for financial relief that the court had no jurisdiction to accept an undertaking by a party in relation to a matter which could not be ordered by the court. There is anecdotal evidence of district judges adopting this view following *Re B*. However it is absolutely clear from the House of Lords judgment in *Livesey v Jenkins* [1985] AC 424 that it is in precisely the circumstances where the court cannot make an order that a party may undertake to perform such an obligation (see eg 444F). It appears therefore from the authorities *Re B* must be viewed as applying narrowly to care and supervision orders under the CA 1989.
2 In *Livesey v Jenkins* Lord Brandon suggested that the repayment of a mortgage may conveniently form part of an undertaking.
3 The enforcement provisions for an undertaking are the same as those for an injunction: CCR Ord 29, rr 1 and 1A.
4 In *Roberts v Roberts* [1990] 2 FLR 111 Butler-Sloss LJ had said that it was important for parties in matrimonial disputes to appreciate that an undertaking had all the force of an injunction. See also *Hussain v Hussain* [1986] 2 FLR 271.

5 The general form of undertaking in Form N117 contains a warning that a consequence of a breach of an undertaking might be imprisonment for contempt.

Undertakings and pitfalls in the drafting of consent orders

4.147 Care should be taken to avoid 'limping dismissals' of a party's claims for financial relief, for example one party's application for a lump sum not being dismissed until he has complied with an undertaking which is by its nature a continuing obligation[1]. The danger is that the lump sum claims remain and there is no clean break in those circumstances.

1 Such as to pay the monthly premiums relating to a life insurance policy.

The agreements contained in the draft order

4.148 It is considered good practice for the parties to recite in the draft order any substantial terms which have been agreed and implemented prior to the order being made. So if the former matrimonial home has been sold and the proceeds distributed between the parties, there will be a recital explaining the proportion of sale proceeds paid to either party. Consent orders are often examined[1] many years after the event, and it can be difficult to understand exactly what happened when a case was compromised unless the order encapsulates the entire agreement.

1 For example, on variation applications.

Agreements rather than undertakings

4.149 The agreement section of the draft order is convenient because it provides the parties with an opportunity to recite all manner of matters that they may have agreed. So if they agree that it will be reasonable for the wife to exercise her earning capacity in a certain number of years' time, there is no reason why that should not be recited in an order (and indeed the respondent may wish this to happen, so that he can rely on it in any future variation application which he may seek to make)[1]. The other function of the agreements in the recitals to the consent order is to set out the matters which the parties should not be allowed to undertake to do. For example, if parties agree that the applicant will not apply for periodical payments to be varied, it will be inappropriate for the party giving that promise to be made to undertake not to make an application for variation of the periodical payments order. The reason for this is that statute gives the applicant the possibility of applying for a variation under the MCA 1973, s 31, and the court will not accept an undertaking to oust its own jurisdiction to make orders. In the same way, if no application is made by a party under the Married Women's Property Act 1882, it will not be possible as a matter of law for that party's rights to make an application under that Act to be dismissed; the court's jurisdiction to make orders under that Act cannot be ousted (and so the most that can happen is that the parties can agree that neither will make an application under that Act).

1 An alternative to including such agreements in the recitals is to refer in the draft order to a side-letter which itself contains the relevant terms. The side-letter should be filed

at the court with the draft order. See *N v N (Consent Order: Variation)* [1993] 2 FLR 868, in which the Court of Appeal disapproved of the failure to show the side-letter to the judge who made the order.

Documents to be filed at court when applying for the consent order

4.150 At the same time as the petitioner applies for decree nisi[1], or at any time thereafter, a party applying for financial relief under the MCA 1973, ss 23, 24 and 24A should file at court the following documentation:

(a) two copies of the draft consent order;

(b) the petitioner's application in Form M13 for such financial relief as has not been requested in the petition;

(c) Form M11 filed on behalf of the respondent, requesting such financial relief that he has not already applied for in any answer;

(d) a statement (or statements) of information which complies with the FPR 1991, r 2.61;

(e) any side-letter incorporating any terms agreed in addition to the terms which are contained in the minutes of consent order[2].

1 The draft orders relating to financial provision in the case of neglect to maintain under the MCA 1973, s 27, and maintenance pending suit under s 22, will of course be filed before this stage.
2 See para 4.149, n 1.

The draft consent order

4.151 The FPR 1991, r 2.61(1) states that two copies of a draft of the order in the terms sought, one of which shall be endorsed with a statement signed by the respondent to the application signifying his agreement, should be filed at the same time as a consent order is applied for[1]. The rule states that at least one of the copies should be signed by the respondent to the application signifying his agreement[2]. It is best practice to get both petitioner and respondent to sign the minutes, not least so as to signify that they actually agree and understand the terms contained in the document[3].

1 The point of filing two copies of the document is to enable the court to approve, and keep on the court file, one of the copies of the minutes; and send out the other (to be endorsed by the district judge, dated and stamped), together with a spare copy of it, to the parties' solicitors.
2 The wording of the rule is misleading because it implies that there is only one respondent to 'the application'. In fact invariably both parties will be making applications for financial relief and both parties should sign the document. Despite the strict wording of the rule (requiring personal signing of the document by a party himself), the rule is sufficiently complied with (where it has not been possible to get a party to sign a document, or no undertakings have been given) if the solicitors themselves alone, and not their clients, sign the document.
3 And see para 4.146 concerning undertakings.

120 *Maintenance and Property Distribution*

The applications in Forms M11 and M13

4.152 Normally the petitioner will have applied for the totality of financial relief in a petition, and there will not therefore be any requirement for her to file Form M13, applying for financial relief, when the draft order is filed. If the respondent has not applied for all forms of financial relief in an answer, or has not already made an application for financial relief in Form M11, he should file Form M11 at the court, applying for the orders which are dealt with in the draft order[1].

> 1 Otherwise the district judge may object that there is no jurisdiction to make orders for which no application has been made; this is the approach of the district judges at the Principal Registry of the Family Division (file Form A in pilot scheme cases).

The rule 2.61 statement of information

Completion of the statement

4.153 The standard forms prescribed by the FPR 1991 enable one statement of information to be completed by both parties. Frequently however each party completes his own form and so separate forms are filed at the court. The statement may be signed by the party himself, or by his solicitor. Note there is no provision in the rules for the FPR 1991, r 2.61 statement to be served on the other party[1]. Either party may however make it a term of the overall agreement that the kind of disclosure which is going to feature on the r 2.61 statement is revealed in advance to the other party.

> 1 The document will however be on the court file and so easily obtainable by the other party's solicitors.

The drafting of the r 2.61 statement

4.154 The points to bear in mind are as follows:

(a) The district judge will peruse and consider the contents of the statement[1] when approving the draft minutes of order. The reason for the statement is to encapsulate the disclosure of a party so as to enable the district judge to take a view about the reasonableness, or otherwise, of the settlement[2]. If the district judge is not satisfied that the agreement is fair to a party, based on the disclosure which is provided in the r 2.61 statement, he may adjourn consideration of the draft order to an inter partes hearing at which he will be able to investigate the matter with the parties and their legal representatives.

(b) The r 2.61 statement contains the up-to-date disclosure of the parties as at the date of the order. It is the vehicle for disclosing a party's up-to-date financial position, updating any affidavits that may have been filed already in the action.

(c) It is possible that the matter will go back to court on a variation application in the future. If there is any material inaccuracy in the r 2.61 statement, it may be highlighted at that later stage by the applicant;

(d) A r 2.61 statement may erroneously omit disclosure of special significance which could enable a party to appeal out of time against the consent order, or apply to the court for the consent order to be set aside.

1 The r 2.61 statement may be made in more than one document and may therefore have a number of different attachments, as the 'boxes' on the prescribed form are very small. Most firms of solicitors have the r 2.61 statement readily available on the word processor and therefore it is easier to expand the size of the relevant 'boxes' to fit the information which is going to be endorsed on it.
2 In accordance with the court's duty under the MCA 1973, s 33A(1).

Contents of the statement

4.155 The contents of the r 2.61 statement, in any application for a consent order under any of the MCA 1973, ss 23, 24 or 24A, are as follows[1]:

1 FPR 1991, r 2.61(1)(a) to (f).

DURATION OF MARRIAGE ETC[1]

4.156 The duration of the marriage, and the age of each party and of any minor or dependent child of the family have to be explained.

1 FPR 1991, r 2.61(1)(a).

CAPITAL RESOURCES AND NET INCOME[1]

4.157 An estimate in summary form of the approximate amount or value of the capital resources and net income of each party and of any minor child of the family is to be provided[2]. To enable the district judge easily to understand what is supposed to happen under the terms of the order when the assets are disclosed in the r 2.61 statement, the form requires an explanation to be given of the net equity in any property concerned, and the effect of its proposed distribution. The summary of capital assets will also take into account the amount of debt in a case.

1 FPR 1991, r 2.61(1)(b).
2 If a party has a business interest which has not been valued, it may be recited on the statement that the party has a shareholding in business, the accounts of which have been disclosed to the other party in the course of the case.

ACCOMMODATION[1]

4.158 What arrangements are intended for the accommodation of each of the parties and any minor child of the family? The answer that the parties will give to this question will assist the district judge to perform the s 25 duty of considering, under s 25(1), the welfare while a minor of any child of the family who has not attained the age of 18. The question may if necessary be answered in vague terms – there is no reason for a party to set out the address where he or she may be living and indeed for reasons of confidentiality this may be the last thing that one of the parties wishes to do.

1 FPR 1991, r 2.61(1)(c).

REMARRIAGE/CO-HABITATION[1]

4.159 Has either party remarried or has he/she any present intention of marrying or co-habiting with another person[2]? The reason for this question is to ensure that a party provides a truthful account of this particular aspect of financial disclosure[3]. The printed form does not provide a box for someone who is actually co-habiting with another person at the time when the statement is completed. In those circumstances, it is necessary to amend the category of answer so that it reads that the party is actually co-habiting with another person.

1 FPR 1991, r 2.61(1)(d).
2 The means of the co-habitee/new spouse being a relevant financial resource under the MCA 1973, s 25(2)(a).
3 Arguably the boxes which a party has to tick are misleading; they require the party to indicate, with a tick in a box, whether he or she intends to marry, or whether he or she intends to co-habit with another person. Sometimes clients ask how the form should be completed bearing in mind the fact that they certainly wish to co-habit or to remarry at some stage in the future, albeit that they have no 'candidate' in mind at the present! In those circumstances, despite the wording of the standard form, it would be correct for that party to say that he has no *present* intention to marry or to co-habit (although he does as a matter of fact intend to marry or to co-habit at some stage in the future). The clients who 'overnight' with someone else often ask what 'co-habitation' actually means or entails. As a rule of thumb, work on the fact that if your client is spending more than three nights per week with his girlfriend, that counts as co-habitation and should be disclosed.

ORDERS RELATING TO PENSION

4.160 Where the order imposes any requirement on the trustees of a pension scheme by virtue of s 25B or s 25C[1], a statement must be provided confirming that those trustees have been served with notice of the application and that no objection to such an order has been made by them within 14 days from such service.

1 Inserted by the Family Proceedings (Amendment) (No 2) Rules 1996, r 4(1) relating to petitions filed on or after 1 July 1996 as r 2.61(1)(dd).

TRANSFER OF PROPERTY[1]

4.161 Where the terms of the order provide for a transfer of property, a statement must be provided which confirms that any mortgagee of that property has been served with notice of the application, and that no objection to such a transfer has been made by the mortgagee within 14 days from such service. Under the FPR 1991, r 2.59(4), a copy of the Form M11 or M13 requesting the property adjustment order should be served on any mortgagee, and it is good practice to make service of the form on a mortgagee a reflex action whenever the application is issued. There is therefore a risk that the final hearing may be adjourned, or the draft order may have to be returned, because Form M11 or M13 has not been duly served on the mortgagee (and there will be costs consequences for a solicitor arising out of failure to serve the notice and out of the consequent adjournment of any hearing that has been fixed)[2].

1 FPR 1991, r 2.61(1)(e).

2 Experience shows that there are district judges whose first question at any final hearing is whether the FPR 1991, r 2.59(4) has been complied with.

ANY OTHER ESPECIALLY SIGNIFICANT MATTERS[1]

4.162 If there is any particular point which a client wishes to point out to the district judge approving the draft order, or to be put down as a marker in the case of any future application for variation, this is the opportunity for recording the matter[2].

1 FPR 1991, r 2.61(1)(f).
2 For example, if a respondent persuades an applicant to accept a clean break in circumstances in which she could have held out for continued maintenance payments, it is good practice for the respondent to explain how the maintenance payments are being capitalised, eg by payment of a certain capital sum in addition to the applicant's housing requirements (if that is not already recited in the preamble to the draft order). It is best then to highlight, for the benefit of the district judge, that consideration has been given to the matter.

The form of the statement in a variation/interim periodical payments application[1]

4.163 When the order simply varies an order for periodical payments, or relates to interim periodical payments, the statement of information only needs to include the information relating to net income. The following points arise:

(a) If the respondent is, on a variation application, capitalising the applicant's periodical payments[2], the statement of information should contain the complete information required by the FPR 1991, r 2.61(1), ie the information set out at para 4.156 ff, rather than simply the material permitted under r 2.61(2).

(b) Sometimes parties enter into consent orders for nominal maintenance payments to be made to the children, as an artificial device to exclude the jurisdiction of the Child Support Agency. In these circumstances, a full r 2.61 statement complying with r 2.61(1) will also be required[3].

(c) In a variation application which relates to an order which has been made relating to a pension under s 25B or s 25C, it is necessary to certify that the trustees have not objected, in a like manner to that provided under r 2.61(1)(dd).

1 FPR 1991, r 2.61(2).
2 For example, by imposing a *Duxbury* payment – see para 4.41.
3 Experience suggests that a party should also explain on the statement why that kind of order is being requested.

Erroneous completion of the statement

4.164 If a party completes the statement in a way which his solicitor knows to be false the solicitor should neither sign the statement on behalf of his client, nor should he file it at court. It is likely that the solicitor would have to come off the record if he or she knew the client was seeking to mislead the court.

Agreements and deeds of separation

The status of agreements between the parties

4.165 A question which commonly arises is the status of an agreement made between the parties, which does not form the subject of a court order[1]. A contract made between parties in matrimonial proceedings, if it is to be enforceable, should comply with the requirements of the law of contract generally. It must be established that there was an intention to create a legal relationship[2]. Consideration should pass between the parties, and if there is any doubt about that the agreement should be executed as a deed. The agreement itself may deal with a whole range of matters relating to financial relief, and matters relating to the children, in exactly the same way as draft orders[3].

1 For useful precedents of separation deeds, reconciliation deeds, pre-marital contracts, memorandum of prior oral agreement, and deeds of variation, see *Precedents – Agreements between Husband and Wife* published by the Solicitors Family Law Association, August 1993.
2 *Balfour v Balfour* [1919] 2 KB 571; *Gould v Gould* [1969] 3 All ER 728.
3 See further *Matrimonial Consent Orders and Agreements* Encyclopaedia of Forms and Precedents (Butterworths, 5th edn) vol 16(2) Family.

The relationship between agreements and orders, and the Edgar *principle*

4.166 The agreement will commonly state that the parties intend it to be in full and final satisfaction of any order that the court could make in any proceedings in the future, and that they intend it to be incorporated into the terms of a court order when proceedings are issued. Occasionally one of the parties may change his mind about the terms of the agreement even after the terms have been fully negotiated (and perhaps even when the terms have been incorporated into a draft consent order which has not yet been filed at the court). The question that then arises is what approach the court will take to agreements that have been negotiated between the parties in these circumstances. In general, the court will wish the parties to adhere to the bargain that they have struck in the past[1]. The court has however, in certain circumstances been willing to make an order in terms that are different (and even significantly different) from the agreement between the parties in special circumstances, such as, for example:

(a) where a party has received no, or very poor, legal advice[2];

(b) where the parties' circumstances as at the date of the order are wholly different from their circumstances at the time when they made an agreement[3];

(c) where there has been material non-disclosure or fraud by a party in the negotiations leading up to the agreement[4].

There is therefore a tension between the desire of the court on the one hand to respect agreements freely negotiated by them and bring about a clean break between parties, in the broad sense of resolving their financial differences between them; and on the other hand, the parental character of the court shown in circumstances where the court endeavours to protect a weaker party[5,6].

1 See *Edgar v Edgar* [1980] 1 WLR 1410. The Court of Appeal in that case concluded that the MCA 1973, s 25 places the court in the same position as it was under earlier legislation: spouses may not, by their own agreement preclude the court from excising jurisdiction over their financial arrangements (*Hyman v Hyman* [1929] AC 601; *Wright v Wright* [1970] 1 WLR 1219). However, 'in a consideration of what is just to be done in the exercise of the courts' powers under the [MCA 1973] in the light of the conduct of the parties, the court must, I think, start from the position that a solemn and freely negotiated bargain ... ought to be adhered to unless some clear and compelling reason, such, for instance, as a drastic change of circumstances, is shown to the contrary' (per Oliver LJ at 1424E and F). Both Oliver and Ormrod LJJ stressed that reaching an agreement was a factor to be taken into account as conduct within the terms of s 25(2) (as it now is).
2 See, eg *Camm v Camm* (1983) 4 FLR 577, and the test of the 'independent bystander'. 'If any independent by-stander had been asked to consider the arrangement that was being put forward in 1975 [at the time of the agreement], he would have been bound to say that it was an unfair arrangement so far as the wife was concerned' (per Sir Roger Ormrod at 585D).
3 See, eg *Beach v Beach* [1995] 2 FLR 160: 'I do not regard this as being an *Edgar* case in simple classification. The classic *Edgar* case contains a litigant who seeks to depart unreasonably or capriciously from a fairly negotiated formal settlement ... Here I contemplate circumstances which are totally different from the circumstances contemplated by the contracting parties .... My conclusion, therefore, is that although the agreement of 20 February 1990 is of importance, it is only of importance of part of the developing history. My essential duty is to determine this application upon the criteria contained in s 25, as amended'. per Thorpe J at 168A to F.
4 See, eg *Livesey v Jenkins* [1985] 1 All ER 106.
5 This was highlighted by Hoffman LJ in *Pounds v Pounds* [1994] 1 FLR 775, who drew attention to the unsatisfactory state of the law under which an 'agreement may be held to be binding, but whether it will be can be determined only after litigation and may involve, as in this case, examining the quality of the advice which was given to the party who wishes to resile. It is then understandably a matter for surprise and resentment on the part of the other party that one should be able to repudiate an agreement on account of the inadequacy of one's own legal advisors, over whom the other party had no control and of whose advice he had no knowledge' (at 791E to F).
6 There is a useful article on the status of agreements, by David Burrows, Solicitors' Journal, 31 March 1995, pp 294, 295.

Application for notice to show cause why the agreement should not be made into an order

4.167 A remedy in the hands of a party who wishes to convert the terms of an agreement as to the terms of an order into an order itself may be to apply to the court for an order to be made in the agreed terms. This may be possible when the agreement seeks to compromise the party's claim for financial relief and is intended by the parties to become an order. The party who wants to convert a draft order into an order after the other party has resiled from it should make application in Form M11 or M13 the effect of which is to require the other party to show cause why the agreement should not be converted into an order. The application should be supported by an affidavit sworn by the applicant explaining the background to the application and setting out the terms of the proposed order agreed between the parties. The application is often the trigger which enables the terms of the agreement, or terms very similar to them, to be ratified by the court. It will only be possible to make the application if all the terms have been agreed; if some of the terms have not been agreed then there will be no true overall agreement which the court will be able to convert into a court order[1].

1 By analogy with the general law of contract and in accordance with the principle that an overall agreement is not severable into its constituent parts.

Full application for financial relief

4.168 In any case where a party is not prepared to adhere to the overall terms of financial relief contained in a separation deed or other agreement, the aggrieved party may alternatively exhibit the terms of the agreement to an affidavit filed at court. This will be relied on by the applicant in the course of his application for financial relief; and the respondent's behaviour in relation to the agreement may be 'conduct' within the items of the MCA 1973, s 25(2)(g)[1].

1 And see *Edgar v Edgar* [1980] 1WLR 1410.

Agreements reached in mediation

4.169 A question which has become apposite since the increased use of mediation is the status of a mediation agreement, ie an agreement reached between the parties as a result of, or during, a mediation session with a specialised mediator or mediators. The agreement will commonly be negotiated on the basis that it has to be converted into the legal language of a draft order by solicitors instructed by the parties. An openly mediated agreement will be, like any other agreement between the parties, a factor to be taken into account under the MCA 1973, s 25(2) if one of the parties then stops the agreement being made into a court order.

Agreement to oust the jurisdiction of the court

4.170 An agreement by the parties to oust the jurisdiction of the court to make orders for financial relief is void[1], but may be upheld precisely because it has been agreed by the parties and is reasonable on *Edgar* principles. The parties may negotiate an agreement between themselves that the applicant will not, for instance, apply to extend the periodical payments order made in her favour for a fixed period of years (perhaps subject to an extreme or extraordinary change in her circumstances). The question that then arises is the extent to which the applicant will be able to get out of that agreement. It may be argued on the respondent's behalf that the agreement of the applicant not to apply for an extension of the periodical payments is an integral part of the negotiated agreement between the parties, and that she should therefore be stopped from making an application for variation[2]. A respondent can never assume that the agreement of the parties to oust the court's jurisdiction will be binding on the applicant, and the agreement is simply one of those s 25(2) circumstances which the court will take into account in the variation/extension application itself.

1 Eg MCA 1973, s 34(1).
2 Such an argument (viz that the wife should not be able to extend periodical payment beyond a fixed term), was upheld in *N v N (Consent Order: Variation)* [1993] 2 FLR 868; the order did not contain a s 28(1A) direction, but the wife had agreed in a side

letter, which was not shown to the district judge who made the original order, that she would not apply for an extension. In the circumstances of this case, the Court of Appeal held the wife to the agreement not to extend, on *Edgar* principles. Contrast, first, *Richardson v Richardson* [1994] 1 FLR 286, where the wife applied for an extension of the periodical payments which had been fixed for a period of three years whereupon there was to be a clean break; Thorpe J ruled that the outcome was 'finely balanced', but that the omission of the s 28(1A) direction was the crucial aspect and that the term should be extended; and second, *B v B (Consent Order: Variation)* [1995] 1 FLR 9, another application by a wife for extension of a maintenance term, and a case in which she had agreed not to apply to extend albeit that there was no s 28(1A) direction. Here the poor quality of the wife's legal advice at the time of the consent order was the crucial aspect which persuaded Thorpe J to allow the maintenance term to be extended for a period of the parties' joint lives. Again the *Edgar* principles were brought to bear upon the decision.

Agreements between the parties recited in the minutes of order

4.171 The question which then arises is the extent to which a party can be sure of enforcing an agreement about a matter which cannot form the subject of a court order. In these circumstances parties can enter into a deed of covenant, which may even be referred to in the draft order, providing specified relief to one of the parties. For example, the applicant may only agree to her claims being compromised on specific terms if the respondent agrees to make a maintenance 'allowance' to her even after she has co-habited or remarried, and this obligation may be put into a deed. The payee will wish this kind of obligation to be binding on the payer's estate. She will then be in a position to take proceedings in the Chancery Division to enforce the agreement if the respondent does not comply with his obligations in the deed.

INJUNCTIONS AND FINANCIAL RELIEF

Introduction

4.172 The circumstances in which the practitioner will consider making an application for an injunction in cases relating to financial relief will be where:

(a) there is a realistic possibility that a party will not disclose, or has not disclosed, documents or items relating to the application which may be removed or destroyed by the respondent unless the other party is able to obtain a search and find order relating to those documents/items;

(b) one party may be endangering the financial status quo, for instance, by selling an asset with the intention of dissipating the proceeds, dissipating the contents of a bank account, or transferring money out of the jurisdiction to make it difficult to find and attack in the financial relief proceedings.

The types of order available

4.173 The following relief is available in applications within proceedings for divorce, nullity and judicial separation:

(a) orders made under the MCA 1973, s 37;

(b) orders made under the inherent jurisdiction of the court, and under the Supreme Court Act 1981, s 37, being injunctions known as Mareva[1] injunctions and Anton Piller[2] orders;

(c) an order *ne exeat regno*[3].

1 *Mareva Cia Naviera SA v International Bulkcarriers SA, The Mareva* [1980] 1 All ER 213n.
2 *Anton Piller KG v Manufacturing Processes Ltd* [1976] Ch 55, [1976] 1 All ER 779.
3 These orders are extremely rare in financial relief cases, and can only be used with the utmost caution. See, eg *Bayer v Winter* [1986] 1 WLR 497. See further para 4.188. For an analogous order, made under the inherent jurisdiction, see *Re S (Financial Provision: Non-Resident)* [1996] 1 FCR 148, where Thorpe J ordered a non-resident to lodge his passport in secure deposit pending the hearing of an interim application.

Obtaining undertakings rather than orders

4.174 At the outset of a matter, it may often be good practice to request the other party to volunteer an undertaking not to alter his or her financial position in any material way without your client's written consent or court order. That will not stop the other party dissipating his assets, but it will facilitate the obtaining of any ex parte order which may be required later in the case, should there be evidence that the other party has breached the undertaking; and if the undertaking has been given to the court[1], it will be possible to apply for the other party's committal.

1 Either in Form N117 (see CCR Ord 29, r 3); a similar form may be used in the High Court, or the undertaking may be contained in a court order.

Avoidance of transactions intended to prevent or reduce financial relief

4.175 The MCA 1973, s 37 has two functions: first, it enables an order to be made which stops a party defeating the other party's claim for financial relief by disposing of assets or transferring them out of the jurisdiction; secondly, it can set aside any disposition that has been made by a party who has dealt with matrimonial assets in such a way as to attempt to defeat the other party's claims. It is the power of setting aside a disposition that is a particularly useful weapon in financial relief proceedings, going beyond the mere 'freezing' of assets by Mareva injunctions or under the inherent jurisdiction of the court.

Financial relief

4.176 An application under the MCA 1973, s 37 can only be made in a case where proceedings for financial relief are brought by one person against another. Financial relief is defined[1] for the purposes of the MCA 1973, s 37 as relief under any of the provisions of the MCA 1973, ss 22, 23, 24, 27, 31 (except subsection (6)) and 35. Any reference in s 37 to defeating a person's claim for financial relief is a reference to:

(a) preventing financial relief from being granted to that person, or to that person for the benefit of a child of the family; or

(b) reducing the amount of any financial relief which might be so granted; or

(c) frustrating or impeding the enforcement of any order which might be or have been made at his instance under any of the above provisions[2].

The MCA 1973, s 37 is therefore designed, for example, to prevent a party giving money away, or putting it into the hands of a third party, to reduce the other party's ability to obtain proper financial relief. A s 37 order will not be made unless an intention to defeat a claim for financial relief is proved. The intention does not have to be the sole or dominant intention of the party, provided that it plays a substantial part in his intentions as a whole[3]. The court will not grant an order unless the intention to defeat claims is proved[4].

1 In the MCA 1973, s 37(1).
2 Ibid, s 37(1).
3 See *Kemmis v Kemmis (Welland Intervening)* [1988] 1 WLR 1307.
4 See eg *Shipman v Shipman* [1991] 1 FLR 250. Here the judge held that a husband was not intending to deal with property in such a way as to defeat the claims of the other party; and so a s 37 order was not appropriate. However in the circumstances of the case, in which the husband lived and had his assets outside the jurisdiction, an order would be made under the inherent jurisdiction freezing the relevant assets.

The orders which can be made

4.177 Under the MCA 1973, s 37(2), where proceedings for financial relief are brought by one person against another[1], the court may make orders as follows:

(a) If it is satisfied that the other party to the proceedings is, with the intention of defeating the claim for financial relief, about to make any disposition or to transfer out of the jurisdiction or otherwise deal with any property, the court may make such order as it thinks fit for restraining the other party from so doing or otherwise protecting the claim[2]. The kind of order that can be made is that money should be frozen in a bank account, and therefore this order is akin to a Mareva injunction. A party will rely on this protection when there are grounds for thinking that this kind of disposition may be made by the other party before the conclusion of the financial relief proceedings. This subsection is sufficiently wide for it to apply to any course of dealing with property, even if the property in question has not yet been purchased. The order is directed against a party (or third party) personally and may relate to assets held out of the jurisdiction[3].

(b) The court may, if it is satisfied that the other party has, with the intention set out in the MCA 1973, s 37(2)(a), made a reviewable disposition and that if the disposition were set aside financial relief or different financial relief would be granted to the applicant, make an order setting aside the disposition. For example, if a party were to obtain a second mortgage over a property during proceedings for financial relief, and dissipate the proceeds, the other party may seek to set the mortgage aside.

(c) If the court is satisfied, in a case where an order for financial relief has been obtained by the applicant against the other party, that the other party has, with the intention set out in the MCA 1973, s 37(2)(a), made a reviewable disposition, it may make an order setting aside the disposition. This part of the subsection is designed to assist a party in a case where the other party is trying to frustrate the enforcement or operation of the court order. An order made under s 37(2)(b) or (c) will contain such directions as may be required to give effect to the order. For example, if a husband gives money to a third party which is proved to be a disposition intended to defeat the claims of the wife, the court may order the third party (who may be represented at a s 37 hearing) to pay that money to the wife, or as the case may be[4]. As a matter of practice the final hearing of the the MCA 1973, s 37(2)(b) application takes place at the same time as the final hearing.

1 See para 4.176.
2 In *Shipman* the husband unsuccessfully argued that he could not be restrained from purchasing a property out of severance pay that he had not yet received. It was also unsuccessfully argued in the case that to apply cash towards payment of a debt was not a disposal of funds for the purpose of s 37(2)(a).
3 See, eg *Hamlin v Hamlin* [1986] 1 FLR 61. Careful thought about enforcement has to be given before attempting to freeze a bank account out of the jurisdiction. The order may not be enforceable in the overseas jurisdiction and therefore the very serving of the order will alert the respondent to the relief which the applicant is seeking, and he may therefore be able to frustrate the intended effect of the order.
4 MCA 1973, s 37(3).

What is a reviewable disposition?

4.178 Under the MCA 1973, s 37(4), any disposition made by the other party to the proceedings for financial relief (whether before or after commencement of those proceedings) is a reviewable disposition unless it was made for valuable consideration (other than marriage) to a person who, at the time of the disposition, acted in relation to it in good faith and without notice of any intention[1] on the part of the other party to defeat the applicant's claim for financial relief. There is a presumption that recent dispositions have been made with the intention of defeating the applicant's claim for financial relief; this is spelled out in the MCA 1973, s 37(5), which takes in any disposition which took place less than three years before the date of the application[2]. Any such disposition will be presumed by the court to be made with the intention of defeating the applicant's claim if (in a case falling within s 37(2)(a) or (b)) the disposition or other dealing would (apart from s 37) have the consequence of defeating the applicant's claim for financial relief; or (in a case falling within s 37(2) (c) above), the disposition has had that consequence.

The object of this provision is to prevent a husband who hears of his wife's intention to bring divorce proceedings from disposing of assets to defeat her claims.

1 For an example of what constitutes notice of intention, see eg *Kemmis v Kemmis*: notice meant actual or constructive notice (and was not limited in the case of dispositions of registered to the statutory substitute for notice in the Land Registration Act 1925). See also, *B v B (P Ltd Intervening)(No 2)* [1995] 1 FLR 374. The husband in this case obtained mortgage finance over a property in which his wife was not living but over which she had registered a class F land charge (which was a nullity as she did not live in the property; she should have registered a caution). The solicitor acting for the mortgagees (interveners in the proceedings) worked in the same firm as the husband's solicitors in the matrimonial case, but notice of the wife's claims in the financial relief proceedings was not thereby to be imputed to the interveners' solicitor.
2 Any disposition made more than three years before the application may be proved by the applicant to have been made in bad faith, but that will be a question of evidence.

Disposition

4.179 Under the MCA 1973, s 37(6) 'disposition' does not include any provision contained in a will or codicil but, with that exception, includes any conveyance, assurance or gift of property of any description, whether made by an instrument or otherwise.

Procedure

Application

4.180 The applicant files the application under the MCA 1973, s 37[1] and the affidavit in support at the same county court at which the petition has been filed. The district judge has jurisdiction to deal with the application[2] but may refer the matter to a judge[3]. The contents of the affidavit, and the service requirements, are set out in the FPR 1991, r 2.59. If an ex parte order has been obtained, it will be served on the respondent and on any relevant third party. If however the application is on notice rather than ex parte, the application will be endorsed with a return date and will then have to be served, with a copy of the affidavit in support, on the respondent.

1 In Form N16A in the county court; in the High Court, by summons. The proceedings will normally be dealt with in the High Court if they are interlocutory applications involving Mareva injunctions, or if they involve directions as to dealing with assets out of the jurisdiction or are sufficiently complex: see *Practice Direction of 5 June 1992* [1992] 2 FLR 87.
2 FPR 1991, r 2.68.
3 Ibid, r 2.65.

Affidavit

4.181 The affidavit by the applicant must contain full particulars of the property to which the disposition relates, and of the person in whose favour the disposition is alleged to have been made. In the case of a disposition alleged to have been made by way of settlement, the affidavit will contain full particulars of the trustees and beneficiaries of the settlement, so far as is known to the applicant[1]. A copy of the application and supporting affidavit must be served on any person in whose favour the disposition is alleged to have been made[2], the application having identified any land that may be involved in the application and giving the same particulars relating to it as have to be supplied on the filing of the application for a property adjustment order[3]. Any third party who has received the applicant's affidavit in relation to the MCA 1973, s 37 application may within 14 days after service or receipt file an affidavit in answer[4].

1 FPR 1991, r 2.59(1)(c).
2 Ibid, r 2.59(3).
3 Ibid, r 2.59(2).
4 Ibid, r 2.59(5).

Directions

4.182 At the directions appointment which will be fixed following the filing of the application, the following directions may commonly be made:

(a) an order for the filing of affidavit evidence in reply to the applicant's affidavit by the respondent, and by any third party who may be involved in the application (if this has not already happened by operation of r 2.59);

(b) leave may be given to the third party to intervene in the proceedings as Intervener. In these circumstances, if the intervener is represented, his solicitors will file notice of acting at the court;

(c) the applicant may be given the opportunity to file an affidavit in response to the respondent's affidavit and the intervener's affidavit;

(d) the court will (in any case which has not involved an immediate s 37 order, for example freezing a bank account) direct that the s 37 application be heard on the return date of the final hearing.

Interveners

4.183 It may be possible to short-circuit any s 37 application by the giving of suitable undertakings in the proceedings which may then limit the need for the intervener to appear in the proceedings. For example, if a respondent to a s 37 application has created a trust over a property owned by him, with the intervener as beneficiary of that trust, and the trust is then attacked under s 37, the intervener could undertake in the s 37 proceedings that he or she would consent to any dealing in the property which may be required as a result of the final order in the financial relief proceedings. The intervener may, for instance, co-operate in the taking out of a mortgage on the property, to enable the respondent to pay such lump sum to the applicant as may be ordered. In these kinds of circumstances, the court could order that the s 37 application be adjourned generally, and that the intervener be excused attendance at the hearing of the application for financial relief. This will then serve to save the costs which would otherwise be incurred by the Intervener in being represented at any final hearing.

Costs

4.184 The court will make such order relating to the costs of the s 37 application as may be deemed justified when the judge has had the opportunity of dealing with all the evidence at the final hearing. If the s 37 application is proved to have been fruitless the applicant will frequently have a costs order made against her which could make significant inroads into any costs order that she may obtain at the final hearing.

Mareva injunctions

4.185 As noted above, a Mareva injunction is more invasive than an order made under the MCA 1973, s 37, because it is not necessary for the applicant to prove an intention by the respondent to defeat an applicant's claim for financial relief in obtaining a Mareva order. A Mareva injunction may restrain a party from disposing of, charging or dealing with assets both within and outside the jurisdiction[1]. The injunction may also include an order that the defendant disclose his assets, therefore supplementing the disclosure requirements within the matrimonial proceedings themselves[2].

1 For authority as to the obtaining of a Mareva injunction applying to assets worldwide, see *Derby & Co Ltd v Weldon (No 6)* [1990] 1 WLR 1139. The Court of Appeal in this case expressed the view that a worldwide injunction may be granted only in exceptional cases and subject to strict undertakings or provisos as the injunction could prove to be more oppressive to the defendant than beneficial to the applicant. A Mareva injunction is a draconian measure and therefore case law and Practice Directions have established a number of protective measures, which are described in para 4.187 ff. It has been held that in a financial relief application an injunction should not extend to all the assets of the other parties; the injunction should be limited to the size of the fund which the applicant could reasonably regard as an issue: see *Ghoth v Ghoth* [1992] 2 FLR 300.
2 See, eg the FPR 1991, r 2.58(3).

The jurisdiction for the making of Anton Piller and Mareva injunctions

4.186 The relevant jurisdiction is the Supreme Court Act 1981, s 37[1]. Under s 37(1) of that Act, the High Court may by order (whether interlocutory or final) grant an injunction in all cases in which it appears to the court to be just and convenient to do so. Under s 37(2) of the 1981 Act, any such order may be made either unconditionally or on such terms and conditions as the court thinks fit. The injunction operates *in personam*, that is against the person who is on the receiving end of the injunction wherever he or she may be. Pursuant to s 37(3) of the 1981 Act, the power of the High Court under subsection (1) to grant an interlocutory injunction restraining a party to any proceedings from removing from the jurisdiction of the High Court, or otherwise dealing with, assets located within that jurisdiction shall be exercisable in cases where that party is, as well as in cases where he is not, domiciled, resident or present within that jurisdiction.

1 Although such orders may also be made under the inherent jurisdiction of the court (see, eg *Shipman v Shipman* [1991] 1 FLR 250). A district judge also has jurisdiction to grant an injunction under the inherent jurisdiction (CCR Ord 13, r 6(2); CCR Ord 21, r 5(2B)).

Grounds for seeking Mareva and Anton Piller orders

Procedural requirements – both orders[1]

4.187 An application for an Anton Piller and Mareva injunction must have the following components[2]:

(a) The applicant must make a full and frank disclosure of all matters within his knowledge which are material to the application[3]. There will be costs, penalties, and possibly damages, against a party who has obtained an ex parte injunction on a false basis. The applicant may have to provide an undertaking to pay damages in the preamble to the order[4]. The applicant must therefore be aware of the nature and meaning of this undertaking; for example where the applicant is trying to 'paralyse' the respondent's business activities by freezing accounts or removing necessary working papers.

(b) The applicant must give particulars of his claim against the respondent, stating the grounds for his claim.

(c) The applicant must give grounds for believing that there is a risk that the assets will be dissipated before the satisfaction by the respondent of the applicant's overall claim.

(d) The applicant must state his grounds for believing that the respondent has the relevant assets. He may have evidence that the assets exist, and be able to exhibit bank statements. Alternatively, the respondent may already have filed an affidavit of means in which the existence of the assets is admitted.

1 See generally the *Practice Direction of 28 July 1994* [1994] 2 FLR 704, [1994] 1 WLR 1233. See also *Practice Direction of 28 October* (1996) Times, 31 October. The former sets out the relevant procedural requirements, and the latter amends and annexes standard forms of Anton Piller orders, world-wide Mareva injunctions, and Mareva injunctions limited to assets within the jurisdiction.
2 These components were considered by the Court of Appeal in *Third Chandris Shipping Corpn v Unimarine SA* [1979] QB 645.
3 See *R v Kensington Income Tax Comrs, ex p Princess Edmond de Polignac* [1917] 1 KB 486.
4 See *Practice Direction of 28 July 1994* [1994] 2 FLR 704, [1994] 1 WLR 1233.

Anton Piller orders

4.188 Anton Piller orders are rare in matrimonial cases. These orders are in the character of search warrants[1]. There will however be matters where the applicant is so concerned that the respondent may dispose of items or documents without disclosing them in the financial relief proceedings that an order may be justified[2].

1 In the *Anton Piller* case, Lord Denning MR described the order as such.
2 In *Emanuel v Emanuel* (1982) 3 FLR 319, [1982] 2 All ER 342, the court authorised the wife's solicitors to enter the husband's and third party's property to look for, inspect and remove all documents relating to the husband's financial position. This is an extremely serious step to take, because it could paralyse a husband's business. For another example of an Anton Piller order made in matrimonial proceedings, refer to *Kepa v Kepa* (1983) 4 FLR 515. Refer also to *Burgess v Burgess* [1996] 2 FLR 34: such orders are only to be used in exceptional cases in family proceedings.

Additional components of any Anton Piller application

4.189 In addition to the factors to be taken into account in any Mareva and Anton Piller applications, the applicant for an Anton Piller order will have to show the following:

(a) that there is a serious risk that unless the order is made items/articles will be destroyed or removed;

(b) the damage for the applicant will be very serious if the injunction is not made[1];

(c) there is clear evidence that the respondent has in his possession the incriminating documents;

(d) there is a real possibility that they may be destroyed before a full application can be made in the proceedings.

1 There is a balance to be struck between the interests of the applicant and the interests of the respondent. Per Scott J in *Columbia Picture Industries v Robinson* [1987] Ch 38: 'A decision whether or not an Anton Piller order should be granted requires a balance to be struck between the plaintiff's needs that the remedies allowed by the civil law for the breach of his rights should be attainable and the requirement of justice that a defendant should not be deprived of his property without being heard'.

The documentation required to make an application for Anton Piller and Mareva orders

4.190 The applicant will need to file at court:

(a) the draft petition for divorce, judicial separation or nullity (if this has not already been issued);

(b) the application (in the High Court this will be by summons)[1];

(c) an affidavit in support setting out the facts and reasons why the injunction is needed;

(d) draft order[2].

In cases of especial urgency it will be possible to attend before the judge without any of those documents, but in those circumstances the applicant will have to undertake to file the documents. Where an appearance in front of the duty judge out of hours is required, it will be necessary to telephone the emergency telephone number provided by the local court[3].

1 And in the county court by application in Form N17A. Invariably however the application will be made to the judge in the High Court rather than to a district judge (see *Practice Direction of 5 June 1992* [1992] 2 FLR 87), notwithstanding that the district judge has jurisdiction to make orders under the inherent jurisdiction under CCR Ord 13, r 6(2), CCR Ord 21, r 5(2B).
2 In the county court this will be in Form N16. Where possible also provide a disk containing the draft in Wordperfect 5.1 for DOS (Practice Direction of 28 October 1996).
3 The relevant number for the High Court in London is 0171 936 6000.

Acting for parties to injunction applications

The applicant

4.191 The applicant should ensure, so far as is possible, that a full and frank disclosure is provided in the affidavit. It will be necessary to serve the order immediately both on the respondent and on any third party, such as a bank, which may be involved in the injunction (it is likely, if the standard form of order annexed to the Practice Direction of 28 July 1994 is used, that only such parts of the order as refer to the third party will need to be served on that party). In the case of an Anton Piller order[1]:

(a) A woman should go along to any premises where the premises are occupied by a woman alone.

(b) Entry to the premises must be between 9.30 am and 5.30 pm (so that the respondent can immediately obtain legal advice), otherwise entry can be refused.

(c) Service of the order should be undertaken, and the order executed and supervised by a solicitor experienced in Anton Piller cases and from a firm other than that of the applicant's solicitor[2].

(d) No item should be removed from premises until the item is listed (to prevent any future dispute on what was taken; the applicant may also need to insure any items of value which are removed).

(e) Search for a removal of items should only be in the presence of the respondent (again to prevent any future dispute about what transpired while the order was being executed).

1 In respect of the following conditions, the authorities are contained in the *Practice Direction of 28 July 1994* [1994] 2 FLR 704, [1994] 1 WLR 1233.
2 See *Universal Thermosensors Ltd v Hibben* [1992] 1 WLR 840.

The respondent

4.192 As far as practicable, any application for the discharge or variation of the order should be dealt with on the return date supplied by the judge when making the ex parte application, rather than beforehand. It is specifically provided in the Practice Direction that if an Anton Piller order or Mareva injunction is discharged on the return date, the judge should also consider whether it is appropriate that he should assess damages at once and direct immediate payment by the applicant. The court's jurisdiction is extraordinarily wide and the respondent's solicitors may be called to provide a very rapid response to overturn or vary an excessive order.

Third party

4.193 A third party who, when aware of the injunction, breaches it is guilty of contempt of court and could be committed to prison. Therefore, for example, if a solicitor permits a sum to be paid out on an account such as his client account that has been frozen by an injunction, he may face serious consequences including, at the very least, suspension from practice.

FINANCIAL PROVISION IN THE CASE OF NEGLECT TO MAINTAIN

4.194 A spouse can make an application under the MCA 1973, s 27 on the ground that the other party has failed to provide reasonable maintenance for the applicant, or has failed to provide, or to make a proper contribution towards, reasonable maintenance for any child of the family[1]. The application can only be made during the marriage and before the institution of any decree proceedings. This kind of relief is, however, useful for a party who does not want to commence decree proceedings and whose spouse is failing to provide adequate financial assistance, and practitioners often threaten to make such applications, knowing that the threat of an application may help their client.

1 MCA 1973, s 27(1).

Jurisdiction

4.195 Jurisdiction is defined by the MCA 1973, s 27(2) which provided that:

(a) either party should be domiciled in England and Wales on the date of the application; or

(b) the applicant should be habitually resident in England and Wales throughout the period of one year ending with the date of the application; or

(c) the respondent is resident in England and Wales on the day of the application.

Relevant considerations in determining a s 27 application

4.196 The court adopts a broad test in determining what kind of relief should be made available to an applicant for financial provision in case of neglect to maintain. All relevant factors including, but not limited to, the s 25(1) and (2) factors will be taken into account (for example, the needs, financial resources and ages of the parties)[1].

1 MCA 1973, s 27(3) and in cases involving children of the family, s 27(3A).

Orders made under MCA 1973, s 27

4.197 If the court is satisfied that reasonable maintenance has not been paid, it can make orders of a capital and of an income nature for the benefit of a spouse or a child of the family (in the case of a child, subject to the Child Support Act 1991, s 8(3) and to restrictions on the making of orders in favour of a child over 18)[1]. The specific orders that can be made are set out in the MCA 1973, s 27(6) and are for periodical payments[2] (which may be of an interim nature[3]), secured periodical payments[4], and orders for a lump sum[5]. Section 27 is most likely to be used when there is an income need. However the facility for the obtaining of a lump sum order is available, for example, against a husband refusing to discharge a sizeable tax bill for which the wife is legally liable; or to discharge mortgage arrears or other liabilities. Indeed s 27(7) specifically provides that a lump sum order may be made for the purpose of enabling any liabilities or expenses reasonably incurred in maintaining the applicant or any child of the family before the making of the application to be met[6].

1 MCA 1973, s 29(1) and (3).
2 Ibid, s 27(6)(a).
3 Ibid, s 27(5).
4 Ibid, s 27(6)(b).
5 Ibid, s 27(6)(c).
6 Ibid, s 27(7)(a) – compare s 23(3).

Procedure for making an application under s 27

4.198 The relevant procedure for an application is set out in the FPR 1991, r 3.1:

(a) The application is made by originating application in Form M19[1] and may be filed at any divorce county court.

(b) It is supported by an affidavit by the applicant (and copies of the documents for service on the respondent)[2].

(c) The applicant's affidavit must provide prescribed[3] information such as full particulars of her property and income (and also of the respondent's property and income so far as may be known to the applicant). The affidavit will need to establish her grounds for an application under the MCA 1973, s 27, ie explaining the basis of the court's jurisdiction in the matter, formal details relating to the marriage of the parties such as appears in a petition, and particulars of the failure to provide reasonable maintenance.

1 FPR 1991, r 3.1(1).
2 Ibid, r 3.1(2).
3 Ibid, r 3.1(3).

Service on respondent

4.199 The respondent has to be served with a copy of the application, a copy of the affidavit, and a notice in Form M20 with Form M16. Within 28[1] days the respondent has the following options:

(a) either to file an affidavit in reply (stating whether he admits failure to maintain, or otherwise and full particulars of his property and income)[2]; or

(b) within the same timescale to file an affidavit setting out the grounds of any challenge to the court's jurisdiction. An affidavit contesting the jurisdiction then freezes the respondent's obligation to file the affidavit of means[3].

1 Ie within 14 days of the 14 days allowed for filing the acknowledgment of service (FPR 1991, r 3.1(5)).
2 FPR 1991, r 3.1(5).
3 Ibid, r 3.1(8). The applicant's affidavit in response to that affidavit should be served within 14 days of receiving the respondent's affidavit (FPR 1991, r 3.1(9)).

Procedural matters

4.200 Procedural issues concerning discovery, disclosure and investigation by the court are available under the FPR 1991, r 3.1 as in ancillary relief cases[1]. If settled by a consent order, the parties will have to comply with the requirements of the FPR 1991, r 2.61[2].

1 FPR 1991, r 3.1(10); for a consideration of ancillary relief procedural issues see paras 2.18 ff (eg r 2.63 questionnaires, para 2.51; production appointments; para 2.53).
2 FPR 1991, r 3.1(10).

MATRIMONIAL AND FAMILY PROCEEDINGS ACT 1984, PART III

Introduction

4.201 An additional layer of financial relief was introduced into the law of England and Wales by Part III of the Matrimonial and Family Proceedings Act 1984, enabling parties who have legally separated, have been divorced or whose marriages have been annulled overseas to make an application for financial relief in this jurisdiction. The legislation was intended to introduce a measure of fairness to a spouse divorced outside this jurisdiction[1]. The case law since this legislation was introduced shows that the courts have been concerned to prevent the legislation from enabling parties to re-apply[2] when they have already obtained satisfactory financial relief in overseas proceedings[3]. Prima facie the order of the foreign court should prevail save in exceptional circumstances[4].

1 The authors know of Islaamic courts in which a wife who has committed adultery has a maximum lump sum entitlement equivalent to £2,000 irrespective of all other factors in a case.

2 This phrase is quoted from the judgment of Thorpe J in *M v M (Financial Provision After Foreign Divorce)* [1994] 1 FLR 399, at 405H. The legislation did not envisage England becoming the 'court of appeal' when parties have exhausted the legal processes in their own jurisdiction.
3 Per Butler-Sloss LJ in *Hewitson v Hewitson* [1995] 1 FLR 241, at 244B to C.
4 Per Russell LJ in *Holmes v Holmes* [1989] 2 FLR 364.

Uses of Part III

Jurisdiction race

4.202 A party may initiate a divorce in England and Wales and find that her spouse has started proceedings in another jurisdiction under which he is able to progress to the divorce and dissolution before she is able to obtain a decree absolute in this country. The wife's entitlement to financial relief under the overseas divorce may be much more restricted than it would have been under proceedings in this jurisdiction. In those circumstances, she may be able to make an application for financial relief in this country under the 1984 Act.

No financial relief in the overseas proceedings

4.203 If a party is left without an effective remedy in the overseas proceedings, she may wish to pursue proceedings under Part III of the 1984 Act[1].

1 Provided that she fulfils the criteria in para 4.204. The Court of Appeal in *Lamagni v Lamagni* [1995] 2 FLR 452 gave leave to the applicant to pursue a claim because she had not obtained any financial provision in a Belgian divorce which had taken place some 14 years earlier. In *M v M*, Thorpe J was sufficiently concerned about the future financial position of the former wife under the French proceedings that, whilst not dismissing her application for leave to apply under the Matrimonial and Family Proceedings Act 1984, he adjourned it generally with liberty to the wife to restore in exceptional circumstances – there is a suggestion at 244D and E of *Hewitson v Hewitson* that Butler-Sloss LJ did not necessarily agree with that aspect of the judgment.

The filter of leave

4.204 Statute has ensured that it is only possible to pursue an application for substantive financial relief[1] in this jurisdiction under the 1984 Act if the applicant obtains the leave of the court to apply for financial relief. The granting of leave is a substantial matter for the court to consider, as the court only grants leave if it considers that there is substantial ground for the making of an application for a financial relief order[2], ie there has to be some forward-thinking by the court to the kind of order that it would make at any final hearing[3].

1 It is appreciated that even if orders are made under the Matrimonial and Family Proceedings Act 1984, the applicant is faced with problems of enforcing the order but that is no different from the party's position if she had obtained orders in the course of the divorce proceedings in this jurisdiction.
2 As in *Hewitson v Hewitson* [1995] 1 FLR 241; the test is 'stringent'.
3 See *Z v Z (Financial Provision: Overseas Divorce)* [1992] 2 FLR 291; this was approved in *Hewitson v Hewitson*: in considering whether there is substantial ground for making

an application the likely outcome of the application, if made, has to be highly relevant (per Butler-Sloss LJ at 243H).

The procedure for obtaining leave to make an application for financial relief

4.205 The procedure is set out in the FPR 1991, r 3.17 and is, briefly, as follows:

(a) The application for leave is made ex parte[1] by originating summons in Form M25. It is issued out the Principal Registry of the Family Division, and must be supported by an affidavit by the applicant. The affidavit will state the facts relied on in support of the application and must refer in particular to the facts set out in s 16(2) of the 1984 Act, those being the matters which the court is under a duty to consider before granting leave.

(b) The affidavit must give the various particulars set out in the FPR 1991, r 3.17(2)[2].

(c) The applicant then receives notice of the date, time and place fixed for the hearing of the application by a judge in chambers. The respondent does not receive notice of the application[3].

(d) It may seem to the judge hearing the application for leave that the applicant or any child of the family is in immediate need of financial assistance. In those circumstances (save in cases where the only ground for jurisdiction under the 1984 Act is that either party has an interest in a dwelling house situated in England or Wales which was at some stage during the marriage a matrimonial home of the parties to the marriage) the court may make an interim order for maintenance[4].

1 The ex parte procedure has been criticised robustly by both judges and counsel in Part III Matrimonial and Family Proceedings Act 1984 cases. It was criticised both by the Court of Appeal and by the judge at first instance in *Hewitson v Hewitson* (and see the article by Mark Everall QC at [1984] Fam Law 549).
2 Including the names of the parties, the date and place of the marriage, the occupation and residence of each of the parties, etc.
3 In *M v M*, the respondent's solicitors knew that an application was going to be made and the applicant's solicitors were criticised by Thorpe J for not answering their enquiries about the date of the application.
4 Matrimonial and Family Proceedings Act 1984, s 14(1).

Progressing the application after leave has been granted

4.206 If the judge grants leave to the applicant to apply for financial relief, the applicant will progress her application for financial relief using the procedure set out in the FPR 1991, r 3.18. The following points arise:

(a) The affidavit in support of the application for an order may well repeat the contents of the affidavit filed in support of the application for leave. The applicant is required under r 3.18(1) to ensure that the affidavit in support of the application gives full particulars of his property and income. This may therefore go beyond the scope of the affidavit filed in support of the application for leave, which is obliged to contain an estimate in summary form of the appropriate amount or value of the capital resources and net income of each party and of any minor child of the family[1].

(b) It may be that the parties have already filed affidavits in divorce proceedings in this jurisdiction, in a case where the respondent has been pursuing proceedings for divorce simultaneously in another jurisdiction[2]. It is possible to ask the court direct that the affidavits filed in the divorce proceedings should stand as affidavits within the proceedings under Part III of the 1984 Act. The divorce matter and the Matrimonial and Family Proceedings Act 1984 matter will be consolidated.

(c) An application under the 1984 Act will be prosecuted in the same kind of way as any application for financial relief under the MCA 1973. For example, it is specifically provided for by the FPR 1991, r 3.18(3) that a party can put in a questionnaire as under FPR 1991, r 2.63; and the court may order the attendance of any person for the purpose of being examined or cross-examined and the discovery and production of any document.

1 FPR 1991, r 3.17(2)(e).
2 In this kind of a case, ensure (if acting for a wife) that any Class F protection over the former matrimonial home is appropriately extended before the overseas divorce.

The substantive orders which may be made under Part III

4.207 These orders are set out in the Matrimonial and Family Proceedings Act 1984, s 17 and include financial provision, property adjustment and s 24A orders[1] under the MCA 1973.

1 Matrimonial and Family Proceedings Act 1984, s 23.

Avoidance of transactions intended to defeat applications for financial relief[1]

4.208 The Matrimonial and Family Proceedings Act 1984 provides relief analogous to the relief available under the MCA 1973, s 37. The procedure relating to any application under the Matrimonial and Family Proceedings Act 1984, s 23 is as set out in the FPR 1991, r 3.18.

1 Subject to the restrictions referred to in s 20 of the 1984 Act.

FAMILY LAW ACT 1996

4.209 When the Family Law Act 1996 is in force[1], the parties will not be able to obtain separation or divorce orders unless the financial matters have been resolved, or one of the parties has declared to the court that it would be otiose for any financial arrangement to be made. In the vast majority of cases, therefore, the divorce/separation proceedings and the financial proceedings will proceed together and financial orders will not be made (as is common under the present law) months or even years after the divorce.

1 See para 3.27 ff.

Amendments made by the Family Law Act 1996

4.210 The following general points may be made about the way in which the law relating to financial relief is being changed.

Nullity

4.211 Since the procedures for obtaining a decree of nullity are not being amended, broadly speaking the financial relief available on nullity remains the same.

Timing of orders

4.212 There is now going to be more flexibility in relation to the financial orders made in divorce/separation proceedings[1]. It will be possible for lump sum and property adjustment orders to be made and to become effective before the divorce/separation order. Further, the courts will be able to make interim lump sum orders.

1 A suggestion made by the Law Commission, and taken up in the Government's Green and White Papers.

Variation/discharge of capital orders

4.213 There is a new procedure which will enable lump sum and property adjustment orders to be varied or discharged on the joint application of parties. This is intended to cater for parties who reconcile and want to unscramble the orders made on divorce/separation.

Pensions

4.214 Most controversially, the court may ultimately have power to split pensions.

Family Law Act 1996, Part I

4.215 The court and any person[1] in exercising the functions set out in Parts II and III of the FLA 1996 will have regard to the general principles set out in Part 1 of the Act. The matters which are most likely to be relevant to the practitioner dealing with financial matters, and which undoubtedly inform any amending rules which will come into force in tandem with the new law, will be designed to reflect the general principles that:

(a) questions should be dealt with in a manner designed to promote as good a continuing relationship between the parties and any children affected as is possible in the circumstances[2]; and

(b) costs should not be unreasonably incurred in connection with the procedures leading to divorce/separation[3].

1 Including, of course, the legal advisers of the parties.
2 FLA 1996, s 1(c)(ii).
3 Ibid, 1(c)(iii). And see para 4.28, n 1 about the pilot changes to ancillary relief procedures introduced in October 1996.

Family Law Act 1996, s 15 and Sch 2

4.216 The FLA 1996, Sch 2 amends substantially the MCA 1973, ss 23 and 24[1]. The main object of Sch 2 is:

(a) to provide that, in the case of divorce or separation, an order for financial provision may be made under the MCA 1973 whether a divorce order or separation order is made; but

(b) to retain (with certain changes) the provision under the MCA 1973 where marriages are annulled.

1 See paras 4.53 ff.

The financial provision orders made on divorce and separation

4.217 Sections 22A and 22B are inserted into the MCA 1973, and set out the financial provision orders available on divorce or separation (and a new s 23 is substituted for the old s 23, dealing with the financial provision available in nullity cases).

Timing of financial provision order

4.218 A financial provision order (redefined in a new s 21 which does not substantively amend the old s 21 definitions) may be made at any time after the statement of marital breakdown has been received by the court[1]. It may therefore be possible for a financial provision order to be made within a much shorter timescale than is available under the present divorce system.

1 Subject to the limitations set out in s 22A(2) and the general restrictions set out in s 22B.

Interim orders

4.219 The financial provision orders may either be interim orders (maintenance pending suit under the MCA 1973, s 22 will be repealed under Sch 10) or they will be 'full' and final orders. The court under the Act will have the flexibility of making interim orders not only for periodical payments but also for the payment of a lump sum in favour of a party or a child. The jurisdiction to make interim orders will be exercisable by the court if the court 'would not otherwise be in a position to make a financial provision order in favour of a party or child of the family'[1].

1 MCA 1973, s 22A(4).

The occasions for interim orders

4.220 Only an interim order may take effect before the making of the divorce/separation order, unless the court is satisfied[1] that the circumstances of the case are exceptional; and that it would be just and reasonable for the order to be so made. This new jurisdiction will therefore cater for those occasions when under the present law an application is made for *Barry* or *F v F* orders reallocating matrimonial assets amongst the parties before a final order[2]. It would be better for a party seeking a lump sum on an interim basis to obtain an interim lump sum order rather than a full financial provision order taking effect, in exceptional circumstances, before the divorce/separation order: only one lump sum order is available to a party in the proceedings.

1 MCA 1973, s 22B(1).
2 See para 4.55.

Different orders on different occasions

4.221 Normally the court would make financial provision orders at the same time, but it will be able to make a separate order on different occasions[1].

1 MCA 1973, s 22A(3).

Directions as to payment of lump sum order

4.222 The MCA 1973, s 22A provides, like its predecessor, for payments of a lump sum to be made by instalments[1]; the instalments of a lump sum order may be secured[2]; and by way of order made at any time after the lump sum order, for interest to be paid on the lump sum order[3].

1 MCA 1973, s 22A(5)(a).
2 Ibid, s 22A(5)(b).
3 Ibid, s 22A(7) and (8) thereby avoiding the trap in *L v L (Lump Sum: Interest)* [1994] 2 FLR 324.

Financial provision orders after divorce/separation orders

4.223 There will be exceptional circumstances when a party will apply for a financial provision order after the divorce/separation order has been obtained; such as that a party's application for a lump sum has been adjourned; or where a party believes that the other party had no significant assets and did not intend to make an application for financial provision[1] – there then being a dramatic change in the financial circumstances of the other party. In these circumstances it may in fact be rather more difficult under the new law for the applicant to launch an application. Under the present law, so long as the applicant had made an application for financial relief in his petition or answer, he would not need leave to pursue the application following a divorce. In the future an applicant will have to get within the s 22B(4) criterion of leave.

1 And so falling within the FLA 1996, s 9(2)(d).

Financial provision and property adjustment in nullity cases

4.224 A new s 23 is substituted which applies to the financial provision orders available on nullity only. It does not substantively amend the financial relief available on nullity under the existing law. There is not going to be the facility in nullity cases to obtain the interim lump sum orders which are available in divorce/separation cases. This does not affect the ability of a party to nullity proceedings attempting to obtain a *Barry* order in appropriate circumstances.

4.225 The property adjustment orders available in nullity proceedings are in a new s 24[1]. Again, this repeats the existing law, but now specifies that the court shall exercise its powers to make property adjustment orders, so far as is practicable, by making on one occasion all such provision as can be made by way of one or more property adjustment orders in relation to the marriage as it thinks fit[2].

1 FLA 1996, Sch 2 para 6.
2 The new s 24(2).

Property adjustment orders on divorce and separation

4.226 The new law is contained in the MCA 1973, s 23A and s 23B, as a result of which the court may make one or more property adjustment orders. The property adjustment orders are the same four types of orders available under the present law (they are redefined at s 21(2) of the amended Act). As is the case with financial provision orders, only one property adjustment order may be made in favour of the same party in the marital proceedings. The court will normally deal with a party's claim for property adjustment orders on one occasion, so far as is practicable[1].

1 MCA 1973, s 23A(3).

Timing of property adjustment order

4.227 As is the case with full financial provision orders, normally no property adjustment order may be made under s 23A so as to take effect before the making of a divorce or separation order[1]. It will however be possible[2] to obtain a property adjustment order with immediate effect, so long as the court is satisfied: that the circumstances of the case are exceptional; and that it would be just and reasonable for the order to be so made. It will not be possible to obtain interim property adjustment orders unless the circumstances of the case are exceptional[3].

1 The new s 23B(1). That is because interim orders are sticking plaster relief. The case for a jointly owned property to be transferred into the name of only one of the parties to the marriage before the final order will hardly ever be made out, as (subject to the capital gains tax points made at paras 2.44 ff) there is rarely any practical requirement for it to happen. The occupation of the property will be regulated as set out in paras 4.73 ff above.
2 The new s 23B(4).
3 The new s 23B(1).

4.228 As with financial provision orders, no property adjustment orders may be made after divorce/separation, except in response to an application made before the divorce order or separation order was made; or on a subsequent application made with the leave of the court[1].

1 The new s 23B(4).

The period of secured and unsecured periodical payments orders

4.229 Paragraph 7 amends the MCA 1973, ss 28 and 29, in respect of the commencement date and duration of secured and unsecured periodical payments orders. Where the court is making a secured or unsecured periodical payments order in favour of a spouse after a statement of marital breakdown, whether before or after an application for a separation or divorce order has been made by reference to that statement, then that order may be backdated to the date when the statement of marital breakdown was received by the court[1]. Different backdating provisions will apply when the order is being made in circumstances such as the conversion from separation to divorce, or an application for a divorce order following cancellation of the order preventing divorce[2].

1 See the new s 28(1)(a)(i).
2 Ibid, s 28(1)(a)(ii).

Variations etc following reconciliation

4.230 Section 31A is inserted into the MCA 1973, giving an entirely new variation power which will apply when parties reconcile and want to unscramble lump sum and property adjustment orders. The application has to be made jointly by the parties to the marriage, and the court has power to make such supplementary directions as they require to bring the variation or discharge into effect. The variation will not be ordered unless it appears to the court that there has been a reconciliation between the parties[1] and the order will not be made unless it appears to the court that the order will not prejudice the interests of any child of the family; or a third party who has acquired any right or interest in consequence of the property adjustment order and is not a party to the marriage or a child of the family[2].

1 MCA 1973, s 31A(6).
2 Ibid, s 31A(7)(a) and (b).

Pension-splitting orders[1]

4.231 The concept of pension-splitting is included in s 16, which amends the MCA 1973 by adding provisions to s 25B and s 25D, which provide for the division of pension rights between parties. This legislation is enabling legislation only: the Government will have to consult widely on the complex issues such as tax treatment which will result from pension-splitting. There will be the usual consultation process of a Green Paper[2] followed by a White Paper and then the introduction of detailed regulations. When s 16 becomes effective, it is certain that pension-splitting orders are going to be made as a matter of course, and it will be negligent for a practitioner not to consider the possibility of enabling clients to benefit from such an order. There may, however, be cases where the other assets in the case are such that the wife can receive a fair share of the entire pot without any pension-splitting order being made.

1 The concept of pension-splitting was made part of the Family Law Bill during the Report Stage in the House of Lords in February 1996. The financial memorandum preceding the published Bill brought from the Lords on 11 March 1996 plaintively comments that Clause 15 of the FLB 'would lead to additional public expenditure by way of administration costs for public service pension schemes and could result in a substantial loss of tax revenue'.
2 Published in July 1996.

Minor and consequential amendments to the MCA

4.232 The FLA 1996, Sch 8 operates to make a number of consequential amendments to the MCA 1973 consequent on the changes to the Act which were noted above.

Capital orders on variation applications

4.233 There is a significant amendment to the s 31 powers which enables the court where, after the dissolution of a marriage, the periodical payments order or secured periodical payments order is discharged; or where the court varies such an order so that payments under the order are required to be made or secured only for such further period as determined by the court; to make a supplemental order for the payment of a lump sum or one or more property adjustment orders. The court is therefore given the power which it lacks under the MCA 1973 to fix the lump sum which capitalises the maintenance entitlement of a wife[1]. A husband may be concerned that there is no mechanism which ties the calculation of the lump sum to the maintenance entitlement. It is therefore theoretically possible for the court to make a punitive lump sum or property adjustment order which is out of proportion to the periodical payments order. It is a chink in the clean break.

1 Thereby dealing with the problem highlighted in *S v S* [1986] 3 All ER 566.

The date when the clean break may become effective

4.234 Where the court is considering an application for financial provision in relation to a divorce before the granting of a divorce order, any direction given by the court which has effect of operating the clean break principle shall only come into effect on the making of a divorce order.

TAX CONSIDERATIONS

4.235 The relevance of tax considerations in financial relief is highlighted as follows.

Income tax

4.236 There is a distinction to be made between old maintenance orders and agreements on the one hand, and orders/agreements made since 15 March 1988 on the other hand.

Old rules: pre-30 June 1988 obligations

4.237 The old rules apply:

(a) to court orders made before 15 March 1988;

(b) to court orders which were applied for on or before 15 March 1988, and made by 30 June 1988;

(c) to maintenance agreements made before 15 March 1988. For tax relief to continue under the old rules for payments made on or after 15 March 1988, a copy of the agreement must have been received at the Tax Office by 30 June 1988. If it was not, the new rules apply to all payments due on or after 15 March 1988;

(d) to replacement court orders and agreements, including assessments made by the Child Support Agency, which amend payments under arrangements to which the old rules apply, and where there is no change in the person(s) to whom the payments are made[1].

1 Finance Act 1988, s 36(4).

TAX RELIEF

4.238 So far as the old orders are concerned, they enable the payer of periodical payments for the benefit of a spouse, former spouse, or child of the family under the age of 21[1], to obtain a measure of tax relief in respect of the maintenance payments due under the order. The relief is pegged (under the Finance Act 1988, s 38(3)) by the relief which the payer was receiving during the tax year to 5 April 1989, and the relief will consist of: a deduction from the payer's total taxable income of the total amount of maintenance as spousal maintenance and for all relevant children; or £1,790 (in both cases during the tax year 1996/97, at 15%) whichever is the lesser[2]. If the spouse through whom the child maintenance payments are being made remarries, the payer will lose the extra tax allowance even though the payments are still being made for the benefit of a child or children.

1 The Finance Act 1994, s 79(2) excludes from tax relief payments made to children when they reach their 21st birthday on or after 6 April 1994.
2 Income and Corporation Taxes Act 1988, s 347B, inserted by the Finance Act 1988, s 36.

150 *Maintenance and Property Distribution*

THE PAYEE

4.239 The maintenance payments are made gross to the payee, who will then have to pay income tax at her appropriate marginal rate on the maintenance payments (albeit that she will be able to apply her personal allowance against the maintenance payments and other income which she may be receiving).

INCREASES IN MAINTENANCE

4.240 Tax relief is *not* available for any payments made by the payer over and on top of the tax relievable maintenance payments pegged during 1988/89. Therefore any additional amount of maintenance, payable because of a subsequent variation whether by consent or otherwise, will be paid on a tax neutral basis, without tax relief being received by the payer on those additional amounts and without tax having to be paid on those amounts by the payee.

New rules – payments

4.241 The position under the new rules is that the qualifying[1] payments are tax neutral, save that the payer is able to apply the additional relief[2] to his single person's allowance[3], or the amount of the payment if that is less than the additional relief. The payee pays no income tax on the maintenance payments which she receives on that basis.

1 The payments will qualify for tax relief if all the following four conditions are satisfied: The payer must be making payments under:
  (a) a United Kingdom court order, or a United Kingdom written agreement which is legally enforceable, or an assessment made by the Child Support Agency (for payments due and made on or after 6 April 1993), or a court order made under the Social Security Acts ordering maintenance to be paid to the DSS (for payments due and made on or after 6 April 1993);
  (b) the payments are made to the divorced or separated husband or wife of the payer, or although paid to the DSS, are treated as if made to him or her;
  (c) he or she has not remarried;
  (d) the payments are for his or her own maintenance, *or* for his or her maintenance of a child under 21 of whom both the payer and the payee are the parents, or who have been treated as a child of the family.
2 £1,790 during 1996/1997.
3 £3,765 during 1996/1997.

Election for new rules

4.242 It is possible for a payer under the old rules to elect to apply the post–1988 rules to the payment of maintenance[1]. The election has to be made by the end of the tax year to apply for the preceding year and any future years. The election has to be submitted to the Revenue and served on the payee within 30 days of its being made[2].

1 The Finance Act 1988, s 39, which consequently applies to the Finance Act 1988, s 36, and disapplies the Finance Act 1988, s 37 and s 38.
2 It will be rare for anyone to want to come off the old rules on to the new rules, but there are circumstances where it might be in the payer's best interests for this to happen. It may be, for example, that a payer of maintenance under a pre–1988 order will not actually be receiving any tax relief on the maintenance payments that he makes (for instance because he was domiciled outside the United Kingdom during the

tax year to 5 April 1989) but the payee is deemed by the Revenue to be liable to income tax on the periodical payments, and this fairly eccentric scenario has been known to occur. In these circumstances the payer is not prejudiced by going on to the new rules, and the payee gains by saving the tax which she would otherwise have to pay on the maintenance payments.

Tax paid in another jurisdiction

4.243 Special attention has to be paid to the tax treatment of spouses (for example Americans) who are obliged to pay tax in another jurisdiction. The maintenance payments may be taxable in their hands[1]. A trap for the unwary is that even the payment of a *Duxbury* sum may[2] prove to be taxable in another jurisdiction. The assistance of an accountant in drafting any consent order in these circumstances is advisable.

1 But the payer may be entitled to tax relief on those payments: this does not necessarily entail the payee having to pay tax on the maintenance; it will be a question of applying the relevant tax domicile rules.
2 See para 4.41.

Capital gains tax

4.244 No capital gains tax will be chargeable on transfers between a husband and wife who have not separated[1]. Where, however, the parties have separated, capital gains tax is going to be chargeable in relation to the gain on any transaction made between the parties (subject to the matrimonial homes exception[2]) unless the transaction takes place in the tax year during which the parties separated and before the decree absolute[3].

1 Taxation of Chargeable Gains Act 1992, s 58(1).
2 See para 4.245.
3 This is conceded as a matter of practice by the Inland Revenue, despite the fact that s 58(1) does not make the position absolutely clear. It may be necessary to consider making tax-effective transfers between the parties in cases where overall terms of settlement have not been agreed. These transfers can be made on the basis that they are without prejudice to the overall terms of settlement.

The matrimonial home – extra-statutory concession dated 22 October 1973, D36

4.245 This operates so as to exempt from capital gains tax the disposition of a party's interest in the matrimonial home or former matrimonial home to the other party, provided that the transferee spouse has continued to live in the house as his or her only or main residence; and provided that the transferring party has not elected for any other property to be his main residence for capital gains tax purposes during the period from the date when he left the property to the date of transfer of his interest[1].

1 It may be better to rely on the three-year rule (under which absence from the property during the last three years of ownership is always disregarded: Taxation of Chargeable Gains Act 1992, s 223(1)); the problem with the extra-statutory concession is that the transferor spouse will lose the capital gains exemption in relation to the new property owned by him or her for such time as the extra-statutory concession applies.

Maintenance and Property Distribution

Principal private residence exemption

4.246 The transfer of a party's interest in the former matrimonial home may in any case be exempt from capital gains tax by virtue of the fact that it is the transferring party's principal private residence (PPR)[1]. The PPR exemption applies (under the current law) for a period of three years from the date of separation. However the period was increased from three years because of the recession in housing prices, and so may be altered at some stage. The common experience of practitioners is that, with the operation of the extra-statutory concession, the PPR relief, and indexation allowance[2], a transferring party is rarely liable to capital gains tax on transfer of his or her share in the property to the other spouse. The amount of the gain will in any case be reduced by the amount which is exempt from capital gains tax each year[3].

1 Taxation of Chargeable Gains Act 1992, s 222(1).
2 Indexation allowance applies the increase in the Retail Prices Index from the date the asset was acquired or 31 March 1982 (if later) until the date of disposal. The current position is regulated by the Finance Act 1988.
3 £6,300 during 1996/97.

INDEMNITIES RELATING TO CAPITAL GAINS TAX

4.247 If there is any question of capital gains tax arising on any transfers between the parties, it is necessary to consider whether or not the transferring spouse will want to be indemnified by the other spouse as to the tax that will be payable. If so, incorporate an indemnity into any order[1].

1 See, eg Precedent 16 in the *Precedents for Consent Orders* published by the SFLA.

Stamp duty

4.248 The relevance of this subject is that whenever there is a transfer of property following a court order, the transfer will to be exempt from stamp duty under paragraph H of the Stamp Duty (Exempt Instruments) Regulations 1987, SI 1987/516[1].

1 Which relates to conveyances or transfers of property within s 83(1) of the Finance Act 1985 (transfers in connection with divorce etc).

BANKRUPTCY AND FAMILY BREAKDOWN

4.249 In 1995 there were 21,933 bankruptcies in England and Wales. When these figures are set against a divorce rate presently set for 41% there are likely to be many instances when the problems associated with the breakdown of a marriage will be exacerbated by the previous or subsequent bankruptcy of a partner to the marriage. The problems commonly arising in such situations and in particular, the impact of the provisions of the Insolvency Act 1986 on the breakdown as regards maintenance and property distribution are considered here. Those situations when an individual's insolvency results in an individual voluntary arrangement are not touched on since the Insolvency Act 1986 only has limited application to such arrangements. For the purposes of this exercise it is assumed that it is the husband who becomes the subject of the bankruptcy order. All references to section numbers and rules relate to the Insolvency Act 1986 unless stated otherwise.

Effect of bankruptcy

4.250 By s 306 the bankrupt's estate vests (without conveyance, assignment or transfer) in his trustee in bankruptcy immediately on his appointment taking effect, or in the case of the Official Receiver, on his becoming trustee. It is then the trustee's duty under s 385 to realise and distribute the bankrupt's estate amongst those creditors who will have proved for their debts, in the order prescribed by the Insolvency Act 1986. The trustee, in most cases, has within three years from the bankruptcy order to complete this task after which the bankrupt husband will be automatically discharged. On discharge, the bankrupt is released from all his bankruptcy debts and restrictions other than certain narrow classes of debt including family proceedings awards, the significance of which is considered below. By this stage however, the bankrupt's assets ought to have been realised by the trustee for the creditors' benefit.

The matrimonial home

4.251 In most cases, by far the most significant of the bankrupt's assets will be the matrimonial home. By s 306, if the matrimonial home is in the husband's sole name, the whole legal and beneficial interest will vest in his trustee. If the home is held in joint names, only the bankrupt's beneficial share under the trust for sale will vest. Common practical concerns arising from this are:

(a) If the home is solely owned by the husband, what steps can the wife take to stay in the property or prevent a sale by the trustee?

(b) If, on the face of it, the property is in the bankrupt husband's sole name, in what circumstances can the wife establish a beneficial interest and if successful, what can she do to protect such interest?

(c) If jointly owned, what is the wife's position? How can her interest be protected?

The solely owned matrimonial home

4.252 The provisions of ss 336 and 337 operate effectively to prevent the sale of the matrimonial home for 12 months provided it is occupied by the bankrupt's spouse and/or by the bankrupt with minor children. By the Matrimonial Homes Act, 1983, s 1, the wife, who otherwise has no beneficial interest in the home, will possess a statutory right of occupation which means that, except will leave of the court, she cannot be evicted from the matrimonial home if in occupation or if not, prevented from entering and occupying the home. If the wife possesses this right, it should be protected by prompt registration; by a Class F Land Charge if the property is unregistered, by a notice if registered. This protection does of course come to an end on decree absolute and so the wife's right should be re-registered at such time.

4.253 The trustee can seek to terminate the wife's right of occupation in the first 12 months after the husband's bankruptcy by applying under the Matrimonial Homes Act 1983 where the matrimonial home is vested in the husband's sole name. Where such an application is made, the court under s 336(4) must take the following factors into consideration:

(a) the interests of the husband's creditors;

(b) the degree to which the wife's conduct contributed to the husband's bankruptcy;

(c) the financial resources and needs of the wife;

(d) the needs of any children; and

(e) all the circumstances of the case other than the needs of the bankrupt husband.

The bankruptcy court must make its order on the basis of what is just and reasonable having considered the above, mainly competing, interests. As regards an application made by the trustee during the 12 month period following the bankruptcy order, the wife will, in most cases, be successful in resisting the application. However, after this period the position changes by virtue of s 336(5) which states that unless the circumstances of the case are exceptional, the interests of the bankrupt's creditors will outweigh all other considerations. At this point the bankrupt husband's right of occupation provided for by s 337 will also end. On this basis, if by this stage, the husband and his wife have separated and the wife remains in the property, in what circumstances might she be able to demonstrate that exceptional circumstances exist?

CASE LAW GUIDANCE

4.254 Guidance from case law on this question is very limited but such that exists suggests that the wife's interest might prevail if the house is say, adapted specially for a handicapped child or if either the spouse or the child is terminally ill. The prospect of the wife and her children being rendered homeless will not amount to exceptional circumstances[1]. In the vast majority of cases therefore, the trustee's application will succeed.

1 *Re Citro* [1990] 3 All ER 952.

4.255 It may be, of course, that the trustee decides to delay seeking an order after the expiration of the 12 month period. This has been quite common in recent years when trustees have postponed the sale process in the hope that property prices will increase. However, once the 12 months has elapsed and exceptional circumstances do not exist, the trustee can make his application under the Matrimonial Homes Act 1983 to terminate the wife's statutory right of occupation and seek an order for possession. Pending such order, the trustee can seek an order under s 1(3) of the Matrimonial Homes Act 1983 for an order that the wife either makes a payment in respect of the occupation or is obliged to repair and maintain the property. Whether such an order is made will depend on the wife's own financial circumstances.

Establishing a beneficial interest

4.256 If the property is in the bankrupt husband's sole name the entire legal and equitable interest will vest automatically in the trustee. If the wife is not in occupation at the time, the protection afforded by s 336 will not bite and the trustee will be able to move immediately to sell the property. If the wife remains in occupation the trustee is unlikely to initiate the sale process until after the 12 month period elapses. In either case, if the wife can demonstrate a beneficial interest in the property, the trustee will be bound by the wife's right.

4.257 The wife's ability to demonstrate such an interest will in each case turn on the facts.

(a) She will succeed if she can demonstrate that she has contributed towards the acquisition of the property whether by contributing towards the deposit or subsequent mortgage payments. In such circumstances a resulting trust arises and the wife, as the contributing party, will receive a sum proportional to the amount she originally contributed[1].

(b) In some cases she may succeed on the basis of her conduct. Until recently this depended on there having been, prior to the purchase of the property, an agreement between the husband and the wife that the property was to be shared beneficially and the wife then acted to her detriment in reliance on such agreement[2]. Such action might include renovating or decorating the house, working in its grounds, or meeting household expenses. However following the decision in *Midland Bank v Cooke*[3] the position now is that the necessary constructive trust can be established by the wife's conduct alone. Thus the wife's contribution to the upbringing of the children and the maintenance and improvement of the matrimonial home can now be sufficient to result in her being awarded with an interest in the property under a constructive trust.

1 *Dyer v Dyer* (1788) 2 Cox Eq Cas 92; *Cowcher v Cowcher* [1972] 1 All ER 943.
2 *Eves v Eves* [1975] 1 WLR 1338, CA; *Pettitt v Pettitt* [1970] AC 777; *Gissing v Gissing* [1971] AC 886; *Lloyds Bank v Rosset* [1990] 2 FLR 155, HL.
3 *Midland Bank v Cooke* [1995] 4 All ER 562.

SIGNIFICANCE OF ESTABLISHING A BENEFICIAL INTEREST

4.258 The importance of establishing a beneficial interest lies in the consequent improvement to the wife's financial position. However, although it will mean that the wife occupies the matrimonial home as of right, rather than by the virtue of the Matrimonial Homes Act 1983, s 1 this does not mean that she will be in a better position to prevent the trustee from obtaining an order for sale. In such circumstances, the trustee's application for an order for possession and sale is made under the Law of Property Act 1925, s 30 and again the court must take into consideration the provisions of both ss 336(4) and 336(5) in reaching its decision. Given the difficulty in demonstrating the existence of exceptional circumstances, this will mean that, in all but a few cases, after the initial 12 month period, the wife will find it difficult to resist the trustee's application despite having successfully asserted a beneficial interest. This will also be the case where the wife's interest in the property is a legal one.

The jointly owned matrimonial home

4.259 If the matrimonial home is jointly owned and the husband and wife hold the property as joint tenants the husband's bankruptcy will automatically sever the joint tenancy. The husband's share then vests in the trustee.

4.260 The determination of both parties' respective shares in the property can on occasions either be unclear or disputed. Assuming this is not the case, how can the wife, whether divorced or not, protect her position? As considered before, after the husband's interest has vested, the trustee may decide upon postponing the sale process. Alternatively he may obtain an order for possession and then apply to the court for a charge over the property but in either case the wife has little control over these decisions.

4.261 As far as the sale of jointly owned property is concerned, if the wife refuses to sell, the trustee will have to apply under the Law of Property Act, s 30 for an order. Again, on such application the s 336(4) factors considered above will have to be taken into account. Because of the uphill struggle the trustee will face in obtaining an order within the first twelve months of the husband's bankruptcy, he will almost certainly defer his application until the expiry of this period, after which the point he will probably succeed given the effect of s 336(5).

EQUITY OF EXONERATION

4.262 There is however one other way in which the wife can seek to improve her position following her husband's bankruptcy. This is by asserting her right of exoneration[1]. By this doctrine where jointly held property has been mortgaged for the husband's debts, the wife can insist that the husband's share is used first. The wife will not succeed, however, where the trustee is able to prove that the wife has benefited from the husband's debt, however indirectly. An example of indirect benefit would be where a husband mortgages his share in the matrimonial home as security for his business. It has been held that in such circumstances the wife did benefit from the husband's debt because the mortgage enabled the husband to continue to draw funds from the company from which he met household expenses and supported his wife's lifestyle. In practice, it follows that the circumstances in which the wife will be able to successfully assert her right of exoneration will be relatively limited.

1 *Re Pittortou* [1985] 1 All ER 285.

Reviewable transactions

4.263 Consideration so far has only been given to the fate of the matrimonial home from a post-bankruptcy perspective. What about the transfer of the home or any interest in it prior to the husband's bankruptcy, in particular where such transfer is made to the wife? At first glance, this ought not to merit much attention. If the husband has previously transferred his interest in the matrimonial home to his wife or any other party prior to his bankruptcy there will be nothing to vest in the trustee under s 306. However, this ignores the provisions of the MCA 1973, s 39 which enables a property transfer order to be set aside by the Bankruptcy Court if s 339 or s 340 of the Insolvency Act 1986 applies. Given the extremely serious consequences this is likely to have on the wife, it is important for the practitioner to identify any transaction which might fall within s 339 or the other two sections considered below.

Transactions at an undervalue

4.264 Section 339 concerns transactions at an undervalue. The husband will enter into a transaction at an undervalue if he makes a gift to someone for which he receives either no consideration or consideration that is significantly less than the consideration provided by him. An impecunious husband may well be tempted to transfer his interest in the matrimonial home to his wife on such basis if there is a likelihood of him being made bankrupt in the not too distant future. Being unaware of s 339 he might believe that such action would prevent the home from falling into the clutches of his creditors after his bankruptcy. However this belief would be mistaken. In such circumstances, the bankrupt husband's trustee can apply to the court to set aside such a transaction if it has been made within the relevant time. This will be either within five years prior to the presentation of the bankruptcy petition or two years if the pre-existing presumption that the bankrupt was insolvent or became insolvent due to the transaction arising from the transfer to his wife is rebutted. If the trustee seeks to set aside the transaction made between the husband and his wife within the two to five year period prior to the presentation of the bankruptcy petition, the wife has to prove that her husband was not or did not become insolvent as a result of the transfer. If the trustee applies within the two year period before the presentation of the Petition, no proof is needed of the insolvency requirements. It will be sufficient for the trustee to demonstrate to the court that the transaction was at an undervalue.

CASE LAW

4.265 The principal cases on this subject have centered around the question of consideration and whether the surrender, by the wife, of her financial claims against her husband in exchange for the transfer of the matrimonial home into her name is proper consideration. The present position would seem to be that such compromise can amount to consideration in money or money's worth but only if the right given up is measurably similar to the value of the interest transferred to her under the court order[1]. If the trustee's application is successful, the court has wide powers under s 425 which include the vesting of the transferred property in the trustee.

1 *Re Abbott* [1983] Ch 45; *Re Kumar* [1993] 2 FLR 382.

Voidable preferences

4.266 The trustee can also seek the same order by demonstrating that the husband has given a preference. By s 440, this will be given where the husband, at the relevant time, does anything, or allows anything to be done which has the effect of putting the recipient in a better position than would have been the case had that thing not been done and the recipient is one of the bankrupt's creditors or a guarantor of one of his debts or liabilities. If the wife falls within any of these classes (typically where she has guaranteed the husband's business) and the preference is given within the relevant period before the presentation of the petition (which, in this case, is two years where the preference given is to the bankrupt's 'associate' or six months otherwise) the trustee may obtain relief under s 425. By s 435 the husband's spouse is an associate.

4.267 It is generally less likely that a trustee will obtain an order on the basis of a transfer of the matrimonial home from husband to wife constituting a preference because the wife would have to be either a creditor or guarantor of the husband. The trustee must also satisfy the court that the outcome of the transaction was the desired result which influenced the bankrupt to enter into the transaction. Although this can be difficult to demonstrate in some circumstances, the case of transfer of the matrimonial home to the husband's wife, it is presumed that the bankrupt had this intention unless this can be rebutted.

Transactions defrauding creditors

4.268 The final way in which a trustee can set aside a transaction relating to the home or indeed any other property is provided for by s 443 which relates to transactions defrauding creditors entered into at an undervalue. This covers a gift or transaction that provides for no consideration to be received, a transaction in consideration of marriage or a transaction which takes place at an undervalue. The distinction between this section and s 339 is that there must be an intention to put the assets beyond the reach of the trustee or otherwise prejudice his interests. If it is proved, the court can restore the position to what it would have been if the transaction had not taken place or otherwise protect the interests of those on the receiving end of the transaction. In this case, there is no time limit prescribed. However, given the necessity to demonstrate an intention, the trustee is again more likely to go down the s 339 route unless the transfer took place more than five years before the bankruptcy in which case, he will have no other option.

4.269 One curious distinction between s 339 and s 340 is highlighted by s 340(6) which states that even if a transfer takes place pursuant to a court order this by itself will not prevent such transfer from constituting a preference. Although s 339 is silent on this, the same point would seem to apply to transactions at an undervalue and transactions defrauding creditors. This does mean that a situation could arise where a property adjustment order made during the course of divorce proceedings, effected during the relevant period and which satisfied the other conditions prescribed by any of the reviewable transactions provisions could subsequently be set aside by a trustee. For this reason, the practitioner advising the wife should be alert to this possibility on advising on the relief sought in divorce proceedings particularly as it would now seem to be the case that if the transfer follows a court order, no distinction will be made between an order made by consent or the result of a contested application[1]. In such circumstances the only realistic option for the wife may be to pursue the husband for maintenance.

1 *Re Flint* [1993] 1 FLR 763.

Other property

4.270 As with the matrimonial home, the bankrupt's interest in any other property, whether jointly or entirely owned, will vest automatically in the trustee on his bankruptcy. In the case of jointly owned property, the wife will again have to establish a pre-existing beneficial interest based on a contribution to the purchase or improvements made as discussed above.

Household items

4.271 In the case of household items owned solely by the bankrupt husband there may be more available for division with the wife on a subsequent divorce than at first might be thought. By s 283(2)(b) 'such clothing, bedding, household furniture, equipment and provisions as are necessary for satisfying the basic needs of the bankrupt and its family' are excluded from the estate. However, in reality, the trustee will not enforce this provision to the point where the bankrupt is only left with such items. The reason for this is a practical one. The costs of moving and auctioning many items outside this limited class tend to be disproportionately high which, together with the low value of second-hand goods, means that the bankrupt in practice will usually tend to retain rather more of his possessions than those listed under s 283(2)(b).

4.272 However any particularly valuable items owned by the bankrupt husband will almost certainly be claimed by the trustee. Where such property exists, by s 308 'where ... the realisable value of ... that property exceeds the cost of a reasonable replacement ... the trustee may by notice in writing claim that property'. The trustee has within 42 days of acquiring knowledge of items such as antiques or expensive cars to serve the appropriate notice which operates to vest such property in the trustee. He must then provide the bankrupt with a replacement which must be reasonably adequate to meet the same needs.

After acquired property

4.273 There will be situations when property is acquired by or devolves upon the bankrupt husband after the commencement of his bankruptcy. In such cases he must give notice of this to his trustee within 21 days of the acquisition (r 6.200). Curiously, such property does not vest automatically in the trustee who has, by s 307, to claim notice of such property for the estate within 42 days of learning of the property. This post-discovery period should operate to thwart any move on the wife's behalf to lay claim to such property or any interest in it.

Maintenance

4.274 The bankruptcy order does not itself affect the bankrupt's earnings although it may provide grounds for the variation or suspension of a maintenance order. However by s 310 the trustee can apply for an income payments order claiming a specified amount of the bankrupt's income for his estate. That said, an order under this section cannot reduce the bankruptcy income below what is 'necessary for meeting the reasonable domestic needs of the bankrupt's family'. It is worth noting, however, that s 385 defines 'family' as dependants living with the bankrupt. Therefore, maintenance paid to a divorced wife living separately, whether for herself and/or their children, will not be taken into consideration when the bankrupt's income needs are assessed.

4.275 Whether or not an income payments order is made, a maintenance order is still technically possible. However, there will be few situations where it is worthwhile seeking a maintenance order given that a trustee ought to have already exercised his powers under s 310 if the level of the bankrupt's income merited such action. Moreover, if steps are taken to seek a maintenance order, they are likely to be frustrated given the provisions of s 285 which enable the court to stay proceedings against a bankrupt at any time after the time of the presentation of the bankruptcy petition.

Effect of bankruptcy order on maintenance order

4.276 The bankruptcy order does not automatically affect an existing maintenance order. However the realities of a bankruptcy will usually lead to the variation or suspension of an order granted prior to bankruptcy. It is worth noting that despite the operation of r 12(3) which states that any obligation arising under an order in family proceedings is not provable in the husband's bankruptcy, arrears under a pre-existing maintenance order will survive the bankrupt's discharge. This means that the wife, unlike most other creditors of her bankrupt husband, is able technically to pursue the husband after his discharge.

Lump sum orders

4.277 Given the automatic effect of s 306, lump sum orders in practice cannot be effective after a bankruptcy order has been made as all the husband's assets will have vested in his trustee. There can be no exception to this rule which means that the wife's application for a lump sum order will have to be postponed until after the husband's discharge.

4.278 A lump sum order made in the period between the presentation of the husband's bankruptcy petition and the date on which his property vest in his trustee is also likely to be ineffective. Under s 284 where a person is adjudged bankrupt, any disposition of property made in this period is void except to the extent that it was made with the court's consent or was subsequently ratified by the court. On the face of it therefore a lump sum order made in such period is likely to fall foul of s 284, particularly if payment under the order is made during this period (the point is made because in *Burton v Burton*[1] a distinction was made between the order itself, which was not held to constitute a disposition and the subsequent payment which would have been).

1 *Burton v Burton* [1986] 2 FLR 419.

4.279 There will however be situations when s 284 will not apply to a payment made. In *Mordant v Halls*[1] for example, a lump sum order made after the presentation of the husband's petition and before the bankruptcy order was upheld due to the fact that the lump sum order followed an order by the court that funds held by the husband abroad should be paid to his solicitors. It was held in this case that such payment had the effect of a payment into court so that the sum paid was no longer part of the husband's estate.

1 *Re Mordant, Mordant v Halls* [1996] 1 FLR 334.

4.280 In *Mordant v Halls* the position of lump sum orders pre-existing the husband's bankruptcy was also addressed. In this case the building society to whom the husband owed money had asserted that by s 382 and r 12(3) the wife was not entitled to the sum paid to the husband's solicitors because she was unable to prove in his bankruptcy (by that stage a bankruptcy order had been made). This contention failed because of the judge's view of the status of the monies paid to the solicitors. However the building society's argument did point to an apparent inconsistency in the insolvency legislation which had been particularly focused on in *Woodley v Woodley*[1].

1 *Woodley v Woodley* [1992] 2 FLR 417.

4.281 Although s 382 which defines bankruptcy debts, would seem to cover such a lump sum order, the wife is nevertheless unable to prove for it in her husband's bankruptcy given the wording of r 12(3). However, in *Woodley v Woodley* doubt was cast on the validity of r 12(3) given its apparent inconsistency with the Act. If the rule in the future is held to be ultra vires it would then mean that the wife would be entitled to prove a lump sum order in her husband's bankruptcy. However, as matters stand, the wife is in a state of limbo over the enforcement of lump sum orders awarded prior to the husband's bankruptcy until the husband's discharge. Whether this operates at the end of the day to the wife's detriment or advantage will vary in each case, depending on the degree of the husband's indebtedness (which would determine the dividend she would receive if her claim were provable) and his financial position post discharge.

Chapter Five

Financial Provision outside the Matrimonial Causes Act

Stephen Wildblood

Introduction 163
Relationships Defined 163
Parental Responsibility for Children 164
Financial Disputes in General 165
The Law of Trusts 168
Personal Property 180
Procedure 182
Financial Provision for Children 186

INTRODUCTION

5.1 The nature of a relationship governs the availability of legal rights and remedies. There remains a significant distinction between the position in law of those who have married and those who have not. That distinction is seen in its most clamant form in the realms of:

(a) the parental responsibility of parents to their children;

(b) the method by which rights and claims relating to property are determined;

(c) the rights of occupation within the family home[1].

1 See para 11.36 et seq and Appendix 1.

5.2 To a limited extent the law has extended greater recognition and remedies to people who are or have been engaged. That recognition is likely to be extended further with the passing of the Family Law Act 1996 (FLA 1996).

RELATIONSHIPS DEFINED

5.3 The classic definition of marriage is that it is 'the voluntary union for life of one man and one woman to the exclusion of all others'[1]. There is no such thing under the law of England and Wales as a common law marriage; people are either married or they are not.

A marriage will be void ab initio if it infringes the provisions specified in s 11 of the MCA 1973[2]; it will be voidable (ie capable of being declared void) if the grounds specified in s 12 of that Act are satisfied[2].

1 See *Hyde v Hyde and Woodmansee* (1866) LR 1 P & D 130.
2 See *Butterworths Family Law Service*, Division G.

5.4 An engagement is an agreement between two people of the opposite sex to marry; beyond that there are no specific requirements under existing law that must be satisfied before an engagement will be held to have taken place[1]; the FLA 1996 will contain a definition of engagement for the purposes of its provisions.

1 In the case of *Shaw v Fitzgerald* [1992] 1 FCR 162, [1992] 1 FLR 357 it was held that there could be an engagement for the purposes of s 2 of the Law Reform (Miscellaneous Provisions) Act 1970 even if one party was already married to someone else.

5.5 At present there is no legal definition of co-habitees (or co-habitants) although the FLA 1996 will include such a definition for the purposes of its provisions. Under the Domestic Violence and Matrimonial Proceedings Act 1976 relief may be sought where a man and woman are 'living with each other in the same household as husband and wife'[1].

1 See *Butterworths Family Law Service*, Division G.

PARENTAL RESPONSIBILITY FOR CHILDREN

5.6 The scope, meaning and acquisition of parental responsibility is considered in para 7.02. However, here reference is made to the CA 1989, s 2(1) and (11) by which it is provided that:

(a) Where a child's father and mother were married to each other at the time of his birth[1], they shall each have parental responsibility for the child;

(b) Where a child's father and mother were not married to each other at the time of the birth[1]:

  (i) the mother shall have parental responsibility for the child;

  (ii) the father shall not have parental responsibility for the child, unless he acquires it in accordance with the provisions of the CA 1989[2].

1 This must be read with s 1 of the Family Law Reform Act 1987 which extends the meaning of the phrase 'father and mother were married to each other at the time of his birth'.
2 For example, by a parental responsibility agreement or order under s 4 of the CA 1989, by adoption or by a residence order (under s 12(2) of that Act).

FINANCIAL DISPUTES IN GENERAL

Between people who have married

5.7 In most instances financial disputes between people who have married will be determined by the use of specific statutory provisions. Where divorce, judicial separation or nullity proceedings have been issued, financial issues should be dealt with under the MCA 1973 unless there is a good reason for not doing so[1]. Where the marriage subsists, issues relating to lump sums and maintenance will be dealt with under the available statutes (eg the MCA 1973 or the Domestic Proceedings and Magistrates' Courts Act 1978). However, it may still be necessary to determine the beneficial interests of a married couple in a property. Where, for instance:

(a) the marriage subsists;

(b) one of the parties is declared bankrupt;

(c) a party to a former marriage remarries without issuing an application for ancillary relief[2];

(d) declarations about property ownership are necessary in order to determine liability to capital gains tax[3].

1 See *Suttill v Graham* [1977] 3 All ER 1117, [1977] 1 WLR 819; *Kowalczuk v Kowalczuk* [1973] 2 All ER 1042; and *Griffiths v Griffiths* [1974] 1 All ER 932, [1974] 1 WLR 1350.
2 See MCA 1973, s 28(3) and the case of *Robin v Robin* (1983) 4 FLR 632.
3 See eg *B v B* [1988] 2 FLR 490.

Engaged couples

5.8 The link between the remedies available to married people and those available to people who are or have been engaged, occurs through the Law Reform (Miscellaneous Provisions) Act 1970, s 2. It provides that:

> (1) Where an agreement to marry is terminated, any rule of law relating to the rights of husbands and wives in relation to property in which either or both has or had a beneficial interest, including any such rule as explained by section 37 of the Matrimonial Proceedings and Property Act 1970, shall apply, in relation to any property in which either or both of the parties to the agreement had a beneficial interest while the agreement was in force, as it applies in relation to property in which a husband or wife has a beneficial interest.

> (2) Where an agreement to marry is terminated, section 17 of the Married Women's Property Act 1882 and section 7 of the Matrimonial Causes (Property and Maintenance) Act 1958 (which confers power on a judge of the High Court or the county court to settle disputes between husband and wife about property) shall apply, as if the parties were married, to any dispute between, or claimed by, one of them in relation to property in which either or both had a beneficial interest while the agreement was in force; that an application made by virtue of this section to the judge under the said section 17, as originally enacted or as

extended by the said section 7, shall be made within three years of the termination of the agreement.

In the case of *Mossop v Mossop*[1] it was held that the above provision does not mean that the court has powers under the MCA 1973, s 24 where an agreement to marry is terminated. Specific note should be taken of the time limit in s 2(2).

1 [1989] Fam 77, [1988] 2 All ER 202.

Other couples

5.9 People who have neither married nor agreed to marry will have to rely upon the general law of trusts and property to resolve financial disputes[1].

1 See para 5.13 et seq.

Married Women's Property Act 1882, s 17

5.10 This section provides that:

In any question between husband and wife as to the title to or possession of property, either party may apply by summons or otherwise in a summary way to the High Court or such county court as may be prescribed and the court may, on such application (which may be heard in private), make such order with respect to the property as it thinks fit. In this section 'prescribed' means prescribed by rules of court and rules made for the purposes of this section may confer jurisdiction on county courts whatever the situation or value of the property in dispute.

The main points to note about this section are:

(a) It is procedural and declaratory only. It does not permit the court to adjust property rights[1]. Thus on an application under this section, the issue is to whom does this property belong rather than to whom in fairness should this property be awarded. Save to the extent provided by statute, this involves determining the parties' beneficial interests in property under the general trust and property law.

(b) It may be used to resolve disputes about property that is outside England and Wales. However, the court will not exercise its powers under this section in relation to such property if the order would be ineffective[2].

(c) It is available to parties who were formerly married provided the application is brought within three years from the date upon which the marriage was dissolved or annulled[3].

(d) It is available where an agreement to marry is terminated on an application that is brought within the time limit specified in the Law Reform (Miscellaneous Provisions) Act 1970, s 2(2)[4].

Financial Disputes in General 167

(e) There are no monetary restrictions on the jurisdiction of the county court under this section (and the application may be heard by a district judge or circuit judge in that court).

(f) It is extended by the Matrimonial Causes (Property and Maintenance) Act 1958, s 7.[5]

(g) The procedure is governed by the FPR 1991, rr 3.6 and 3.7. This includes the procedure for obtaining any necessary injunctions.

1 *Pettitt v Pettitt* [1970] AC 777, [1969] 2 All ER 385.
2 *Hamlin v Hamlin* [1986] Fam 11, [1985] 2 All ER 1037; and *Razelos v Razelos* [1969] 3 All ER 929, [1970] 1 WLR 390.
3 Matrimonial Proceedings and Property Act 1970, s 39.
4 See para 5.08.
5 See para 5.11.

Matrimonial Causes (Property and Maintenance) Act 1958, s 7

5.11 This section[1] extends the Married Women's Property Act 1882, s 17 so as to enable the court:

(a) to make orders in relation to:

  (i) money to which or to a share of which, the applicant spouse was beneficially entitled (whether by reason that it represented the proceeds of property to which, or to an interest in which she was beneficially entitled, or for any other reason),

  (ii) property (other than money) to which, or to an interest in which, the applicant was beneficially entitled;

(b) to trace any such money or property[2];

(c) to make orders for sale under the Married Women's Property Act 1882, s 17[3].

1 For the full text of the section see the County Court Practice (the 'Green Book') in that part that relates to 'Husband and Wife'.
2 Section 7(4).
3 Section 7(7).

Improvements to the matrimonial home

5.12 Under the Matrimonial Proceedings and Property Act 1970, s 37, it is provided that:

> Where a husband or wife contributes in money or money's worth to the improvement of real or personal property in which or in the proceeds of sale of which either or both of them has or have a beneficial interest, the husband or wife so contributing shall, if the contribution is of a substantial nature and subject to any agreement to

the contrary, express or implied, be treated as having then acquired by virtue of his or her contribution a share or an enlarged share as the case may be in that beneficial interest of such an extent as may have been agreed, or in default of such agreement, as may seem in all the circumstances just to any court before which the question of any existence or extent of the beneficial interest of the husband or wife arises (whether in proceedings between them or in any other proceedings).

The main points of note under this section are:

(a) it relates to issues between spouses and formerly engaged couples (under the Law Reform (Miscellaneous Provisions) Act 1970, s 2);

(b) the contribution may be in money or money's worth (ie the claimant may have paid for the improvement or done it herself[1]);

(c) one or both of the parties must have a beneficial interest in the property in issue (thus this section cannot be used to claim a share in a property that is wholly owned by a third party);

(d) the contribution must be of a substantial nature[2];

(e) the claim may be defeated by a contrary agreement.

1 See *Harnett v Harnett* [1973] Fam 156 at 167.
2 See *Re Nicholson* [1974] 2 All ER 386, [1974] 1 WLR 476 (provision of a gas fire insufficient).

THE LAW OF TRUSTS

Checklist

5.13 Subject to limited statutory provisions, the beneficial interests in a property will be determined by the general law of trusts and property. Under the LPA 1925, ss 35 and 36 any jointly owned property will usually be held upon the statutory trusts for sale provided by those sections. When the practitioner is faced with an application relating to beneficial interests under such a trust it is suggested that the following checklist is considered (each item in the checklist is considered below):

(a) Bring all outstanding claims before the court by way of a consolidated action at the same time.

(b) Consider the statutory provisions that apply.

(c) Examine the documents of title.

(d) Consider what express agreements, arrangements or understandings were made at the time of purchase.

(e) Decide whether there is basis for inferring a common intention that the claimant should have a beneficial interest in particular by:

   (i) discovering who paid what towards the purchase,

    (ii) discovering what arrangements were made in respect of the mortgage.
(f) Consider who carried out what improvements to the property and the basis upon which the improvements were carried out.
(g) Consider any issues relating to estoppel and the 'equity of exoneration'.
(h) Ascertain the size of the share claimed in the property.
(i) Consider the date for the valuation of that share.
(j) Consider the question of sale.
(k) Consider any issues relating to chattels or other items of property.
(l) Consider the jurisdiction of the court in relation to the intended application.

The above checklist is considered in more detail in the paragraphs that follow.

Bringing outstanding claims together

5.14 In the case of *Hammond v Mitchell* [1991] 1 WLR 1127 at 1138, [1992] 1 FLR 229, Waite J said:

> 'Whatever form the proceedings take in cases of this kind and whatever the High Court Division or the county court in which the process is initiated, it must be a matter of prime concern to the parties' advisers and to the district judge or magistrate[1] before whom they come in the first instance to see that all possible issues, including those of maintenance, are raised at the earliest stage so that an informed judgment can be made as to the form and the procedure which will provide the quickest and most effective means of resolving them.'

It is most likely that the practitioner will have to give consideration to some or all of the following:

(a) seeking declaratory relief in respect of property ownership[2];

(b) seeking orders for sale in respect of jointly owned property[3];

(c) seeking orders in respect of chattels[4];

(d) seeking orders for financial provision in respect of children under the CA 1989, Sch 1;

(e) seeking any other necessary financial orders (for instance, relating to a jointly owned endowment policy).

---

1 This comment must be considered in the light of the Child Support Act 1991, s 8(3) (see para 1.05) which will make it very rare indeed that any financial application will come before the magistrate.
2 Under the Married Women's Property Act 1882, s 17 or under the court's general equitable jurisdiction.
3 Under the LPA 1925, s 30 (or the Married Women's Property Act 1882, s 17 as extended by the Matrimonial Causes (Property and Maintenance) Act 1958, s 7(7)).

4 Either under the court's general equitable jurisdiction or under the LPA 1925, s 188 (that section provides that, where any chattels belong to persons in undivided shares, persons interested in a moiety or upwards may apply to the court for an order for the division of the chattels or any of them, according to a valuation or otherwise).

Statutory provisions

5.15 It is plainly important to ensure that the correct and necessary procedure is followed from the outset. This will involve giving consideration to the nature of the relationship between the couple. Different statutory provisions will apply in respect of:

(a) parties who are married[1];

(b) parties who were engaged[2];

(c) parties who were neither engaged nor married[3].

In identifying the nature of the claim it is, amongst other things, necessary to differentiate between:

(i) a claim that a constructive trust exists (based upon the actual or imputed intention of the parties); and

(ii) a claim that a resulting trust exists (based upon contributions to the purchase of the property)[4].

1 See paras 5.10 to 5.12.
2 See para 5.08.
3 See para 5.09.
4 See *Drake v Whipp* [1996] 2 FLR 296.

Documents of Title

5.16 In the case of *Pettitt v Pettitt*[1] Lord Upjohn said:

'In the first place, the beneficial ownership of the property in question must depend upon the agreement of the parties determined at the time of its acquisition. If the property in question is land, there must be some lease or conveyance which shows how it was acquired. If that document declares not merely in whom the legal title is to vest but in whom the beneficial title is to vest, that necessarily concludes the question of title as between spouses for all time, and in the absence of fraud or mistake at the time of the transaction the parties cannot go behind it at any time thereafter even on death or the break up of the marriage.'

The primary importance of the documents of title has been stressed in many subsequent cases[2]. It also has its basis in the provisions of the LPA 1925, s 53[3]. This may raise some or other of the following issues:

(a) Sometimes it is not possible to obtain a copy of the documents of title in respect of the property. For instance, where the legal title and the mortgage in respect of the property are vested in the sole name of the proposed respondent and the proposed respondent declines to produce the documentation. In those circumstances, the practitioner acting for the applicant is well advised to write to the respondent indicating that unless the documents of title are produced within a certain period the applicant will proceed with the claim and refer to the request upon the issue of costs.

(b) A solicitor acting on a joint purchase should investigate with the proposed purchasers the intended beneficial interest in the property and ensure that any intended beneficial interests are declared in the documents of title[4].

(c) Where there is a declared beneficial joint tenancy within the documents of title, the parties will hold the property on trust for themselves as beneficial tenants in common in equal shares following any severance of the beneficial joint tenancy[5] (in the absence of any claim for rectification or rescission)[6].

(d) Where title to the property is registered, the property may have become vested in the purchaser through the use of a standard form of transfer. Where the standard form of transfer contains a declaration that 'the survivor of them can give a valid receipt for capital money arising on the disposition of the land' that declaration alone is not sufficient to constitute a declaration of the parties' beneficial interests in the property[7].

1 [1970] AC 777 at 813.
2 For example, *Bernard v Josephs* (1982) 4 FLR 178 at 186.
3 The LPA 1925, s 53 reads as follows:
   '(1) Subject to the provisions hereinafter contained with respect to the creation of interests in land by parol–
   (a) no interest in land can be created or disposed of except by writing signed by the person creating or conveying the same, or by his agent thereunto lawfully authorised in writing, or by will, or by operation of law;
   (b) a declaration of trust respecting any land or any interest therein must be manifested and proved by some writing signed by some person who is able to declare such trust or by his will;
   (c) a disposition of an equitable interest or trust subsisting at the time of the disposition, must be in writing signed by the person disposing of the same, or by his agent thereunto lawfully authorised in writing or by will.
   (2) This section does not affect the creation or operation of resulting, implied or constructive trusts.'
4 *Cowcher v Cowcher* [1972] 1 All ER 943 and *Bernard v Josephs* (1982) 4 FLR 178.
5 See David Burrows 'Joint Property' [1995] Sol Jo 1176 where the subject of severance of joint tenancy is considered fully.
6 *Goodman v Gallant* [1986] Fam 106 in which it was said 'In the absence of any claim for rectification or rescission, the provision in a conveyance of an express declaration of trust conclusively defines the parties' respective beneficial interests; accordingly, the provision that the plaintiff and the defendant hold the property in trust for themselves as joint tenants entitles them on severance to the proceeds of sale in equal shares'.
7 See *Huntingford v Hobbs* [1993] 1 FLR 736 and *Harwood v Harwood* [1991] 2 FLR 274. In the case of *Huntingford v Hobbs* it was held that 'in deciding whether or not the declaration in the transfer constituted a declaration of trust, the meaning of the words used was alone material, and since the words used, though entirely consistent with the existence of a beneficial joint tenancy, were no less consistent with the parties holding the property as trustees for a third party, it follows that it was impossible

to read the declaration as constituting a declaration of beneficial interest'; the court therefore went on to consider the parties' respective beneficial interests on other grounds, having decided that the transfer did not record a declaration of trust. These two cases have to be compared with the case of *Re Gorman* [1990] 2 FLR 284 where Vinelott J and Mervyn Davies J had a case where the transfer contained a declaration stating that the transferees were 'entitled to the land for their own benefit and that the survivor of them could give a valid receipt for capital monies arising on the disposition of the land' it was held on that wording that there was a declaration that the parties held as beneficial joint tenants.

Express agreement, arrangements or understandings

5.17 The principles arising under this area were enunciated by Lord Bridge in the case of *Lloyds Bank v Rosset* [1991] 1 AC 107 in which he said at 132:

'The first and fundamental question which must always be resolved is whether, independently of any inference to be drawn from conduct of the parties in the course of sharing the house as their home and managing their joint affairs, there has at any time prior to acquisition or exceptionally at some later date, been any agreement, arrangement or understanding reached between them that the property is to be shared beneficially. The finding of an agreement or arrangement to share in this sense can only, I think, be based on evidence of express discussion between the partners, however imperfectly remembered and however imprecise their terms may have been. Once a finding to this effect is made, it will only be necessary for the partner asserting a claim to a beneficial interest against a partner entitled to the legal estate to show that he or she had acted to his or her detriment or significantly altered his or her position in reliance on the agreement, in order to give rise to a constructive trust or a proprietary estoppel.'

In order to substantiate a claim to a beneficial interest relying upon this principle, the following points need to be considered:

(a) The relevant contention of the parties must be a shared intention that was expressly communicated between them. It cannot mean an intention which either happened to have in his or her own mind but had never communicated to the other[1].

(b) In pleading a case where this principle is relied upon, the express discussions to which the court's initial enquiries will be addressed should be set out in the greatest detail, both as to language and to circumstances[2]. This therefore means that the practitioner must take detailed and careful instructions at the outset in respect of what was said between the parties. Examples of such cases are *Eves v Eves*[3] and *Grant v Edwards*[4];

(c) The detrimental reliance should be of the kind considered in the case of *Grant v Edwards*. In that case Nourse LJ said that the type of conduct that was required to show detrimental reliance was 'conduct on which the woman could not reasonably have been expected to embark unless she was to have an interest in the house'. Browne-Wilkinson VC put the matter thus:

'As at present advised, once it has been shown that there was a common intention that the claimant should have an interest in the house, any act done by her to her detriment relating to the joint lives of the parties is, in my judgment, sufficient detriment to qualify. The acts do not have to be inherently referable to the house: see *Jones v Jones* [1977] 1 WLR 438 and *Pascoe v Turner* [1979] 1 WLR 431'[5].

1 *Springette v Defoe* [1992] 2 FCR 561 at 567.
2 *Hammond v Mitchell* [1991] 1 WLR 1127, [1992] 1 FLR 229.
3 [1975] 1 WLR 1338.
4 [1986] Ch 638, [1987] 1 FLR 87.
5 *Grant v Edwards* [1987] 1 FLR 87 at 95B and 100B – D.

Inferred common intention

5.18 In *Lloyds Bank v Rosset* Lord Bridge says[1], having considered cases where there is an express agreement, arrangement or understanding that the parties should have a shared beneficial interest in the property:

'In sharp contrast with this situation is the very different one where there is no evidence to support a finding of an agreement or arrangement to share, however reasonable it might have been for the parties to reach such an agreement if they had applied their minds to the question and where the court must rely entirely on the conduct of the parties both as the basis from which to infer a common intention to share the property beneficially and as the conduct relied upon to give rise to a constructive trust. In this situation direct contributions to the purchase price by the partner who is not the legal owner whether initially or by payment of mortgage instalments, will readily justify the inference necessary for the creation of a constructive trust. As I read the authorities it is at least extremely doubtful whether anything less will do.'

The above passage represents a somewhat narrower approach to the issue of an inferred common intention than that which has been adopted elsewhere[2]. In considering whether there is sufficient to base a claim to a beneficial interest upon an inferred common intention it is necessary to consider:

(a) contributions to the purchase price;

(b) arrangements that were made in respect of the mortgage;

(c) whether there is any other basis for contending that there is sufficient evidence to contend that a common intention to share the property should be inferred[3].

1 [1991] 1 AC 107 at 133.
2 In *Grant v Edwards* [1987] 1 FLR 87 at 97H Browne-Wilkinson VC said:
'Lord Diplock in *Gissing v Gissing* [1971] AC 886 points out that, even where parties have not used express words to communicate their intention and therefore there is no direct evidence, the court can infer from their actions an intention that they shall both have an interest in the house. This part of his speech concentrates on the types of evidence from which the courts are most often asked to infer such an intention, viz contributions (direct and indirect, the deposit, the mortgage instalments

or general housekeeping expenses). In this section of his speech he analyses what types of expenditure are capable of constituting evidence of such common intention; he does not say that if the intention is proved in some other way such contributions are essential to establish a trust'. In *Savill v Goodall* [1994] 1 FCR 325 Nourse L J refers to 'a second category such as *Gissing v Gissing* ... where the necessary common intention can only be inferred from the conduct of the parties, usually from the expenditure incurred by them respectively'.
3 *Midland Bank v Cooke* [1995] 2 FLR 915.

Contributions to the purchase price other than through the mortgage

5.19 It is well established that, in the absence of any express declaration or agreement as to beneficial interests, the parties' contributions to the purchase price will determine their share in the equity[1]. Where part of the purchase price for the property is made up by a council house discount, that council house discount is likely to be treated as a contribution to the purchase price by the person to whom the discount was afforded[2]. Where part of the purchase price was paid as a result of a gift from a third party, it is necessary to determine to whom the gift was made in order to ascertain the identity of the person who contributed the money from the gift to the purchase of the property[3].

1 *Bernard v Josephs* (1982) 4 FLR 178; *Crisp v Mullings* (1975) 239 Estates Gazette 119; and *Walker v Hall* [1984] FLR 126.
2 *Springette v Defoe* [1992] 2 FCR 561.
3 See, for instance, *McHardy v Warren* [1994] 2 FLR 338 in which the Court of Appeal was prepared to assume that a wedding present made by one spouse's parents was in fact a gift to both spouses jointly and therefore the money that had been used to buy a property represented a joint contribution by the spouses to the purchase price. This case was followed in the Court of Appeal decision in *Halifax Building Society v Brown* [1996] 1 FLR 103. There is, however, some authority for the suggestion that gifts from the relatives of one spouse are to be presumed to be gifts only to that spouse and not to both (see *Samson v Samson* [1960] 1 All ER 653).

Mortgages: the two approaches

5.20 In the case of *Marsh v Von Sternberg*[1] the late Bush J identified that the Court of Appeal had adopted two different approaches to the issue of the creation of a beneficial interest arising out of mortgage arrangements. Those two approaches are:

(a) the approach by which a person's mortgage liability is treated as a contribution to the purchase of a property thereby conferring a beneficial interest (see below);

(b) the approach by which a person's contributions to the mortgage payments form the basis of the inference that the beneficial ownership is jointly held (see below).

1 [1986] 1 FLR 526.

Mortgages: the liability approach

5.21 An example of this approach would be as follows:

(a) Hopeless Hall was bought in 1985 for £100,000 in the joint names of Mr Rich and Miss Poor (there was no expressed declaration of trust and no expressed agreement as to the beneficial interest).

(b) Mr Rich paid £50,000 in cash towards the purchase. The balance of £50,000 was paid by a mortgage in the joint names of Mr Rich and Miss Poor.

(c) At the time of purchase, therefore, Mr Rich contributed 75% of the gross purchase price and Miss Poor contributed 25%.

(d) Hopeless Hall sells in 1994 for £175,000 (after solicitors' and estate agents' fees). The mortgage is still £50,000.

(e) The share of Miss Poor is 25% × £175,000 = £43,750. However, she is responsible for one half of the mortgage debt, ie one-half of £50,000 = £25,000. She, therefore, receives £43,750 – £25,000 = £18,750.

(f) Mr Rich receives 75% × £175,000 = £131,250. However, he is also responsible for one-half of the mortgage. He therefore receives £131,250 – £25,000 = £106,250.

This approach was adopted in cases such as *Marsh v Von Sternberg*[1] and *Huntingford v Hobbs*[2]. It is entirely consistent with the approach that a person's beneficial interest in a property will be determined by the amount the person contributes to the purchase price (in the absence of express declaration or agreement). It can only be of relevance where the claimant has assumed a liability for the mortgage (and not where the claimant has made payments towards someone else's liability).

1 [1986] 1 FLR 526.
2 [1993] 1 FLR 736.

Mortgages: contributions to payments

5.22 The way in which mortgages are paid may provide the basis of establishing a person's beneficial interest in a property[1], that is by having regard to actual contributions towards the mortgage payments. This approach proceeds upon the basis that there is nothing inherently improbable in the parties acting on the understanding that the claimant should be entitled to a share which is not to be quantified immediately upon the acquisition of the home but should be left to be determined when the mortgage was repaid or the property disposed of, on the basis of what would be fair having regard to the total contributions, direct or indirect, which each spouse had made by that date[2]. The approach does not preclude the possibility that, while initially there was no intention that the claimant should have any interest in the property, circumstances may subsequently arise from which the intention to confer an equitable interest on the claimant may arise[3]. This approach has been criticised as creating a 'wavering equity'[4].

1 See *Midland Bank v Cooke* [1995] 2 FLR 915.
2 *Gissing v Gissing* [1971] AC 886 at 906.
3 *Passee v Passee* [1988] 1 FLR 263.
4 In *Marsh v Von Sternberg* [1986] 1 FLR 526, Bush J.

Other evidence of inferred intention

5.23 In the case of *Burns v Burns*[1] Fox LJ said:

'What is needed, I think, is evidence of a payment or payments by the plaintiff which it can be inferred was referable to the acquisition of the house ... a payment can be said to be referable to the acquisition of the house if, for example, the payer either:

(a) pays part of the purchase price, or

(b) contributes regularly to the mortgage instalments, or

(c) pays off part of the mortgage, or

(d) makes a substantial financial contribution to the family expenses so as to enable the mortgage instalments to be paid.

But if a payment cannot be said to be, in a real sense, referable to the acquisition of the house, it is difficult to see how, in such a case as the present, it can base a claim for an interest in the house[2].'

In *Lloyds Bank v Rosset* Lord Bridge doubts whether anything other than direct contributions to the purchase price or the mortgage instalments will be sufficient to justify the inference necessary to the creation of a constructive trust[3]. It is suggested that the answer to this may well lie in the following propositions:

(a) If it is suggested that a payment is to cause the creation of a trust relating to a property, the payment must genuinely relate to its acquisition.

(b) A broader approach may be adopted to words and actions that will be sufficient to permit the court to find that there was an express 'understanding' (or agreement or arrangement) that parties were to share a property beneficially; it may be suggested that the cases of *Eves v Eves* and *Grant v Edwards* are in fact examples of this broader approach[4].

(c) Once it is established that a claimant has a beneficial interest, the size of that beneficial interest will be determined on a broad spectrum of evidence[5].

1 [1984] FLR 216.
2 At 226.
3 [1991] 1 AC 107 at 113.
4 In *Eves v Eves* [1975] 1 WLR 1338 the male partner had told the female partner that the only reason that the property was to be acquired in his name alone was because she was under 21 and that, but for her age, he would have had the house put into their joint names. He admitted in evidence that this was simply an excuse. That evidence was held

to be sufficient to indicate that it was the intention of the parties that the claimant should have a beneficial interest in the property. In *Grant v Edwards* [1986] Ch 638 the female partner was told by the male partner that the only reason for not acquiring the property in joint names was because she was involved in divorce proceedings and that, if the property were acquired jointly, this might operate to her prejudice in those proceedings; that was sufficient for there to be a finding that it was the parties' common intention that she should have a beneficial interest in the house.

5 See *Midland Bank v Cooke* [1995] 2 FLR 915.

Improvements to property

5.24 Where parties were married or engaged, the Matrimonial Proceedings and Property Act 1970, s 37 will have to be considered[1]. However, in the absence of available statutory provisions, it is settled law that the mere fact A has expended money or labour on B's property does not entitle A to an interest in the property, in the absence of either an express agreement or of a common intention to be inferred from the conduct of the parties and of any question of estoppel[2].

1 See para 5.12.
2 *Thomas v Fuller-Brown* [1988] 1 FLR 237. In *Pettitt v Pettitt* [1970] AC 777 it was held that in the absence of agreement and any question of estoppel, one spouse who does work or spends money on the property of the other has no claim whatever upon the property of the other.

Proprietary estoppel

5.25 The courts have recently drawn together the principles relating to constructive trusts and those relating to estoppel[1]. There is an obvious similarity between the principles that arise on a claim to a beneficial interest on the grounds of an express agreement, arrangement or understanding and those that arise on a claim based on proprietary estoppel. There remains, however, a line of authority whereby equitable rights have arisen through the application of the principles relating to estoppel. Sometimes the courts have applied a narrow approach to the circumstances in which such a claim may arise[2]; other courts have been more liberal. This more liberal approach has been most recently adopted in the Court of Appeal[3]. The narrow interpretation of proprietary estoppel requires that five elements are shown:

(a) the plaintiff must have made a mistake as to his legal rights;

(b) the plaintiff must have expended some money or done some act on the faith of his mistaken belief;

(c) the defendant must know of the existence of his own right which is inconsistent with the right claimed by the plaintiff;

(d) the defendant must know of the plaintiff's mistaken belief in his right; and

(e) the defendant must have encouraged the plaintiff in the expenditions of money, or in the other acts which he has done, either directly or by abstaining from asserting his legal right[4].

The relief afforded by the courts will be the minimum equity to do justice to the parties; on the facts of the case of *Pascoe v Turner*[5], this was interpreted as meaning that the man must transfer the property to the woman (he had promised that the house would belong to her and she had made improvements to it). Where the claimant has adopted a course of conduct which is prejudicial or otherwise detrimental to her, there is at least a rebuttable presumption that she adopted that course of conduct in reliance on the assurances[6]. In *Coombes v Smith*[7], it was held that the plaintiff's conduct in leaving her husband and moving in with the defendant was insufficient to base a claim of estoppel.

1 See *Lloyds Bank v Rosset* [1991] 1 AC 407 at 132 and *Grant v Edwards* [1987] 1 FLR 87 at 99.
2 See, for instance *Coombes v Smith* [1986] 1 WLR 808.
3 See *Wayling v Jones* [1995] 2 FLR 1029 and *Re Basham* [1987] 1 All ER 405, [1986] 1 WLR 1498. This more liberal approach would appear more consistent with the cross-fertilisation with constructive trusts referred to in *Grant v Edwards* [1987] 1 FLR 87 at 99.
4 See *Crabb v Arun* [1976] Ch 179.
5 [1979] 2 All ER 945, [1979] 1 WLR 431
6 Compare *Coombes v Smith* [1986] 1 WLR 808 at 821B–E with *Greasley v Cooke* [1980] 1 WLR 1306 at 1311H and 1313.
7 [1986] 1 WLR 808. Per contra see *Wayling v Jones* [1995] 2 FLR 1029, CA where a man who moved in to live with the owner of a hotel was held to benefit from a proprietory estoppel on the death of the owner.

Equity of exoneration

5.26 Where a property is jointly owned and it is charged to secure the debts of only one of the joint owners, the other owner is entitled to have that secured indebtedness discharged out of the debtor's interest in the property (in the absence of a contrary intention). In the case of *Re Pittortou*[1] the husband and wife owned a property in their joint names. A second mortgage was taken out to secure the husband's indebtedness to the bank; that indebtedness arose under a bank account that was used partly for his business and partly to meet household expenses. It was held that insofar as the husband's debts to the bank arose from his business, that indebtedness was to be met only from the husband's share in the property; however, the indebtedness arising from household expenditure was a debt that fell on the property as a whole.

1 [1985] 1 All ER 285, [1985] 1 WLR 58.

The size of the share claimed

5.27 In quantifying shares there are a number of possibilities:

(a) Where the parties' shares are declared in the documents of title, those shares cannot be altered in the absence of a claim for rectification or rescission. The documents of title (or the separate written declaration of trust or notice of severance of it[2]) will determine the parties' shares in the property.

(b) Where there is an express arrangement, agreement or understanding, prima facie the parties will have the beneficial interests that they intended. However, there have been instances where the court has been prepared to find a lesser beneficial interest than that expressed orally between the parties on the grounds of flexibility[3].

(c) Where the intention to create a beneficial interest is implied, the court may apply a broad brush to determine the parties' shares[4].

(d) Where the property is bought without a mortgage and joint beneficial interests arise through joint contributions to the purchase price, the parties' beneficial interest in the property will reflect their contributions to its purchase (in the absence of express declarations or agreement, arrangements or understandings).

(e) The quantification of shares where a claim is established through the mortgage liability has already been described[5];

(f) Where mortgage repayments form the basis of the creation of the beneficial interest, the court may make an overall assessment of the domestic arrangements in order to determine the shares[6] in the property.

(g) Where a claim is based upon improvements alone, the share of the claim will be calculated on the basis of the cost of the improvements or the amount by which the value of the property increased as a result of those improvements, whichever is the less[7].

1 For consideration of trusts see para 5.13 et seq.
2 *Goodman v Gallant* [1986] 1 FLR 513.
3 In *Grant v Edwards* [1986] Ch 638 Brown-Wilkinson VC said: 'Whereas in this case, the existence of some beneficial interest in the claim has been shown, prima facie the interest of the claimant will be that which the parties intended. ... In *Eves v Eves* Brightman J at p 755A plainly felt that a common intention that there should be a joint interest pointed to the beneficial interest being equal. However, he felt able to find a lesser beneficial interest in that case without explaining the legal basis on which he did so. With diffidence, I suggest that the law of proprietary estoppel may again provide useful guidance. If proprietary estoppel is established, the court gives effect to it by giving effect to the common intention so far as may fairly be done between the parties. For that purpose, equity is displayed at its most flexible'. However, in the case of *Saville v Goodall* [1994] 1 FCR 325 at p 331 it was said: 'It was submitted that an intention that a house should be owned jointly could nevertheless mean that it could be owned in unequal shares. I am quite unable to accept that solution. Mr Saville and Mrs Goodall are not lawyers. If an ordinary sensible couple without more declare an intention to own their home jointly they can only be taken to intend that they share it equally'.
4 *Drake v Whipp* [1996] 1 FLR 826, CA.
5 See paras 5.21 and 5.22.
6 A more recent case concerning the quantification of a share on the approach adopted in *Passee v Passee* is the case of *Midland Bank v Cooke* [1995] 2 FLR 915.
7 *Re Pavlou* [1993] 3 All ER 145.

Date for quantification of shares

5.28 As a result of a succession of cases it is now well established that the appropriate date for the valuation of parties' shares in property, in the absence of express contrary agreement as to the date of valuation, should be the date of sale of the property or realisation of the shares[1].

1 *Gordon v Douce* [1983] 2 All ER 228; *Turton v Turton* [1987] 2 All ER 641; *Walker v Hall* [1984] FLR 126; and *Passee v Passee* [1988] 1 FLR 263.

Sale

5.29 Often an application for a declaration that a trust exists in respect of a property will be joined in an application for an order that a property should be sold. In respect of husbands and wives (or couples who have been engaged) that application for sale may be made under the Married Women's Property Act 1882 as extended by the Matrimonial Causes (Property and Maintenance) Act 1958, s 7. Otherwise the application for an order for sale will be under the LPA 1925, s 30[1]. On an application for an order for sale, it does not always follow that a court will make an immediate order that the property be sold. An order for sale will be made where it is considered just and equitable so to order. The court will have regard to the underlying purpose of the trust for sale, including any secondary purpose that arises from the responsibility to care for children. The court has a discretion upon the issue of sale[2]. Examples of where orders for sale have been refused have been:

(a) Where the mother has custody of a child who is living in the home and the father sought an order for sale. His application was dismissed (not adjourned), the court concluding that it was an irresistible inference that the parties had bought the property as a family home for themselves and the children for the indefinite future (there was no evidence that the father had any immediate need to realise his investment)[3].

(b) Where a spouse required time to find alternative accommodation[4].

(c) Where there was a prospect of divorce proceedings in the future[5].

1 And see Trusts of Land and Appointment of Trustees Act 1996 when in force.
2 *Re Evers's Trust* [1980] 1 WLR 1327.
3 Ibid.
4 *Niven v Niven* [1970] 1 WLR 955.
5 *Danchevsky v Danchevsky* [1975] Fam 17, [1974] 3 All ER 934, although on appeal an order for sale was made on the facts of this particular case.

PERSONAL PROPERTY

Married Women's Property Act 1882

5.30 Under s 1 of the Married Women's Property Act 1882 it is provided that:

'If any question arises as to the right of a husband or wife to money derived from any allowance made by the husband for the expenses of the matrimonial home or for similar purposes, or to any property acquired out of such money, the money or property shall in the absence of any agreement between them to the contrary, be treated as belonging to the husband and wife in equal shares.'

The primary points under that section are:

(a) The money in issue must arise from an allowance made for 'expenses of the matrimonial home or for similar purposes'. Thus, for instance, if the husband were to pay to the wife an allowance from which she paid the mortgage that would suffice.

(b) The section also extends to any property that is acquired out of any such allowance (for instance, if the wife buys personal property from the money given to her, the section would apply).

(c) The section can be rebutted by a contrary agreement.

(d) The section applies to people who have married or to people who have been engaged[1].

1 See the Law Reform (Miscellaneous Provisions) Act 1970, s 2.

Law of Property Act 1925, s 188

5.31 This section provides that, where any chattels belong to persons in undivided shares, persons interested in a moiety or upwards may apply to the court for an order for the division of the chattels or any of them, according to a valuation or otherwise. The court may make such order and give any consequential directions as it thinks fit. A county court has jurisdiction where the capital value of the property does not exceed the county court limit[1].

1 The county court limit is currently £30,000: see the High Court and County Courts Jurisdiction Order 1991, art 2(3).

Other personal property

5.32 Other issues relating to the ownership of personal property will have to be determined through the application of the general considerations that relate to the ownership of property. Thus it will be important to identify:

(a) whether there was any express agreement, arrangement or understanding in relation to the property ownership;

(b) where the money came from that was used to buy the personal property;

(c) who owned any chattels given in part exchange for the chattel in issue.

As to bank accounts, sums held in a jointly owned bank account will usually be divided equally between the parties. If both parties contribute to a bank account held in one partner's name, the law of trusts will have to be examined to see whether the other party can claim a share in that account. In the case of *Paul v Constance*[1] the issues related to money held in a bank account in the sole name of the man; the woman gave evidence that there had been express discussions confirming that the money was regarded as belonging equally to the parties; there was also evidence that both parties used the money held in the account. The woman sought a declaration that she was entitled to half the money in the account as a result of an express trust that had been fashioned out of the words that had been used between the couple. The woman succeeded in her claim. The Court of Appeal upheld her claim, finding that there was sufficient evidence of an express declaration of trust.

1 [1977] 1 All ER 195, [1977] 1 WLR 527.

PROCEDURE

Married Women's Property Act 1882

The relevant rules

5.33 The procedure under the Married Women's Property Act 1882, s 17 is laid down in the FPR 1991, r 3.6.

Which court?

5.34 Both the High Court and the county court have jurisdiction under the Married Women's Property Act 1882, s 17 whatever the value of the property in question may be (in this respect the jurisdiction under this Act is similar to the jurisdiction of the county court in relation to claims for ancillary relief on a divorce, judicial separation or decree of nullity). Where the application is made to a county court, the application should be filed:

(a) subject to (b) below, in the court for the district in which the applicant or respondent resides, or

(b) in the divorce county court in which any pending matrimonial cause has been commenced by or on behalf of either the applicant or the respondent, or in which any matrimonial cause is intended to be commenced by the applicant[1].

In the High Court the proceedings may be issued out of the principal registry or any district registry[2].

1 FPR 1991, r 3.6(3).
2 Ibid, r 3.6(1).

Form of application

5.35 In the High Court the proceedings are started by an originating summons. In the county court the application is started by an originating application. In both the High Court and the county court the application is to be made in Form N23 and is to be supported by an affidavit[1]. An order under s 17 may be made in any ancillary relief proceedings upon the application of any party thereto in Form N11 by notice of application or summons[2].

1 FPR 1991, r 3.6(1).
2 Ibid, r 3.6(2).

Particulars of property and mortgage

5.36 Where the application concerns the title to or possession of land, the originating summons or application shall:

(a) state whether the title to the land is registered or unregistered and, if registered, the Land Registry title number; and

(b) give particulars so far as known to the applicant of any mortgage of the land or interest therein[1]. The applicant is under a duty to serve a copy of the originating summons or application upon any mortgagee and any person so served may apply to the court in writing within 14 days after service, for a copy of the affidavit in support. Within 14 days of receiving such an affidavit, the mortgagee may file an affidavit in answer and should be entitled to be heard on the application[2].

1 FPR 1991, r 3.6(4).
2 Ibid, r 3.6(6).

The respondent

5.37 The originating summons or application has to be served on the respondent, together with a copy of the affidavit in support and an acknowledgment of service in Form N6[1]. If the respondent intends to contest the application he must file within 14 days after the time allowed for sending the acknowledgment of service, an affidavit in answer to the application setting out the grounds on which he relies, and lodge in the Court Office a copy of the application for service on the applicant[2]. If the respondent fails to file the necessary affidavits, the applicant may apply for directions; and the district judge may give such directions as he thinks fit, including a direction that the respondent shall be barred from defending the application unless an affidavit is filed within such time as the district judge may specify[3].

1 FPR 1991, r 3.6(5).
2 Ibid, r 3.6(7).
3 Ibid, r 3.6(8).

Other procedural provisions

5.38 A district judge may grant an injunction in proceedings under s 17, if, but only so far as, the injunction is ancillary or incidental to any relief sought in those proceedings[1]. Further, the following specific rules apply to applications under s 17[2]:

(a) Rule 2.62(4) which provides that 'at the hearing of an application for ancillary relief, the district judge shall, subject to rr 2.64, 2.65 and 10.10 investigate the allegations made in support of and in answer to the application, and may take evidence orally and may at any stage of the proceedings, whether before or during the hearing, order the attendance of any person for the purpose of being examined or cross-examined and order the discovery and production of any document or require affidavits'.

(b) Rule 2.62(5) which provides 'that the district judge may at any stage of the proceedings give directions as to the filing and service of pleadings and as to the further conduct of the proceedings'.

(c) Rule 2.62(6) which provides that 'Where any party to such an application intends on the day appointed for the hearing to apply for directions, he shall file and serve on every party a notice to that effect'.

(d) Rule 2.63 which provides that 'any party to an application for ancillary relief may by letter require any other party to give further information concerning any matter contained in any affidavit filed by or on behalf of that other party or any other relevant matter, or to furnish a list of relevant documents or to allow inspection of any such document, and may, in default of compliance by such party, apply to the district judge for directions'.

(e) Rule 2.64 which provides that at the conclusion of his investigation, the district judge may make such order as he thinks fit and, pending such final determination, may make an interim order upon such terms as he thinks fit. The provisions of RSC Ord 31, r 1 (power to order sale of land) apply to applications under s 17.

(f) Rule 2.65 which provides that the district judge may refer an application under s 17 to a judge for his decision.

(g) Rule 2.66 which specifies the arrangements that are to be made for the hearing of the application. In particular, that the hearing shall, unless the court otherwise directs, take place in chambers and that a judge shall have the same powers as a district judge[3].

Subject to the express provisions of r 3.6, the FPR 1991 apply to an application under the Married Women's Property Act, s 17 (with the necessary modifications) as if the application were a cause, the originating summons or application a petition, and the applicant a petitioner[4].

1 FPR 1991, r 3.6(9).
2 Ibid, r 3.6(10).
3 Ibid, r 3.6(11).

Section 17 in the principal registry

5.39 The FPR 1991, r 3.7 makes specific provisions in respect of applications under s 17 in the Principal Registry. In particular:

(a) where the application under s 17 is to be linked with proceedings for divorce, nullity or judicial separation that either are or will be pending in the Principal Registry, the application under s 17 may be made to the Principal Registry as if it were a county court[1];

(b) where proceedings under s 17 are to be heard in the Principal Registry, the Matrimonial and Family Proceedings Act 1984, s 42 will apply (this is the statutory provision that governs the county court proceedings in the Principal Registry of the Family Division)[2]. CCR Ord 4(8) and FPR 1991, r 3.6(3) (both of which relate to the venue of the proceedings) shall not apply[3];

(c) FPR 1991, r 1.4(1) will apply (which relates to whether proceedings in the Principal Registry will be treated as pending in a divorce county court or in the High Court)[4].

1 FPR 1991, r 3.7(1).
2 See *Butterworths Family Law Service*, Division G.
3 See ibid, Division H.
4 See ibid, Division H.

Procedure under the Law of Property Act 1925

5.40 By reason of the High Court and County Courts Jurisdiction Order 1991, art 2 the county court has jurisdiction under the LPA 1925, s 30 'whatever the amount involved in the proceedings and whatever the value of any fund or asset connected with the proceedings'. Where proceedings are brought only under this section, the application should be made in the county court by originating application or in the High Court by originating summons.

County court jurisdiction: declarations of trust

5.41 The county court's general equitable jurisdiction is specified by the County Courts Act 1984, s 23. The current equitable jurisdiction is £30,000[1]. That jurisdiction limit applies, amongst other things, to proceedings 'for a declaration that a trust subsists'[2]. The value of the property to be dealt with provides the criterion by which it is to be determined whether a county court possesses jurisdiction (except in cases of a sale where the jurisdiction is decided by the amount of the purchase money or in cases relating to foreclosure or redemption of any mortgage or for enforcing any charge or lien). In many instances, therefore, that general jurisdiction will be exceeded where there are applications relating to property. The jurisdiction may be extended by agreement the County Courts Act 1984, s 24. If there is any doubt about the county court's jurisdiction, it is well worth agreeing that a memorandum under the County Courts Act 1984, s 24 should be signed before any proceedings are initiated. If there is likely to be a contested issue as to whether an engagement took place (and, therefore, a contested issue about whether there is jurisdiction under the Married Women's Property Act 1882 as a result of the Law Reform (Miscellaneous Provisions) Act 1970, s 2) it is wise for a memorandum under the County Courts Act 1984, s 24 to be signed before the proceedings are issued if the property in question is likely to exceed the county court's equitable jurisdiction (in this way, if it is found by the court that the engagement did not take place, the county court would still have jurisdiction to deal with the matter under its general equitable jurisdiction).

1 County Courts Jurisdiction Order 1981.
2 County Courts Act 1984, s 23(b)(ii).

General procedure in the county court

5.42 An application for a declaration that a trust subsists should be made by originating application. The originating application should set out the orders the court is requested to make; it should also give sufficient particulars of the basis of the claim to justify the orders that are sought. The originating application is lodged with the request for issue. The court will usually provide a return date for a pre-trial review. At the pre-trial review directions will be given; these directions will usually require an affidavit or answer to be filed by the respondent (and for valuations of the property to be secured). The application will be heard by the circuit judge in the light of the district judge's limited jurisdiction of £5,000 under CCR Ord 21, r 5. However, the jurisdiction of the district judge may be extended by leave of the judge and with consent of the parties[1].

1 CCR Ord 21, r 5(1)(d).

Procedure in the High Court

5.43 In the High Court proceedings for a declaration of trust are started by originating summons either in the Family Division or in the Chancery Division. The originating summons is to be supported by an affidavit; a notice to proceed will be issued. The court will then arrange for a return day at which directions will be given.

FINANCIAL PROVISION FOR CHILDREN

Children Act 1989, s 15 and Sch 1

5.44 The provisions of the CA 1989, s 15 and Sch 1 have, to a very large extent, replaced the previous statutory provisions that related to financial applications in respect of children[1]. The CA 1989 now contains a unified code for dealing with such applications. However, applications in respect of children may still be made under certain other statutes[2].

1 For instance, the Family Law Reform Act 1987 and the Affiliation Proceedings Act 1957.
2 For instance under the MCA 1973 and the Domestic Proceedings and Magistrates' Courts Act 1978.

Joinder with other applications

5.45 Often it will be necessary to give consideration to joining together applications that relate to the property of co-habitees with applications for financial relief under the CA 1989, Sch 1. Where possible such applications should be heard together before the same court[1]. The separate applications may well have to be issued in different formats; however, orders for them to be heard before the same court at the same time can be made at the stage at which directions are sought (for instance at the first appointment of the originating application where an application is made to the court for a declaration of a beneficial interest in a jointly owned home or at the first directions appointment in respect of the application under Schedule 1 of the CA 1989).

1 *Hammond v Mitchell* [1991] 1 WLR 1127 (which has been further considered at para 5.14).

The Child Support Act 1991

5.46 By reason of the Child Support Act 1991 the court's powers to make maintenance orders in respect of children have been severely curtailed[1]. The court may still retain jurisdiction to make child maintenance orders in some limited circumstances, however[2].

1 Under the Child Support Act 1991, s 8(3) no court may exercise any power which it would otherwise have to make, vary or revise any maintenance order in relation to the child and absent parent concerned where a child support officer would have jurisdiction to make a maintenance assessment with respect to a qualifying child and an absent parent of his on an application duly made by a person entitled to apply for such an assessment with respect to that child (see para 10.5).
2 For instance under the transitional provisions of the Child Support Act 1991, where a consent application follows written agreement between the parties (see the Child Maintenance (Written Agreements) Order 1993, where a parent is resident abroad or where the application relates to school fees, etc (Child Support Act 1991, s 8(6)–(8); and para 10.5)

When Schedule 1 orders may be made

5.47 An order under the CA 1989, Sch 1 may be made on an application by a parent or guardian of a child or by any person in whose favour a residence order is in force with respect to a child[1]. Further, the court may make an order under the CA 1989, Sch 1 when it makes, varies or discharges a residence order, even though no application has been made for an order under the Schedule[2]. The child has a limited right to apply[3].

1 Schedule 1(1).
2 Schedule 1(6).
3 See para 5.57.

Orders that may be made in a High Court or a county court

5.48 The High Court or county court may make any of the following orders:

(a) An order requiring either or both parents of a child to make periodical payments either to the applicant for the benefit of the child or to the child himself. The order may be for such term as may be specified in it.

(b) An order requiring either or both parents of a child to secure periodical payments to the applicant for the benefit of the child or to the child himself. Again, the order may be for such term as is specified in it.

(c) An order requiring either or both parents of a child to make a lump sum payment either to the applicant for the benefit of the child or to the child himself.

(d) An order requiring a settlement to be made for the benefit of the child, and to the satisfaction of the court of property:

    (i) to which either parent is entitled (either in possession or in reversion);

    (ii) which is specified in the order.

(e) An order requiring either or both parents of a child to transfer such property to which the parent is, or the parents are, entitled (either in possession or reversion) as may be specified in the order. The transfer to the applicant, for the benefit of the child, or to the child himself[1].

1 CA 1989, Sch 1(2). And see further provisions regarding lump sums at para 5.55.

Orders that may be made by the magistrates' court

5.49 A magistrates' court may only make the orders that are set out in (a) and (c) in the above paragraph (that is to say the magistrates' court may only make periodical payment orders or lump sum orders)[1]. The amount of any lump sum that a magistrates' court may order may not exceed £1,000 (or such larger amount as the Secretary of State may fix)[2].

1 CA 1989, Sch 1, para 1(1)(b).
2 Ibid, Sch 1, para 5(2).

Parent

5.50 The word 'parent' is defined as including any party to a marriage (whether or not subsisting) in relation to whom the child concerned is a child of the family[1]. However, this definition does not apply to Sch 1, para 2 (orders for financial provision for persons over 18) or Sch 1, para 15 (which relates to local authorities' contributions to child's maintenance). Thus, a co-habitant who is not a parent of the child cannot be treated as a parent for the purposes of this Schedule[2]; Whilst, step-parents will be caught by the definition where the child concerned was a child of the family[3] and the step-parent has married one of the child's parents.

1 CA 1989, Sch 1, para 16(2).
2 *J v J* [1993] 2 FLR 56.
3 'Child of the family' is defined by the CA 1989, s 105(1) in similar terms to the MCA 1973 and includes children 'treated as children of the family'.

Child

5.51 A child[1] means a person under the age of 18, subject to para 16 of Sch 1. Paragraph 16 of Sch 1 provides that 'child' includes, in any case where an application is made under paras 2 or 6 in relation to a person who has reached the age of 18, that person[2].

1 CA 1989, s 105(1) defines a 'child'.
2 Paragraph 2 relates to orders for financial relief for a person over 18. Paragraph 6 relates to the variation of orders for periodical payments.

Child of the family

5.52 Child of the family is defined in the CA 1989, s 105 in relation to the parties to a marriage as:

(a) a child of both of those parties;

(b) any other child, not being a child who is placed with those parties as foster parents by a local authority or voluntary organisation, who has been treated by both of those parties as a child of their family.

Factors which the court is to take into account

5.53 In deciding whether to exercise its powers to make a financial provision order, and, if so, in what manner, the court must have regard to all the circumstances including:

(a) the income, earning capacity, property and other financial resources of any parent of the child, applicant or any other person in whose favour the court proposes to make an order, has or is likely to have in the foreseeable future;

(b) the financial needs, obligations and responsibilities which any of the above persons may have or is likely to have in the foreseeable future;

(c) the financial needs of the child;

(d) the income, earning capacity, if any, property and other financial resources of the child;

(e) any physical or mental disability of the child;

(f) the manner in which the child was being, or was expected to be educated or trained[1].

A court may make an order against a bankrupt parent[2].

1 CA 1989, Sch 1, para 4(1).
2 *Re G (Children Act 1989: Schedule 1)* [1996] 2 FLR 171.

Liability of person who is not mother or father

5.54 In deciding whether to exercise its powers against a person who is not the mother or father of a child (and if so in what manner) the court must have regard in addition to the following:

(a) whether that person has assumed responsibility for the maintenance of the child and, if so, the extent to which and basis on which he assumed that responsibility and the length of the period during which he met that responsibility;

(b) whether he did so knowing that the child was not his child;

(c) the liability of any other person to maintain the child[1].

Where an order is made against a person who is not the father of the child, the court must record in the order that the order was made on the basis that the person against whom the order is made is not the child's father[2].

1 CA 1989, Sch 1, para 4(2).
2 Ibid, Sch 1, para 4(3).

Lump sums

5.55 Futher provision as to the making of lump sum orders are provided as follows[1]:

(a) An order for a lump sum may be made for the purpose of enabling any liabilities or expenses to be met which were:

    (i) incurred in connection with the birth of the child or in maintaining the child; and

    (ii) reasonably incurred before the making of the order,

to be met.

Though, this provision does not limit the generality of the court's power to make a lump sum order as it sees fit, having regard to the factors specified in Sch 1, para 4.

(b) The magistrates' court may currently only order a lump sum of up to £1,000.

(c) Where the court varies or discharges an order for periodical payments or secured periodical payments, it also has the power to make an order for the payment of a lump sum.

(d) An order may be made for the payment of a lump sum by instalments.

(e) An order for payment by instalments may be varied as to the number of instalments, the amount of any instalments payable and the date on which any instalment becomes payable.

1 CA 1989, Sch 1, para 5.

Other capital orders

5.56 In respect of a tenancy it has been held that the court has power under Sch 1 to direct that the father shall transfer to the mother the tenancy since to do so would confer benefit to the child[1]. The phrase 'for the benefit of the child' should be given a wide import[1]. However, in respect of other property adjustment orders it has been held that they should not ordinarily be made to provide benefits for the child after he has attained his independence. In those circumstances, any settlement of property is likely to be made on the basis that provision is only made for the child whilst the child is dependent; this has been considered in two particular cases:

(a) In *A v A*[2] the father was a very wealthy man who lived outside the United Kingdom. He was the father of only one of the three children who lived with the mother. The mother sought an outright transfer of the property that the father had acquired through an off-shore company as a home for the mother and the children. Ward J held that the proper order was to require a settlement to be made for the benefit of the child and to the satisfaction of the court of the relevant property. The terms of the settlement should be that the nominees of the mother and father were to hold the property for the child for a term which would terminate six months after the child had attained the age of 18, or six months after she had completed her full-time education (which included her tertiary education), whichever was the latest.

(b) In *T v S*[3] Johnson J held that 'in the striking words of Booth J in *Kiely v Kiely*'[4] the statutory scheme should be construed as enabling the court to make proper financial provision 'for children as children or dependants'. He went on to say that there may be circumstances in which it is necessary for the court to make provision for children based upon their having a continuing need after they have attained their majority and, indeed, after they have left full-time education, but such circumstances would be 'special'[5].

1 *K v K* [1992] 2 FLR 220, [1992] 2 FCR 253.
2 [1994] 1 FLR 657.
3 [1994] 1 FCR 743, [1994] 2 FLR 883.
4 [1988] 1 FLR 248.
5 Following the terminology of Scarman LJ in *Chamberlain v Chamberlain* [1974] 1 All ER 33, CA.

Financial relief for persons over 18

5.57 A person who has attained the age of 18 may apply for :

(a) an order that either or both of his parents pay him periodical payments; or

(b) an order requiring either or both of his parents to pay a lump sum[1].

A court will only make such an order if:

(c) an applicant is, will be or (if an order were made under this paragraph) would be receiving instruction at an educational establishment or undergoing training for a trade, vocation or profession, whether or not while in gainful employment; or

(d) that there are special circumstances which justify the making of such an order[2].

There are the following additional restrictions to the powers of the court:

(e) An application may not be made for such an order if, immediately before the applicant reached the age of 16, a periodical payments order was in force with respect to him;

(f) no such order may be made at a time when the parents are living with each other in the same household[3].

1 CA 1989, Sch 1, para 2(2).
2 Ibid, Sch 1, para 2(1).
3 Ibid, Sch 1, para 2(3) and (4).

Variation and discharge

5.58 Under Sch 1, para 1(4) the court may vary or discharge an order for periodical payments or secured periodical payments (subject to the limitations on the court's powers as a result of the Child Support Act 1991). The order for variation or discharge may be made on the application of any person by or to whom payments were required to be made under the existing order. Further provision in respect of the variation of such orders is set out in Sch 1, para 6. These additional provisions include the power of a child who has reached the age of 16 to apply himself for the variation of an order for periodical payments[1].

1 CA 1989, Sch 1, para 6(4).

Retrospective and continuing powers

5.59 The provisions of Sch 1 are retrospective (therefore an application may be made under Sch 1 even if the applicant would have been out of time under statutory provisions that existed before the Act came into force, such as the Affiliation Proceedings Act 1957[1]). The powers under Schedule 1 may be exercised at any time[2].

1 *H v O* [1992] 1 FLR 282.
2 CA 1989, Sch 1, para 1(3).

Procedure

5.60 The procedure for such applications is laid down in the FPR 1991 (for the High Court and county court) and in the Family Proceedings Courts

Financial Provision for Children 193

(Children Act 1989) Rules 1991 (in respect of the magistrates' court). The procedure is as follows:

(a) The application is made in Forms C1 and C10. It must be accompanied by a statement of means in Form C10A: see FPR 1991, r 4.4 and FPC (CA 1989) R 1991, r 4.

(b) The respondents are every person with parental responsibility, every person who had parental responsibility immediately before any care order relating to the child and any person whom the applicant believes is interested in or affected by the proceedings. Additionally, if a local authority is providing accommodation for the child or a person is caring for the child in a refuge, service must be effected on that local authority or person.

(c) Every respondent must file an acknowledgment in Form T7 within 14 days of the service of the application.

(d) A directions hearing will be held in accordance with FPR 1991, r 4.14 or FPC (CA 1989) R 1991, r 14.

(e) Although there is no specific prescribed form for an order under Sch 1, it is incumbent upon the court to make findings of fact[1]. Further, where the court is asked to make an order by consent it should do so because such an order was to the benefit of the child in case of future difficulties and also may have tax benefits[2].

1 *Re C* [1994] 2 FCR 1122.
2 *K v H* [1993] 2 FLR 61.

Appeals

5.61 An appeal from a magistrates' court against an order under the CA 1989, Sch 1 will be to the High Court under s 94 of that Act. Such an appeal will include an appeal from the refusal of justices to remit arrears which had accrued under a child periodical payments order made under the 1989 Act[1]. Appeals in the High Court and the county courts will follow the procedure in the FPR 1991, r 8.1 (to judge) and then RSC Ord 59 (judge to Court of Appeal).

1 *S v S* [1993] 1 FLR 606.

Chapter Six

Inheritance

Robert Purdie

Succession 195
Family Provision 202

SUCCESSION

Introduction

6.1 This chapter covers the more important aspects of succession in the context of family law and as a background to family provision.

The effect of marriage

6.2 Subject to certain exceptions, a will is revoked by the subsequent marriage of the testator[1]. This applies where the marriage is valid in English law[2] and also where the marriage is voidable[3]. A void marriage does not revoke a will because there never was a marriage[4]. There is an exception for wills exercising a power of appointment[5], which provides that a disposition in a will in exercise of a power of appointment takes effect despite the subsequent marriage of the testator unless the property so appointed would, in default of appointment, pass to the testator's personal representatives.

1 Wills Act 1837, s 18(1).
2 *Mette v Mette* (1859) 1 Sw & Tr 416.
3 *Re Roberts* [1978] 3 All ER 225, [1978] 1 WLR 653, CA. For the grounds on which a marriage celebrated after 31 July 1971 is voidable see the MCA 1973, s 12, and para 3.8.
4 *De Reneville v De Reneville* [1948] P 100, [1948] 1 All ER 56; the decree is merely declaratory. For the grounds on which a marriage celebrated after 31 July 1971 is void see the MCA 1973, s 11 and para 3.8.
5 Wills Act 1837, s 18(2).

Wills in expectation of marriage

6.3 Where it appears from a will that at the time it was made, the testator was intending to be married to a particular person and he intended that the will (or a disposition in the will) should not be revoked by his marriage to that person, then the will is not revoked by the subsequent marriage and the disposition takes effect despite the subsequent marriage[1]. Furthermore, where it appears that a disposition in a will was not to be revoked by marriage to a particular person, any other disposition in the will takes effect, notwithstanding the marriage, unless it appears from the will that the testator intended the disposition to be revoked by the marriage[2]. In this respect *Re Coleman*[3] has been reversed, as the amendments to the Wills Act 1837 relate to dispositions rather than to the will as a whole.

1 Wills Act 1837, ss 18(3), (4) (as substituted).
2 Ibid, s 18(4)(b).
3 [1976] Ch 1, [1975] 1 All ER 675 a decision on the previous legislation; LPA 1925, s 177.

The effect of divorce or nullity

6.4 Where a decree absolute of divorce or nullity pronounced in England or Wales, or a similar foreign decree is made that would be entitled to recognition in England and Wales[1] special provisions apply in respect of an appointment of a former spouse as executor or trustee, or a gift to a former spouse[2]. The date of the will or termination of marriage is immaterial, the important date is that of the death of the testator. In respect of deaths after 1982 and before 1996 (except in so far as a contrary intention appeared in the will), the will takes effect as if any appointment of the former spouse as executor or trustee were omitted[3] and any devise or bequest to the former spouse lapses[4]. In this context 'lapse' meant that the subject matter of the devise or bequest became part of the residue, or where there was no effective gift of residue, it passed on intestacy[5]. In respect of deaths after 1995 the effect of divorce or nullity changed, subject to a contrary intention in the will. After 1995 provisions in the will appointing executors or trustees or conferring a power of appointment, if they so appoint or confer power on the former spouse, take effect as if the former spouse had died on the date on which the marriage was dissolved or annulled[6]. Any property (or an interest in property) devised or bequeathed to the former spouse, passes as if the former spouse had died on the date on which the marriage was dissolved or annulled[7].

1 Under the FLA 1986, Part II.
2 Wills Act 1837, s 18A inserted by the Administration of Justice Act 1982 and as amended by the FLA 1986 and the Law Reform (Succession) Act 1995.
3 Wills Act 1837, s 18A(1)(a).
4 Ibid, s 18A(1)(b).
5 *Re Sinclair* [1985] Ch 446, [1985] 1 All ER 1066, CA, overruling *Re Cherrington* [1984] 2 All ER 285, [1984] 1 WLR 772.
6 Wills Act 1837, s 18A(1)(a), as substituted.
7 Ibid, s 18A(1)(b), as substituted.

The effect of judicial separation

6.5 A decree of judicial separation has no effect on the will of either spouse. In respect of deaths on or after 1 August 1970, where a decree of judicial separation is in force and the separation is continuing, then where either party to the marriage dies leaving a total or partial intestacy, the property in respect of which he or she died intestate devolves as if the other spouse were already dead[1].

1 MCA 1973, s 18(2).

Intestate succession (including partial intestacy)

6.6 An intestacy occurs where a deceased does not leave a valid will. A partial intestacy occurs where a testator leaves a will but does not fully dispose of all his property. A statutory trust for sale arises[1] in cases of total and partial intestacy. Section 33(1) of the Administration of Estates Act 1925 directs the personal representatives to get in the assets with a power to postpone. Subsection (2) directs the personal representatives to pay funeral, testamentary and administration expenses, debts and other liabilities (which would include inheritance tax), to set aside a fund to pay pecuniary legacies (in the case of a partial intestacy) and then hold the residuary estate to be distributed in accordance with s 46. Where the will of a testator leaves a life interest to his spouse but is silent as to the interest in remainder the question arises as to when the partial intestacy arises. In *Re McKee*[2] it was held that the partial intestacy arose on the death of the wife and so her estate was entitled to the statutory legacy. In *Re Bowen-Buscarlet*[3] it was held that the partial intestacy was immediate and so the spouse was entitled to an immediate payment of the statutory legacy, subject to hotchpot. It seems to be accepted that the approach in *Re Bowen-Buscarlet* is to be preferred to that in *Re McKee*.

1 By operation of the Administration of Estates Act 1925, s 33.
2 [1931] 2 Ch 145, CA.
3 [1972] Ch 463, [1971] 3 All ER 636 (following *Re Douglas's Will Trusts* [1959] 2 All ER 620, [1959] 1 WLR 744).

Spouse: qualification

6.7 There are two elements: the spouse must be a spouse and must survive the deceased.

(a) *Marriage*. The spouse must be a spouse as a result of a valid marriage, or a voidable marriage that has not been avoided at the time of death of the deceased; ie it must be subsisting at the date of death. A marriage ceases to subsist when it is dissolved or annulled by decree absolute. Where decree absolute and the death of one of the parties occurs on the same day, the exact time of each event must be considered[1]. The FPR 1991[2] provide that a decree absolute is indorsed with the precise time at which it was made. A party to a void marriage is not a surviving spouse as there never was a marriage[3]. There is no direct authority as to the status of a surviving spouse or spouses to a polygamous marriage. An indirect authority is *Re Sehota*[4] where a wife in an actually polygamous marriage was held to be a spouse for the purposes of an application under the Inheritance (Provision for Family and Dependants) Act 1975.

(b) *Survival.* In order to benefit on intestacy, the spouse must survive the intestate. This is a question of fact. The Administration of Estates Act 1925, s 46(3) provides that in the case where an intestate and his or her spouse die in circumstances rendering it uncertain which of them survived the other, they are deemed to have died at the same time[5]. In respect of deaths on or after 1 January 1996, s 43(2A)[6] provides that where an intestate's spouse survived the intestate but died within 28 days of the intestate, the estate of the intestate is distributed as if the spouse had not so survived.

1 *Re Seaford* [1968] P 53, [1968] 1 All ER 482, CA.
2 Rule 2.51.
3 *De Reneville v De Reneville* [1948] P 100, [1948] 1 All ER 56.
4 [1978] 3 All ER 385, [1978] 1 WLR 1506.
5 In cases of *commorientes* (where two or more persons have died in circumstances rendering it uncertain which of them survived the other or others) the normal rule contained in the LPA 1925, s 184 that such deaths are presumed to have occurred in order of seniority (ie the younger are deemed to have survived the elder) does *not* apply to husband and wife on intestacy.
6 Inserted by the Law Reform (Succession) Act 1995.

Spouse: Entitlement

6.8 This depends upon the classes of relatives that survive the intestate. See Table 2 in Appendix 2.

(a) *Personal chattels.* The surviving spouse is absolutely entitled to the personal chattels of the intestate as defined by the Administration of Estates Act 1925, s 55(1)(x). The value of items is not relevant in determining whether they are personal chattels; likewise a collection of items may be personal chattels whether kept in the intestate's house, stored or on loan to a museum[1].

(b) *Fixed net sum.* The surviving spouse is absolutely entitled to the fixed net sum (otherwise called the 'statutory legacy'). This is currently £125,000 where there is issue and £200,000 where there is no issue in respect of deaths on or after 1 December 1993[2]. For previous amounts of the fixed net sum: see Table 2 in Appendix 2. Interest is payable on the statutory legacy from the date of death until payment; the current rate of interest is 6%[3]. Previous rates are shown in Table 3 in Appendix 2. The interest is payable out of income but charged upon corpus[4].

(c) *Life interest.* Subject to personal chattels and the fixed net sum, where the intestate leaves issue, the surviving spouse is entitled to half of the balance of the estate for life[5]. The surviving spouse is entitled to capitalise the life interest in accordance with the statutory provisions[6]. The election to redeem the life interest must be made within 12 months of the grant of representation[7].

(d) *Matrimonial home.* Where the title to the matrimonial home is held by the intestate and spouse as beneficial joint tenants, the surviving spouse is entitled to the whole property by operation of law under the right of survivorship. Accordingly the deceased's severable share does not form part of the net estate[8]. Where the title to the matrimonial home is held in the sole name of the intestate, it must be determined whether the surviving spouse has a beneficial interest in the property[9]. Third parties may have a beneficial interest in the matrimonial home on the same basis or under proprietory estoppel[10]. The surviving spouse has a right to appropriate the intestate's interest in the matrimonial home in or towards satisfaction of any absolute interest of the surviving spouse in the real or personal estate of the intestate[11]. The surviving spouse must have been resident in the matrimonial home at the time of death of the intestate[12]. The election must be exercised within 12 months of the grant of representation[13]. The value of the matrimonial home is taken as at the date of the appropriation[14]. The words 'in or towards satisfaction of any absolute interest of the surviving spouse' mean that the surviving spouse can only have the house if the value of the house is less than any absolute interest. However the provisions of Schedule 2, paragraph 5(2) of the Administration of Estates Act 1925 allow the personal representatives to appropriate the matrimonial home to the surviving spouse provided he or she returns to the estate any excess value over and above the absolute interest[15].

1 *Re Crispin* [1975] 1 Ch 245, [1974] 3 All ER 772, CA.
2 SI 1993 2906.
3 SI 1983 1374.
4 *Re Saunders* [1929] 1 Ch 674.
5 Administration of Estates Act 1925, s 46(1)(i), Table, paras (2), (3).
6 Ibid, s 47A and the Intestate Succession (Interest and Capitalisation) Order 1977, art 3 and the Table in the Schedule.
7 Administration of Estates Act 1925, s 47A(5).
8 Ibid, ss 1(1) and 3(4).
9 See the Matrimonial Proceedings and Property Act 1970, s 37 and cases on implied resulting and constructive trusts such as *Pettitt v Pettitt* [1970] AC 777, [1969] 2 All ER 385, HL; *Gissing v Gissing* [1971] AC 886, [1970] 2 All ER 780, HL; and *Lloyds Bank plc v Rossett* [1991] 1 AC 107, [1990] 1 All ER 1111, HL.
10 See eg *Re Basham* [1987] 1 All ER 405, [1986] 1 WLR 1498.
11 Intestate Estates Act 1952, s 5 and Sch 2.
12 Ibid, Sch 2, para 1(1).
13 Ibid, Sch 2, para 3(1)(a).
14 *Robinson v Collins* [1975] 1 All ER 321, [1975] 1 WLR 309.
15 *Re Phelps* [1980] Ch 275, [1979] 3 All ER 373, CA.

Issue: Qualification

6.9 The position of the various categories of children must be considered to see if they qualify.

(a) *Legitimate children.* These are issue and comprise children of a valid or voidable marriage (whether or not the marriage has been annulled), and include a child en ventre sa mère at the date of the father's death.

(b) *Children of a void marriage.* A child of a void marriage (whenever born) is treated as legitimate if at the time of insemination or conception (or marriage if later) either or both parties reasonably believed that the marriage was valid[1]. A child is only a child of a void marriage if born after the ceremony of marriage, although insemination or conception may have taken place previously[2]. The words 'whenever born' indicate that the Act applies to children born before or after commencement[3]. In *Hashmi v Hashmi*[4], children of a polygamous marriage (then void under English law) were declared to be legitimate because the marriage was valid according to the law of the husband's domicile.

(c) *Legitimated children.* A legitimated child is within the meaning of issue in respect of deaths on or after 1 January 1976[5]. An illegitimate child is legitimated by the subsequent marriage of his parents during his life as from the date of the marriage provided the father is domiciled in England and Wales at the date of the marriage[6] or is domiciled in a country at the date of the marriage by the law of which the child is legitimated[7]. Legitimation under a foreign law may include legitimation by a polygamous marriage[8].

(d) *Illegitimate children.* At common law an illegitimate child was unable to take on intestacy. This has now been modified in two stages:

   (i) in respect of deaths on or after 1 January 1970 an illegitimate child had the same rights on the intestacy of his parents as if born legitimate. The parents had the same rights on the intestacy of their illegitimate children as if born legitimate. This was limited to the relationship of parents and children and did not apply to siblings, grandparents and remoter issue[9];

   (ii) in respect of deaths after 3 April 1988 an illegitimate child is entitled to take on an intestacy as if legitimate. On the intestate death of an illegitimate child, all relatives are entitled as if the child had been born legitimate[10].

Under the Family Law Reform Act 1969[11] the father was presumed to have predeceased the illegitimate child, unless the contrary was proved. Under the Family Law Reform Act 1987[12] it is presumed that the father and all relations on the father's side have predeceased the illegitimate child, unless the contrary is proved.

(e) *Adopted children.* The Adoption Act 1976 provides that as from 1 January 1976, an adopted child is treated as the legitimate child of the adopter or adopters and of no-one else[13]. Where the adopters are a married couple, the child is a brother or sister of the whole blood to other children of the marriage, including other adopted children[14]. Where the adopter is a single person the child is a brother or sister of the half-blood to any other children of the adopter[15]. See s 42 for rules of construction.

(f) *Human Fertilisation and Embryology Act 1990*. The woman who gives birth to the child is, in law, the mother[16]. In respect of a relevant procedure, carried out on or after 1 August 1991 in respect of a married woman, her husband (if he is not the donor) is treated as the father, unless he did not consent to the procedure[17]. Where licensed treatment is provided for a man and a woman (not married to each other) the man is treated as the father[18]. A man, whose sperm is used after his death, is not to be treated as the father[19].

1 Legitimacy Act 1976, s 1.
2 *Re Spence* [1990] Ch 652, [1990] 2 All ER 827, CA. This case contains a useful analysis of the differences between legitimated children and children treated as legitimate.
3 Ibid.
4 [1972] Fam 36, [1971] 3 All ER 1253.
5 Legitimacy Act 1976, s 5. In respect of deaths after 1925 but before 1976 see Legitimacy Act 1926, ss 3–5 (now repealed with savings).
6 Legitimacy Act 1976, s 2.
7 Legitimacy Act 1976, s 3.
8 *Bamgbose v Daniel* [1955] AC 107, [1954] 3 All ER 263, PC.
9 FLRA 1969, s 14.
10 FLRA 1987, ss 1 and 18.
11 Section 14(2).
12 Section 18(2).
13 Adoption Act 1976, s 39.
14 Ibid, s 39(1)(a).
15 Ibid, s 39(1)(b).
16 Human Fertilisation and Embryology Act 1990, s 27.
17 Ibid, s 28(2).
18 Ibid, s 28(3), (4).
19 Ibid, s 28(6)(b).

Issue: Entitlement

6.10

(a) *Where surviving spouse*. Half of the residue goes to issue on the statutory trusts plus the reversion of the other half following the life interest of the surviving spouse, subject to the surviving spouse's rights to capitalisation.

(b) *Where no surviving spouse*. All goes to issue on the statutory trusts. If issue of the intestate die before distribution or during the lifetime of the surviving spouse, the children of the deceased issue take their parents share per stirpes and equally if more than one.

Other relatives

6.11 See Table 1 in Appendix 2 for the order of entitlements of relatives where the intestate is survived by neither spouse, nor issue. Where issue or other relatives disclaim their entitlement, the residue is held on trust for the next following class of relatives[1].

1 *Re Scott* [1975] 2 All ER 1033, [1975] 1 WLR 1260.

FAMILY PROVISION

Introduction

6.12 The Inheritance (Provisions for Family and Dependants) Act 1975[1] limits the testamentary freedom of a testator by enabling family and dependants to apply to the court for financial provision out of the net estate of the deceased. The jurisdiction of the court depends upon the deceased being domiciled in England and Wales at the date of death[2]. Certain categories of persons[3] are entitled to apply. An application under the Act is personal to the applicant and does not pass to his personal representatives on death[4]. Between former spouses or those judicially separated, the court deciding on ancillary relief or financial relief after foreign divorce may order that the parties are not entitled to apply under the Act[5].

1 All statutory references are to the Inheritance (Provisions for Family and Dependants) Act 1975 unless otherwise stated.
2 Section 1(1).
3 See those categories listed in s 1(1) as amended by the Law Reform (Succession) Act 1995.
4 *Whytte v Ticehurst* [1986] Fam 64, [1986] 2 All ER 158. Thus an application by a widow under the Act abated on her death prior to determination.
5 Sections 15 and 15A. See *Whiting v Whiting* [1988] 2 All ER 275, [1988] 1 WLR 565, CA.

Classes of applicants

6.13 The following classes of persons are entitled to apply under the Act. Each category must be considered in turn to determine the extent of the category.

Spouse

6.14 The surviving wife or husband of the deceased[1]. This means a surviving husband of wife as a result of a valid marriage (not dissolved) or a voidable marriage that has not been avoided. It includes a judicially separated spouse (subject to an order under s 15). It includes a spouse in an actually polygamous marriage[2]. It includes a party to a void marriage (that has not been dissolved or annulled) provided the applicant entered the marriage in good faith[3].

1 Section 1(1)(a).
2 *Re Sehota* [1978] 3 All ER 385, [1978] 1 WLR 1506.
3 Section 25(4). A person who contracted a void marriage with the deceased otherwise than in good faith might well be a co-habitant within s 1(1)(ba) or a dependant within s 1(1)(e). However, public policy might prevent such a claim: *Whiston v Whiston* [1995] Fam 198, [1995] 2 FCR 496, CA.

Former spouse

6.15 This means a person whose marriage to the deceased has been dissolved or annulled as being voidable *and* who has not remarried. A party to a marriage that has been annulled as being void is a former spouse provided he or she has not remarried. Remarriage includes entering into a void or voidable marriage[1].

1 Section 25(5).

Co-habitant

6.16 Although the Act does not use the word 'co-habitant', a person who for the whole of the two years immediately preceding the death of the deceased, lived with the deceased in the same household as husband and wife, is a qualified applicant[1]. This only applies in respect of deaths after 1995[2]. This provision overcomes some of the difficulties faced by co-habitants in coming within the category of dependants[3] as, for example where there was a pooling of resources rather than dependency. The use of the word 'household' is significant because it is an abstract rather than physical concept[4]. Thus it is possible for persons to remain in the same household, even if physically apart, such as where one is in hospital or a nursing home.

1 Sections 1(1)(ba), 1(1A), inserted by the Law Reform (Succession) Act 1995. A spouse or former spouse who qualifies under s 1(1)(a) or (b) does not qualify under s 1(1)(ba).
2 Ibid.
3 Under s 1(1)(e).
4 *Santos v Santos* [1972] Fam 247, [1972] 2 All ER 246, CA.

Children

6.17 A child of the deceased is a qualified applicant[1]. This means legitimate children, illegitimate children[2], adopted children, children as conceived as a result of procedures under the Human Fertilisation and Embryology Act 1990[3] and would include a child of the deceased en ventre sa mère at the date of death of the deceased[4]. A natural child of the deceased ceases to be his child on adoption by another by reason of the Adoption Act 1976, s 39(2) and cannot apply[5]. The Act does not distinguish between minor children and adult children; each is equally qualified to make a claim[6].

1 Section 1(1)(c).
2 Section 25(1).
3 Where a parental order has been made under s 30, then the provisions of the Adoption Act 1976, ss 39(1)(a), (2), (4) and (6) apply with appropriate modifications.
4 Section 25(1).
5 *Re Collins* [1990] Fam 56, [1990] 2 All ER 47.
6 It is more difficult for adult children to succeed.

Step-children

6.18 A person who, in the case of any marriage to which the deceased was at any time a party, was treated by the deceased as a child of the family in relation to that marriage, is a qualified applicant[1]. Thus the deceased must have married the parent of the applicant *and* treated the applicant as a child of the family in relation to that marriage. As with children, the Act does not distinguish between minor step-children and adult step-children; each is equally qualified to make a claim. The provision may be very wide indeed; the treatment as a child of the family need not have occurred during the marriage, provided it was in relation to the marriage[2]. The applicant may never have been a minor during the marriage[3].

1 Section 1(1)(d).
2 *Re Debenham* [1986] 1 FLR 404. For matrimonial cases on the meaning of 'treatment as a child of the family' see: *A v A (Family: Unborn Child)* [1974] Fam 6, [1974] 1 All ER 755; *M v M (Child of the Family)* (1981) 2 FLR 39, CA; and *D v D (Child of the Family)* (1981) 2 FLR 93, CA.
3 *Re Leach* [1986] Ch 226, [1985] 2 All ER 754, CA where the applicant was aged 32 when her father remarried. On the father's death his estate passed to the step-mother. On analysis of the facts it was held that the step-mother had treated the applicant as a child of the family by assuming the position of a parent with its attendant responsibilities and privileges; as a child gets older, the parent's privileges may increase and the responsibilities diminish.

Other dependants

6.19 A person (not within previous categories) who immediately before the death of the deceased was being maintained wholly or partly by the deceased is a qualified applicant[1]. Such a person is treated as being maintained by the deceased, either wholly or partly, if the deceased (other than for full valuable consideration) was making a substantial contribution in money or money's worth towards the reasonable needs of the applicant[2]. These requirements are cumulative, both must be satisfied[3]. The fact that the deceased has provided for the applicant is prima facie evidence of an assumption of responsibility[4]. The words 'immediately before the death of the deceased' have caused problems of interpretation[5]; the period leading up to death is looked at given that in the period immediately before death, roles may have been reversed where the applicant nurses the deceased. The provision of free accommodation by the deceased for the applicant is an important consideration, but the pooling of resources by the deceased and the applicant does not establish dependency[6]. 'Full valuable consideration' has caused problems for the courts. A contractual relationship is not necessary[7]. It is difficult to quantify domestic services in financial terms[8]. If the flow of benefits was broadly commensurate then there is full valuable consideration[9]; however, extra devoted care and attention, particularly when the other is in ill health does not disadvantage an applicant[10]. A relationship between the applicant and the deceased is insufficient to establish a claim; the applicant must establish some sort of obligation[11]. However, the length of a relationship is a relevant consideration, in conjunction with the level of support provided by the deceased[12]. 'Valuable consideration' does not include marriage or a promise of marriage[13].

1 Section 1(1)(e).
2 Section 1(3).
3 *Re Beaumont* [1980] Ch 444, [1980] 1 All ER 266.
4 *Jelley v Illife* [1981] Fam 128, [1981] 2 All ER 29, CA and *Bishop v Plumley* [1991] 1 All ER 236, [1991] 1 WLR 582, CA overruling on this point *Re Beaumont*, above.
5 See *Re Beaumont*, above and *Bishop v Plumley*, above.
6 *Bishop v Plumley*, above.

7 *Re Beaumont*, above.
8 *Re Wilkinson* [1978] Fam 22, [1978] 1 All ER 221.
9 *Bishop v Plumley*, above.
10 Ibid.
11 *Williams v Johns* [1988] 2 FLR 475, a case of an adult adopted child but the case emphasises the need for obligation.
12 *Malone v Harrison* [1979] 1 WLR 1353, see also *Harrington v Gill* (1983) 4 FLR 265 where eight years co-habitation showed sufficient dependency.
13 Section 25(1).

Threshold conditions

6.20 The ground for making an order under the 1975 Act is that the disposition of the estate of the deceased under the will or intestacy (or a combination of both) failed to make reasonable financial provision for the applicant[1]. 'Reasonable financial provision' is defined by s 1(2). In the case of a surviving spouse (except those judicially separated and the separation was continuing) it means such financial provision as it would be reasonable in all the circumstances for the spouse to receive, whether or not that provision is required for his or her maintenance[2]. In all other cases it means such financial provision as it would be reasonable in all the circumstances for the applicant to receive for his maintenance[3]. 'Maintenance' means more than subsistence or just enough to get by but is not as wide as anything reasonably desirable. The test has a subjective element in that the standard of living of the applicant must be considered. Maintenance means payments which relate directly or indirectly to the cost of day-to-day living[4]. A capital sum to enable an applicant to meet inheritance tax on an inter vivos gift from the deceased is not within the meaning of 'maintenance'[5]. Where an applicant, other than a spouse, does not benefit from the estate of the deceased, it is necessary for the applicant to establish that it was unreasonable for the deceased not to provide for him or her[6].

1 Section 1(1).
2 Section 1(2)(a).
3 Section 1(2)(b).
4 See *Re Coventry* [1980] Ch 461, [1979] 3 All ER 815, CA.
5 *Re Dennis* [1981] 2 All ER 140.
6 *Re Coventry*, above.

Statutory criteria

6.21 Section 3 provides the criteria which the court must consider in determining whether the disposition of the estate of the deceased made reasonable financial provision for the applicant[1]. If the applicant fails to get over this initial hurdle the application will be dismissed. If the court is satisfied that the disposition of the deceased's estate did not make reasonable financial provision for the applicant, then the court applies the criteria in s 3 to determine what orders should be made. The statutory criteria in s 3(1)(a)–(g) are of general application together with additional matters depending upon the class of applicant. The general criteria are:

(a) the financial resources and financial needs which the applicant has or is likely to have in the foreseeable future;

(b) the financial resources and financial needs[2] which any other applicant for an order under section 2 of this Act has or is likely to have in the foreseeable future;

(c) the financial resources and financial needs which any beneficiary of the estate of the deceased has or is likely to have in the foreseeable future;

(d) any obligations and responsibilities which the deceased had towards any applicant for an order under the said section 2 or towards any beneficiary of the estate of the deceased;[3]

(e) the size and nature of the net estate of the deceased;[4]

(f) any physical or mental disability of an applicant for an order under the said section 2 or any beneficiary of the estate of the deceased;

(g) any other matter, including the conduct[5] of the applicant or any other person, which in the circumstances of the case the court may consider relevant.

1 Section 3(1).
2 'Financial needs' means reasonable requirements: *Harrington v Gill* (1983) 4 FLR 265. The court may consider the applicant's standard of living while the deceased was alive and the extent to which the deceased contributed to such standard.
3 This requires the court to balance the claims of applicants and beneficiaries: *Kusminow v Barclays Bank Trust Co Ltd* [1989] Fam Law 66.
4 Where the estate is small it is more difficult for an applicant to establish a claim: *Re Gregory* [1971] 1 All ER 497, [1971] 1 WLR 1455 (a case under the old law). See *Moody v Stevenson* [1992] Ch 486, [1992] 2 All ER 524, CA where Waite J commented that the task of judging the reasonableness of a testator's posthumous provision for his dependants is seldom easy, and becomes even more difficult when the estate is small and the resources available to answer the competing calls on the deceased's bounty are limited.
5 The question of conduct should probably be considered in the same way as under the MCA 1973, s 25(2)(g); see *Re Snoek* (1983) 13 Fam Law 18.

Spouse

6.22 Where the applicant is the spouse of the deceased, the court must additionally consider the age of the applicant and the duration of the marriage[1], and the contribution made by the applicant to the welfare of the family of the deceased, including any contribution made by looking after the home and caring for the family[2]. In addition, unless at the date of death a decree of judicial separation was in force and the separation was continuing, the court must have regard to the provision that the applicant might reasonably have expected to receive if the marriage had been terminated by divorce rather than by death[3]. The divorce analogy is difficult to apply because the situation is radically different on death. The income position will differ because the deceased has no income. The capital position may be altered by payment of death-in-service benefits or maturity of a life policy. On divorce the aim is to provide a home for each of the parties – on death only the survivor needs to be housed[4]. A life interest in the majority of the estate for a surviving spouse was considered to be reasonable financial provision[5]. The divorce analogy did not really help because, although on divorce the wife would have been awarded free capital, in that case she had the use of most of the estate for life. The leading case is still probably *Re Besterman*[6], although the requirement on divorce (so far as possible) to place the parties in the position as if the marriage had not broken down has been repealed[7]. In addition it is a 'big money' case and not easily related to more modest circumstances. The so-called 'cushion' has not always been followed[8]. Where the will of the deceased makes substantial provision for charities, s 3(1)(d) will usually require the obligations and responsibilities of the deceased to the applicant to be given priority[9]; however more difficult questions arise where the other beneficiaries are people with claims on the deceased. The provision for a surviving spouse is not limited to an amount required for maintenance[10], but what is reasonable in all the circumstances.

1 Section 3(2)(a). This is similar to the MCA 1973, s 25(2)(d). See para 4.24.
2 Section 3(2)(b). This is similar to the MCA 1973, s 25(2)(f). See para 4.27.
3 Section 3(2), often called the divorce analogy. Where a spouse dies within 12 months of a decree of judicial separation without an order for ancillary relief being made, the court may treat the surviving spouse for the purposes of the application as if the decree had not been made: s 14(1) and see para 6.14. If the separation was not continuing, the normal test relating to a spouse applies: ss 3(2), 14(2).
4 See *Moody v Stevenson* [1992] Ch 486, [1992] 2 All ER 524 where the difficulty was discussed. *Re Krubert* [1996] 27 LS Gaz R 28, CA it was pointed out that the 'divorce analogy' is only one factor to be considered and the overriding consideration is what is reasonable in all the circumstances.
5 *Davis v Davis* [1993] 1 FLR 54, CA. See also *Moody v Stevenson*, above, where a surviving spouse was given a life interest in the matrimonial home.
6 [1984] Ch 458, [1984] 2 All ER 656, CA; the approach of Oliver LJ was approved in *Re Krubert* above. See also *Re Bunning* [1984] Ch 480, [1984] 3 All ER 1.
7 Matrimonial and Family Proceedings Act 1984.
8 *H v H (Financial Provision: Capital Allowance)* [1993] 2 FLR 335 and see *Dart v Dart* [1996] 2 FLR 286, CA. However see *Jessop v Jessop* [1992] 1 FLR 591 where a widow was given a capital reserve for future contingencies and *Davis v Davis*, above where a life interest was held to be sufficient.
9 *Re Besterman* [1984] Ch 458, [1984] 2 All ER 656, CA.
10 Section 1(2)(a).

Former spouse

6.23 The court additionally is to have regard to the age of the applicant, the duration of the marriage, and contributions of the applicant[1]. Where spouses have settled their financial affairs on divorce (whether by agreement or order) there is a heavy burden on the applicant to establish a claim under the 1975 Act, particularly where the estate is small[2]. Where a surviving former spouse is in receipt of periodical payments from the deceased it will generally be appropriate to make some provision out of the estate, although the differences in the statutory criteria on ancillary relief and under the Act must be considered[3].

Where a party to a marriage dies within 12 months of a decree absolute of divorce, nullity or a decree of judicial separation and an application for ancillary relief has either not been made[4], or if made has not been determined[5], then the court shall, if it thinks just to do so, treat the applicant for the purposes of the application as if the relevant decree had not been pronounced[6]. It should be noted that a spouse who remarries after making an application for ancillary relief but before the application is determined, will be debarred from applying under the Act[7]. The provisions of s 14 do not enable a person to apply when barred from applying by remarriage.

1 Section 3(2).
2 *Re Fullard* [1982] Fam 42, [1981] 2 All ER 796, CA. See also *Brill v Proud* [1984] Fam Law 59.
3 *Re Crawford* (1982) 4 FLR 273. See also *Re Farrow* [1987] 1 FLR 205.
4 Section 14(1)(a).
5 Section 14(1)(b).
6 Section 14(1).
7 See also the MCA 1973, s 25(2).

Co-habitants

6.24 The court is additionally required[1] to have regard to the age of the applicant and the length of time during which the applicant and the deceased lived together as husband and wife in the same household[2]. Further the court must consider the contribution made by the applicant to welfare of the family of the deceased, including contribution made by looking after the home or caring for the family[3]. As yet there is no case law on this class of applicant. The policy seems to be to facilitate claims that would not be possible under s 1(1)(e) where the applicant gave full valuable consideration by the pooling of resources. It is submitted that a reasonably generous approach may be adopted by the courts, but in all such cases the crucial factor will be balancing the needs of the applicant as against the needs of beneficiaries.

1 Section 3(2A), inserted by Law Reform (Succession) Act 1995, s 2(4).
2 Section 3(2A)(a).
3 Section 3(2A)(b).

Children

6.25 The court is additionally required to have regard to the manner in which the applicant was being or might expect to be educated or trained[1]. Such factors really only apply to minors and those in their late teens or early twenties. Generally it is difficult for an adult child to bring a claim in the absence of special circumstances[2]. Section 3(1)(d) and (g) cannot be construed to include legal obligations and responsibilities which the deceased had failed to discharge during his son's minority many years before[3]. An application by an adult son was dismissed where he had received an inter vivos gift from the deceased but needed a lump sum to pay capital transfer tax on the gift[4]. The impecuniosity of the applicant coupled with continuing parental affection on the part of the deceased is insufficient to give rise to a claim[5]. A 19 year old girl claiming social security was awarded £5,000 out of an estate of £35,000[6]. The receipt of state benefit is not relevant to considering whether the disposition of the estate made reasonable financial provision[7]. On the facts, the husband (who took on intestacy, notwithstanding a decree nisi) had been violent to the deceased; accordingly s 3(1)(d) was an important factor in the exercise of discretion.

1 Section 3(3).

2 *Re Coventry* [1980] Ch 461, [1979] 3 All ER 815, CA.
3 *Re Jennings* [1994] Ch 286, [1994] 3 All ER 27, CA.
4 *Re Dennis* [1981] 2 All ER 140.
5 *Williams v Johns* [1988] 2 FLR 475.
6 *Re Collins* [1990] Fam 56, [1990] 2 All ER 47.
7 Ibid, but local authority means tested benefits did not fall to be considered on the facts of the case.

Step-children

6.26 The court is additionally required to have regard to whether and if so on what basis the deceased assumed responsibility for the applicant and the length of time for which such responsibility was discharged[1]. Further, whether the deceased knew that the applicant was not his child; and, the court must consider whether any other person is liable to maintain the applicant. As with children, the actual or expected manner or education or training is to be considered. These factors are more appropriate to cases where the applicant is a minor or in late teens or early twenties. Adult step-children are equally entitled to apply. In one case[2] the judge balanced the obligations and responsibilities of the deceased to the adult applicant step-child against those to his sisters who were entitled on intestacy. An important factor was that much of the deceased's estate had been derived by inheritance from the applicant's mother. Similar approaches have been adopted[3].

1 Section 3(3)(a)–(c).
2 *Re Callaghan* [1985] Fam 1, [1984] 3 All ER 790.
3 See eg *Re Leach* [1986] Ch 226, [1985] 2 All ER 754, CA.

Dependants

6.27 The court is additionally required to have regard to the extent to which and the basis upon which the deceased assumed responsibility for the maintenance of the applicant, and the length of time for which the deceased discharged that responsibility[1]. The level of support given by the deceased to the applicant and the length of time are very important. Provision has been made for a mistress (there were others) of the deceased, having regard to the generous level of support and standard to which the deceased had maintained the applicant, and to the length of the relationship[2]. There must be an obligation, often a moral one[3]. Co-habitants have succeeded where there has been a degree of dependancy[4] but not otherwise[5].

1 Section 3(4).
2 *Malone v Harrison* [1979] 1 WLR 1353.
3 In *Re Wilkinson* [1978] Fam 22, [1978] 1 All ER 221, the sister of the deceased successfully claimed; she had given up work to look after her brother.
4 See *Re Haig* (1979) 129 NLJ 420 and *Harrington v Gill* (1983) 4 FLR 265.
5 See *Re Beaumont* [1980] Ch 444, [1980] 1 All ER 266.

Time limits

6.28 An application must be made within six months from the date when the grant of representation of the estate of the deceased is first taken out. An application may be made subsequently, but only with the leave of the court[1]. An application cannot be made unless a grant has been taken out[2]. Where a grant of probate has been replaced by a grant of letters of administration (or vice versa) the six month time limit starts to run from the date of the later grant[3]. In considering an application for leave the court will have regard to whether the claim is likely to succeed[4]. An application for leave to apply by a widow, six years out of time has been granted by reason of exceptional circumstances[5], namely the collapse of interest rates in 1992, and that the widow (aged 85) had no independent advice as to the implications of the will or her right to challenge it. In addition there was no prejudice to the other beneficiaries. The court will also consider whether there is a satisfactory explanation for the delay, efforts to mitigate any effects of delay, whether the estate was distributed before notice of the claim was given[6]. Under the previous legislation, the Inheritance (Family Provision) Act 1938, leave was granted where a widow gave birth to a posthumous child[7] and where an elderly and infirm widow was unaware of her husband's death for some five months after probate had been granted[8]. Applications for leave are decided on the individual facts of each case. Applications for leave on behalf of minor children may well be viewed more leniently than such applications by adults.

1 Section 4.
2 *Re McBroom* [1992] 2 FLR 49; see however *Re Searle* [1949] Ch 73.
3 *Re Freeman* [1984] 3 All ER 906, [1984] 1 WLR 1419.
4 *Re Dennis* [1981] 2 All ER 140.
5 *Stock v Brown* [1994] 1 FLR 840. However see *Escritt v Escritt* (1981) 3 FLR 280 where leave was refused after a delay of three years.
6 *Re Salmon* [1981] Ch 167, [1980] 3 All ER 532.
7 *Re Trott* [1958] 2 All ER 296, [1958] 1 WLR 604.
8 *Re McNare* [1964] 3 All ER 373, [1964] 1 WLR 1255.

Procedure

6.29 The application may be brought in either the High Court or in the county court; both have unlimited jurisdiction. Unlimited jurisdiction was conferred on county courts by the County Courts Act 1984, s 25[1]. Under the High Court and County Courts Jurisdiction Order 1991[2], actions of which the value is less than £25,000 are to be tried in the county court, and actions of which the value is more than £50,000 are to be tried in the High Court, unless in either case the court considers[3] that the action should be tried in the other court. Actions where the value is between £25,000 and £50,000 may be tried in either court. The value of the action is the amount of money that the applicant can reasonably assert to be the worth of the claim[4]. In the High Court the action may be brought in either the Chancery Division or in the Family Division[5].

1 As amended by the High Court and County Courts Jurisdiction Order 1991.
2 Article 7.
3 Having regard to the matters set out in art 7(5).
4 Article 9(1)(b)(i). Thus it is the applicant's reasonable expectation rather than the size of the estate that governs jurisdiction.
5 RSC Ord 99, r 2. In selecting the Division the applicant should consider whether there are related proceedings pending in one Division. Where an action will involve the taking of complex accounts the better practice is to use the Chancery Division.

High Court

6.30 The application is commenced by originating summons[1] issued out of Chancery Chambers, the principal registry of the Family Division or any district registry, supported by an affidavit of the plaintiff[2]. The affidavit must exhibit an official copy of the grant of representation to the deceased's estate and of every testamentary document admitted to proof[3]. A copy of the affidavit must be served on every defendant with the summons[4]. The personal representatives should be made defendants to the summons[5]. The major beneficiaries should be joined as defendants; it is not necessary to join every beneficiary, particularly where there are several pecuniary legatees whose interest is minor compared with the totality of the estate. In every case the plaintiff must carefully consider which beneficiaries should be joined[6]. The court may make orders for the representation of interested persons who cannot or cannot readily be ascertained, persons who are ascertained but cannot be found, and persons who although ascertained and found ought to be represented for the purpose of saving expense[7]. The personal representative defendants must file an affidavit in answer and other defendants, while under no obligation, may file an affidavit in answer[8]. The time for filing such affidavits is within 21 days of service of the summons and plaintiff's affidavit[9]. The affidavit of a personal representative must state full particulars of the value of the deceased's net estate[10], the identity or classes of beneficiaries and the value of their interests so far as ascertained[11], identifying any beneficiary who is a minor or patient[12], and any facts so far as known which might affect the exercise of the court's powers[13].

Affidavit evidence from beneficiaries will usually concentrate on matters raised by the plaintiff and the financial position of the beneficiary so that the court has the information necessary to apply the statutory criteria under s 3. The action may be disposed of in chambers[14] either by a judge or by a master or district judge[15]. Directions may be given during the proceedings for further evidence and discovery, particularly where the court is asked to exercise powers under s 10. At the full hearing, the personal representative must produce to the court the grant of representation[16]; if an order under the Act is made, the grant remains in the custody of the court until a memorandum of the order has been endorsed on or permanently annexed to the grant in accordance with s 19(3)[17].

---

1 RSC Ord 99, r 3(1). The originating summons is in Form 10, Appendix A, ibid r 3(2). The relief sought will be that the plaintiff be granted reasonable financial provision out of the estate. Where leave is sought to bring the action out of time, the summons should seek such leave.
2 RSC Ord 99, r 3(3).
3 Ibid. The plaintiff's affidavit should explain the way in which he is qualified to bring an application under s 1. It should further deal with the relevant matters to which the court will have regard under s 3 when determining the application. A useful checklist is provided in CCR Ord 48, r 2. Where leave is sought to bring the action out of time, the affidavit should address the matters referred to in para 6.28.
4 RSC Ord 99, r 3(3).
5 *Supreme Court Practice 1995*, para 99/4/1.
6 Ibid, para 99/4/2.
7 RSC Ord 15, r 13, applied by Ord 99, r 4(2).
8 RSC Ord 99, r 5(1).
9 Ibid.
10 Ibid, r 5(2)(a).

11 Ibid, r 5(2)(b).
12 Ibid, r 5(2)(c).
13 Ibid, r 5(2)(d). See also *Practice Note (Inheritance: Family Provision)* [1976] 2 All ER 447, [1976] 1 WLR 418; the personal representatives are not obliged to make enquiries or investigations, nor to raise controversial matters. If necessary they may lodge further evidence when the issues are more defined.
14 RSC Ord 99, r 8.
15 Ibid; see also *Practice Note (Inheritance: Family Provision)*, above, para 6.
16 RSC Ord 99, r 7.
17 Ibid.

County courts

6.31 The application is made by originating application[1] issued out of the court for the district in which the deceased resided at death[2]; or if the deceased did not then reside in England and Wales, out of the court for the district in which the respondent, or one of the respondents, resides or carries on business, or in which the estate or part of it is situate[3]; if neither applies, the applicant may issue out of the court for the district in which he resides or carries on business[4]. The originating application must state: the name of the deceased, date of death and domicile at death[5]; the relationship of the applicant to the deceased or other qualification for applying[6]; the date on which representation with respect to the deceased's estate was first taken out and the names and addresses of the personal representatives[7]; whether the disposition of the deceased's estate made any provision for the applicant and if so what provision[8]; to the best of the applicant's knowledge and belief, the persons or classes of persons interested in the deceased's estate and the nature of their interests[9]; particulars of the applicant's present and foreseeable financial resources and financial needs and any other information that he desires to place before the court on the matters that the court is required to have regard under s 3[10]; where appropriate, a request for leave to bring the application out of time and the grounds[11]; and, the nature of the provision sought[12]. An official copy of the grant of representation to the deceased's estate and every testamentary document admitted to proof must be filed with the originating application[13]. The respondents must file and serve an answer to the application within 21 days of service of the originating application[14]. The answer of a personal representative must contain prescribed information[15]. Unless otherwise directed, the return date of the originating application is treated as a pre-trial review[16]. At such hearing the court will give any necessary directions as to the joinder of parties[17] and for the filing of evidence. The question of transfer to the High Court can be considered[18], or if the application remains in the county court directions may be given for mode of trial. The full hearing may be in chambers and before a circuit judge or district judge[19]. As with High Court procedure, the grant must be produced at the hearing and if an order is made, the proper officer sends a sealed copy with a grant to the Principal Registry of the Family Division for a memorandum of the order has been endorsed on or permanently annexed to the grant in accordance with s 19(3)[20].

1 CCR Ord 48, r 2. See Practice Form N423.
2 CCR Ord 48, r 4(1)(a).
3 Ibid, r 3(1)(b).
4 Ibid, r 3(1)(c).

5 Ibid, r 2(a).
6 Ibid, r 2(b).
7 Ibid, r 2(c).
8 Ibid, r 2(e).
9 Ibid, r 2(f).
10 Ibid, r 2(g).
11 Ibid, r 2(h).
12 Ibid, r 2(i).
13 Ibid, r 3(2).
14 Ibid, r 5.
15 Ibid, r 5(a)–(d). This information is the same as a personal representative is required to give by affidavit in the High Court under RSC Ord 99, r 5.
16 CCR Ord 48, r 3(3).
17 Ibid, r 4, similar to RSC Ord 99, r 4.
18 An order for transfer will specify whether the same is to the Chancery Division or the Family Division: CCR Ord 48, r 9.
19 Ibid, r 7.
20 Ibid, r 8.

Net estate defined

6.32 Section 25(1) defines the 'net estate'. The following dispositions are automatically included in the net estate.

(a) *Powers of appointment.* An unexercised general power of appointment (not exercisable by will) is included, automatically.

(b) *Nominations.* Nominations under an enactment are automatically treated as forming part of the net estate[1]. A nomination of death benefits under a pension scheme is not a nomination under an enactment[2].

(c) *Donationes mortis causa.* Donationes mortis causa are automatically treated as forming part of the net estate[3].

1 Section 8(1).
2 *Re Cairnes* (1982) 4 FLR 225.
3 Section 8(2).

Joint tenancies

6.33 These do not form part of the net estate[1]. The court may make an order that the deceased's severable share form part of the net estate for the purpose of facilitating the making of financial provision for the applicant[2]. The value of the deceased's severable share must be taken at the value immediately before his death. Thus a mortgage must be taken into account. In addition, although the value is taken immediately before death, regard must be had to the imminent death and to any life policy that will pay off the deceased's share of the mortgage[3].

1 Section 9(1).
2 See *Jessop v Jessop* [1992] 1 FLR 591, CA where the deceased's share of a house owned jointly with his mistress was severed to provide for the widow.
3 *Powell v Osbourne* [1993] 1 FLR 1001, CA.

Anti-avoidance provisions

6.34 Certain provisions in the 1975 Act permit the court to order that assets be brought into the net estate of the deceased. Where the court makes an order which augments the net estate, the property so added is not to be treated any differently from the rest of the net estate[1].

1 *Re Crawford* (1982) 4 FLR 273.

Inter vivos dispositions

6.35 The court may order the donee to bring money or property into the estate where a disposition was made within six prior to death. The court must be satisfied that:[1]

(a) the deceased must have intended to defeat an application for financial provision under the Act. The intention to defeat need not be the sole intention;[2]

(b) the donee did not give full valuable consideration;

(c) the exercise of the powers would facilitate the making of financial provision for an applicant.

Once an application under s 10(1) is made, the donee or any applicant can apply for other dispositions to be similarly treated provided they were made within six years of death with an intention to defeat, and full valuable consideration was not given.

1 Section 10(2).
2 *Re Dawkins* [1986] 2 FLR 360.

Contracts

6.36 Where:

(a) the deceased entered into a contract to leave property by will on or after 1 April 1976,

(b) the deceased intended[1] to defeat an application for financial provision under the Act,

(c) the donee did not give or promise to give full valuable consideration, and

(d) the exercise of the powers would facilitate the making of financial provision the court can make orders under s 11(2)(i) and (ii) effectively bringing the property into the estate[2].

1 The intention to defeat need not be the sole intention: *Re Dawkins* [1986] 2 FLR 360.
2 Section 11(2)(a)–(d).

Types of order

6.37 The court can make any of the orders specified in s 2(1)(a)–(f)[1]. There is considerable flexibility in the way in which the orders can be used to achieve a just result, balancing all the relevant claims and factors in s 3. Orders for periodical payments are rare because of the costs of administration. It is far more common to have an order for a lump sum of transfer of property[2]. The purchase of a matrimonial home in the joint names of the parties to a marriage is a post-nuptial settlement[3]; it can thus be varied under s 2(1)(f). The court may exercise its powers under s 2(1)(d) to settle part of the estate on protective trusts for the benefit of the applicant[4]. Orders may contain consequential and supplemental provisions for giving effect to the order and for the purpose of securing that the order operates fairly between the beneficiaries[5].

1 The orders are: (a) periodical payments, (b) lump sum, (c) transfer of property, (d) settlement, (e) acquisition out of property comprised in the estate and transfer or settlement, and (f) variation of settlement.
2 See *Moody v Stevenson* [1992] Ch 486, [1992] 2 All ER 524.
3 *Brown v Brown* [1959] P 86, [1959] 2 All ER 266, CA.
4 *Re Abram* [1996] 2 FLR 379.
5 Section 2(4).

Part IV

Children

Chapter Seven

Children

Stephen Wildblood

Introduction 219
Parental Responsibility 219
Guardians 223
Child Defined 227
Wardship and the High Court's Inherent Jurisdiction 231
Surrogacy and Embryology 237
Legitimacy 241
Blood Tests 243
Adoption 245
Who may Apply to Adopt? 250
Who may be Adopted? 253
Parental Agreement to Adoption 255
Freeing for Adoption 259
Adoption Procedure 261

INTRODUCTION

7.1 This chapter examines various aspects of the relationships that a child may have, particularly the child's relationships with those who care for the child. At the forefront of any such examination must be the nature of a child's relationship with his parents. Since the advent of the CA 1989 there has been a shift of focus from parents' rights to the new concept of parental responsibility.

PARENTAL RESPONSIBILITY

Definition

7.2 The CA 1989 gives only a limited definition of parental responsibility. By s 3 of the Act it is defined as 'all the rights, duties, powers, responsibilities and authority which by law a parent of a child has in relation to a child and his property'[1]. However, the term represents a thread that runs through much of

219

the legislation relating to children. Essentially it means the responsibility that a parent has to care for and nurture a child[2]. Features of parental responsibility are that a parent with such responsibility has at least the following rights, duties and responsibilities in respect of a child:

(a) the right to object to the child's emigration[3];

(b) the right to name the child and object to any changes in the child's name[4];

(c) the right to decide upon any medical treatment for the child (which has to be read in the light of the Family Law Reform Act 1969, s 8 that relates to consent to medical treatment of a child who has attained the age of 16);

(d) the right to consent to the child's marriage;

(e) the right to object to adoption of the child[5];

(f) the right to decide the child's religion or education;

(g) the responsibility to protect and maintain the child;

(h) the right to appoint a guardian of the child.

Parental responsibility also extends to guardianship of the child since its meaning includes the rights, powers and duties which a guardian of the child's estate (appointed before the commencement of the CA 1989, s 5 to act generally) would have had in relation to the child and his property; these rights include the right of the guardian to receive or recover in his own name, for the benefit of the child, property of whatever description and wherever situated which the child is entitled to receive or recover[6].

Subject to any provision of the CA 1989, a person who is caring for a child but does not have parental responsibility for him may do what is reasonable for the purpose of safeguarding or promoting the child's welfare[7].

1 CA 1989, s 3(1).
2 And see, eg Lord Scarman's analysis of the subject prior to the CA 1989 in *Gillick v West Norfolk and Wisbech Area Health Authority* [1986] AC 112, [1985] 3 All ER 402, [1986] 1 FLR 224.
3 CA 1989, s 13(1)(b).
4 Ibid, s 13(1)(a).
5 Ibid, s 12(3).
6 Ibid, s 3(1).
7 Ibid, s 3(5).

7.3 Section 2(1) and (2) of the Act stipulates which parents will have parental responsibility[1]. However, in addition to the mother of a child and father who is married to the mother the following also have or acquire parental responsibility:

(a) adoptive parents[2];

(b) a person with a residence order in relation to the child[3];

(c) a local authority that has a care order in relation to the child[4];

(d) a guardian of the child[5].

The Act specifically provides that more than one person may have parental responsibility for the child at the same time[6] (which is perhaps not surprising since most children will be born to two married parents). The Act further specifically provides that:

(i) A person who has parental responsibility for a child at any time shall not cease to have that responsibility solely because some other person subsequently acquires parental responsibility for the child[7].

(ii) Where more than one person has parental responsibility for a child, each of them may act alone and without the other (or others) in meeting that responsibility; save where any enactment requires the consent of more than one person in a matter affecting the child[8].

(iii) The fact that a person has parental responsibility for a child shall not entitle him to act in any way which would be incompatible with any order made with respect to the child under the Act[9].

(iv) A person who has parental responsibility for a child may not surrender or transfer any part of that responsibility to another but may arrange for some or all of it to be met by one or more persons acting on his behalf[10].

(v) The making of any such arrangement shall not affect any liability of the person making it which may arise from any failure to meet any part of his parental responsibility for the child concerned[11].

1 And see further para 5.6.
2 Adoption Act 1976, s 12.
3 CA 1989, s 12(2).
4 Ibid, s 33(3)(a).
5 Ibid, s 3(6)(a).
6 Ibid, s 2(3).
7 Ibid, s 2(6).
8 Ibid, s 2(7).
9 Ibid, s 2(8).
10 Ibid, s 2(9).
11 Ibid, s 2(6)–(11).

Acquisition of parental responsibility by father

Generally

7.4 Where a father is not married to the mother of a child he does not automatically have parental responsibility. He may acquire it either by a parental responsibility agreement[1] or a parental responsibility order[2]. Like any other individual, he might also acquire parental responsibility as a result of residence by:

(a) a residence order[3];

(b) an appointment as a guardian[4];

(c) an adoption order[5].

1 CA 1989, s 4(1)(b).
2 Ibid, s 4(1)(a).
3 Ibid, s 12(2) which requires that a person who has a residence order will acquire parental responsibility.
4 CA 1989, s 5.
5 Under the Adoption Act 1976, s 12(1); but note that under s 14(2) (see para 7.66) an unmarried couple cannot together adopt a child.

Parental responsibility agreement

7.5 A parental responsibility agreement must be made in the prescribed form[1]. The form prescribed is that set out in the Parental Responsibility Agreement Regulations 1991[2]. The form itself specifies how it must be completed and witnessed and must then be filed with the Principal Registry.

1 CA 1989, s 4(2).
2 SI 1991/1478 as substituted by SI 1994/3157.

Parental responsibility order

7.6 A father may apply to the court for a parental responsibility order where he does not already have it[1]. The application may be started at any level of court and will be made upon the standard forms provided by either the Family Proceedings Rules 1991 (in the county court or High Court) or the Family Proceedings Courts (Children Act 1989) Rules 1991 (in the magistrates' court). In deciding whether or not to grant a parental responsibility order the court should consider:

(a) the degree of commitment which the father has shown to the child;

(b) the degree of attachment between the father and the child;

(c) the reasons of the father for applying for the order[2].

Where a father has shown the necessary degree of attachment and commitment to his child, it is prima facie in the interests of the child for there to be a parental responsibility order (so that the child benefits from the dual protection of having two parents both of whom have responsibility for him)[3]. Sometimes the making of a parental responsibility order is opposed because it is suggested by the mother that the father would use the grant of such an order to question aspects of the children's upbringing unnecessarily. In the case of *Re P*[4] it was held that an order for parental responsibility does not give the father the right to interfere in matters within the day-to-day management of the child's life nor to override the mother (the mother's residence order gave her the responsibility to decide upon day-to-day issues affecting the child and a parental responsibility order would not authorise the father to interfere in those decisions). It is rare for the courts to refuse an application for a parental responsibility order although, in appropriate circumstances, it will do so[5]. The fact that parental responsibility might not be exercisable at the time the order is sought does not preclude the making of a parental responsibility order[6]. The essence of a parental responsibility order is that it confers status (and the conferment of status should be the focus of the court's concentration sooner than the acquisition of rights)[7]. The court should not withhold a parental responsibility order so as to force a father to meet his financial responsibilities to the child[8].

1 CA 1989, s 4(1)(a).
2 See, eg *Re H* [1993] 1 FLR 484, [1993] 1 FCR 85; *S v R* [1993] 1 FCR 331; *Re CB* [1993] 1 FLR 920, [1993] 1 FCR 440; *Re W* [1993] 2 FCR 427. The factors are not, however, intended to be exhaustive but merely an indication of factors which are relevant in this type of application: *Re G* [1994] 1 FLR 504.
3 *Re E* [1995] 1 FLR 392.
4 [1994] 1 FLR 578 per Wilson J. See also *Re S* [1995] 2 FLR 648.
5 See eg *Re T* [1993] 1 FCR 973, [1993] 2 FLR 450.
6 See *W v Ealing London Borough Council* [1994] 1 FCR 436 and *D v Hereford and Worcester County Council* [1991] Fam 14, [1991] 1 FLR 205.
7 See *Re S* [1995] 2 FLR 648 and also *Re G (Child care: Parental involvement)* [1996] 1 FLR 857.
8 See *Re H (Parental responsibility: Maintenance)* [1996] 1 FLR 867.

Termination of parental responsibility

7.7 A parental responsibility order or a parental responsibility agreement may only be brought to an end by an order of the court made on the application:

(a) of any person who has parental responsibility for the child[1]; or

(b) with the leave of the court, of the child himself[2].

Where the child seeks leave to make such an application, the court may only grant leave if it is satisfied that the child has sufficient understanding to make the application[3].

1 *Re P* [1995] 1 FLR 1048. In this case Singer J had an application to revoke a parental responsibility agreement (after making the agreement, the mother discovered that the father had abused the child). The court revoked the agreement, holding that it was in the interest of the child to do so and that it would be wrong for the mother and father to have equal status in respect of the child.
2 CA 1989, s 4(3).
3 Ibid, s 4(4).

GUARDIANS

Appointment

7.8 A guardian of a child may only be appointed in accordance with the provisions of the CA 1989[1]. The provisions governing the appointment are specified in s 5. The appointment may be made either:

(a) by the court[2]; or

(b) by a parent with parental responsibility[3]; or

(c) by another guardian[4].

1 CA 1989, s 5(13).
2 Ibid, s 5(1).
3 Ibid, s 5(3).
4 Ibid, s 5(4).

Appointment by the court

7.9 The court may appoint a guardian of a child in the circumstances described in the CA 1989, s 5(1). Under that section it is provided that a court may appoint an individual to be the guardian of a child if:

(a) the child has no parent with parental responsibility for him; or

(b) a residence order has been made with respect to the child in favour of a parent or guardian of his who has died while the order was in force (however, by reason of s 5(9), this does not apply if the residence order was also made in favour of a surviving parent, ie there was a joint or shared residence order between the dead parent and the surviving parent).

The order may be made on the application of 'any individual' or, in any family proceedings, of the court's own motion[1].

1 CA 1989, s 5(1) and (2).

PROCEDURE

7.10 The main points concerning procedure are as follows:

(a) The application is made in the standard Form C1 prescribed for general applications to the court (in the magistrates' court by the Family Proceedings Court (Children Act 1989) Rules 1991 and in the county court and High Court by the Family Proceedings Rules 1991).

(b) Once an application has been made it may only be withdrawn with the leave of the court (by reason the FPR 1991, r 4.5 and FPC(CA 1989)R 1991, r 5).

(c) The application may be made to any court.

(d) The FPC(CA 1989)R 1991, Sch 2 and the FPR 1991, Appendix 3 define the respondents to the application.

The power of the High Court to exercise its inherent jurisdiction to appoint a guardian is restricted by the CA 1989, s 5(11) and (12). There does not appear to be any reason why the court should not appoint more than one guardian.

Appointment by a parent

7.11 A parent with parental responsibility for a child may appoint another individual to be the guardian of the child in the event of the parent's death[1]. The appointment must be made in the way specified in s 5, that is it must be made in writing and must be dated and signed by the person making the appointment or:

(a) in the case of an appointment made by will which is not signed by the testator, is signed at the direction of the testator in accordance with the requirements of the Wills Act 1837[2]; or

(b) in any other case, is signed at the direction of the person making the appointment, in his presence and in the presence of two witnesses who each attest the signature[3].

1 CA 1989, s 5(3).
2 See *Butterworths Family Law Service,* Division G, Vol 2.
3 CA 1989, s 5(5).

Appointment by a previous guardian

7.12 A guardian of a child may appoint another individual to take his place as the child's guardian in the event of his death. For the appointment to be valid it must satisfy the provisions of s 5(5)[1].

1 Those provisions are set out in para 7.11.

The effect of an appointment

7.13 The effect of an appointment as a guardian is to confer parental responsibility for the child upon the individual appointed[1].

1 CA 1989, s 5(6).

When the appointment takes effect

7.14 The appointment will either take effect:

(a) upon the death of the person making the appointment (where on that person's death the child has no parent with parental responsibility for him or where the person that died had a residence order in his favour in relation to the child at the time of his death)[1]; or

(b) when the child no longer has a parent with parental responsibility for him (where on the death of the person making the appointment the child has a parent with parental responsibility for him and the dead person did not have a residence order in relation to the child in his favour at the time of his death)[2].

1 CA 1989, s 5(7). If there was a shared or joint residence order the appointment will not take effect until the death of both parents: see s 5(9).
2 CA 1989, s 5(7)(a).

Revocation of the appointment

7.15 An appointment of a guardian under s 5(3) or (4) of the CA 1989 will be revoked:

(a) by a subsequent appointment under either of those subsections if the appointment is made by the same person in respect of the same child (unless it is expressly or impliedly clear that the purpose of the later appointment is to appoint an additional guardian)[1];

(b) if the person who made the appointment revokes the appointment by a written and dated instrument (which is either signed by him or at his direction in the presence of two witnesses who each attest the signature)[2];

(c) (save where the appointment was made by a will or codicil) if the person who made the appointment destroys the document by which the appointment was made or causes it to be destroyed[3].

An appointment under a will or codicil is revoked if the will or codicil is revoked.

1 CA 1989, s 6(1).
2 Ibid, s 6(3).
3 Ibid, s 6(4).

Disclaimer of guardianship

7.16 There may well be circumstances in which a person who has been appointed a guardian does not wish to take up the responsibility placed upon him/her. Under the CA 1989, s 6(5) a person who has been appointed a guardian may disclaim that guardianship by an instrument in writing signed by him and made within a reasonable time of his first knowing that the appointment has taken effect. Section 6(6) makes provision for such disclaimers to be in a form that is to be prescribed by statutory instrument; at the time of writing no such form has been prescribed, however, once such a form is prescribed, no disclaimer will take effect unless it is in the correct form. The Act does not define the period within which the disclaimer must be made, other than as stated above (within a reasonable time of the person appointed first knowing that the appointment has taken effect). If the disclaimer is made outside this period, it is probably necessary for the person wishing to disclaim to apply to the court for an order revoking the guardianship (see next paragraph).

Court revocation of guardianship

7.17 The court may revoke an appointment of a guardian 'at any time' upon an application brought by:

(a) any person who has parental responsibility for the child (this would include the person who has been appointed a guardian where the appointment has taken effect);

(b) the child concerned (with leave of the court).

Further, the court may revoke the appointment of a guardian in any family proceedings of its own motion[1]. In this way a person who would not otherwise be able to apply for the revocation of the guardianship may be able to secure its revocation by the issue of family proceedings, such as an application by a relative of the child to be appointed a guardian (followed by an invitation to the court to use its own powers to revoke the existing guardianship of the other person). On an application to revoke an appointment, the welfare of the child will be the court's paramount consideration, but the welfare checklist in s 1(3) of the Act will not apply (since it relates to section 8 orders and to orders under Part IV of the Act).

1 CA 1989, s 6(7).

CHILD DEFINED

The age of majority

7.18 The age of majority is specified in s 1 of the Family Law Reform Act 1969 as 18[1]. However, the law recognises that as children grow older their views, wishes and rights require greater recognition[2]. Therefore, increasing notice is paid to the wishes of children as they approach majority[3].

1 'A person shall attain full age on attaining the age of 18'.
2 See, eg the analysis of this by Sir Thomas Bingham MR in *Re S* [1994] 2 FLR 1065.
3 See, eg the welfare checklist in the CA 1989, s 1 by which the court has to have regard to 'the ascertainable wishes and feelings of the child concerned' (considered in the light of his age and understanding).

Child defined: Children Act and Adoption Act

7.19 The general provisions of both of these Acts define children as those who have not attained the age of 18[1]. The old term 'minor' (or 'infant') has been superceded by the CA 1989 but remains in, for example the FPR 1991, Parts V – IX[2] (which is partly derived from certain pre-Children Act rules).

1 The CA 1989 defines 'child' in s 105 as 'subject to paragraph 16 of Schedule 1 (which relates to financial applications), a person under the age of 18'. the Adoption Act 1976 defines 'child' in Section 72 as meaning 'except where used to express a relationship, a person who has not attained the age of 18'.
2 Derived from RSC Ord 90.

When does a child acquire independent rights?

7.20 In at least two cases it has been held that a foetus does not have an independent right of action until born alive:

(a) In the case of *C v S*[1] it was held an injunction should not be granted on the application of a prospective father to prevent the pregnant woman from having an abortion on the basis that in the light of the limited length of the pregnancy the foetus could not be said to be capable of independent life but also because the foetus did not have an independent right of action.

(b) Similar views had been expressed in the earlier case of *Paton v British Pregnancy Advisory Service Trustee*[2]. However, it has been held that a child can sue for pre-birth injuries[3].

1 [1987] 1 All ER 1230.
2 [1978] 2 All ER 987.
3 *Hunt v Severs* [1993] QB 815 at 842.

The 16 year old

7.21 The law recognises the right of a 16 year old to make many major decisions for himself. This is reflected, for instance in the following provisions:

(a) the right of a child aged 16 to marry (with the appropriate consents)[1];

(b) the right to give an effective consent to medical treatment[2];

(c) the right to make decisions about local authority accommodation, irrespective of the wishes of a person with parental responsibility[3];

(d) the right not to be subjected to orders under s 8 of the CA 1989 (ie for residence, contact, prohibited steps or specific issues orders) save in exceptional circumstances[4].

1 See the Marriage Act 1949, s 3 as amended.
2 See the Family Law Reform Act 1969, s 8 (below).
3 See s 20 of the Children Act 1989
4 Save for an order varying or discharging such a s 8 order – see s 9(7) of the Children Act 1989

Family Law Reform Act 1969, s 8

7.22 Section 8(1) of the Family Law Reform Act 1969 provides that:

> The consent of a minor who has attained the age of 16 to any surgical, medical or dental treatment which, in the absence of consent, would constitute a trespass to his person, shall be as effective as it would be if he were of full age; and where a minor has by virtue of this section given an effective consent to any treatment it shall not be necessary to obtain any consent for it from his parent or guardian.

For the purposes of that subsection 'treatment' includes any diagnostic or ancillary procedure (eg a pre-operative examination or an anaesthetic)[1]. This section does not, however, provide that the child aged 16 or over with the absolute right to refuse medical treatment. The court, parents or others with parental responsibility may override the child's refusal and may give consent to treatment. This was demonstrated in the case of *Re W*[2]. In that case a 16 year old refused to consent to treatment for anorexia nervosa. Under the inherent jurisdiction of the High Court[3], the Court of Appeal ordered that the treatment should continue. In deciding upon an application for orders relating to medical treatment the court's paramount consideration will be the welfare of the child (where the application is for a specific issues order the welfare checklist under the CA 1989, s 1(3) will have to be considered).

1 Family Law Reform Act, s 8(2).
2 [1992] 4 All ER 627.
3 And see further para 7.27ff.

Limitations on proceedings for older children

7.23 The 17 year old is protected from care proceedings in that no care order or supervision order may be made in respect of a child who has reached the age of 17 (or 16, in the case of a child who is married). No s 8 order can be made to run beyond a child attaining 16 save in exceptional circumstances[2].

1 CA 1989, s 31(3).
2 Ibid, s 9(7).

Gillick **competence**

7.24 The statutory dividing lines that establish a child's legal status do not always provide the simple solution[1]. Section 8 of the Family Law Reform Act 1969 deals with the position in respect of children who have attained the age of 16 but not those under that age. These issues came before the House of Lords in the *Gillick* case[2]. The mother sought an assurance from the health authority that it would not provide contraceptive or abortion treatment to her children (who were under 16) without her consent. This case, therefore, raised difficult issues relating to medical and legal practice; it would be an assault if medical treatment were to be given without appropriate consent. The House of Lords held that parental rights diminish as a child develops sufficient understanding and maturity to make decisions for himself. The point at which a child may decide matters for himself is not resolved by the child attaining a certain age; it is resolved by having regard to the welfare of the individual child and, in particular, the maturity of that individual child. Lord Fraser was of the opinion that a doctor would be entitled to provide contraceptive advice and treatment to the child under 16 without the consent or knowledge of the parents if the doctor was satisfied that:

(a) the child would understand his advice;

(b) he could not persuade the child either to inform the parents or to let him inform them;

(c) the child was likely to begin or continue to have sexual intercourse with or without contraceptive advice;

(d) unless the child received such advice or treatment her physical and/or mental health were likely to suffer;

(e) the child's best interests required him to give her the advice and/or treatment without the parents' knowledge or consent[3].

1 See *Gillick* and *Re S*.
2 *Gillick v West Norfolk and Wisbech Area Health Authority* [1986] AC 112, [1985] 3 All ER 402, [1986] 1 FLR 224.
3 At 174 of the AC report (413 of the All ER report).

Emergency treatment

7.25 Even where the child does not have *Gillick* competence there may be exceptional circumstances where a doctor may treat a child without first obtaining the consent of a parent. Such circumstances might be:

(a) where emergency treatment is necessary;

(b) where the parents cannot be found;

(c) where the parents have abandoned the child;

(d) where the court has ordered the treatment.

Save in dire circumstances, the court's authority should be sought for such treatment (either through the use of the inherent jurisdiction of the High Court or an application for a specific issue order)[1].

1 In most instances the better course will be, eg for the local authority or the health authority to apply under the inherent jurisdiction.

Cases subsequent to *Gillick*

7.26 Subsequent to the *Gillick* decision the courts have held that:

(a) the court, parents and people with parental responsibility for the child have power to override the refusal of the *Gillick* competent child to undergo treatment and to consent to the treatment[1];

(b) the court may veto medical treatment to which the child has consented[2], even where the natural parents do not have that power[3];

(c) whenever the competence of the child arises, the court must take account of the wishes of the patient in respect of the proposed treatment[4].

1 See *Re R* [1992] Fam 11, [1991] 4 All ER 177.
2 See *Re W* [1992] 4 All ER 627.
3 See *Re R* above.
4 See *Re S* [1994] 2 FLR 1065.

WARDSHIP AND THE HIGH COURT'S INHERENT JURISDICTION

Introduction

7.27 Prior to the advent of the CA 1989 frequent use was made of the High Court's inherent jurisdiction in relation to children and, in particular, to the High Court's wardship jurisdiction. The effect of the CA 1989 has been to reduce the number of such applications considerably. The inherent jurisdiction of the High Court is not limited to wardship[1]. Therefore, in order to invoke the inherent jurisdiction of the High Court it is not necessary always to issue wardship proceedings.

1 See *Re W* [1993] 1 FLR 1.

Basis of jurisdiction and effect of wardship

7.28 The inherent jurisdiction of the High Court in respect of children is an aspect of the Crown's role as parens patriae. The inherent jurisdiction has developed through the Chancery Court and is now exercised by the Family Division of the High Court. The effect of making the child a ward of court is that the court assumes responsibility for all major matters in the child's life. Thus, no major decision may be made in respect of the child who is a ward of court without the prior leave of the court[1].

1 *Re CB (a minor)* [1981] 1 All ER 16.

Limitations due to age and presence of child

7.29 An unborn child has no rights of its own and therefore cannot be made a ward of court[1] (and in all probability cannot be made the object of an order under the court's inherent jurisdiction). The wardship and inherent jurisdictions can only be exercised in respect of children[2]. If within wardship proceedings orders are sought under other statutory provisions, any limitations upon the making of orders under those provisions will also apply.

Further, the jurisdiction may be exercised only with respect to any child who is either:

(a) a British subject, whether or not he is within the jurisdiction;

(b) physically present in England and Wales; or

(c) resident in England and Wales[3].

1 *Re F* [1988] 2 FLR 307.
2 Ie child as defined by Family Law Reform Act 1969, s 1 (ie a person who has not attained the age of 18).
3 *Re P (GE) (an infant)* [1965] Ch 568, [1964] 3 All ER 977 and *Harben v Harben* [1957] 1 All ER 379.

Limitations on the jurisdiction

Local authorities

7.30 Section 100 of the CA 1989 imposes restrictions on the use of the wardship jurisdiction as follows:

(a) The power of the High Court to make a care order within wardship proceedings under s 7 of the Family Law Reform Act 1969 is abolished[1].

(b) The court may not exercise the High Court's inherent jurisdiction in respect of children:

  (i) so as to require a child to be placed in the care, or put under the supervision of, a local authority;

  (ii) so as to require a child to be accommodated by or on behalf of the local authority;

  (iii) so as to make a child who is the subject of a care order a ward of court;

  (iv) for the purpose of conferring on any local authority the power to determine any question which has arisen, or which may arise, in connection with any aspect of parental responsibility for a child[2].

(c) A local authority may not apply for any exercise of the High Court's inherent jurisdiction in respect of children without the prior leave of the court. The court may only grant leave if it is satisfied that:

  (a) the result which the authority wish to achieve could not be achieved through the making of an order other than one under the Court's inherent jurisdiction for which the local authority is entitled to apply; and

  (b) there is reasonable cause to believe that if the Court's inherent jurisdiction is not exercised with respect to the child he is likely to suffer significant harm[3].

1 CA 1989, s 100(1).
2 Ibid, s 100(2).
3 Ibid, s 100(3).

Uses of the inherent jurisdiction

7.31 Thus it has been held that the CA 1989 has specifically preserved the exercise by the High Court of its inherent jurisdiction with respect to children[1]. It has circumscribed it and hedged round it but it has not removed the court's power to exercise that jurisdiction. It would take very clear words which cannot be found in the Act to take away that power completely. The inherent jurisdiction has been held to be correctly invoked to protect children at risk where it was not sought to remove them from home[2].

Devon County Council v *S*[2] where the mother had had nine children by a number of different men. Y was a family friend and a frequent visitor to the home (he was not the father of any of the children). Y had convictions for sexual offences against children. The courts concluded that Y represented a grave risk to the children. The mother did not perceive Y to be a risk to the children. The local authority sought to invoke the inherent jurisdiction of the High Court in order to secure orders preventing Y from having contact with the children. The district judge refused leave to the local authority to invoke that jurisdiction. On appeal it was held that any member of the family could have applied to the court to exercise its inherent power to protect the children at risk. Since no member of the family had done so, it was quite wrong that a restrictive interpretation of s 100 should prevent the local authority from doing so;

Re S[3] where the father had sexually assaulted his step-child. Assurances were given to the local authority that the father was living away from home but those assurances proved untrue. Accordingly, the local authority sought the leave of the court to pursue an application for an order excluding the father from the home under the inherent jurisdiction of the court pursuant to the CA 1989, s 100. The court held that interim care orders (which were suggested by the guardian ad litem) together with an order under s 34 (authorising the local authority to refuse contact between the children and the father) would not achieve the result desired by the local authority. This was because if the mother did not co-operate with such an order the children would be removed from her care, contrary to what was seen as being in their best interests. Further, an order under s 34 was designed to promote reasonable contact between the children and the parents and was not an appropriate method of obtaining an ouster order. Therefore, since no other alternative order had been suggested, the case came within the ambit of s 100(4)(a). Since, on the facts, the court had reasonable cause to believe that if the court's inherent jurisdiction was not exercised the children were likely to suffer significant harm, it followed that the court was empowered by s 100 to grant, under the inherent jurisdiction, the order sought by the local authority;

Re DB and CB[4]. Section 100(2) of the CA 1989 should not be interpreted in such a way as to prevent or discourage local authorities from exercising the right, potentially valuable to the children they serve, of having recourse to the inherent jurisdiction in cases where their general powers under Part IV of the Act may be found, for exceptional reasons, to be insufficient to enable them to carry out their duty under s 17 to safeguard and promote the welfare of the child in need within their area.

Practice Note[5]. The sterilisation of a minor will in virtually all cases require the prior sanction of a High Court judge. Applications in respect of a minor should be made in the Family Division of the High Court within proceedings either under the inherent jurisdiction or the CA 1989, s 8(1) (a specific issue order). The Official Solicitor's view is to prefer applications under the inherent jurisdiction.

Re O[6]. The inherent jurisdiction of the High Court is the most appropriate legal framework within which to consider a contested issue relating to emergency medical treatment for a child.

---

1 *South Glamorgan County Council v W and B* [1993] 1 FLR 574, [1993] 1 FCR 626, CA per Douglas Brown J; upheld in *Re W* [1992] 4 All ER 627 (see para 7.27).

234 *Children*

2 [1994] 1 FLR 355.
3 [1994] 1 FLR 623, [1994] 2 FCR 986.
4 [1993] 2 FCR 607.
5 [1996] 2 FLR 111.
6 [1993] 1 FCR 925, [1993] 2 FLR 149. This decision was also considered in *Re R* [1993] 2 FLR 757, [1993] 2 FCR 544.

Other limitations on court's powers

7.32 In addition to the above there are further limitations on the exercise by the High Court of its inherent or wardship jurisdictions such as:

(i) where the use of wardship is being used in an attempt to obviate immigration legislation[1];

(ii) where the orders sought are outside the ambit of the Court's powers – such as an attempt to attach a power of arrest to an injunction[2].

1 *Re F* [1990] Fam 125, [1989] 1 FLR 233.
2 *Re G* (1982) 4 FLR 538.

Wardship to challenge local authorities' decisions

7.33 It is extremely unlikely that the wardship or inherent jurisdictions can be used to review decisions made by a local authority in the provisions of services or accommodation under statutory duties imposed upon the local authorities[1]. Remedies under the CA 1989 are now much wider (eg contact with children in care) and despite the CA 1989, the courts will maintain the new view that a statutory code is already provided for challenge to local authorities[2]. Judicial review is the only proper course for challenge; and in judicial review the court can contest the motion to use wardship as appropriate[3].

1 See the pre-Children Act cases of *Re W* [1985] FLR 879, *W v Nottinghamshire County Council* [1986] 1 FLR 565 and *A v Liverpool City Council* [1982] AC 363, 1981 2 All ER 385.
2 *A v Liverpool City Council*, above.
3 RSC Ord 53 (and see chapter 9).

Uses of wardship

7.34 The following can only be examples of circumstances in which the use of High Court's inherent wardship jurisdictions may be considered:

(a) where it is necessary to obtain declaratory relief in respect of intended medical treatment[1];

(b) where it is necessary to consider obtaining injunctions to prevent publicity of details relating to a child[2];

(c) where it is necessary to obtain injunctions to secure the removal of an adult from the child's household;

(d) where it is necessary to obtain orders for the protection of a child (such as the removal of the child from the jurisdiction, although most of such orders may be obtained as prohibited steps orders under the CA 1989, s 8);

(e) where it is necessary to obtain declarations relating to the withholding of medical treatment[3];

(f) in private law proceedings where a party seeks an order for care and control and also seeks the greater protection of the High Court's involvement through wardship proceedings.

1 See, eg *Re W* [1992] 4 All ER 627.
2 See, eg *Re S* [1994] 1 FLR 623, [1994] 2 FCR 986.
3 See, eg *Re J (A minor – Wardship: Medical Treatment)* [1991] Fam 33, [1991] 1 FLR 366 where a child was born with so serious physical injuries that his life would be unbearable, the court directed that treatment need not be given to prolong his life.

Wardship proceedings

7.35 The procedure for making a child a ward of court is laid down in the FPR 1991, r 5.1. That rule provides as follows:

(a) the application is to be made by originating summons and is to be supported by an affidavit unless the court otherwise directs (r 5.1(1));

(b) where a local authority seeks leave to issue a wardship application under the CA 1989, s 100(3), it should comply with the FPR 1991, r 4.3. Under r 4.3 the application for leave should be made in writing setting out the reasons for the application and there should be a draft of the proposed originating summons submitted with the written request for leave. The procedure for considering an application for leave is set out in r 4.3(2) to (4);

(c) where there is no person other than the minor who is a suitable defendant, an application may be made ex parte to a district judge for leave to issue either an ex parte originating summons or an originating summons with the minor as a defendant. Except where such leave is granted, the minor is not to be made a defendant to the originating summons in the first instance (r 5.1(3));

(d) particulars of any originating summons that has been issued in the district registry are to be sent by the proper officer of the district registry to the Principal Registry for recording in the Register of Wards (r 5.1(4));

(e) the originating summons must state the child's date of birth (unless otherwise directed). Further the originating summons must be accompanied by the child's birth certificate (or the entry in the Adopted Children Register relating to the child). If that certificate is not filed the plaintiff must seek directions as to the proof of birth of the child at the first hearing of the originating summons (r 5.1(5));

(f) the plaintiff must give a brief description in the body of the summons of his interest in or relation to the child (r 5.1(6));

(g) the originating summons should state the whereabouts of the child or should state that the plaintiff is unaware of the child's whereabouts, unless the court otherwise directs (r 5.1(7));

(h) a defendant who is served with the originating summons must lodge 'forthwith' in the relevant registry a notice stating the address of the defendant and the whereabouts of the child (or that he is unaware of the child's whereabouts). The defendant must serve upon the plaintiff a copy of this notice, unless the court otherwise directs. Where the child is himself a defendant, this requirement need not be satisfied (r 5.1(8));

(i) notice must be given by any party other than the child of any change in his address or if he becomes aware of any change in the whereabouts of the child. Such notice must be given forthwith and must be lodged with the relevant registry (see r 5.1(9)). The defendant must be informed of the requirements of r 5.1(8) and (9) by notice in the originating summons.

Defendants to wardship

7.36 In considering who should be a defendant to a wardship originating summons the following points need to be borne in mind:

(a) if the intention of the proceedings is to resolve a disagreement, that the parties to the proceedings should clearly be the parties to that disagreement (save in the circumstances set out in (iii) below);

(b) otherwise, the parties to the proceedings should be those who have an interest in the child;

(c) where the proceedings are issued so as to prevent an undesirable association between the child and another person (for instance where a girl is associating with a male adult abuser) that person should not be joined as party to the proceedings but should be made a defendant to the application for an injunction by which the association is desired to be terminated[1];

(d) a person who wishes to be joined into the proceedings may, of course, make an application to this effect to the court. In order to be joined into the proceedings it is necessary for such an applicant to show a genuine interest[2];

(e) a child should only be joined into the proceedings if there is a special reason. Where this is intended, the guidance of the Official Solicitor should be sought before the issue of the proceedings. If the child becomes a party he must act by a next friend or guardian ad litem who will in most circumstances be the Official Solicitor.

1 *Practice Direction* [1983] 2 All ER 672, 4 FLR 640.
2 *A v Berkshire County Council* [1989] 1 FLR 273.

Procedure under the court's inherent jurisdiction

7.37 An application for an order under the High Court's inherent jurisdiction in respect of children should be made in a similar way to that referred to above in respect of wardship proceedings[1]; Save that the application should be headed 'in the ...'[2].

1 See *Re F (Sterilisation Mental Patient)* [1989] 2 FLR 376.
2 Acts of wardship.

SURROGACY AND EMBRYOLOGY

7.38 With the advances that have been made in medical science, it has been necessary for the law to encompass the developments within the fields of surrogacy and embryology. The complexity of issues that arise through surrogacy were identified in the case of *Re C*[1]. As a result of that case, the Warnock Report was commissioned. Following that report the Surrogacy Arrangements Act 1985 was passed.

1 [1985] FLR 846.

The Surrogacy Arrangements Act 1985

7.39 The purpose of the act was to regulate surrogacy arrangements. The act defines a 'surrogate mother' as 'a woman who carries a child in pursuance of an arrangement:

(a) made before she began to carry the child, and

(b) made with a view to any child carried in pursuance of it being handed over to, and parental responsibility being met (so far as practicable) by, another person or other persons'[1].

The Act provides that a woman begins to carry a child at the time of the insemination that results in her carrying the child (or of the placing in her of an embryo, of an egg in the process of fertilisation or of sperm and eggs that results in her carrying the child)[2]. Thus the above sections envisage a woman carrying a child with a view to handing it over to someone else.

1 Surrogacy Arrangements Act 1985, s 1(2).
2 Ibid, s 1(6).

Enforceability of arrangements and offences

7.40 The Surrogacy Arrangements Act 1985 specifically provides that a surrogacy arrangement is unenforceable by or against any of the persons making it[1]. The Act also specifies certain offences which may be committed in respect of surrogacy (the punishment for which is provided by s 4 of the Act). The offences cover a wide range of activities relating to:

(a) involvement in surrogacy on a commercial basis[2];

(b) advertising the availability of surrogacy arrangements[3].

The Act does not seek to prevent all surrogacy arrangements; the focus of the offences is upon commercial activity. This aspect of the Surrogacy Arrangements Act 1985 is further demonstrated by the provision that specifies that an offence under s 2(1) of the Act (which relates to offences for negotiating surrogacy arrangements on a commercial basis etc) is not committed where:

(i) a woman, with a view to becoming a surrogate mother herself, does any act mentioned in sub-section 2(1) or causes such an act to be done; or

(ii) any person, with a view to a surrogate mother carrying a child for him, does any act or causes any act to be done as is mentioned in s 2(1) of the Act[4].

1 Surrogacy Arrangements Act 1985, s 1A.
2 Ibid, s 2.
3 Ibid, s 3.
4 Ibid, s 2(2).

Whose child is it?

7.41 The Human Fertilisation and Embryology Act 1990 seeks to define who will be treated as the parents of the child where the child has been born as a result of surrogacy, *in vitro* fertilisation or donation. The Act provides the following definition of 'mother':

> 'The woman who is carrying or has carried a child as a result of the placing in her of an embryo or of sperm and eggs, and no other woman, is to be treated as the mother of the child.'

The Act therefore specifies that it is the woman who carries (ie gives birth to) the child that will be treated as the mother. However, this definition relates only to the case where a child has been carried 'as a result of the placing in the woman of an embryo or of sperm and eggs' (the Act does not specify what is to happen where the woman carries a child through the donation of eggs alone).

The above definition of 'mother' does not apply to a child where the child is subsequently adopted (for in those circumstances the child will become the child of the adopters)[1]. The Act specifically states that the above definition of mother applies whether the woman was in the United Kingdom or elsewhere at the time of the placing in her of the embryo or the sperm and eggs[2].

Section 28 of the Act provides a definition of 'father' in respect of a child who is being or who has been carried by a woman as a result of the placing in her of an embryo or of sperm and eggs or her artificial insemination. The Act provides:

(a) where the surrogate mother was married, her husband will be treated as the father of the child, unless it is shown that he did not consent to the placing in her of the embryo or the sperm and eggs or to her insemination (these provisions do not apply where the child is subsequently adopted or where the child is treated at common law as a legitimate child of the parties to a marriage);

(b) if the above does not apply, but 'treatment services' were provided for the surrogate mother and another man (who did not himself provide the sperm) that man will be treated as the father of the child (again, subject to the limitations relating to adoption and legitimacy that are referred to above).

Where a person is treated as the father of the child as a result of one of the above two definitions, no other person is to be treated as the father of the child[3].

1 Human Fertilisation and Embryology Act 1990, s 28(2) and (5).
2 Ibid, s 28(3).
3 Ibid, s 28(4). See *Re B (Parentage)* [1996] 2 FLR 15.

Parental orders

7.42 Section 30 of the Human Fertilisation and Embryology Act 1990 makes provision for 'parental orders' to be made in favour of the 'gamete donors' (ie the people who donated the egg cell or the sperm cell). A parental order provides for a child to be treated in law as the child of the applicant's marriage[1]. The order may be made if the following conditions are satisfied:

(a) the child must have been carried by a woman other than the wife as the result of the placing in her of an embryo or sperm and eggs or her artificial insemination[2];

(b) the gametes of the husband or the wife, or both, must have been used to bring about the creation of the embryo[3];

(c) the husband and wife must apply for the order within six months of the birth of the child (or within six months of the coming into force of the Act (1 November 1994[4]);

(d) at the time of the application and of the making of the order the child's home must be with the husband and the wife and the husband or the wife or both of them must be domiciled in the United Kingdom or in the Channel Islands or the Isle of Man[5].

(e) at the time of the making of the order both the husband and the wife must be at least 18[6];

(f) the court must be satisfied that both the father of the child (where he is not the husband) and the woman who carried the child have freely and with full understanding of what is involved, agreed unconditionally to the making of the order, unless the person whose agreement is required cannot be found or is incapable of giving agreement. Agreement of the woman who carried the child is ineffective if given by her less than six weeks after the child's birth[7].

(g) the court must be satisfied that no money or other benefit (other than expenses reasonably incurred) has been given or received by the husband or the wife for or in consideration of:

  (i) the making of the order,

  (ii) any agreement required by subsection (5),

  (iii) the handing over of the child to the husband and the wife, or

  (iv) the making of any arrangements with a view to the making of the order, unless authorised by the court[8].

1 Human Fertilisation and Embryology Act 1990, s 30(1).
2 Ibid, s 30(1)(a).
3 Ibid, s 30(1)(b).
4 Ibid, s 30(2).
5 Ibid, s 30(3).
6 Ibid, s 30(4).
7 Ibid, s 30(5) and (6).
8 Ibid, s 30(7).

Procedure

7.43 The application for an order under the Human Fertilisation and Embryology Act 1990, s 30 is made on Form C51 to the magistrates' court but may be transferred to the county court under the Children (Allocation of Proceedings) Order 1991[1]. Procedure is governed by the FPR 1991, Part IVA and the FP(CA 1989)R, rr 21A-J. The applicants are the husband and the wife and the respondents are the birth parents (unless application is made under s 30(6) to dispense with their consent) and any other person with parental responsibility. The appointment of a guardian ad litem should be considered as the order is in Form C53 (if granted) or Form C54 (if refused).

1 Article 7.

If no parental order

7.44 If a parental order is not sought or is not available, consideration may have to be given to possible applications, for instance under the CA 1989 or the Adoption Act 1976.

LEGITIMACY

Introduction

7.45 On the 4 April 1988 the Family Law Reform Act 1987 came into effect. The Act was intended to remove the words 'legitimate' and 'illegitimate' from legal vocabulary. However, the Act does not abolish the concept and status of legitimacy and illegitimacy. That concept is still seen, in particular, in the parental responsibility that is afforded to the fathers of children when they are married to the mother[1] (but is not afforded as of right to the unmarried father)[2]. The Family Law Reform Act 1987 provides that:

> 'References (however expressed) to any relationship between two persons shall, unless the contrary intention appears, be construed without regard to whether or not the father and mother of either of them, or the father and mother of any person through whom the relationship is deduced, had or have been married to each other at any time[3].'

Thus, in describing the relationship between a child and his father, that relationship is to be construed without regard to whether the parents of the child were married. The terminology that the Act introduces is that of 'a person whose father and mother were (or were not) married to each other at the time of his birth'[4]. Because there are now many different ways in which a child may be conceived, the time of a person's birth is specifically defined as beginning with:

(a) the insemination resulting in his birth; or

(b) where there was no such insemination, his conception, and (in either case) ending with his birth[5].

1 CA 1989, s 2(1).
2 Ibid, s 4 enables fathers to obtain parental responsibility; and see para 5.6.
3 Family Law Reform Act 1987, s 1(1).
4 Ibid, s 1(2).
5 Ibid, s 1(4).

Legitimacy at common law

7.46 The basic English language definition of 'legitimacy' is 'born in wedlock'. The common law recognises a child as legitimate when the child is born during the lawful marriage of his parents. The common law also presumes that a child born to a married woman is the child of her husband (and therefore the child is legitimate). Both parents will have parental responsibility in respect of their child born during their marriage. The presumption of legitimacy at common law (or by statute) is rebuttable on the balance of probabilities[1]. The presumption of legitimacy will also apply where a child is born not later than the usual period of gestation after the marriage has been dissolved (on the basis that it will be presumed that the child was conceived during the marriage[2]).

1 Family Law Reform Act 1969, s 26 which provides that 'any presumption of law as to the legitimacy or illegitimacy of any person may in any civil proceedings be rebutted

by evidence which shows that it is more probable than not that that person is illegitimate or legitimate, as the case may be, and it shall not be necessary to prove that fact beyond reasonable doubt in order to rebut the presumption'.
2 *Re Overbury* [1954] 3 All ER 308.

Legitimacy by statute

Artificial insemination

7.47 Under the Family Law Reform Act 1987, s 27 a child who is born to a married woman by artificial insemination will be treated in law as the child of the parties to that marriage unless:

(a) at the time of insemination the marriage had been dissolved or annulled;

(b) the husband did not consent to the insemination.

For the purposes of this provision 'a marriage' will include a void marriage if at the time of the insemination either or both of the parties to the marriage reasonably believed that the marriage was valid (and it will be presumed, unless the contrary is shown, that one of the parties did so believe)[1].

1 Family Law Reform Act 1987, s 27(2).

Subsequent marriage

7.48 Where the parents of an illegitimate child marry one another, the marriage will render the child legitimate from the date of the marriage if the father of the child is at the date of the marriage domiciled in England and Wales[1]. If the father is not domiciled in England and Wales at the time of the marriage, the child may still be recognised as legitimate in England and Wales if the law of the country in which the father is domiciled recognises the legitimation of the child by the marriage[2].

1 Legitimacy Act 1976, s 2.
2 Ibid, s 3.

Void and voidable marriages

7.49 Where a child is born from a void marriage, the child will still be treated as legitimate if at the time of the child's conception or of the insemination resulting in the birth, both or either of the parties to the marriage reasonably believed that the marriage was valid (that belief being presumed by reason of s 1(4) of the Act)[1]. This, however, will only apply where the father of the child was domiciled in England and Wales at the time of the birth or, if he died before the birth, was so domiciled immediately before his death[2]. A voidable marriage remains valid until it is declared a nullity; therefore, a child born or conceived during the marriage will be treated as legitimate even if it is subsequently annulled[3].

1 Legitimacy Act 1976, s 1(1).
2 Ibid, s 1(2).
3 MCA 1973, s 16.

Adoption

7.50 Under the Adoption Act 1976, s 39 an adopted child will be treated as the legitimate child of the adopters if they are a married couple.

Declarations of parentage, legitimacy or legitimation

7.51 The Family Law Act 1986 introduced statutory powers by which a person could apply for declarations as to his parentage, legitimacy or legitimation. The Act provides that 'any person' may apply to the court[1] for a declaration:

(a) that a person named in the application is or was his parent[2];

(b) that he is the legitimate child of his parents[3];

(c) that he has become a legitimated person[4];

(d) that he has not become a legitimated person[5].

The court will only have jurisdiction to entertain an application if the applicant is either domiciled in England and Wales on the date of the application or has been habitually resident in England and Wales throughout the period of one year ending with that date[6]. The application must be made to the High Court or county court[7]. Where a declaration is made by the court, the prescribed officer of the court will notify the Registrar General of the making of the declaration. The procedure for such applications is specified the FPR 1991, rr 3.13 and 3.14.

1 Family Law Act 1986, s 56.
2 Ibid, s 56(1A).
3 Ibid, s 56(1B).
4 Ibid, s 56(2A).
5 Ibid, s 56(2)(b).
6 Ibid, s 56(3).
7 Ibid, s 63.

BLOOD TESTS

Family Law Reform Act 1969, s 20

7.52 The power of the court to order blood tests is derived from the Family Law Reform Act 1969, s 20. The court may order such tests in any civil proceedings in which paternity is at issue upon the application of any party to those proceedings[1]. Where an order is made, the order will specify the person who is to carry out the tests (the applicant should specify in her application who she suggests should do the tests)[2]. Following the direction, the person who carries out the tests will make a report giving the results of the tests[3]. The report is to be in a prescribed form and 'shall be received by the court as evidence in the proceedings'.

1 Family Law Reform Act 1969, s 20(1).
2 Ibid, s 20(1A).
3 Ibid, s 20(2)

Consents

7.53 A blood test taken following an order under s 20 may not be taken from a person without his consent. (And for these purposes a child who has attained the age of 16 may give a valid consent[2].) A blood sample may be taken from a person under the age of 16 years (who is not a mental patient) if the person who has 'care and control' consents[3].

1 Family Law Reform Act 1969, s 21(1) and (2).
2 Ibid, s 21(3).
3 Ibid, s 2.

Failure to comply with directions for blood tests

7.54 Where a person fails to comply with a direction for a blood test, the court may draw such inferences, if any, from the fact that appears proper in the circumstances. In *Re F*[1] Balcombe LJ said after referring to *W v W*[2]:

(a) the presumption of legitimacy merely determines the onus of proof;

(b) public policy no longer requires that special protection shall be given by the law to the status of legitimacy;

(c) the interests of justice will normally require that available evidence be not suppressed and that the truth be ascertained wherever possible. In many circumstances, the interests of the child are also best served if the truth is ascertained;

(d) however, the interests of justice may conflict with the interests of the child. In general the court ought to permit a blood test of a young child to be taken unless satisfied that that would be against the child's interests; it does not need to be satisfied that the outcome of the tests will be for the benefit of the child;

(e) it is not really protecting the child to ban a blood test on some vague and shadowy conjecture that it may turn out to be to its disadvantage; it may equally well turn out to be for its advantage or at least do it no harm;

(f) a blood sample may not be taken from a person under the age of 16 years without the consent of the person having his or her care and control. Without such consent, it may not be proper for the court to order that a blood test of the child be taken[3].

1 [1993] 1 FLR 598.

2 *W v W* [1972] AC 24.
3 At 601.

7.55 In *Re A (A Minor: Paternity Refusal of Blood Tests)*[1] the Court of Appeal had to consider the inferences that should be drawn from a refusal to comply with a direction for blood tests. The court held that:

(a) Section 23 of the 1969 Act was untouched by the CA 1989. The result is that all issues of paternity now fall to be resolved within the framework of the CA 1989 by courts which are given statutory freedom (at all levels of the Family Court jurisdiction) to deal with the evidence at large, and (specifically) to reach their own determination as to the significance to be attached to and the inference to be drawn from the circumstances that a person has refused to consent to a scientific test directed by the court under the amended s 20 of the 1969 Act.

(b) The former authorities on the requirements of corroboration for the purposes of Affiliation Act proceedings ceased to be in point after the abolition of the bastardy jurisdiction on 1 January 1989.

(c) The court's powers of inference under s 23(1) of the 1969 Act are fully enlarged and unconfined. They are amply wide enough to extend to any inference drawn as to the very fact which is in issue in the proceedings, namely the child's actual paternity.

(d) Any man who is unsure as to whether the child he is alleged to have fathered might be that of another man had it within his powers to set all doubts at rest by submitting to a test. Against that background of law and scientific advance, it followed in justice and in commonsense that if a mother claimed against one of the possible fathers, and he chose to exercise his right not to submit to be tested, the inference that he was the father of the child would be virtually inescapable. He would have to advance very clear and cogent reasons for his refusal to be tested.

In *Re G (A Minor: Blood Test)* it was held that it would not be sufficient to refuse to make a direction for blood tests simply because a mother indicated that she would not comply[2]; and now see *Re H (Paternity: Blood Test)*[3].

1 [1994] 2 FLR 463.
2 [1994] 1 FLR 495.
3 [1996] 2 FLR 65.

ADOPTION

Introduction

7.56 The law of adoption in this country is a creation of statute. The first such statute was the Adoption of Children Act 1926. The current statutory provisions are to be found in the Adoption Act 1976. The main procedural provisions are: the Adoption Rules 1984[1]; the Magistrates' Courts (Adoption) Rules 1984[2]; and the Adoption Agencies Regulations 1983[3].

1 SI 1984/265.
2 SI 1984/611.
3 SI 1983/1964.

The effect of adoption

7.57 Adoption of a child has the following effects in law:

(a) The child is prevented from being illegitimate[1].

(b) The child is treated in law as if it were not the child of any person other than the adopters or adopter (although in the case of a child who is adopted by one of its natural parents as the sole adoptive parent this provision has no effect as respects entitlement or anything else that is dependent upon the relationship to that parent)[2].

(c) Where the adopters are a married couple, the child will be treated as if it had been born as a child of that marriage (whether or not he was born before or after the marriage actually took place)[3].

(d) Where the adopters are not a married couple, the child will be treated as if he had been born to the adopter 'in wedlock' (although this will not cause the child to be treated as if he were a child of any actual marriage of the single adopter)[4].

(e) The adopters will acquire parental responsibility for the adopted child[5] (although this will not be the case so far as parental responsibility is concerned for any period before the order was made)[6].

(f) The making of the adoption order will extinguish:

 (i) the parental responsibility which any person has for the child immediately before the making of the order;

 (ii) any order under the CA 1989;

 (iii) any duty that arises by virtue of an agreement or order of the court to make payments, so far as the payments are in respect of the child's maintenance or upbringing for any period after the making of the order (subject to any terms of a trust or agreement)[7].

1 Adoption Act 1976, s 39(4).
2 Ibid, s 39(2) and (3).
3 Ibid, s 39(1)(a).
4 Ibid, s 39(1)(b).
5 Ibid, s 12(1).
6 Ibid, s 12(2).
7 Ibid, s 12(3) and (4).

Other consequences of adoption

7.58 An adoption order will have the following additional consequences:

(a) The child will acquire British citizenship, provided that at least one of the applicants is a British citizen[1].

(b) The name of the child may be changed. The intended new name may be stated in the application for an adoption order. In the application for an adoption order there is a standard paragraph which provides: 'If an adoption order is made in pursuance of this application, the child is to be known by the following names ...'. In the adoption order itself, the order will state the names by which the child is to be known[2].

(c) The child will still be prevented from marrying a member of his birth family who is within the prohibited degrees. The child's previous relationship with his birth family will still apply for the purposes of ss 10 and 11 (incest) of the Sexual Offences Act 1956[3].

(d) Adoption will not affect any interest or expectant interest vested in possession before the adoption[4].

(e) The adoption will be recorded in the Adopted Children's Register by the Registrar General[5].

1 British Nationality Act 1981, s 1(5).
2 In the magistrates' court the forms are set out in Sch 1 of the Magistrates' Courts (Adoption) Rules 1984 (Form 6: application; Form 13 : order). In the High Court and county court the forms are set out in Schedule 1 of the Adoption Rules 1984 (Form 7: application; Form 15: order).
3 Adoption Act 1976, s 47.
4 Ibid, ss 42–46.
5 Ibid, s 50 and Sch 1.

Adoption agencies

7.59 The Adoption Act makes provision for the establishment of an adoption service by every local authority[1]. Every local authority is under a duty to establish and maintain within their area a service designed to meet the needs, in relation to adoption, of :

(a) children who have been or may be adopted,

(b) parents and guardians of such children,

(c) persons who have adopted or may adopt a child.

The duty is on every local authority either to provide that service itself or to secure that the services are provided by approved adoption societies. So as to avoid duplication, omission or avoidable delay, the Act requires that those services are to be provided in conjunction with the local authority's other social services and with approved adoption societies in their area[2]; the idea is to ensure that there is full inter-agency co-operation in respect of adoption. The extent of the duty is wide and specifically includes a requirement that the local authority shall:

(i) provide temporary board and lodging where needed by pregnant women, mothers or children;

(ii) make arrangements for assessing the children and prospective adopters, and placing children for adoption;

(iii) provide counselling for people with problems relating to adoption[3].

When a local authority or an approved adoption society is providing this service, the local authority or the society may be referred to as 'an adoption agency'[4].

1 Adoption Act 1976, s 1(1).
2 Ibid, s 1(3).
3 Ibid, s 1(2).
4 Ibid, s 1(4).

Regulation of adoption agencies

7.60 The Adoption Agencies Regulations[1] specify the manner in which adoption agencies are to conduct themselves. The Regulations provide amongst other things for:

(a) approval of an adoption society to be given by the Secretary of State upon an application to him[2];

(b) annual reports and information to be given by approved adoption societies to the Secretary of State[3];

(c) the establishment of an adoption panel and the appointment of members to it[4];

(d) the adoption agencies to make written arrangements for their adoption work and, in particular, to satisfy themselves that social work staff employed in adoption work have had sufficient experience and qualifications for the task[5];

(e) the adoption agency to preserve case records in a way that will ensure their confidentiality[6] save as set out in reg 15.

Beyond that where an adoption is intended the Regulations impose duties on local authorities to the child, the parents and/or guardians and the prospective adopters[7]. These are considered later in this chapter.

1 SI 1983/1964.
2 Regulation 2.
3 Regulation 3.
4 Regulation 5.
5 Regulation 6.
6 Regulation 14.
7 Regulations 7 – 9.

Placement for adoption

7.61 The intention of the Adoption Act 1976 is to secure that adoption orders take place primarily as a result of placements made by adoption agencies. The Act specifically provides that a person other than an adoption agency may not make arrangements for the adoption of a child or place a child for adoption, unless :

(a) the proposed adopter is a relative of the child, or

(b) he is acting in pursuance of an order of the High Court[1].

The Act defines the word 'relative' as meaning in relation to a child 'a grandparent, brother, sister, uncle or aunt, whether of the full-blood or half-blood or by affinity and includes, where the child is illegitimate, the father of the child and any person who would be a relative within the meaning of this definition if the child were the legitimate child of his mother and father'[2]. The Act creates offences where these provisions are ignored[3]. Where a child is placed for adoption in breach of s 11, the adoption application will not necessarily fail[4].

1 Adoption Act 1976, s 11.
2 Ibid, s 72.
3 Ibid, s 11(3).
4 See *Re S (Arrangements for Adoption)* [1985] FLR 579; *Gatehouse v Robinson* [1986] 1 FLR 504; and *Re G (Adoption: Illegal Placement)* [1995] 1 FLR 403.

Non-agency placements

7.62 Notwithstanding the provisions of s 11 of the Adoption Act 1976 (see above) there are circumstances in which a child will have been placed with people who apply to adopt other than by the adoption agency. Such circumstances might be, for instance:

(a) where the child had genuinely been place with someone under a private fostering arrangement[1] and, following that initial arrangement for fostering, the people caring for the child wish to adopt;

(b) where the proposed adoption arises out of surrogacy arrangements;

(c) where the adoption is sought in respect of a foreign child (where the child's country of origin is not one that is party to a specific convention or treaty);

(d) where local authority foster parents apply for an adoption order without the local authority having approved them as prospective adopters of a child.

1 The provisions for private fostering are in the CA 1989, s 76.

How to get to placement stage

7.63 Save in circumstances such as those set out above, the 'placement stage' in respect of an adoption will usually be achieved as a result of a decision by an adoption agency where a child is either in the care of a local authority pursuant to a care order or is being accommodated by a local authority under its duties in Part III of the CA 1989. Where it is proposed that a ward of court should be placed for adoption, the prior sanction of the court will be necessary[1].

> 1 See *Re F (Wardship: Adoption)* [1984] FLR 60. Where such leave is sought the court will have to consider whether the adoption application has a reasonable chance of succeeding: see *F v S* [1973] Fam 203, [1976] 1 All ER 722.

Notice where non-agency placement

7.64 The Adoption Act requires notice to be given to an adoption agency of an intended adoption application where the placement was not made by that agency[1]. The intention of these provisions is to ensure that a local authority has ample opportunity to investigate such a proposed adoption. The Act makes the following requirements in respect of that notice:

(a) the notice must be given to the local authority within whose area the applicant has his home[2];

(b) the notice must be of the applicant's intention to apply for an adoption order in respect of the child[3];

(c) the notice must be given at least three months before the date of the proposed adoption order[4];

(d) the notice must be given within the period of two years preceding the making of the application[5].

On the receipt of the notice, the local authority is under a duty to investigate the proposed adoption[6] and to submit a report to the court. Where the notice relates to a child whom the local authority knows is looked after by another authority, the authority receiving notice must inform the other local authority in writing that they have received notice from the proposed adopters[7].

> 1 Adoption Act 1976, s 22.
> 2 Ibid, s 22(1).
> 3 Ibid, s 22(1).
> 4 Ibid, s 22(1).
> 5 Ibid, s 22(1A).
> 6 Ibid, s 22(2) – (4).
> 7 Ibid, s 22(4)

WHO MAY APPLY TO ADOPT?

7.65 A single person may adopt a child if he satisfies the following conditions[1]:

(a) he must have attained the age of 21;
(b) he must either not be married or, if he is married, the court must be satisfied that:
    (i) his spouse cannot be found, or
    (ii) the spouses have separated and are living apart, and the separation is likely to be permanent, or
    (iii) his spouse is by reason of ill-health, whether physical or mental, incapable of making an application for an adoption order;
(c) he must either be domiciled in a part of the United Kingdom or in the Channel Islands or the Isle of Man (or the application must be for a convention adoption order in which case s 17 of the Adoption Act 1976 must be complied with)[2].

1 Adoption Act 1976, s 15.
2 Ibid, s 17.

7.66 An adoption order may be made on the application of more than one person if[1]:

(a) the application is made by a married couple where both the husband and wife have attained the age of 21 years (or, where one of the applicants is the father or mother of the child, that person must have attained the age of 18 years and the other spouse must have attained the age of 21 years);
(b) one or both of them must be domiciled in the United Kingdom or in the Channel Islands or the Isle of Man (or the application must be for a convention adoption order and s 17 of the Adoption Act must be complied with).

Thus couples not married cannot adopt jointly.

1 Adoption Act 1976, s 14.

7.67 An adoption order may not be made on the application of the mother or father of the child alone unless the court is satisfied that[1]:

(a) the other natural parent is dead or cannot be found, or by virtue of s 28 of the Human Fertilisation and Embryology Act 1990, there is no other parent; or
(b) there is some other reason justifying the exclusion of the natural parent (and where such an order is made, the reason justifying the exclusion of the other natural parent must be recorded by the court).

1 Adoption Act 1976, s 15(3).

Child to live with adopters

7.68 The Act imposes the following requirements in respect of the time during which the child must have lived with the adopters before the court may make an adoption order[1]:

(a) Where the applicant or one of the applicants is a parent, step-parent or relative of the child[2] or the child was placed with the prospective adopters by an adoption agency or in pursuance of an order of the High Court, the adoption order may not be made unless the child is at least 19 weeks old and at all times during the preceding 13 weeks had his home with the applicants or one of them.

(b) Where the above does not apply (for instance where the child was placed with the prospective applicant under a private fostering arrangement that has graduated to a prospective adoptive placement), the adoption order may not be made unless the child is at least 12 months old and at all times during the preceding 12 months had his home with the applicants or one of them.

(c) By way of a catch all provision, an adoption order may not be made unless the court is satisfied that sufficient opportunity to see the child with the applicant or applicants in the home environment has been afforded to the adoption agency (where the child was placed by an agency) or in any other case to the local authority within whose area the prospective adoptive home is[3].

1 Adoption Act 1976, s 13.
2 See s 72 for the definition of 'relative'.
3 Adoption Act 1976, s 13(3).

Application following prior refusal

7.69 The Act also places restrictions upon the ability of people who wish to adopt to make repeated applications to the courts. Those restrictions arise because it is provided that[1] a court may not proceed to hear an application for an adoption order where a previous application for a British adoption order by the same person in respect of the same child was refused by a court unless:

(a) in refusing the previous application the court directed that this restriction should not apply; or

(b) it appears to the court that because of a change in circumstances or for any other reason it is proper to proceed with the application.

1 Adoption Act 1976, s 24(1).

Adoption for money

7.70 The Act also prohibits the making of an adoption order in relation to a child unless the court is satisfied that the applicants have not given any payment or reward for or in consideration of the adoption of the child, the grant of consent to the adoption, the handing over of the child with a view to adoption or the making of any arrangements for the adoption of a child[1].

1 Adoption Act 1976, ss 24(2) and 57.

WHO MAY BE ADOPTED?

7.71 The adoption order must relate to a child who has never married[1]. For the purposes of the Act a child is defined as a person who has not attained the age of 18 years (except where the word is used to express relationship)[2]. An application to adopt may be made in respect of a child who is not a British citizen, although in those circumstances notice must be given to the Home Office by the applicants with the proposed adoption application[3]. An adoption order may be made notwithstanding that the child is already an adopted child[4].

1 Adoption Act 1976, s 12(5).
2 Ibid, s 72(1).
3 See *Re W* [1986] Fam 54, [1986] 1 FLR 179 and *Re K* [1994] 2 FLR 557.
4 Adoption Act 1976, s 12(7).

Adoption agency's duties to child, parents or guardian

7.72 The Adoption Agencies Regulations 1983 provide that an adoption agency has duties when considering adoption for a child. Those duties in respect of the child's parents or guardian (and also in respect of the child, having regard to his age and understanding) are to do the following in so far as is reasonably practicable[1]:

(a) to provide a counselling service for them;

(b) to explain to them (and provide them with written information about) the legal implications of and procedures in relation to freeing for adoption.

After satisfying the above requirements, an adoption agency that is considering adoption for a child must then:

(i) Set up a case record in respect of the child and place on it any information obtained in respect of the proposed adoption.

(ii) Obtain, so far as is reasonably practicable such particulars of the parents or guardian (and having regard to his age and understanding, the child) as are set out in the schedules to the Adoption Agencies Regulations 1983 together with any information that may be requested by the Adoption Panel.

(iii) Arrange and obtain a written report by a registered medical practitioner in respect of the child (unless a recent report is available).

(iv) Arrange any other examinations and screening procedures in respect of the child and (so far as is reasonably practicable) his parents to the extent that may be advised by the adoption agency's medical adviser.

(v) Prepare a written report containing the agency's observations as a result of their enquiries.

The Regulations also impose duties on the local authority in respect of the father of the illegitimate child[2]. These include a requirement that the agency shall, so far as it considers reasonably practicable and in the interests of the child, ascertain whether the natural father intends to apply for 'custody' of the child[3].

1 Adoption Agencies Regulations 1983, reg 7.
2 Ibid, reg 7(3).
3 Ibid, reg 7(2)(c).

Adoption agency's duties in respect of prospective adopters

7.73 The Regulations provide that an adoption agency that is considering whether a person might be a suitable adoptive parent must:

(a) provide a counselling service for the prospective adopter;

(b) explain to him (and provide him with written information about) the legal implications of the procedure in relation to adoption.

After complying with the above, an adoption agency that is still considering the prospective adopter must:

(i) Set up a case record in respect of him and place on it any information obtained about him.

(ii) Obtain a medical report on the prospective adopter.

(iii) Obtain a written report about the premises that the prospective adopter intends to use as his home if he adopts a child.

(iv) Obtain written reports following the interview with two referees that the prospective adopter has nominated on his behalf.

(v) Obtain a written report from the prospective adopter's local authority in relation to him.

(vi) Prepare a written report containing the results of the agency's investigations.

1 Adoption Agencies Regulations 1983, reg 8.

Referral to Adoption Panel

7.74 After completing its investigations in respect of the child, the natural parents, the guardian and the prospective adopter the adoption agency must refer the matter to the Adoption Panel. The Adoption Panel will then consider the matter in accordance with the Regulations. The provisions of those Regulations are in regs 9 and 10 of the Adoption Agencies Regulations.

Post Panel

7.75 Following the referral to the Adoption Panel, the adoption agency must decide whether to proceed with the intended adoption. If it does decide to proceed it must then:

(a) notify in writing the parents of the child (including the father of an illegitimate child) if it considers that adoption is in the child's best interests and whether it intends to issue an application to free the child for adoption;

(b) inform the prospective adopter of its decision as to whether it considers him to be a suitable adoptive parent in general and, in particular, a suitable adoptive parent for the particular child[1].

1 Adoption Agencies Regulations 1983, reg 11.

PARENTAL AGREEMENT TO ADOPTION

7.76 The act provides that an adoption order shall not be made unless:

(a) the child is free for adoption by order of the court;

(b) each parent or guardian of the child freely and with full understanding of what is involved, agrees unconditionally to the making of an adoption order (whether or not he knows the identity of the applicants); or

(c) his agreement to the making of the adoption order is dispensed with on a ground specified in s 16(2) of the Act[1].

1 Adoption Act 1976, s 16(1).

Consent

7.77 The following are the main points arising over the issue of consent:

(a) An agreement to adoption is ineffective if it is given by the mother less than six weeks after the child's birth[1]. The intention of this is to allow the mother a period of adjustment following the birth before any major decisions are made.

(b) The Act defines 'parent' as meaning in relation to a child, any parent who has parental responsibility for the child under the CA 1989[2]. Therefore, the consent of a father who does not have parental responsibility is not a necessary precondition to an adoption order.

(c) The consent must be unconditional.

(d) The agreement to adoption may be given orally or in writing[3]. The Act provides that agreement 'may be given in writing' and, if the document signifying the agreement or consent is witnessed in accordance with the Rules, it shall be admissible in evidence without further proof of the signature of the person by whom it was executed[4].

(e) The agreement to adoption may be withdrawn at any time up to the hearing. However, where agreement has been given and is subsequently withdrawn, this may have an effect upon whether the court will be prepared to dispense with the agreement of that parent to adoption[5].

(f) The provisions of s 16(1) do not apply where the child is not a United Kingdom national and the application is for a Convention Adoption Order[6].

1 Adoption Act 1976, s 16(4).
2 Ibid, s 72(1).
3 *Re T (Adoption: Consent)* [1986] Fam 160, [1986] 1 All ER 817 and *Re LW (A Minor – Adoption or Custodianship)* [1991] FCR 867.
4 See the Adoption Act 1976, s 61. The Rules are r 20 of the Adoption Rules 1984 and of the Magistrates' Courts (Adoption) Rules 1984.
5 See *Re H* [1977] 2 All ER 339n, [1977] 1 WLR 471n and *Re W* [1982] 3 FLR 75.
6 Adoption Act 1976, s 16(3).

Dispensing with agreement

7.78 In the next paragraph consideration is given to the law relating to when a court will dispense with the agreement of a parent or guardian to the adoption of a child. The ground most frequently used is that specified in s 16(2)(b) of the Act (that is, that the parent or guardian is withholding his agreement unreasonably). The grounds will, however, be considered in the order that they appear in s 16(2).

Cannot be found or is incapable of giving agreement

7.79 If, under this ground[1], it is contended that a parent cannot be found it is necessary to show that every reasonable step has been taken to find the parent or guardian. This will include making enquiries through the Department of Social Security and the taking of any other steps that may lead to the discovery of the parent or guardian's whereabouts[2]. Where it is contended that a parent is incapable of giving agreement, this will have to be proved on evidence before the court. The inability may relate to physical or mental inability. The inability may also arise where the parents are living in a totalitarian country so that any communication to them would place them in jeopardy[3].

1 Adoption Act 1976, s 16(2)(a)
2 *Re F* [1970] 1 QB 385, [1969] 3 All ER 1101.
3 *Re R* [1966] 3 All ER 613, [1967] 1 WLR 34.

Withholding agreement unreasonably

7.80 There has been a wealth of authority on the interpretation of this provision[1]. The following are the main points that arise when this section is considered:

(a) The test is reasonableness and not anything else[2].

(b) Although welfare is not the test, in considering the reasonableness of the parents' refusal the court will take into account that a reasonable parent pays regard to the welfare of his child. Welfare may be decisive in those cases where an unreasonable parent would regard it as such[3].

(c) The question in any given case is whether a parental veto comes within the band of possible reasonable decisions and not whether it is right or mistaken. There is a band of decisions within which no court should seek to replace the individual parent's judgment with its own[4]. A reasonable parent has in mind the interests of the child, the natural parent and the adoptive family[5].

(d) The wishes of the prospective adopters to achieve security and any need of the child for stability will inevitably be a material factor for the court to consider[6].

(e) The prospects of rehabilitation and of any beneficial contact will also be material[7].

(f) A sense of grievance or injustice held by the natural parent will not of itself be material save to the extent to which it is necessary to examine the basis of that of grievance or injustice[8].

(g) The desire of the natural parent to retain a relationship between the relevant child and other children may be a relevant factor[9].

(h) Where a parent gives agreement and then retracts it, this may also be a relevant factor[10].

1 Adoption Act 1976, s 16(2)(b).
2 *Re W* [1971] AC 682 at 698 (this should be read in the light of what is said in *Re H* (1983) 4 FLR 614).
3 *Re W*, above.
4 *Re W*, above.
5 *O'Connor v A and B* [1971] 2 All ER 1230.
6 *Re F* [1982] 1 All ER 321 and *Re EL – G* (1987) 4 FLR 589.
7 See, eg *Re M* [1985] FLR 921 and *Re P* [1994] 2 FLR 1000.
8 *Re BA* [1985] FLR 1008 and *Re E* [1990] 2 FLR 397.
9 *Re E* [1989] 1 FLR 126.
10 *Re H* [1977] 2 All ER 339n.

Has persistently failed without reasonable cause to discharge his parental responsibility for the charge

7.81 In order to satisfy this ground the failure must be permanent and to such an extent that there can be no advantage to the child in keeping contact with the natural parent[1].

1 See *Re D* [1973] Fam 209, [1973] 3 All ER 1001.

Has abandoned or neglected the child

7.82 In order to satisfy this ground the parent or guardian must have abandoned or neglected the child in a way that would be criminal[1].

1 See *Watson v Nikolaisen* [1955] 2 QB 286 (for abandonment) and *Re P (Infants)* [1962] 3 All ER 789 (for neglect).

Has persistently ill-treated the child

7.83 The word 'persistently' denotes permanent ill-treatment, although the period over which the ill-treatment continues need not be lengthy[1]. The ill-treatment must, of course, relate to the child in issue.

1 *Re A (A Minor)* (1979) 2 FLR 173 where the ill-treatment occurred over three weeks.

Seriously ill-treated

7.84 This ground does not apply unless (because of the ill-treatment or for some other reasons) the rehabilitation of the child within the household of the parent or guardian is unlikely[1]. One act of ill-treatment would be sufficient for this provision, as long as that act could be regarded as serious ill-treatment[2].

1 See the Adoption Act 1976, s 16(5).
2 See *Re PB (Application to Free For Adoption)* [1985] FLR 394.

The adoption order

7.85 The form of the adoption order is specified within the Rules[1]. The Act provides that an adoption order may contain such terms and conditions as the court thinks fit. In respect of that power:

(a) The court will only attach conditions to an adoption order in exceptional circumstances[2].

(b) Since adoption proceedings are 'family proceedings' for the purpose of the CA 1989, an alternative to imposing a condition may be to make an order under the 1989 Act (although this will still be very rare)[3].

(c) It will be particularly rare that conditions will be opposed against the wishes of the prospective adopters[4].

(d) It has been held to have been unnecessary to make an order for contact where the prospective adopters agreed that there should be a level of contact[5].

1 Adoption Rules 1984, r 15 and the Magistrates Courts (Adoption) Rules 1984, r 13.
2 *Re C* [1989] AC 1, [1988] 1 All ER 705.
3 CA 1989, s 8.
4 *Re D* [1992] 1 FCR 461.
5 *Re T* [1995] 2 FLR 251.

FREEING FOR ADOPTION

Introduction

7.86 An order freeing a child for adoption confers parental responsibility for the child on the adoption agency[1]. It is the method by which an adoption agency may resolve any issues relating to the parents' agreement to adoption with a view to securing the smooth running of the adoption process for the adopters.

1 Adoption Act 1976, s 18(5).

Pre-conditions for freeing order

7.87 Before a child may be freed for adoption the following need to be satisfied:

(a) Either each parent or guardian of the child must freely and with a full understanding of what is involved, agree generally and unconditionally to the making of an adoption order or the agreement of each parent or guardian must be dispensed with on a ground specified in s 16(2) of the Adoption Act 1976[1].

(b) An application must have been made by the adoption agency either with the consent of a parent or guardian of the child or the adoption agency must have applied to dispense with the agreement of each parent or guardian of the child and the child must be in the care of the adoption agency[2].

(c) If an application is made to dispense with the agreement of a parent or guardian, the child must already be placed for adoption or the court must be satisfied that it is likely that the child will be placed for adoption[3].

(d) The court must be satisfied that each parent or guardian has been given a opportunity to make a declaration that he prefers not to be involved in future questions concerning the adoption of the child (and any such declaration is to be recorded by the court)[4].

(e) Before making an order freeing a child for adoption where the father of the child does not have parental responsibility for him, the court must be satisfied, in relation to any person claiming to be the father, that:

(i) he has no intention of applying for parental responsibility under the CA 1989, s 4 or for a residence order under s 10 of that Act; or

(ii) if he did may any such application it would be likely to be refused[5].

1 Adoption Act 1976, s 18(1).
2 Ibid, s 18(2).
3 Ibid, s 18(3).
4 Ibid, s 18(6).
5 Ibid, s 18(7).

Freeing and contact

7.88 An application for a freeing order may be heard at the same time as a cross-application by a natural parent for contact. This invariably raises difficult issues for the court. The following represents some of the judicial guidance that has been given:

(a) A court may make a contact order at the same time as a freeing order[1].

(b) A court should not bind prospective adopters at the freeing stage to accept contact as a condition of an adoption order[2].

(c) A local authority should be cautious about applying for a freeing order where contact is continuing[3].

1 *Re A* [1993] 2 FLR 645.
2 *Re P (Adoption Freeing Order)* [1994] 2 FLR 1000.
3 *Re E* [1990] FCR 921, [1990] 2 FLR 397 (which must be read in the light of *Re A* and *Re P* above).

Adoption agency action post-freeing

7.89 Where a natural parent has not made a declaration that he prefers not to be involved in future questions concerning the adoption of a child[1] the adoption agency must:

(a) within 14 days following the date 12 months after the making of the freeing order (unless the agency has previously by notice to the former parent told him that an adoption order has been made in respect of the child) give notice to the former parent telling him whether an adoption order has been made in respect of the child and if not whether the child has been placed for adoption[2];

(b) if, following the above notice, the child is adopted or placed for adoption (or indeed ceases to have his home with a person with whom he was placed for adoption) the adoption agency must notify the former parent[3].

The natural 'former' parent may at any time notify the adoption agency that he prefers not to be involved in future questions concerning the adoption of the child[4].

1 Adoption Act 1976, s 18(6).
2 Ibid, s 19(2).
3 Ibid, s 19(3).
4 Ibid, s 19(4).

Revocation of freeing order

7.90 If an adoption order has not been made in respect of the child and if the child has not been placed for adoption, a 'former parent' may apply to revoke the freeing order at any time more than 12 months after the making of the order[1].

1 Adoption Act 1976, s 20.

ADOPTION PROCEDURE

In the High Court or county court

7.91 The procedure is laid down in the Adoption Rules 1984, rr 14 to 25. The main points are as follows:

(a) If the applicant wishes his identity to be kept confidential, he may apply, before commencing the proceedings for a serial number to be assigned to him (r 14).

(b) the proceedings are commenced by an originating summons (in the High Court) or an originating application (in the county court) in Form 6 as set out in the Schedule to the Adoption Rules.

(c) The applicant is the proposed adopter. The respondent is:

  (i) each parent or guardian (not being an applicant of the child, unless the child is free for adoption);

  (ii) any adoption agency having parental responsibility for the child be virtue of ss 18 or 21 of the Act;

  (iii) any adoption agency named in the application or in any form of agreement to the making of the adoption order having taken part in the arrangements for the adoption of the child;

  (iv) any local authority to whom the applicant has given notice under s 22 of the Act of his intention to apply for an adoption order;

  (v) any local authority or voluntary organisation which has parental responsibility for, is looking after, or is caring for the child;

  (vi) any person liable by virtue of any order or agreement to contribute to the maintenance of the child;

  (vii) where the applicant is a single person who is separated from his spouse (and where the separation is likely to be permanent) the spouse of the applicant must be a respondent;

  (viii) in the High Court, the child.

The court may direct that any other person or body (except, in the county court, the child) be made a respondent (r 15).

(d) On the filing of the application, the court will examine it and may refer it to the judge or district judge for directions (r 16).

(e) The court will then appoint a reporting officer (if the parent or guardian agrees to the adoption order) or a guardian ad litem (if the parent or guardian is unwilling to agree: rr 17 and 18) who will file a report[1].

(f) Where the parent or guardian is unwilling to agree to adoption, the applicant must file a statement of facts (which shall be framed in such a way as not to disclose the identity of the applicant in a case where a serial number has been assigned). The statement of facts must set out 'the facts on which the applicant intends to rely' (r 19).

(g) The proper officer of the court will list the case for hearing by a judge as soon as practicable after the originating process has been filed (r 21).

(h) The adoption agency or local authority will file a report under Sch II of the Adoption Rules 1984 (r 22). As to the duty to consult the unmarried father for the purposes of this report, see *Re P*[2].

(i) The arrangements for the hearing are to be in accordance with r 23.

1 As to the confidentiality of the report see *Re D (Minors) (Adoption Reports Confidentiality)* [1996] AC 593.
2 *Re P (Adoption) (Natural Fathers Rights)* [1994] 1 FLR 771.

Procedure in freeing applications

7.92 The procedure on an application to free a child for adoption in the High Court and county court is specified in rr 4 to 13 of the Adoption Rules 1984. The procedure is similar to that which applies on an application for an adoption order.

Procedure in the magistrates' court

7.93 The procedure in the magistrates' court is laid down in the Magistrates Courts (Adoption) Rules 1984 and is similar to that in the High Court and county court.

Overseas adoptions

7.94 An overseas adoption is an adoption made in a country that is specified in the Adoption (Designation of Overseas Adoptions) Order 1973[1]. Article 4 of the 1973 Order specifies how proof of adoption may be given.

1 SI 1973/19.

Convention adoption

7.95 The provisions of s 17 of the Adoption Act 1976 (which relate to convention adoptions) have very limited application. The convention referred to is the Hague Convention on Jurisdiction, Applicable Law and Recognition of Decrees Relating to Adoption[1]. The Convention so far has only been ratified by the United Kingdom, Austria and Switzerland. The procedure in relation to Convention adoption is set out in rr 27 to 36 of the Adoption Rules 1984.

1 Cmnd 7342.

Recognition at common law

7.96 In limited circumstances an adoption that took place abroad may be recognised in this country under the common law. However, this recognition is not well defined. It is probable that a foreign order would be recognised at common law if one of the applicant's was domiciled in the country which made the order (although it is possible that both applicants might have to be domiciled in that country).

Other international adoptions

7.97 If the adoption order does not attract recognition in this country, it will be necessary for an adoption order to be secured in this country for that adoption to be recognised. For an adoption order to be made in those circumstances, it will be necessary for the applicants to satisfy the usual requirements in respect of an adoption order. That may well raise difficulties in respect of the evidence that will be available as to the consent of the natural parents. Those who seek to adopt a child in these circumstances would be well advised to secure the necessary consent in the form specified by the Adoption Rules before leaving the foreign country with the child[1].

1 See, eg the Adoption Rules 1984, rr 8 and 20.

International adoptions

7.98 The Adoption Act 1976 defines 'adoption' as meaning adoption:

(a) by an adoption order;
(b) by an order made under the Children Act 1975, the Adoption Act 1958, the Adoption Act 1950 or any enactment repealed by the Adoption Act 1950;
(c) by an order made in Scotland, Northern Ireland, the Isle of Man or in any of the Channel Islands;
(d) which is an overseas adoption; or

(e) which is an adoption recognised by the law of England and Wales and effected under the law of any other country[1].

1 Adoption Act 1976, s 38.

7.99 Thus, certain adoptions which took place outside the jurisdiction of England and Wales will be recognised as having created an adoption. Automatic recognition will therefore apply to:

(a) orders made in Scotland, Northern Ireland, the Isle of Man and the Channel Islands;

(b) overseas adoptions – this is defined in the Act as meaning an adoption of a description as the Secretary of State may by order specify, being a description of adoption of children appearing to him to be affected under the law of any country outside Great Britain, and an order under this section may contain provision as to the manner in which evidence of an overseas adoption may be given[1];

(c) Convention adoptions[2].

In addition to adoptions that are recognised on any of the above three bases, recognition may be afforded at common law.

1 Ibid, s 72(2).
2 Ibid, s 17.

Chapter Eight

Children Proceedings

Stephen Wildblood

Introduction   265
The Welfare of the Child   266
Welfare and Social Work Reports   270
Section 8 Orders   273
Statutory Restriction on Making Section 8 Orders   283
Applicants for Section 8 Orders   285
Section 8 Orders with Conditions   292
Family Assistance Orders   293
The Threshold Criteria   293
Evidence and Procedure   299
Disposal of Applications   302
Supervision Orders   304
Contact with Children in Care   305
Section 37 Reports   311
Discharge and Variation of Care and Supervision Orders   312
Guardians Ad Litem   312
Protection of Children   314
Child Assessment Orders   315
Child Assessment Orders/Emergency Protection Orders   316
Emergency Protection Orders   316
Prohibition against further Applications without Leave   322
Appeals   322
Practice and Procedure   324

INTRODUCTION

8.1 The Children Act 1989 came into force on the 14 October 1991[1]. It represented a thorough revision of most aspects of the law relating to children. The Act is often regarded as being divided into two areas; provisions relating to private law (being the law relating to the responsibilities and proceedings of private individuals in respect of children) and public law (the law relating to the responsibilities and proceedings in respect of children in which public bodies are involved)[2]. The Act contains transitional provisions[3].

1 Save the CA 1989, s 5(11) and (12) which relate to guardians.
2 Private law is in Part II of the Act; public law in Parts III onwards of the Act.

3 See CA 1989, Sch 14 and *Re C (Transitional Provisions)* [1992] 1 FCR 169, [1992] 1 FLR 628 and *Re H (Transitional Provisions)* [1992] Fam Law 383. For the position where interim orders were made permitting a child into the care of the local authority, see the Children Act 1989 (Amendment and Transitional Provisions) (No 2) Order 1991, SI 1991/1990.

THE WELFARE OF THE CHILD

8.2 The welfare of the child preserves a primacy of place within the Act. Section 1(1) of the Act provides that:

> When a court determines any question with respect to:
>
> (a) the upbringing of the child; or
>
> (b) the administration of a child's property or the application of any income arising from it,
>
> the child's welfare shall be the court's paramount consideration.

It has been held that:

(a) where proceedings involve more than one child, it is the child who is the subject of the proceedings whose welfare is paramount[1];

(b) the decision of the House of Lords in *Richards v Richards* has not been overruled by the provisions of the CA 1989[2].

1 See *Birmingham City Council v H* [1994] 2 AC 212, [1994] 1 All ER 12, [1994] 1 FLR 224, HL where the mother of the relevant child was aged 16. See also *F v Leeds City Council* [1994] 2 FLR 60 where, again, the mother and child were both minors. See also *Re T and E (Proceedings Conflicting Interests)* [1995] 1 FLR 581 (where the father sought a residence order in respect of a child and a local authority sought orders freeing both children for adoption).
2 See *Gibson v Austin* [1993] 1 FCR 638, [1992] 2 FLR 437; *Richards v Richards* [1984] AC 174.

Delay

8.3 The Act positively discourages delay in proceedings relating to children. It is provided that:

> In any proceedings in which any question with respect to the upbringing of a child arises, the court shall have regard to the general principle that any delay in determining the question is likely to prejudice the welfare of the child[1].

This can be read in conjunction with the requirement that cases under the CA 1989 should be subject to timetables established through the direction of the court[2]. It has been held that:

(a) Practitioners and courts have a duty to avoid delay in children cases, even where delay is perceived to be in the interests of one of the adult parties. Open-ended orders concerning hearing dates should not be made[3].

(b) Directions appointments are of vital importance. The court must take a firm grip of every child case. It must build in reviews of progress and set stringent timetables[4].

(c) Although delay is ordinarily inimical to the welfare of the child, a planned and purposeful delay may be appropriate. Where a care order is made, the court transfers control of issues relating to children to the local authority (save to the extent that continuing court involvement is provided by the Act, for instance over matters of contact or discharge of the care order). The point at which a court should pass that control to the local authority by the making of a final care order invariably raises difficult issues. Ultimately, it is for the court to determine, in the exercise of its discretion, when that point has been reached and that determination will vary according to different circumstances of different cases[5].

1 CA 1989, s 1(2).
2 Ibid, s 11(1).
3 *B v B* [1994] 2 FLR 489, [1994] 2 FCR 667.
4 *Re A and B (No 2)* [1995] 1 FLR 351, [1995] 3 FCR 449.
5 These issues are considered in a number of cases: see *Re L* [1996] 1 FLR 116, CA; *Re C* [1992] 2 FCR 341 (Ward J); *Hounslow London Borough Council v A* [1993] 1 FCR 164 (Booth J); *Re CN* [1992] 2 FCR 401 (Eubank J); *Re J (Minors – Care Plan)* [1994] 1 FLR 253 (Wall J); *Cheshire County Council v P* [1993] 2 FCR 397, CA; and *Buckinghamshire County Council v M* [1994] 1 FCR 860, [1994] 2 FLR 506, CA.

The welfare checklist

8.4 The court is obliged to consider the welfare checklist[1] in the following circumstances[2]:

(a) when the court is considering whether to make, vary or discharge a s 8 order[3], and the making, variation or discharge of the order is opposed by any party to the proceedings; or

(b) the court is considering whether to make, vary or discharge an order under Part IV[4].

The welfare checklist requires the court to have particular regard to:

(i) the ascertainable wishes and feelings of the child concerned (considered in the light of his age and understanding);

(ii) his physical, emotional and educational needs;

(iii) the likely effect on him of any change in his circumstances;

(iv) his age, sex, background and any characteristics of his which the court considers relevant;

(v) any harm which he has suffered or is at risk of suffering;

(vi) how capable each of his parents, and any other person in relation to whom the court considers the question to be relevant, is of meeting his needs;

(vii) the range of powers available to the court under the CA 1989 in the proceedings in question.

The court should give consideration to the welfare checklist in any case where the statute requires this to be done[5].

1 CA 1989, s 1(3).
2 Ibid, s 1(4).
3 Section 8 orders are ordered for residence, contact, prohibitive steps or specific issues.
4 Orders under Part IV of the Act are orders for care, supervision, parental contact with child in care, educational supervision orders, interim care and supervision orders, discharge and variation of care orders and supervision orders and orders pending appeals in such cases: CA 1989, ss 31 – 42.
5 In *Re D (Contact: Interim Order)* [1995] 1 FLR 495 Wall J held that it is unacceptable for any court to make a bland statement that it has considered all aspects of the welfare checklist without further particularisation; unless, elsewhere in the course of its judgment, it has, in considering the evidence or in making findings, dealt in detail with the relevant aspects of the checklist, thereby demonstrating that it has applied its mind to the relevant facts (see also *Re H* [1993] 1 FLR 440). In *H v H* [1995] 1 FLR 529n the Court of Appeal (which included Wall J) stated that the welfare checklist should not be equated with the list of checks that a pilot has to perform before taking off; statute does not say that the judge has to read out the seven items in s 1(3) and pronounce his conclusion on each.

The wishes and feelings of the child

8.5   In the early days following the introduction of the CA 1989, this part of the welfare checklist became the object of judicial comment and scrutiny. It has been held that:

(a) Although the wishes and feelings of the child may be the first of the various heads in the checklist under s 1(3) of the Act, it has no priority over all the others. A court has a duty to listen and to ascertain the wishes and feelings of the child as to his future but the court is not to be constricted by those wishes and should disregard them if the child's future welfare appears to diverge from his express wishes[1].

(b) Where children do express clear wishes and are of a mature age and understanding, the court should pay more than lip service to their ascertainable wishes and feelings[2].

(c) Although a judge has a discretion to see children privately, that discretion should be exercised cautiously and only after hearing submissions from the parties. Normally, children's feelings and wishes should be recorded through the guardian ad litem or the court welfare officer. It should only be in rare and exceptional cases that magistrates should themselves see a child in private where a guardian ad litem or welfare officer is involved. Where judges or justices do see a child in private, it is crucial that they should make known to the parties any matter that the child has told them which may affect their own views or which may influence the decision that they are likely to reach[3].

1 *Re W (Minors – Residence Order)* [1992] 2 FCR 461 and *Re W (A Minor – Medical Treatment Court Jurisdiction)* [1993] Fam 64, [1992] 4 All ER 627.
2 *M v M* [1993] 1 FCR 5, [1993] Fam Law 396.
3 *B v B* [1994] 2 FCR 667, [1994] 2 FLR 489; *Re M (Minors)* [1993] 2 FLR 706, [1993] 2 FCR 721 and *Re R* [1993] 2 FLR 163, [1993] 2 FCR 525.

The needs of the child

8.6 A child's needs will cover a broad spectrum of factors that will vary from case to case. Needs may include the need for a child to undergo a blood test to ascertain whether the child is HIV positive[1].

1 *Re W (A Minor: HIV Test)* [1995] 2 FCR 184.

Change of circumstances

8.7 Variations in the arrangements for children may add to a child's sense of instability during a time when the family is being restructured. The relevance of the 'status quo' (ie retention of existing arrangements) has been considered in a succession of cases[1].

1 *D v M* [1983] Fam 33, [1982] 3 All ER 897; *S v W* (1981) 11 Fam Law 81; and *Allington v Allington* [1985] FLR 586.

The age of the child

8.8 There is no presumption of law that a child of any given age is better off with one parent or the other. The only legal principle involved is that the welfare of the child is paramount. However, no court will be ignorant of what would be the natural position if all other things were equal. A very young baby will normally be with his/her mother. It has therefore been held that there is rebuttable presumption of fact (not law) that the best interests of the baby are served by being with its mother (although different considerations may well apply when moving on to whatever age it might be appropriate to describe the baby as having become a child)[1].

1 See *Re W (Residence Order: Baby)* [1992] 2 FLR 332, [1992] 2 FCR 603. See also, eg *Re A* [1991] 2 FLR 394, [1991] FCR 569 and *Re S* [1991] 2 FLR 388, [1991] FCR 155.

Harm

8.9 Harm means ill-treatment or the impairment of health or development[1]. Development, health and ill-treatment are all defined within the Act[2]. For the risk of harm see *Re M and R*[3].

1 CA 1989, ss 31(a) and 105(1).
2 Ibid, s 31(9).
3 [1996] 2 FLR 195. See also *Re P (Sexual abuse: Standard of proof)* [1996] 2 FLR 333.

Capability

8.10 It is not only the capability of the child's parents that the court will have to consider but also the capability of any other relevant person. This may, for instance, include a step-parent or other relative who will play a major part in the child's life.

Range of powers

8.11 In private law proceedings this may involve the court considering, for example, whether there should be a joint residence order made or a restriction against further proceedings[1]. In public law proceedings this may involve considering whether a care order or a supervision order is more appropriate.

1 CA 1989, s 91(14).

No order

8.12 The court must not make an order under the Act in respect of the child unless it considers that doing so would be better for the child than making no order at all[1]. It has been held that:

(a) In the absence of an issue upon which it is necessary for the court to intervene, the court will usually decline to make an order (even if the order was sought by consent). However, where a child is living with a grandparent who does not have the status of enjoying parental responsibility, it would be better for the child if a residence order was made than making no order at all[2].

(b) Where the court decides to make no order, an order of the court should be drawn up setting out that the court has made no order[3].

(c) Where an application has merit, a court should usually make an order (and not leave it to the parties to accommodate themselves to the court's perception of the child's welfare)[4].

(d) Where the court is invited to make a periodical payments order under Sch 1 of the Act by consent, the court should make an order to that effect as invited[5].

1 CA 1989, s 1(5).
2 *B v B* [1992] 2 FLR 327, [1993] 1 FCR 211.
3 *S v R* [1993] 1 FCR 331.
4 *Re S* [1996] 1 FLR 158 where the grandparent's application for contact had overwhelming merit.
5 *K v H* [1993] 2 FLR 61.

WELFARE AND SOCIAL WORK REPORTS

Welfare reports – the Act

8.13 The Act provides that a court, when considering any question with respect to a child under the Act, may ask a probation officer or a local authority to report to the court on such matters relating to the welfare of the child as are required[1]. Where the report is to be made by the local authority, the court may ask that it is prepared either by an officer of the authority or by such other person (other than a probation officer) as the authority considers appropriate.

Welfare and Social Work Reports

The Act provides the report may be made in writing or orally (as the court requires)². Where the court makes such a request it is the duty of the person or authority requested to comply³. The court may take account of any statement or evidence in a report, regardless of any enactment or rule of law, which would otherwise prevent it from doing so (eg hearsay evidence)⁴.

1 CA 1989, s 7(1).
2 Ibid, s 7(3).
3 Ibid, s 7(5).
4 Ibid, s 7(4).

Who should report?

8.14 The Act provides that the report may be requested from a probation officer or a local authority. Welfare officers may have special expertise in relation to court proceedings that is not possessed by many social workers. Therefore, in a more complex case, it may be more appropriate that the report is prepared by a welfare officer¹. However, this may have to be balanced against the need to avoid delay (in areas where the preparation of welfare reports is greatly delayed). Where a welfare report is to be prepared by a local authority, enquiries will have to be made of that authority to ascertain the facilities that exist for compliance with any order that it prepares a report. The fixing of a hearing date for the final hearing should not be deferred until the welfare report is received². On an application for contact, the court does not have the power to order a local authority under s 7 to instruct a child psychiatrist to prepare a report for the court's consideration³.

1 *Re W (A Minor) (Welfare Reports)* [1995] 3 FCR 793, [1995] 2 FLR 142.
2 *Re A and B (Minors No 2)* [1995] 3 FCR 449.
3 See *Re K (Contact Psychiatric Report)* [1995] 2 FLR 432. The intervention of a psychiatrist could have been achieved by the parties being invited to instruct a psychiatrist jointly or by invoking RSC Ord 40 under the FPR 1991, r 1.3(1), the County Courts Act 1984 s 6 and CCR Ord 2, r 6.

Welfare officers' recommendations

8.15 A court is free to exercise its discretion contrary to the recommendation of a welfare officer but it is well settled practice that the court should give an explanation which is sufficiently detailed to explain why it is doing so¹.

1 See *M v C* [1993] 1 FCR 264, *Re L* [1995] 2 FLR 445 and *Re V* [1995] 2 FLR 1010.

Welfare officers' attendance

8.16 The court may order the welfare officer to attend¹. If it does not, there will be no requirement for the attendance of the welfare officer. Therefore, a party who wishes the welfare officer to attend should secure such an order. Where an order is made for the attendance of the welfare officer, it is for the

272 Children Proceedings

court to inform the welfare officer of the direction (unless the welfare officer is present at the hearing when the order is made for his attendance)[2]. The following has been said concerning the welfare officer's attendance:

(a) In many circumstances it will be wrong for a judge to proceed to form conclusions directly contrary to the recommendations of a welfare officer without availing himself of the opportunity of receiving further assistance from the welfare officer in the form of evidence[3].

(b) The above should not be regarded as a hard and fast rule in all circumstances (particularly where the welfare officer either makes no firm recommendation or only a tentative one)[4].

1 FPR 1991, r 4.13 and FP(CA1989)R 1991, r 13.
2 Ibid, r 4.13(3) and r 13(3).
3 *Re CB (A Minor Access)* [1992] 1 FCR 320.
4 *Re C* [1995] 1 FLR 617 and *Re H* [1994] 2 FLR 969.

Welfare reports – confidentiality

8.17 Difficult issues may arise where a welfare officer is told something by a person who wishes that information to remain confidential to the court (and not be disclosed to a particular party). It has been held that:

(a) A judge is entitled to receive confidential information in those rare cases where he is fully satisfied, judicially, that real harm to the child might otherwise ensue.

(b) The court has a discretion to receive and act on evidence adduced by one party or emanating from a welfare officer, which has not been disclosed to the other party. The power should only be exercised in the most exceptional circumstances.

(c) Before ordering non-disclosure, the court should consider the evidence itself[1].

(d) Informants who make allegations against an applicant for a residence order should not be given undertakings by the welfare officer that their confidentiality would be respected. The question is one for the court[2].

1 The principles to be applied were laid down by the House of Lords in *Official Solicitor v K* [1965] AC 201. The principles in that case apply to cases relating to children who are not wards of court: see *Re C* [1991] FCR 308; *Re B* [1992] 2 FCR 617; and *Re M* [1994] 1 FLR 760. In adoption proceedings governed by the Adoption Rules 1984, r 53(2), the considerations of those laid down in *Re D* [1995] 2 FLR 687.
2 *Re G* [1993] 2 FLR 293, [1994] 1 FCR 37.

Welfare officers and conciliation

8.18 Many courts have now introduced formal mediation into the court process. It has been held that:

(a) Where a welfare officer requires the opportunity to mediate between the parents, it would be appropriate to adjourn the application for a fixed period to enable this to be done[1].

(b) Given the public importance of conciliation in matrimonial proceedings concerning children, statements made by either of the parties in the course of meetings held or communications made for the purposes of conciliation could not be disclosed in proceedings under the CA 1989, save in the exceptional case that such a statement indicated that the maker had in the past caused, or was likely in the future to cause, serious harm to the well-being of the child[2].

1 *S v R* [1993] 1 FCR 331.
2 *Re D* [1993] 2 All ER 693, [1993] 1 FCR 877.

SECTION 8 ORDERS

Section 8 orders defined

8.19 A 'section 8 Order' is defined by the Act as any order mentioned in s 8(1) of the Act or any order varying or discharging such an order[1]. Those orders are:

(a) a residence order, which means an order settling the arrangements to be made as to the person with whom a child is to live;

(b) a contact order, which means an order requiring the person with whom a child lives, or is to live, to allow the child to visit or stay with the person named in the order, or for that person and the child otherwise to have contact with each other;

(c) a prohibited steps order, which means an order that no step which could be taken by a parent in meeting his parental responsibility for a child, and which is of a kind specified in the order, shall be taken by any person without the consent of the court;

(d) a specific issue order, which means an order giving directions for the purpose of determining a specific question which has arisen, which may arise, in connection with any aspect of parental responsibility for a child[2].

1 CA 1989, s 8(2).
2 Ibid, s 8(1).

Residence orders

8.20 A residence order is not an order which connotes possession in respect of the child or which in any sense excludes another parent. It is an order of the court which may be required to regulate where children are to live during a particular period[1]. Other statutory provisions relating to the duration and effect of a residence order are:

(a) A residence order will cease to have effect if two parents with parental responsibility resume co-habitation for a continuous period of more than six months[2].

(b) If a residence order is made in favour of a father who would not otherwise have parental responsibility for the child, the court must also make an order granting him parental responsibility[3].

(c) Where a residence order is made in favour of a person who is not the parent or guardian of the child concerned, that person will have parental responsibility for the child while the residence order remains in force.

(d) Where a residence order is in force in respect of a child, no person may cause the child to be known by a new surname or remove the child from the United Kingdom, without either the written consent of every person who has parental responsibility for the child or the leave of the court[5] (although this will not prevent the removal of the child for the period of less than one month by the person in whose favour the residence order is made)[6].

1 *Re W* [1992] 2 FCR 461.
2 CA 1989, s 11(5).
3 Ibid, s 12(1).
4 Ibid, s 12(2). See the limitations on the extent of this parental responsibility imposed by s 12(3).
5 Ibid, s 13(1).
6 Ibid, s 13(2).

Residence orders – case law

8.21 There is a wealth of authority concerning the residence (and previously, the custody) of children. The following are some of the main points that have emerged:

(a) *Parental preference*. There is a strong supposition that, other things being equal, it is in the interests of a child that it shall remain with its natural parents, but this may have to give way to particular needs in particular circumstances. Various courts have pronounced upon this principle in different ways and with varying degrees of force of expression[1].

(b) *Age of child*. There is no presumption of law that a child of any given age is better off with one parent or the other. However, there is a rebuttable presumption of fact that the interests of a baby will be served by being with its mother[2].

(c) *Children together*. Wherever possible, siblings should be kept together[3].

(d) *Status quo*. The maintenance of the status quo may be an important factor[4].

(e) *Religion*. The child's religious beliefs may be of significance. The courts have had to consider the position of Jehovah's Witnesses and Scientologists in particular[5].

(f) *Homosexuality* will be a factor to be taken into account but does not necessarily render a parent unfit to look after a child[6].

(g) *Family arrangements unsettled.* Where the family arrangements are unsettled, it may be more appropriate to make an interim order and to hold a review once the family was more settled[7].

(h) *Ancillary relief.* Where the decision concerning the arrangements for the children and the decision relating to the matrimonial home impinge upon each other, it is desirable that those two decisions should be dealt with by the same court at the same time[8].

1 *Re W* [1993] 2 FLR 625; *Re H* [1991] 2 FLR 109; *Re K* [1990] 2 FLR 64; and *Re KD* [1988] 2 FLR 139.
2 *Re W* [1992] 2 FLR 332, [1992] 2 FCR 603; *Re S* [1991] 2 FLR 388, [1991] FCR 155; and *Re A* [1991] 2 FLR 394, [1991] FCR 569.
3 *C v C (Custody of Children)* [1988] 2 FLR 291, [1988] FCR 411, compare this with *Re B(T) (A Minor)* [1995] 2 FCR 240 where the court had to balance the status quo against the importance of siblings being placed together.
4 See *D v M* [1983] Fam 33, [1983] 4 FLR 247; and *Allington v Allington* [1985] FLR 586; and *Re J* [1989] 2 FLR 304, [1990] FCR 135; and see para 8.7.
5 The position of Jehovah's Witnesses was considered in *Re H (Custody: Religious Upbringing)* (1980) 2 FLR 253 and in *Re R* [1993] 2 FLR 163. The position of Scientologists was considered in *Re B and G* [1985] FLR 134.
6 See *C v C* [1991] 1 FLR 223, [1991] FCR 254 and *B v B* [1991] FCR 1.
7 *Re S* [1992] 1 FCR 158.
8 *Re B* [1991] FCR 414 and *B v B* [1994] 2 FLR 489, [1994] 2 FCR 667.

Application after wardship orders

8.22 In some circumstances the CA 1989 may afford parents a technical opportunity to re-open issues that were resolved in proceedings prior to the introduction of the Act. This had led to consideration being given to the extent to which the court will entertain oral evidence on an application for orders under that Act, in particular for residence and contact. It has been held that the court has a broad discretion to determine the extent to which it will entertain oral evidence. In appropriate circumstances, a court may dismiss an application without such evidence[1].

1 See *Cheshire County Council v M* [1993] 1 FLR 463, [1992] 2 FCR 817; *W v Ealing London Borough* [1993] 2 FLR 788, [1993] 1 FCR 436; and *Re B* [1994] 2 FLR 1, [1994] 2 FCR 812.

Ex parte orders

8.23 Ex parte residence orders may cause a grave injustice to a person who sees the removal of a child from him/her without being afforded the opportunity of making representations to the court that made the order. Practice appears to vary from area to area, however the authority emanating from the higher courts does not. The rules now make provision for ex parte interim residence orders to be made[1]. However, the following are the stated principles that should apply:

(a) An ex parte application for an interim residence order should only be made in 'exceptional' or 'compelling' circumstances[2].

(b) The better procedure is to apply inter partes on short notice[3].

(c) Even where it is right to make an order ex parte, a return day should be arranged as soon as possible where the matter could be heard inter partes[4].

(d) The right procedure by which to challenge an ex parte order is to apply to the court below inter partes for the ex parte order to be discharged or varied (sooner than to appeal)[5].

1 FPR 1991, r 4.4(4) and FPC(CA1989)R 1991, r 4(4).
2 *Re G* [1992] 2 FCR 720 and *M v C* [1993] 1 FCR 264.
3 *Croydon London Borough Council v A (No 3)* [1992] 2 FLR 350 and *Re P* [1993] 2 FCR 417.
4 *Re Y* [1993] 2 FCR 422 and *Re O* [1993] 1 FLR 172.
5 *Re H* [1994] Fam Law 422.

Contact orders

8.24 The contact that a court may order may take many forms. Amongst the forms of order are orders for:

(a) *Direct contact*. This phrase is used to mean where the child and the person concerned meet. The contact may be 'staying' or 'visiting'.

(b) *Indirect contact*. Such contact would include letters and telephone calls.

(c) *Supervised contact*. This generally is used to mean where a third party (not necessarily a social worker or welfare officer) is present for part of the contact. A lesser degree of supervision is sometimes referred to as 'monitored'.

An order for parental contact will cease to have effect if the parents live together for a continuous period of more than six months after the order[1].

1 CA 1989, s 11(6).

The importance of contact

8.25 Since well before the CA 1989, the courts have stressed the importance of contact in private law proceedings. The principles applied by the courts were stated as long ago as 1962 in *S v S*[1]. The principles were clearly stated again in *Re H*[2]. Those principles are:

(a) In deciding whether contact should cease or should be reintroduced the same principles apply.

(b) No court should deprive a child of contact with either parent unless it is wholly satisfied that it is in the interests of the child that contact should cease (and that is a conclusion at which the court should be extremely slow to arrive).

(c) Where parents have separated and one of them has the care of the child, contact to the other often results in some upset to the child, but that upset is usually minor and superficial and is heavily outweighed by the long-term advantage to the child of keeping in touch with the parent concerned.

(d) Save in exceptional circumstances, to deprive a parent of contact is to deprive a child of an important contribution to his emotional well being in the long-term.

(e) The correct test is for the judge to ask himself whether there are cogent reasons why the child should be denied the opportunity of contact with its father[3].

1 [1962] 2 All ER 1.
2 [1992] 1 FLR 148.
3 In the case of *Re D* [1993] 2 FLR 1, the Court of Appeal held that *Re H* still applied after the introduction of the CA 1989. In the case of *Re M* [1995] 1 FLR 274 it was held that the test in *Re H* had not been extended by recent authority (in the case of *Re W* [1994] 2 FLR 441, the President had said that contact is a fundamental right which should be observed unless there were 'wholly' exceptional circumstances, but this is not an extension of *Re H*).

Implacable hostility

8.26 In some cases the implacable hostility of the residential parent may form the basis of a refusal of contact (for instance, where the court is left in the position that to ignore that hostility would cause harm to the child)[1]. However, the court will not allow there to be 'a selfish parent's charter' whereby a parent can make such a fuss that the other parent is stopped from seeing the child[2]. The court cannot be put in a position where a parent tells the court 'I shall not obey an order of the court'[3]. It may be that where a case of this nature arises, assistance can be provided by more court control, lawyer co-operation with the attempts at resuming contact, the avoidance of delay, strength of recommendation from welfare officer and ensuring that a case comes before the correct level of court[4].

1 See, eg *D v D* [1993] 1 FCR 964, [1993] 2 FLR 1.
2 *Re H* [1994] 2 FLR 776.
3 *Re W* [1994] 2 FLR 441.
4 *D v D* [1994] 1 FCR 694 in which it was said, although magistrates should not automatically decline jurisdiction where termination of contact is in issue, consideration should be given to transferring the case to a higher court.

Examples of refusal of contact

8.27 Examples of cases where a court has been prepared to refuse contact to a parent are:

(a) where a father behaves irresponsibly towards the child[1];

(b) where the child is of a mature age and does not wish to have contact[2];

(c) where the parent seeking contact is a transsexual (although this is not an automatic prohibition)[3];

(d) where contact would have a destabilising effect upon the mother's new household[4];

(e) where the father has sexually abused the child (although again this will not necessarily cause all contact to cease)[5].

A father who is genuinely fond of his children but who exhibits eccentric, bizarre behaviour capable of baffling or distressing a child, should not be prevented from having defined contact to his children, provided there is no suggestion of violence, verbal aggression or risk to the children[6]. For a case concerning a child born by artificial insemination see *Re CH (Contact: Parentage)*[7].

1 *Re T* [1993] 1 FCR 973 (the father removed the young child from the mother and had no understanding of the effect of his actions upon the child) and *Rashid v Rashid* (1978) 9 Fam Law 118 (breach of court orders and removal from jurisdiction).
2 See, eg *Re M* [1995] 1 FLR 274 where, in fact, the children were only 9 and 8.
3 See *Re F* [1993] 2 FLR 677 and *L v C* [1995] 2 FLR 438, [1995] 3 FCR 125.
4 *Re SM* [1991] 2 FLR 333 and *Re H* [1993] 1 FLR 484.
5 See *Re R* [1988] 1 FLR 206, *S v S* [1988] 1 FLR 213; *Re P* [1988] 2 FLR 209; and *H v H* [1989] 1 FLR 212.
6 *Re B* [1992] 1 FLR 140.
7 [1996] 1 FLR 569.

Contact – no knowledge of father

8.28 Particularly difficult issues will arise where a child has not had contact with its father and believes that someone else is the father. In a case where this arose, the Court of Appeal held that:

(a) the child had a right to know about her paternity[1].

(b) it was unrealistic and dangerous to try and re-introduce the father without prior information being given to the child;

(c) the mother, step-father and the child needed skilled help in overcoming the first stage of letting the child know about her paternity. That help was best provided by a child psychiatrist[2].

1 *Re H (Paternity: Blood Test)* [1996] 2 FLR 65, CA.
2 *Re R* [1993] 2 FLR 762, [1993] 1 FCR 954.

Indirect and infrequent contact

8.29 In the case of *Re O*[1] a judge had ordered that a mother should:

(a) send the father photographs of the child every three months;

(b) send the father progress reports when the child began nursery school or playgroup;

(c) inform the father of any significant illness and send medical reports;

(d) accept delivery of cards and presents for the child via the public postal service of the family court welfare service and read and show any such communication to the child and deliver any such present to him.

The mother appealed against the order, relying upon the decision in *Re M*[2]. The

Court of Appeal overruled *Re M* and held that the judge was entitled to make the order. In the case of *Re P*[3] the Court of Appeal held that the practice of according contact to a parent only three or four times a year might well deserve close scrutiny; a child who is old enough to enjoy the company of his natural father might find that contact inadequate.

1 [1995] 2 FLR 124.
2 [1994] 1 FLR 272.
3 [1992] 1 FCR 91.

Contact – other relatives

8.30 The principles that apply in respect of a parent having contact with a child, do not extend to other relatives[1]. In particular, they do not apply to grandparents[2] or step-parents[3].

1 *Re A* [1995] 2 FLR 153.
2 *Re A*, above.
3 *Re H* [1994] 2 FLR 776.

Adoption and contact

8.31 Where there are competing applications for contact and adoption, it is desirable that they should be heard together[1]. This also applies where there is an application for a freeing order as well as an application for contact (although in those circumstances the application for contact will be made under the CA 1989, s 34[2]). Where adoptive parents are ready and willing to agree to contact, it is unnecessary and wrong for the court to order the adoptive parents to permit it[3].

1 *G v G* [1993] Fam 253, [1993] FLR 306.
2 *Re A* [1993] 2 FLR 645, [1994] 1 FCR 104.
3 *Re T* [1995] 2 FLR 251.

Interim contact

8.32 The court will be cautious about making interim contact orders where the principle of contact is in dispute and there is a substantial factual issue relating to the child[1]. This may be particularly so where it is suggested that the applicant is either dangerous or unstable[2]. In appropriate circumstances, however, the court should be prepared to make an interim order so that the contact may be tested or observed[3].

1 *Re D* [1995] 1 FLR 495.
2 *Re NW* [1993] 2 FLR 591, [1994] 1 FCR 121.
3 *Re B* [1994] 2 FLR 269.

Paper dismissal

8.33 Although the court has the discretion to determine the extent of the oral evidence that it will hear[1] it may be wrong for a court to consider a contact application without hearing oral evidence[2].

1 See *Re B* [1994] 2 FLR 1, [1994] 2 FCR 812.
2 *Re M* [1995] 1 FLR 1029.

Contact and the checklist

8.34 In *Re M*[1] Wilson J said:

> 'I personally find it helpful to cast the principles (relating to contact) into the framework of the checklist of considerations set out in s 1(3) of the Children Act 1989 and to ask whether the fundamental emotional need of every child to have an enduring relationship with both his parents (s 1(3)(b)) is outweighed by the depth of harm which, in the light, inter alia of his wishes and feelings (s 1(3)(a)) this child would be at risk of suffering (s 1(3)(e)) by virtue of a contact order.'

1 *Re M (Contact: Welfare Test)* [1995] 1 FLR 274.

Local authority involvement

8.35 Where a local authority is ordered to carry out an investigation under the CA 1989, s 37 and decides not to seek care or supervision orders, it will not have any right to become a party to private law contact proceedings[1].

1 See *F v Cambridgeshire County Council* [1995] 2 FCR 804.

Prohibited steps orders

8.36 The Act itself imposes various restrictions on the powers of the court to make orders under s 8 of the Act[1]. These are considered in the paragraph relating to that section. However, in addition to the statutory restrictions, there are the following examples of restrictions about the use of prohibited steps applications that arise from case law:

(a) It is not open to a court to make a prohibited steps order prohibiting parents from having any contact with each other (since such an order did not impinge upon the parental responsibility of the parents concerned but impinged only upon contact between the parents themselves)[2].

(b) A court cannot make an order that 'neither the local authority nor the police shall take any further step in relation to the welfare of the children without referring to the court'. Such an order was beyond the powers of the court under the CA 1989, s 8[3].

(c) Where one parent acts without consulting the other (eg by placing a child in a new school without the other's agreement) the court will not necessarily make a prohibited steps order pending a hearing inter partes[4].

(d) It is very doubtful whether a prohibited steps order can in any circumstances be used to oust a father from the matrimonial home nor can it be used to prevent one parent assaulting the other[5].

1 CA 1989, s 9.
2 *Croydon London Borough Council v A* [1992] 2 FLR 341, [1992] 1 FCR 522.
3 *D v D (County court jurisdiction: injunctions)* [1993] 2 FLR 802.
4 *Re G* [1994] 2 FLR 964.
5 *Nottinghamshire County Council v P* [1994] Fam 18, [1993] 3 All ER 815 and *M v M* [1994] Fam Law 440.

Prohibited steps and jurisdiction

8.37 An application to prevent a parent from removing a child permanently from the jurisdiction may be made by way of prohibited steps application[1]. Where such an application is made, it need not necessarily be heard in the High Court (it should be transferred for determination either in the county court or in the High Court, depending on the complexity and difficulty of the decision)[2].

1 *Re WB (Residence Orders)* [1995] 2 FLR 1023, [1993] 1 FCR 231 and *Re L* [1993] 1 FCR 325.
2 *MH v GP* [1995] 2 FLR 106.

Removal from jurisdiction

8.38 Applications in respect of the lawful removal from the jurisdiction of children may come before the court in private law proceedings either on an application for a prohibited steps order (ie to prohibit the removal) or by way of a specific issue application (to remove the child). The principles that a court will apply were distilled by Thorpe LJ in this way:

> 'An application for leave to take a child out of the jurisdiction is to be considered on the premise that the welfare of the child is the first and paramount consideration, but that leave should not be withheld unless the interests of the child and those of the custodial parents are clearly found to be incompatible. So the approach of the court is to sanction the realistic proposal of the custodial parent, unless that proposal is inconsistent with the child's welfare[1].'

Those principles arise from a succession of cases[2]. In deciding upon the application of those principles to a particular case, the following particular points arise from the cases:

(a) The implementation of the CA 1989 has not changed the test that is to be applied, but has merely emphasised that the checklist is to be applied when considering welfare[3].

(b) Frequently, the balance will be between the wish of the residential parent to emigrate against the effect upon the contact that the other parent will have with the children[4].

(c) The adjournment of an application may be wrong and it may add to the stresses and strains upon the family as a whole and in particular the children[5].

(d) The person applying to remove children permanently from the jurisdiction should be in a position to show the arrangements that are proposed for the housing and education of the children and any other major matters relating to their future welfare[6].

1 *Re K* [1992] 2 FLR 98.
2 *Poel v Poel* [1970] 1 WLR 1469; *A v A* (1979) 1 FLR 380; *Hurwitt v Hurwitt* (1979) 3 FLR 194; *Chamberlain v De La Mare* (1982) 4 FLR 434; *Lonslow v Hennig* [1986] 2 FLR 378; *Belton v Belton* [1987] 2 FLR 343; *Re F* [1988] 2 FLR 116; *Tyler v Tyler*

[1989] 2 FLR 158; *K v K* [1992] 2 FLR 98; *M v M* [1992] 2 FLR 303; *M v A* [1993] 2 FLR 715; *Re G* [1994] 2 FLR 301; *MH v GP* [1995] 2 FLR 106.
3 *M v A* [1993] 2 FLR 715.
4 *Tyler v Tyler* [1989] 2 FLR 158.
5 *Belton v Belton* [1987] 2 FLR 343.
6 *Re K*, above.

Prohibited steps orders against non-party

8.39 Under the CA 1989, s 8 a prohibited steps order can be made against a person who is not a party to the proceedings and is not present in court if it is needed to protect the children and no other means of achieving the same object exists[1].

1 *Re H (Minors: Prohibited Steps)* [1995] 1 FLR 638.

Specific issue orders

8.40 Specific issue orders may relate to a wide range of activity. However, the question to be determined by the application must relate to an aspect of parental responsibility for a child. Examples of cases where such orders have been made are:

(a) Applications to permit the removal of a child from the jurisdiction (see the paragraph above).

(b) Applications for the sterilisation of a minor (although the preferred view may well be that such applications be made within the inherent jurisdiction of the High Court)[1].

(c) Applications for leave for children to be interviewed in respect of alleged criminal activity[2].

(d) Applications for orders permitting HIV tests in respect of children[3].

Applications for the change of a child's surname are free standing applications (and not applications for a specific issue order)[4]. Under s 13(1)(a) where a residence order is in force with respect to a child, no person may cause the child to be known by a new surname without either the written consent of every person who has parental responsibility or the leave of the court. Applications for the change of surname should not be taken lightly for they raise important matters relating to a child's welfare[5].

1 See the *Practice Note* [1993] 2 FLR 222 and *Re HG* [1993] 1 FCR 553, [1993] 1 FLR 587.
2 *Re F* [1995] 1 FLR 819 and *Re M* [1995] 1 FLR 825.
3 See *Re HIV Tests* [1994] 2 FLR 116.
4 *Re B (Change of surname)* [1996] 1 FLR 791.
5 See *Re F* [1993] 2 FLR 837n, [1994] 1 FCR 110 referring to *W v A* [1981] Fam 14. Such orders should only be made on an ex parte application in exceptional circumstances (see *Re J* [1993] 1 FLR 699, [1993] 1 FCR 74).

Limitations on specific issue orders

8.41 It has been held that the court has no jurisdiction under the CA 1989 to make a specific issue order compelling a local authority to provide services on behalf of the child in need¹. A specific issue order which provided that children be returned from a father to the mother was contrary to s 9(5) of the Act which prohibits the making of a specific issue order with a view to achieving a result which could be achieved by a residence order². The sterilisation of a minor is better dealt with under the court's inherent jurisdiction³.

1 *Re J* [1995] 1 FLR 669, [1995] 3 FCR 799.
2 *M v C* [1993] 1 FCR 264 (although there appears to be some debate about this, see *Re D* [1992] 1 All ER 892 and compare with *Re B* [1992] Fam 162, [1992] 3 All ER 867.
3 *Practice Note (Official Solicitor: Sterilisation)* [1996] 2 FLR 111.

STATUTORY RESTRICTION ON MAKING SECTION 8 ORDERS

8.42 The CA 1989 contains a number of restrictions on the making of section 8 orders. The following restrictions apply to the making of any section 8 order:

(a) No court may make any order under s 8 which is to have effect for a period which will end after the child has reached the age of 16 unless the court is satisfied that the circumstances of the case are exceptional¹.

(b) A court may not make a section 8 order (other than one varying or discharging a section 8 order) with respect to a child who has reached the age of 16 unless it is satisfied that there are exceptional circumstances².

(c) A person who is or was at any time within the last six months a local authority foster parent of a child may not apply for leave to apply for a section 8 order with respect to the child unless:

   (i) he has the consent of the authority;

   (ii) he is a relative of the child (see s 105 for the definition of relative);

   (iii) the child has lived with him for at least three years preceding the application³.

1 CA 1989, 9(6).
2 Ibid, s 9(7).
3 Ibid, s 9(3).

8.43 There are, in addition, the following further restrictions:

(a) *Residence or contact.* A local authority may not apply for a residence or contact order and no court may make such an order in favour of a local authority¹.

(b) *Orders other than residence.* A court may not make any section 8 order, other than a residence order, with respect to a child who is in the care of a local authority².

(c) *Prohibited steps order and specific issue order.* A court may not exercise its powers to make a specific issue order or prohibited steps order:

   (i) with a view to achieving a result which could be achieved by making a residence or contact order; or

(ii) in any way which is denied to the High Court (by s 100(2)) in the exercise of its inherent jurisdiction with respect to children[3].

1 CA 1989, s 9(2).
2 Ibid, s 9(1).
3 Ibid, s 9(5).

Restrictions on local authority

8.44 If a local authority declines to take steps under Part IV of the CA 1989 for the protection of children at risk, the court will be powerless to act and will be deprived of an opportunity to make an appropriate order. Where a local authority applied for a prohibited steps order, requiring that a father should not live in the same household as his daughters and should not have any contact with them, the application was bound to fail because it was an attempt by the local authority to achieve a 'no contact' order for which the local authority could not apply for such an order[1]. It is suggested that in most instances the resolution of this difficulty may lie in Part IV of the Act or resort to the High Court's inherent jurisdiction[2].

1 *Nottinghamshire County Council v P* [1993] 2 FLR 134.
2 See *Devon County Council v S* [1994] 1 FLR 355 and *Re S* [1994] 1 FLR 623, [1994] 2 FCR 986.

Power of court to make section 8 orders

8.45 A court may make a section 8 order in any 'family proceedings'[1] concerning the welfare of a child if:

(a) the court has before it an application for an order in respect of the child; or

(b) the court considers that the order should be made, even though there is no such application before it[2].

The court, therefore, has the power to make any section 8 order within family proceedings of its own motion. It has been held that legal advisers should ensure that their clients are made well aware of the powers of the court in family proceedings to make a wide range of orders under the Act of its own motion[3].

1 Family proceedings are defined in s 8(3) and (4) as meaning any proceedings under the inherent jurisdiction of the High Court in relation to children and any proceedings under:
   (a) Parts I, II and IV of the CA 1989,
   (b) the MCA 1973,
   (c) the Domestic Violence and Matrimonial Proceedings Act 1976,
   (d) the Adoption Act 1976,
   (e) the Domestic Proceedings and Magistrates' Courts Act 1978,

(f) the Matrimonial Homes Act 1983, ss 1 and 9,
(g) Part III of the Matrimonial and Family Proceedings Act 1984.
2 CA 1989, s 10(1).
3 *Re SW* [1993] 2 FLR 609, [1993] 1 FCR 896.

APPLICANTS FOR SECTION 8 ORDERS

Applications without leave

8.46 The Act lists those who may apply for section 8 orders without the prior leave of the court. Some classes of people are entitled only to apply for specific orders. The people who may apply for orders without leave (and the orders that they may seek) are:

(a) *Any section 8 order.* Any parent or guardian of the child or any person in whose favour a residence order is in force with respect to the child may apply for any section 8 order without leave[1].

(b) *Residence or contact.* Residence or contact orders may be sought without leave of the court by the following:

  (i) any party to a marriage (whether or not subsisting) in relation to whom the child is a child of the family (as defined by the CA 1989, s 105);

  (ii) any person with whom the child has lived for a period of at least three years;

  (iii) any person who:

   (a) in any case where a residence order is in force with respect to the child, has the consent of each of the persons in whose favour the order was made;

   (b) in any case where the child is in the care of a local authority, has the consent of that authority; or

   (c) in any other case, has the consent of each of those (if any) who have parental responsibility for the child[2].

(c) *Variation or Discharge of a section 8 order.* Anyone other than those set out above, may apply for the variation or discharge of a section 8 order if that order had been made on his application or (in the case of a contact order) he is named in the order[3].

1 CA 1989, s 10(4).
2 Ibid, s 10(5).
3 Ibid, s 10(6).

Applications for leave (other than by child)

8.47 Where a person is not entitled to apply for a section 8 order as of right, that person will need to secure the leave of the court for the making of any such application. The Act sets out the provisions that are to be considered by the court on an application for leave[1]. In any application for leave the applicant must show an arguable case. On an application for leave by a person other than the child concerned, the court must have particular regard to:

(a) the nature of the proposed application for the section 8 order;

(b) the applicant's connection with the child;

(c) any risk there might be of that proposed application disrupting the child's life to such an extent that he would be harmed by it; and

(d) where the child is being looked after by a local authority:

    (i) the authority's plans for the child's future; and

    (ii) the wishes and feelings of the child's parents.

On such an application the child's welfare will not be the court's paramount consideration. The court will have to consider the provisions of s 10(9) and also determine whether there are reasonable prospects of the application succeeding[2]. When considering any risk[3] that might arise from the application, the court is not only concerned with the effects of the application itself being made, but also with the effect that the making of the application might have upon the child's life. The fact that s 10(9) of the Act requires particular matters to be taken into account does not exclude consideration of other potentially relevant matters, including the wishes of the child[4].

1 CA 1989, s 10(9).
2 *Re A* [1992] 2 FLR 154.
3 CA 1989, s 10(9)(c).
4 *A v A and Newham London Borough Council* [1993] 1 FCR 870.

Cases concerning particular applicants

8.48 Applications by various classes of applicant have come before the court. The following are examples:

(a) *Aunt.* An aunt applied to a court in care proceedings for leave to be joined as a party so that she could seek a residence or contact order. The magistrates rejected her application on the grounds of the welfare of the child. On appeal it was held that the magistrates had applied the wrong test[1].

(b) *Natural parents of adopted children.* The natural parent of a child who had been adopted is not a parent within the meaning of the CA 1989. Therefore, such a person requires the prior leave of the court before making an application for a contact order. Such an application should either be started in or transferred to the High Court. The Official Solicitor should be invited to act as amicus curiae and as respondent to the application. Notice of the application should be given to the local authority. No notice should be given to the adopters. If the court considers there is a prima facie case, the adopters should be given notice. In a rare case where a judge was satisfied that there was a sufficient case for the contact application to proceed, the notice to the adopters should not be served through the court but should be left to the Official Solicitor to communicate[2].

(c) *Natural parent after freeing order.* A natural parent is not entitled to apply for a section 8 order following the making of a freeing order without the prior leave of the court[3].

(d) *Foster parents.* Even where a foster parent has authority from a local authority to make an application under s 9(3) it will still be necessary for the foster parent to secure the leave of the court. The court rejected an application by a foster mother, where there were serious charges against her and where the children were opposed to returning to the foster mother[4]. In another case the foster parents (with the local authority's support) were granted leave, notwithstanding the objections of the parents[5].

(e) *Grandparents.* A grandparent needs the leave of the court before making an application for a section 8 order[6]. Although grandparents ought to have a special place in any child's affection worthy of being maintained by contact[7], there is no presumption that a grandparent should have contact unless there were cogent reasons. Further, even if leave to apply is granted, it cannot be said that the grant of leave shifts the burden of proof to the party objecting to the making of a contact order[8].

(f) *Elder brother.* If an elder brother has no point of view or argument to put forward which is separate from those which may be advanced by other parties to the proceedings, there will be no value in him being joined as a party and separately represented[9].

1 *G v Kirklees Metropolitan Borough Council* [1993] 1 FCR 357, [1993] 1 FLR 805.
2 *Re S(J)* [1993] 2 FCR 193.
3 *M v C and Calderdale Metropolitan Borough Council* [1993] 1 FLR 505, [1993] 1 FCR 431.
4 *JR v Merton London Borough Council* [1992] 2 FCR 174.
5 *C v Salford County Council* [1992] 2 FLR 926.
6 *Re A* [1995] 2 FLR 153 and *Re F and R* [1995] 1 FLR 524 (where it was held that the magistrates should have heard evidence from the main parties in order to enable them to form a view on disputed facts).
7 *Re M* [1995] 3 FCR 550, [1995] 2 FLR 86.
8 *Re A* [1995] 2 FLR 153.
9 *North Yorkshire County Council v G* [1994] 1 FCR 737.

Applications for leave by children

8.49 Where it is proposed that an application should be made by a child, two considerations will generally arise:

(a) should the child be granted leave to make the application;

(b) should the child take part in any proceedings with the benefit of a next friend or guardian ad litem.

Children – the grant of leave

8.50 The Act specifies that the court may grant leave to a child to make a section 8 order if the court is satisfied that the child has sufficient understanding to make the proposed application for the section 8 order[1]. In applying for leave the child must show an arguable case. This provision has been considered in a number of cases as follows:

(a) An application for leave by a child raises issues which should be determined in the High Court. If the proceedings are started elsewhere, they should be transferred to that court[2].

(b) Section 10(9) of the Act does not apply to applications by children which are governed by s 10(8). The court should approach such applications cautiously and should have regard to the likelihood of success of the application[3].

(c) There is a divergence of view about whether the interests of the child are paramount on such an application or whether they are matters of importance only[4].

1 CA 1989, s 10(8).
2 *Practice Direction* [1993] 1 FLR 668, [1993] 1 FCR 584, [1993] 1 All ER 820, [1993] 1 WLR 313. See also *Re AD* [1993] 1 FCR 573.
3 *Re C* [1995] 1 FLR 927.
4 See *Re C* [1995] 1 FLR 927; *Re C* [1994] 1 FLR 26; and *Re SC* [1994] 1 FLR 96, [1994] 1 FCR 837.

Representation of the child

8.51 In deciding upon the representation of a child, it is necessary to distinguish between proceedings that are 'specified' and those which are not. Specified proceedings are defined[1] as any proceedings:

(a) on an application for a care order or supervision order;

(b) in which the court has given a direction under s 37(1) and has made, or is considering whether to make, an interim care order;

(c) on an application for the discharge of a care order or the variation or discharge of a supervision order;

(d) on an application under the CA 1989, s 39(4).

(e) in which the court is considering whether to make a residence order with respect to a child who is the subject of a care order;

(f) with respect to contact between a child who is the subject of a care order and any other person;

(g) under Part V of the CA 1989;

(h) on an appeal against:

(i) the making of, or refusal to make, a care order, supervision order or any order under s 34;

(ii) the making of, or refusal to make, a residence order with respect to a child who is the subject of a care order; or

(iii) the variation or discharge, or refusal of an application to vary or discharge, an order of a kind mentioned in sub-paragraph (i) or (ii) above;

(iv) the refusal of an application under the CA 1989, s 39(4) (to substitute a supervision order for a care order);

(v) the making of or refusal to make an order under Part V; or one which is specified by rules of court.

1 CA 1989, s 41(6).

Representation of child in specified proceedings

8.52 In specified proceedings (as defined above) the child will be represented by a guardian ad litem in accordance with the CA 1989, s 41 and the FP(CA 1989)R 1991, r 10 (in the High Court or county court) and the FP(CA1989)R 1991, r 10 (in the magistrates' court). Those rules set out the full extent of the guardian's duties in respect of the child. The duties of a solicitor acting on behalf of the child are set out in rr 4.12 and 12 respectively.

In non-specified proceedings

8.53 In non-specified proceedings, the representation of children is dealt with in the FPR 1991, rr 9.1–9.3 (there are no corresponding provisions in the FP(CA1989)R 1991 for the magistrates court). Under those rules, the following points are worthy of specific mention:

(a) A person's name may not be used in any proceedings as next friend of a child unless that person is the Official Solicitor or unless specific documents are filed (as to those documents, see below).

(b) Unless a child is prosecuting or defending proceedings under r 9.2A (see next paragraph) no notice of intention to defend may be given or answer or affidavit in answer filed by or on behalf of the child, unless the person giving the notice or filing the answer or affidavit is the Official Solicitor or has filed the documents referred to below.

(c) The documents referred to above (in respect of a child who is not also a patient under the Mental Health Act 1983) are:

(i) a written consent to act by the proposed next friend or guardian ad litem;

(ii) a certificate by the solicitor acting for the child:

(a) that the solicitor knows or believes that the person to whom the certificate relates is a minor,

(b) that the person named in the certificate as next friend or guardian ad litem has no interest in the cause or matter in question adverse to that of the person under disability and that he is a proper person to be next friend or guardian.

The above impose a responsibility upon the solicitor acting on behalf of the child. The solicitor needs to give careful thought to whether he is in a position to give the certificate (which may attract attention during the course of the hearing). It may be very difficult for the solicitor to give the appropriate certificate where the proposed next friend of a child has been held to have failed to pay regard to the child's welfare in the past (eg in a previous judgment of the court).

Child without next friend/guardian

8.54 Rule 9.2A of the FPR 1991 provides that, in non-specified proceedings, a child may begin, prosecute or defend proceedings without a next friend or guardian ad litem:

(a) where he has obtained the leave of the court; or

(b) where a solicitor:

(i) considers that the child is able, having regard to his understanding, to give instructions in relation to the proceedings; and

(ii) has accepted instructions from the child to act for him in the proceedings and where the proceedings have begun, in so acting[1].

1 FPR 1991, r 9.2(a)(i).

8.55 A child may apply for leave without a next friend or guardian ad litem either by filing a written request for leave (which should set out the reasons for the application) or by making an oral request for leave at any hearing in the proceedings[1]. These provisions were considered by the Court of Appeal in *Re S*[2]. That case makes the following particular points:

(a) The test under the Rules is framed with reference to the child's understanding, not his age. The child's understanding has to be assessed relative to the issues in the proceedings. Where any sound judgment on the issues calls for insight and imagination which only maturity and experience can give, both the court and the solicitor should be slow to conclude that the child's understanding is sufficient.

(b) The court may revoke leave after it has been granted if the court considers that the child's understanding is insufficient to justify the continuation of that leave[3].

(c) The Rules do not provide what is to happen where the child is being represented by a solicitor other than as a result of the leave of the court and the court is of the opinion that a next friend or guardian is necessary. The answer seems to lie in the appointment of a guardian under the FPR 1991, rr 4.14(2)(d) and 9.5(1).

(d) By reading r 9.2(a)(iv) and (vi) conjunctively, a court has the power to remove a next friend or guardian.

(e) The judge in that case had been plainly right to regard the parents as parties whom he should hear on the question of the child's application for leave.

The court should be slow to question the solicitor's assessment of the child's understanding but has power to do so[4]. Where a child ceases to be represented by the Official Solicitor as his guardian ad litem, the form of order may be that made in *Re MH*[5]. Children intervening in family applications in the High Court ought, for practical reasons, to be made parties in order to make their position clear and to obviate any difficulties over who represented them[6].

1 FPR 1991, r 9.2(a)(ii).
2 *Re S* [1993] Fam 263, [1993] 2 FLR 437.
3 FPR 1991, r 9.2(a)(viii).
4 *Re CT* [1992] 2 FCR 92.
5 [1993] 2 FCR 437.
6 *Re L v L* [1994] 1 FLR 156.

The role of the Official Solicitor

8.56 Fresh guidance has been given as to the appointment of the Official Solicitor as guardian ad litem or next friend in family proceedings[1].

1 See *Practice Note* [1995] 2 FLR 479, [1996] 1 FCR 78.

Shared residence orders

8.57 Under the CA 1989, s 11(4) a residence order may be made in favour of two or more people who do not themselves all live together. Where this happens the order may specify the periods during which the child is to live in the different households concerned. Under the law that existed prior to the introduction of the CA 1989, orders for shared care and control were very rare indeed[1]. Following the implementation of the CA 1989, it appeared at first as though that philosophy would continue[2]. However, attitudes appear to have softened through a succession of cases such as:

(a) *A v A*[3]. In that case the Court of Appeal held that although a shared residence order was an unusual order to be made in unusual circumstances, there was not a test of 'exceptional circumstances' in respect of such orders.

(b) *Re H*. A shared residence order may be used for the purposes of conferring parental responsibility on a step-father in circumstances where he would not otherwise have it and where the welfare of the child justified the order (particularly because the order was of important practical therapeutic effect)[4].

(c) *Re R*. A judge made a shared residence order so that an existing arrangement could continue whereby the child spent time in both households (both parents worked). The judge attached weight to the financial disadvantage that would result if the mother gave up her job and drew state benefits and child support was payable by the father. The Court of Appeal upheld his decision[5].

(d) *Re AB*. This is an example of an unusual case where an unmarried foster father applied for an adoption order (he and his partner were not able to make a joint application to adopt due to the Adoption Act 1976, s 14). The court made an adoption order in favour of the foster father and a joint residence order in respect of both foster parents[6].

1 (1986) 150 JP 439.
2 *Re H* [1994] 1 FLR 717, [1993] 1 FCR 671.
3 [1994] 1 FLR 669.
4 *Re H* [1995] 2 FLR 883 (see also *Re WB* [1995] 2 FLR 1023).
5 *Re R* [1995] 2 FLR 612.
6 *Re AB* [1996] 1 FLR 27.

SECTION 8 ORDERS WITH CONDITIONS

8.58 Section 11(7) of the Act provides that a section 8 order may:

(a) contain directions about how it is to be carried into effect;

(b) impose conditions which must be complied with by any person:–

    (i) in whose favour the order is made;

    (ii) who is a parent of the child concerned;

    (iii) who is not a parent of his but who has parental responsibility for him; or

    (iv) with whom the child is living,

and to whom the conditions are expressed to apply;

(c) be made to have effect for a specified period, or contain provisions which are to have effect for a specified period;

(d) make such incidental, supplemental or consequential provision as the court thinks fit.

Where there are grounds for an interim care order, that form of order may be more appropriate than an order under s 8 together with conditions under s 11(7)[1].

1 *Birmingham City Council v H* [1993] 1 FCR 247, [1992] 2 FLR 323. Compare this with *C v Solihull Metropolitan Borough Council* [1993] 1 FLR 290.

FAMILY ASSISTANCE ORDERS

8.59 These orders are intended to give short-term support to a family in need[1]. The order provides that a probation officer or a local authority officer shall advise, assist (and where appropriate befriend) any person named in the order[2]. The order may name the following people:

(a) any parent or guardian of the child;
(b) any person with whom the child is living or in whose favour a contact order is in force with respect of the child;
(c) the child himself[3].

The order can only be made with the consent of every person named in the order and where the circumstances are exceptional[4]. The order may last for no more than six months[5]. Where the order requires a local authority to make an officer of their's available, the authority must agree or the child concerned must be a child who either lives or who will live within their area[6]. Where a court wants to arrange for supervised contact within private law proceedings, the appropriate way to do so is to make a family assistance order under s 16 of the Act sooner than seeking to achieve that end by way of provision under s 11(7)(d) of the Act[7]. Alternatively, a supervision order might be made where the threshold criteria are satisfied[8].

1 CA 1989, s 16.
2 Ibid, s 16(1).
3 Ibid, s 16(2).
4 Ibid, s 16(3).
5 Ibid, s 16(5).
6 Ibid, s 16(7).
7 *Leeds City Council v C* [1993] 1 FLR 269, [1993] 1 FCR 585.
8 *Re DH* [1994] 1 FLR 679.

THE THRESHOLD CRITERIA

8.60 The 'threshold' criteria form the basis upon which a court will consider an application for care or supervision orders. However, on such applications the threshold criteria do not represent the only statutory factors that a court must consider. A flowchart representing the court's considerations is shown in Table 1 (below).

Section 31

8.61 Section 31 of the CA 1989 contains the threshold criteria. That section provides[1]:

TABLE 1

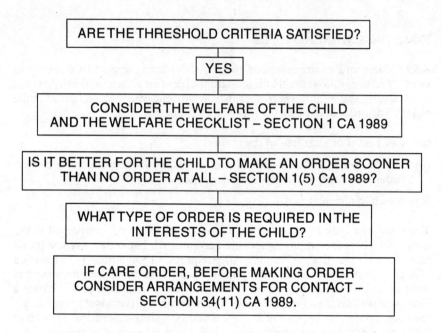

'(1) On the application of any local authority or authorised person, the court may make an order:

  (a) placing the child with respect to whom the application is made in the care of a designated local authority; or

  (b) putting him under the supervision of a designated local authority or of a probation officer.

(2) A court may only make a care order or supervision order if it is satisfied:

  (a) that the child concerned is suffering, or is likely to suffer, significant harm; and

  (b) that the harm, or likelihood of harm, is attributable to:

    (i) the care given to the child, or likely to be given to him if the order were not made, not being what it would be reasonable to expect a parent to give to him; or

    (ii) the child being beyond parental control.'

The Act goes on to define 'harm' in a way that has been described as resembling a Russian doll. The Act provides[2]:

'Harm means ill-treatment or the impairment of health or development; development means physical, intellectual, emotional, social or behavioural development; health means physical or mental health; and ill-treatment includes sexual abuse and forms of ill-treatment which are not physical.'

The Act also provides that[3]:

'Where the question of whether harm suffered by a child is significant turns on the child's health or development, his health or development shall be compared with that which could reasonably be expected of a similar child.'

1 CA 1989, s 31(1)(2).
2 Ibid, s 31(9).
3 Ibid, s 31(10).

Restrictions on the making of care and supervision orders

8.62 The Act itself imposes various restrictions upon the making of such orders. In particular:

(a) The order can only be made upon the application of any local authority or authorised person[1].

(b) The application may be made on its own or in any other family proceedings[2].

(c) No care or supervision order may be made with respect to a child who has reached the age of 17 (or 16 in respect of a child who is married)[3].

(d) An application may not be made if at the time that it is made the child is already subject to an unresolved application for a care order or supervision order or is already the subject to such an order[4].

1 CA 1989, s 31(1).
2 Ibid, s 31(4).
3 Ibid, s 31(3).
4 Ibid, s 31(7).

The effect of a care order

8.63 The effect of a care order is specified in the CA 1989, s 33. That section provides that:

(a) Where a care order has been made, the local authority is under a duty to receive the child into its care and to keep him in its care while the order remains in force[1].

(b) The local authority designated by the care order will have parental responsibility for the child and will have the power to determine the extent to which any parent or guardian of the child may meet his parental responsibility for him (but in determining the extent to which a parent or guardian may exercise parental responsibility the local authority must be satisfied that it is necessary to do so to safeguard or promote the child's welfare)[2]. Any such limitation imposed by a local authority upon the exercise by a parent or guardian of his parental responsibility will not prevent a parent or guardian, who has care of the child, from doing what is reasonable in all the circumstances in the child's welfare[3].

(c) While the care order is in force, the local authority may not:
- (i) cause the child to be brought up in any religious persuasion other than that in which he would have been brought up if the order had not been made; or
- (ii) have the right:
    - (a) to consent or refuse to consent to the making of an application for an order freeing the child for adoption;
    - (b) to agree or refuse to agree to the making of an adoption order, or an order under the Adoption Act 1976, s 55 (adoption of children abroad);
    - (c) to appoint a guardian of the child[4].

(d) While a care order is in force no person may:
- (i) cause the child to be known by a new surname, or
- (ii) remove the child from the United Kingdom,

without either the written consent of every person who has parental responsibility for the child or the leave of the court (although the removal of the child from the United Kingdom will not be prevented for a period of less than one month. The making of arrangements for a child in care to live outside the United Kingdom is governed by Sch 2, para 19 of the Act[5]).

1 CA 1989, s 33(1).
2 Ibid, s 33(3) and (4) of the Children Act 1989.
3 Ibid, s 33(5).
4 Ibid, s 33(6).
5 Ibid, s 33(7) and (8).

Timetable

8.64 The Act requires that a timetable should be drawn up by the court with a view to disposing of the application without delay. There is a requirement, also, that a court gives such directions as it considers appropriate for the purpose of ensuring, so far as is reasonably practicable, that the timetable is adhered to[1].

1 CA 1989, s 32.

Care/supervision

8.65 On an application for a care order the court may make a supervision order. On an application for a supervision order, the court may make a care order[1].

1 CA 1989, s 31(5).

The two limbs of the threshold criteria

8.66 The House of Lords have considered both limbs of the threshold criteria. In the case of *Re M*[1] the House of Lords held that:

(a) The natural construction of the conditions in s 31(2) is that where, at the time the application is disposed of, there are in place arrangements for the protection of the child by the local authority on an interim basis (which protection has been continuously in place for sometime) the relevant date with respect to which the court has to be satisfied was the date at which the local authority initiated the procedure for protection under the Act from which those arrangements followed.

(b) If, after a local authority has initiated protection arrangements, the need for them has terminated (because the child's welfare has been satisfactorily provided for otherwise) it would not be possible to found jurisdiction in any subsequent proceedings.

(c) The above does not preclude the court from taking into account at the date of the hearing all the relevant circumstances.

In the case of *Re H and R (Sexual Abuse Standard of Proof)*[2] the House of Lords stated that the word 'likely' when used in the CA 1989, s 31(2) is being used 'in the sense of a real possibility, a possibility that cannot sensibly be ignored having regard to the nature and gravity of the feared harm in the particular case'. 'Likely' does not mean 'probable'.

1 *Re M (A Minor) (Care Order Threshold Conditions)* [1994] 2 AC 424, [1994] 3 All ER 298, [1994] 2 FLR 577, [1994] 2 FCR 871.
2 *Re H and R* [1996] 1 All ER 1, [1996] 1 FLR 80. In *Newham London Borough Council v AG* [1993] 1 FLR 281, [1992] 2 FCR 119, the Court of Appeal had held that the phrase 'likely to suffer' should not be equated with 'on the balance of probabilities'; in looking to the future the court has to assess risk.

Fact finding

8.67 During the course of a hearing a court will have to decide upon the facts that are established within a given case. Once the court has determined the relevant facts, it can then apply those facts to the relevant statutory criteria (such as the threshold criteria in s 31). In making findings of fact in family proceedings:

(a) the burden of proof rests upon the person who makes the assertion (eg the applicant for a care order);

(b) the standard of proof is the general civil standard of proof, the 'preponderance of probability'[1]. However, the more serious the allegation, the stronger should be the evidence that the court requires before concluding that the allegation is established on the balance of probability[2].

If there is insufficient evidence to prove a fundamental fact upon which the applicant relies, it may be impossible for the court to find the threshold criteria are satisfied[3].

1 Per Lord Nicholls.
2 *Re H and R* [1996] 1 All ER 1 at 16.
3 See, eg *Re P* [1994] 2 FLR 751 (dispute between experts as to whether a child's death was due to non-accidental injury or natural causes); *Re H and R,* above (dispute about whether sexual abuse had been proved).

Care orders and conditions

8.68 Where a court makes a care order, it has no power to add any direction to the order. Once an order is made, the responsibility for the child is placed with the local authority and the responsibility of the court for the child ceases. Accordingly, it has been held:

(a) A court's direction that a guardian ad litem should be allowed to have a continuing involvement was not permissible[1].

(b) An order directing a review of the progress of the care plan and of contact six months after the making of a care order was 'manifestly ultra vires'[2].

(c) The local authority's care plan should be scrutinised by the court carefully. If the court does not agree with the care plan, it can refuse to make the care order[3].

1 *Re CN* [1992] 2 FCR 401 and *Re T* [1994] 2 FLR 423.
2 *Re B* [1993] 1 FLR 421.
3 *Re KDT* [1994] 2 FCR 721.

Care plan

8.69 For the reasons set out in the previous paragraph, the court will scrutinise every care plan carefully. The care plan should, as far as reasonably possible, comply with the *Children Act 1989 Guidance Regulations* Vol 3, Ch 2, para 2.62[1]. The following additional guidance has been given in respect of care plans:

(a) The care plan should be made before the final hearing and in consultation with the parents and other parties, or should at least take their views and wishes into account[2].

(b) The local authority's care plan should set out its plans for the child in as objective a manner as possible and in neutral, unemotive language[3].

(c) Wherever possible, evidence should be available in support of the care plan (including as to the feasibility of any long-term proposals made by the local authority)[4].

1 *Manchester City Council v F* [1993] 1 FLR 419n, [1993] 1 FCR 1000; *Re J* [1994] 1 FLR 253. In *Re R* [1994] 2 FCR 136 Wall J sets out in full the provisions of para 2.62 of Vol 3 of the *Guidance Regulations* at 143 of the judgment.

2 *Re J* [1994] 1 FLR 253.
3 *Re DH* [1994] 1 FLR 679.
4 *Re R* [1994] 2 FCR 136.

Orders by consent

8.70 Where the parties are agreed whether care orders should be made, issues may arise as to the extent to which a court should make findings of fact beyond those agreed between the parties. The court has to be satisfied that the requirements of the CA 1989, s 31 are made out[1]. However, the profundity of any investigation must reflect the reality where there is a consensus amongst the parties, particularly when the parties include a public authority with statutory duties and a guardian ad litem on behalf of the child[2]. Where all the parties are agreed upon the terms of the appropriate order, magistrates should be slow to discard the arrangements so negotiated[3]. Where sufficient findings of fact are agreed for the purposes of satisfying the threshold criteria, the court may regard it as inappropriate for there to be investigations on oral evidence of further facts[4]; however, it has been said that a court hearing an application under s 31 must always be free, where necessary, to investigate and make findings on the facts relating to any alleged abuse of the child[5].

1 *Re G* [1994] 2 FLR 69.
2 *Devon County Council v S* [1992] 2 FLR 244, [1992] 1 FCR 550.
3 *S v E* [1993] 1 FCR 729 and *M v Warwickshire County Council* [1994] 2 FCR 121.
4 *Stockport Metropolitan Borough Council v D* [1995] 1 FLR 873.
5 *Re G* [1994] 2 FLR 69.

Withdrawal of application

8.71 As with any other application under the CA 1989, an application may only be withdrawn with leave of the court[1]. The guardian ad litem should personally be present on the hearing of an application for leave to withdraw care proceedings[2]. The welfare checklist does not specifically apply to such an application but the fundamental question upon an application to withdraw care proceedings is whether the withdrawal will promote or conflict with the welfare of the child concerned[3].

1 FPR 1991, r 4.5 and FP(CA1989)R 1991, r 5.
2 *Re F* [1993] 2 FLR 9, [1993] 1 FCR 389.
3 *Re DB and CB* [1993] 2 FCR 607.

EVIDENCE AND PROCEDURE

Disclosure of expert reports

8.72 In wardship proceedings it has been held that there was power to order disclosure of adverse medical evidence[1]. Initially, it was held that, under the CA 1989, there was no power to override legal and professional privilege and order disclosure of a medical report on which a party did not intend to rely[2].

However, it has subsequently been held and confirmed that legal professional privilege which attaches to medical reports must yield to the overriding principle that the interests of a child are paramount. That overriding principle would be defeated if a party were to suppress an unfavourable report. Therefore, there is a positive professional duty on representatives to disclose material that effects the welfare of a child[3].

1 *Re A* [1991] 2 FLR 473.
2 *Re B* [1993] 2 FCR 241.
3 *Oxfordshire County Council v M* [1994] 1 FLR 175; *Essex County Council v R* [1994] 1 FCR 225; and *Re DH* [1994] 1 FLR 679. See also *Re L (Police investigation: privilege)* [1996] 1 FLR 731 where the point was left open. For the retention of legal professional privilege see *R v Derby Magistrates' Court, ex p B* [1996] 1 FLR 513.

Inter-agency disclosure

8.73 The CA 1989 provides that a statement or admission made in proceedings under Part IV or V of the Act shall not be admissible in evidence against the person making it or his spouse in proceedings for an offence other than perjury[1]. The leave of the court is required before any document in proceedings under the CA 1989 can be disclosed to a person other than a party to the proceedings, a welfare officer or the Legal Aid Board[2]. This had led to the following decisions:

(a) *Oxfordshire County Council v P*[3] where it was held that a guardian ad litem was wrong to inform the social worker of the mother's confession to the guardian ad litem that the mother had injured the child (the social worker then informed the police and as a result criminal proceedings were taken).

(b) *Re C*[4] in which it was held that the disclosure of the guardian ad litem's report following the making of a care order should be strictly controlled and should only be allowed once the court had been told for whom the distribution of the report is required. On the facts of that case, disclosure of the report to a family centre which was connected with social services and which offered therapeutic treatment to the children concerned was permitted but no more.

(c) *Re G*[5], this case examines the extent of the social worker's duties of confidentiality during care proceedings and should be read in conjunction with *Cleveland County Council v F* [1995] 1 FLR 797. The decision of the Plymouth County Court in *Re T* [1995] Fam Law 603 would appear to be in some doubt.

(d) The court has had to consider applications by the police for disclosure of papers in the case of *Re EC (Disclosure of material)*[6]. There have also been applications by parties to care proceedings for disclosure against the police[7].

1 CA 1989, s 38(2).
2 FPR 1991, r 4.23 and FP(CA1989)R 1991, r 23.
3 *Oxfordshire County Council v P* [1995] 1 FLR 552.

4 *Re C* [1996] 1 FLR 61.
5 *Re G (Social Worker: Disclosure)* [1996] FLR 276.
6 [1996] 2 FLR 123
7 *Cleveland County Council v F* [1995] 1 FLR 797 and *Nottinghamshire County Council v H* [1995] 2 FCR 365. See also the House of Lords in *Re L (Police investigation: privilege)* [1996] 1 FLR 731 and *Re A (Criminal proceedings: Disclosure)* [1996] 1 FLR 221.

Orphans

8.74 Where a child is left with no adult having parental responsibility for him, the local authority may wish to have the control that is afforded by a care order. In the case of *Birmingham City Council v JD, ID and CM*[1] it was held that it would be artificial to hold that the threshold criteria under s 31 had been met; therefore a care order was not made on the facts of that case. In the subsequent case of *Re SH*[2] the court held that there was sufficient evidence on the facts of the case to justify the making of a care order.

1 [1994] 2 FLR 502.
2 [1995] 1 FLR 746, [1996] 1 FCR 1.

Care and criminal proceedings

8.75 In *Re S*[1] the Court of Appeal had held that it would be preferable for a criminal trial to be heard first before care proceedings unless there were exceptional circumstances. However, in *Re TB*[2] it was held that it should not be assumed that care proceedings should be adjourned automatically in every case where a parent was the defendant in criminal proceedings; each case has to be considered on its own facts and on its own merits and the welfare of the child has to take priority over the detriment to the parents who were to be tried in a criminal court.

1 [1995] 1 FLR 151.
2 [1995] 2 FLR 801, [1996] 1 FCR 101.

Issue estoppel

8.76 There may be instances where a party to proceedings wishes to challenge an earlier finding of fact. There may be circumstances where the court will be prepared to permit an investigation of antecedent findings, but these circumstances would be rare[1]. The doctrine of issue estoppel may be important to children's cases but only to a limited extent[2].

1 *Re S* [1995] 2 FLR 639.
2 *Re S (Discharge of Care Order)* [1995] 2 FLR 639.

DISPOSAL OF APPLICATIONS

Is a care order or supervision order more appropriate?

8.77 Where the threshold is crossed, the court may have to decide whether to make a care order or a supervision order. The difference between the two has been considered in a number of cases[1]. The factors to take into account are:

(a) There is no way to enforce conditions attached to a supervision order under Sch 3 of the Act save by applying to vary or discharge the supervision order.

(b) A supervision order lasts, in the first instance, for only a year but a care order may last during the child's minority.

(c) A care order gives the local authority parental responsibility and enables them to limit the exercise by the parents of their parental responsibility.

(d) The child may still be placed at home with the parents under a care order as a result of the Placement of Children with Parents etc Regulations 1991, if the local authority is satisfied that the conditions in those Regulations are met.

(e) The primary concern in any consideration as to whether to make a supervision order or a care order must be to afford protection for the child.

1 *Re D* [1993] 2 FLR 423, [1993] 2 FCR 88; *Re R and G* [1994] 1 FLR 793; *Re S* [1993] 2 FCR 193; and *Re T* [1994] 1 FLR 103, [1994] 1 FCR 663; *Re S (Care or supervision order)* [1996] 1 FLR 753; *Re V (Care or supervision order)* [1996] 1 FLR 776.

Care and residence applications

8.78 If there is a reasonable alternative to a care order by a placement of a child within the family, it should be taken[1]. Wherever possible, competing applications should be heard together[2]. Even though threshold criteria applicants of s 1(1) and (3) might still not dictate the need for an order.

1 *Re H* [1994] 2 FLR 80, [1994] 3 FCR 183.
2 *W v Wakefield City Council* [1994] 2 FCR 564.

Arrangements by local authority for children to live abroad

8.79 The Act makes provision governing the arrangements that a local authority may make for children to live outside England and Wales[1]. It differentiates between:

(a) children who are in the care of the local authority[2]; and

(b) children who are looked after by the local authority[3].

1 CA 1989, Sch 2, para 11.

2 Ibid, Sch 2, para 19(1). By reason of s 105(1) any reference to a child who is in the care of a local authority is a reference to a child who is in their care by virtue of a care order. 'Care order' is defined in s 31(11) of the Act as meaning an order under s 31(1)(a) (and it includes an interim care order under s 38).
3 CA 1989, Sch 2, para 19(2). The meaning of 'a child who is looked after by a local authority' is given in s 22(1) of the Act.

Emigration of child in care

8.80 A local authority may only arrange for or assist in arranging for any child in their care to live outside England and Wales with the approval of the court[1]. The court may not give its approval unless it is satisfied that:

(a) living outside England and Wales would be in the child's best interests;

(b) suitable arrangements have been made, or will be made, for his reception and welfare in the country in which he will live;

(c) the child has consented to living in that country; and

(d) every person who has parental responsibility for the child has consented to his living in that country[2].

However, that list of conditions is qualified as follows:

(i) Although the above list includes a requirement that the child must consent to living in that country, where the court is satisfied that the child does not have sufficient understanding to give or withhold its consent, it may disregard that requirement and give its approval for the child to live in the country concerned with a parent, guardian or other suitable person[3].

(ii) Although the above list specifies that the consent of every person with parental responsibility is a pre-condition to the granting by the court of approval, the Act goes on to provide[4] where such a person has failed to give his consent, the court may disregard that provision and give its approval if it is satisfied that that person:

(a) cannot be found;

(b) is incapable of consenting; or

(c) is withholding his consent unreasonably[5].

Where a court gives leave, it may order that its decision is not to have effect during the appeal period[6]. A child in care may emigrate if every person with parental responsibility consents. The FPR 1991, r 4.24 provides that consent shall be given either orally in court or in writing to the court signed by the person giving his consent.

1 CA 1989, Sch 2, para 19(1).
2 Ibid, Sch 2, para 19(3).
3 Ibid, Sch 2, para 19(4).
4 Ibid, Sch 2, para 19(5).

5 For the interpretation of these words see *Re G* [1994] 2 FLR 301, [1994] 2 FCR 359 and *Re W* [1994] 2 FLR 1087, [1994] 3 FCR 242.
6 The 'appeal period' is defined in the CA 1989, Sch 2, para 19(8).

Emigration of child looked after by local authority

8.81 A local authority may, with the approval of every person who has parental responsibility for the child, arrange for, or assist in arranging for, any child looked after by them to live outside England and Wales[1]. This provision relates to children who are not in the care of the local authority under a care order.

1 CA 1989, Sch 2, para 19(2).

SUPERVISION ORDERS

Effect of supervision orders

8.82 The Act[1] imposes a duty upon the supervisor:

(a) to advise, assist and befriend the supervised the child;

(b) to take such steps as are reasonably necessary to give effect to the order; and

(c) where:

    (i) the order is not wholly complied with, or

    (ii) the supervisor considers that the order may no longer be necessary, to consider whether or not to apply to the court for its variation or discharge.

1 CA 1989, s 35.

Duration of supervision order

8.83 The initial duration of a supervision order will be for a period of up to one year beginning with the date on which it was made[1]. The court may make a supervision order for an initial period of less than 12 months[2]. An application may be made to extend the supervision order beyond the initial one year period[3]. On such an application the court does not have jurisdiction to make a care order (other than on the application of a local authority for such an order) and it is for the local authority to justify to the court that the welfare of the child requires the supervision order to continue and for it to be extended[4]. The extension may not be beyond the period of three years beginning with the date upon which the order was made[5].

1 CA 1989, Sch 3, para 6(1).
2 *M v Warwickshire County Council* [1994] 2 FLR 593.
3 CA 1989, Sch 3, para 6(3).

4 *Re A* [1995] 1 FLR 335, [1995] 2 FCR 114.
5 CA 1989, Sch 3, para 6(4).

Conditions to be attached to a supervision order

8.84 The conditions that may be attached to a supervision order are set out in Sch 3 of the Act. That Schedule specifies:

(a) the extent of the power of the supervisor to give directions in relation to the child[1];

(b) the conditions that may be attached to a supervision order with the consent of any 'responsible person'[2].

(c) orders that may be made for psychiatric and medical treatment of the supervised child[3].

An undertaking (or condition outside Schedule 3) may not be attached to a supervision order[4].

1 CA 1989, Sch 3, para 1(2).
2 Ibid, Sch 3, para 3. The 'responsible person' is defined in Sch 3, para 1 as 'any person who has parental responsibility for the child and any other person with whom the child is living'.
3 The case law upon the extent to which conditions may be imposed see: *Nottinghamshire County Council v P* [1993] 1 FLR 514 (ie the decision of Ward J at first instance); *Croydon London Borough Council v A* [1992] 2 FLR 341; *Re H* [1994] 2 FLR 979, [1994] 2 FCR 1; and *Hereford and Worcester County Council v R and G* [1994] 2 FCR 981.
4 *Re B (Supervision order: Parental undertaking)* [1996] 1 FLR 676; *Re V (Care or supervision order)* [1996] 1 FLR 776.

CONTACT WITH CHILDREN IN CARE

The general requirement for reasonable contact

8.85 Where a child is in the care of a local authority, the authority must allow the child reasonable contact with the following people (subject to the limitations set out in the next paragraph):

(a) his parents;

(b) any guardian of his;

(c) where there was a residence order in force with respect to the child immediately before the care order was made, the person in whose favour the order was made; and

(d) where, immediately before the care order was made, a person had care of the child by virtue of an order made in the exercise of the High Court's inherent jurisdiction with respect to children, that person[1].

It is to be noted that the requirement is for there to be reasonable contact; this is not the same as contact at the discretion of the local authority[2].

1 CA 1989, s 34(1).
2 *Re P (Contact with Children in Care)* [1993] 2 FLR 156.

Limitations on reasonable contact

8.86 The Act makes provision for the following limitations upon the right of reasonable contact:

(a) *Order permitting refusal.* On the application of the local authority or the child, the court may make an order authorising the authority to refuse to allow contact between the child and any of the persons set out in (a) to (d) of the previous paragraph who are named in the order[1].

(b) *Defined contact.* On an application made by the local authority or the child, the court may make such order as it considers appropriate with respect to the contact which is to be allowed between the child and any named person[2].

(c) *Withholding contact.* A local authority may refuse to allow the reasonable contact provided by s 34(1) or by an order under s 34, if:

  (i) the authority is satisfied that it is necessary to do so in order to safeguard or promote the child's welfare, and

  (ii) the refusal:

   (a) is decided upon as a matter of urgency, and

   (b) does not last for more than seven days[3].

1 CA 1989, s 34(4).
2 Ibid, s 34(2).
3 Ibid, s 34(6). Where the local authority decides to withhold contact in such circumstances, the provisions of the Contact with Children Regulations 1991 should be satisfied (these require that the child must agree if of sufficient understanding and the authority must send written notice of the withholding of contact to people who are specified in the Regulations).

Orders for contact by parent, etc

8.87 An application may be made to the court for an order for contact with a child in care by any of the following[1]:

(a) a parent of the child;

(b) a guardian of the child;

(c) a person who had a residence order in respect of the child immediately before the care order was made;

(d) a person who had the care of the child pursuant to an order of the High Court under its inherent jurisdiction immediately before the making of the care order;

(e) any person who has obtained the leave of the court to make the application. Where such an application is made the court may make such order as it considers appropriate 'with respect to the contact which is to be allowed between the child and that person'[2].

As with any other order for contact under this section the court may attach conditions[3].

1 CA 1989, s 34(3).
2 Ibid, s 34(3).
3 Ibid, s 34(7).

Case law on court orders

8.88 Contact applications made by parents usually fall within two categories:

(a) those which ask for contact as such with no suggestion that the applicant wishes to take over the care of the child. In such a case the issue of contact would often depend on whether contact will frustrate long-term plans for the child;

(b) applications for contact, which represent an attempt to set aside the care order itself. In such a case the court will obviously take into account the failure to apply to discharge the care order, but the provisions of the CA 1989, s 1 have to be considered and the local authority has the task of justifying the cessation of contact (if that is sought).

8.89 In an earlier decision, the court had expressed reluctance to order contact if it represented an interference with the local authority's care plan for the child[1]. However, under s 34 the correct test is:

(a) The Act provides a presumption in favour of continuing reasonable contact.

(b) That presumption of contact has to be balanced against any issues relating to the welfare of the child. If a judge concludes that the benefits of contact outweigh the advantages of disrupting any of the local authority's long-term plans (where the plans are inconsistent with such contact) then the judge must refuse any application by the local authority to terminate contact. This is not to monitor or scrutinise the local authority's plans but to discharge the duty under s 34 of the Act.

(c) Even when the CA 1989, s 31 is satisfied, contact may be of singular importance to the long-term welfare of the child. It may give the child the security of knowing that his parents love him and are interested in his welfare; it may avoid any damaging sense of loss to the child in seeing himself abandoned by his parents. Contact may also enable the child to commit himself to a substitute family with the seal of approval of his natural parents and give the child the necessary sense of family and personal identity. Contact, therefore, is capable of reinforcing and increasing the chances of success of a permanent placement[2]. In the light of the wording of the section, an order for 'reasonable contact' is otiose (because it merely repeats the requirements of s 34). The court cannot impose obligations upon parents for them to accept contact[3]. Where an interim care order is made, contact should generally be maintained save in circumstances of exceptional and severe risk[4].

1 *Re B* [1993] 1 FLR 543, [1993] 1 FCR 363 and *Re E* [1994] 1 FLR 146, [1994] 1 FCR 584.
2 *Re S* [1994] 2 FLR 222.
3 *Re F* [1995] 1 FLR 510, [1994] 2 FCR 1354.
4 *A v M and Walsall Borough Council* [1993] 2 FLR 244.

When may an order be made?

8.90 An order may be made in respect of contact with a child in care:

(a) on the making of a care order or in any family proceedings in connection with a child who is in the care of a local authority (even though no application for such an order has been made)[1];

(b) upon the application of a person entitled to seek the order[2].

1 CA 1989, s 34(5). The order for contact may be made either at the same time as the care order is made or later (s 34(11)). Before making a care order, the court is obliged to consider the arrangements which are proposed for contact and invite the parties to comment upon those arrangements (s 34(11)).
2 CA 1989, s 34(3).

Application for leave

8.91 The provisions of s 10(9) of the Act are not specifically stated to apply to an application for leave under s 34. However, it has been said that it would be anomalous were the court not to take into account the criteria laid out in section 10(9) when considering the grant of leave under s 34[1]. Although the child has the right to make an application in respect of contact without leave, in most circumstances it would be more appropriate for the application to be made by the local authority itself upon the child's behalf.

1 *Re M (Contact Leave to Apply)* [1995] 3 FCR 550, [1995] 2 FLR 86.

Variation or discharge

8.92 The court may vary or discharge any order for contact to a child in care on the application of the local authority, the child concerned or the person named in the order[1].

1 CA 1989, s 34(9).

Education supervision order

8.93 Education supervision orders may be made if a court is satisfied that the child concerned is of compulsory school age and is not being properly educated[1]. Such proceedings are not specified proceedings within s 41(6) of the Act and therefore it is not open to the court to appoint a guardian ad litem for the child under that section[2]. Such orders represent the first step to secure the attendance of a child at school; if that step is unsuccessful, the education authority should notify the appropriate local authority; that local authority would then have to consider whether to apply for care or supervision orders. If a child is not attending school, it may not be difficult to satisfy the threshold criteria under s 31[3].

1 CA 1989, s 36.
2 *Essex County Council v B* [1993] 1 FLR 866, [1993] 1 FCR 145.
3 *O v Berkshire County Council* [1992] 1 FCR 498.

Interim care/supervision orders

Grounds for making interim order

8.94 An interim care or supervision order may not be made unless the court is satisfied that there are 'reasonable grounds for believing that' the threshold criteria in s 31(2) of the Act are met[1]. The court may make such an order in any proceedings for care or supervision orders (where the proceedings are adjourned) or where the court gives a direction under s 37(1)[2]. Where the grounds specified in s 38 for the making of an interim order are satisfied, the court must then go on to consider s 1 of the Act before deciding to make an order[3].

1 CA 1989, s 38(1) and (2).
2 In appropriate circumstances, an interim care order may be made where a local authority's care plan is insufficiently clear or where there is a need for further assessment: see *Re B* [1993] 1 FLR 815, [1993] 1 FCR 565; *Re C* [1994] 1 FCR 447; *Hounslow London Borough Council v A* [1993] 1 FCR 164; *Re C* [1992] 2 FCR 341; *Re R* [1994] 2 FCR 136; *Re L* [1996] 1 FLR 116 (approving *Re J* [1994] 1 FLR 253); and *Re CN* [1992] 2 FCR 401. In *Cheshire County Council v P* [1993] 2 FCR 397 the Court of Appeal held that it was the court's duty under the CA to determine questions relating to the child's upbringing as they arise and to do so with finality and as much speed as is consistent with justice and the welfare of the child; it would seldom if ever be right for the court to make continued use of its powers of adjournment under s 38 of the Act.
3 *Humberside County Council v B* [1993] 1 FCR 613, [1993] 1 FLR 257.

Duration of interim order

8.95 The maximum period for the first interim order is eight weeks[1]. Subsequent orders may be made for up to four weeks (or for up to eight weeks from the beginning of the first interim order)[2]. There is no limit in principle to the number of interim orders which the court can make.

1 CA 1989, s 38(4) and (5).
2 *Gateshead Metropolitan Borough Council v N* [1993] 1 FLR 811, [1993] 1 FCR 400.

Medical or psychiatric examination

8.96 On the making of an interim care or supervision order, the court may give directions with regard to the medical or psychiatric examination or other assessment of the child[1]. In particular, the court may order that there shall be no such examination or assessment (or that there should be no such examination or assessment unless the court orders to the contrary)[2]. Such orders may be made at any time while an interim order is in force and may be subsequently varied[3]. If the child concerned is of sufficient understanding to make an informed decision, he may refuse to submit to the examination or assessment[4]. The above provisions confer upon the court power to make a direction with which even a local authority, having the interim care of the child, is bound to comply; therefore, the order may compel the local authority to arrange for a medical or psychiatric examination[5].

1 CA 1989, s 38(6).
2 Ibid, s 38(7).
3 Ibid, s 38(8).
4 Ibid, s 38(6).
5 *Re O* [1993] 1 FLR 860, [1992] 2 FCR 394. See also *Berkshire County Council v C* [1993] 1 FCR 608.

Judicial guidance on interim orders

8.97 Judicial guidance has been given as to how magistrates should approach applications for interim orders[1]. That guidance includes the following:

(a) Justices have to bear in mind that an interim care order is a holding order until the substantial hearing. Nevertheless, they should consider all the relevant risks pending at the time of the hearing and ensure that the substantive issues are heard at the earliest possible date.

(b) Justices should be prepared to transfer proceedings laterally to an adjacent Family Proceedings court if they find that they have insufficient time to hear the application.

(c) On an interim application, justices should rarely make findings on disputed facts (which should be left to the final hearing).

(d) Justices should be cautious about changing a child's residence on an interim order. The preferred course should be to leave the child in his current residence with a direction for safeguard together with an early hearing date. Where an interim order would lead to a substantial change in the child's position, oral evidence should be permitted (albeit limited).

(e) Justices should ensure that they have the written advice of the guardian ad litem. A party who is opposed to a recommendation by a guardian ad litem should be given the opportunity of putting questions to the guardian.

(f) Justices must comply with the mandatory requirements of the Family Proceedings Courts (Children Act 1989) Rules 1991, especially r 21. They should read any documents filed under r 17 before the hearing. There should be an appropriate written record of the hearing kept by the clerk and there should be findings and reasons given in support of the ultimate decision.

(g) The proceedings should not be conducted in an adversarial way.

(h) If justices are obviously about to make an error in law or in procedure, it is the duty of advocates to advise them of that error.

1 *M v Hampshire County Council* [1993] 1 FCR 23 and *Re F* [1994] 1 FLR 240, [1994] 1 FCR 729.

SECTION 37 REPORTS

8.98 The court may order a local authority to make a report in respect of a child. The conditions that must be satisfied before the court may make such an order are:

(a) An issue must have arisen in family proceedings with respect to the welfare of a child[1].

(b) It must appear to the court that it may be appropriate for a care or supervision order to be made in respect of the child[2]. The court's order is directed towards the local authority in whose area the child is ordinarily resident or (where the child is not ordinarily resident in the area of the local authority) the authority within whose area any circumstances arose in consequence of which the direction is being given[3].

1 CA 1989, s 37(1).
2 Ibid, s 37(5).
3 Ibid, s 37(2).

8.99 Following the making of such an order the local authority must:

(a) Undertake the investigation.

(b) Consider whether they should apply for a care order or a supervision order with respect to the child, provide services or assistance for the child or his family, or take any other action with respect to the child.

(c) Where the local authority decides not to apply for care or supervision orders in respect of the child, it must inform the court (within eight weeks of the date of the direction unless the court otherwise orders) of the local authority's reasons for so doing and any service or assistance which they have provided (or intend to provide) for the child and his family[1].

(d) Where the authority decides not to apply for a care or supervision order with respect to the child, it must consider whether it would be appropriate to review the case at a later date (and if they decide that it would be, the authority must determine the date on which the review is to begin)[2].

(e) A court should not order a local authority to carry out an investigation under s 37 unless it appears that it might be appropriate to make a public law order (in purely private law proceedings, an independent investigation may be conducted by the court welfare officer)[3].

The procedure where the court gives a direction under s 37 is set out in the FPR 1991, r 4.26 and the FP(CA 1989)R 1991, r 27.

1 CA 1989, s 37(3) and (4).
2 Ibid, s 37(6).
3 *Re C E (a minor) (Section 37 Direction)* [1995] 1 FLR 26. The court has the power to direct that as part of the investigation under s 37, the local authority should investigate what help of a psychiatric or counselling nature might be available: *Re H* [1993] 2 FCR 277.

DISCHARGE AND VARIATION OF CARE AND SUPERVISION ORDERS

8.100 Section 39 sets out the provision for the variation and discharge of care and supervision orders. A care order may be discharged by the court on the application of:

(a) any person who has parental responsibility for the child;

(b) the child himself; or

(c) the local authority designated in the order[1].

The test to be applied on an application to discharge an order is the welfare test specified in s 1 of the Act; the applicant bears the burden of satisfying that test. There may be instances where the court will question previous findings of fact made in earlier proceedings, but such instances will be rare[2]. A supervision order may be varied or discharged by the court on the application of:

(i) any person who has parental responsibility for the child;

(ii) the child himself; or

(iii) the supervisor[3].

1 CA 1989, s 39(1).
2 *Re S* [1995] 2 FLR 639.
3 CA 1989, s 39(2).

GUARDIANS AD LITEM

8.101 The appointment of guardians ad litem takes place in specified proceedings (as defined by CA 1989, s 41(6)) as a result of the CA 1989, s 41. The section also makes provision for the appointment of solicitors to represent the child[1]. The duties of a solicitor so appointed are specified within the rules[2]. A guardian ad litem has the right at all reasonable times to examine and take copies of:

(a) any records of, or held by, a local authority or an authorised person which were compiled in connection with the making, or proposed making, by any person of any application under this Act with respect to the child concerned;

(b) any records of, or held by, a local authority which were compiled in connection with any functions which stand referred to their Social Services Committee under the Local Authority Social Services Act 1970, so far as those records relate to that child; or

(c) any records of, or held by, an authorised person which were compiled in connection with the activities of that person, so far as those records relate to that child[3].

Where the guardian takes a copy of any such record, it will become evidence before the court if referred to in the guardian's report or evidence[4]. The following cases have given guidance on issues relating to guardians ad litem:

(i) *Re S*[5]. Although a court may ask for a welfare report in both private and public law proceedings, there need to be special circumstances before a welfare report will be ordered in addition to a guardian ad litem's report.

(ii) *R v Cornwall County Council*[6]. A local authority cannot interfere with a manner in which guardians ad litem consider it necessary for the carrying out of their duties. Although the local authority is bound by the Guardians Ad Litem and Reporting Officers (Panels) Regulations 1991 to set up a panel of guardians, the guardians are independent.

(iii) *R v Hereford and Worcester County Council*[7]. Where a local authority is considering the removal of the child from a foster parent, it has a duty to consult the guardian ad litem and should consult the foster parent before making a decision.

(iv) *Re M*[8]. Where an emergency protection order expires and there are no pending care proceedings, a person who has been appointed guardian ad litem cannot continue to act in the capacity of guardian. However, where appropriate such a person could apply for leave to make a section 8 order.

(v) *Devon County Council v S*[9]. As a result of the provisions of the FPR 1991, r 4.10(7) and the FP(CA 1989)R 1991, r 10(7), a guardian ad litem may not be a serving probation officer (except that a probation officer who has not in that capacity been previously concerned with the child or his family and who is employed part-time may, when not engaged in his duties as a probation officer, act as a guardian ad litem). Welfare officers are probation officers.

(vi) *Re T (A Minor) (Guardian ad litem Case Record)*[10]. Where social service records include Form F (a case record prepared by the authority, giving detailed information concerning prospective adopters) the guardian should be entitled to see that document.

(vii) *Oxfordshire County Council v P*[11]. If a mother confesses to a guardian ad litem that she has injured the child, the guardian should regard that information as confidential. The confession should not be reported to the police without the prior leave of the court.

(viii) *Re C (Disclosure)*[12]. It can never be proper for a guardian ad litem to promise a child that information will be withheld from the court. Issues concerning the withholding of information are more suited to the High Court.

(ix) *Re N (Child Abuse: Evidence)*[13]. A guardian ad litem is ill-equipped to diagnose sexual abuse.

1 CA 1989, s 41(4).
2 FPR 1991, r 4.12 and FP(CA1989)R 1991, r 12; and see the *Family Law Act Guide to Good Practice for Solicitors Acting for Children* (published annually).
3 CA 1989, s 42(1).
4 Ibid, s 42(2).
5 [1993] 1 FLR 110, [1992] 2 FCR 554.
6 [1992] 1 WLR 427, [1992] 1 FLR 270.
7 [1992] 1 FLR 448, [1992] 1 FCR 497.
8 [1993] 1 FLR 275, [1993] 1 FCR 78, see also *Re S* [1996] 1 FLR 158.
9 [1993] 1 FLR 842, [1993] 2 FCR 36.
10 [1994] 1 FLR 632; *Manchester City Council v T* [1994] Fam 181, [1994] 2 All ER 526
11 [1995] 1 FLR 552.
12 [1996] 1 FLR 797.
13 [1996] 2 FLR 214.

PROTECTION OF CHILDREN

Duty to investigate

8.102 A local authority is under a statutory duty to make (or cause to be made) such enquiries as they consider necessary to enable them to decide whether they should take any action to safeguard or promote a child's welfare where:

(a) the authority is informed that a child who lives, or is found, in its area is the subject of an emergency protection order or is in police protection; or

(b) the authority has reasonable cause to suspect that a child who lives, or is found, in its area is suffering or is likely to suffer significant harm[1].

1 CA 1989, s 47(1).

8.103 This duty includes:

(a) Considering whether the authority should make any application to the court or exercising any other power under the CA 1989 in respect of the child[1].

(b) Considering whether the child should be provided with accommodation[2].

(c) The taking of such steps as are reasonably practicable to obtain access to the child or to ensure that access is obtained to him by a person authorised by the local authority (unless the local authority is satisfied that it has sufficient information with respect to the child)[3].

(d) Consulting with the local education authority if the enquiries lead to a suggestion that matters relating to the child's education need to be investigated[4].

(e) Applying for an emergency protection order, a child assessment order, a care order or a supervision order if access to the child is removed or information about his whereabouts denied (unless the authority is satisfied the child's welfare can be satisfactorily safeguarded without such application being made)[5].

(f) If, following the enquiries, the authority decides not to apply for orders, considering whether to hold a review of the case at a later date (and if so, decide the date upon which that review is to begin)[6].

(g) Taking any necessary action to safeguard or promote the child's welfare, if the authority decides that such action is necessary[7].

1 CA 1989, s 47(3)(a).
2 Ibid, s 47(3)(b).
3 Ibid, s 47(4).
4 Ibid, s 47(5).
5 Ibid, s 47(6).
6 Ibid, s 47(7).
7 Ibid, s 47(8).

CHILD ASSESSMENT ORDERS

8.104 The purpose of a child assessment order is to direct a short-term assessment of the needs of the child. The application for such an order is made by the local authority or an 'authorised person'[1]. The grounds upon which a child assessment order may be made are:

(a) the applicant has reasonable cause to suspect that the child is suffering, or is likely to suffer, significant harm;

(b) an assessment of the state of the child's health or development, or of the way in which he has been treated, is required to enable the applicant to determine whether or not the child is suffering, or is likely to suffer, significant harm; and

(c) it is unlikely that such an assessment will be made, or be satisfactory, in the absence of an order under this section[2]. The order must specify the date by which the assessment is to begin and it is for a maximum period of seven days[3]. The child may only be kept away from home under such an order if the order directs that this should be so and it is necessary for the purpose of the assessment (in which event the order must itself specify how long the child may be kept away from home and the contact that the child is to have with 'other persons' while away from home)[4].

1 'Authorised person' is defined in the CA 1989, s 31(9). It means a local authority or the NSPCC (until such time as the Secretary of State extends its meaning by regulation).
2 CA 1989, s 43(1).
3 Ibid, s 43(5).
4 Ibid, s 43(9) and (10).

CHILD ASSESSMENT ORDERS/EMERGENCY PROTECTION ORDERS

8.105 When a case comes before the court on an application for a child assessment order, it may be that the court will form the view that the concerns in respect of the child are greater than originally imagined. The Act, therefore, specifically provides that a court may treat an application for a child assessment order as an application for an emergency protection order[1]. Further, the court is prohibited from making a child assessment order if it is satisfied that there are grounds for making an emergency protection order and that it ought to make such an order rather than a child assessment order[2].

1 CA 1989, s 43(3).
2 Ibid, s 43(4).

Compliance

8.106 The Act contains provisions to ensure compliance with the child assessment order[1]. However, it is also provided that if a child is of sufficient understanding to make an informed decision, he may refuse to submit to a medical or psychiatric examination or any other assessment[2].

1 CA 1989, s 43(6) and (7).
2 Ibid, s 43(8).

EMERGENCY PROTECTION ORDERS

Grounds for application

8.107 The Act specifies three grounds upon which the court may make an emergency protection order.

The first ground[1]

8.108 This ground is available on the application of 'any person' (therefore it is not confined to applications by a local authority or an authorised person). The first ground is that the court is satisfied that there is reasonable cause to believe that the child is likely to suffer significant harm if:

(a) he is not removed to accommodation provided by or on behalf of the applicant; or

(b) he does not remain in the place in which he is then being accommodated.

The following points arise under this ground:

(i) In order to satisfy this ground, the court (and not the applicant) must be satisfied that the grounds are met.

(ii) There must be evidence of significant harm (as to the likelihood of significant harm see *Re H and R*[2]). It is suggested that there must also be evidence that is sufficient to justify the removal of the child quickly from his current circumstances.

1 CA 1989, s 44(1)(a).
2 [1996] 1 FLR 80, [1996] 1 All ER 1.

The second ground[1]

8.109 This ground relates to an application by a local authority. On such an application the court may make an emergency protection order if satisfied that:

(a) enquiries are being made with respect to the child under the CA 1989, s 47(1)(b); and

(b) those enquiries are being frustrated by access to the child being unreasonably refused to a person authorised to seek access and that the applicant has reasonable cause to believe that access to the child is required as a matter of urgency.

1 CA 1989, s 44(1)(b).

The third ground[1]

8.110 This ground relates to an application by an authorised person (ie a local authority or the NSPCC as defined by the CA 1989, s 31(9)). The grounds for the making of the order are:

(a) the applicant has reasonable cause to suspect that a child is suffering, or is likely to suffer, significant harm;

(b) the applicant is making enquiries with respect to the child's welfare; and

(c) those enquiries are being frustrated by access to the child being unreasonably refused to a person authorised to seek access and the applicant has reasonable cause to believe that access to the child is required as a matter of urgency.

The Act defines a person authorised to seek access as:

(i) in the case of an application by a local authority, an officer of the local authority or a person authorised by the authority to act on their behalf in connection with the enquiry;

(ii) in the case of an application by an authorised person, that person (the authorised person must produce some evidence of his identity when seeking access)[2].

1 CA 1989, s 44(1)(c).
2 Ibid, s 44(2)(b) and (3).

Effect of an emergency protection order

8.111 The effect of an emergency protection order is as follows:

(a) It operates as a direction to any person who is in a position to do so to comply with any request to produce the child to the applicant[1].

(b) It authorises the removal of the child at any time to accommodation provided by or on behalf of the applicant and his being kept there (in so far as is necessary to safeguard the welfare of the child)[2].

(c) It authorises the prevention of the child's removal from any hospital, or other place, in which the child was being accommodated immediately before the order was made[3], in so far as this is necessary to safeguard the welfare of the child[4].

(d) It gives the applicant parental responsibility for the child, but the applicant may only take such action in meeting his parental responsibility for the child as is reasonably required to safeguard or promote the welfare of the child (having regard to the duration of the order).

1 CA 1989, s 44(4)(a).
2 Ibid, s 44(4)(b)(i) and (5)(a).
3 Ibid, s 44(4)(b)(ii) and (5)(a).
4 Ibid, s 44(4)(c) and (5)(b).

Additional directions with emergency protection order

8.112 Where a court makes an emergency protection order, it may also give directions with respect to:

(a) the contact which the child is or is not to be allowed with any named person; and

(b) the medical or psychiatric examination or other assessment of the child. However, if the child is of sufficient understanding to make an informed decision, the child may refuse to submit to the examination or other assessment[1].

1 CA 1989, s 44(6).

8.113 Subject to any such direction from the court, the applicant for an emergency protection order is under a duty to allow the child reasonable contact with:

(a) his parents;

(b) any person who is not a parent of his but who has parental responsibility for him;

(c) any person with whom he was living immediately before the making of the order;

(d) any person in whose favour a contact order is in force with respect to him;

(e) any person who is allowed to have contact with the child by virtue of an order under s 34; and

(f) any person acting on behalf of any of those persons[1].

Where the court makes a direction in respect of examination or assessment, it may order that there should be no such examination or assessment (or none without the court's prior direction)[2].

1 CA, s 44(13).
2 Ibid, s 44(8).

Return of the child

8.114 Where a child is removed by the applicant from accommodation following the making of an order or is prevented by the applicant from being removed from a hospital or other place, the applicant is under a duty to return the child to the accommodation (or to permit the removal of the child from the hospital or other place) when it appears to the applicant that it is safe for this to be done[1]. However, where the applicant does return the child in these circumstances, he may again exercise his powers with respect to the child at any time whilst the emergency protection order remains in force if it appears to him that a change in the circumstances of the case makes it necessary for him to do so[2].

1 CA 1989, s 44(10) and (11).
2 Ibid, s 44(12).

Duration of emergency protection order

8.115 An emergency protection order shall have effect for no more than eight days, although the order may subsequently be extended for up to seven days (if the court is satisfied that it has reasonable cause to believe that the child is likely to suffer significant harm if the order is not extended)[1]. If the day upon which the order would otherwise end is a public holiday (ie Christmas Day, Good Friday, a bank holiday or a Sunday) the order may specify a period which ends at noon on the first day after the eight day period which is not a public holiday[2]. If the child is in police protection and the police officer applies for an emergency protection order, the eight day period will start from the day that the child was taken into police protection[3].

1 CA 1989, s 45(1), (4) and (6).
2 Ibid, s 45(2).
3 Ibid, s 45(3).

Procedure for emergency protection order

8.116 The application is made on Form C1 together with Form C11[1]. The application is made to the magistrates' court except in circumstances laid down by regulation. The application will often be made ex parte. A copy of the application must be served within 48 days of the making of an order on each party, any person who has actual care of the child and the local authority in whose area the child lives or is found[2] (as well as a parent). If the court refuses the application ex parte it may direct that it should be heard inter partes[3]. The court may take into account any hearsay evidence in a report[4].

1 FP(CA1989)R 1991, Sch 1.
2 See the Children (Allocation of Proceedings) Order 1991.
3 FP(CA1989)R 1991, r 21(8).
4 Ibid, r 4(5).

Discharge of emergency protection order

8.117 An application for the discharge of an emergency protection order may be made by:

(a) the child;

(b) a parent of the child;

(c) any person who is not a parent of the child but who has parental responsibility for him;

(d) any person with whom the child was living immediately before the making of the order[1].

No application for the discharge of an emergency protection order may be heard by the court before the expiry of 72 hours, beginning with the making of the order[2].

1 CA 1989, s 45(8).
2 Ibid, s 45(9).

Appeals

8.118 There is no appeal that may be made against:

(a) the making of, or refusal to make, an emergency protection order;

(b) the extension of, or refusal to extend, the period during which such an order is to have effect;

(c) the discharge of, or refusal to discharge, such an order; or

(d) the giving of, or refusal to give, any direction in connection with such an order[1].

1 CA 1989, s 45(10). See *Essex County Council v F* [1993] 1 FLR 847, [1993] 2 FCR 289.

Discovery of child

8.119 Section 48 of the CA 1989 includes provisions intended to assist in the discovery of children who may be in need of emergency protection. Where it appears to a court making an emergency protection order that adequate information about the child's whereabouts:

(a) is not available to the applicant for the order; but

(b) is available to another person,

it may include in the order a provision requiring that other person to disclose, if asked to do so, by the applicant, any information that he may have as to the child's whereabouts. In addition, an emergency protection order may authorise the applicant to enter premises specified by the order and search for the child with respect to whom the order is made[1].

1 CA 1989, s 48(1) and (3).

Other protective measures

8.120 Under the CA 1989, s 46, where a constable has reasonable cause to believe that a child will be otherwise likely to suffer significant harm, he may:

(a) remove the child to suitable accommodation and keep him there; or

(b) take such steps as are reasonable to ensure that the child's removal from any hospital, or other place, in which he is then being accommodated is prevented.

The section then sets out the duties of the police constable following such action. A child may not be kept in police protection for more than 72 hours[1]. Section 50 includes provisions for the recovery of abducted children[2].

1 CA 1989, s 46(6).
2 Section 50(1) provides that where it appears to the court that there is reason to believe that a child to whom the section applies:
   (a) has been unlawfully taken away or is being unlawfully kept away from the responsible person;
   (b) has run away or is staying away from the responsible person; or
   (c) is missing,
   the court may make a recovery order.

PROHIBITION AGAINST FURTHER APPLICATIONS WITHOUT LEAVE

8.121 Under the CA 1989, s 91(14) it is provided that:

> 'On the disposing of any application for an order under this Act, the court may (whether or not it makes any other order in response to the application) order that no application for an order under this Act of any specified kind may be made with respect to the child concerned by any person named in the order without the leave of the court.'

Such orders should not be made as a run-of-the-mill type of order; they should be used sparingly. They may be appropriate where applications were being made too often or where the other party and the child were suffering harm[1]. Cases where this section have been considered are:

(a) *Berkshire County Council v Y*[2]. In exceptional circumstances it is possible to apply the prohibition contained in this sub-section to future applications for contact to a child in care, despite the fact that the application being disposed of is the first brought by the party to whom the prohibition subsequently applies.

(b) *Re S*[3]. A judge should give a warning that he is considering making an order under this sub-section.

(c) *Re F*[4]. Where a prohibition has been imposed, it may be removed by the court subsequently. In this case the Court of Appeal gave guidance to the approach of removal of a prohibition.

(d) *Re G and M*[5]. In this case a prohibition was imposed because of the harm that was being experienced by the other party and the child and the need for the respondent mother to be protected against the destabilising affect of such applications.

1 *Re F* [1992] 2 FCR 433 and *Re H* [1991] FCR 896. See also *Re G (Child care: Parental involvement)* [1996] 1 FLR 857.
2 [1994] 2 FLR 699.
3 [1994] 2 FLR 1057.
4 [1995] 1 FLR 956, [1996] 1 FCR 81.
5 [1995] 3 FCR 514.

APPEALS

8.122 The Act provides for a statutory right of appeal to the High Court against:

(a) the making by a magistrates' court of any order under the act; or

(b) any refusal by a magistrates' court to make such an order[1].

On an appeal the High Court may make any order as may be necessary to give effect to its determination of the appeal and may make such incidental or consequential orders as appear to it to be just². The procedure in respect of such appeals is laid down in the FPR 1991, r 4.22 (as supplemented by RSC Ord 55). The procedure is further developed in a *Practice Direction*³. That Practice Direction states that:

(i) Such appeals should be commenced by filing the documents referred to in r 4.22(2) in the Registry which is also a care centre, nearest to the court in which the order appealed from was made.

(ii) The appeal will be heard and determined by a High Court judge of the Family Division who will normally sit in open court.

(iii) The hearing will take place as directed at the nearest convenient High Court centre. The procedure in respect of appeals is again further dealt with in the Administrative Direction⁴.

1 CA 1989, s 94(1).
2 Ibid, s 94(4) and (5).
3 [1992] 1 FLR 463, [1992] 1 FCR 432.
4 [1992] 2 FLR 503, [1992] 2 FCR 601.

Principles governing an appeal

8.123 The principles in *G v G*¹ should broadly apply to appeals under s 94². Those principles, in summary, are that an appellate court reviewing the decision of a judge in the exercise of his discretion is bound by the principle that before it could intervene, it had to be satisfied, not merely that the judge had made a decision with which the appeal court might reasonably disagree, but that his decision was so plainly wrong that the only legitimate conclusion was that he had erred in the exercise of his discretion³. These principles have to be borne very much in mind before an appeal is attempted. Hopeless appeals may result in orders for costs or wasted costs orders⁴.

1 [1985] 2 All ER 225, [1985] 1 WLR 647, [1985] FLR 894.
2 *Re M (Section 94 Appeals)* [1995] 1 FLR 546.
3 See *Re M* at 548F.
4 See *Re N* [1995] 2 FLR 230.

The time for an appeal

8.124 The time for an appeal under s 94 is specified in the FPR 1991, r 4.22(3). The time for an appeal is:

(a) 14 days after the determination against which the appeal is brought, or

(b) in the case of an appeal against an interim care or supervision order under the CA 1989, s 38(1), within seven days after the making of the order, or

(c) with the leave of the court to which, or the judge to whom, the appeal is to be brought, within such other time as that court or judge may direct.

Case law concerning appeals

8.125 The following cases have been reported concerning the appeal provisions:

(a) *R v Oxfordshire County Council*[1]. Where there is an appeal from a decision of the Family Proceedings Court in a secure accommodation order case (or in any other urgent case) it is the duty of the appellant's solicitor to make the district registry aware of the need for urgency and to invite the district registry or the district judge to list the matter at the nearest court where an early hearing can take place before a High Court judge.

(b) *Re W and S*[2]. It is essential that all documentation, including the notes of evidence in respect of an appeal, should be provided in legible typescript.

(c) *Essex County Council v B*[3]. It is no part of the function of the district judge to engage himself in some sort of vetting procedure, only allowing those appeals from magistrates to proceed which he thinks are worthwhile. It is the duty of the district judge to arrange for a hearing before a High Court judge, either at the nearest High Court centre or, if time does not permit, at the Royal Courts of Justice or some other convenient centre. The district judge has power under the FPR 1991[4] only when application is made to him.

(d) *Re U (T) (a minor)*[5]. On an appeal from magistrates, the documents which should be filed and served under the FPR 1991, r 4.22(2), should include the statements which form the basis of the evidence of witnesses together with any reports including the report of the guardian ad litem.

(e) *Re M*[6]. It is inappropriate to appeal interim orders unless the situation provided by the interim order is intolerable.

1 [1992] 1 FLR 648.
2 [1992] 2 FCR 665.
3 [1993] 1 FLR 866, [1993] 1 FCR 145.
4 The district judge has powers under the FPR 1991, r 4.22(7) to:
   (a) permit the withdrawal of the appeal,
   (b) have the appeal dismissed with the consent of all the parties, or
   (c) give leave for the grounds of appeal to be amended.
5 [1993] 2 FCR 565.
6 [1992] 1 FCR 313.

PRACTICE AND PROCEDURE

Introduction

8.126 The main procedural provisions relating to the CA 1989 are found in the FPR 1991 (for the High Court and county court)[1] and in the FP(CA 1989)R 1991[2].

1 SI 1991/1247.
2 SI 1991/1395.

Family Proceedings Rules 1991

8.127 The main provisions relating to procedure under the CA 1989 are found in Part IV of those Rules. The Rules cover the following provisions:

Rule 4.1:	Interpretation and application of the Rules.
Rule 4.2:	Prescribed matters for the purposes of the Act.
Rule 4.3:	Applications for leave to commence proceedings.
Rule 4.4:	The method by which applications are to be made.
Rule 4.5:	Withdrawal of application.
Rule 4.6:	The transfer of applications between courts.
Rule 4.7:	The parties to proceedings.
Rule 4.8:	Service of documents.
Rule 4.9:	Acknowledgment of application.
Rule 4.10:	The appointment of guardians ad litem in specified proceedings.
Rule 4.11:	The powers and duties of the guardian ad litem.
Rule 4.12:	The solicitor for the child.
Rule 4.13:	The welfare officer.
Rule 4.14:	Directions.
Rule 4.15:	Timing of proceedings.
Rule 4.16:	Attendance at directions appointments and hearing.
Rule 4.17:	Documentary evidence.
Rule 4.18:	Expert evidence – examination of child.
Rule 4.19:	Amendment of documents.
Rule 4.20:	Oral evidence.
Rule 4.21:	The hearing.
Rule 4.21A:	The attachment of a penal notice to a section 8 order.
Rule 4.22:	Appeals.
Rule 4.23:	The confidentiality of documents.
Rule 4.24:	Notification of consent.
Rule 4.25:	Secure accommodation – evidence.
Rule 4.26:	Investigations under s 37.
Rule 4.27:	Direction to a local education authority to apply for an education supervision order.
Rule 4.28:	Transitional provisions.

Family Proceedings Courts (Children Act 1989) Rules 1991

8.128 These Rules follow the same format and numbering as the FPR 1991 (save for the omission of the first '4') up to r 21 (which relates to hearings).

The allocation of proceedings

8.129 The allocation of proceedings under the CA 1989 is dealt with in the Children (Allocation of Proceedings) Order 1991[1].

1 SI 1991/1677.

Case management

8.130 At the beginning of 1995 the President of the Family Division published a Practice Direction setting out the method by which greater court control over cases would be exercised. The Practice Direction[1] can be summarised thus:

(a) Failure by practitioners to conduct cases economically will be visited by appropriate orders for costs, including wasted costs orders.

(b) The court will limit discovery, the length of opening and closing oral submissions, the time allowed for the examination and cross-examination of witnesses, the issues on which it wishes to be addressed, the reading aloud of documents and authorities.

(c) Unless otherwise ordered, every witness statement or affidavit will stand as evidence in chief of the witness concerned. The statements should contain the witness's evidence without prolixity. The statement must be confined to material matters of fact and not (except in the case of evidence of professional witnesses) of opinion. If hearsay evidence is to be adduced, the source of the information must be declared or a good reason given for not doing so.

(d) The duty of full and frank disclosure should be observed in Children Act cases both by the parties and by their legal representatives.

(e) The parties and their advisers must use their best endeavours to confine the issues and the evidence called to what is reasonably considered to be essential for the proper presentation of their cases, to reduce or eliminate issues for expert evidence and to agree which of the issues are the main issues (in advance of the hearing). A bundle should be agreed and prepared for use by the court and should be in A4 format where possible and suitably secured. The bundle should be lodged with the clerk at least two clear days before the hearing. Bundles must be paginated, indexed and wholly legible. They should be arranged chronologically.

(f) In cases estimated to last for five days or more and in which no pre-trial review has been ordered, an application should be made for a pre-trial review. The pre-trial review should be listed at least three weeks before the hearing and be conducted by the judge or district judge before whom the case is to be heard. The pre-trial review should be attended by the advocates who are to represent the parties at the hearing. Whenever possible, statements of evidence and all reports should be filed before the date of the review and in good time for them to be considered by all the parties.

(g) Whenever practicable and in any matter estimated to last five days or more, the parties should lodge chronologies and skeleton arguments not less than two clear days before the hearing. Skeleton arguments should be brief.

(h) In advance of the hearing, upon request, or otherwise in the course of the opening, parties should be prepared to furnish the court, if there is no core bundle, with a list of documents essential for a proper understanding of the case.

(i) The opening speech should be succinct. At its conclusion, the parties may be invited briefly to amplify those skeleton arguments. In a heavy case, the court may in conjunction with final speeches require written submissions, including the findings of fact for which each party contends.

1 [1995] 1 FLR 456.

Time estimates

8.131 The court has given guidance on the preparation of time estimates. Where any hearing is expected to last one day or more, the parties should give a written time estimate. It should be signed by the solicitor and by counsel, if instructed. A suitable form is available from the court. If the parties' time estimate changes, the court must be notified[1]. The time estimate must include judicial reading time and time for the delivery of a temporary judgment[2]. There is no good reason why the approach of Sedley J in *Vernon v Bosley (No 2)*[3] should not be adopted in Children Act proceedings (part of that process will involve a direction that an expert attend on a given date for a period of x hours and that the time for examination, cross-examination and re-examination be defined).

1 *Practice Direction* [1994] 1 FLR 108.
2 *Re MD and TD* [1994] 2 FLR 336, [1994] 2 FCR 94; See also *Re JC* [1995] 2 FLR 77.
3 [1995] 2 FLR 78 (and see *Re T and E* [1995] 1 FLR 581).

Experts

8.132 Considerable guidance has been given by the court for the use of experts in proceedings under the CA 1989[1]. The full extent of that guidance is not set out her; however, some of the main points are:

(a) Experts should be fully instructed. The letter of instruction should always set out the context in which the expert's opinion is sought and should define carefully the specific questions the expert is being asked to address.

(b) The expert's letter of instruction should be disclosed to the other parties. Experts should always be invited to confer with each other before the trial in an attempt to reach agreement or limit the issues.

(c) Generalised orders giving leave for the papers to be shown to 'an expert' should never be made. In each case the expert or area of expertise should be identified.

(d) If the medical evidence points overwhelmingly to non-accidental injury, an expert who advises the parents and the court that the injury had an alternative and innocent causation has a very duty upon him to ensure that he has considered carefully all the available material. Experts should normally give an opinion upon each set of competing facts.

(e) The expert reports should be collated by a co-ordinator and a schedule should be prepared for the court.

(f) For the right of an expert to give evidence on the 'ultimate issue' before the court see *Re M and R (Child Abuse: Evidence)*[2].

1 *Re DH (A Minor – Child Abuse)* [1994] 1 FLR 679; *Re M (Minors – Care Proceedings – Child's Wishes)* [1994] 1 FLR 749; *Oxfordshire County Council v M* [1994] 1 FLR 175; *Re G* [1994] 2 FCR 106; *Re AB (A Minor – Medical Issues Expert Evidence)* [1995] 1 FLR 181; *Re C (Expert Evidence – Disclosure Practice)* [1995] 1 FLR 204; *Re CS (Expert Witnesses)* [1996] 2 FLR 115; *Re B (Care: Expert Witnesses)* [1996] 1 FLR 667.
2 [1996] 2 FLR 195

Justices' reasons

8.133 Justices are required to state their reasons for making orders. There are certain minimum findings and reasons which must be stated so that the parties in the appellate court can see how the justices have approached their task[1]. The court of first instance cannot communicate with the appellate court in order to improve the reasons given[2]. If justices fail to express their reasons adequately, their decision will be regarded as unsafe and incapable of being relied upon (and therefore may be set aside on appeal, depending upon the facts of the given case)[3].

1 *R v Oxfordshire County Council* [1992] 3 All ER 660, [1992] 1 FLR 648.
2 *N v B* [1993] 1 FCR 231, reported as *Re WB* [1995] 2 FLR 1023.
3 *Re W (A Minor Contact)* [1994] 1 FLR 843 and *W v Hertfordshire County Council* [1993] 1 FLR 118.

Chapter Nine

Children and Judicial Review

Judith Hughes

Duties of the Local Authority to Children in their Area 331
Judicial Review 341

DUTIES OF THE LOCAL AUTHORITY TO CHILDREN IN THEIR AREA

Introduction

9.1 It is the duty of every local authority to safeguard and promote the welfare of children within their area who are in need and to promote the upbringing of such children by their families so far as is consistent with that duty by providing a range and level of services appropriate to those children's needs including providing for any member of his family[1]. Assistance may be in kind or, in exceptional circumstances, in cash. Assistance may be unconditional or subject to conditions as to the repayment for the assistance but before giving assistance or imposing any conditions the local authority should have regard to the means of the child concerned and each of his parents[2].

1 CA 1989, s 17(1).
2 Ibid, s 17(6)(7) and (8).

A child in need defined

9.2 A child is to be taken to be in need if:

(a) he is unlikely to achieve or maintain, or to have the opportunity of achieving or maintaining, a reasonable standard of health or development without the provision for him of services by a local authority under this Part;

(b) his health or development is likely to be significantly impaired or further impaired without the provision for him of such services; or

(c) he is disabled[1];

and family in relation to such a child, includes any person who has parental responsibility for the child and any other person with whom he has been living[2].

1 'Disabled' is defined by the CA 1989, s 17(11) as 'blind, deaf or dumb or suffering from mental disorder of any kind or is substantially and permanently handicapped by illness, injury or congenital deformity or such other disability as may be prescribed'. 'Development' means physical, intellectual, emotional, social or behavioural developments; 'health' means physical or mental health.
2 CA 1989, s 17(10). This does not extend to a relative to whom the child is close but with whom the child is not living.

9.3 The local authority has to maintain a Register of Disability which may be kept by means of a computer[1]. The needs of the child have to be assessed by the local authority and this may be done at the same time as other statutory assessments are carried out[2].

1 CA 1989, Sch 2, Part I, para 2.
2 Ibid, Sch 2, Part I, para 3.

What services must the local authority provide?

For children living with their families

9.4 With respect to children in need[1] living with their families the local authority should provide (as they consider appropriate) advice, guidance and counselling; occupational, social, cultural or recreational activities; home help (including laundry facilities); facilities for or assistance with travelling from home to take advantage of any of the provisions and assistance to enable the child concerned and his family to have a holiday[2]. Facilities provided may include family centres[3], such day care for children under five in need in their area as appropriate either through a placement in a local authority day nursery or by the local authority providing a private day nursery place or paying for the services of a child minder[4]. The local authority must keep a register of child minders[5]. It must provide care outside school hours or during school holidays[6]. It must review the provision of day care which it makes for the under eights together with the extent to which there are services available in the locality of childminders and day nurseries once within 12 months of the implementation of the Act and then once every three years[7]. The local authority shall make such use of services available for children cared for by their own parents as appears to it reasonable in his case[8].

1 See para 9.2.
2 CA 1989, Sch 2, Part I, para 8.
3 Ibid, Sch 2, Part I, para 9.
4 Ibid, s 18.
5 Ibid, s 71; a childminder is defined as a person who looks after two or more children under the age of eight for more than two hours per day.
6 CA 1989, s 18(5).
7 Ibid, s 19(5).
8 Ibid, s 22(3)(b).

9.5 Some local authorities may be able to provide every service its children in need require itself but others do not have the resources to do so. Provision is accordingly made in the CA 1989 for a local authority to seek the help of another local authority[1], education authority, local housing authority, health authority or National Health Service Trust or any person authorised by the Secretary of State for the purposes of the section[2]. The authority whose help is so requested should comply with the request if compatible with their own statutory or other duties and obligations and does not unduly prejudice the discharge of any of their functions[3].

1 Help is only likely to be provided by another local authority in the unlikely event of there being sufficient resources: CA 1989, s 27(2).
2 CA 1989, s 27(1) and (3).
3 Ibid, s 27(2).

For children looked after by local authorities

9.6 The local authority must offer accommodation to every child in need in their area who appears to require accommodation either as a result of no-one having parental responsibility for him; his being lost or having been abandoned or because the person who has been caring for him is being prevented (whether or not permanently, and for whatever reason) from providing him with suitable accommodation or care[1]. This was voluntary and not intended to be a backdoor route into care[2]. A child who is accommodated under this provision of the CA 1989 is described as an accommodated child[3].

1 CA 1989, s 20(1)(a)–(c).
2 Ibid, s 20(8).
3 Ibid, s 22.

9.7 The local authority must provide accommodation for any child in need within their area who has reached 16 and whose welfare the authority consider is likely to be seriously prejudiced if they do not provide him with accommodation. The local authority may also provide accommodation for a person between the ages of 16 and 21 if they consider that would safeguard or promote his welfare[1]. Where a local authority is looking after a child it must safeguard and promote its welfare[2]. When a local authority is trying to determine where a child accommodated by them or who is in their care is to live, then the local authority may provide accommodation and maintenance for any child by placing them in one of a wide range of living situations including a family, a relative of his, any other suitable person, or in a community, voluntary, or registered children's home or by making such other arrangements as appear appropriate to them[3]. It must also provide alternative accommodation to that where the child may be living if necessary[4] and that accommodation can either be with his family, a relative or other suitable person or by maintaining him in a community home, a voluntary home, a children's home or by such other arrangements as seem appropriate to them. The local authority can provide for his maintenance as appropriate[5]. The local authority should also provide advice, assistance and befriending to a child living in its accommodation with a view to promoting the child's welfare when the local authority ceases to look after him[6]. The local authority can provide funds to enable him to continue his education or training and can continue to provide this even when the young person attains the age of 21 before completing his course[7].

1 CA 1989, s 20(5).
2 Ibid, s 22(3)(a).
3 Ibid, s 23(2)(a).
4 Ibid, ss 20 and 21 and Sch 2, Part I, para 5.
5 Ibid, s 23.
6 Ibid, s 24.
7 Ibid, s 24 (8) and (9).

Placement of children

9.8 Where a child is placed with a family, a relative or other person considered suitable by the local authority it will be on such terms as to payment and otherwise as the authority may decide[1]. Where a child is so placed, the person(s) with whom he lives will be deemed to be a 'local authority foster parent'[2] unless he is a parent, has parental responsibility or where the child is in care under a care order and he is living with the person in whose favour there is a residence order in force[3]. By reason of s 23(6) of the CA 1989 the local authority should first try to place the child with his parents or a relative before seeking a placement outside the family. That person may be paid at the discretion of the local authority[4]. If the child is to be placed with a foster family it should be one near his home and, if he is to be placed with a sibling, in a home where they can be accommodated together[5]. All foster placements are subject to regulations which have been made by the Secretary of State[6]. The regulations provide for records of the placement to be kept, visits to the foster home to be made by representatives of the local authority and for agreements with the parents of the child, if practicable, to provide for the type of accommodation available for the child, the name of the person responsible for the child in the local authority, the number of visits of the parents, the services to be provided by the local authority to the child, the duration of the arrangement and so forth. Matters which have to be agreed with the foster parents include provision as to support and training, procedure for review of approval of a foster parent and the respective obligations of the local authority and its foster parents. The foster parents must undertake to keep the local authority informed if the child becomes ill when in their care and must, for example, not administer corporal punishment to them.

1 CA 1989, s 23(2)(a).
2 Ibid, s 23(3).
3 Ibid, s 23(4).
4 Ibid, Sch 1, para 15.
5 Ibid, s 23(7)(a).
6 The Arrangements for Placement of Children (General) Regulations 1991 and the Foster Placement (Children) Regulations 1991.

Foster parents seeking residence orders

9.9 A foster parent can apply for a residence order of a child under s 8 of the CA 1989 if a child has been living with them for more than three years[1] and may do so where the child has resided with them for less than three years with the leave of the local authority[2]. Where the local authority is refusing to give such leave the only course would be to encourage a child to apply for a residence order under ss 8 and 10 of the Act. Where a foster parent obtains a residence order there is a discretion in the local authority to pay a residence order allowance[3].

1 CA 1989, s 9(3)(c).
2 Ibid, s 9(3)(a).
3 Ibid, Sch 1, para 15.

Children residing in children's homes

9.10 A local authority caring for a child may provide for his accommodation and maintenance by placing him in a community home[1]. Every authority has the duty to maintain community homes and ensure that they are available for the care of children looked after by them[2]. The community home may be run by the local authority or by a voluntary organisation[3]. A voluntary organisation has the same duty to a child living in its home while he is living there and to advise, assist and befriend him with a view to promoting his welfare when he ceases to be so accommodated[4].

1 CA 1989, s 23(2)(b).
2 Ibid, s 53.
3 Ibid, s 53(4).
4 Ibid, s 61(1).

Appointment of an independent visitor

9.11 Where a local authority is caring for a child who has not been visited by any parent or person with parental responsibility within the previous 12 months or the child only has infrequent communication with that person, the authority is required to appoint an independent visitor if that is in the child's best interests[1]. The visitor should visit, advise and befriend the child. He may claim his expenses from the local authority[2]. The appointment may be terminated if the visitor notifies the local authority of his wish to resign or it is terminated by the local authority or the child, having sufficient understanding, objects to the appointment[3].

1 CA 1989, Sch 2, Part II.
2 Ibid, Sch 2, para 17(2).
3 Ibid, Sch 2, para 17(5).

Secure accommodation

9.12 A local authority has to provide secure accommodation which is accommodation provided for the purpose of restricting liberty[1]. There are criteria which must be met, namely that the child:

(a) has a history of absconding and is likely to abscond from any other description of accommodation; and if he absconds, he is likely to suffer significant harm; or

(b) if he is kept in any other description of accommodation he is likely to injure himself or other persons[2].

A child may be detained in secure accommodation for up to 72 hours, whether consecutive or not within a period of 28 consecutive days[3]. Where the period is likely to exceed 72 hours then the local authority or health authority or other relevant holding body[4] must seek the authority of the court[5]. The court must determine whether any relevant criteria for keeping the child in secure accommodation are satisfied in the case of the child and, if so, it must specify the maximum period for which he may be so kept[6]. The order runs from the date when it is made and not the date when the child is actually placed in secure accommodation[7]. No court should make a decision without the child being represented unless the child, having been informed of his right to apply for legal aid and having had the opportunity to do so, has refused or failed to apply[8]. If the child whose liberty it is sought to restrict is under the age of 13 it would seem that the case should be discussed with the Social Services Inspectorate and thereafter a formal written submission should be made to the Secretary of State setting out the reasons why secure accommodation is considered the only way of dealing with the child[9].

1 CA 1989, s 25(1).
2 Ibid, s 25(1)(a) and (b).
3 Ibid, s 25(2)(a) and the Children (Secure Accommodation) Regulations 1991, reg 10.
4 Children (Secure Accommodation) Regulations 1991, reg 7(3)(a) and (b) and the Children (Secure Accommodation) (No 2) Regulations 1991, reg 2.
5 CA 1989, s 25(2).
6 See ibid, s 25(3) and (4). Under the Children (Secure Accommodation) Regulations 1991 the maximum initial period is three months (reg 11) and a court may order a further period not exceeding six months (reg 12) at any one time.
7 *Re B (A Minor) (Secure Accommodation)* [1994] 2 FLR 707.
8 CA 1989, s 25(6); it is not necessary for the child to be present at court. See *Re W (Secure Accommodation Order: Attendance at Court)* [1994] 2 FLR 1092.
9 *The Children Act 1989 Guidance and Regulations* 1991, (HMSO) vol 4.

Reviews

9.13 All children who are being looked after by a local authority must have their situations reviewed pursuant to regulations laid down under the CA 1989. The first review must be within four weeks of the date the children first start to be looked after by the local authority and the second review no more than three months after the first. Subsequent reviews are to be carried out not more than six months after the date of the previous review[1]. There must be written arrangements governing the manner in which each child's case will be reviewed and these must be drawn to the attention of the child, his parents, and anyone with parental responsibility or whose views the local authority consider to be relevant[2]. When conducting the review the local authority must consider a range of issues as set out in the regulations[3]. The local authority is also required under the review procedure to explain to the child any steps which the child may take under the Act including his right to apply with leave for a section 8 order, his right when he is in care to apply for the discharge of the care order and the availability of the procedure established under the Act for considering representations[4].

1 Review of Children's Cases Regulations 1991 (as amended by the Children (Representations, Placements and Reviews) (Miscellaneous Amendments) Regulations 1991).
2 Review of Childrens' Cases Regulations 1991, regs 4(1), 7.
3 Review of Children's Cases Regulations 1991, reg 5 and Sch 2.
4 CA 1989, Sch 1, para 5(a)(c).

Review of case where child in secure accommodation

9.14 In addition to the duties for review of the case of each child being looked after by the local authority, in respect of each child who is in secure accommodation the local authority must establish a review panel and must appoint three people, at least one of whom must not be employed by the local authority, who shall review the keeping of the child in secure accommodation[1]. Consideration must be given to whether the criteria continue to apply and whether there is any other accommodation for the child which would be more appropriate[2]. Records must be kept relating to important details of children in secure accommodation pursuant to the Act[3].

1 Children (Secure Accommodation) Regulations 1991, regs 15 and 16.
2 Ibid, r 16(1).
3 Ibid, r 17.

Representations

9.15 There is a procedure laid down in the CA 1989 for representations (including complaints) to be made by any child who is being looked after by them or not being looked after by them but is in need, or a parent of his, or by any person who is not a parent but who has parental responsibility for him, or by local authority foster parents or any other person whom the local authority consider has sufficient interest in the child's welfare to warrant his representations being considered by them about the discharge by the authority of their functions under Part III of the Act[1]. The procedure shall ensure that at least one person who is not a member or officer of the authority takes part in the consideration and any discussions which are held by the authority about the action (if any) to be taken in relation to the child in the light of the consideration². Where any representation has been considered under the procedure established by a local authority under this section, the authority shall (a) have due regard to the findings of those considering the representation and (b) take such steps as are reasonably practicable to notify in writing the person making the representation, the child (if the authority considers he has sufficient understanding), and such other persons, if any, as appear to the authority to be likely to be affected, of the authority's decision in the matter and the reasons for taking that decision and of any action which they have taken or propose to take³. Where any complainant remains dissatisfied as a result of the determination he has the right to have a panel convened which must have one independent member who may be the same independent member as was earlier involved in the decision⁴. They must consider taking action against the local authority possibly for breach of statutory duty or for judicial review.

1 CA 1989, s 26(3).
2 Ibid, s 26(4).
3 Ibid, s 26(7).
4 Representations Procedure (Children) Regulations, 1991, reg 8.

Education

9.16 It is beyond the scope of this book to give other than a broad outline about the obligation of the local authority to provide educational facilities for children in its area and the remedies for dissatisfied parents or those with parental responsibility for a child[1]; and since these paragraphs went to press, the Education Act 1996 has come into force (1 November 1996). The statutory system of education in England and Wales was established by the Education Act 1944. The Education Acts 1944 to 1988 provide for compulsory education for all children aged 5 to 16 in primary and secondary education in maintained schools[2]. The Education Act 1981 requires the Secretary of State for Education and Science to promote the education of the people of England and Wales and to secure the effective execution by local authorities, under his control and direction, of a varied and comprehensive education service in every area[3]. It is the duty of the local authority to contribute towards the spiritual, moral, mental and physical development of the community by securing efficient education throughout the primary, secondary and further education[4]. Clearly local authorities have many duties including inter alia maintaining schools, arranging transport, co-operating with parents to enable them to express a preference as to which of the schools their child attends and to enforce school attendance. The governors of a school maintained by the local education authority are in partnership with the Secretary of State, the local authority and the parents in carrying out the national policy for education. The parents have a duty to cause their child to receive efficient full-time education suitable to his ability, age and aptitude and to any special educational needs he may have by regular attendance at school or otherwise[5]. Parental wishes as to the school the child should attend and what he is to be taught there should prevail in so far as the same is in accordance with provision of sensible instruction and prudential public spending[6].

1 A 'child' for the purposes of the Education Act 1981 includes any person who has not attained the age of 19 years and is registered as a pupil at a school: see the Education Act 1981, s 20(1).
2 A maintained school means any grant maintained school, any county or voluntary school and any maintained special school which is not in a hospital.
3 Education Act 1944, s 1 as amended by the Secretary of State for Education and Science Order 1964.
4 Ibid.
5 Ibid.
6 Ibid, s 76.

Appeals

9.17 Every local authority must make arrangements for parents to appeal their decision as to the school at which education is to be provided for their child and any decision made by or behalf of governors refusing to admit a child to a county[1], controlled or special agreement school[2]. In the case of the first two the appeal is to an appeal committee of either three, five or seven members appointed by the authority and in the case of special agreement schools is to an odd numbered appeal committee of between three and seven members nominated by the governors from among persons appointed by the governors[3]. Local authorities must also make arrangements for appeals to be made against decisions excluding pupils from schools in the authority and allowing any governing body of such a school to appeal against the direction of the local authority to reinstate any pupil who had been previously excluded. The appeals are to an appeal committee[4]. The decision of an appeal committee on any such appeal is binding on the persons concerned. Where the appeal committee decides that the pupil should be reinstated it must direct either that he be reinstated immediately or that he be reinstated by such date as is specified in the direction[5]. There is also provision in the Education Acts for appeals to be made in respect of children with special educational needs[6].

1 A primary or secondary school established and maintained by an education authority or former education authority: see the Education Act 1944, s 9(2).
2 A voluntary school which the Secretary of State has directed to be a 'controlled school' see the Education Act 1944, s 15.
3 Education Act 1980, s 7(4) and Sch 2, Part I.
4 Ibid, s 7(4), Sch 2, Part I and the Education (No 2) Act 1986, Sch 3.
5 Education (No 2) Act 1986, s 26(5).
6 Education Act 1981 and the Education Act 1980, Sch 2, Part I.

A child with 'special needs'

9.18 Where a local authority considers that a child for whom they are responsible has, or probably has, special education needs[1] which call for the authority to determine the special educational provision which should be made for him, the authority must make an assessment of his needs[2]. Before making such assessment the authority must serve notice on the child's parents informing them (a) of their intention to make such an assessment and the reasons for their decision; (b) of the procedure to be followed in making it; (c) of the name of the officer of the authority from whom further information may be obtained; and (d) of the parents' right to make representations and submit written evidence within such period (not less than 29 days from the service of the notice) as may be specified in the notice[3]. The authority must then, having considered any such representations, assess the educational needs of the child concerned[4]. For the purposes of making an assessment, an educational authority is required to seek, and take account of educational, medical and psychological advice from prescribed persons[5] subject to an exception in respect of a child who has moved from one authority to another and in respect of whom an assessment has been made in the last three years[6]. If the child is under the age of two years the local authority may make an assessment to determine the special educational provision that should be made for him if the parents consent. If the parents of such a child request such assessment, the local authority should make one[7].

1 A child has special educational needs if he has a learning difficulty which calls for special educational provision to be made for him: Education Act 1989, s 1(1). A child has a 'learning difficulty' if (1) he has a significantly greater difficulty in learning than the majority of children of his age or (2) if he has a disability which either prevents or hinders him from making use of educational facilities of a kind generally provided in schools for children of his age or (3) he is under five and likely to fall within (1) and (2) above when over that age: Education Act 1981, s 1(2).
2 Education Act 1981, s 5(1). An exception is when the local education authority concludes it is not necessary to make an assessment when the High Court in wardship has decided what educational provision should be made for the child. See *Re D (A Minor)* [1987] 3 All ER 717, [1987] 1 WLR 1400.
3 Education Act 1981, s 5(3).
4 Ibid, s 5(4).
5 Education (Special Educational Needs) Regulations 1994, regs 6–9.
6 Ibid, r 12.
7 Education Act 1981, s 6(1).

9.19 If the authority decides, after assessment, that they are not required to determine the special educational provision that should be made for the child, the parent has the right to appeal in writing to the Secretary of State[1] and the authority must inform the parent of that right[2]. On any such appeal the Secretary of State may, if he thinks fit, direct the authority to reconsider that decision[3].

1 Education Act 1981, s 5(6).
2 Ibid, s 5(7).
3 Ibid, s 5(8).

Statement of special needs

9.20 Where a child's special educational needs have been assessed and the local authority considers that they should determine the special education provision that should be made for him, they must make and maintain a statement[1] of the child's special educational needs. Before doing so they must serve the proposed statement on the parent and also a written explanation of the procedure for making representations[2] about the statement and for attending meetings to discuss the statement with the local authority[3]. The local authority is not obliged to make a statement where, following an assessment it concludes that the special educational needs of the child are being met satisfactorily[4].

1 Education (Special Educational Needs) Regulations 1994, reg 10 which sets out the contents required to be included therein.
2 Education Act 1981, s 7.
3 Ibid, s 7(6).
4 *R v Secretary of State for Education and Science, ex p Lashford* (1988) 86 LGR 13, [1988] 1 FLR 72, CA per Nicholls LJ.

Appeals against special education needs

9.21 Every local education authority must make arrangements to enable the parent of a child for whom they maintain a statement to appeal against the specialist education provision in the statement[1]. Such an appeal is to an appeal committee[2] which can confirm the special provision[3] or remit the case to the authority for reconsideration in the light of their observations[4]. Where the case is remitted to the local authority they must reconsider it and must inform the appellant in writing of their decision[5]. In a case where an appeal committee confirms the decision the appellant may appeal to the Secretary of State[6]. In those cases where an appeal is made the Secretary of State may, after consulting the local education authority concerned (a) confirm the special educational provision in the statement, (b) amend the statement in so far as it deals with provision of education and make such other consequential amendments to the statement as he considers appropriate or (c) direct the local education authority to cease to maintain the statement[7].

1 Education Act 1981, s 8(7).
2 Constituted in accordance with the Education Act 1980, s 7(4), Sch 2, Part I; Education Act 1981, s 8(2).
3 Education Act 1981, s 8(4)(a).
4 Ibid, s 8(4)(b).
5 Ibid, s 8(5).
6 Ibid, s 8(6).
7 Ibid, s 8(7).

JUDICIAL REVIEW

What is judicial review?

9.22 Judicial review replaced the former prerogative remedies of certiorari, mandamus and prohibition in 1977. The changes were originally made on the recommendation of the Law Commission by changes to RSC Ord 53. Later the Supreme Court Act 1981 gave statutory backing to these changes[1]. Judicial review can lie only if there is an enforceable right or duty and can only operate if there is a decision to review. The purpose of judicial review has been said to be to:

'ensure that the individual is given fair treatment by the authority ... it is no part of that purpose to substitute the opinion of the judiciary or individual judges ... the function of the court is to see that lawful authority is not abused by unfair treatment and not to attempt itself the task entrusted to that authority by the law[2]'.

1 Supreme Court Act 1981, s 31.
2 *Chief Constable of the North Wales Police v Evans* [1982] 1 WLR 1155 per Hailsham LC at 1160.

The procedure

9.23 The procedure which has to be followed is clearly set out in the Supreme Court Practice[1]. An application may not be made unless leave of the court has been obtained[2]. The reason that leave is required is that the court will wish to ensure that the applicant has sufficient standing to commence the application and the case has some prospect of success. An application for leave must be made ex parte to the judge by filing in the Crown Office a notice in Form 86A and an affidavit which verifies the fact relied on or by seeking an oral hearing on Form 86A. The judge may deal with the application on the papers[3]. In the event leave is refused, the applicant may seek leave in open court from the single judge[4]. Where leave is refused by the single judge it may be renewed by applying in any criminal cause or matter to a Divisional Court of the Queen's Bench Division and in any other case to a single judge sitting in open court, provided that no application for leave may be renewed in any non-criminal cause or matter in which the judge has refused leave after a hearing[5]. The hearing of the renewed leave to appeal will be heard ex parte unless the court otherwise directs. The court may allow an applicant hearing an application for leave to amend his statement, whether by specifying different or additional grounds or relief or otherwise on such terms as the court things fit[6]. It is not possible to appeal against the refusal of leave where renewal of the application is permitted[7]. If the renewed application is refused by a single judge in open court or a Divisional Court then, in a civil case, the applicant can renew the application to move for judicial review before the Court of Appeal by an application lodged with the Civil Appeals Office within seven days of the refusal from the Court of Appeal. Where leave is granted then if the relief sought is an order of prohibition or certiorari and the court so directs, the grant of leave operates as a stay of the proceedings to which the application relates. Generally, cases in which judicial review is sought are heard in the Queen's Bench Division but it is quite possible to request in the application that they should be heard by a judge of the Family Division[8].

1 RSC Ord 53. The notes to Ord 53 contain a very helpful introduction to the whole subject.
2 RSC Ord 53, r 3.
3 Ibid.
4 Ibid.
5 Ibid, r 3(4).
6 Ibid, r 3(6).
7 Ibid, r 13.
8 Ibid, r 7.

Who may apply?

9.24 Any person with a 'sufficient interest in the matter to which the application relates' may apply for judicial review[1]. However if there is an alternative relief to be obtained by way of appeal the courts will only exceptionally grant the applicant relief by way of judicial review[2]. If the applicant has a direct personal interest in the relief which he is seeking he may well be considered to have sufficient interest in the application to which the matter relates. If, however, his interest is general or public it will be a question for the determination of the court whether his interest is sufficient to enable him to proceed. Even if leave is granted on an ex parte basis it is open to the court on a subsequent inter partes hearing to reconsider the standing of the applicant[3].

1 Supreme Court Act 1981, s 31(3) and RSC Ord 53, r 3(7).
2 See eg *R v Chief Constable of Merseyside Police, ex p Calveley* [1986] QB 424, [1986] 1 All ER 257 where it was held there were exceptional circumstances to allow judicial review to five police officers who had been disciplined at a disciplinary hearing and who had not exhausted the remedies available under the Police Act 1964 but where there had been an abuse of the process which had prejudiced the officers and justified the grant of judicial review.
3 See, eg *R v Secretary of State for the Home Department, ex p Rukshanda Begum* [1990] COD 107, CA.

Against whom can judicial review proceedings be brought?

9.25 Judicial review enables the High Court to exercise its supervisory jurisdiction to review the validity and legality of the decisions of all inferior courts, which in practice means the magistrates' and county courts hearing public law cases, tribunals or other persons or bodies exercising administrative powers whether of a legislative, executory, judicial or adjudicatory character. It is not an appeal system. It was used successfully to review a decision of the Foreign Secretary who had refused to issue the applicant with a passport[1] but not, for example, against a decision taken by the Jockey Club of Great Britain[2].

1 See *R v Secretary of State for Foreign and Commonwealth Affairs, ex p Everett* [1989] QB 811.
2 See *R v Disciplinary Committee of the Jockey Club, ex p Aga Khan* [1993] 1 WLR 909 in which the Court of Appeal refused an appeal by the Aga Khan from the Divisional Court which had held that the decision of the Jockey Club was not susceptible to judicial review because its powers derived from the contractual relationship between the club and those agreeing to be bound by the Rules of Racing; that such powers were enforceable by private action for injunction, damages and declaration.

Discharge of leave

9.26 It is open to a respondent to apply for the discharge of leave, where leave to apply for judicial review has been granted ex parte; although it is suggested that this course should only be taken where the respondent can show that the substantive hearing is likely to fail[1].

1 RSC Ord 53, r 14(1).

Once leave has been granted

9.27 Where leave to move for judicial review has been granted either by the judge or the Court of Appeal the applicant must initiate a substantive application for judicial review. The substantive application is made by originating motion (unless the court has directed, at the leave stage, that it be commenced by originating summons to a judge in chambers). Notice of motion must be issued within 14 days of grant of leave[1]. The applicant must serve the originating motion (or summons) together with a copy of the statement he lodged with his leave application on 'all persons directly affected'[2] and where the application seeks relief against a court or an officer of the court[3] it must also be served on the clerk or registrar of that court. It is not necessary under the rules for any affidavit to be served with the motion or summons but it is advisable to do it because a copy must be supplied to any party on demand[4]. It is also necessary for the applicant to enter an application for hearing by lodging with the Crown Office an affidavit of service and a copy of the originating motion[5].

1 RSC Ord 53, r 5(5).
2 RSC Ord 53, r 5(3).
3 Judicial review lies only against inferior courts, not against the High Court or Court of Appeal: RSC Ord 53, r 14(12).
4 RSC Ord 53, r 6(4).
5 RSC Ord 53, r 5(5).

Interim orders

9.28 It is possible to apply for interim relief, such as for example, a stay pending the hearing of an application for judicial review[1] or an interlocutory injunction[2]. It is also possible to apply for discovery, interrogatories or leave to cross-examine a deponent[3].

1 RSC Ord 53, r 3(10)(a).
2 RSC Ord 53, rr 3(10)(b) and 8.
3 RSC Ord 53, rr 3(10)(b) and 8.

Steps to be taken by a respondent

9.29 If a respondent wishes to rely on affidavit evidence he must file his affidavit(s) within the Crown Office within 56 days after service on him of the applicant's motion (or summons[1]). The 56 day time limit is strictly enforced[2].

1 RSC Ord 53, r 6(4).
2 RSC Ord 53, r 14(42).

Scope of judicial review

9.30 The remedy of judicial review is concerned with reviewing, not the merits of the decision in respect of which the application for judicial review is made, but the decision-making process itself. Where a local authority has been given by Parliament a discretion in any decision-making process, then provided it does not make any mistakes in law in reaching its decision and that its decision is reasonable, the court cannot interfere by way of judicial review[1]. A decision of a court or public authority may be quashed where that body acted without jurisdiction or exceeded its jurisdiction or failed to comply with the rules of natural justice or where there is an error of law on the face of the record or where the decision is unfair[2] or such that no such person or body properly directing itself on the relevant law and acting reasonably could have reached that decision[3]. The function of the court is to see that lawful authority is not abused by unfair treatment. The court has power to grant orders of mandamus, prohibition and certiorari, to grant declarations and injunctions and to award damages[4]. Certiorari is an order which brings up into the High Court the decision of an inferior court or tribunal or a local authority and quashes it. Where the court subsequently grants an order of certiorari it may remit the matter to the original decision-making body with a direction to reconsider and reach a decision in accordance with the findings of the High Court[5]. Prohibition restrains an inferior court, tribunal or local authority from acting outside its jurisdiction and although it operates prospectively it prevents a decision maker from taking a decision or putting it into effect. Mandamus is an order requiring an inferior court or tribunal to carry out its judicial or other public duty. It can be granted where an inferior court or tribunal is obliged to state a case and is refusing to do so. There are also statutory provisions for mandamus, requiring a case to be stated which may be directed to the Crown Court or magistrates' court[6].

1 See *Devon County Council v George* [1989] AC 573 and *R v Essex County Council, ex p Washington* [1987] 1 FLR 148.
2 See eg *Council of Civil Service Unions v Minister for the Civil Service* [1985] AC 374.
3 See *Associated Provincial Picture Houses Ltd v Wednesbury Corpn* [1948] 1 KB 223, [1947] 2 All ER 680 per Lord Greene MR.
4 RSC Ord 53.
5 Supreme Court Act 1981, s 31(5).
6 Ibid, s 29(3) and the Magistrates' Courts Act 1980, s 111(6).

When should judicial review be invoked?

9.31 It should generally be sought within three months of the decision which it is sought to review[1] unless the applicant can show good cause to extend the time limit[2]. The court will then consider whether the grant of an extension of time for applying for judicial review will be likely to cause substantial hardship or prejudice, not only to the instant parties, but to a wider public[3].

1 RSC Ord 53, r 4(1) and see also the Supreme Court Act 1981, s 31(6); but see *R v London Borough of Greenwich, ex p Patterson* [1993] 2 FLR 886.
2 RSC Ord 53, r 4(1). Where an application is made to extend the time under r 4 notice of the application for leave must be given to the person who will be respondent to the motion: see *R v Ashford Kent Justices, ex p Rickley* [1955] 1 WLR 562.
3 See *R v Stratford-on-Avon District Council, ex p Jackson* [1985] 3 All ER 769, [1985] 1 WLR 1319, CA.

Judicial review in family proceedings

9.32 It has been said that in family proceedings recourse to judicial review is and ought to be rare:

> 'Unlike other areas of judicial review, the considerations are not limited to the individual who may have been prejudiced and the tribunal or organisation being criticised. In this field unusually there is a third component of enormous importance: the welfare of the child which is the purpose of the entry on the register. In proceedings in which the child is the subject his or her welfare is paramount[1].'

However, there are circumstances in which procedural or administrative error by the local authority is alleged, when judicial review is an appropriate remedy. In the majority of cases where judicial review is sought in family proceedings the decision which falls to be challenged is that made by a local authority relating to children who are 'in need'[2] or who are, or should be, accommodated by the local authority[3].

1 *Re T (Accommodation by Local Authority)* [1995] 1 FLR 159, [1995] 1 FCR 517.
2 CA 1989, s 17.
3 CA 1989, ss 20 and 22.

Examples of successful use of judicial review in children cases

9.33 In a case when the local authority failed to disclose to parents medical examinations and reports relating to their children who were the subject of the proceedings and refused to permit the parents to instruct their own medical consultant to examine the child those decisions were subject to judicial review and quashed[1]. Where the local authority failed to provide accommodation for a 17 year old the decision was subject to judicial review[2], and in cases when decisions were made by the local authority to close children's homes without sufficient regard to the interests of the children living in them[3], orders for judicial review were granted. Decisions taken at case conferences are subject to judicial review when the question is whether the conduct of the conference was unfair or unreasonable. So, for example, where a case conference proceeds on unsubstantiated allegations without giving the parent concerned the chance to deal with the allegations, the decision of the conference not to rehabilitate the child to the parent may be quashed[4]. Similarly, a foster mother who was removed from the local authority's panel of foster parents for alleged sexual interference with a child in her charge was held to be entitled to know the substance of the allegations and to be given the opportunity to answer them in accordance with the rules of natural justice[5]. Moreover, an order of certiorari was made to quash the decision by a local authority taken at a case conference to place the name of an alleged 'known child abuser' on the child abuse register without giving him notice of the allegations or opportunity to deal with them[6]. Where the local authority decided to disclose the name of the applicant, one of its foster parents, as an alleged sexual abuser of a child to the present carers of a number of children previously fostered by the applicant an order of certiorari was granted to quash the decision[7]. Where in proceedings in the magistrates' court a party was served with a guardian ad litem's report on the morning of the hearing and he was not given an adjournment to enable answers to be made, judicial review of the magistrates' court order was granted and the care order discharged[8]. In *R v Willesden Justices, ex p Brent London Borough*[9] directions were given on an application for judicial review as to the presence of a social worker in court. Judicial review was successfully used when a child was removed from its aunt without explanation and placed for adoption prior to full hearing and without the opportunity being given to the aunt to answer the guardian ad litem who supported the local authority[10]. Examples of other circumstances in which judicial review has been successfully used are when the failure by a local authority to inform the guardian ad litem of its plans for a child[11], failure by the magistrates' court to give any reasons for the dismissal of an application to discharge a care order[12] and failure by an aggrieved party to make representations as to the venue for trial[13]. Judicial review was also granted where maintenance arrears were remitted without giving the payee an opportunity to be heard[14].

1 See eg *R v Hampshire County Council, ex p K* [1990] 2 QB 71, [1990] 2 All ER 129.
2 See eg *R v Solihul Metropolitan Borough Council, ex p C* [1984] FLR 363; *R v Avon County Council, ex p K* [1986] 1 FLR 443; and *Re T (Accommodation by Local Authority)* [1995] 1 FLR 159, [1995] 1 FCR 517.
3 See eg *R v Derbyshire County Council, ex p T* [1990] 1 FLR 237, CA; *R v Secretary of State for Home Department, ex p Brassey* [1989] 2 FLR 486.
4 See eg *R v Bedfordshire County Council, ex p C* [1987] 1 FLR 239, [1987] Fam Law 55; *R v Herfordshire County Council, ex p B* [1987] 1 FLR 239, [1987] Fam Law 55.
5 See *R v London Borough of Wandsworth, ex p P* [1989] 1 FLR 387, [1989] Fam Law 185.
6 *R v Norfolk County Council, ex p X* [1989] 2 FLR 120.
7 *R v London Borough of Wandsworth, ex p P* [1989] 1 FLR 387.
8 See *R v West Malling Juvenile Court, ex p K* [1986] 2 FLR 405.
9 [1988] 2 FLR 95.
10 *R v Hereford and Worcester County Council, ex p D* [1992] 1 FLR 448.
11 See eg *R v North Yorkshire County Council, ex p M* [1989] 1 FLR 203.
12 *R v Worcester City Juvenile Court, ex p F* [1989] 1 FLR 230, [1989] 1 All ER 500.
13 *R v Wareham Magistrates' Court, ex p Seldon* [1988] 1 All ER 746.
14 *R v Dover Magistrates' Court, ex p Kidner* [1983] 1 All ER 475, [1983] 13 Fam Law 208.

Use of judicial review in private law cases

9.34 Although judicial review is more likely to occur in public law cases involving the local authority it can be used to correct procedural errors in private law cases. So, for example, where the deputy clerk to the justices refused to transfer contact and parental responsibility proceedings to the county court that decision was subject to judicial review and an order of certiorari granted[1]. Judicial review was also used successfully to quash the decision of justices to imprison a person for default in paying a sum due under the Magistrates' Courts Act 1980 where there was no evidence that the magistrates considered alternatives to imprisonment[2].

1 See *R v South East Hampshire Family Proceedings Court, ex p D* [1994] 1 WLR 611.
2 See *R v Luton Magistrates' Court, ex p Sullivan* [1992] 1 FCR 475, [1992] 2 FLR 196; *R v Slough Justices, ex p Lindsay* (1996) Times, 14 November, Sir Stephen Brown P.

Wardship and judicial review

Before 14 October 1991

9.35 The High Court had power to use its inherent jurisdiction to ward a child who was the subject of a successful judicial review[1]. Even before the coming into force of the CA 1989 it appeared that the case needed to be exceptional for the High Court[2]. A court had wide powers once the wardship jurisdiction was exercised, so for example, it had power to review the decision of a local authority not to allocate a social worker to a particular case[3].

1 See eg *R v N Yorkshire County Council, ex p M (No 3)* [1989] 2 FLR 82, [1989] FCR 403.
2 See *R v North Yorkshire County Council, ex p M (No 3)* above.
3 See *B (Wards) (Local Authority: Directions)* [1988] 1 FLR 484.

After the 14 October 1991

9.36 The court cannot use the wardship jurisdiction with regard to a child who is in the care of the local authority after 14 October 1991[1]. Provided that the child is not in the authority's care it could be warded and thereby enable the High Court to give directions as to how the case should proceed and also monitor the ward's progress.

1 CA 1989, s 100(2)(c).

Refusal of judicial review

9.37 Judicial review has been refused where children were placed on the At Risk Register after a case conference which the mother was not invited to attend[1], to review a local authority's decision to place a child for adoption with people other than the short-term foster parents who had cared for him for two years and wished to adopt him[2] and by a guardian ad litem who wished to attend the local authority's adoption panel to explain in person her written report[3].

1 *R v Harrow London Borough, ex p D* [1990] Fam 133; *R v East Sussex County Council, ex p R* [1991] 2 FLR 358, [1990] FCR 873.
2 *R v Lancashire County Council, ex p M* [1992] 1 FLR 109.
3 *R v North Yorkshire County Council, ex p M (No 2)* [1989] 2 FLR 79.

Judicial review and the representation of the child under the Children Act 1989

9.38 In *R v Cornwall County Council, ex p Cornwall and Isles of Scilly Guardians ad Litem and Reporting Officers Panel*[1] the President of the Family Division, Sir Stephen Brown J, granted the applicants, who were members of the Panel of Guardians ad Litem and Reporting Officers an order of certiorari against the local authority who had tried to impose a scheme to limit the time and thereby cost of the enquiries undertaken by them. It was held by the court that the role of the guardians ad litem was of primary importance under the CA Act 1989. Their independence in carrying out their duties should be clearly recognised and understood. It was vital that their position should not be compromised, that the courts should have confidence in their independence and that the guardians themselves should feel confident of their independent status. He found the imposition of any scheme limiting their independence against their wishes arbitrary and unreasonable and an abuse of power.

1 [1992] 1 FLR 270.

Chapter Ten

Child Support

Judith Hughes

The Law Before the Child Support Act 1991   351
The Child Support Legislation   352
The Child Support Agency   355
Reviews and Appeals   379
Collection and Enforcement   385

THE LAW BEFORE THE CHILD SUPPORT ACT 1991

10.1 Before 1990 the only forum for decisions on quantum of child maintenance were the courts. Pursuant to the MCA 1973, s 23, the divorce court had power to grant periodical payments, secured provision and lump sum or sums to a child of the family[1]. A child of the family was defined[2] as: (a) a child of both parties, and (b) any other child (not being a child who has been boarded out with those parties by a local authority or voluntary organisation), who has been treated by both those parties as a child of their family. For example, where the child of a previous marriage has accompanied one parent into another marriage and there is treated as a child of the family, a child can be a child of more than one family.

1 1 MCA 1973, ss 23(1)(d), (e) and (f).
2 Ibid, s 52(1).

10.2 It was also possible before the Child Support Act 1991 came into force to seek maintenance orders in the magistrates' court[1]. Moreover, public bodies such as the Department of Social Security could make a complaint to a magistrates' court in cases where income support was claimed by or in respect of a person whom another person is liable to maintain and the court could order that other person to pay such sum as it considered appropriate.

1 In respect of legitimate children under the Domestic Proceedings and Magistrates Court Act 1978 or under the Guardianship of Minors Acts 1971–1973 and in respect

of illegitimate children under the Affiliation Proceedings Act 1957 and thereafter under the Guardianship of Minors Act 1971 as amended by the Family Law Reform Act 1987 and then under the CA 1989, s 15 and Sch 1 for periodical payments and lump sums.

THE CHILD SUPPORT LEGISLATION

10.3 The intention to produce a Child Support Act was announced in July 1991 in parallel with existing social security legislation[1]. The Child Support Bill which became the Child Support Act was published on 15 February 1991 and it received Royal Assent on 25 July 1991. It came into force on 5 April 1993. The long title of the Act is:

> An Act to make provision for the assessment, collection and enforcement of periodical maintenance payable by certain parents with respect to children of theirs who are not in their care; for the collection and enforcement of certain other kinds of maintenance; and for connected purposes.

The Act provided that much of the detailed provisions would be dealt with in regulations. After the Act was introduced concern was expressed about the inflexibility of the formula and the resulting high levels of maintenance with the result there was an enquiry into its workings by the Social Security Committee of the House of Commons which reported in December 1993. Pursuant to their recommendations the Amendment Regulations of February 1994 were introduced. However, following further concern, there were Amendment Regulations in February 1995 and the Child Support Act 1995 was passed into law in July 1995. Some of it is still not in force.

The main changes introduced by the 1995 Act have been the provision for departure directions, and a child maintenance bonus and job seeker's allowance. Numerous regulations have been made emanating from the Department of Social Security. Various rules and orders have come from the Lord Chancellor's Department.

1 Social Security Act 1986, s 24 and its successor the Social Security Administration Act 1992.

The duty to maintain

10.4 Section 1 of the 1991 Act sets out the basic principle underlying the whole Act, namely that both natural parents[1] have an obligation to maintain their children. The section also deals with how that obligation may be discharged[2]. Therefore, when an obligation to maintain has been quantified and paid there is no further liability to maintain under the Act. For the first time, the Act introduced a formula whereby the quantum of maintenance was calculated[3]. It must be borne in mind that the Act is only concerned with child support; spousal maintenance continues to exist and to be dealt with by the courts.

1 'Parent' in relation to any child means any person who in law is the mother or father of the child so it includes an adoptive parent but not a step-parent: CSA 1991, s 54.
2 CSA 1991, s 1(1), 1(2) and 1(3).
3 Ibid, s 11.

The Child Support Legislation 353

Child maintenance: situations which fall outside the 1991 Act

10.5 Wherever the child support officer would have jurisdiction to make a maintenance assessment in respect of a child[1], no court may exercise any power it might otherwise have to make, vary or revive any maintenance order in respect of the child[2]. Nor may the court vary any maintenance agreement in respect of such a child[3]. However, the court may make consent orders provided that there is a written agreement[4]. There are situations where the Child Support Agency does not have jurisdiction such as in respect of:

(a) children who are not the natural, or adopted, children of the parents;
(b) in respect of sums required for educational expenses[5];
(c) in respect of children over 19 or those between 17 and 19 who are not in full-time education;
(d) in making lump sum or property adjustment orders for children[6]; and
(e) to provide payment of expenses for a disabled child[7].

Where the absent parent is a high earner and the higher additional element of the formula provides insufficient maintenance for the child it is possible to approach the court for a top up order after the assessment has been made[8]. Equally where additional education expenses, or expenses for blind and disabled children, are required it will be necessary to seek these through the courts[9]. Where the person with care or the absent parent or the child is habitually resident abroad there is no jurisdiction to involve the agency and application can only be made through the courts[10].

1 CSA 1991, s 8(1).
2 Ibid, s 8(3).
3 Ibid, s 9(5).
4 CSA 1991, s 8(5); Child Maintenance (Written Agreements) Order 1993, art 2.
5 CSA 1991, s 8(7).
6 Eg under the MCA 1973, s 23 or the CA 1989, Sch 1.
7 CSA 1991, s 8(8).
8 Ibid, s 8(6).
9 CSA 1991, s 8(7) and (8).
10 CSA 1991, s 44 (which defines the jurisdiction of the child support officer).

10.6 In all these cases applications are made to the court either under the MCA 1973[1] or under the CA 1989[2]. Where there is an existing order application can only be made to the court which made that order [3].

1 See para 10.1, n 1.
2 CA 1989, s 15 and Sch 1.
3 CSA 1991, s 8(3A).

Essential terminology

10.7 There are certain phrases used in the Act which it is necessary to understand.

(a) A 'qualifying child' is defined as a child either under 16 or between 16 and 19 in full-time education or who is 16 or 17 and has recently left school[1], one or both of whose parents is/are in relation to him an absent parent. A person is not a child if he has been married or celebrated a marriage which is void or in respect of which a decree of nullity has been granted[2].

(b) The parent of a child is an 'absent parent' in relation to the child, if

   (i) that parent is not living in the same household with the child; and

   (ii) the child has his home with a person who is, in relation to him, a person with care.

(c) A 'person with care' is defined as a person

   (i) with whom the child has his home,

   (ii) who usually provides day-to-day care for the child (whether exclusively or in conjunction with any other person); and

   (iii) who does not fall within a prescribed category of person[3]. Under this section the Secretary of State may prescribe categories of persons who are not capable of being a person with care, and thus unable to apply for a maintenance assessment. Since they may not include the people listed in s 3(4) of the Act, those persons, namely parents, guardians, persons in whose favour residence orders under the CA 1989, s 8 are in force are always capable of being a 'person with care'. Those prescribed persons who may not be persons with care include a local authority, a person with whom a child who is looked after by the local authority is placed by that authority under the CA 1989[4].

(d) A person with care must be distinguished from the occasional use of 'parent with care' (eg in section 6 applications[5]) which restricts the class of applicant in this category.

(e) 'Child support maintenance' is the term used in the Child Support Act for periodical payments which are required to be paid in accordance with a maintenance assessment[6].

(f) 'Day-to-day care' is defined as

   (i) care of not less than 104 nights in total during the 12 month period ending with the relevant week, or

   (ii) where in the opinion of the child support officer a period other than 12 months but ending with the relevant week is more representative of the current arrangement for the care of a child in question, and where the child is a boarder at a boarding school or is an in-patient in a hospital, the person who, but for those circumstances, would otherwise provide day-to-day care of the child, shall be treated as providing day-to-day care during the periods in question[7]. A parent may be providing 'day-to-day' care for a qualifying child and still be an absent parent[8].

The Child Support Legislation 355

(g) The 'effective date'[9] which is crucial to the working of the child support scheme is defined in the regulations as 'the date on which a maintenance assessment takes effect'[10].

  (i) Where the person with care made the application, the effective date is the date the maintenance enquiry form was sent to the other person.

  (ii) Where the application is made by an absent parent, it is the date on which an effective maintenance form is received by the Secretary of State.

  (iii) Where there is an existing court order, the effective date is two days after the assessment is complete[11].

(h) The 'relevant week' is for the person making the application, the seven days immediately preceding the submission of the form to the Child Support Agency and, for the person receiving it, the seven days immediately prior to his receipt of it[12].

---

1 CSA 1991, s 3.
2 Ibid, s 55(2).
3 Ibid, s 3.
4 Child Support (Maintenance Assessment Procedure) Regulations 1992, reg 51.
5 See para 10.43.
6 CSA 1991, s 3(6).
7 See the Child Support (Maintenance Assessments and Special Cases) Regulations 1992, reg 1.
8 CS(MASC)R 1992, reg 18(2)(a)(ii).
9 (Child Support(Maintenance Assessment Procedure) Regulations 1992, reg 30.
10 Ibid, reg 1(2) and CS(MASC)R 1992, reg 1(2). These provisions also apply where there is a written maintenance agreement: Child Support (Maintenance Arrangements and Jurisdiction) Regulations 1992, reg 4(2).
11 Child Support (Maintenance Arrangements and Jurisdiction) Regulations 1992, reg 2(5).
12 CS(MASC)R, reg 1(2).

The welfare of the child

10.8 By s 2 of the Act where in any case which falls to be dealt with under the Act, the Secretary of State or any child support officer is considering the exercise of any discretionary powers conferred by the Act he must have regard to the welfare of any child likely to be affected by his decision: that is to say, not just any qualifying child or child of the family.

THE CHILD SUPPORT AGENCY

10.9 The Child Support Agency, or CSA, is staffed by child support officers under the direction of the Chief Child Support Officer whose duty is to advise officers on their functions, to keep under review the operation of the Acts and to make annual written reports to the Secretary of State. The Secretary of State shall publish in such manner as he considers appropriate, any such written report. Child support officers are appointed to perform certain functions, namely to trace absent parents, to assess maintenance payable and to collect and enforce child maintenance payments[1].

1 CSA 1991, s 4(1).

The assessment

10.10 Once the child support officer has the completed maintenance application form and the maintenance enquiry form he will have the data needed to enable him to complete the assessment. The aim of the assessment is to calculate a figure which is considered appropriate for the absent parent to pay as child support maintenance. Much of the assessment will be based on income support allowances and premiums balanced against each parent's income net of income tax and half pension payments, the ages of qualifying children, offset by expenses such as housing costs. Income support figures are index-linked annually.

The formula

10.11 The formula for the calculation of maintenance payment consists of four basic elements namely: the maintenance requirement, assessable income, the deduction rate, and protected earnings. It is arrived at by reference to s 11 of the Child Support Act and the assessment is determined in accordance with the provisions of Part 1 of Schedule 1 of the 1991 Act[1].

1 CSA 1991, s 11(2).

The maintenance requirement

10.12 The maintenance requirement is defined[1] as the minimum amount necessary for the maintenance of the qualifying child or, if there is more than one qualifying child, all of them. The formula is [**MR = AG − CB**]. The maintenance required (**MR**) is based on income support (IS) rates less child benefit (**CB**). It is the aggregate (**AG**) of the amounts to be taken into account under the income support legislation to arrive at the basic day-to-day costs of supporting the children and this is calculated[2] by adding

(i) the child personal allowance for each qualifying child set at income support levels (from April 1997, under 11 years £16.90, 11–15 years £24.75, 16–17 years £29.60 and 18 years £38.90);

(ii) the amount of any income support family premium (currently £10.80);

(iii) the amount of income support lone parent premium where the person with care has no partner (currently £4.95); and

(iv) the adult over 25 income support personal allowance as adjusted (currently £49.15).

One hundred per cent is allowed where at least one qualifying child is under 11years of age, 75% aged 11, 12 and 13 and 50% if the youngest child is aged 14 or 15. There is no allowance where the youngest child is aged 16 or over. From this must be deducted the child benefit (**CB**) payable but excluding single parent supplement for the child. The child benefit deducted for the eldest child is higher (£11.05) than for second and subsequent children (currently £9.00). If the eldest child in the family is not one of the subjects of assessment the £10.80 will be attributable to him and the sum for each child in the assessment will be £8.80.

1 See CS(MASC)R 1992, Part II.
2 CSA 1991, Sch 1, para 5(1).

EXAMPLE 1

10.13 Jack and Jill have two children aged 14 and 10, Jackie and Jilly. Jack and Jill separate and Jack moves to a rented flat while Jill has no partner and lives with the children in the former matrimonial home.
Calculation of MR is (per week)

Personal allowance for Jill		49.15
Jackie (14)		24.75
Jilly (10)		16.90
Family premium		10.80
Lone parent premium		4.95
		106.65
Less child benefit (CB)		
Jackie	– 11.05	
Jilly	– 9.00	20.05
Thus MR =		**86.60**

The assessable income

10.14 The assessable income of the absent parent is $[A = N - E]$ where A is the income available to him or her, N is the net income and E is his or her allowable expenditure[1]. The formula for calculating the assessable income of the caring parent is $[C = M - F]$ where C is the income of the carer, M is the net income and F are the allowable deductions[2]. M is calculated exactly as N is for the absent parent[3]. With regard to F, this should be calculated in the same way as the calculation for E but with references for absent parent being replaced with references to a parent with care[4]. Detailed lists of items which may be taken into account in the assessment in respect of both an employed person[5] and in respect of a self-employed person[6] are included in the regulations.

358 Child Support

Earnings specifically do not include various items which are also specified in the regulations[7] examples of which are expenses wholly and necessarily received in the course of employment, occupational pension, advance of a loan to an employee, payments in kind. Payments received by an absent parent by way of state benefits are initially taken into account and then some of them are disregarded[8]. In order to calculate N^9, it is necessary to add to income from employment:

(a) any benefits[10] paid to the relevant parent,

(b) any other income he or she may have[11],

(c) any income of a child of the parent who is a member of his family[12], and

(d) any sum which is treated as his income[13].

There are 48 categories of items which it is possible to disregard provided for in the regulations, such as income tax, compensation for personal injury, disability allowance, child benefit not exceeding the basic rate[14]. Moreover, where the absent parent's income consists only of youth training allowance, student grant or prisoners pay it should be disallowed[15]. Exempt income,[16] is the aggregate of any of the following items to which the absent parent may be entitled: income support, personal allowance for a single claimant aged not less than 25, an amount of his housing costs determined in accordance with the regulations[17], lone parent premium where the absent parent has a child living with him, income support disability premium, income support severe disability premiums or income support carer allowances, income support family premium and the income support allowance for each relevant child or half that sum if reg 9 (2) applies[18]. Sometimes a notional income will be credited to a parent if the child support officer believes that the parent has worked for no payment or an unrealistically low payment and that his intention in doing that work or avoiding receipt of that income was to reduce his assessable income for the purposes of the Act[19]. Moreover, where a payment is made in kind other than school fees or under certain trusts for the benefit of the absent parent the child support officer may take that into account[20]. Where the child support officer concludes that a person has deprived himself of capital the amount taken into account therefrom should be reduced on an annual basis by the amount of income calculated to have arisen from that source[21].

1 CSA 1991, Sch 1, para 5(1).
2 Ibid, Sch 1, para 5(2).
3 Ibid.
4 CS(MASC)R 1992.
5 Ibid, Sch 1, paras 1 and 2.
6 Ibid, Sch1, para 1(2).
7 Ibid, Sch 1, para 1(2).
8 Ibid, Sch 1, para 6.
9 Ibid, Sch 1, paras 7 and 9.
10 Ibid, Sch 1, paras 6 ff.
11 Ibid, Sch 1, paras 8 ff.
12 Ibid, Sch 1, paras 17 ff.
13 Ibid, Sch 1, para 25.
14 Ibid, Sch 2, paras 1–48.

15 Ibid, reg 7(3).
16 Ibid, reg 9(1).
17 Ibid, regs 14–18 and see para 10.15.
18 Ibid, reg 9(2) and see para 10.16.
19 Ibid, Sch 1, paras 26 and 27.
20 Ibid, Sch 1, para 31.
21 Ibid, Sch 1, para 30.

Exempt income: housing costs

10.15 It is impossible in a work such as this to go into minute detail with regard to each and every element which must be taken into account when calculating the assessable income. However, a person's housing costs are to be taken into account and they shall be the aggregate of the eligible costs paid in respect of his home although they may not be allowed in full[1]. The categories which are eligible to be taken into account are rent, mortgage interest, interest payments on loans for repairs and improvements to the home[2], mesne profits and so forth. Categories which fall outside allowed housing costs include meals, cleaning of rooms, laundry and sports facilities[3]. Housing costs are only allowable if they are incurred in relation to the home and he or a member of his family are liable for them and that the person to whom the cost has to be paid is not a member of the same household. If the parent in question is meeting costs for which he is not liable, those costs are only eligible if his paying them determines he retains the accommodation.

1 CS(MASC)R 1992, reg 15.
2 Ibid, Sch 3, para 2.
3 Ibid, Sch 3, para 6.

Exempt income: excessive housing costs

10.16 The amount of housing costs of an absent parent which are to be taken into account shall not exceed the greater of £80 or half the amount of **N** as calculated above or £80 or half of the absent parent's protected income[1]. However this does not apply if:

(a) the absent parent has day-to-day care of a child;

(b) if he receives housing benefit or a disability premium;

(c) if he remains in his former matrimonial home and has paid the housing costs for the period of 52 weeks before the date of the application for child support maintenance and there has been no increase in the costs other than increase in mortgage interest levels; or

(d) the absent parent is deprived of the equity in his former home which is still occupied by his former partner and therefore he has higher housing costs than he would otherwise have[2].

1 CS(MASC)R 1992, reg 18.
2 Ibid, reg 18(2).

Exempt income: travel costs

10.17 An allowance for the employed may be claimed within **E** of 10 pence per mile for every mile of work travel over 150 miles per week (measured in a straight line from the employee's house to his place of work) for which the employee is unable to claim expenses from the employer. These include cost of fuel, travel tickets and payments to another to provide transport[1].

1 Child Support (Miscellaneous Amendments) Regulations 1995, Sch 3.

Exempt income: pre-April 1993 transfers

10.18 Where before 5 April 1993 parents had made a transfer of capital in lieu of child maintenance a 'scale allowance' is provided for[1]. Any transfer of property will be deemed to qualify unless it was made expressly to compensate the other parent for giving up her right to apply for maintenance to the court, but while transfers expressly made as child maintenance compensation are taken at their full value, any other qualifying transfer is only allowed at 50%.

1 Child Support (Miscellaneous Amendments) Regulations 1995, Sch 3A.

EXAMPLE 2

10.19 Jill earns £866.66 per month, £200 per week net. She pays £120 per month mortgage in respect of the former matrimonial home. Jack earns £866.66 net per month, £200 per week net and he pays rent of £325 per month, £75 per week.

(1) $A = N - E$

Jack's net income (N)		200.00
less housing costs	75.00	
IS allowance	49.15	124.15
Jack's assessable income (A) is		75.85

(2) $C = M - F$

Jill's net income (M)		200.00
less housing costs	27.69	
IS allowance	49.15	
lone parent premium	4.95	
family premium	10.80	
Jackie (14)	24.75	
Jilly (10)	16.45	133.79
Jill's assessable income (C) is		66.21

The general rule

10.20 Assessment is under the general rule for lower income families. It is always necessary to do the basic formula calculation, however high the parties' incomes, firstly to eliminate the possibility of the lower figures applying and, secondly because data from the basic formula are used in the higher income calculations. The general rule formula is expressed[1] as $[(A + C) \times P]$, where **A** is the absent parent's assessable income, **C** is the assessable income of the caring parent and **P** is a number between 0 and 1 as may be prescribed. **P** has been prescribed at 0.5[2]. Where the result is an amount which is equal to or less than the amount of the maintenance requirement for the qualifying child or children the amount the absent parent should pay is $[A \times P]$. Therefore, when the **MR** is equal to not more than half of his assessable income he will pay no more than **MR**. The formula for the basic element formula $[BE = A \times G \times P]$ where **A** and **P** remain as described above. **G** is defined as

$$G = \frac{MR}{(A + C) \times P}$$

1 CSA 1991, Sch 1, para 2.
2 CS(MASC)R 1992, reg 5(b).

EXAMPLE 3

10.21 In the case of Jack and Jill, the MR is £86.60.
A is £75.85 and C is £66.21. $A + C \times .5 = £71.03$
£71.03 is less than £86.60 per week.
Therefore Jack pays child maintenance of $75.85 \times .5 = £37.92$ per week.

Nil and no assessable income

10.22 Where a person's assessable income is a negative figure, it is to be taken at nil[1]. Where the absent parent is on income support (IS) the formula is not used to assess the child maintenance payable. Instead there will be a minimum payment deducted from the state benefits to show recognition that there is a child for whom support should be provided[2]. The deduction amounts to 10% of the adult personal allowance for those 25 and over, currently £4.70 per week[3]. There is provision for payment due to be deducted from the absent parent's benefits[4].

1 CSA 1991, Sch1, para 5(3).
2 CSA 1991, s 43.
3 CSA 1991, Sch 1, para 7; CS(MASC)R 1992, reg 13.
4 CS(MASC)R 1992, reg 28.

The additional element in the case of higher income families

10.23 However, in the case of wealthier parents, their contribution should not be confined to the basic element (**BE**) and an additional element (**AE**) will be payable. In that case the maintenance to be paid is determined by the formula [**BE + AE**]. **AE** is the smaller figure produced by the following two calculations:

(a) **AE = 1 – G × A × R** where R is the number of qualifying children being 0.15, 0.20 or 0.25 depending on whether the assessment relates to one, two or three qualifying children respectively, and the other elements remain as already described; or

(b) **AE = [Z × Q1 + (Q2 × number of children)] × [A divided by (A + C)]** where **Q1** is the sum of the child allowance mentioned above in the calculation of MR, **Q2** is the family premium for each child and **Z** is 1.5.

So, where the absent parent has income to meet the additional element it is limited to 3/2 the family premium and 3/2 the child's personal allowance reduced by the ratio of the respective incomes of the parents.

EXAMPLE 4

10.24 If, in example 2, Jill's figures remain the same but instead of a weekly net income of £200, Jack has £600 per week net and a monthly rental of £325 as before, the calculations will be as follows:

Jill's assessable income (C) remains at 68.11

Jack's income is		600.00
Less		
Housing costs	75	
IS allowance	49.15	124.15
Jack's assessable income (A) is		475.85

The calculations are as follows:

(1) $(A + C) \times P = (475.85 + 66.21) \times .5 = 542.06 \times .5 = 271.03$
271.03 is greater than 86.60 (MR)
Where the resulting figure is greater than MR, proceed to basic and additional element calculations.

(2) Basic element calculation
(a) $G = \dfrac{86.60}{(475.85 + 66.21) \times .5} = .32$
(b) $BE = A \times G \times P = 475.85 \times .32 \times .5 = 76.14$

(3) Additional element calculations
$AE = (1 - G) \times A \times R = .68 \times £475.85 \times .2 = 64.72$

or $\quad AE = Z \times Q \times \dfrac{A}{(A+C)}$

$\quad = 1.5 \times (10.80 + 24.75 + 10.80 + 16.90) \times \dfrac{475.85}{(475.85 + 66.21)} = 83.29$

(4) The first calculation yields the lesser result

The maintenance assessment is BE + the lesser sum so in this example the payment would be 76.14 + 64.72 = £140.86 per week.

Protected income

10.25 In order to ensure that the absent parent is left with a minimum amount of income to cover his own needs there is provision that the amount of any assessment should be adjusted so as not to reduce his income below that level, known as 'protected income level'. At this stage the whole family's income and expenses are taken into account, including those related to a new partner and step-children by adding together the relevant income support allowances; a basic sum of £30; housing costs, the parent's council tax, any work travel allowance and a safety margin of 15% of the difference between the sum reached by this style of the calculation and his net income. From 15 April 1995 no absent parent is expected to pay more than 30% of his own net income. However, any adjustment may not result in him paying less than the minimum payment currently £4.70 per week, unless this is a special case[1].

1 See the CS(MASC)R 1992, reg 13 as amended from 5 April 1996 to 10%.

Special cases

10.26 There are a number of categories of special cases which cover situations where a family does not comprise a carer and an absent parent but where, for example, a grandmother is caring for the children away from the parents. 'Special case' is not defined by the Act but in general terms it means a case to which the usual rules of assessment of child support maintenance do not apply or only apply as amended by the regulations.

Both parents are absent

10.27 Where both parents are absent and their qualifying child is being cared for by another carer or in an institution, both parents are liable for assessment and application will be made in respect of each of them[1] unless one of them cannot be found, is dead or outside the jurisdiction of the child support officer[2]. Where the income of the second parent is not known it will be assumed to be nil until that information is available[3]. The person with care may apply for a child maintenance assessment provided that there is no court order or written maintenance agreement made before 5 April 1993. The amount of the maintenance requirement will be calculated in the usual way for each parent

364 *Child Support*

except that if the child is in the care of an institution as opposed to an individual there will be no lone parent premium.

1 Child Support (Maintenance Assessment Procedure) Regulations, reg 5(1).
2 Ibid, reg 19(2)(a) and (b).
3 CS (MASC)R 1992, reg 19 (3).

EXAMPLE 5

10.28 Janet and John leave their two children aged 8 and 4 with her mother, a widow who does not work, while they work in another town. Janet earns £200 net per week and John earns £250 net per week. Janet and John are living in a rented flat costing £80 per week. Janet's mother applies for an assessment. She is entitled to claim the child benefit as she is the person responsible for the children[1].

(1) MR is $16.90 + 16.90 + 49.15 + 15.75 - 20.05 = 78.65$

(2) A (Janet) $= 200 - (49.15 + 80) = 70.85$

(3) C (John) $= 250 - (49.15 + 80) = 120.85$

(4) $(70.85 + 120.85) \times .5 = 95.85$

£95.85 is more than MR (£78.65)

(5) $G = \dfrac{78.65}{95.85} = .82$

(6) Janet's higher income calculation:

$BE = 70.85 \times .82 \times .5 = 29.05$

$AE = 70.85 \times .18 \times .2 = 2.55$

Thus child support payable by Janet is $29.05 + 2.55 = 31.60$ per week.

(7) John's higher income calculation:
$BE = 120.85 \times .82 \times .5 = 49.55$
$AE = 120.85 \times .18 \times .2 = 4.35$

Thus the child support payable by John is $49.55 + 4.35 = 53.90$ per week.

(8) The total to be paid by Janet and John to her mother is the aggregate of 31.60 and 53.90 — £85.50 per week.

1 Social Security Contributions and Benefits Act 1992, ss 141 and 143.

Persons treated as absent parents[1]

10.29 Where two or more persons who do not live in the same household each provide day to day care for the same qualifying child; and at least one of those persons is a parent of the child the case is a special case for the purposes of the Act. The criterion in this category is day-to-day care which is defined[2] as periods averaging over one year of not less than two nights per week. Complex calculations can be done in order to calculate the appropriate payment due from the person who provides care on a substantial number of days per year. The relevant formula is

$$T = X - \left(\frac{(X+Y) \times J}{7 \times L}\right)$$

Where T is the proportion which the parent will be assessed to pay; X is the amount of child support which would have been payable ignoring the protected income and minimum amount provisions by the absent parent; Y is the amount of child support maintenance payable by the other parent as if they were an absent parent with C being the assessable income of the parent under assessment, or, if there is no such parent, Y is nil; J is the total average weekly number of nights for which day to day care is provided for each child concerned calculated to two decimal places and L is the number of children in the assessment.

1 Child Support (Maintenance Assessment Procedure) Regulations 1992, reg 20.
2 Ibid, reg 1(2).

EXAMPLE 6

10.30 Benjamin and Flopsy have two children, Mopsy and Cottontail who are aged 10 and 8. The children have lived with their grandmother Mrs Rabbit, a widow, for some years but then recently returned to live with their parents. Unfortunately Benjamin and Flopsy's marriage could not survive the return of the children and they separated. Benjamin earns £290 net per week and lives in rented accommodation in The Burrows costing £80 per week and Flopsy lives in a tree house and earns £175 net per week and she has a mortgage of £70 per week. Mopsy sees Benjamin once a week for the day and stays with him for one night a month and for a week in the holidays, 19 nights in all per year. Cottontail stays with Benjamin every other week-end and for one half of the school holidays making a total of 146 nights per year.

I Calculation of X

(1) MR = 78.65 per week (calculated as in Example 5 above).

(2) A = 290 − (49.15 + 80) = 160.85

(3) C = 175 – (70 + 49.15 + 16.90 + 16.90 + 15.75) = 6.30
(4) 160.85 + 6.30 = 83.57

£83.57 is more than MR (£78.65)

(5) $G = \dfrac{78.65}{83.57} = .94$

(6) BE = 160.85 × .94 × .5 = 75.60
(7) AE = 160.85 × .06 × .2 = 1.93
(8) X = 77.53

II Calculation of Y

As above with A and C reversed. This will be the position where (A + C) × P is more than MR but where it is less A × P will vary according to which parent is being assessed.

G will be the same for each in the BE/AE calculation

(1) BE = 6.30 × .94 × .5 = 2.96
(2) AE = 6.30 × .06 × .2 = 0.08
(3) Y = 3.04

III Calculation of J

As Mopsy stays for less than 104 nights per year she is not included in the calculation of J. Cottontail stays for 146 nights per year so the calculation is 146/52 = 2.80 days per week.

IV Calculation of T

(1) $T = X - \left(\dfrac{(X+Y) \times J}{7 \times L} \right)$

(2) $T = 77.53 - \left(\dfrac{(77.53 + 3.04) \times 2.8}{7 \times 2} \right)$

(3) T = 77.53 – (80.57 × .2)
(4) T = 77.53 – 16.11
(5) T = 61.42

That is the sum of child support maintenance payable by Benjamin

Note: T can be subject to protected income and minimum payment calculations in appropriate cases[1].

1 CS(MASC)R 1992, reg 20(6).

One parent is absent and the other is treated as absent

10.31 Where the child is living with a person with care and the person with care is not a parent, where one parent is absent and the other parent has extensive contact or shared residence arrangements with the person with care[1]. Where, for example, a 10 year old lives with her grandmother and visits her mother who is cohabiting with a man the child dislikes. The child stays with her mother for 140 nights per annum. The mother would be treated as an absent parent. In assessing child support maintenance the assessment is carried out treating the mother as if she were the person with care. Her liability to child support maintenance would be assessed under reg 20(4)[2].

1 CS(MASC)R 1992, reg 21.
2 CS(MASC)R 1992.

Multiple applications involving one absent parent

10.32 Where an absent parent has children by two or more parents and two or more of them have sought an assessment, the absent parent's assessable income is worked out in the normal way. It is shared between the different applications based on the comparative size of the maintenance requirements

EXAMPLE 7

10.33 Rat is the father of Faith's daughter Hope and also of Charity's sons Roberto and Roland. The MR for Hope is 67.50 and for Roberto and Roland it is £82.45 (therefore the total maintenance requirement is £149.95). Rat has assessable income of £110. The amount of his assessable income used for Hope will be

$$\frac{67.50 \times 110.00}{149.95} = 49.51$$

The amount of Rat's assessable income which will be used for assessing maintenance for Roberto and Roland will be

$$\frac{82.45 \times 110}{149.95} = 60.48$$

The amount of maintenance Rat can afford to pay for Hope with assessable income of 49.51 can be worked out, using the appropriate formulae. Assuming Faith has no income of her own it will be 49.51 × 50% = 24.75. Similarly the amount of maintenance he has to pay for Roberto and Roland can be worked out and will be 30.24 if their mother has no assessable income. Therefore he pays a total of £55 by way of child maintenance which is 50% of his assessable income. If an absent parent has to pay the minimum amount of maintenance this is apportioned between the different applications based on the comparative size of the maintenance requirements (MR)[1].

1 CS(MASC)R 1992, regs 13, 26, 28 and Sch 4.

Person caring for children of more than one absent parent

10.34 To assess MR in a case where a person is caring for two or more qualifying children and at least two have different parents who are absent or treated as absent it is necessary to divide AG by the number of absent parents or parents–save that where both of a child's parents are absent or treated as such they count as one[1]. The calculations can be long and complex and it is not thought necessary to include one in this text[2].

1 CS(MASC)R 1992, reg 23.
2 For an excellent and detailed example the reader may wish to consult *The Child Support Act 1991 A Practitioner's Guide* by David Burrows (1993) p 77 ff.

Persons with part time care

10.35 Two or more people not living in the same household and not treated as absent parents can apply individually for an assessment in respect of a qualifying child for whom they each provide day-to-day care[1]. Where only one applies she is entitled to receive the full amount of any child support maintenance[2]. The Secretary of State may apportion the amount paid between the carers in the same ration in which they provide such care for the child[3] but before doing so he must consider all the circumstances of the case, particularly the interests of the child and the day to day arrangements for his care[4].

1 CS(MASC)R 1992, reg 24(1).
2 Ibid, reg 24(2)(a).
3 Ibid, reg 24(2)(b).
4 Ibid, reg 24(2)(c).

Care provided in part by the local authority

10.36 Where the local authority provides part-time care the child support maintenance is calculated by the usual means and then the daily rate calculated by dividing the maintenance figure by seven. For each night that day to day care is provided for the child other than by the local authority the daily rate is payable by the absent parent[1].

1 CS(MASC)R 1992, reg 25.

Cases where child support maintenance is not to be payable

10.37 There are a number of situations set out in reg 26 in which child support is not payable, not even the minimum amount and it is treated as nil. These include where the income of the absent parent includes one or more state benefits or would do so but for some overlapping with some other benefit and these benefits include sickness, maternity, disability, invalidity and military disablement pensions. Also where the absent parent is a child or a prisoner.

Where child in boarding school or in hospital

10.38 Where children are at boarding school or in hospital as an in-patient, although the school or hospital will provide day-to-day care whilst the child is with them, the person with care does not cease to be that because of the child being away from her or him in these circumstances. Child support will remain payable whilst the child is away from home and even if the absent parent is paying boarding school fees[1].

1 CS(MASC)R 1992, reg 27.

Parent with whom child is placed by the local authority

10.39 Where the child is placed with his parent under the CA 1989, s 23(5) they are to be regarded as his parents with care[1]. Thus where the local authority places a child home on trial with one parent she can apply for an assessment, even though parental responsibility remains vested in the local authority while the care order continues.

1 CS(MASC)R, reg 27A inserted by the Child Support (Miscellaneous Amendments) Regulations 1993, reg 25.

Tax relief

10.40 Child support maintenance qualifies for tax relief but only on the payments up to a maximum limit of the difference between the single person's and married couple's tax allowance. The absent parent makes the payment and claims tax relief up to this level. The amount of maintenance due in the tax year up to this limit is deducted from the absent parent's taxable income subject to a limit of 15% from April 1995[1].

1 CSA 1991, s 8.

The procedure

Who may apply?

10.41 A person who is an absent parent or a person with care (whether or not a parent) of a qualifying child[1] can apply for a maintenance assessment. No application may be made for an assessment if there is in force a maintenance assessment made in response to an application under s 6[2]. A local authority is excluded from the definition of a person with care so a local authority is not able to apply for a maintenance assessment even where the child is in their care[3].

1 See para 10.7.
2 CSA 1991, s 4 (9).
3 Child Support (Maintenance Assessment Procedure) Regulations 1992, reg 51(1).

10.42 More than one person may be a person with care in relation to a qualifying child. Where more than one application is made the Act provides that regulations may provide for two or more applications to be treated as a single application and for replacement of an assessment made on the application of that or any other person. Regulations[1] provide for the treatment of more than one application and deal with priority of applications where, for example, two or more applications are made in respect of the same child or children.

1 CS(MAP) Regs 1992.

Authorisation for recovery of child support maintenance

10.43 A parent who is caring for the child and is supported by prescribed state benefits[1] claimed by her or another on her behalf cannot apply for an assessment under s 4 but the Secretary of State require a parent to make such an application under s 6 of the Act and this requirement operates whether or not an order or agreement is in force. Any court order in existence will come to an end two days after an assessment is made[2]. Moreover the parent with care shall, so far as reasonable, give the CSA the information which it needs to trace the absent parent, make an assessment and recover the relevant amount from that absent parent[3]. The only exception to this is if the Secretary of State decided there would be a risk of her or children living with her suffering harm or undue distress as a result[4]. If the Secretary of State is not satisfied as to this and the parent with care refuses to co-operate he may give a 'reduced benefit direction'[5] in respect of that parent.

1 Ie, income support, family credit and disability working allowance: CSA 1991, s 6(1), Child Support (Maintenance Assessment Procedure) Regulations 1992, reg 34.
2 Child Support (Maintenance Arrangements and Jurisdiction) Regulations 1992, reg 3(5).
3 CSA 1991, s 6(9).
4 Ibid, s 6(2).
5 See para 10.51.

The application

10.44 Whether under s 4 or s 6 the application follows the same procedure which is governed by the Child Support (Maintenance Assessment Procedure) Regulations 1992. Application is made on a maintenance application form (MAF). Once this has been fully completed it is sent to the Secretary of State who must pass it to the child support officer for determination[1]. If the rules are not complied with the CSA allows an applicant to correct any errors, and, provided he does so within 14 days the application is treated as if it had been correctly submitted on the date of submission of the defective application[2].

1 CSA 1991 s 11(1).
2 Child Support (Maintenance Assessment Procedure) Regulations 1992, reg 2.

Fees

10.45 Where application is made for an assessment, a fee becomes payable on the date it is made and therefore it is payable on each anniversary of that date[1]. There is a fee for assessment and for collection. The fee is presently £44 for assessment and £34 for collection[2]. No fees are payable by persons receiving state benefits, any person whose assessable income is nil, any absent parent whose income is within the protected level, and any person under 16 or under 19 in full time education and training[3].

1 Child Support Fees Regulations 1992.
2 Ibid, reg 4.
3 Ibid, reg 3(5).

The assessment

10.46 Once the MAF has been lodged the child support officer sends out to the absent parent or parents a maintenance enquiry form (MEF) and a written request that the form be completed and returned[1]. There is no fixed time for the sending out of the form but that date is critical for the date from which the payments run is the date on which the form was despatched to the absent parent. Notice to an absent parent must specify the effective date of the maintenance assessment if applicable and in general terms the provisions relating to interim maintenance assessments. In respect of absent parents, the rules about amendments are the same as the rules for the completion of the form itself[2]. Unless there is a dispute about paternity made by the absent parent the CSA then proceeds to carry out the assessment. Initially, a member of the CSA staff collects the information and enters it on a computer. If more information is required that will be sought. It generally takes several weeks from the date of the lodging of the MAF for the assessment. Where a qualifying child dies before an application for an assessment has been determined, the child support officer shall treat the application as if it had not included that child. If the assessment has been made, but the parent or person with care has not been notified of the result of that assessment, then a new assessment will be made as if the original application had not included that child. In the unlikely event of the death of all the qualifying children in an application, the application should be treated as not having been made[3].

1 CS(MAP)R 1992, reg 5.
2 Ibid, reg 6.
3 Ibid, reg 7 as amended by the Child Support and Income Support (Amendment) Regulations (CSIS(A)R) 1995.

Maintenance periods

10.47 All periods of child support maintenance are expressed in weekly amounts and are payable in respect of successive maintenance periods of seven days[1]. The first maintenance period is the date of the first maintenance assessment[2], whatever day of the week that falls. Thereafter if an assessment is replaced by a fresh assessment the new rate of payment dates back to the beginning of the maintenance period in which the effective date of the new assessment occurs[3].

1 CS(MAP)R 1992, reg 33.
2 Ibid, reg 33(2).
3 Ibid, reg 33(4).

Interim assessments

10.48 It is possible for an interim assessment to be made and this will remain in force while the additional information is collected[1]. In making any interim assessment the child support officer must have regard to the welfare of the children likely to be affected by the decision. He must give notice if considering making an interim assessment to the absent parent concerned, the person with care concerned and, in Scotland, to the child concerned[2]. Where such notice is served the officer may not make the proposed interim assessment before the expiry of a warning period of 14 days[3]. The intention in making an interim assessment is to penalise the parent who has failed to comply with the request for information made by the CSA. There are four categories of interim assessment:

(a) Category A where the absent parent has failed to provide information about his own means and under this category the interim assessment is set at one and a half times MR[4];

(b) a Category B interim maintenance assessment may be made where the child support officer needs information about the income of the absent parent or parent with care's partner or other member of the family's income and it has not been provided. In such cases E will be worked out on the assumption the partner's income exceeds the prescribed limit thus halving the family premium and child allowance;

(c) a Category C interim assessment is appropriate where the absent parent is self-employed and he cannot provide the required information at once but he expects to do so within a reasonable time. A Category C interim assessment is a maximum of £30 although it is in the discretion of the child support officer where on the scale he or she pitches it;

(d) a Category D interim maintenance assessment can be made where it appears to the child support officer on the information available that a maintenance assessment would be higher than an existing Category A interim maintenance assessment.

1 CSA 1991, s 12 as substituted by s 11 of the 1995 Act.
2 Ibid, s 12(4).
3 CS(MAP)R 1992, reg 8(1) as amended by the CSIS(A)R 1995.
4 Ibid, reg 8(2) as amended by the CSIS(A)R 1995.
5 Ibid, reg 8(2)(e) as amended by the CSIS(A)R 1995.

Cancellation of interim assessments

10.49 Interim assessments may be cancelled by an officer if he believes the delay in the provision of information was unavoidable[1].

1 CS(MAP)R 1992, reg 8(6) as amended by the CSIS(A)R 1995.

Final assessments

10.50 Once the child support officer has all the information he needs the assessment will be made in accordance with the formula. Application may also be made to the agency to arrange for the collection and enforcement of the child support maintenance once it has been assessed[1].

1 CSA 1991, s 29(1)(b).

A reduced benefit direction

10.51 Where there is no co-operation from the person with care of the child providing information as to the absent parent and the Secretary of State does not find that there would be harm to her or any children living with her as the result of complying with the request for information by the CSA and where he gives the 'reduced benefit direction' that in practice means that there will be 20% of the income support personal allowance for the 26 weeks following immediately the issue of the direction and then 10% of that allowance for the next 52 weeks[1]. A reduced benefit direction will come into effect on the first day of the second benefit week following the review[2]. There is provision for the termination of a reduced benefit direction

(a) where the parent complies with the obligation to reveal information about the absent parent;

(b) where further information is given to the Agency as to why there should not be a reduced benefit direction;

(c) where the welfare of the child is brought into question; or

(d) in Scotland when a child made the application.

1 CS(MAP)R 1992, reg 36.
2 Ibid, reg 36(4).

'The departure direction'

10.52 Under the Child Support Act 1991 there was no discretion given to the CSA to depart from the result of the application of the formula save in the circumstances of the special cases[1]. In the face of much criticism the White Paper, 'Improving Child Support'[2] conceded that there should be a system giving discretion in operation. The provisions introducing this are to be found in the Child Support Act 1995[3]. The 1995 Act introduces three steps which must be followed to ascertain whether the departure direction would be appropriate in any case. The steps are:

(a) that the case falls within one or more of the cases set out in s 4B or the regulations under them;

(b) that it is just and equitable that a departure direction be made; and

(c) that specified general principles are observed.

The departure scheme is intended to be introduced in 1997 but some pilot schemes have been introduced in the Home Counties[4].

1 See paras 10.26 ff.
2 January 1995, Cm 2745.
3 CSA 1995, ss 1–9, Sch 1 and 2.
4 Child Support Departure Direction (Anticipatory Application) Regulations 1996.

10.53 By s 1 of the 1995 Act it is provided that 'where a maintenance assessment is in force either the person with care or the absent parent or, in Scotland, either of them or the child could apply to the Secretary of State for a departure direction.' Pursuant to this section the departure direction is inserted into the 1991 Act at new s 28F. The application must be made in writing and must state whether it is based on the effect of the current assessment or a material change in the circumstances of the case since the current assessment was made. An application may be made for a departure direction even though an application has been made for a review under ss 17 or 18 of the 1991 Act or a child support officer is conducting a review of the current assessment under ss 16 or 19[1]. The Secretary of State may by regulations provide for the question whether a change of circumstance is material to be determined in accordance with the regulations[2].

1 See paras 10.30 ff.
2 CSA 1995, s 1.

10.54 By s 2 of the Child Support Act 1995 there is inserted into the 1991 Act a new s 28B which details the preliminary consideration which the Secretary of State must give to the application for a departure direction. Where he does so, he may reject the application if it appears to him that there are no grounds on which a departure direction could be given in response to application or that the difference between the amount of child support maintenance fixed by the current assessment and the amount of child support maintenance which would be fixed if a fresh maintenance assessment were to be made as a result of a departure direction allowing the departure allowed for. Before completing any preliminary consideration, the Secretary of State may refer the current assessment to a child support officer to be reviewed as if an application for review had been made pursuant to ss 17 and 18 of the 1991 Act. Where, as the result of a review of a current assessment a fresh maintenance assessment is made, the Secretary of State shall notify the applicant and such other persons prescribed by regulations and may direct that the application is to lapse, unless, before the end of such period as may be prescribed, the applicant notifies the Secretary of State that he wishes it to stand[1].

1 CSA 1995, s 2.

Regular payment condition

10.55 Where an application for a departure direction is made by an absent parent the Secretary of State may impose on him a regular payments condition. The conditions are that the applicant must make the payments of child support maintenance fixed by the current assessment and must make such reduced payments of child support maintenance as may be determined in accordance with regulations made by the Secretary of State. Where the Secretary of State imposes a regular payments condition he shall give written notice to the absent parent and person with care concerned of the imposition of the condition and of the effect of failure to comply with it. The condition ends on determination of the application. It is also provided in this section[1] that an application for a departure direction fails if it is withdrawn or lapses or it is rejected by the Secretary of State on a preliminary consideration[2]. Where an absent parent has failed to comply with a regular payments condition the Secretary of State may refuse to consider the application and in prescribed circumstances[3] the application shall lapse. It is for the Secretary of State to consider whether an absent parent has failed to comply with a regular payments condition and he then must give that absent parent and the person with care written notice of his decision.

1 CSA 1995, s 3.
2 Ibid, s 3(5).
3 Regulations are awaited in which these circumstances will be defined.

10.56 The Secretary of State must determine an application for a departure direction which has not failed[1] or refer it to a child support appeal tribunal for the tribunal to determine. That tribunal has the same powers as the Secretary of State would have were he to determine the application[2]. In determining the application the Secretary of State must have regard both to the fact that parents have an obligation for maintaining their children whenever they can afford to do so and where a parent has more than one child his obligation to maintain them should be no less of an obligation than his obligation to maintain any other of them. When determining the application the Secretary of State should have regard to any representations made to him by the person with care or absent parent, or in Scotland, either of them or the child concerned. In determining any application for a departure direction, no account shall be taken of the fact that any part of the income of the person with care is or would be if a departure direction is made derived from any benefit or that some or all of any child support maintenance might be taken into account in any manner in relation to any entitlement to benefit.

1 That is to say which has not withdrawn or lapsed or been dismissed by the Secretary of State on a preliminary consideration.
2 CSA 1995, s 4.

10.57 By s 6 it is provided that the Secretary of State should give a departure direction if he is satisfied the case merits it and falls within the requirements. In considering whether it would be just and equitable to give such a direction the Secretary of State should take into account the income of the absent payer, the financial circumstances of the person with care and the welfare of any child likely to be affected by the direction[1].

1 CSA 1995, s 6.

10.58 Where a departure direction is given, it shall be the duty of the child support officer to whom the case is given to comply with the direction as soon as practicable. A departure direction may last for a specified period or until the occurrence of a specified event. Regulations may be made for the cancellation of a departure direction in prescribed circumstances and also to make provision as to when a departure direction is to take effect, even from a date earlier than that on which the direction is given[1].

1 CSA 1995, s 7. Regulations are in draft.

The child maintenance bonus

10.59 One of the new proposals introduced by the 1995 Act was the payment of a child maintenance bonus. When the calculation of council tax, family credit and housing benefit is undertaken, the first £15 of maintenance is disregarded. The Secretary of State may make provision of a child maintenance bonus to persons who are or have been in receipt of child maintenance and to or in respect of whom income support or a job seeker's allowance is or has been paid. The bonus is to be treated for all purposes as payable by way of income support or a job seeker's allowance. For each week in which maintenance is paid, the parent will receive a credit of £5 which will be payable as a lump sum when she leaves income support or job seeker's allowance to take up work of 16 hours or more each week. These provisions have not yet come into force[1].

1 CSA 1995, s 10.

The role of inspectors

10.60 Inspectors are appointed under the Act[1] and provided with a certificate of appointment which he must produce if required on applying for admission to premises. The inspector has power to enter premises, question and require information. He may not enter premises which are used solely as a dwelling-house[2]. He may also enter Crown premises provided he is satisfied that the Sovereign is not in residence[3]. Any occupier, employee, person carrying on a trade, profession, vocation or business or their employee or agent can be interviewed by the inspector[4]. The inspector can report anyone who fails to answer questions or provide documents when required without lawful excuse and that person shall be guilty of an offence and liable on summary conviction to a fine[5].

1 CSA 1991, s 15.
2 Ibid, s 15(4)(a).
3 Child Support (Information, Evidence and Disclosure) Regulations 1992, reg 7.
4 CSA 1991, s 15(6).
5 Ibid, s 15(7).

Review of decisions for change of circumstances

10.61 If the person with care knows of a change of circumstances affecting the eligibility of the case for child maintenance between the time of sending in the information and receiving the assessment, the CSA must be informed. However, if either party has any other relevant change of circumstances there is a choice as to whether to request a change of circumstances review[1]. If a review is requested the date of the request determines the date that any change might come into effect. This applies even where an assessment is awaited[2]. If a review is requested the application[3] should be made to the Secretary of State who should refer any application under this section to a child support officer[4]. If a review is requested the child support officer can retain the existing assessment, terminate the assessment completely or make a fresh assessment if the change is significant[5], but where the original assessment has ceased to have effect he may continue the review as if the application for a review related to the original assessment and any subsequent assessment[6]. The child support officer is only obliged to take into account a change of circumstances of which he has been notified in advance or one he knows has taken place[7]. In completing a review of any maintenance assessment made after the original assessment with the same persons as the original assessment under this section, the child support officer concerned shall make a fresh maintenance assessment but only in the circumstances already described[8]. If he is satisfied that the original maintenance assessment was not validly made he may cancel it with effect from the day it took place[9].

1 CSA 1991, s 17(1).
2 Ibid, Sch 1, para 15.
3 CSA 1995, s 12.
4 Ibid, s 12.
5 CSA 1991, s 17(6).
6 CSA 1995, s 12(4).
7 Ibid, s 12(5).
8 Ibid, ss 12(7) and (8).
9 Ibid, s 14.

Termination of assessments: mandatory

10.62 An assessment ceases to have effect on the death of the absent parent or of the person with care[1] with respect to whom it was made; on there no longer being a qualifying child with respect to whom it would have effect[2]; attains the age of 16 or finishes full-time education; when the absent parent ceases to be the parent of the child (eg the child is adopted or dies); when the absent parent and the parent with care have been living together for a continuous period of six months[3], or where a new maintenance assessment is made with respect to any qualifying child with respect to whom the assessment in question was in force immediately before the making of the new assessment. It also ceases where the person with care, the absent parent or the qualifying child with respect to whom an assessment is in force ceases habitually to be resident within the United Kingdom[4].

1 CSA 1991, Sch 1, para 16(1)(a).
2 Ibid, Sch 1, para 16(1)(c).
3 Ibid, Sch 1, para 16(1)(d).
4 Ibid, s 44(3).

Termination of assessments: discretionary

10.63 A maintenance assessments can be cancelled in several circumstances. It can be cancelled where the child support officer conducting a review is satisfied that the assessment was not validly made[1], where a child support officer is conducting a review of a s 6 application under ss 16, 17, 18 and 19 and it appears that the person with care has failed to provide him with sufficient information to complete the review, and the person with care has ceased to fall into the provisions of s 6[2]. It can be cancelled from the date on which in the opinion of the child support officer the person with care ceases caring for the qualifying child[3] or where both the absent parent and the person with care ask for it to be cancelled, provided the child support officer is satisfied that they are living together[4].

1 CSA 1991, s 18(10A).
2 Ibid, Sch 1, para 16(6).
3 Ibid, Sch 1, para 16(4).
4 Ibid, Sch 1, para 16.

Disputes as to parentage

10.64 An absent parent may dispute paternity. If he does so, unless the child support officer is satisfied that any of the exceptions are met[1] before the application can proceed this issue will have to be determined as only an absent 'parent' can be obliged to support his child and 'parent' is defined as the mother or father of the child[2]. In the event of a dispute, the person with care or the Secretary of State may apply to the court for a declaration as to whether or not the alleged parent is one of the child's parents[3]. The court to which the application for a declaration is made is the magistrates' court[4]. The matter may be transferred to the High Court or county court in which event directions must be given[5]. The court can direct that bodily samples be taken either on its own motion or on the application of any party to the proceedings and may draw such inferences in the absence of compliance with such an order as may appear proper in the circumstances[6]. If on hearing any application the court is satisfied that the alleged parent is, or is not, the parent of the child in question it should make a declaration to that effect. The declaration has effect only for the purposes of the Act⁷. An appeal involving an issue of parentage proceeds through the courts⁸.

1 CSA 1991, s 26(2) and see para 10.26 ff.
2 CSA 1991, s 54.
3 Ibid, s 27.
4 Children (Allocation of Proceedings) Order 1991.
5 FPR 1991, r 3.21 inserted by the Family Proceedings Amendment Rules 1993, r 4.
6 Family Law Reform Act 1969, ss 20, 21 and 23 as amended by the CA 1989 and the Family Law Reform Act 1987.
7 CSA 1991, s 27(3).
8 Child Support Appeals (Jurisdiction of Courts) Order 1993.

10.65 There can be no dispute as to paternity and the assessment proceeds in the following circumstances[1]: where the alleged parent is a parent of the child in question by virtue of having adopted him; where the alleged parent is a parent of the child in question by virtue of an order under s 30 of the Human Fertilisation and Embryology Act 1990 (parental orders in favour of gamete donors); where there is a declaration of parentage in existence under s 56 of the Family Law Act 1986 or a declaration by a court in Scotland that the alleged parent is a parent of the child in question and the child has not subsequently been adopted. Further exceptions are that a declaration has been made under s 27 of this Act and the child has not been subsequently adopted or there has been a finding in affiliation proceedings or in other relevant proceedings that the alleged parent is the father of the child in question.

1 CSA 1991, s 26.

DNA testing

10.66 It has been held recently[1] that proceedings under s 27 amounted to civil proceedings for the purposes of the Family Law Reform Act 1969, s 20(1) and, as a result, the court has power to order scientific testing to take place to enable the question of paternity to be answered. Where the parent has a direction made against him but decides to exercise his right not to submit to the test then such refusal will entitle the court to draw appropriate inferences, which almost inevitably will be that that person is the parent[2].

1 *Re E* [1994] 2 FLR 548, Stuart White J.
2 *Re A (A Minor) (Paternity)* [1994] 2 FLR 463.

REVIEWS AND APPEALS

Introduction

10.67 The Act introduced a system of reviews which are internal to the Child Support Agency, and of independent appeals. Reviews are conducted by child support officers from which there is an appeal to child support appeal tribunals.

Reviews

10.68 Reviews can take place in one of four forms:

(a) annual reviews conducted by the child support officer[1];

(b) review by way of change of circumstances[2];

(c) review by another child support officer of a decision to refuse assessment or review under s 17[3]; or

(d) internal review on discovery of a defective assessment[4]. Where a child support officer is satisfied that a maintenance assessment is defective by reason of having been made in ignorance of a material fact, having been based on a mistake as to a material fact or being wrong in law he may make a fresh maintenance assessment on the assumption that the person in whose favour the original assessment was made has made a fresh application for a maintenance assessment[5].

1 CSA 1991, s 16.
2 Ibid, s 17.
3 Ibid, s 18.
4 Ibid, s 19.
5 Ibid, s 19(1).

Fresh application

10.69 Reviews under ss 16 and 17 are conducted as if a fresh application for a maintenance assessment had been made[1] and so, by implication is a review under ss 18 and 19[2]. For reviews under ss 17 and 18 all relevant persons unless they exist on income support must give the child support officer information as to their current circumstances[3]. Where a child support officer is not conducting a review as sought by the parties for change of circumstances but is nevertheless satisfied that it is appropriate to make a fresh maintenance assessment, he may do so[4]. Before doing so, he must give notice to the parties.

1 CSA 1991, ss 16(3) and 17(5).
2 Ibid, ss 18(9) and 19(3).
3 CS(MAP)R 1992, regs 17(5) and 19(2).
4 CSA 1991, s 19(2).

Effective date of fresh maintenance assessments

10.70 Where a review results in a change in the amount of child support maintenance, a fresh assessment is issued. It will depend on the type of the review as to effective date of the assessment[1].

[1] CS(MAP)R 1992, reg 31; following a review under s 16 it is 52 weeks from the date of the original assessment (s 16(5)(a)) and under s 17 it is the date of the application (reg 31(2)).

Procedure on review

10.71 The child support officer must give notice to all relevant persons 14 days before he conducts a review under s 16 and before he requests current information on their circumstances subject to the exception for those on income support. Under s 17 either an absent parent or a person with care can apply for the review but any application must state the grounds for asserting that there is a change of circumstance and provide sufficient information to forestall the child support officer rejecting the application on grounds that he would be unlikely to make a fresh assessment. If the child support officer decides to proceed he does so as if with a fresh application[1].

1 CSA 1991, s 17(5) and the Child Support (Maintenance Assessment Procedure) Regulations 1992, reg 19.

10.72 The review should be considered de novo. This means that all powers available for the conduct of the original assessment may be used again. Even if the result is exactly the same as it was previously a fresh assessment must be issued. Detailed provisions as to the dates of maintenance assessments following reviews are to be found in the regulations[1].

1 Child Support (Maintenance Assessment Procedure) Regulations 1992, reg 31.

Reviews of a child support officer's decision

10.73 It is open to the person who has made an application for a maintenance assessment or the review thereof which has been refused to apply to the Secretary of State for the refusal to be reviewed. It is also open to the absent parent or person with care or in Scotland for either of them or the child concerned to apply to the Secretary of State for review. It is also open to an appropriate person[1] to apply for review where the maintenance assessment is cancelled or where cancellation of a maintenance assessment is refused[2]. Moreover, a person in receipt of a reduced benefit direction may also seek a review[3]. The application for review must be made to the Secretary of State and received within 28 days of the date of the notification to the applicant of the decision against which review is sought although the Secretary of State may refer a late application if he is satisfied the delay was unavoidable[4]. Any application for review must be in writing and must give reasons why it is being made[5]. The Secretary of State must refer to a child support officer any application for review made in writing. The child support officer must then conduct the review unless in his opinion there are no reasonable grounds for supposing that the refusal, assessment or cancellation in question was made in ignorance of a material fact, was based on a mistake as to a material fact or was wrong in law[6].

1 Defined by s 18(12) as the absent parent or person with care with respect to whom the maintenance assessment in question was or remains in force or in Scotland those people and the child.

2 CSA 1991, s 18.
3 Child Support (Maintenance Assessment Procedure) Regulations 1992, reg 41.
4 Ibid, reg 24.
5 CSA 1991, s 18(5).
6 CSA 1991, s 18(6).

Appeals to child support appeal tribunals

10.74 The right to appeal arises where any person is aggrieved after a review under s 18 of the Child Support Act 1991 has been refused or a review has taken place[1]. It is also possible for a person who is aggrieved by a reduced benefit direction to appeal against that decision[2]. Each type of appeal should be brought within 28 days of the decision appealed against unless leave of the chairman of a child support appeal tribunal is given to appeal out of time[3]. The child support appeal tribunal must decide the correctness or otherwise of the relevant assessment or reduced benefit direction. It has no power to modify assessments. An appeal may be lodged but lapse before a decision is made if the officer in charge of the review decides that if every ground of appeal were to succeed the decision would be the same as that he made on review, but, in all other circumstances the appeal must proceed.

1 CSA 1991, s 20.
2 Ibid, s 46(7).
3 Ibid, s 29(2).

10.75 Any person with care or absent parent could appeal to a child support appeal tribunal in respect of the decision on a departure direction[1]. Except with the leave of the chairman of a child support appeal tribunal, no appeal shall be brought after the period at the end of 28 days beginning with the date on which notification of the decision was given[2]. On an appeal the tribunal should consider the matter and have regard to any representations made by the Secretary of State and confirm the decision or replace it with such decision as the tribunal thinks appropriate[3].

1 CSA 1991, s 28H.
2 CSA 1995, s 8.
3 Ibid, s 8(4).

Procedure

10.76 Regulations[1] govern the procedure at child support appeal tribunals. They are comprehensive and deal with such matters as time limits, service of documents or notice, directions, striking out of proceedings, withdrawal of appeal, postponement, summoning of witnesses, and adjournments. By reg 11 it is provided that a tribunal shall hold an oral hearing of every appeal and may hold an oral application of any hearing. Each party to the proceedings must be given not less than 10 days' notice of the hearing. At any hearing any party to the proceedings shall be present and heard and may address the tribunal and call witnesses. Any hearing shall be in private unless the chairman directs the hearing or part of it shall be in public. A child support appeal tribunal will consist of a chairman and two other persons who must not all be of the same sex unless the chairman rules it is not reasonably practicable to comply with that requirement in those proceedings[2]. The decisions are taken by the majority and all decisions must be given in writing[3]. The regulations provide[4] for the setting aside of any decision of the child support appeal tribunal where it may be just to do so on the ground of non-receipt of documents, non-attendance by a party or his representative or some procedural irregularity or mishap.

1 Child Support Appeal Tribunals (Procedure) Regulations 1992.
2 CSA 1991, s 3(2).
3 Child Support Appeal Tribunals (Procedure) Regulations 1992, reg 13.
4 Ibid, reg 15.

Successful appeals

10.77 In the event that an appeal is allowed, the tribunal must remit the case to the Secretary of State who must arrange for it to be dealt with by a child support officer[1]. By s 20(4), the child support appeal tribunal may in remitting the case, give such directions as it considers appropriate.

1 CSA 1991, s 20(3).

Appeals to child support commissioners

10.78 If either the parent with care or the absent parent does not agree with the decision of the child support appeal tribunal it is possible to appeal to a child support commissioner but only on a point of law[1]. It is necessary to obtain leave to appeal from the chairman of the child support appeal tribunal or, failing that, from a child support commissioner[2].

1 CSA 1991, s 24(1).
2 Ibid, s 24(6). Child Support Commissioners (Procedure) Regulations 1992, Part II.

10.79 The Chief Child Support Commissioner and other child support commissioners must have a ten year general qualification[1]. A child support commissioner will sit alone unless it appears that an appeal which is due to be heard by one of the child support commissioners involves a question of law of special difficulty and he may direct that the appeal be dealt with by a tribunal consisting of any three of the child support commissioners.

1 Courts and Legal Services Act 1990, s 71.

Procedure

10.80 Regulations[1] now govern the appeals under s 24 and these provide for time limits, the form of notice of application for leave and for notice of appeal, the time limits and directions as well as the form of hearings.

1 Child Support Commissioners (Procedure) Regulations 1992.

10.81 If a child support commissioner holds that the decision appealed against was wrong in law he shall set it aside and when so doing he can either make findings, give the decision which he feels should have been given by the child support appeal tribunal without making further findings, or he may refer the case with directions for its determination to a child support appeal tribunal or to a child support officer[1]. Unless an appeal can be brought from the decision of the child support commissioners under s 25 of the Child Support Act[2], their decision is final.

1 CSA 1991, ss 24(2) and (3).
2 See para 10.82.

Appeals from child support commissioners on a point of law

10.82 An appeal lies from a child support commissioner on a point of law only. No appeal may be brought except with the leave of the child support commissioner who gave the decision or another child support commissioner or with the leave of the appropriate[1] court if the child support commissioner refuses leave. An application for leave to appeal may only be made by a person who was party to the proceedings in which the original decision or appeal was given, the Secretary of State or any person authorised to do so by regulations made by the Lord Chancellor[2]. It must be made in writing and made within three months of the date the applicant was given notice of the decision[3]. The Chief Commissioner may appoint a different commissioner than the one who gave the decision to determine the application for leave to appeal if he is satisfied that it is impracticable or would cause delay if the same commissioner determined the application.

1 Defined in s 25(4) as the Court of Appeal unless the child support commissioner directs that the appropriate court is the Court of Session.
2 CSA 1991, s 25.
3 Child Support Commissioners (Procedure) Regulations 1992, reg 25.

Appeals to the Court of Appeal

10.83 Appeals to the Court of appeal will follow normal procedure[1] and are not provided for in the Child Support Act. In the event of leave being granted an appeal could be made from the Court of Appeal to the House of Lords on a point of law.

1 RSC Ord 59.

Other appeals

10.84 By s 45 of the Child Support Act 1991 the Lord Chancellor may make such provision as he considers necessary to secure that appeals or such class of appeals as he may specify may be made to a court[1] instead of to a child support appeals tribunal or made in such circumstances as may be specified.

1 Defined as the High Court, a county court or magistrates' court, or in Scotland the Court of Session or the Sheriff's Court. Thus appeals from a deductions from earnings order are to a magistrates' court: see para 10.91.

Judicial review

10.85 In principle, it may be possible to seek judicial review of the decisions of the Secretary of State. It is not an appellate jurisdiction and before it is invoked other appeal procedures must normally have been exhausted. To succeed in an application an applicant must show one or more of the following in relation to a public body: excess or want of jurisdiction, breach of duty to act fairly or that no body or person in performance of their public duties properly directing themselves on the relevant law and acting reasonably, could have reached the decision in question[1]. Thus decisions in the Act vested in the Secretary of State may be assessable to judicial review; whereas decisions of a child support officer will normally only be assessable to appeal to a child support appeal tribunal.

1 In accordance with *Associated Provincial Picture Houses Ltd v Wednesbury Corpn* [1948] 1 KB 223, [1947] 2 All ER 680; and see *R v Secretary of State for Social Security, ex p Biggin* (considered further at para 10.91).

COLLECTION AND ENFORCEMENT

Collection

10.86 The role of the Child Support Agency differs in the case of a parent with care who is receiving state benefits and one who is not. A parent receiving benefit is obliged to authorise the Secretary of State to take action to recover child maintenance from the absent parent[1] while a person with care, the absent parent who is not receiving benefit can apply to the Secretary of State for a maintenance assessment and may ask the Secretary of State to arrange collection of the child support maintenance in accordance with the assessment and the enforcement of the obligation to pay[2]. Complete discretion is given to the Agency[3], although in a benefit case proceeding under s 6 the responsibility for collection and enforcement will automatically be assumed by the Agency[4].

1 CSA 1991, ss 6(1) and 29(1).
2 Ibid, s 4.
3 Ibid, s 29(1).
4 Ibid, s 29(1)(a).

10.87 The regulations governing the collection of child support are to be found in Part II of the Child Support (Collection and Enforcement) Regulations 1992 and these provide for the method of payment, the identity of the payee, with what regularity and the giving to the payer an opportunity to make representation about these matters.

10.88 By s 30 of the Act there is power for the Secretary of State to collect periodical payments and secured periodical payments 'of a prescribed kind to or for the benefit of any person who falls within a prescribed category and also which are payable for the benefit of a child even though he is arranging for the collection of child support maintenance with respect to that child.' There is no definition of periodical payments or secured payments in the Act[1]. Regulations[2] provide for the categories of maintenance which may be collected and how they should be collected. At present the agency is empowered to collect any top up payments ordered by the court[3], school fees[4] and disability maintenance[5] where it is already collecting child support[6]. The Agency has not yet taken up these powers.

1 So we assume the words have the same meaning as in the MCA 1973, ss 23–24.
2 See the Child Support (Collection and Enforcement) Regulations 1992.
3 CSA 1991, s 8(6).
4 Ibid, s 8(7).
5 Ibid, s 8(8).
6 Child Support (Collection and Enforcement of Other Forms of Maintenance) Regulations 1992, reg 2.

Enforcement

10.89 In the event that an absent parent fails to pay under the maintenance assessment there are various methods of enforcement provided by the Act namely by deduction from earnings orders, liability orders and enforcement by distress each of which will be considered in turn.

By deduction from earnings orders

10.90 The Secretary of State may make a deduction from earnings order against a liable person to secure the payment of any amount due under the maintenance assessment in question to secure the payment of arrears of child support maintenance payable under the assessment; or current payments or both[1]. A deductions from earnings order is a question entirely for the discretion of the Secretary of State[2]. No grounds for imposing the order need be established nor need reasons for it be given. It is directed at an employer who has the liable person in his employment and this can include employees of the Crown[3] and shall have effect from such date as may be specified in the order. It can only be made when the person against whom the order is made has earnings[4] which can be attached. It operates as an instruction to the employer to make deductions from the liable persons earnings and to pay the amounts deducted to the Secretary of State. The order must be served on both the employer and the liable person and the employer must co-operate with the order from seven days after it has been served on him[5]. The employer must notify the Secretary of State in writing when served with an order on the assumption he is the employer and the named employee is not in his employment, if he becomes aware there is a deduction of earnings order in existence in respect of one of his employees, and further when the employee changes employment[6].

1 CSA 1991, ss 31 and 32.
2 Ibid, s 31(2).
3 Ibid, s 32(2)(1)(a).
4 Defined by CS(MASC)R 1992, reg 8(3)–(5) as including wages or salary (including bonus commission and overtime pay), pension and statutory sick pay.
5 CSA 1991, s 31(4)–(7).
6 Child Support (Collection and Enforcement) Regulations 1992, reg 16.

APPEALS

10.91 It is also provided that a person who is aggrieved by the making of a deduction from earnings order against him may appeal to a magistrates' court though the court should not question the maintenance assessment[1]. A liable person may appeal to the magistrates' court by way of complaint within 28 days of the dates on which the matter appealed against arose[2]. The appeal may only be made on one or both of two very limited grounds namely that (a) the deduction from earnings order is defective, or (b) that the payments in question do not constitute earnings[3]. In *R v Secretary of State for Social Security, ex p Biggin*[4] the Divisional Court dismissed an appeal of an absent parent who had appealed to the magistrates' court and from there to the Divisional Court against a deduction from earnings order claiming that the Child Support Agency had failed to consider the welfare principle in making that order and that the justices should quash it. The magistrates had decided that there was no evidence that the Child Support Agency had failed to consider the welfare principle and the complaint should be dismissed. It was suggested that judicial review might lie against the decision for failing to consider the welfare principle.

1 CSA 1991, s 31(5).
2 Child Support (Collection and Enforcement) Regulations 1992, reg 22(1).
3 Ibid, reg 22(3); and see *Secretary of State for Social Security v Motton* (1996) Independent, 30 January.
4 [1995] 1 FLR 851, Thorpe J.

PENALTIES FOR NON-COMPLIANCE WITH A DEDUCTIONS FROM EARNINGS ORDER

10.92 In the event that either the employer or the employee fails to comply with a deduction from earnings order he shall be liable to criminal sanctions[1]. It is a defence for a person charged with an offence under this subsection to prove that he took all reasonable steps to comply with the requirements in question[2]. The penalty on summary conviction is a fine not exceeding level two on the standard scale[3].

1 CSA 1991, s 32(8).
2 Ibid, s 32(10).
3 Ibid, s 32(11).

By liability orders

10.93 In the event that a liable person fails to make one or more of the child support maintenance payments and it appears to the Secretary of State that it is inappropriate to make a deduction from earnings order against him (because, for example, he is not employed) or, although a deduction of earnings order has been made against him, it has proved ineffective as a means of securing that payments are made in accordance with the maintenance assessment in question, the next step is that the Secretary of State may apply to a magistrates' court for a liability order against the liable person. This is only a step towards further means of enforcement. Where the Secretary of State applies for a liability order, the magistrates' court shall make the order if satisfied that the payments in question have become payable by the liable person and have not been paid. If an application for a liability order is made the court shall not question the maintenance assessment under which the payments of child support maintenance fell to be made[1].

1 CSA 1991, s 33.

10.94 Regulations[1] provide that the Secretary of State must give the payer at least seven days' notice of his intention to apply for a liability order. Such notice shall set out the amount of child support maintenance which it is claimed has become payable by the liable person and has not been paid and the amount of any interest in respect of arrears payable. If any part of the amount is paid leaving some outstanding it is not necessary to give the payer a further notice[2].

1 Child Support (Collection and Enforcement) Regulations 1992, Part IV.
2 Ibid, reg 27.

ENFORCEMENT OF LIABILITY ORDERS BY DISTRESS

10.95 Where a liability order has been made against a payer the Secretary of State may levy the appropriate amount by distress and sale of the liable person's goods[1]. The appropriate amount is the extent in respect of which the order remains unpaid and an amount in respect of the charges connected with the distress[2]. In exercising his powers the Secretary of State may seize any of the liable person's money, bank notes, bills of exchange, promissory notes, bonds, or securities for money belonging to the liable person and his goods except his tools of trade and basic domestic items such as are necessary for satisfying his basic domestic needs including those of any member of his family with whom he resides[3]. No person levying distress is to be taken as a trespasser[4] and anyone who sustains special damage by reason of any irregularity in levying a distress under this section may recover full satisfaction for the damage by proceedings in trespass[5]. The section also provides that regulations may be made providing for the locations in which distress may be levied, provides that such distress shall not be deemed unlawful on account of any defect or want of form in the liability order; provides for appeal to the magistrates' court by a person aggrieved by an attempt to levy distress and makes provision as to the powers of the court on an appeal[6].

1 CSA 1991, s 35(1).

2 Ibid, s 35(2).
3 Ibid, s 32(3).
4 Ibid, s 35(5).
5 Ibid, s 35(6).
6 Ibid, s 36(8).

Enforcement of liability orders in county courts

10.96 Another form of enforcement of a liability order open to the Secretary of State is to seek to recover the amount due through a county court as if it were a judgment or order of the county court. By s 36 it is provided that where a liability order has been made to the extent that it remains unpaid, if a county court so orders, it shall be recoverable by means of garnishee proceedings or a charging order, as if it were payable under a county court order.

Enforcement by committal to prison

10.97 Where the Secretary of State has sought to levy an amount by distress under the Child Support Act 1991 or to recover an amount in the county court under s 36 and any part of the sum due remains unpaid he may apply to a magistrates' court for the issue of a warrant committing the liable payer to prison[1]. In such event the court must enquire into the liable person's means and whether there has been wilful refusal or culpable neglect on his part[2]. Only in the event that the court is of the opinion there has been wilful refusal or culpable neglect on the part of the liable person, and he is over 18 years of age[3], it may issue a warrant for committal against him or fix a term of imprisonment and postpone the issue of the warrant until such time and on such conditions as it thinks just[4]. Any warrant shall be made in respect of an amount equal to the aggregate of the amount mentioned in s 35(1) or so much of it as remains outstanding and an amount in respect of costs of commitment and the warrant must state the total amount. A warrant issued under the section shall order the liable person to be imprisoned for a specified period which is a maximum of six weeks and allow for him to be released upon the payment of the amount stated in the warrant. The warrant may be directed to such person or persons as the court issuing it thinks fit. Regulations provide that the period of imprisonment is lessened with part payment, the form of warrant, the procedure to be adopted and for the form of means enquiry which may take place[5].

1 CSA 1991, s 40(1).
2 Ibid, s 40(2)(b).
3 Ibid, s 40(5).
4 Ibid, s 40(3)(b); and now see *R v Slough Justices, ex p Lindsay* (1996) Times, 14 November, Sir Stephen Brown P for what may amount to 'culpable neglect to pay' .
5 Child Support (Collection and Enforcement) Regulations 1992, regs 33 and 34.

Arrears

10.98 Where the Secretary of State recovers arrears from the liable payer he may retain them if he is satisfied that the amount of any benefit paid to the person with care of the child or children in question would have been less had the absent parent not been in arrears with his child support maintenance[1].

Regulations² provide for the Secretary of State to make an agreement with the absent parent enabling him to pay all outstanding money due on agreed dates and in agreed amounts³. If the parent does enter such an agreement the Agency should serve a schedule of dates and amounts of payments and send it to anyone it deems appropriate⁴. Any such agreement contains an implied term that current maintenance is to be paid on its due date⁵. If the agency has delayed in enforcing arrears it may consider not enforcing arrears more than six months old. There is a ceiling to the amount that can be claimed as no absent parent should pay more than 33.33% of his income on current maintenance and arrears.

1 CSA 1991, s 41(5).
2 Child Support (Arrears, Interest and Adjustment of Maintenance Assessments) Regulations 1992.
3 Ibid, reg 5(1).
4 Ibid, reg 5(2).
5 Ibid, reg 5(7).

Interest

10.99 Where the Agency has been authorised to collect maintenance under ss 4(2) or 7(3) of the Act where under s 6 of the Act it is collecting maintenance in a benefit case and the absent parent has failed to make one or more payments of maintenance then the absent parent shall, in accordance with the Arrears Regulations, be liable to pay interest set at 1% over bank base rate with respect to the arrears¹.

1 CSA 1991, s 4(1)(3) and (4) and Arrears Regulations 1992 regs 2 and 3.

10.100 However, interest will not be payable if the arrears arise in a period which terminated before the date 14 days earlier than the service of the arrears notice¹. Other circumstances in which they are not payable are where a fresh assessment is made but before it is notified to the absent parent arrears arise under it²; where arrears arise after 17 April 1995³; where the arrears arose on or before 17 April 1995 and the absent parent did not know, or could not have been reasonably expected to know that they existed⁴. Also where within 28 days of the due payment date an arrears agreement was entered into and where its terms have been complied with, in respect of the arrears to which the agreement related⁵; and finally where an arrears agreement was entered into later than within 28 days of the due date of payment, and where the terms of that agreement have been complied with, those arrears in respect of any period which post dates the agreement⁶.

1 Arrears Regulations, reg 3(2).
2 Ibid, reg 3(6).
3 Ibid, reg 4(1)(a).
4 Ibid, reg 4(1)(b).
5 Ibid, reg 5(3).
6 Ibid, reg 5(4).

Part V

Domestic Violence

Chapter Eleven

Domestic Violence

Robert Purdie

Introduction 393
Procedure 402
Restraint of Molestation 417
Exclusion Injunctions 420
Re-entry to the Matrimonial Home 431
Power of Arrest 433

INTRODUCTION

11.1 An injunction is a court order whereby someone, usually a party to the proceedings, is restrained from doing a specific act or acts[1] or is required to do a specific act or acts[2].

The injunction has its origins in the courts of equity and until 1854 the courts of common law had no general power to grant an injunction[3]. Since 1875 all divisions of the High Court have had jurisdiction to grant injunctions[4].

The High Court may grant an injunction, either interlocutory or final, in all cases in which, to do so, is just and convenient[5]. The jurisdiction of the county court is similar[6]. An injunction will only be granted in support of a legal right[7], or to protect children[8].

There must be a close nexus between the substantive proceedings and the claim to the interlocutory injunction so that the application for the injunction arises out of, or is incidental to, the action[9]. For example, there is no power to grant a non-molestation injunction in proceedings under the Inheritance (Provision for Family and Dependants) Act 1975[10].

---

1 A prohibitory injunction.
2 A mandatory injunction.
3 Common Law Procedure Act 1854, s 79.
4 Supreme Court of Judicature Act 1873, now replaced by Supreme Court Act 1981, s 37(1).
5 Supreme Court Act 1981, s 37(1).
6 County Courts Act 1984, ss 38 and 39.

7 *Montgomery v Montgomery* [1965] P 46, [1964] 2 All ER 22 and *Robinson v Robinson* [1965] P 39, [1963] 3 All ER 813.
8 *Stewart v Stewart* [1973] Fam 21, [1973] 1 All ER 31; *Phillips v Phillips* [1973] 2 All ER 423, [1973] 1 WLR 615; *Quinn v Quinn* (1983) 4 FLR 394, CA. See also *Beard v Beard* [1981] 1 All ER 783, [1981] 1 WLR 369, CA, where the exceptional nature of the jurisdiction to protect children was emphasised.
9 *Des Salles d' Epinoix v Des Salles d'Epinoix* [1967] 2 All ER 539, [1967] 1 WLR 553, CA; *F v F (Exclusion Order)* (1980) 3 FLR 202, Eastham J; *McGibbon v McGibbon* [1973] Fam 170, [1973] 2 All ER 836; see also *Winstone v Winstone* [1960] P 28, [1959] 3 All ER 580. Cf *The Siskina* [1979] AC 210, [1977] 3 All ER 803, HL at 256 and 824f–h, per Lord Diplock.
10 *Andrew v Andrew* [1990] 2 FLR 376.

Domestic Violence and Matrimonial Proceedings Act 1976

County courts

11.2 The Act gives jurisdiction to every county court to grant certain injunctions whether or not any other relief is sought in those proceedings upon an application by a party to a marriage[1]. This provision ended the need for a husband or wife seeking such injunctive relief to bring proceedings for trespass or assault claiming not only an injunction but also damages.

The marriage to which the applicant must be a party would include not just a valid marriage but also any marriage celebrated outside England and Wales which the court would recognise. It is not clear whether or not the Act applies to parties to actually polygamous marriages[2]. It would probably apply to potentially polygamous marriages[3]. The language[4] of s 1 appears to presuppose a monogamous relationship. If the Act does not apply to polygamous marriages the court would nonetheless have jurisdiction if the parties came within the meaning of the phrase 'living with each other in the same household as husband and wife'[5].

On the granting of a decree absolute, whether of divorce or nullity, the parties cease to be husband and wife and therefore the court would not have jurisdiction to entertain an application from a former spouse because he or she would no longer be a party to a marriage. Where an injunction is sought by one former spouse against the other, it is usually more appropriate to seek the injunction in the matrimonial cause[6], than to commence new proceedings.

A decree of judicial separation does not bring to an end the status of husband and wife although it does relieve the petitioner of the obligation to cohabit with the respondent[7]. It follows that husbands and wives who are judicially separated from each other may apply to the court under the provisions of the Domestic Violence and Matrimonial Proceedings Act 1976.

1 Section 1(1), as therein defined; see paras 11.8 and 11.9.
2 See however *Re Sehota* [1978] 3 All ER 385, [1978] 1 WLR 1506, a case under the Inheritance (Provision for Family and Dependants) Act 1975.
3 *Hussain (Aliya) v Hussain (Shahid)* [1983] Fam 26, [1982] 3 All ER 369, CA.
4 Section 1(1)(*a*) refers to 'the other party to the marriage' while s 1(1)(*b*) and (*c*) refers to 'the other party'.
5 See paras 11.8 – 11.9.
6 As to whether or not injunctions can be granted in matrimonial causes after decree absolute see para 11.4.
7 MCA 1973, s 18(1); *Hutchinson v Hutchinson* [1947] 2 All ER 792, Denning J.

High Court

11.3 The question of whether the High Court has jurisdiction to entertain proceedings to grant relief under s 1(1) of the Domestic Violence and Matrimonial Proceedings Act 1976 where no other relief is sought in the proceedings is not without difficulty. Section 1(1) of the 1976 Act is expressed to be 'without prejudice to the jurisdiction of the High Court'. It follows that the Act does not extend the jurisdiction of the High Court[1].

In *Crutcher v Crutcher*[2] it was held that s 1(1) of the 1976 Act did not enlarge the jurisdiction of the High Court to grant an injunction and if it was desired to obtain such an injunction in the High Court, proceedings for some substantive relief must have been commenced or there must be the usual undertaking to commence proceedings forthwith. It was held further that the words in the Act 'whether or not any other relief is sought in the proceedings' referred to an application in the county court. Thus although it would appear that the powers of the Family Division to grant an injunction similar to those available under s 1(1) of the 1976 Act are limited to cases where there are already proceedings in that division for divorce, judicial separation or nullity, or wardship, the court in *Crutcher v Crutcher* does not appear to have considered the effect of the Rules of the Supreme Court[3]. These Rules made with the authority of Parliament[4] prescribe the procedure to be followed on an application by a party to a marriage[5] for an injunction containing any of the relief set out in s 1(1) of the 1976 Act. It is prescribed[6] that the application should be made by originating summons. It is submitted that the decision of *Crutcher v Crutcher* was reached without consideration of the Rules and is therefore *per incuriam*; consequently the Family Division of the High Court may grant such injunctions in summary proceedings virtually in exactly the same way as the county court.

However, it remains in doubt whether the High Court has jurisdiction where the parties are not married but are living together as husband and wife in the same household[7]. Whilst it is submitted that the High Court has jurisdiction to entertain such applications, it is to be emphasised that the overwhelming majority of such applications will be made in the county court rather than the High Court. Unless there is any special reason for commencing the proceedings in the High Court applications should be made in the appropriate county court if for no other reason than that of saving costs.

1 See *Davis v Johnson* [1979] AC 264 at 332B, [1978] 1 All ER 1132 at 1143a–b, HL per Viscount Dilhorne.
2 (1978) 128 NLJ 981, per Payne J.
3 FPR 1991, r 3.9 previously RSC Ord 90, r 30.
4 Matrimonial and Family Proceedings Act 1984, s 40(1) as amended by Courts and Legal Services Act 1990.
5 RSC Ord 90, r 30(1) used the phrase 'a party to a marriage within the meaning of section 1(1), Domestic Violence and Matrimonial Proceedings Act 1976.' From this it is likely that the High Court may entertain applications from persons who come within the meaning of the phrase 'a man and a woman who are living with each other in the same household as husband and wife'.
6 FPR 1991, r 3.9(2).
7 *Seray-Wurie v Seray-Wurie* [1987] Fam Law 124, CA, but on the question of the jurisdiction of the High Court see [1986] CA Transcript 259.

Interlocutory relief in a matrimonial cause

11.4 From the date on which the petition is presented[1] until a decree absolute of divorce or nullity or a decree of judicial separation, the court has power[2] to enjoin one spouse for the benefit of the other.

The court on an application made ex parte before the presentation of a petition, may grant a non-molestation or ouster injunction on the proposed petitioner's undertaking to file a petition for divorce, nullity or judicial separation[3]. The jurisdiction of the court is different after the suit has been determined[4]. The court will grant an order restraining molestation after a final decree[5], however; the grant of an ouster injunction after decree absolute is by no means as easy, from the point of view of the jurisdiction of the court, as is the grant of a non-molestation injunction. In general, an ouster injunction will only be granted, after decree absolute, in support of either a proprietary right[6] or for the welfare of the children[7]. Where there are no children and the spouse seeking the order has no proprietary right in the matrimonial home, the court has no jurisdiction to do more than make a non-molestation order[8]. The appropriate remedy to resolve disputes about property may be to apply in the suit for ancillary relief and not to apply for injunctive relief[9].

The right of a spouse to apply for a transfer of property order by way of ancillary relief in the suit is not a proprietary right and cannot be protected by a mandatory injunction ordering the other spouse to leave the matrimonial home[10]. The court has adequate power[11] to preserve matrimonial assets so that any orders of the court made in this context will not be defeated. After decree absolute the court has jurisdiction[12] to protect the interests of children and where the children require somewhere to live, the court will grant an injunction ordering a spouse to vacate the former matrimonial home, should this be necessary. It is submitted that injunctions should not be granted after decree absolute restraining the use of the former matrimonial home by reason only of the fact that there are children of the family to whom the MCA 1973, s 41 applies who are living in that home but that injunctions should only be granted where they are required for the protection of such children.

The Court of Appeal[13] has condemned as 'extremely undesirable and a complete abuse of the process of injunctive relief in this context' the practice of ousting a spouse in order to present the court with a *fait accompli* on the hearing of an application for ancillary relief.

In cases involving the protection of children, the court will act even after the passage of some time since the grant of a decree absolute. In *Beard v Beard*[14] the judge at first instance, a year after decree absolute as an emergency measure for the protection of children ordered the wife to leave the former matrimonial home in which she had been looking after the children and granted interim care and control to the father. On appeal this decision was upheld and the Court of Appeal emphasised that the court has jurisdiction to make such orders for the protection of children, in emergency, during the continuance of the emergency and for the period of the emergency[15]. It is to be emphasised however that this decision was wholly exceptional and in order to invoke it the circumstances must justify the application of the term 'emergency'. It was made clear that the propositions advanced were not to be interpreted as throwing any light at all upon the jurisdiction of the court in situations other than such extreme emergency[16]. The jurisdiction of the High Court and divorce county courts to grant interlocutory injunctions are identical[17]. As a matrimonial cause can only be commenced in a divorce county court[18] any application, ex parte, before the issue of proceedings must be made in a county court[19].

1 That is the date on which it is filed at the court office: see FPR 1991, r 2.6(5); *Alston v Alston* [1946] P 203, [1946] 2 All ER 62.
2 County Courts Act 1984, s 38; Supreme Court Act 1981, s 37.
3 See further para 11.11.
4 The suit is determined on pronouncement of a decree absolute of divorce or nullity or a decree of judicial separation. A decree of judicial separation, however, does not end the status of the parties as husband and wife; the petitioner is no longer obliged to cohabit with the respondent. See the MCA 1973, s 18(1). Other rights and obligations may continue; see 22 *Halsbury's Laws* (4th edn) 1105 HUSBAND AND WIFE.
5 *Robinson v Robinson* [1965] P 39, [1963] 3 All ER 813; *Montgomery v Montgomery* [1965] P 46, [1964] 2 All ER 22; *Webb v Webb* [1986] 1 FLR 541, CA; *Ruddell v Ruddell* (1967) 111 Sol Jo 497. After decree absolute a former spouse, with no proprietory rights in the former matrimonial home cannot rely on the inherent jurisdiction of the court to exclude his or her former spouse from the home as the applicant has no more rights than an independent adult licensee. *O'Malley v O'Malley* [1982] 2 All ER 112, [1982] 1 WLR 244, CA. It is an abuse of process to use the remedy of injunction to set the scene for ancillary relief, ibid. The decision in *O'Malley v O'Malley* does not derogate from the inherent jurisdiction of the court to grant injunctions, after decree absolute, for the protection of children: *Quinn v Quinn* (1983) 4 FLR 394, CA; *Beard v Beard* [1981] 1 All ER 783, [1981] 1 WLR 369, CA; see also *Waugh v Waugh* (1981) 3 FLR 375, CA, the actual decision in *Waugh v Waugh* might be different now by reason of Housing Act 1985, s 91(3)(b).
6 *Brent v Brent* [1975] Fam 1, [1974] 2 All ER 1211, Dunn J.
7 *Stewart v Stewart* [1973] Fam 21, [1973] 1 All ER 31; *Phillips v Phillips* [1973] 2 All ER 423, [1973] 1 WLR 615; *Quinn v Quinn* (1983) 4 FLR 394, CA.
8 *Webb v Webb* [1986] 1 FLR 541, CA.
9 *Grace v Grace* [1980] CA Transcript 418.
10 *Brent v Brent* [1975] Fam 1, [1974] 2 All ER 1211, per Dunn J (obiter) which was a decision immediately after the pronouncement of a decree nisi where Dunn J held that as the decree would be made absolute in six weeks time, the position after decree absolute should be considered: following *Montgomery*, above, he held the court had not jurisdiction after decree absolute to exclude a husband from premises owned wholly by him or before decree absolute to make such an order the purpose and effect of which was to produce that result.
11 Under the MCA 1973, s 37.
12 *Stewart v Stewart*, above.
13 *Grace v Grace*, above. See also *O'Malley v O'Malley* [1982] 2 All ER 112, [1982] 1 WLR 244, CA, but see *Quinn v Quinn* (1983) 4 FLR 394, CA.
14 [1981] 1 All ER 783, [1981] 1 WLR 369, CA.
15 [1981] 1 All ER 783 at 787d-h, [1981] 1 WLR 369 at 373B-E.
16 Ibid at 787d and 373B.
17 Supreme Court Act 1981, s 37(1): County Courts Act 1984, s 38.
18 Matrimonial and Family Proceedings Act 1984, s 33(3).
19 See further para 11.11.

Matrimonial Homes Act 1983

11.5 The Act[1] gives jurisdiction to the High Court[2] and county courts[3] to grant injunctions[4] relating to the occupation of a dwelling house[5] which is or has been the matrimonial home[6]. The parties must be married[7] and the marriage may have been entered into under a law which permits polygamy[8]. Where both spouses have a legal[9] interest in the matrimonial home they are each entitled to occupy the same[10] but not to the exclusion of the other. Where the title to the matrimonial home is in the sole name of one spouse he or she is entitled to occupy the same[11] and the other spouse has rights of occupation[12] namely: if in occupation, a right not to be evicted or excluded by the other except with the leave of the court[13]; if not in occupation, a right to enter and occupy the home with the leave of the court[14].

Where the matrimonial home is in the joint names of the parties either spouse may apply to the court, during the subsistence of the marriage[15], for an order prohibiting, suspending or restricting the exercise by the other's right to occupy the home[16]. Where the matrimonial home is in the sole name of one spouse either spouse may apply, during the subsistence of the marriage[17], for an order declaring, enforcing or terminating those rights[18]; prohibiting, suspending or restricting the exercise of those rights[19]; or, requiring the other spouse to permit the applicant to exercise his or her rights[20] of occupation.

Rights of occupation end on the death[21] of one spouse or on the termination of the marriage[22] unless in the event of a matrimonial dispute or estrangement[23] the court directs otherwise by an order[24] made during the subsistence of the marriage. Therefore unless such a direction has been made under the Matrimonial Homes Act 1983, s 1 before decree absolute, a spouse who has no proprietary interest in the matrimonial home has difficulty in obtaining an injunction in respect of the occupation of the matrimonial home against the other[25].

Although the Act only applies to spouses[26] where, on an application under the Act, one party alleges that there never has been a marriage, the court may treat the marriage as binding[27] unless the contrary is shown when the issue is properly determined by the court[28].

1 Matrimonial Homes Act 1983.
2 Ibid, s 1(9).
3 Ibid.
4 Ibid, s 1(2).
5 As defined in ibid, s 10(1).
6 Ibid, s 1(10).
7 Ibid, s 1. The Act uses the word 'spouse'.
8 Ibid, s 10(2).
9 As opposed to equitable.
10 By virtue of joint ownership, recognised by the Matrimonial Homes Act 1983, s 9.
11 By virtue of the legal interest in the property whether freehold, leasehold or rented.
12 Matrimonial Homes Act 1983, s 1(1).
13 Ibid, s 1(1)(a).
14 Ibid, s 1(1)(b).
15 Ie before it is ended by a decree absolute of divorce or nullity.
16 Matrimonial Homes Act 1983, s 9.
17 Ie before it is ended by a decree absolute of divorce or nullity.
18 Matrimonial Homes Act 1983, s 1(2)(a).
19 Ibid, s 1(2)(b).
20 Ibid, s 1(2)(c).
21 Ibid, s 2(4)(a).
22 Ibid, s 2(4)(b), ie a decree absolute of divorce or nullity.
23 The term 'matrimonial dispute or estrangement' is not defined but by reason of the fact that the order must be made under Matrimonial Homes Act 1983, s 1, it would seem to be limited to proceedings under the Matrimonial Homes Act 1983 or

interlocutory relief in a matrimonial cause. It might include proceedings under the Domestic Violence and Matrimonial Proceedings Act 1976.

24 Under Matrimonial Homes Act 1983, s 1.
25 See para 11.4.
26 Matrimonial Homes Act 1983, s 1.
27 *Seray-Wurie v Seray-Wurie* [1987] Fam Law 124, CA.
28 Where there is no marriage the court would have jurisdiction under the Domestic Violence and Matrimonial Proceedings Act 1976 if the parties came within the meaning of the phrase 'living with each other in the same household as husband and wife'. See further paras 11.2, 11.8 and 11.9.

Wardship

11.6 The wardship jurisdiction of the High Court is inherent and derives from the protection given by the Crown to its subjects. Those who are minors[1] are more vulnerable than adults and are given the special protection of the Crown as *parens patriæ*[2].

Any minor who is a British subject or who is present in England or Wales may be made a ward of court[3] although the court may refuse to exercise the jurisdiction[4].

A judge exercising the wardship jurisdiction has limitless power to protect the ward from any interference with his or her welfare, direct or indirect[5]. It is unfruitful to seek to define any limits to the jurisdiction[6]. The exercise of the wardship powers is discretionary[7]. The interests of the ward are the paramount consideration[8]. In the exercise of their discretionary powers, judges should keep a proper balance between the protection of their wards and the rights of outside parties (those parties not in a family or personal relationship with the ward) whether such rights arose by common law or statute[9].

1 A minor is a person under the age of 18: Family Law Reform Act 1969, s 1(1).
2 *Re P (GE) (an infant)* [1965] Ch 568, [1964] 3 All ER 977, CA.
3 A minor becomes a ward upon the issue of the originating summons: FPR 1991, r 5.1.
4 Child in the care of the local authority, see *A v Liverpool City Council* [1982] AC 363, [1981] 2 All ER 385, HL. Minor whose parent claims diplomatic immunity, see *Re C (an infant)* [1959] Ch 363, [1958] 2 All ER 656. Child refused entry by the immigration authorities, see *Re Mohammed Arif (an infant)* [1968] Ch 643, [1968] 2 All ER 145, CA; see also *Re S (minors)* (1980) 11 Fam Law 55, CA. No jurisdiction to grant a bare declaration of paternity: *Re JS (a minor)* [1981] Fam 22, [1980] 1 All ER 1061, CA. The above examples are not exhaustive.
5 *Re X (a minor) (Wardship: Restriction on Publication)* [1975] Fam 54, [1975] 1 All ER 702, CA; *Re R (MJ) (a minor)* [1975] Fam 89, [1975] 2 All ER 749; *Re D (a minor) (Wardship: Sterilisation)* [1976] Fam 185, [1976] 1 All ER 326; *Re J (a minor)* [1984] FLR 535, [1984] Fam Law 308.
6 Ibid.
7 Ibid.
8 Ibid and see the CA 1989, s 1(1).
9 Ibid.

11.7 The Children Act 1989 gives the High Court and county courts, inter alia, power to make residence orders, contact orders, prohibited steps orders and specific issue orders[1]. In proceedings for a residence order the court may grant an ancillary injunction in respect of an infringement of the exercise of parental responsibility[2] or any other right in relation to the child[3]. Such an injunction may be granted as interlocutory relief without the issue of separate proceedings[4]. It would seem that an ouster injunction may be granted as interlocutory relief in section 8 proceedings, but only where the conditions in the Domestic Violence and Matrimonial Proceedings Act 1976 or the Matrimonial Homes Act 1983 are satisfied. Although the question of where a child should live will usually be suitable for determination by a specific issue order, such an order may not interfere with proprietory rights of occupation[5].

1 Section 8.
2 'Parental responsibility' is defined by s 3.
3 *M v M (Residence Order: Ancillary Injunction)* [1994] Fam Law 440, Johnson J; *C v K (Inherent Powers: Exclusion Order)* [1996] 2 FLR 506, Wall J.
4 Ibid. This is consistent with *Re W (a minor)* [1981] 3 All ER 401, 11 Fam Law 207, CA; *Ainsbury v Millington* [1986] 1 All ER 73, [1986] 1 FLR 331, CA; see also *D v Q* [1990] Fam Law 302.
5 *Pearson v Franklin (Parental Home: Ouster)* [1994] 1 FLR 246, CA. See also *Re D (Prohibited Steps Order)* [1996] 2 FLR 273.

Unmarried couples

11.8 The 1976 Act[1] provides remedies for unmarried as well as married couples. If the language of s 1(2) of the 1976 Act were to be interpreted strictly, its meaning would be greatly restricted since the literal meaning of the words suggest that both the parties to an application must be living together with each other at the time when an application is made. Such a literal interpretation would deprive the Act of much of its effect and rationale. On the other hand, according to the wording a wider meaning might result in serious difficulties in interpreting facts[2].

This was finally resolved in *Davis v Johnson*[3]; it was held that the Act gave jurisdiction to county courts to grant exclusion injunctions where the parties, whether married or living together unmarried, had shared accommodation irrespective of any right of property vested in the person excluded whether as owner, tenant or joint tenant in the same circumstances that such an injunction would be granted under the terms of the Act to a married woman. In effect, unmarried persons living together in the same household as husband and wife are treated by the Act as if they were married[4]. The Act extends protection to households in which a man and a woman live irrespective of whether or not they bring up children at the same time. Difficult questions of fact arise where the relationship has ended, and some time has elapsed before an application to the court is made. The question which has to be answered in such a case is when the relationship between the man and woman concerned is to be treated as having come to an end. It has been indicated that the longer the period of time that has elapsed between the cessation of the relationship between the parties and the issue of the summons is, the more difficult it will be for an applicant to bring himself within the section[5]. The words in the Domestic Violence and Matrimonial Proceedings Act 1976, 'living with each other in the same household as husband and wife', should be interpreted as referring to the relationship existing immediately before the incident (or series of incidents) giving rise to the application[6]. This question is one of fact and it is submitted that where there has been delay for which there is a good explanation, this should not be fatal to the application.

It is a question of fact whether on the circumstances of any particular case, a man and woman are properly to be held as living in the same household as husband and wife. The court deciding the issue must look at all the facts and ask itself whether it can be said that the parties are living together in the same household as husband and wife. In answering that question there are many different factors which must be taken into account; it will depend on the domestic relationship between the parties; their ages; the accommodation that is available and in general upon their manner of life together[7].

Decisions and interpretations of the words 'living with each other in the same household'[8] provide some assistance in the interpretation of the Act of 1976. The phrase 'household' has an abstract meaning[9] rather than referring to something physical. Mere physical absence from the matrimonial home is not fatal to the suggestion that the parties are 'living together' unless it can also be shown that one or other of the parties has made up his or her mind that he or she will not renew the relationship of living together in the same household with the other party. Even where the parties continue to share the premises in which they had lived together, it is not certain that they can be described as living together for the purposes of the Act. So for example where two parties continue to live in a house but occupy different rooms in the property; do not speak to each other and do not take their meals together it is unlikely that they will be held to be living together for the purposes of the Act[10].

1 Domestic Violence and Matrimonial Proceedings Act 1976, s 1(2).
2 *B v B (Domestic Violence: Jurisdiction)* [1978] Fam 26, [1978] 1 All ER 821. See also *McLean v Burke* (1980) 3 FLR 70, CA.
3 [1979] AC 264, [1978] 1 All ER 1132, HL answering some of the questions raised in *B v B (Domestic Violence: Jurisdiction)* above and *Cantliff v Jenkins* [1978] Fam 47n, [1978] 1 All ER 836, CA.
4 Ibid at 334E and at 1145a, per Viscount Dilhorne approved and followed by the Court of Appeal in *McLean v Nugent* (1980) 1 FLR 26, CA.
5 *McLean v Nugent* (1980) 1 FLR 26, CA per Ormrod LJ.
6 *McLean v Burke* (1980) 3 FLR 70, CA.
7 *Hills v Bushby* [1977] CA Transcript 398b.
8 Divorce Reform Act 1969, ss 2(5) and 3(6), repealed and replaced by the MCA 1973, s 2(6).
9 *Santos v Santos* [1972] Fam 247, [1972] 2 All ER 246, CA.
10 *Hollens v Hollens* (1971) 115 Sol Jo 327, Wrangham J.

11.9 The words 'in the same household' are to be regarded as words of limitation the effect of which is to treat persons living with each other as living apart unless they are 'in the same household'[1]. Courts construing the statute should not lose sight of the practicalities of such relationships and should be reluctant to find artificial and separate households in circumstances where the practicalities of the accommodation prevent the reality of two separate households[2]. The question is one of degree and the whole of the physical circumstances have to be looked at to determine whether the degree of separation is such as to justify the finding of two separate households. Whilst cases decided under the old law may provide some guidance, it is to be borne in mind that the old decisions were the product of judicial stretching of the law designed to get over the impossible position in which a couple had ceased to communicate altogether but neither of the parties was able to leave the home they had formerly shared together because of the absence of alternative accommodation[3]. Just as it was necessary to stretch the law for the purposes of practical necessity in those cases, it may be necessary to take a quite contrary approach when determining applications under the 1976 Act, regard having been had to the fact that one or other of the parties may not be able to leave because of the impracticality of obtaining alternative accommodation in circumstances where, by reason of the proximity of the parties and the disintegration of their relationship, protection may most be needed.

The phrase 'living with each other as husband and wife' also acts as a phrase of limitation by excluding from the protection of the Act any case in which a man and a woman simply share living accommodation for the purposes of reducing their individual expenses.

For the test of living together as husband and wife for the purposes of certain state benefits regard is had to various factors such as whether the parties are members of the same household, the stability of the relationship, the extent of any financial support, the presence of a sexual relationship, whether the couple have children and whether they represent that they are married. These matters are only indications and the main factor is that of the parties' general relationship[4].

Where the parties are not married and do not come within the definition of 'living with each other in the same household as husband and wife' recourse must be had to common law actions in tort for trespass or assault[5].

1 *Mouncer v Mouncer* [1972] 1 All ER 289 at 291f, per Wrangham J and see *Hills v Bushby* [1977] CA Transcript 398b.
2 *Adeoso v Adeoso* [1981] 1 All ER 107 at 110d–f, [1980] 1 WLR 1535 at 1537F–H, CA, per Ormrod LJ.
3 Ibid at 109d–f and at 1537F–H.
4 *Re J (Income Support: Cohabitation)* [1995] 1 FLR 660.
5 *Hills v Bushby* [1977] CA Transcript 398b.

PROCEDURE

Applications for ex parte injunctions and orders

Applications to county courts under the Domestic Violence and Matrimonial Proceedings Act 1976

11.10 Such applications should be made to the county court for the district in which the applicant or the respondent resides or for the district in which the matrimonial home[1] is situate[2]. The application is made in the prescribed form supported by affidavit[3]. The affidavit must explain why the application is made ex parte[4]. In a case of great urgency, an application may be made before the issue of the originating application[5] upon an undertaking to issue such by the party making the application or if the party is represented, then by the solicitors acting for him or her[6].

1 'Matrimonial home' means premises in which the husband and wife live; or in the case of an unmarried couple the premises in which they live together in the same household as husband and wife: Domestic Violence and Matrimonial Proceedings Act 1976, s 1(2).

2 FPR 1991, r 3.9(2).
3 CCR Ord 13, r 6(3), (3A). It should be noted that an affidavit sworn by an applicant in support of an ex parte application for an injunction must disclose all material facts to the extent that an applicant must act *uberrima fides* or he will disentitle himself to the relief sought. This requirement is imposed by the court for its own protection and to ensure so far as is possible that the ex parte application procedure is not abused; see *R v Kensington Income Tax General Comrs, ex p Princess de Polignac* [1917] 1 KB 486.
4 CCR Ord 13, r 6(3A). For example the applicant may fear a violent response to the service of an application and accordingly needs immediate protection. See further para 11.20.
5 CCR Ord 13, 6(4).
6 A time limit will be fixed for the issue of the originating application. The time allowed will, in general, not exceed 24 hours and may be shorter depending upon the prevailing circumstances.

Applications to county courts for interlocutory relief in a matrimonial cause

11.11 Where a cause is pending an application should be made to the court in which that cause is pending. Where no matrimonial proceedings have been commenced then an application may be made to any divorce county court[1]. The application is made in the prescribed form supported by affidavit[2].

In cases of great urgency, the application may be made before the cause is commenced[3]. The court will require an undertaking that a matrimonial cause will be commenced[4]. Where a proposed petitioner is frightened of the other spouse and does not wish to disclose his present residence to the proposed respondent, leave may be obtained[5] for his or her address not to be included within the petition. Application for such leave should be made upon the application for an ex parte injunction the reasons for it being set out in the affidavit which is used to support the application for an ex parte relief.

1 FPR 1991, r 2.6(1).
2 CCR Ord 13, r 6(3), (3A).
3 CCR Ord 13, r 6(4).
4 An undertaking must be given to present a petition for divorce, judicial separation or nullity. A time limit will be fixed for the filing of such documents which, in general will not exceed 24 hours in respect of the petition. Longer periods of time may be allowed to file the supporting documents which are:

> In the case of petition for divorce, judicial separation or nullity (a) the marriage certificate; (b) statement as to the arrangements for children; (c) certificate with regard to reconciliation FPR 1991, r 2.6(2), (3), (5).

5 FPR 1991, r 2.3; see *Practice Direction* [1975] 2 All ER 384, [1975] 1 WLR 787.

Applications to county courts under the Matrimonial Homes Act 1983

11.12 The application, which is made in the prescribed form supported by affidavit[1], is made to the court for the district in which the matrimonial home is situate[2]. In cases of urgency, the application may be made before the issue of the originating application[3], upon an undertaking to issue the same[4]. Where a matrimonial cause has been commenced, or is about to be commenced, an application for relief under the Matrimonial Homes Act 1983 must be made as interlocutory relief in such proceedings[5].

1 CCR Ord 13, r 6(3), (3A).

2 CCR Ord 4, r 8(a)(ii).
3 CCR Ord 13, r 6(4), (4A).
4 A time limit will be fixed for the issue of the originating application. The time allowed will, in general, not exceed 24 hours and may be shorter depending upon the circumstances.
5 FPR 1991, r 3.8(3).

Applications to county courts under the Children Act 1989

11.13 The application, which is made in the prescribed form supported by affidavit[1], may be made to any county court[2]. However, where a matrimonial cause is pending applications under the CA 1989, Parts I and II, in relation to a child of the family must be made in the cause[3]. In cases of urgency, application may be made at the same time as an ex parte application for a section 8 order[4].

1 CCR Ord 13, r 6(3), (3A).
2 FPR 1991, Part IV does not limit the jurisdiction of courts by the residence of the parties of the children.
3 FPR 1991, r 2.40(1); leave to intervene is not necessary for applications by non-parties.
4 An ex parte application for a s 8 order is permitted by FPR 1991, r 4.4(4) but such an order will be very exceptional, see *Re B (minors) (Residence Order)* [1992] Fam 162, [1992] 3 All ER 867, CA.

Applications to the High Court under the Domestic Violence and Matrimonial Proceedings Act 1976

11.14 Such application may be made either at the Principal Registry in London or any district registry of the High Court[1]. The application, which is made by affidavit[2], may be made before the issue of an originating summons[3] upon an undertaking to issue the same[4].

1 FPR 1991, r 3.9(2).
2 RSC Ord 29, r 1(2).
3 RSC Ord 29, r 1(3).
4 The time limit will be fixed for the issue of originating summons. The time allowed will in general not exceed 24 hours and may be shorter depending upon the prevailing circumstances.

Applications to the High Court for interlocutory relief in a matrimonial cause

11.15 As a matrimonial cause cannot be commenced in the High Court[1] there will already be proceedings pending at the time any application for interlocutory relief is made to the High Court. The application for such relief should be made either at the Royal Courts of Justice or at the appropriate district registry depending upon whether the suit is pending in the Principal Registry or a district registry. The application is made by affidavit[2].

1 Matrimonial and Family Proceedings Act 1984, s 33(3).
2 RSC Ord 29, r 1(2).

Applications to the High Court under the Matrimonial Homes Act 1983

11.16 The application is made either at the Principal Registry[1] or at any district registry of the High Court[2]. The application which is made on affidavit[3] may, in cases of urgency, be made before the issue of the originating summons[4] upon an undertaking to issue such originating summons[5]. Where a matrimonial cause has been commenced, or is about to be commenced, an application for relief under the Matrimonial Homes Act 1983 must be made by an interlocutory application in such proceedings[6].

1 Defined as the Principal Registry of the Family Division by the FPR 1991, r 1(2).
2 FPR 1991, r 3.6(1) as applied by r 3.8(2).
3 RSC Ord 29 r 1(2).
4 RSC Ord 29 r 1(3).
5 A time limit will be fixed for the issue of the originating summons. The time allowed will, in general, not exceed 24 hours and may be shorter depending upon the prevailing circumstances.
6 FPR 1991, r 3.8(3).

Applications to the High Court under the Children Act 1989

11.17 The application, which is made in the prescribed form supported by affidavit[1], may be made to the Principal Registry or any district registry[2]. Unless there is good reason to issue in the High Court, application should be made to a county court. However, where a matrimonial cause is pending applications under the CA 1989, Parts I and II, in relation to a child of the family must be made in the cause[3]. In cases of urgency, application may be made at the same time as an ex parte application for a section 8 order[4].

1 RSC Ord 29, r 1(2).
2 FPR 1991, Part IV does not limit the jurisdiction of courts by the residence of the parties of the children.
3 FPR 1991, r 2.40(1); leave to intervene is not necessary for applications by non-parties.
4 An ex parte application for a s 8 order is permitted by FPR 1991, r 4.4(4) but such an order will be very exceptional; see *Re B (minors) (Residence Order)* [1992] Fam 162, [1992] 3 All ER 867, CA.

Applications in wardship proceedings in the High Court

11.18 Applications for interlocutory relief in wardship proceedings may be made either at the Principal Registry in London or at any district registry of the High Court[1]. The application is made by affidavit[2]. The application may be made before the issue of the originating summons[3] upon an undertaking to issue the originating summons[4]. Since the CA 1989 came into force the use of wardship proceedings has diminished. Unless there is good reason to issue wardship proceedings, application should be made under the CA 1989.

1 FPR 1991, r 5.1.
2 RSC Ord 29, r 1(2).
3 RSC Ord 29, r 1(3).
4 A time limit will be fixed for the issue of the originating summons. The time allowed will in general not exceed 24 hours and may be shorter depending upon the prevailing circumstances.

Procedure upon the hearing of ex parte applications

11.19 Applications for injunctions restraining molestation, exclusion injunctions and injunctions requiring the respondent to permit the applicant to enter and remain in the home or to return children and thereafter not to remove children from the care and control of a particular parent must be made to a judge or district judge of either the High Court or the county court[1].

Most courts have at least one day in each week when urgent ex parte applications can be made[2]. Applications at the Royal Courts of Justice are heard at 10.30 am and 2 pm each week day[3]. Urgent applications at other times may be made by arrangement with the Clerk of the Rules.

Where an applicant's solicitors notify the respondent's solicitors of an intended ex parte application and fail to notify them of its withdrawal they may be personally liable for costs incurred by those parties of attendance at the abortive hearing[4].

The application should be made on affidavit, except in a case of great urgency when the judge may exceptionally hear oral evidence. The affidavit should be as full and complete as possible.

Only in exceptional circumstances should an applicant for a non-molestation or ouster injunction be asked to give an undertaking in respect of damages sustained by the respondent[5]. In general such an undertaking is unnecessary and inappropriate in matrimonial and children's cases involving personal conduct. The undertaking should not be recited automatically in the order as drawn up by the court.

Applications are heard in chambers[6] though a judge may direct the matter to be heard in open court at his discretion.

Where an ex parte injunction is made, a return date will be specified at which time an inter partes hearing will take place. The return date should be made as soon as possible after the ex parte hearing[7]. The reason is that on an ex parte application, the court will be unable to reach a rational and balanced decision[8] with the result that delay in hearing the respondent's side of the matters which are alleged to have necessitated the application may cause him or her great injustice and inconvenience.

An ex parte injunction together with any supporting affidavit should be served on the respondent as soon as possible[9]. Furthermore, where the injunction has been obtained on an undertaking to issue substantive proceedings the originating document should be served at the same time or if this is not possible, as soon as possible thereafter. Where an undertaking is given to issue substantive proceedings 'as soon as reasonably practical' this means the same as 'forthwith'[10]. It is important that there should be no default in compliance with such an undertaking[11]. It is to be emphasised that before an injunction can be enforced by committal to prison the order must have been endorsed with a penal notice and served personally upon the respondent irrespective of whether a solicitor is on the record as acting on behalf of the respondent.

1 FPR 1991, rr 3.8(4), 3.9(10).
2 This may be at 10.30 am or at 2 pm or both. Some courts hear ex parte applications at 4 pm. The practice varies from court to court and details can always be obtained by telephoning the court office.
3 See also Notice in Daily Cause List.
4 *Re F* (1984) Times, 25 August.
5 *Practice Direction* [1974] 2 All ER 400, [1974] 1 WLR 576.

6 FPR 1991, r 3.9(2), *Practice Direction* [1974] 2 All ER 1119, [1974] 1 WLR 936.
7 *Ansah v Ansah* [1977] Fam 138, [1977] 2 All ER 638, CA. See also *Morgan v Morgan* (1978) 9 Fam Law 87, CA; *Loseby v Newman* [1995] 2 FLR 754, CA.
8 *Rennick v Rennick* [1978] 1 All ER 817, [1977] 1 WLR 1455, CA, per Ormrod LJ, obiter.
9 This must be done for two reasons: firstly so that he or she becomes aware of the order and is then able to comply with it and secondly so that the order may be enforced by committal. Furthermore service must be effected so as to give the respondent at least two clear days' notice of the return date.
10 *PS Refson & Co Ltd v Saggers* [1984] 3 All ER 111, [1984] 1 WLR 1025.
11 Ibid.

Principles applicable to the determination of ex parte applications

11.20 In general, an application for an injunction, under the Acts of 1976 or 1983 or as interlocutory relief in a matrimonial suit, should only be made or granted ex parte where there is a real immediate danger of serious injury or irreparable damage[1]. The 1976 Act was created and designed to provide an emergency procedure to cope with the crisis incidents in domestic life[2] and it follows that only exceptional cases falling within either of the two categories will justify a departure from the normal procedure particularly where orders are sought which may have the effect of depriving a respondent of a roof over his head. Almost every application for a non-molestation order, an order ousting the other party from the matrimonial home or an order that the applicant be permitted to re-enter the matrimonial home inevitably will involve a degree of emergency but such 'normal emergency' does not justify an application made ex parte. It is to be emphasised that whilst the power of the court to intervene immediately and without notice to the other party in a family dispute is essential to the administration of justice, the power must be used with great caution and only in circumstances where it is really necessary to act immediately[3]. Whilst the court is generally reluctant to grant an injunction ex parte except in the clearest cases, because to do so may result in an injustice to the respondent which will have the effect of damaging the court's authority, the court is in particular reluctant to make orders which would involve the ousting of a respondent from the matrimonial home without the opportunity of his having been heard[4].

Where such a radical remedy is sought, it is important to reach a rational and balanced decision[5]. It has been emphasised by the courts on numerous occasions that the most urgent of applications when onerous relief is claimed, can be dealt with on two days' notice in matrimonial proceedings pending in the Divorce Registry for hearing at the Royal Courts of Justice[6] and the corresponding procedure in divorce county courts where a suit is pending or is about to be commenced or in which an undertaking to file can be given. Urgent applications for relief under the Act of 1976 between co-habitees or between husband and wives with no present intention of divorcing or judicially separating may be treated with equal speed.

More generally, circumstances may arise when prior notice cannot be given to the respondent in particular, where the one parent has disappeared with the children or a spouse is so frightened of the other that some protection must be provided against a violent response to service of the proceedings but in all such cases, the court must be satisfied that such protection is genuinely necessary before it will be persuaded to act[7].

1 See *Practice Direction* [1978] 2 All ER 919, [1978] 1 WLR 925. The contents of the Practice Direction and the need for following it was emphasised by the Court of Appeal in *Smollen v Smollen* [1979] CA Transcript 794 (14 December). See also *Beese v Woodhouse* [1970] 1 All ER 769, [1970] 1 WLR 586, CA.
2 *McLean v Nugent* (1980) 1 FLR 26, CA, per Ormrod LJ.
3 *Ansah v Ansah* [1977] Fam 138 at 142H, [1977] 2 All ER 638 at 642b–c, per Ormrod LJ.
4 See *G v G (Ouster: ex parte application)* [1990] 1 FLR 395, CA and *Masich v Masich* (1977) 7 Fam Law 245, CA.
5 *Rennick v Rennick* [1978] 1 All ER 817, [1977] 1 WLR 1455, CA.
6 See *Practice Direction* [1972] 2 All ER 1360, [1972] 1 WLR 1047. The procedure is also set out in the Daily Cause List under the heading 'Matrimonial Causes and Matters – Urgent Applications'.
7 *Ansah v Ansah* [1977] Fam 138 at 143 C [1972] 2 All ER 638 at 642e, per Ormrod LJ.

Time limits

11.21 Once the court, in its discretion, grants an ex parte injunction, the order, when drawn up, must clearly state the terms of the injunction and must moreover, specify the return date when the matter will be considered further by the court in the presence of both parties. The return date even if that date is only for a preliminary hearing of the matter must be as soon as practicable and should normally be a matter of days rather than weeks away from the date of the ex parte order.

In order to prevent injustice to the respondent, an order obtained ex parte must state expressly the date on which it expires[1]. Where, exceptionally, it is anticipated by the party obtaining an order ex parte that there will be difficulty in serving the other side, it may be permissible for the court to fix a longer period before the return date and to protect the respondent's interest sufficiently by incorporating into the order a liberty in the respondent to apply to the court upon short (usually 24 hours) notice to discharge any or all of the orders made by the court on the ex parte application[2].

It is to be emphasised that in no circumstances should an order be made upon an ex parte application which is expressed to operate 'until further order'. To make such an order upon an application made ex parte is wholly unjustifiable and improper[3].

1 *Ansah v Ansah* [1977] Fam 138 at 143D–F, [1972] 2 All ER 638 at 642f–h, per Ormrod LJ.
2 Ibid.
3 *Morgan v Morgan* (1978) 9 Fam Law 87, [1978] CA Transcript 423, per Bridge LJ; a case concerning an appeal from a non-molestation order made on the ex parte application of a husband against his wife.

Power of arrest

11.22 In order for the court to have power to impose a power of arrest upon an order made ex parte, it will be necessary for the court to be satisfied, as it is necessary to satisfy it on all such applications, that not only has the respondent caused actual bodily harm to the applicant but also that he or she is likely to do so again[1]. Whilst there may be little or no difficulty in satisfying a judge on an application properly made ex parte that an applicant has suffered actual bodily harm at the hands of the respondent, it may well be very difficult or impossible to establish ex parte that the respondent is likely to do so again[2]. It follows, that even where the court is prepared to make an order upon an application made ex parte, it may well not be prepared to make an order endorsed with a power of arrest unless it is possible to establish on affidavit any reason for supposing that a respondent is likely to commit further actual bodily harm upon the applicant. Evidence which might support such an application and which should be included in any affidavit in support of an application made ex parte where it is intended to apply to the court for a power of arrest to be attached to any order made on the application would include the allegations that previous orders of the court that had been made were flouted; that criminal convictions of violence had been recorded against the respondent prior to the incidents complained of; that by committing the offences in question, the respondent will be in breach of probation orders, suspended sentences, conditional discharges or other orders of the court should process for enforcement be taken or that the history of the particular relationship is one of persistent and protracted violence.

1 *Lewis v Lewis* [1978] Fam 60, [1978] 1 All ER 729, CA.
2 *Morgan v Morgan* (1978) 9 Fam Law 87, [1978] CA Transcript 423.

Applications inter partes for injunctions

Applications to the county court under the Domestic Violence and Matrimonial Proceedings Act 1976

11.23 Such applications are made by originating application[1] to the county court for the district in which the applicant or the respondent resides or in which the matrimonial home[2] is situate[3].

The applicant must swear an affidavit setting out the grounds upon which he or she seeks the relief claimed[4]. The originating application together with the supporting affidavit should be served personally[5] on the respondent at least two clear days before the hearing[6]. An affidavit of service of these documents should be sworn by the person serving them[7].

Having been served with the originating application and affidavit in support, the respondent should file an affidavit in answer. The affidavit should admit or deny, as appropriate, the allegations in the affidavit of the applicant and should set out any other relevant matters upon which the respondent relies such as the availability of alternative accommodation for either himself or the applicant.

In general, applications will be heard by a judge or district judge[8] in chambers[9] although the court may direct that the matter be heard in open court.

Except in a case of urgency the applicant, before the hearing, should prepare a draft of the injunction sought[10]. If the application is granted the draft should be submitted to the judge who will settle the terms of the injunction[11]. When settled the injunction will be forwarded to the proper officer[12] for filing[13] who will issue a copy to the applicant's solicitor for service. The order thus issued should be endorsed with a penal notice[14] and should be served personally[15] so that the same may be enforced by committal for breach. It is good practice for the person serving the order endorsed with the penal notice upon the respondent personally to swear an affidavit of service immediately after which exhibits the order served and sets out the circumstances of service so that it can be retained on file by the applicant's solicitors for use in the event of breach in an application to commit.

1 FPR 1991, r 3.9(2) in Form N16A.
2 'Matrimonial home' means the premises in which a husband and wife live; in the case of an unmarried couple the expression means premises in which they live together in the same household as husband and wife. See the Domestic Violence and Matrimonial Proceedings Act 1976, s 1(2).
3 FPR 1991, r 3.9(2).
4 CCR Ord 13, r 6(3).
5 Personal service is desirable in case the respondent does not attend the hearing; see CCR Ord 13, r 1(2), (3). However it should be borne in mind that where a solicitor is on the record of the court as acting for the respondent, service upon that solicitor will be good service.
6 FPR 1991, r 3.9(5).
7 This is to prove personal service in case the respondent does not attend the hearing. The requirement in CCR Ord 7, r 6(1)(b) that an affidavit of service should be sworn is directory and not mandatory: see *Savage v Savage* [1979] CA Transcript 537. It follows that where service has been effected oral evidence of good service is admissible.
8 FPR 1991, r 3.9(10).
9 FPR 1991, r 3.9(2).
10 CCR Ord 13, r 6(6).
11 CCR Ord 13, r 6(6).
12 For the meaning of 'proper officer' see CCR Ord 1, r 3.
13 CCR Ord 13, r 6(7).
14 CCR Ord 29, r 1(2), (3).
15 CCR Ord 29 r 1(2), (3).

Applications to county courts for interlocutory relief in a matrimonial cause

11.24 An application for an injunction in a matrimonial cause is made by notice of application[1] and should be supported by an affidavit sworn by the applicant. The application together with the affidavit in support should be served at least two clear days before the date of hearing[2]. The application and supporting affidavit should be served personally[3] and the process server should swear an affidavit of service exhibiting the documents served and setting out the circumstances in which they were served[4].

The application is made to a judge or district judge[5]. The application like applications made ex parte and inter partes for relief under the 1976 Act may be heard by the judge in chambers[6].

Upon being served with the applicant's affidavit and application, the respondent should then file an affidavit in answer. The affidavit should admit or deny as appropriate the allegations contained in the affidavit in support of the application and should set out any other relevant matters which will be relied upon by the respondent at the hearing of the application.

Except in a case of urgency the applicant, before the hearing, should prepare a draft of the injunction sought[7]. If the application is granted the draft should be submitted to the judge who will settle the terms of the injunction[8]. When settled the injunction will be forwarded to the proper officer⁹ for filing¹⁰ who will issue a copy to the applicant's solicitor for service. The order should be endorsed with a penal notice¹¹ and the copy issued by the court to the applicant's solicitors should be served personally¹² on the respondent in order that, in the event of breach, it may be enforced by committal. It is good practice for the person serving the order personally upon the respondent to prepare and swear an affidavit of service setting out the circumstances in which it was served and exhibiting the documents served which should then be retained on file by the solicitors acting for the applicant so that in the event of a committal hearing, the contemporaneous affidavit is available.

1 FPR 1991, r 10.9 and CCR Ord 13, 4 1.
2 CCR Ord 13, rr 1(2),(3), as applied by FPR 1991, r 10.9.
3 Personal service is desirable in case the respondent does not attend the hearing. However, service may be effected by post to a solicitor on the record or to a party in person; see FPR 1991, r 10.17. It is to be emphasised that where a solicitor is on the record as acting for a respondent, service upon that solicitor is good and effective service until such time as that solicitor is removed from the record as acting in accordance with the Rules of Court.
4 This is to prove personal service in case the respondent does not attend the hearing. The requirement in CCR Ord 7, r 6(1)(b) that an affidavit of service should be sworn is directory and not mandatory: see *Savage v Savage* [1979] CA Transcript 537. The effect is that where an affidavit of service is not available at the hearing, oral evidence to prove service is admissible.
5 FPR 1991, rr 3.8(4), 3.9(10).
6 *Practice Direction* [1974] 2 All ER 1119, [1974] 1 WLR 936.
7 CCR Ord 13, r 6(6).
8 CCR Ord 13, r 6(6).
9 For the meaning of 'proper officer' see CCR Ord 1, r 3.
10 CCR Ord 13, r 6(7).
11 CCR Ord 29, r 1(2)(3).
12 CCR Ord 29, r 1(2)(3).

Applications to county courts under the Matrimonial Homes Act 1983

11.25 The application is made by originating application¹ to the county court for the district in which the applicant or respondent resides². Where matrimonial proceedings are pending between the parties, an application under ss 1 or 9 must be made as an interlocutory application in such proceedings³. The applicant must swear an affidavit setting out the grounds of the application⁴. The originating application and supporting affidavit should be served personally⁵ on the respondent at least two clear days before the return date⁶. On issue of the originating application the proper officer will have fixed the return date⁷.

Having been served with the originating application and affidavit in support the respondent should swear and file an affidavit in answer, admitting or denying the allegations, as appropriate, and setting out all relevant matters that will be relied upon at the hearing.

Where the application is for an ouster injunction it will be heard by a judge or district judge⁸. However, where it is sought to terminate the respondent's rights of occupation⁹ and it appears to the court, on an ex parte application, that the respondent is not in occupation and his whereabouts cannot, after reasonable inquiries, be ascertained, the court may dispense with service and hear and determine the application¹⁰.

The application will be heard in chambers unless otherwise directed.

Except in a case of urgency, the applicant, before the hearing, should prepare a draft of the injunction sought[11]. If the injunction is granted the draft should be submitted to the judge, who will settle the terms of the injunction[12]. When settled, the injunction will be forwarded to the proper officer for filing[13], who will issue a copy to the applicant's solicitors for service.

The order, thus issued, should be endorsed with a penal notice[14] and served personally[15] on the respondent so that the same may be enforced by committal if it is breached. It is good practice for an affidavit of service to be made by the person serving the order, and filed with the court, so that it is ready in the event of an application to commit.

1 FPR 1991, rr 3.6(1)(b), 3.8(2).
2 FPR 1991, rr 3.6(3), 3.8(2).
3 FPR 1991, r 3.8(3).
4 FPR 1991, rr 3.6(1), 3.8(2).
5 Personal service is desirable in case the respondent does not attend the hearing. CCR Ord 13, r 1(5) permits the court to proceed in the respondent's absence. Where the respondent has a solicitor on the record as acting, service on his solicitor is good service: CCR Ord 7, r 6(1)(b). An affidavit of service should be sworn and filed where personal service has been effected.
6 CCR Ord 13, r 1(2).
7 CCR Ord 3, r 4(4)(a).
8 FPR 1991, r 3.8(4).
9 See the Matrimonial Homes Act 1983, s 1(2)(a).
10 FPR 1991, r 3.8(5).
11 CCR Ord 13, r 6(6).
12 CCR Ord 13, r 6(6).
13 CCR Ord 13, r 6(7).
14 CCR Ord 29, rr 1(2),(3).
15 CCR Ord 29, rr 1(2),(3).

Applications to the High Court under the Domestic Violence and Matrimonial Proceedings Act 1976

11.26 The application made by a party to a marriage[1] to the High Court for an injunction under the 1976 Act is, if no other relief is sought in the proceedings, made by originating summons[2] issued out of the Principal Registry[3] or out of a district registry[4] of the High Court[5]. Where a cause or proceedings under the FPR 1991, Part III are pending, an application under s 1 of the 1976 Act by a party to the other proceedings, may be made as an interlocutory application in such proceedings[6].

The originating summons should contain a concise statement of the relief or remedy claimed[7]. The parties to the originating summons are described as plaintiff and defendant[8]. On the issue of the originating summons, the plaintiff may apply for the date of the hearing to be fixed[9].

The originating summons must be served not less than four clear days[10] before the date fixed for the hearing[11]. If the plaintiff wishes to adduce evidence in support at the hearing, he must do so by affidavit[12] which must be served on the defendant not less than four clear days before the hearing[13].

The time for the defendant to acknowledge service of the originating summons expires on the next day but one before the date of hearing fixed[14].

Although the originating summons and memorandum of acknowledgement of service may be served by post[15] it is desirable that they should be served personally together with the affidavit in support[16]. The process server should swear an affidavit deposing to the fact of personal service and exhibiting any documents served upon the respondent[17].

The defendant should swear an affidavit in answer to the application admitting or denying as appropriate, the allegations made by the plaintiff and, in addition, setting out any other relevant matters which the respondent will rely upon at the hearing of the application.

Unless directed otherwise by the judge, the application will be heard in chambers[18].

If an injunction is granted then the order, duly endorsed with a penal notice[19] should be served personally on the defendant[20] so that the same may be enforced by committal. The person serving the order thus endorsed with the penal notice, should, as a matter of practice swear an affidavit immediately following service in which he deposes to the circumstances of personal service and exhibits the documents served which should then be retained on the file of solicitors acting for the applicant so as to be available should the need arise for an application to commit the respondent for breach of the order.

1 This includes a man and a woman who are living with each other in the same household as husband and wife: see Domestic Violence and Matrimonial Proceedings Act 1976, s 1 (2).
2 FPR 1991, r 3.9(2). The originating summons is as in Form 10 in Appendix A of the Rules.
3 This means the Principal Registry of the Family Division.
4 This means any district registry having a divorce county court within its district: FPR 1991, r 1.2.
5 FPR 1991, r 3.9(2).
6 FPR 1991, r 3.9(3).
7 RSC Ord 7, r 3(1).
8 RSC Ord 6, r 2(2).
9 RSC Ord 28, r 2(2). This should be done so that the matter can be heard promptly.
10 The use of the word 'clear' has the result that both the date from which the period commences and the date when the act is done are excluded from the computation, see *Supreme Court Practice 1997*, para 3/2/8.
11 RSC Ord 28, r 3(2).
12 RSC Ord 28, r 3(3).
13 RSC Ord 28, r 3(3).
14 RSC Ord 28, r 2(2).
15 RSC Ord 10, rr 1(2), 5.
16 So that actual knowledge can be proved if the defendant fails to attend the hearing.
17 Stating by whom the document was served; the day of the week and the date on which it was served; where and how: RSC Ord 65, r 8.
18 See *Practice Direction* [1974] 2 All ER 1119, [1974] 1 WLR 936.
19 RSC Ord 45, r 7(4); the text of the penal notice is as at para 45/7/6 of the *Supreme Court Practice 1997*.
20 RSC Ord 45, r 7(2).

Applications to the High Court for interlocutory relief in a matrimonial cause

11.27 The application is made by summons[1] supported by an affidavit. The application is made to a judge or district judge[2]. The summons and supporting affidavit should be served personally[3] at least two clear days[4] before the date of hearing[5]. An affidavit of service of the summons and supporting affidavit should be sworn by the process server[6].

The respondent should swear an affidavit in answer to the application admitting or denying as appropriate the allegations contained in the affidavit in support of the application and furthermore setting out any other relevant matters which he intends to rely upon at the hearing of the application.

The application will be heard in chambers by a judge or district judge[7] unless otherwise directed[8].

If the judge grants the injunction then the same, duly endorsed with a penal notice[9] should be served personally[10] on the respondent so that the same may be enforced by committal. The person serving the order endorsed with the penal notice should swear an affidavit of service immediately after the event of service which deposes to the circumstances in which service was effected on the respondent personally and which exhibits the documents that were served. The affidavit thus sworn should be retained by solicitors acting for the applicant for use in the event of an application to commit the respondent for breach of the order.

1 RSC Ord 29, r 1(2); FPR 1991, r 10.9(b).
2 FPR 1991, rr 3.8(3), 3.9(10).
3 Personal service is desirable in case the respondent does not attend the hearing. However, where a solicitor is on the record as acting, the summons may be served upon him by post: see FPR 1991, r 10.2. Once a solicitor is on the record of the court as acting, service may be effected upon him until substitution of another solicitor on the record or if the party is acting in person has been effected: see *Supreme Court Practice 1997*, para 67/1/5.
4 See *Supreme Court Practice 1997*, para 3/2/8.
5 RSC Ord 32, r 3.
6 This is to prove personal service in case the respondent does not attend the hearing. The requirement is directory not mandatory; see *Savage v Savage* [1979] CA Transcript 537. The effect is that if it becomes necessary to prove service, oral evidence is admissible in the event of an affidavit of service not being available to the court.
7 FPR 1991, rr 3.8(3), 3.9(10), 10.9(a).
8 *Practice Direction* [1974] 2 All ER 1119, [1974] 1 WLR 936.
9 RSC Ord 45, r 7(4); *Supreme Court Practice 1997*, para 45/7/6.
10 RSC Ord 45, r 7(2).

Applications to the High Court under the Matrimonial Homes Act 1983

11.28 The application is made by originating summons[1], issued out of the Principal Registry or a district registry supported by affidavit.

The originating summons, and supporting affidavit should be served personally on the respondent[2], together with a form of acknowledgement of service[3]. The respondent should acknowledge service as directed. If the respondent intends to contest the application, he must, within 14 days after the time allowed for acknowledging service[4], file an affidavit in answer[5] setting out the grounds on which he relies[6]. If he does not do so the registrar may order him to do so[7] and, in default, debar him from defending[8].

As the timetable prescribed does not provide for an early hearing of the application it is more appropriate to proceed in the county court[9]. Where proceedings are brought in the High Court an application may be made to the district judge, on issue of the originating summons, to reduce the time limits and to expedite the hearing[10].

Where the application is for an ouster injunction it may be heard by a judge or district judge[11]. Where it is sought to terminate the respondent's rights of occupation[12] and it appears to the district judge on an ex parte application, that the respondent is not in occupation and that his whereabouts cannot, after reasonable inquiries, be ascertained, the district judge may dispense with service, and hear and determine the application[13].

The application will be heard in chambers unless otherwise directed.

If the judge grants the injunction then the same, duly endorsed with a penal notice[14], should be served personally[15] on the respondent so that the same may be enforced by committal if breached. It is good practice for an affidavit of service to be made by the person serving the order and filed with the court so that it is ready in the event of an application to commit.

Where a cause[16] is pending between the parties in the High Court an application for relief under the Matrimonial Homes Act 1983 must be made by interlocutory summons in those proceedings[17].

1 FPR 1991, rr 3.6(1), 3.8(2).
2 This is to prove service in case the respondent does not attend the hearing. An affidavit of service should be sworn and filed.
3 FPR 1991, rr 3.6(5), 3.8(2).
4 14 days; FPR 1991 r 10.8(2)(b).
5 FPR 1991, rr 3.6(7), 3.8(2).
6 Ibid.
7 FPR 1991, rr 3.6(8), 3.8(2).
8 Ibid.
9 See para 11.25.
10 FPR 1991, rr 2.62(5), 3.6(10), 3.8(2).
11 FPR 1991, r 3.8(4).
12 See Matrimonial Homes Act 1983, s 1(2)(a).
13 FPR 1991, r 3.8(5).
14 RSC Ord 45, r 7(4).
15 RSC Ord 45, r 7(2).
16 Ie a matrimonial cause.
17 FPR 1991, r 3.8(3).

Applications to the High Court in wardship proceedings

11.29 Wardship proceedings are commenced by originating summons issued out of the Principal Registry or a district registry of the High Court supported by the plaintiff's affidavit[1]. Immediately on issue of the originating summons the minor becomes a ward[2]. An application for an injunction is made by summons[3] and may be made whether or not a claim for an injunction was included in the originating summons[4].

The summons should be supported by an affidavit, both of which should be served personally[5], not less than two clear days before the hearing[6]. The respondent to the application should file evidence in answer[7] as appropriate.

The application is made to a judge[8] and will be heard in chambers[9]. If the judge grants the injunction the same, duly endorsed with a penal notice[10] should be served personally[11] on the respondent so that the same may be enforced by committal if breached. It is good practice for an affidavit of service to be made by the person serving the order. The affidavit should then be filed with the court so that it is ready in the event of an application to commit.

1 FPR 1991, r 5.1(1).
2 Supreme Court Act 1981, s 41. The minor will cease to be a ward if no appointment for directions is taken out within 21 days of the issue of the originating summons unless otherwise ordered; FPR 1991, r 5.3(1).
3 FPR 1991, r 10.9.
4 RSC Ord 29, r 1(1). See also *Re N (infants)* [1967] Ch 512, [1967] 1 All ER 161.
5 Personal service is desirable in case the respondent does not attend the hearing. Where the respondent has solicitors on the record as acting for him service on them is good service, RSC Ord 65, r 5. Although the parties to an originating summons are described as *Plaintiff* and *Defendant*, RSC Ord 7 r 2(2), the term *respondent* is used to indicate the respondent to the summons for the injunction who might be either plaintiff or defendant.
6 RSC Ord 32, r 3.
7 See *Practice Direction (Family Division: Filing Affidavits)* [1984] 1 All ER 684, [1984] 1 WLR 306.
8 RSC Ord 32, 11(1)(d), save that a district judge may grant an injunction by consent RSC Ord 32, r 11(2).
9 The court sits in chambers as a matter of practice; when wardship was assigned to the Chancery Division the practice was to hear matters in camera. The wardship jurisdiction is confidential. See Administration of Justice Act 1960, s 12.
10 RSC Ord 45, r 7(4).
11 RSC Ord 45, r 7(2). For the importance of serving third parties affected by an injunction, see *Re L (a minor)* [1988] 1 FLR 255.

Urgent applications procedure at the Royal Courts of Justice

11.30 A matrimonial cause pending in the divorce registry is treated as pending in a divorce county court, and not in the High Court, and a particular procedure applies for making urgent applications for injunctions.[1] Under this procedure, the applicant selects any day at noon on which the court is sitting as the date and time on which the application is to be made; provided that two days' notice can be given to the respondent. The applicant must serve a notice of application of such hearing on the respondent, giving him two days' notice. The applicant must send at the same time, a copy of such notice to the Clerk of the Rules, giving the title and number of the proceedings. The matter is then listed in the Cause List for hearing on the day so selected by the applicant.

This procedure does not apply to matrimonial causes pending in the High Court[2]. In such cases it is recommended that the applicant issues a summons specially fixed; the Clerk of the Rules will, on request fix the hearing for the earliest date available[3].

1 *Practice Direction* 10 July 1972, [1972] 2 All ER 1360, [1972] 1 WLR 1047. See further the Notice in the Daily Cause List.
2 *Practice Direction* 10 July 1972, above.
3 *Practice Direction* 10 July 1972, above.

Adjournments

11.31 As has already been seen most applications, inter partes, for injunctions require only at least two clear days' notice. It frequently happens that a respondent is unable to instruct a solicitor to represent him at the hearing, that his solicitor is unable to obtain a grant of an emergency legal aid certificate, or that his solicitor is unable to draft a full affidavit in answer to the application. All these matters may give rise to an application to adjourn the hearing of the application.

The court has power to adjourn the hearing of the application either to a fixed date[1] or generally[2]. An adjournment may be granted on terms[3]. The power to grant an adjournment is a matter for the discretion of the judge[4]. As such the Court of Appeal will not interfere with the exercise on the judge's discretion unless it can be shown that he has exercised his discretion on improper grounds[5].

Where there is no degree of urgency and an adjournment is sought to adduce evidence crucial to the issues to be decided by the court then an adjournment should be granted[6]. However where both parties are before the court and each has sworn a full affidavit the court may well feel that it has sufficient information to decide the issues, particularly as both parties may be cross-examined on their affidavits.

1 RSC Ord 32, r 4; CCR Ord 13, r 3.
2 Ibid. Such a course would probably only be taken where the parties wished to attempt to effect a reconciliation.
3 Such as by the grant of a non-molestation injunction or a re-entry injunction pending the full hearing. In many cases a respondent will offer undertakings in order to persuade the applicant to agree to an adjournment.
4 *Pearson v Pearson* (1981) 3 FLR 137, CA. See also *Joyce v King* (1987) Times, 13 July, CA.
5 The appellant must show that the judge has considered an irrelevant matter, failed to consider a relevant matter or that the effect of his order is plainly wrong.
6 *Pearson v Pearson*, above.

RESTRAINT OF MOLESTATION

Jurisdiction

11.32 The Domestic Violence and Matrimonial Proceedings Act 1976 gives the court power to grant an injunction restraining one party to a marriage (as therein defined) from molesting the other[1] and restraining one party from molesting a child living with the other[2]. In a matrimonial cause, the court has power to grant injunctions restraining molestation between spouses and to restrain either spouse from molesting any child of the family[3]. There is power in wardship[4] and under the CA 1989[5] to restrain molestation of the minor or molestation of any person having care and control of the minor[6]. A husband has no right to discipline his wife by 'reasonable chastisement' or to confine her to enforce his rights to consortium[7]. An injunction will not be granted under the 1976 Act to an applicant who is and intends to continue in cohabitation with the respondent. The purpose of such an injunction is to protect the application for the purpose of enabling him or her to free himself or herself from the relationship and thereafter to remain free from such cohabitation. The court does not have jurisdiction to grant an injunction where the applicant is willing to continue the cohabitation only if the respondent ceases violence and molestation[8].

1 Section 1(1)(a).
2 Section 1(1)(b).
3 Child of the family is defined by the MCA 1973, s 52(1).
4 *Re V (a minor) (wardship)* (1979) 123 Sol Jo 201, Baker P.
5 The court may grant an injunction restraining molestation or to prevent the infringement of the exercise of parental responsibility or any other right in relation to a child: *M v M (Residence Order: Ancillary Injunction)* [1994] Fam Law 440, Johnson J. See also *Re W (a minor)* [1981] 3 All ER 401, CA; *Ainsbury v Millington* [1986] 1 All ER 73 [1986] 1 FLR 331, CA, cases under the previous law.
6 For power to protect a person having care and control of a minor see *X County Council v A* [1985] 1 All ER 53, sub nom *Re X (a minor) (Wardship Injunction)* [1984] 1 WLR 1422.
7 *R v Jackson* [1891] 1 QB 671, CA.
8 *F v F (Protection from violence: continuing cohabitation)* [1989] 2 FLR 451.

Meaning of molestation

11.33 The meaning of molestation was considered in *Vaughan v Vaughan*[1] where it was held that molestation has a very wide meaning. In the absence of any authority[2] the court considered definitions of molestation in the *Concise Oxford Dictionary*[3] and approved the definition in the *Shorter Oxford Dictionary*[4] which is in the following terms: 'To cause trouble; to vex; to annoy; to put to inconvenience'.

It is very difficult to lay down any conclusive definition of molestation but it should be recognised that it is very wide. It includes acts and threats of violence[5] and 'a multitude of other things'[6]. It could include attempted intercourse without consent of the other party[7] and would also include vexatious communication by one spouse towards another. Oral harassment, which can not be strictly classes as a threat, is actionable if it causes physical or psychiatric illness to the victim[8]. Where there is a risk that the cumulative effect of such harassment might cause such illness, a quia timet injunction may be granted[9]. The jurisdiction of the court is not limited to the restraint of conduct that is in itself tortious or otherwise unlawful[10].

1 [1973] 3 All ER 449, [1973] 1 WLR 1159, CA.
2 Apart from one indirect authority: *Phillips v Phillips* (1905) Times, 19 December.
3 5th edn, 'meddle hostilely or injuriously with (person)'.
4 3rd edn.
5 *Davis v Johnson* [1979] AC 264 at 341A, [1978] 1 All ER 1132 at 1150d per Lord Salmon.
6 Ibid. See also *Horner v Horner* [1982] Fam 90, [1982] 2 All ER 495, CA. Harassment by sending threatening messages by post and making frequent pestering phone calls is molestation. Such *might* be criminal, see the Malicious Communications Act 1988, sending indecent or grossly offensive letters intended to cause distress or anxiety; the Telecommunications Act 1984, s 43, sending grossly offensive, obscene or menacing communications; the Public Order Act 1986, s 4A, causing intentional harassment, alarm or distress. See also *Burnett v George* [1992] 1 FLR 525, CA; *R v Ireland* [1996] 3 WLR 650, CA; *R v Johnson* (1996) 160 JP 605, CA.
7 *Paton v British Pregnancy Advisory Service Trustees* [1979] QB 276 at 280 E–F, [1978] 2 All ER 987 at 990g per Baker P. The so called 'marital exemption' to rape has been abolished: *R v R* [1992] 1 AC 599, [1991] 4 All ER 481, HL.
8 *Khorasandjian v Bush* [1993] QB 727, [1993] 3 All ER 669, CA.
9 Ibid.
10 *Burris v Azadani* [1995] 4 All ER 802, [1995] 1 WLR 1372, CA.

Principles on which the court acts

11.34 The court will not grant an injunction restraining molestation unless it is proved that the respondent has in the past committed acts of molestation[1]. The purpose of such injunctions is to protect the other spouse and children and to ensure that no undue pressure is put upon them while proceedings are pending and during the breakup of the marriage[2].

It is unclear as to whether or not the court must, in addition to past acts of molestation, find that the respondent is likely to commit acts of molestation in the future. The seriousness or otherwise of past acts will assist the court in deciding whether or not future acts are likely to be committed. It is submitted that an applicant is entitled not to be molested and that it is unnecessary for the court to find that acts of molestation are likely to be committed in the future. This is particularly so where the application is for an order restraining molestation of a child where an important consideration is that of the child's welfare and as such, the court is concerned with the protection of the child. As the only remedy for breach of a non-molestation injunction is an order for committal, an application for an injunction should not be made lightly[3].

1 *Spindlow v Spindlow* [1979] Fam 52, [1979] 1 All ER 169, CA.
2 *Paton v British Pregnancy Advisory Service Trustees* [1979] QB 276 at 280C, [1978] 2 All ER 987 at 990e–f, per Baker P.
3 *Freedman v Freedman* [1967] 2 All ER 680n, [1967] 1 WLR 1102.

Undertakings

11.35 The overwhelming majority of applications for injunctions restraining molestations are disposed of by one party giving an undertaking to the court not to molest the applicant or child[1] or by each party giving a cross-undertaking not to molest the other or the child as the case may be. An undertaking is a promise to the court which can be enforced in exactly the same way as injunction, namely by committal[2]. The court must be satisfied that the undertaker is making a genuine promise[3].

In general, an undertaking should be given if asked for as it does not involve the party giving the undertaking making any admission whatsoever that he or she has in the past assaulted or molested the applicant. Furthermore, it does not infringe the rights of the person giving the undertaking. If he or she intends in the future to assault or molest the applicant or the child, then he or she ought to be restrained; conversely, if he or she does not intend in the future to assault or molest the applicant or child then there is no harm in promising to the court not to do so. It is to be emphasised that a power of arrest cannot be attached to an undertaking[4]. It follows that where the applicant considers that it is necessary for a power of arrest to be attached to any order made it will be necessary for the respondent to submit to the injunction.

Disposing of such matters by way of undertakings has the advantage of saving costs and time, of easing the court lists and of avoiding bitter battles in court. Where an application for a non-molestation injunction is only part of the relief sought, as for example where the real issue is that of ousting a spouse from the matrimonial home, disposing of part of the application by way of undertakings has the additional advantage of clarifying the real issues before the court.

A party who has given an undertaking to the court may apply, on notice, for the same to be discharged or for the terms thereof to be varied, on good grounds, provided that there has not been a disposal of the application which gave rise to the giving of the undertaking[5]. An application is not disposed of where undertakings are given until further order, or where the application is adjourned generally. However, where the application which gave rise to the giving of the undertaking has been stood over, adjourned to a fixed date, or otherwise disposed of, the court will not, pending the adjourned hearing (if any), entertain an application for discharge from or to vary the terms of the undertaking[6].

1 The usual wording of such an undertaking is 'not to use violence against [the applicant or named child] and not to threaten, harass or pester [the applicant or named child]'.
2 *Hipgrave v Hipgrave* [1962] P 91, [1962] 1 All ER 75. See also *Hussain v Hussain* [1986] Fam 134, [1986] 1 All ER 961, CA: 'Let it be stated in the clearest possible terms that an undertaking to the court is as solemn, binding and effective as an order of the court in the like terms and that the contrary has never been suggested', per Sir John Donaldson MR.
3 The court may well be reluctant to accept an undertaking not to drink from a person who is alleged to have serious drink problems: see *Ancliffe v Ancliffe* [1980] CA Transcript 520 (12 June), per Brandon LJ.
4 *Carpenter v Carpenter* [1988] 1 FLR 121, CA.
5 *Butt v Butt* [1987] 3 All ER 657, [1987] 1 WLR 1351.
6 Ibid, and see *Chanel Ltd v FW Woolworth & Co Ltd* [1981] 1 All ER 745, [1981] 1 WLR 485, CA.

EXCLUSION INJUNCTIONS

General

11.36 Prior to the decision in *Richards v Richards*[1] it was thought that the power of the court to exclude a spouse from the matrimonial home was derived from the general jurisdiction of the court to grant injunctions[2]. An exclusion injunction was always regarded as a drastic remedy[3] and would not be granted where there was merely unpleasantness, tension and inconvenience[4] in the matrimonial home. The test was that a spouse should only be excluded where it was fair, just and reasonable that he or she should be so excluded[5].

In several cases the court regarded the welfare of children of the family as the first and paramount consideration[6]. Furthermore where it was clear that the marriage had broken down irretrievably the problem was often one of 'who was to go' and the solution to that was to be found in the children[7] and on the balance of hardship[8].

A conflict of authority, in decisions of the Court of Appeal, developed as to the test to be applied on an application for an exclusion injunction. In *Myers v Myers*[9] an injunction was refused as the applicant's unwillingness to return to the matrimonial home, while her husband remained, was unreasonable, although actuated by genuine fear. In *Samson v Samson*[10] it was held that the court should consider first the welfare of any children and then have regard to the interests of the parties. It was further held that a court should not consider whether the applicant was justified in leaving the matrimonial home (if that had happened) as such a consideration would often be based on inadequate material.

This conflict has now been resolved, so far as spouses are concerned, by *Richards v Richards*[11] where it was held that during the subsistence of the marriage, applications for exclusion injunctions are to be brought under the provisions of the Matrimonial Homes Act 1983.

1 [1984] AC 174, [1983] 2 All ER 807, HL.
2 Supreme Court Act 1981, s 37; County Courts Act 1984, s 38.
3 *Bassett v Bassett* [1975] Fam 76, [1975] 1 All ER 513, CA.
4 *Hall v Hall* [1971] 1 All ER 762, [1971] 1 WLR 404, CA.
5 *Walker v Walker* [1978] 3 All ER 141, [1978] 1 WLR 533, CA. Before such a conclusion could be reached all the circumstances of the case had to be examined including: (i) the behaviour of the applicant and the respondent, (ii) the effect on any children if the respondent stays or goes, (iii) the respondent's personal circumstances, and (iv) the likelihood of injury to the applicant, the respondent, their health either physical or mental; per Geoffrey Lane LJ.
6 *Rennick v Rennick* [1978] 1 All ER 817, [1977] 1 WLR 1455, CA; *Spindlow v Spindlow* [1979] Fam 52, [1979] 1 All ER 169, CA.
7 *Bassett v Bassett*, above.
8 Ibid.
9 [1982] 1 All ER 776, [1982] 1 WLR 247, CA; applying *Elsworth v Elsworth* (1978) 1 FLR 245, CA.
10 [1982] 1 All ER 780, [1982] 1 WLR 252, CA; following *Bassett v Bassett*, above, and *Walker v Walker*, above.
11 [1984] AC 174, [1983] 2 All ER 807, HL.

Rights of occupation

11.37 Where a matrimonial home is owned by two spouses by virtue of the legal estate being vested in them jointly[1], by virtue of a contract[2], or by statute[3], they are each entitled to occupy the property[4].

A spouse, in whose sole name, the title to the matrimonial home is vested is entitled to occupy the same by virtue of his or her proprietary right.

Statutory rights of occupation are given to a spouse who has no proprietary rights in the matrimonial home[5]. Where:

(a) one spouse is entitled to occupy a dwelling house by virtue of any estate or interest or contract or by virtue of any enactment giving him or her the right to remain in occupation[6]; and

(b) the other spouse has no legal or equitable title to occupy the matrimonial home[7]; and

(c) the dwelling house is or has been the matrimonial home[8] of the parties; and

(d) the marriage subsists[9];

the spouse without rights has statutory rights of occupation. These are: if in occupation, a right not to be evicted or excluded from the dwelling house or any part thereof except with the leave of the court[10] or, if not in occupation, a right with the leave of the court to enter and occupy the dwelling house[11]. Where one spouse has either of those rights, either spouse may apply to the court for an order declaring, enforcing, restricting or terminating those rights or prohibiting, suspending or restricting the exercise of the right to occupy the dwelling house by the other spouse; or requiring either spouse to permit the exercise by the other of that right[12].

Where each spouse is entitled[13] to occupy such a dwelling house, either may apply, during the subsistence of the marriage, for an order prohibiting, suspending or restricting the exercise of the other's right to occupy[14], or requiring the other to permit the applicant to exercise his or her rights[15].

1 It is immaterial whether they are, in equity, joint tenants or tenants in common.
2 Eg a contractual tenancy, whether protected or not.
3 Eg a statutory tenancy under the Rent Act 1977.
4 This is recognised by the Matrimonial Homes Act 1983. See also *Gurasz v Gurasz* [1970] P 11 at 17, [1969] 3 All ER 822 at 824, CA.
5 Matrimonial Homes Act 1983, s 1. 'Dwelling house' includes any building or part thereof which is occupied as a dwelling, and any yard, garden or outhouse belonging to the dwelling house and occupied therewith: ibid, s 10(1). See *Kinzler v Kinzler* [1985] Fam Law 26, CA, where on the facts the whole of a hotel constituted the matrimonial home.
6 Matrimonial Homes Act 1983, s 1.
7 That spouse will have a common law right enforceable against the other; *Gurasz v Gurasz*, above. See also *Chaudhry v Chaudhry* [1987] 1 FLR 347, CA.
8 Matrimonial Homes Act 1983, s 1(10). See *S v S* (1980) 10 Fam Law 153, 124 Sol Jo 219 for the difficulties which may arise where the dwelling house has not been the matrimonial home. It is an objective test whether or not a dwelling house is the matrimonial home: *Mackintosh v Mackintosh* [1986] CA Transcript 262.
9 Matrimonial Homes Act 1983, s 1(10).
10 Ibid, s 1(1)(a).
11 Ibid, s 1(1)(b).
12 Ibid, s 1(2).
13 By virtue of a proprietary, contractual or statutory right.
14 Matrimonial Homes Act 1983, s 9(1), (3).
15 Ibid.

Matrimonial Homes Act 1983

11.38 The power of the High Court and county courts to grant injunctions requiring a party to a marriage, during the subsistence of the marriage, to vacate the matrimonial home or to restrain a spouse from returning to the matrimonial home, is derived from the Matrimonial Homes Act 1983[1] and the inherent jurisdiction[2] has been absorbed by statute[3]. An application for an exclusion injunction[4] should be drafted by reference to rights of occupation rather than in terms of exclusion or ouster.

On an application for an exclusion injunction the court may make such order as it thinks just and reasonable[5], having regard to:

(a) the conduct of the spouses in relation to each other and otherwise;

(b) their respective needs and financial resources;

(c) the needs of any children; and

(d) the circumstances of the case[6].

The statute does not provide that any one factor is to be given any more weight than another[7]; the weight to be given to each factor is a matter for the judge depending on the facts of each individual case[8]. Decisions of appellate[9] courts on exclusion injunctions given prior to *Richards v Richards* should be regarded with extreme caution as such do not have regard to the criteria laid down by the Matrimonial Homes Act 1983, although they have not necessarily erred on their own facts[10].

An exclusion injunction is a drastic remedy[11] and should only be made where a judge is satisfied that no lesser measure will protect the applicant and any children sufficiently[12]. A lesser measure of protection would include an order whereby the parties would live separately under the same roof[13], although a realistic view must be taken of the possibility and practicality of parties living separately in the same home[14]. Involuntary violence[15] is not a ground for refusing an injunction[16], the actual violence and the consequences to the applicant (and any children) are the important factors[17]. Rape or attempted rape will usually justify excluding the man[18]. The fact that an applicant has been refused a personal protection order[19] in the magistrates' court does not fetter the judge's discretion on an application for an exclusion injunction[20].

Often an application to exclude a party will be heard at the same time as an application for interim residence[21]. It may be that a contested application for residence should be adjudicated upon before the court considers an application to exclude one of the parties[22], even if such means that the matter must be adjourned for a welfare report[23], although where an interim order is made it may be appropriate to exclude the non-residential parent pending the preparation of a court welfare report, if such is in the interests of the children[24]. Where applications for residence, and exclusion, are listed for determination at the same hearing, the judge should decide the issue of residence before dealing with the question of exclusion[25].

1 Formerly the Matrimonial Homes Act 1967.
2 Supreme Court Act 1981, s 37. County Courts Act 1984, s 38.
3 *Richards v Richards* [1984] AC 174, [1983] 2 All ER 807, HL.
4 Commonly called an ouster injunction.
5 Matrimonial Homes Act 1983, s 1(3).
6 Ibid. The importance of applying the statutory criteria was emphasised in *Summers v Summers* [1986] 1 FLR 343, [1986] Fam Law 56, CA.
7 *Richards v Richards* [1984] AC 174 at 222, [1983] 2 All ER 807 at 830, HL, per Lord Brandon. The Guardianship of Minors Act 1971, s 1 which provided, inter alia, that where the legal custody or upbringing of a minor is in question, the court, in deciding that question, must regard the welfare of the minor as the first and paramount consideration, did not apply on an application for an exclusion injunction; *Richards v Richards*, above. On the facts of a particular case it may be that the welfare and needs of minor children should be given great weight; see *Lee v Lee* [1984] FLR 243, [1984] Fam Law 243 CA.
8 *Lee v Lee*, above.
9 [1984] AC 174, [1984] 2 All ER 807, HL.
10 *Richards v Richards*, above, per Lord Hailsham LC. See also *P v P (Ouster)* [1993] Fam Law 283.
11 *Burke v Burke* [1987] 2 FLR 71, CA; see also *Summers v Summers* (1987) Times, 19 May, CA: indeed it has always been regarded as drastic: see *Bassett v Bassett* [1975] Fam 76, [1975] 1 All ER 513, CA.

12 *Reid v Reid* (1984) Times, 30 July, CA. See also *Burke v Burke*, above, exclusion should only be ordered in a case of real emergency.
13 In an appropriate case coupled with a non-molestation injunction and, subject to the statutory criteria, a power of arrest.
14 *Anderson v Anderson* [1984] FLR 566, [1984] Fam Law 183, CA.
15 Eg caused by epilepsy.
16 *Wooton v Wooton* [1984] FLR 871, [1985] Fam Law 31, CA.
17 Ibid. Threats of violence are also important: *Baggott v Baggott* [1986] 1 FLR 377, [1986] Fam Law 129, CA.
18 *E v E (Ouster Order)* [1995] 1 FLR 224.
19 Under the Domestic Proceedings and Magistrates' Courts Act 1978.
20 *O'Brien v O'Brien* [1985] FLR 801, [1985] Fam Law 191, CA.
21 Under the old law orders for interim custody often led to psychological complications in that one parent may feel he has won, whereas the other parent may feel at a disadvantage at the substantive hearing: *Re B (a minor)* (1983) 4 FLR 683, 13 Fam Law 176, CA.
22 *Smith v Smith* (1979) 10 Fam Law 50, CA; *Wood v Wood* (1978) 9 Fam Law 254, [1978] CA Transcript 766; *Mitchell v Mitchell* [1979] CA Transcript 221.
23 A judge may order that the welfare report be expedited, but there must be special factors to justify expedition. Every case involving children is urgent and it must be remembered that the welfare officers are very busy. However an eight-month delay in the preparation of a welfare report is unacceptable: *Elder v Elder* [1986] 1 FLR 610, [1986] Fam Law 190, CA. In most cases it should be possible to decide the question of exclusion without the assistance of a welfare report: *Osborne v Osborne* [1982] CA Transcript 420.
24 *D v D (Injunction: Exclusion Order)* (1982) 4 FLR 82, 12 Fam Law 150, CA.
25 *Re T (a minor: wardship); T v T (Ouster Order)* [1987] 1 FLR 181, [1986] Fam Law 298, CA.

11.39 It is inappropriate to decide the application on a partial view of the evidence[1] or to make an exclusion order where the evidence is limited to a single uncorroborated incident[2]. On a contested application it is important that the court hears oral evidence with cross-examination in order to make findings of fact[3]. A spouse should not be excluded merely because the marriage has broken down and the matrimonial home has become a place of tension[4]. An exclusion order should not be made so as to 'allow the dust to settle' and thereby possibly lead to a reconciliation between the parties[5]. In considering the application the court should have regard to the reasonableness or unreasonableness of the applicant's conduct[6].

In considering the needs of the parties it is relevant to take into account the duty of the local authority to rehouse under Part III of the Housing Act 1985[7]. It is also relevant to take into account alternative accommodation available to the parties[8]. However, merely finding a solution to the housing problem for a child is an irrelevant exercise[9].

Where, in the exercise of the court's discretion, it is decided to grant an exclusion injunction the same should take effect as soon as possible[10] unless there are very compelling reasons to the contrary[11].

In making an exclusion order the court may except from a spouse's right of occupation a part of the dwelling house[12] and in particular, a part of the same used for or in connection with a trade, business or profession of the other spouse[13].

Rights of occupation end on the death of a spouse[14], or other termination of the marriage[15] unless, in the event of a matrimonial dispute or estrangement[16], the court sees fit to direct otherwise[17] by order, during the subsistence of the marriage[18].

Where an exclusion injunction is made it may be limited[19] or be expressed as being 'until further order'[20]. The court should, in every case consider the imposition of a time limit on the operation of the injunction[21]. Where there are no matrimonial proceedings an order without limitation may have the consequence of being, in effect, a summary transfer of property order[22].

1 *Reid v Reid* (1984) Times, 30 July, CA.
2 *Reid v Reid*, above.
3 *Shipp v Shipp* [1988] 1 FLR 345; *Tuck v Nicholls* [1989] 1 FLR 283.
4 *Burke v Burke* [1987] 2 FLR 71, CA, where it was said that an ouster injunction was not simply a routine stepping stone on the way to a divorce emphasised in *Summers v Summers* (1987) Times, 19 May, CA.
5 *Summers v Summers* [1986] 1 FLR 343, [1986] Fam Law 56, CA.
6 *Harris v Harris* [1986] 1 FLR 12, [1986] Fam Law 16, CA. In some cases the court will not be able to decide the reasonableness of the applicant without cross-examination by the respondent.
7 *Thurley v Smith* [1984] FLR 875, [1985] Fam Law 31, CA. However see *Warwick v Warwick* (1981) 3 FLR 393, CA, where it was held that it was manifestly wrong to make an exclusion order where the court had the express knowledge that the applicant would not, in the event of the exclusion injunction sought being granted, return to live in the matrimonial home, but wished to apply for rehousing by way of an exchange.
8 *Baggott v Baggott* [1986] 1 FLR 377, [1986] Fam Law 129, CA.
9 *G v J (Ouster Order)* [1993] Fam Law 341.
10 *Burke v Burke* [1987] 2 FLR 71, CA. It should normally take effect within a week or two and not be left hanging over a man's head 'to bring him to his senses'. There is no such creature as an 'ouster nisi', per Lloyd LJ. In *Burke v Burke*, above the Court of Appeal substituted a two-week period for an eight week one. See also *Chadda v Chadda* (1980) 11 Fam Law 142, CA.
11 *Burke v Burke*, above.
12 Matrimonial Homes Act 1983, s 1(3)(a).
13 Ibid.
14 Ibid, s 2(4)(a).
15 Ibid, s 2(4)(b).
16 The phrase 'matrimonial dispute or estrangement' is not defined but would include an application under the principles of the Matrimonial Homes Act 1983.
17 Matrimonial Homes Act 1983, ss 1, 2(4).
18 Ibid, s 2(4).
19 Ibid, s 1(4).
20 Ibid.
21 *Practice Note* [1978] 2 All ER 1056, sub nom *Practice Direction* [1978] 1 WLR 1123. Where an order suspends right of occupation a time limit is bound to be imposed. An order terminating rights of occupation is final and a time limit cannot be included. Where the order is prohibitive or restrictive in terms of exercise of rights of occupation a time limit should be considered. An order made as interlocutory relief in a matrimonial cause is often made until the hearing of the application for ancillary relief.
22 *Hopper v Hopper* [1979] 1 All ER 181, [1978] 1 WLR 1342n, CA.

Domestic Violence and Matrimonial Proceedings Act 1976

11.40 The procedure under the Domestic Violence and Matrimonial Proceedings Act 1976 is essentially designed to deal with emergencies[1]. The statute is purely procedural[2] and does not affect proprietary rights[3] although a person may be excluded notwithstanding that he or she has a proprietary interest in the home[4], however, an injunction cannot be used permanently to deprive a property owner of his dwelling[5].

On an application for an exclusion injunction under the Domestic Violence and Matrimonial Proceedings Act 1976, s 1(1)(c), the court must make such order as is just and reasonable[6] having regard to the criteria set out in the Matrimonial Homes Act 1983[7], the principles of which apply to applications between unmarried couples[8], equally as to spouses[9]. The provisions of the CA 1989 have not altered the test to be applied[10].

Where an exclusion order is made consideration should be given to imposing a time limit on the operation of the injunction[11]. If no time limit is given then the order may have the effect of being a summary transfer of property order[12]. Between married couples a limit on the injunction provides a period during which it will become clear whether or not the parties will reconcile, and if they do not it will allow time to commence matrimonial proceedings.

Between unmarried couples, where the property is in joint names and the parties are not going to reconcile, a time limit provides an opportunity for them to resolve the question of occupation of the home[13]. Where the property-owning party has been excluded there will be a 'cooling-off' period, during which the applicant can obtain permanent alternative accommodation. Where the non-property-owning party has been excluded it may be appropriate for the injunction to be expressed to last 'until further order'[14].

Where an injunction is limited in time the applicant may apply for an extension if he or she requires protection for a longer period. Likewise a respondent may apply for discharge of an order if the applicant no longer needs protection.

Where parties become reconciled the need for an injunction has gone, and the same should be discharged[15].

1 *Wooton v Wooton* [1984] FLR 871, [1985] Fam Law 31, CA and see *Hopper v Hopper* [1979] 1 All ER 181 [1978] 1 WLR 1342n, CA.
2 *Davis v Johnson* [1979] AC 264, [1978] 1 All ER 1132, HL.
3 Ibid.
4 Ibid, overruling *B v B (Domestic Violence: Jurisdiction)* [1978] Fam 26, [1978] 1 All ER 821, CA, and *Cantliff v Jenkins* [1978] Fam 47n, [1978] 1 All ER 836, CA.
5 *Davis v Johnson*, above.
6 Matrimonial Homes Act 1983, s 1(3).
7 Ibid, s 1(3). The statutory criteria are: (1) the conduct of the parties in relation to each other and otherwise; (2) their respective needs and financial resources; (3) the needs of any children; and (4) all the circumstances of the case.
8 Persons who come within the meaning of the phrase 'living with each other in the same household as husband and wife': see the Domestic Violence and Matrimonial Proceedings Act 1976, ss 1(2), 2(2).
9 *Lee v Lee* [1984] FLR 243, [1984] Fam Law 243, CA.
10 *Gibson v Austin* [1992] 2 FLR 437, CA.
11 *Practice Note* [1978] 2 All ER 1056, [1978] 1 WLR 1123.
12 *Hopper v Hopper* [1979] 1 All ER 181, [1978] 1 WLR 1352n, CA.
13 Eg by commencing proceedings under Law of Property Act 1925, s 30, or being rehoused by the local authority.
14 *Spencer v Camacho* (1983) 4 FLR 662, 13 Fam Law 114, CA. See also *Hills v Bushby* [1977] CA Transcript 398b, CA, where it was held that the Domestic Violence and Matrimonial Proceedings Act 1976 gave the applicant a summary remedy in summary proceedings to enforce her legal rights as owner of her property against anyone going through the more complicated business of applying for a possession order, per Ormrod LJ.

15 *Davis v Johnson* [1979] AC 264, [1978] 1 All ER 1132, HL. It is important that parties are advised that an injunction should be discharged on a reconciliation. A court may well refuse to enforce an injunction by committal after a reconciliation. Applicants whose feelings towards their partners are equivocal should be informed that the courts tend to discourage those who 'blow hot and cold'. The court's protection should not be sought lightly as orders are serious matters; see, by way of analogy, *Freedman v Freedman* [1967] 2 All ER 680n, [1967] 1 WLR 1102, Ormrod J.

Interlocutory relief in a matrimonial cause

11.41 Pending suit[1] an exclusion injunction may be made by way of interlocutory relief under the provisions of the Matrimonial Homes Act 1983[2]. There is no presumption that either spouse has the right to remain in the matrimonial home to the exclusion of the other[3].

In almost every case there will, inevitably, be a degree of unpleasantness, inconvenience and tension consequent upon the breakup of the relationship. In addition if there is to be a divorce[4] the parties must separate, sooner or later; however it is submitted that a court should not lose sight of the statutory criteria to be applied[5]. Where spouses are independent adults, without children, questions of occupation of the matrimonial home should be dealt with on an application for ancillary relief and not by way of injunction[6]. However where, pending suit, a spouse is in need of protection, the absence of children should not deter him or her from applying to exclude the other from the home.

After a decree absolute of divorce or nullity former spouses are unable to apply for relief under the Matrimonial Homes Act 1983[7] but may apply for an injunction under the inherent jurisdiction[8] in support of a legal right[9].

The right of a spouse to apply for a transfer of property order[10] is not a proprietary right and therefore cannot be protected by a mandatory injunction requiring the other party to vacate the former matrimonial home[11]. The court has adequate powers to prevent the dissipation of assets to frustrate the orders that a court might make for ancillary relief[12]. An application for an injunction, after decree absolute, as an attempt to set the scene for proceedings for ancillary relief is improper and an abuse of process[13].

A former spouse, after decree absolute, who does not have a proprietary interest in the matrimonial home, has no more rights than an independent adult licensee and may not apply to exclude his or her former spouse under the inherent jurisdiction[14] unless it be in the interests of the children of the family[15].

Where the title to the former matrimonial home is in the sole name of a former spouse it would seem that he or she would have a legal right to exclude the other. However an injunction to exclude a non-property-owning former spouse from the matrimonial home prior to the hearing of proceedings for ancillary relief might be regarded as molestation and refused in the exercise of the court's discretion. It should be noted that an injunction in matrimonial proceedings may not be used as a substitute for a possession action[16].

1 Ie before decree absolute of divorce or nullity, or before a decree of judicial separation.
2 *Richards v Richards* [1984] AC 174, [1983] 2 All ER 807, HL.
3 *Willmott v Willmott* [1921] P 143, 90 LJP 206.
4 Or a judicial separation or annulment.
5 Matrimonial Homes Act 1983, s 1(3).

6 *Pearson v Pearson* (1981) 3 FLR 137, CA.
7 Matrimonial Homes Act 1983, s 2(4); unless in the event of a matrimonial dispute or estrangement the court sees fit to direct otherwise by order under s 1 during the subsistence of the marriage. Spouses who are judicially separated may apply for relief under the Matrimonial Homes Act 1983.
8 Supreme Court Act 1981, s 37; County Courts Act 1984, s 38. See also *Lucas v Lucas* [1992] 2 FLR 53, CA and *Hennie v Hennie* [1993] 2 FLR 351, CA.
9 *North London Rly Co v Great Northern Rly Co* (1883) 11 QBD 30, 52 LJQB 380, CA. In *Webb v Webb* [1986] 1 FLR 541, CA the crucial factor which enabled the former wife to obtain an injunction to prevent her former husband from going to her property was that she alone had a proprietory interest in the dwelling house.
10 Under the Matrimonial Causes Act, s 24(1)(a).
11 *Brent v Brent* [1975] Fam 1, [1974] 2 All ER 1211, Dunn J obiter.
12 Including under Matrimonial Causes Act 1973, s 37.
13 *Waugh v Waugh* (1981) 3 FLR 375, CA. See also *Grace v Grace* [1980] CA Transcript 418, CA.
14 *O'Malley v O'Malley* [1982] 2 All ER 112, [1982] 1 WLR 244, CA.
15 *Quinn v Quinn* (1983) 4 FLR 394, CA; see also *Beard v Beard* [1981] 1 All ER 783, [1981] 1 WLR 369, CA.
16 *Delorey v Delorey* (1967) 111 Sol Jo 757 and *Jedfield v Jedfield* (1960) Times, 10 November.

Wardship and Children Act 1989

11.42 There is no jurisdiction to make an ouster injunction in proceedings under the CA 1989 where the title to the property is in the joint names of the parties[1]. If the applicant in such proceedings has a proprietary right in the property and the respondent does not, it may be that an exclusion injunction could be made, in the proceedings, ousting the respondent[2], provided that the order was ancillary to an order for residence or care and control[3].

Exclusion injunctions have been made in wardship proceedings although the only reported decision[4] was made well before the decision in *Richards v Richards*[5] and the question of jurisdiction was not apparently investigated in any detail.

Where the circumstances of parties to wardship or CA 1989 proceedings are such that there is jurisdiction to make an application under the Matrimonial Homes Act 1983 or under the Domestic Violence and Matrimonial Proceedings Act 1976 such proceedings may be heard at the same time as the wardship or CA 1989 application.

Where proceedings are heard together a judge may first deal with the question of residence[6], and then decide the issue of ouster taking into account his decision on residence as one of the factors relevant to exclusion[7]. Such a process does not elevate the statutory criterion[8] of the needs of any children[9]. Indeed any other approach[10] would be illogical and might not result in any conclusion[11].

1 *M v M (Residence Order: Ancillary Injunction)* [1994] Fam Law 440, following cases under the (repealed) Guardianship of Minors Act 1971 to 1973; see *Ainsbury v Millington* [1986] 1 All ER 73, [1986] 1 FLR 331, CA; *Re W (a minor)* [1981] 3 All ER 401, 11 Fam Law 207, CA, distinguished. A further appeal in *Ainsbury v Millington* [1987] 1 All ER 929, [1987] 1 WLR 379, HL was dismissed without consideration of the merits. *C v K (Inherent Powers: Exclusion Order)* [1996] 2 FLR 506, Wall J.
2 *Re W (a minor)*, above.

3 As to the requirement that there must be a nexus between the substantive proceedings and an interlocutory injunction para 11.1.
4 *Re V (a minor) (wardship)* (1979) 123 Sol Jo 201, Sir George Baker P.
5 [1984] AC 174, [1983] 2 All ER 807, HL.
6 Where the welfare of the child is the paramount consideration; CA 1989, s 1. For the meaning of 'first and paramount' see *J v C* [1970] AC 668, [1969] 1 All ER 788, HL.
7 *Re T (a minor: wardship)*; *T v T (Ouster Order)* [1987] 1 FLR 181, [1986] Fam Law 298, CA.
8 Matrimonial Homes Act 1983, s 1(3).
9 *Re T*; *T v T*, above.
10 Such as deciding the question of ouster first.
11 *Re T*; *T v T*, above.

Exclusion of third party

11.43 In a matrimonial cause[1] the court has power, to prevent molestation, or for the protection of children, to exclude third parties from the matrimonial home[2]. Each of these cases was concerned with a wife applying to exclude her husband's mistress from the matrimonial home. In *Adams v Adams*[3], it was made clear that although an injunction would only be granted in support of a legal right or for the welfare of children[4], and that the wife had no legal right against the husband's mistress[5] an injunction could be granted for the protection of children whose welfare was in jeopardy.

In *Jones v Jones*[6] the wife sought injunctions ordering the husband and his mistress (who was pregnant by the husband) to vacate the matrimonial home. The husband opposed the injunction on the ground that he was the sole tenant of the property. The court nevertheless held[7] that the husband and his mistress should vacate the home. In this case it should be noted that the children of the family consisted of a girl, aged 18, and a boy, aged 17. The decision appears to be based more on the conduct of the husband being so outrageous[8] as to make it impossible for the parties to live together than on the basis of the welfare of the children.

In *Hense v Hense and Churchill*[9] the court held that a wife should not be expected to put up with the presence of the husband's mistress in the matrimonial home. Although the jurisdiction of the court does not appear to have been in dispute, the view was expressed[10] that the court might not have a discretion to refuse to grant an injunction in such circumstances.

Where a spouse is excluded from the matrimonial home[11] the court should not invite, or accept, any undertaking from the party remaining not to cohabit with another person therein[12], if such an undertaking is offered it should not be accepted[13]. However, where an injunction to exclude the respondent has been refused, and there is tension in the matrimonial home, it is 'altogether reasonable' for a party to be asked to undertake not to invite his/her girlfriend/boyfriend to visit the matrimonial home[14]. An injunction may be granted to prevent relatives of a parent from entering the home where the other parent and children live, to prevent such relatives from interfering in the exercise of parental responsibility by the parent with whom the children reside[15].

1 Ie an action for divorce, nullity or judicial separation; Matrimonial and Family Proceedings Act 1984, s 32.

2 *Adams v Adams* (1965) 109 Sol Jo 899, Baker J; *Jones v Jones* [1971] 2 All ER 737, [1971] 1 WLR 396, CA; *Pinckney v Pinckney* [1966] 1 All ER 121n, Ormrod J; *Hense v Hense and Churchill* [1976] CA Transcript 403, CA.
3 (1965) 109 Sol Jo 899 Baker J.
4 Following *Montgomery v Montgomery* [1965] P 46, [1964] 2 All ER 22, Ormrod J.
5 Except in an action for enticement, if the same could be proved. The cause of action of enticement was abolished by the Law Reform (Miscellaneous Provisions) Act 1970, s 5.
6 [1971] 2 All ER 737, [1971] 1 WLR 396, CA.
7 Following *Silverstone v Silverstone* [1953] P 174, [1953] 1 All ER 556 and *Gurasz v Gurasz* [1970] P 11, [1969] 3 All ER 822, CA.
8 And, therefore, it is submitted, molestation.
9 [1976] CA Transcript 403, CA.
10 Per Sir John Pennycuick.
11 Or gives an undertaking to vacate.
12 *Holtom v Holtom* (1981) 11 Fam Law 249, CA.
13 Ibid.
14 *Miller v Miller* (1983) 4 FLR 115, CA per Sir John Arnold P at 117G–H.
15 *M v M (Residence Order: Ancillary Injunction)* [1994] Fam Law 440, *C v K (Inherent Powers: Exclusion Order)* [1996] 2 FLR 506, Wall J

House other than the matrimonial home

11.44 The Matrimonial Homes Act 1983 does not apply to a dwelling house which has at no time been a matrimonial home of the spouses in question[1]. The Domestic Violence and Matrimonial Proceedings Act 1976[2] likewise only applies to a matrimonial home. In the case of an unmarried couple the term 'matrimonial home' would seem to mean the premises which contain the household in which they live with each other as husband and wife[3].

An application to exclude a party from a property other than the matrimonial home must be based on a legal right that the applicant is entitled to occupy the same while the respondent is not. An injunction might be refused in the exercise of the court's discretion[4].

In order for a spouse to be entitled to go to live in a property, other than the matrimonial home, owned by the other spouse, the applicant must prove an occupational licence[5]. Although a husband has a common law duty to provide a roof over his wife's head[6], such duty may be limited to an existing matrimonial home[7].

1 Section 1(10).
2 Sections 1(1)(c), (d) and 2(1)(c).
3 Sections 1(2), 2(2).
4 Eg where pending suit a husband living in the matrimonial home applied to exclude the wife from their 'holiday home' held in his sole name.
5 *S v S* (1980) 10 Fam Law 153, 124 Sol Jo 219, French J. Such a licence may be implied.
6 *Gurasz v Gurasz* [1970] P 11, [1969] 3 All ER 822, CA.
7 *S v S*, above. See *Chaudhry v Chaudhry* [1987] 1 FLR 347, CA, for the position where the third party has a legal interest in the matrimonial home.

Financial consequences of exclusion

11.45 It is almost inevitable, pending suit, that where the parties to a marriage separate there is insufficient income to maintain two households. The spouse who leaves the matrimonial home needs to finance alternative accommodation; while the spouse who remains will be concerned to see that the outgoings on the matrimonial home are maintained.

Where a court makes an exclusion injunction under the Matrimonial Homes Act 1983 it may order a spouse occupying the dwelling house, by virtue of a right of occupation, to make periodical payments to the other spouse in respect of the occupation[1] or impose on either spouse obligations as to the repair and maintenance of, or the discharge of liabilities in respect of, the dwelling house[2]. Orders may be limited for a period specified in the order, or have effect until further order[3].

Any payment, tender or other thing made or done by a spouse entitled by virtue of this provision to occupy a dwelling house, towards satisfaction of the liability of the other spouse for any rent, rates[4], mortgage payments, or other outgoings is as good as if made or done by the other spouse; and may be treated by the person to whom they are made as having been made by that other spouse[5]. The fact that a payment has been so treated does not affect any claim by that other spouse who made the payment to an interest in the property by virtue of the payment[6]. Occupation by one spouse by virtue of such a right of occupation or order is treated as possession by the other spouse for the purposes of the Rent (Agriculture) Act 1976, the Rent Act 1977[7]; and treated as occupation by the other spouse for the purposes of the Housing Act 1985, Part IV.

A transfer of property order[8] is, of course, available in respect of the former matrimonial home where the legal title is freehold or on a long lease. Such an order may also be made in respect of a private tenancy, where there is no covenant against assignment[9]; or, where there is a covenant against assignment, with the landlord's consent. Furthermore, a transfer of property order may be made in respect of a local authority tenancy[10]. Apart from the jurisdiction under the Matrimonial Causes Act 1973[11] there is an alternative procedure, in some ways more simple, under the Matrimonial Homes Act 1983[12].

1 Matrimonial Homes Act 1983, s 1(3)(b).
2 Ibid, s 1(3)(c).
3 Ibid, s 1(4). The court may make an interim order enforcing a spouse's rights of occupation: *Baynham v Baynham* [1969] 1 All ER 305, [1968] 1 WLR 1890, CA.
4 See below.
5 Matrimonial Homes Act 1983, s 1(5).
6 Ibid, s 1(7).
7 This only applies to the matrimonial home, see *Hall v King* [1988] 1 FLR 376, CA.
8 Made under the MCA 1973, s 24(1)(a).
9 *Hale v Hale* [1975] 2 All ER 1090, [1975] 1 WLR 931, CA.
10 *Thompson v Thompson* [1976] Fam 25, [1975] 2 All ER 208, CA, and see *Regan v Regan* [1977] 1 All ER 428, [1977] 1 WLR 84. See also Housing Act 1985, s 91(3)(b).
11 Made under the MCA 1973, s 24(1)(a).
12 Section 7 and Sch 1.

RE-ENTRY TO THE MATRIMONIAL HOME

11.46 The courts have power, under the Domestic Violence and Matrimonial Proceedings Act 1976[1] and as interlocutory relief in a matrimonial cause to grant a mandatory injunction under the principles of Matrimonial Homes Act

1983[2] requiring the respondent to permit the applicant to enter and remain in the matrimonial home or any specified part of it.

Where an applicant has been excluded from the home, either by being locked out or thrown out, it is proper to apply for re-entry relief ex parte[3] where the applicant has nowhere suitable to stay as the matter will then be one of urgency.

Where children have been excluded from the home it would seem that there is no power under the Domestic Violence and Matrimonial Proceedings Act 1976 to require a respondent to permit the children to re-enter the home[4]; there is power to make such an order in a matrimonial cause or under the Matrimonial Homes Act 1983[5] as parental responsibility may include a duty to protect children[6]. This rather unfortunate lacuna in the statute can, it is submitted, be overcome if the court in addition to granting an order requiring the respondent to permit the applicant to re-enter the home, grants an order restraining the respondent from molesting the children. The meaning of molestation is very wide[7] and it is submitted that a respondent who did not, on request, permit the children to return to the home would be molesting them and therefore in breach of the order and in danger of being committed to prison for such breach on application.

It has never been laid down by an appellate court as to the test to be applied on an application for a re-entry injunction although the matter was considered obiter by Lord Salmon in *Davis v Johnson*[8] in relation to applications under the Domestic Violence and Matrimonial Proceedings Act 1976. Lord Salmon's criteria are either that a party must have been driven from the home by serious[9] molestation or locked out of the home without reasonable justification[10], before a judge could grant a re-entry injunction. The Matrimonial Homes Act 1983 sets out criteria to be considered[11].

Furthermore Lord Salmon went on to say[12] that only in exceptional cases would a re-entry injunction be granted without the court, in addition, excluding the other party from the home. This may well be so on an inter partes application but is not so where an application is made ex parte as a party may only be excluded on an ex parte application in the most exceptional circumstances[13]. However merely because a party is entitled to a re-entry injunction the court should not lose sight of the principles to be applied on an application to exclude a party from the matrimonial home[14].

1 Section 1(1)(d).
2 Section 1(2)(c).
3 See paras 11.19 and 11.20.
4 This would appear to be the result of the wording of s 1(1).
5 This would appear to be the result of the wording of s 1(2)(c).
6 See 5(2) *Halsbury's Laws* (4th edn) para 730.
7 See *Vaughan v Vaughan* [1973] 3 All ER 449, [1973] 1 WLR 1159, CA, and see para 11.33.
8 [1979[AC 264 at 342A, [1978] 1 All ER 1132 at 1151b.
9 Lord Salmon does not seek to define 'serious'.
10 There is no explanation of what would justify locking the other party out of the home. Where the parties are joint owners they each have a legal right to occupy the home. It is submitted that such justification might be more easily found between unmarried couples than between husband and wife. See also *Dennis v McDonald* [1982] Fam 63 at 70B–E and 71E–F. [1981] 2 All ER 632 at 637g–j and 638g–h, per Purchas J. The decision was upheld by the Court of Appeal [1982] Fam 63, [1982] 1 All ER 590, CA. The dicta were not considered.

11 Section 1(3). The court may make such order as is just and reasonable having regard to the specified matters.
12 [1979] AC 264 at 343 B, [1978] 1 All ER 1132 at 1151c.
13 *Masich v Masich* (1977) 7 Fam Law 245, CA.
14 See paras 11.36–11.42.

POWER OF ARREST

Attachment of power of arrest

11.47 The Domestic Violence and Matrimonial Proceedings Act 1976 includes a provision which empowers a judge, in certain circumstances, to attach a power of arrest to certain injunctions.
Section 2 (1) of the Act provides:

Where, on the application by a party to a marriage[1], a judge grants an injunction containing a provision (in whatever terms):

(a) restraining the respondent from using violence against the applicant, or

(b) restraining the respondent from using violence against a child living with the applicant, or

(c) excluding the respondent from the matrimonial home or from a specified area in which the matrimonial home is included, the judge may, if he is satisfied that the respondent has caused actual bodily harm to the applicant or, as the case may be, to the child concerned and considers that he is likely to do so again, attach a power of arrest to the injunction.

It should be noted that the Act does *not* provide for the attachment of a power of arrest to an injunction requiring the respondent to permit the applicant to enter and to remain in the matrimonial home or a part of the matrimonial home.

Before the judge can attach a power of arrest he must be satisfied first that the respondent has caused actual bodily harm to the applicant or to a relevant child; and, second must consider that he or she is likely to do so again. If those conditions are fulfilled then it is a matter for the judge's discretion as to whether or not the power should be imposed[2].

Actual bodily harm, in this context, has the same meaning as in its normal usage, namely criminal law. Actual bodily harm includes[3] any hurt or injury calculated to interfere with the health or comfort of the victim. Furthermore, an injury to the state of the victim's mind for the time being, is within the definition of actual bodily harm[4]. However, there is a need for a sufficient degree of psychological harm[5], or psychiatric injury which must be more than mere emotion such as fear or distress[6].

A power of arrest attached to an injunction is not to be regarded as a routine remedy, but is appropriate only in exceptional situations[7]

The application for injunctions, where a power of arrest is sought, must include a request for a power of arrest to be attached to the injunction(s)[8]. If the application for the injunction(s) does not include a request for a power of arrest a respondent, who would not oppose the grant of an injunction but would oppose the imposition of a power of arrest, might not attend the hearing.

Where a power of arrest is imposed without the respondent being present at the hearing the order should include a provision that the respondent be at liberty to apply on 24 hours' notice to discharge that part of the injunction which relates to the power of arrest[9].

Where a power of arrest is attached to an injunction a judge should consider for what length of time the power of arrest is a necessary for the protection of the applicant or the child[10]. In fixing a time limit, the judge, having found that the respondent is likely to cause actual bodily harm in the future either to the applicant or to a child, must consider for how long the applicant or child is likely to be in danger. Where a power of arrest is discharged, but the injunction remains in force, breach of the order can, of course, be enforced by applying for an order of committal.

A power of arrest may be attached to an injunction granted as interlocutory relief in matrimonial cause, pending in either the High Court or in a divorce county court, in the same way as it may be attached to an injunction granted in proceedings under the Act of 1976[11].

It may also be attached to an injunction restraining trespass or assault in a common law action where the parties are husband and wife, or come within the meaning of the phrase 'living together in the same household as husband and wife'[12].

A power of arrest may only be attached under its terms of the Domestic Violence and Matrimonial Proceedings Act 1976. There is no jurisdiction to impose a power of arrest in wardship proceedings, as a means of enforcement, otherwise than under the statutory provision[13].

It has never been considered by the Court of Appeal whether or not a respondent may consent to the attachment of a power of arrest to injunctions made against him. It is submitted that the court should always be asked to approve such an agreement and that approval may only be given if the statutory pre-conditions have been satisfied.

Where an order is made which includes a power of arrest in the county court the power of arrest is in Form N110. There is no prescribed form for one in the High Court, in practice however, the same form of wording is used.

Where a power of arrest is attached to an injunction the same should nonetheless be endorsed with a penal notice so that it may be enforced by committal if the same should be necessary[14].

A copy of an injunction containing a power of arrest must be delivered to the applicant's local police station[15]. The court will send a copy of the order to the police station. Where the proceedings are heard at the Royal Courts of Justice a copy of the order will be accompanied by Form D462 which gives the police information about the parties' names, addresses and solicitors.

While a power of arrest is in force, if an order is made varying or discharging the injunction, an officer of the court[16] must immediately inform the senior officer at the applicant's local police station. Furthermore, if the applicant's address has changed since the order was made the local police station for the new address must be informed, and a copy of the order must be delivered to them[17]. A power of arrest cannot be attached to an undertaking[18].

1 The words 'party to a marriage' do not apply to parties whose marriage has been dissolved: *White v White* [1983] Fam 54, [1983] 2 All ER 51, CA. Thus a power of arrest cannot be attached to an injunction made against a former spouse unless they come within the meaning of the phrase 'living with each other in the same household as husband and wife'. It is submitted that a court is probably unable to extend the time of operation of a power of arrest, after decree absolute, which was attached to an injunction before decree absolute. In respect of cohabitees the power exists only when the parties are cohabiting (or on an application immediately following the cessation): *Duo v Osborne* [1992] 2 FLR 425, CA.
2 *Lewis v Lewis* [1978] Fam 60, [1978] 1 All ER 729, CA.
3 See Offences Against the Person Act 1861, s 47.
4 *R v Miller* [1954] 2 QB 282 at 292 [1954] 2 All ER 529 at 534c, per Lynsky J. Tenderness and pain is sufficient to constitute actual bodily harm: *R v Reigate Justices, ex p Counsell* (1983) 148 JP 193.
5 *Kendrick v Kendrick* [1990] 2 FLR 107.
6 *R v Chan-Fook* [1994] 2 All ER 552, [1994] 1 WLR 689, CA. See also *R v Ireland* [1996] 3 WLR 650, CA.
7 See *Lewis v Lewis*, above, *per curiam* Ormrod LJ, at 63 and 731, Roskill LJ at 64B and 732c. See also *McLean v Nugent* (1980) 1 FLR 26, CA, per Ormrod LJ.
8 See *Lewis v Lewis*, above and *McLean v Nugent*, above.
9 See *McLean v Nugent*, above.
10 See *Practice Note* [1981] 1 All ER 224, [1981] 1 WLR 27 which states: 'Unless a judge is satisfied that a longer period is necessary in a particular case, the period should not exceed 3 months'. If there is power to extend the operation of a power of arrest, a judge must decide the same by reference to the statutory criteria which apply to the initial attachment. In *Carpenter v Carpenter* [1988] 1 FLR 121, CA the court was split as to whether there must be fresh actual bodily harm since the incidents which led to the initial attachment.
11 See *Lewis v Lewis*, above.
12 See *McLean v Nugent*, above.
13 *Re G (Wardship) (Jurisdiction: Power of Arrest)* (1983) 4 FLR 538, 13 Fam Law 50, CA.
14 RSC Ord 45, r 7(4); CCR Ord 29 r 1(2), (3).
15 FPR 1991, r 3.9(6)(b).
16 In the High Court this is done by a district judge of the Family Division.
17 FPR 1991, r 3.9(7).
18 *Carpenter v Carpenter* [1988] 1 FLR 121, CA.

Arrest for breach

11.48 Where a power of arrest has been attached to an injunction then a constable may, without warrant, arrest a person whom he has reasonable cause for suspecting of being in breach of that injunction. Where the injunction restrains the use of violence, the breach must be the use of violence; and, where the injunction excludes a party from the matrimonial home or an area including the matrimonial home, the breach must be entry into the excluded area[1].

Thus, where an injunction restrains a respondent from 'assaulting, molesting or otherwise interfering with the applicant' and the judge attaches a power of arrest, a person can be in breach of order without using violence. However, it is only for a *violent* breach that he can be arrested.

1 Domestic Violence and Matrimonial Proceedings Act 1976, s 2(3). It is of note that at common law, a licence to enter premises granted by a wife in a domestic dispute cannot be unilaterally revoked by the husband (the subject of the complaint made to the

police) so as to make the police officers trespassers from the moment they are told to go (or as soon afterwards as they can reasonably be expected to leave). It is implied that when a request is made to police in such circumstances, the licence extends to a right not only to enter the home, but also to remain there long enough to take reasonable steps to inquire as to the whereabouts and safety of the complainant and any children, and for the police to be satisfied that there was no reasonable fear of a breach of the peace: *R v Thornley* (1980) 72 Cr App Rep 302.

Committal for breach

11.49 A person arrested under a power of arrest must be brought before a judge within 24 hours of his arrest (without taking into account Christmas Day, Good Friday or any Sunday), and may not be released within the twenty-four hours except on the direction of a judge; but the Act does not authorise detention after the expiry of 24 hours[1].

The arresting constable must forthwith after arrest seek the directions of the court which granted the injunction as to the time and place at which the arrested person is to be brought before the judge[2]. A person arrested for breach of an injunction made in the High Court, when brought before the judge, may be committed to prison notwithstanding that he has not been served with a copy of the injunction under Order 45, r 7(2) and that there is no application for a committal order under Order 53, r 4. A person arrested and brought before a judge in breach of a county court injunction may be committed to prison notwithstanding that he has not been served with a copy of the injunction under CCR Order 29, r 1(4) and that he has not been served with a notice in Form N78.

The power of the court to commit a person to prison, who has been arrested under a power of arrest, is to be used with great care because it is a very draconian provision, intended to get rid of all technicalities and to streamline the procedure so that judges can deal with domestic emergencies[3]. The effect of CCR Ord 47, r 8(7) and (8) when read together is exactly the same as the provisions of FPR 1991, r 3.9(8)[4]. In consequence a judge in the county court has exactly the same power as a judge of the High Court to deal with breaches of injunctions granted under the Domestic Violence and Matrimonial Proceedings Act 1976[5].

The judge, before whom the arrested person is brought, may deal with the question of committal there and then, or may adjourn the proceedings for up to 14 days from the date of arrest[6]. There is no power to detain a contemnor between the finding of contempt and passing sentence at a subsequent date[7].

There is no necessity to commit someone to prison merely because he has breached an order[8]. In a domestic context all the facts must be examined, and it is doubtful whether a judge is justified in sending a spouse to prison without finding out the views of the other spouse[9]. A judge has a very wide discretion as to whether or not to make a committal order where there has been a breach of an injunction[10].

1 Domestic Violence and Matrimonial Proceedings Act 1976, s 2(4). See *Practice Direction* (23 January 1980, unreported).
2 Ibid.
3 *Boylan v Boylan* (1980) 11 Fam Law 76, CA, per Ormrod LJ.

4 Ibid.
5 Ibid.
6 FPR 1991, r 3.9(8), the alleged contemnor must be released. The court may adjourn for evidence to be adduced: *Roberts v Roberts* [1991] 1 FLR 294, CA.
7 *Delaney v Delaney* [1996] QB 387, [1996] 1 FLR 458, CA.
8 See *Smith v Smith* [1988] 1 FLR 179, CA.
9 See *Boylan v Boylan*, above, per Ormrod LJ.
10 See *McLean v Nugent* (1980) 1 FLR 26, CA.

Part VI

Enforcement

Chapter Twelve

Financial Orders

Robert Purdie

Introduction 441
Orders to be Enforced 441
Methods of Enforcement 442

INTRODUCTION

12.1 This chapter considers firstly, the types of order to be enforced and secondly, the various methods of enforcement that are available. It is of great importance that the order to be enforced has been carefully drafted. It is outside the scope of this work to deal with the technicalities of drafting[1]. In this chapter, the term 'creditor' is used to mean the person in whose favour the order has been made and the term 'debtor' is used to mean the person against whom the order has been made.

1 See 6 and 21 *Court Forms* and *Butterworths Family Law Service* for the relevant precedents.

ORDERS TO BE ENFORCED

12.2 The main forms of financial order are as follows:

(a) maintenance pending suit[1];

(b) periodical payments[2];

(c) secured periodical payments[3];

(d) lump sum[4], whether outright or by instalments;

(e) transfer of property[5];

(f) settlement of property[6];

442 *Financial Orders*

(g) variation of settlement[7] and extinguishing[8] or reducing[9] the interest under a settlement.

1 MCA 1973, s 22. See paras 4.125 et seq.
2 MCA 1973, ss 23(1)(a), (d); 27(6)(a), (d); CA 1989, Sch 1, para 1(2)(a); Domestic Proceedings and Magistrates' Courts Act 1978, ss 2(1)(a), (c); Matrimonial and Family Proceedings Act 1984, s 17(1)(a). See paras 4.33 et seq.
3 MCA 1973, ss 23(1)(b), (e); 27(6)(b), (e); CA 1989, Sch 1, para 1(2)(b); Matrimonial and Family Proceedings Act 1984, s 17(1)(a). See paras 4.46 et seq.
4 MCA 1973, ss 23(1)(c), (f); 27(6)(c), (f); CA 1989, Sch 1, para 1(2)(c); Matrimonial and Family Proceedings Act 1984, s 17(1)(a); Domestic Proceedings and Magistrates' Courts Act 1978, ss 2(1)(b), (d), limited to a maximum of £1,000. See paras 4.53 et seq.
5 MCA 1973, s 24(1)(a); CA 1989, Sch 1, para 1(2)(e); including transfer of tenancies; Matrimonial and Family Proceedings Act 1984, s 17(1)(b). See paras 4.61 et seq.
6 MCA 1973, s 24(1)(b); CA 1989, Sch 1, para 1(2)(d); Matrimonial and Family Proceedings Act 1984, s 17(1)(b). See paras 4.68 et seq.
7 MCA 1973, s 24(1)(c); Matrimonial and Family Proceedings Act 1984, s 17(1)(b).
8 MCA 1973, s 24(1)(d); Matrimonial and Family Proceedings Act 1984, s 17(1)(b).
9 MCA 1973, s 24(1)(d); Matrimonial and Family Proceedings Act 1984, s 17(1)(b). See paras 4.77 et seq.

12.3 In addition, the following matters need to be considered:

(a) payment of interest on a lump sum[1];

(b) enforcement of undertakings to pay sums of money[2];

(c) orders for sale of property, both as a substantive order and as a means of enforcement[3].

1 See para 4.59.
2 See paras 12.10 and 12.17.
3 See paras 4.87 and 12.41.

METHODS OF ENFORCEMENT

12.4 The following methods of enforcement will be considered:

(a) judgment summons[1], and complaints under the Magistrates' Courts Act 1980, s 93;

(b) attachment of earnings[2];

(c) garnishee proceedings[3];

(d) means of payment order[4];

(e) charging order[5];

(f) execution of instrument by district judge[6];

(g) directions for settlement of instrument[7];

(h) order for and writ or warrant of possession[8];

(i) sequestration[9];

(j) order for sale of land[10];

(k) directions as to the manner of carrying out a sale[11];

(l) registration in the magistrates' court[12];

(m) writ of ne exeat regno[13];

(n) appointment of a receiver[14].

1 Debtors Act 1869, s 5; FPR 1991, rr 7.4 – 7.6; CCR Ord 28.
2 Attachment of Earnings Act 1971; CCR Ord 27; Magistrates' Courts (Attachment of Earnings) Rules 1971.
3 RSC Ord 49; CCR Ord 30.
4 Maintenance Enforcement Act 1991, s 27.
5 Charging Orders Act 1979; RSC Ord 50; CCR Ord 31.
6 Supreme Court Act 1981, s 39.
7 MCA 1973, s 30.
8 RSC Ord 31, r 1, Ord 45, r 3; CCR Ord 22, r 12, Ord 26, r 17.
9 RSC Ord 46, r 5.
10 MCA 1973, s 24A.
11 RSC Ord 31; CCR Ord 22, r 12.
12 Maintenance Orders Act 1958.
13 For a history of the writ see *Felton v Callis* [1969] 1 QB 200, [1968] 3 All ER 673, Megarry J. See also *Thaha v Thaha* [1987] 2 FLR 142, Wood J.
14 Supreme Court Act 1981, s 38. RSC Ord 51.

Choosing the best method

12.5 Table 1, below, shows the methods of enforcement that are available to enforce a particular type of order. However, the applicant will wish to choose the method that is cheapest and most effective in enforcing a particular order. In many family cases the creditor will have detailed information as to the means of the debtor as a result of affidavits and disclosure as well as from evidence given at any hearing. Thus the creditor may well have sufficient information to decide which method of enforcement will stand a good prospect of success.

Oral examination

12.6 However, where default occurs in respect of continuing maintenance or instalments of a lump sum at a time when the creditor has little current information as to the income and assets of the debtor, consideration should be given to making application for oral examination[1] of the debtor. The disadvantage of such an application is that the debtor is alerted to the actions of the creditor and so a view must be taken in each case as to the risk of dissipation of assets.

1 RSC Ord 48; CCR Ord 25, r 3.

12.7 The creditor may apply ex parte for the oral examination of the debtor at any time after the date for payment[1]. Where the order to be enforced was the High Court, the appropriate court for oral examination is the court that made the order, whether it be the Principal Registry or a district registry[2]. Where the order to be enforced was made by a divorce county court the application for

444 *Financial Orders*

TABLE 1: METHODS OF ENFORCEMENT

ORDERS	Judgment summons	Arrears complaint	Attachment of earnings	Garnishee	Means of payment order	Charging order	Execution of instrument by district judge
Maintenance pending suit	Y	§	Y	Y	Y	—	—
Periodical payments	Y	§	Y	Y	Y	—	—
Secured periodical payments	Y	Q	Y	Y	Y	—	—
Lump sum (outright)	Y	M	Y	Y	—	Y	—
Lump sum (by instalments)	Y	M	Y	Y	Y	Y	—
Transfer of property	—	—	—	—	—	—	Y
Settlement	—	—	—	—	—	—	Y
Variation of settlement	—	—	—	—	—	—	Y
Order for sale of land	—	—	—	—	—	—	Y
Undertaking to pay sums of money	Y	—	?	Y	—	?	—

Key:
Y The method of enforcement is available. **§** The orders for maintenance pending suit and periodical payments can be enforced by an arrears complaint only if the order is registered in a magistrates' court. ***** While it is possible for an order for maintenance pending suit to be registered in a magistrates' court, in practice it is unlikely to happen. **Q** While it is possible for an order for secured periodical payment to be registered in a magistrates' court (and therefore enforceable by an arrears complaint), in practice it is unlikely to

Directions for settlement of instrument	Order for and writ or warrant of possession	Sequestration	Order for sale	Directions as to manner of carrying out a sale	Registration in magistrates' court	Writ of *ne exeat regno*	Appointment of receiver
—	—	Y	—	—	*	Y	Y
—	—	Y	—	—	Y	Y	Y
—	—	Y	—	—	Q	Y	Y
—	—	Y	Y	C	—	Y	Y
—	—	Y	Y	C	—	Y	Y
Y	Y	Y	—	—	—	—	Y
Y	—	Y	—	—	—	—	Y
Y	—	Y	—	—	—	—	Y
Y	Y	Y	X	Y	—	—	Y
—	—	Y	—	—	—	?	—

happen. **M** An arrears complaint can only apply to orders for lump sums made by a magistrates' court. **X** An order for sale of land can be both a substantive order and a means of enforcement. **?** While an undertaking to pay a sum of money can be enforced by judgment summons and garnishee, it is uncertain whether the other methods indicated can be used.

Financial Orders

oral examination is made to the divorce county court that the creditor considers to be nearest to the place where the debtor resides or carries on business[3]. In the High Court the application is made ex parte on affidavit[4]; in the county court it is made by notice in Form N316, supported by affidavit[5]; in either case the grounds of the application should be given. Where interest is claimed, the calculation should be set out in writing; in the county court a copy must be filed[6]. If the order for oral examination is made, it requires the debtor to attend before the district judge or officer of the court at a specified place and time to be orally examined as to his means and may require the production of documentary evidence[7]. A High Court order must be served personally on the debtor[8]. In the county court, the order is served in the same manner as a default summons[9], if the debtor fails to attend the court may make a further order for his attendance[10]. The debtor may request conduct money[11].

1 RSC Ord 48(1); CCR Ord 25, r 3(1).
2 *Supreme Court Practice 1997*, para 48/1–3/2.
3 FPR 1991, r 7.1(5)(a).
4 RSC Ord 48, r 1.
5 FPR 1991, r 7.1(5)(b). Where the court to which application is made, did not make the order, a copy of the order must be exhibited.
6 CCR Ord 25, r 5A; in the High Court the calculation should be included in or exhibited to the affidavit. For interest on lump sums see para 4.59.
7 RSC Ord 48, r 1(1); CCR Ord 25, r 3(1), Form N37.
8 RSC Ord 48, r 1(2).
9 CCR Ord 25, r 3(3). This is usually by post, see ibid Ord 7, r 1.
10 CCR Ord 25, r 3(4), this order in Form N39 will usually be served personally.
11 *Protector Endowment Co v Whitlam* (1877) 36 LT 467; CCR Ord 25, r 3(5A).

12.8 The oral examination is conducted by the district judge or a court officer. In the High Court the examiner causes the evidence of the debtor to be written down, read over to him and signed by him[1]; this practice is followed in county courts. In order for the procedure to achieve anything useful it is essential first, that the creditor is represented otherwise only standard questions will be put to the debtor; second, a realistic time estimate must be given[2]. In the High Court, failure to attend is contempt and punishable by committal[3]. In the county court disobedience to an order in Form N39 is contempt and punishable by committal[4].

1 RSC Ord 48, r 3.
2 This must allow for the lengthy process of writing down the debtor's evidence and reading it back to him; an estimate of two hours or half a day is recommended.
3 Provided sufficient conduct money has been tendered, *Protector Endowment Co v Whitlam* above, and see *Rendell v Grundy* [1895] 1 QB 16. For committal, see chapter 14.
4 CCR Ord 25, r 3(4), (5). For committal, see chapter 14.

Arrears over 12 months old

12.9 Leave of the court is necessary to enforce arrears of payments due under certain orders, where those arrears became due more than 12 months before the commencement of the proceedings to enforce the same[1]. The orders are maintenance pending suit, an interim order for maintenance, or any financial provision order. In a magistrates' court, the general practice is to follow the same principle in exercising a discretion under the Magistrates' Court Act 1980, s 95[2] in deciding whether or not to remit arrears[3]. The philosophy underlying the 12-month rule is that if the creditor has waited for a year before starting to enforce an order he or she has not needed the money or has managed well enough without it[4]. It is therefore most unwise to allow arrears to accrue and become 'stale'. The mere fact that a debtor is an irregular or reluctant payer is not an unusual circumstance justifying a departure from the normal rule[5]. Where the order to be enforced provided for backdating, this may provide justification for departing from the normal rule and allow leave to be granted to enforce arrears beyond the 12-month period[6]. There may well be other circumstances on the individual facts of a case that will allow leave to be granted to enforce beyond 12 months, but the onus is on the creditor to show a good reason for leave, and diligent efforts to attempt enforcement should carry weight. Where a creditor does not know the whereabouts of the debtor, assistance may sometimes be obtained from Government departments[7]. An application for leave should be made in accordance with the Family Proceedings Rules 1991, r 10.9; save where application is made for the issue of a judgment summons[8]. Where application is made for an attachment of earnings order[9], any application for leave must be made at the same time[10].

1 MCA 1973, s 32(1); Domestic Proceedings and Magistrates' Courts Act 1978, s 32(4).
2 See paras 12.14 – 12.16.
3 *Ross v Pearson* [1976] 1 All ER 790, [1976] 1 WLR 224.
4 See *Kerr v Kerr* [1897] 2 QB 439 at 443; see also *Fowler v Fowler* (1979) 2 FLR 141.
5 *Dickens v Pattison* [1985] FLR 610.
6 *Russell v Russell* [1986] 1 FLR 465, CA.
7 *Practice Direction* [1989] 1 All ER 765, [1989] 1 WLR 219.
8 See paras 12.10 – 12.13.
9 See paras 12.17 – 12.23.
10 CCR Ord 27, r 17(3).

Judgment summons

12.10 An application for committal by way of judgment summons is available to enforce those orders specified in the Administration of Justice Act 1970, Sch 8[1]. It is also available to enforce an undertaking to pay a sum of money where it is appropriate to treat an undertaking as 'a periodical or other payment having effect as if made under Part II of the Matrimonial Causes Act 1973'[2]. The request for the issue of a judgment summons is in Form M16[3] and includes provision for an application to be made for leave to enforce any arrears that accrued more than 12 months prior to the issue of the application[4]. The application must be supported by affidavit verifying the amount due under the order and showing how the amount is arrived at[5]. Leave of a judge is necessary to issue a judgment summons where the debtor is in default under an order of commitment made on a previous judgment summons in respect of the same order.

1 Paras 2A, 3 and 4. The orders are orders for periodical or other payments made or having effect as if made under the MCA 1973, Part II, made under the Domestic

Proceedings and Magistrates' Courts Act 1978, Part I, or made or having effect as if made under the CA 1989, Sch 1.
2 See *Symmons v Symmons* [1993] 1 FLR 317.
3 FPR 1991.
4 See para 12.9.
5 FPR 1991, r 7.1(1). The affidavit must exhibit a copy of the order except where the application is made to the court which made the order.

12.11 The application for issue of a judgment summons may be made in respect of a High Court order to the Principal Registry, a district registry or to a divorce county court, whichever is most convenient in the opinion of the judgment creditor[1]; and in respect of a county court order to whichever divorce county court is most convenient in the opinion of the judgment creditor[2]. It is no longer necessary to issue a separate judgment summons in respect of each order, nor to seek leave for a parent to act as next friend of a child in respect of child maintenance[3]. It is only necessary to issue one judgment summons in respect of such orders[4]. The judgment summons is in Form M17[5]. It must be served personally and conduct money must be tendered[6]. The time for service would seem to be not less than 14 days before the hearing[7]. At the hearing the creditor is entitled to cross-examine the debtor as to his means and the reason for non-payment. Where the judge is satisfied[8] that the debtor has or has had since the date of the order, the means to pay but has refused or neglected to pay the same[9], the debtor may be committed to prison for up to six weeks or until earlier payment[10]. An order for committal may be suspended[11] on payment of the debt (often by instalments) and this is the usual course as immediate imprisonment may adversely affect the debtor's ability to pay. Alternatively, the judge may make a new order for payment of the amount due under the original order plus the costs of the judgment summons where the original order was for a lump sum or costs[12], or maintenance pending suit or periodical payments where it appears that the order would have been varied or suspended if the debtor had so applied[13]. Alternatively the judge may make an attachment of earnings order[14]. If the debtor is bankrupt at the date of the hearing, he is unlikely to have the means to pay and a committal order will only be made if his failure to pay before the bankruptcy order deserved punishment[15].

1 FPR 1991, r 7.4(2)(a), regard should be had to the debtor's residence or place of business, irrespective of where the order was made.
2 FPR 1991, r 7.4(2)(b), regard should be had to the debtor's residence or place of business, irrespective of where the order was made.
3 FPR 1991, r 7.4(8).
4 Ibid.
5 FPR 1991, r 7.4(5).
6 Ibid.
7 Although FPR 1991, r 7.4(4) provides for 10 days, r 7.4(6) applies the provisions of CCR Ord 28, r 3 to both High Court and county court judgment summonses. CCR Ord 28, r 3 provides 14 days for service. Accordingly the better practice is to allow 14 days to avoid technical defences.
8 Contempt must be proved beyond reasonable doubt: *Re Bramblevale* [1970] Ch 128, [1969] 3 All ER 1062, CA; *Dean v Dean* [1987] 1 FLR 517, CA; *Woodley v Woodley* [1992] 2 FLR 417, CA.
9 Debtors Act 1869, s 5. There must be evidence that the debtor has or has had the means to pay: *Buckley v Crawford* [1893] 1 QB 105.
10 Debtors Act 1869, s 5.

11 FPR 1991, r 7.4(10).
12 Ibid, r 7.4(9)(a).
13 Ibid, r 7.4(9)(b).
14 Attachment of Earnings Act 1971, s 3(4)(a). See paras 12.17 – 12.23.
15 *Woodley v Woodley (No 2)* [1993] 2 FLR 477, CA. Orders in family proceedings are not debts provable in bankruptcy; see Insolvency Rules 1986, r 12.3(2)(a).

12.12 A creditor who fails to prove that the debtor has or has had the means to pay and has refused or neglected to pay, is liable to be ordered to pay the debtor's costs[1]. In the High Court where no committal order is made, the judge may allow the debtor's costs as a set off against the debt[2]. Unless otherwise directed, the creditor's costs are fixed and allowed without taxation[3]. In county courts, legal aid is not available for the creditor and is not available for the debtor where the only issue is the time and mode of payment[4]. No costs are allowed to the creditor in respect of county court proceedings unless a committal order is made or the debtor pays the debt before the hearing[5]. Costs may be fixed without taxation[6].

1 Form M16, clause 3.
2 FPR 1991, r 7.5(3).
3 FPR 1991, r 7.5(6).
4 Legal Aid Act 1988, Sch 2, Part II, para 5. In practice the debtor will be granted legal aid because the liberty of the subject is involved.
5 CCR Ord 28, r 10(1).
6 CCR Ord 28, r 10(2)(b).

12.13 Imprisonment under the Debtors Act 1869 does not discharge nor satisfy the debt, nor does it prevent the creditor from using any other method of execution that may be available[1].

1 *Re Edgcombe, ex p Edgcombe* [1902] 2 KB 403.

Arrears complaint

12.14 A magistrates' court has power[1] to issue a warrant to commit a person to prison for a maximum of six weeks[2] in respect of default in paying a sum due under a magistrates' court maintenance order[3]. The court may not commit a debtor to prison except by order made on complaint[4] and upon proof[5] that the debtor has, or has had since the date on which the sum was adjudged to be paid, the means to pay the sum or any instalment of it on which he has defaulted, and refuses or neglects, or as the case may be, has refused or neglected to pay[6].

1 Magistrates' Courts Act 1980, s 76(1).
2 Ibid, ss 93(7) and 76(3), Sch 4 para 3.
3 Ibid, s 92(1)(a). 'Magistrates' court maintenance order' means a maintenance order enforceable by a magistrates' court: Magistrates' Courts Act 1980, s 150(1). 'Maintenance order' means any order specified in the Administration of Justice Act 1970, Sch 8 and includes such an order which has been discharged, if any arrears are recoverable thereunder; MCA 1980, s 150(1).

4 The complaint may be made by the person in whose favour the order was made or the clerk of the court: Magistrates' Courts Rules 1981, r 59(1).
5 On the criminal standard.
6 Magistrates' Courts Act 1980, s 96(1).

12.15 The power to commit a debtor to prison is one of extreme severity to be exercised sparingly and only as a matter of last resort[1]. A debtor may not be committed under s 76 unless the following conditions are fulfilled[2]: (a) he is present in court[3]; (b) his default amounts to a deliberate defiance or reckless disregard of the order about which the court has conducted a full enquiry[4]; and (c) the bench is satisfied that all other methods of enforcing payment have been considered and have either proved unsuccessful or were unlikely to be successful[5].

1 *R v Luton Magistrates' Court, ex p Sullivan* [1992] 2 FLR 196.
2 Ibid.
3 Magistrates' Courts Act 1980, s 93(6)(a). Where the debtor fails to appear, a warrant under the Magistrates' Courts Act 1980, s 93(5) should be issued to secure his attendance.
4 Magistrates' Courts Act 1980, s 93(6) as explained in *R v Luton Magistrates' Court, ex p Sullivan* by Waite J. The onus of proof is on the debtor to show that his default is not due to wilful refusal or culpable neglect: *James v James* [1964] P 303, [1963] 2 All ER 465. And see *R v Slough Justices, ex p Lindsay* (1996) Times, 11 November, Sir Stephen Brown J as to the care to be exercised by the justices before committing a debtor to prison.
5 Administration of Justice Act 1970, s 49(1). Following the introduction of a means of payment order under the Maintenance Enforcement Act 1991, imprisonment for arrears should become even rarer.

12.16 On the hearing of the complaint, the court may remit arrears in whole or in part[1]. Imprisonment for arrears does not discharge the debt[2]. Unless otherwise ordered, no arrears accrue while a debtor is in custody for failure to pay a sum due under a magistrates' court maintenance order[3]. Where imprisonment has been imposed, the debtor will be immediately released on payment of the full amount of the debt for which commitment was made together with any costs ordered[4]. The court may order that arrears be paid by instalments[5], and if so, shall make a means of payment order[6].

1 Magistrates' Courts Act 1980, s 95(1).
2 Ibid, s 93(8).
3 Ibid, s 94.
4 Ibid, s 79(1); see also Magistrates' Courts Rules 1981, r 55.
5 Magistrates' Courts Act 1980, s 95(2)
6 Ie one of the orders under the Magistrates' Courts Act 1980, s 59(3)(a)–(d).

Attachment of earnings

12.17 The High Court may make an attachment of earnings order in respect of a High Court maintenance order[1]; a county court may make such an order in respect of a High Court or county court maintenance order[2]; and, a magistrates' court may make such an order in respect of a magistrates' court maintenance order[3]. 'Maintenance order' means an order for periodical or other payments[4]. It is uncertain whether this method is available to enforce an undertaking to make payments of money[5]. Where the payer is in employment, attachment of earnings is usually a good method of enforcement, having the advantage of obtaining any arrears and securing compliance in the future. 'Earnings' includes wages or salary payable under a contract of sevice[6]; pension[7]; and statutory sick pay[8]. 'Earnings' do not include payments by foreign governments[9]; forces pay and allowances (but not forces pensions)[10]; social security pensions[11]; disability pensions or allowances[12]; or guaranteed minimum state pension[13].

1 Attachment of Earnings Act 1971, s 1(1).
2 Ibid, s 1(2)(a).
3 Ibid, 1971, s 1(3)(a).
4 Ibid, 1971, s 2(a). For a full list see Attachment of Earnings Act 1971, Sch 1; the orders are maintenance pending suit, periodical payments, secured periodical payments and lump sum whether outright or by instalments.
5 See *Symmons v Symmons* [1993] 1 FLR 317 and *Gandolfo v Gandolfo* [1981] QB 359, [1980] 1 All ER 833.
6 Attachment of Earnings Act 1971, s 24(1)(a) and includes fees, bonus, commission or overtime.
7 Attachment of Earnings Act 1971, s 24(1)(b) and includes periodical payments by way of compensation for loss of office. In practice, the terms of a pension trust deed may prevent an order being made: *Edmonds v Edmonds* [1965] 1 All ER 379n.
8 Attachment of Earnings Act 1971, s 24(1)(c).
9 Ibid, s 24(2)(a).
10 Ibid, s 24(2)(b). See however Air Force Act 1955, ss 150, 151A; Army Act 1955, ss 150, 151A; Naval Forces (Enforcement of Maintenance Liabilities) Act 1947 and Naval Discipline Act 1957, s 128E.
11 Attachment of Earnings Act 1971, s 24(2)(c).
12 Ibid, s 24(2)(d). This does not include a pension on early retirement as a result of ill health: *Miles v Miles* [1979] 1 All ER 865, [1979] 1 WLR 371.
13 Attachment of Earnings Act 1971, s 24(2)(f).

12.18 In respect of a qualifying periodical maintenance order[1] the court may make an attachment of earnings order at the time of making the maintenance order or in the course of any proceedings relating to it either of its own motion or on the application of the payee or applicant for the order[2]. In respect of other maintenance orders, the payee may apply at any time after the maintenance order has been made[3]; it is not necessary for the payer to be in arrears[4]. The debtor may apply for an order[5].

1 Maintenance Enforcement Act 1991, s 1(1), (3).
2 Ibid, s 1(3).
3 Attachment of Earnings Act 1971, s 3(1).
4 Ibid, s 3(3), (3A).
5 Ibid, s 3(1)(d); CCR Ord 27, r 17(4).

High Court and county courts

12.19 No rules of procedure currently exist in respect of applications to the High Court; accordingly county court procedure should be followed with necessary alterations. An application is made to the county court which made the maintenance order[1]. Where the maintenance order was made by the High Court, the better practice is that an application should be made to the Principal Registry if that was where the order was made or, in respect of orders in district registries, to the county court at the same location as the district registry. Where there are arrears, the creditor must file an affidavit showing how the amount due and any interest are calculated[2]; together with a further copy of the interest calculation[3]. Where there are no arrears, the payee should explain in the affidavit, the grounds of the application. The application together with a form of reply is served as if it were a fixed date summons[4]. Within eight days of service, the debtor is required to file a reply in the form provided[5].

1 CCR Ord 27, r 17(2). The application is in Form N55(A).
2 FPR 1991, r 7.1(1).
3 CCR Ord 25, r 5A.
4 CCR Ord 27, r 5(1) as substituted by Ord 27, r 17(3A); see also Ord 7, r 10.
5 CCR Order 27, r 5(2), which provides that the requirement is imposed by the Attachment of Earnings Act 1971, s 14(4).

12.20 The application is heard by the district judge in chambers[1]. If the debtor fails to attend the hearing the court may adjourn the application and order him to attend at a specified time on another day[2]. If he fails to attend the adjourned hearing the judge may order him to be arrested and brought to court either forthwith or at such other time as the judge directs[3]. Where the debtor fails to attend, or refuses to be sworn or to give evidence, the judge may order his imprisonment for not more than 14 days[4]. The power to order the attendance of the debtor, arrest or imprisonment may be exercised by a district judge, assistant or deputy district judge as well as by a circuit judge[5].

1 CCR Ord 27 r 7(1), as substituted by CCR Ord 27, r 17(5).
2 Attachment of Earnings Act 1971, s 23(1).
3 Ibid, s 23(1A).
4 Ibid, s 23(1).
5 Ibid, s 23(11).

Magistrates' courts

12.21 A magistrates' court has jurisdiction to make an attachment of earnings order if it would have jurisdiction to enforce payment of any arrears under the related maintenance order[1]. The application is made by complaint[2]. The procedure follows the normal course of hearing a complaint[3]. Orders under s 14(1)[4] may be made by a single justice[5]. Where the complainant is present but the defendant fails to appear at the hearing, the court may proceed in his absence[6] or issue a warrant for his arrest[7] provided in each case the court is satisfied by evidence that the summons was served[8], or in the case of an adjourned hearing, that the defendant had adequate notice of the time and place of the adjourned hearing[9].

1 Magistrates' Courts (Attachment of Earnings) Rules 1971, r 4.
2 Ibid; Attachment of Earnings Act 1971, s 19(1).
3 See Magistrates' Courts Act 1980, s 53; Magistrates' Courts Rules 1981, r 14.
4 See para 12.22.
5 Attachment of Earnings Act 1971, s 14(3).
6 Magistrates' Courts Act 1980, s 55(1).
7 Ibid, s 55(2).
8 Ibid, s 55(3).
9 Ibid, s 55(4).

Powers of all courts

12.22 Where a court has power to make an attachment of earnings order it may order the debtor to provide the court within a specified period a signed statement[1] as to the identity of his employer[2], particulars of his earnings, anticipated earnings, resources and needs[3]; and particulars to enable the employer to identify the debtor[4]. An order may be made requiring the debtor's apparent employer to furnish the court within a specified time with a signed statement of the debtor's earnings and anticipated earnings[5].

1 Attachment of Earnings Act 1971, s 14(1)(a).
2 Ibid, s 14(1)(a)(i).
3 Ibid, s 14(1)(a)(ii).
4 Ibid, s 14(1)(a)(iii).
5 Ibid, s 14(1)(b).

Attachment of earnings order

12.23 The order is directed to the debtor's employer and requires him to make periodical deductions from the debtor's earnings[1], and to pay the amounts so deducted to the collecting officer[2] specified in the order[3]. The order must provide for a 'normal deduction rate'[4] which must not exceed the rate necessary for meeting the current payments under the maintenance order[5] and a further sum to secure payment of any arrears within a reasonable time[6]; the court must take account of any obligation to deduct income tax from the payments[7]. The order must specify a 'protected earnings rate' which is the rate below which, having regard to the debtor's needs and resources, the court considers that the debtor's earnings should not be reduced[8]. An order lapses if the debtor changes employment[9]. An order may be varied or discharged[10].

1 Attachment of Earnings Act 1971, s 6(1)(a). Deductions are made in accordance with ibid, Sch 3, Part I.
2 The High Court may designate an officer of the High Court or the proper officer of a county court as collecting officer: CCR Ord 27, r 17(7). In county courts, the collecting officer will be the proper officer. In magistrates' courts the collecting officer will be the justices clerk: Attachment of Earnings Act 1971, s 6(7), (8).
3 Attachment of Earnings Act 1971, s 6(1)(b).
4 Ibid, s 6(5)(a).
5 Ibid, s 6(6)(b)(i).
6 Ibid, s 6(6)(b)(ii).
7 Ibid, s 6(6)(a). This is only relevant in respect of maintenance orders under the old rules; see Taxes Act 1988 and Finance Act 1988.
8 Attachment of Earnings Act 1971, s 6(5)(b).
9 Ibid, s 9(4).
10 Ibid, s 9(1).

Garnishee proceedings

12.24 The court may attach debts by ordering a person[1] who owes money to the debtor to pay it to the creditor instead of to the debtor. This is a generally used to attach a credit balance in a bank or building society account held by the debtor, but it is available to attach any debt that is due and owing to the debtor. The remedy is available in the High Court[2] or county courts[3]. The garnishee must be within England and Wales and the the amount due to the creditor must exceed £50 in the High Court[4] or £25 in county courts[5]. The application is made ex parte with an affidavit[6] stating the name and address of the debtor[7]; identifying the judgment or order, the amount thereof and the balance unpaid[8]; identifying the garnishee and stating that to the best of the deponent's knowledge and belief he is indebted to the debtor[9]; and where the garnishee is a deposit taking institution, stating the name and address of the branch where the debtor's account is believed to be held and the account number(s), or that such information is not known to the deponent[10].

1 Referred to as 'the garnishee'; the creditor is 'the garnishor'.
2 RSC Ord 49; Supreme Court Act 1981, s 40.
3 CCR Ord 30; County Courts Act 1984, s 108.
4 RSC Ord 49, r 1(1).
5 CCR Ord 30, r 1(1).
6 RSC Ord 49, r 2; CCR Ord 30, r 2.
7 RSC Ord 49, r 2(a); CCR Ord 30, r 2(a).
8 RSC Ord 49, r 2(b); CCR Ord 30, r 2(b), (e); FPR 1991, r 7.1(1).
9 RSC Ord 49, r 2(c); CCR Ord 30, r 2(c).
10 RSC Ord 49 r 2(d); CCR Ord 30 r 2(d). Deposit taking institutions may charge up to £30 for administrative and clerical expenses: Supreme Court Act 1981, s 40A, County Courts Act 1984, s 109; Attachment of Debt Expenses Order 1983. Charges may be reduced if full information is given.

Order nisi

12.25 The ex parte hearing is before the district judge[1]. In the first instance the order is one to show cause; pending the return date, the order attaches as much of the debt as is sufficient to meet the arrears and costs of the garnishee proceedings[2]. The order is drawn up by the proper officer of the court[3]. The order must be served on the garnishee at least 15 days before the return date[4], and on the debtor at least seven days after the order has been served on the garnishee and at least seven days before the return date[5]. The order binds in the hands of the garnishee any debt due to the debtor up to the amount specified in the order[6].

1 *W v W* [1961] P 113, [1961] 1 All ER 751.
2 RSC Ord 49, r 1(2); CCR Ord 30, r 1(2).
3 FPR 1991, r 2.43(1)(a), (b); CCR Ord 30, r 3(1).
4 RSC Ord 49, r 3(1)(a); CCR Ord 30, r 3(2)(a).
5 RSC Ord 49, r 3(1)(b); CCR Ord 30, r 3(2)(b).
6 RSC Ord 49, r 3(2); CCR Ord 30, r 3(2).

Defences by the garnishee

12.26 A garnishee may allege that there is no debt to attach because it has not yet become due, or that it has already been paid before the order nisi was served. In the county court, where the garnishee is a deposit taking institution and alleges that it does not owe any money to the debtor[1], it may before the return date give notice to the creditor and the proper office to that effect, whereupon the garnishee proceedings are stayed[2]. Where a creditor disputes an allegation in such a notice, the court on the return date will give directions for the determination of that issue[3].

1 For example because his account is overdrawn.
2 CCR Ord 30, r 5.
3 CCR Ord 30, r 8.

Order absolute

12.27 Where there is no appearance or dispute by the garnishee on the return date, the court may in its discretion make the order absolute[1]. The discretion will normally be exercised to make the order absolute. However, where the debtor applies for a variation of the maintenance order the discretion might be exercised to adjourn the question of making the order absolute until the hearing of the variation application. Once an order absolute is made, the creditor can enforce the debt against the garnishee as an order for the payment of money[2]. Where a garnishee disputes liability[3], the court may summarily determine the issue or give directions for the determination of the issue[4]. Payment under an order absolute is a good discharge of the liability of the garnishee to the debtor[5], even if the garnishee order is subsequently set aside or the judgment reversed.

1 RSC Ord 49, r 4(1); CCR Ord 30, r 7(1).
2 RSC Ord 49, r 4(2); CCR Ord 30, r 7(2).
3 Or gives notice under CCR Ord 30, r 5.
4 RSC Ord 49, r 5; CCR Ord 30, r 9.
5 RSC Ord 49, r 5; CCR Ord 30, r 11.

Means of payment order

12.28 This type of order was introduced by the Maintenance Enforcement Act 1991. Where the High Court or a county court makes a qualifying periodical maintenance order[1] it may at the same time[2] or at any later time[3] make a means of payment order[4] either of its own motion or at the request of the debtor, creditor or applicant for the maintenance order[5].

1 A qualifying periodical maintenance order is a maintenance order (within the meaning of the Administration of Justice Act 1970, Sch 8; see para 12.10 n1) which requires money to be paid periodically by the debtor to the creditor: Maintenance Enforcement Act 1991, s 1(2).
2 Maintenance Enforcement Act 1991, s 1(1).
3 Ibid, s 1(3)
4 Ie an order under the Maintenance Enforcement Act 1991, s 1(4).
5 Maintenance Enforcement Act 1991, s 1(1), (3). The debtor, creditor or applicant for the maintenance order are collectively referred to as 'interested parties': Maintenance Enforcement Act 1991, s 1(10).

Order

12.29 The court may make an attachment of earnings order[1] to secure payments under a qualifying periodical maintenance order[2]. The court may also order that the payments under the qualifying periodical maintenance order be made by the debtor to the creditor by standing order[3], or by any other method which requires the debtor to give his authority for payments of a specific amount to be made from an account of his to an account of the creditor's on specific dates during the period for which the authority is in force and without the need for any further authority from the debtor[4]. The court may give the debtor the opportunity to open a bank account and where the debtor defaults without reasonable excuse, the court may order him to open such an account[5]. In deciding whether to exercise its powers under the Maintenance

Enforcement Act 1991, the court (if practical) must invite representations from all interested parties and take such representations into account[6]. The court may revoke, suspend, vary or revive an order either of its own motion in the course of any proceedings relating to a qualifying periodical maintenance order[7], or on the application of any interested party[8].

1 See paras 12.17 – 12.23.
2 Maintenance Enforcement Act 1991, s 1(4)(b).
3 Ibid, s 1(4)(a), (5)(a).
4 Ibid, s 1(4)(a), (5)(b). It is unlikely that banks would accept a direct debit in favour of a personal creditor, but might accept the same where the maintenance order was assigned to the DSS.
5 Maintenance Enforcement Act 1991, s 1(6).
6 Ibid, s 1(8).
7 Ibid, s 1(7)(b).
8 Ibid, s 1(7)(a).

Charging order

12.30 The court may impose a charge on the debtors interest in land[1], securities[2], or funds in court[3]. This is a method of providing security for the debt, rather than enforcing it, although the court may appoint a receiver of the income generated by the property charged and may order its sale. This is often a good method of enforcement of a lump sum order where the debtor has property; it may be used where one party is ordered to pay a lump sum in return for a transfer of the matrimonial home. Where the order is sought in respect of funds in court, the appropriate court is the court in which the fund is lodged[4]. In respect of a High Court order for maintenance or a lump sum over £5,000, the application is made to the Principal Registry, or the district registry in which the order was made[5]. Additionally, in the case of a High Court order the application may be made to the county court for the district in which the debtor resides or carries on business, or if none to that where the creditor resides or carries on business[6]. In the case of a county court order the application must be made to the county court for the district in which the debtor resides or carries on business, or if none to that where the creditor resides or carries on business[7].

1 Charging Orders Act 1979, s 2(2)(a).
2 Ibid, s 2(2)(b).
3 Ibid, s 2(2)(c).
4 Ibid, s 1(2)(a).
5 Ibid, s 1(2)(b), (c).
6 CCR Ord 31, r 1(1)(c).
7 CCR Ord 31, r 1(1)(b).

12.31 The application is made by filing an affidavit giving the name and address of the debtor, all known creditors of the debtor, details of the asset to be charged, and setting out the amount due and how any interest is calculated[1]. The creditor should identify any other interested person, such as the debtor's spouse. The application is in the first instance ex parte to the district judge who may make a charging order nisi and fix a day for further consideration of the matter[2]; in the meantime the property is charged. The creditor must serve the order nisi and affidavit on the debtor, other creditors[3] and any other person directed by the court[4].

1 RSC Ord 50, r 1(3); CCR Ord 31, r 1(2), Ord 25, r 5A; FPR 1991, r 7(1).
2 RSC Ord 50, r 1(2); CCR Ord 31, r 1(4).
3 In the High Court, if so directed; in county courts, unless otherwise directed.
4 RSC Ord 50, r 2; CCR Ord 31, r 1(6), (9).

12.32 A charging order nisi in respect of land can be registered at HM Land Registry and creditors are well advised to do so. At the further hearing of the application, the court may make the order absolute or discharge the order nisi[1]. Other persons interested in the subject matter of the charge, such as co-owners of land have a right to be heard. The court has a wide discretion[2].

1 RSC Ord 50, r 3; CCR Ord 31, r 2.
2 See *Harman v Glencross* [1986] Fam 81, [1986] 1 All ER 545, CA where the position of third parties as against the creditor was considered.

12.33 After an order absolute is made, the judgment creditor may apply for an order for sale of the property charged. If the debt does not exceed £30,000, such application may be made to the county court[1], in any case, the application may be made by originating summons to the Chancery Division of the High Court[2]. If the interest charged is merely a beneficial interest under a trust for sale, the creditor may apply for the execution of the trust. In such a case, the county court has jurisdiction to entertain the application whatever the amount of the debt or the value of the property[3]. In exercising its discretion to order a sale, the court will have regard to the circumstances and in particular, the relative values of the judgment debt and the value of the property. The court will not readily make an order for sale where the judgment debt is small, or where the sale of the property would realise little value.

1 County Courts Act 1984, s 23(c); CCR Ord 31, r 4.
2 RSC Ord 50, r 9A.
3 LPA 1925, s 30; High Court and County Courts Jurisdiction Order 1991, art 2(1)(a).

Execution of instrument

12.34 Where the High Court has given or made a judgment or order directing a person to execute any conveyance, contract or other document, or to endorse any negotiable instrument, then if that person neglects or refuses to comply with the judgment or order, or after reasonable inquiry cannot be found, the High Court may order execution of that document by a nominated person on such terms and conditions as may be just[1]. The county court has similar jurisdiction[2]. It is normally required that the respondent should have had the opportunity to sign, but this is not necessary if it is clear that he will not do so[3], or if his attitude is to resile from the order[4].

1 Supreme Court Act 1981, s 39.

2 County Courts Act 1984, s 38 which in effect applies the Supreme Court Act 1981, s 39.
3 *Savage v Norton* [1908] 1 Ch 290.
4 *Potter v Potter* [1990] 2 FLR 27, CA.

12.35 This provision is normally used in respect of a contract or transfer in pursuance of an order for sale of transfer of property. It is good practice for such an order to include an undertaking that the parties will execute all such documents as may be necessary or expedient to give effect to the terms of the order. If such an undertaking is refused that is prima facie evidence that an order is necessary; equally failure to comply with the undertaking makes it easier to obtain the order. The nominated person is usually the district judge.

Order for and writ or warrant of possession

12.36 Where the High Court or a county court has made an order for the sale of land any party bound by the order and in possession of the land, may be ordered to deliver up possession to the purchaser or to such other person as the court may direct[1]. This may be used to enforce an order for sale of land or transfer of property order. It has been held that the court has no power under the Matrimonial Causes Act 1973, s 24A to grant a possession order against a spouse in the face of an equitable interest enjoyed by her as a joint tenant in possession[2]; however, the provisions of the Rules of the Supreme Court and the County Court Rules were not considered. In the High Court a writ of possession is issued to the sheriff, and in county courts a warrant of possession is issued to the bailiff; in each case they are required physically to take possession of the land and give it to the person in whose favour the order was made.

1 RSC Ord 31, r 1; applied to county court proceedings by CCR Ord 22, r 12; and see FPR 1991, r 2.64(3) for application of these provisions to sales of land pursuant to orders for sale under MCA 1973, s 24A.
2 *Crosthwaite v Crosthwaite* [1989] 2 FLR 86, CA.

12.37 In the High Court, leave is generally required[1]. In county courts, leave is required if more than six years have elapsed since the date of the order or if there has been a change of parties[2]. Otherwise, the person in whose favour the order was made may issue the writ or warrant as soon as the time for compliance with the order has expired. The court does have a general discretion to stay execution of an order as a result of matters that have arisen since the order was made[3]. In the High Court, an application for leave is made by summons to the district judge if the possession order was conditional, if six years have elapsed since the order was made, or if the person against whom it is to be enforced has changed[4]. In county courts, the application is made ex parte on affidavit, although the district judge may require it to be made on notice[5].

1 RSC Ord 45, r 3(2), Ord 46, r 2.
2 CCR Ord 26, r 5.
3 RSC Ord 45, r 11; CCA 1984, ss 38, 76.
4 RSC Ord 46, r 4; see also Secretary's Circular (unreported) 19 January 1972.
5 CCR Ord 25, r 3.

12.38 In the High Court, the applicant files a praecipe together with the writ for sealing. The sealed writ is then served by the applicant of the under-sheriff for the area in which the land is situate[1]. In county courts, the applicant files a form of request for the issue of the warrant[2]. Where there has been wrongful re-entry on land after the execution of a warrant of possession, a writ or warrant of restitution may be issued with leave[3].

1 RSC Ord 46, r 6.
2 CCR Ord 26, r 1.
3 RSC Ord 46, r 3; CCR Ord 26, r 17(4), (5).

Writ of sequestration

12.39 Sequestration is a process of contempt and as such the writ is normally only available as a means of enforcing a coercive order against someone who has committed a contempt by disobeying the order[1]. It is available to enforce orders for ancillary relief[2], however the high cost of this remedy may outweigh the benefit to the creditor[3].

1 *Pratt v Inman* (1889) 43 Ch D 175.
2 See *Romilly v Romilly* [1964] P 22, [1963] 3 All ER 607; *Hipkin v Hipkin* [1962] 2 All ER 155, [1962] 1 WLR 491; *Capron v Capron* [1927] P 243; *Birch v Birch* (1883) 8 PD 163; and *Sansom v Sansom* (1879) 4 PD 69.
3 See *Clark v Clark* [1989] 1 FLR 174 and the sequel *Clark v Clark (No 2)* [1991] 1 FLR 179.

12.40 In the High Court, the judgment creditor may with leave issue a writ requiring the sequestrators named in the writ to take possession of all the assets of the debtor. Although the county court has similar powers it is more appropriate for the application to be made to the High Court. Leave is required[1] and is generally only granted where the value of the assets will be sufficient to meet the substantial costs of the proceedings and the debt. The application is by motion supported by affidavit[2]. The notice of motion and affidavit must usually be served personally[3]. If leave is granted, the applicant files a praecipe and writ for sealing. The writ is then served on the sequestrators[4].

1 RSC Ord 45, r 5(1)(i).
2 RSC Ord 45, r 5.
3 Ibid.
4 RSC Ord 45, r 6.

Order for sale

12.41 Where in any cause or matter relating to land it appears necessary or expedient for the land to be sold, the court may order that land to be sold[1]. In addition, where the court has made an order for secured periodical payments, lump sum or property adjustment, the court may on making that order or at any time thereafter make an order for the sale of such property as may be specified, being property in which either or both of the parties have a beneficial interest either in possession or reversion[2]. The court may well have had this power prior to the amendment of the Matrimonial Causes Act 1973[3].

1 RSC Ord 32, r 1 applied to county court proceedings by CCR Ord 22, r 12.
2 MCA 1973, s 24A; and see FPR 1991, r 2.64(3).
3 *Ward v Ward and Greene* [1980] 1 All ER 176n, CA.

12.42 Such an order does not come within the meaning of 'ancillary relief'[1], and where the remedy is used as a means of enforcement the application should be to the district judge by summons or notice[2], supported by affidavit.

1 FPR 1991, r 1.2(1).
2 Ibid, r 10.9.

Directions as to the manner of carry out an order for sale

12.43 Where the court has made an order for the sale of land it may give such directions as it thinks fit for the purpose of effecting the sale, including[1]:

(a) appointing the party or person who is to have the conduct of the sale;

(b) fixing the manner of the sale, whether by contract conditional on the approval of the court, private treaty, public auction, tender or some other manner;

(c) fixing a reserve or minimum price;

(d) requiring payment of the purchase price into court or to trustees or to other persons;

(e) settling the particulars and conditions of sale;

(f) obtaining evidence as to the value of the property;

(g) fixing the security (if any) to be given to the auctioneer, if the sale is to be by public auction, and the remuneration to be allowed to him;

(h) requiring an abstract of the title to be referred to conveyancing counsel of the court, or some other conveyancing counsel for his opinion thereon and to settle the particulars and conditions of sale[2].

These powers are very wide and should be sufficient to enable the court to give the tightest directions to ensure that an order for sale is not frustrated. Directions can be given as to the identity of estate agents, display of a 'for sale' board, whether agents may hold a key and as to requirements for viewing by prospective purchasers.

1 RSC Ord 31, r 2(1) applied to county court proceedings by CCR Ord 22, r 12.
2 RSC Ord 31, r 2(2)(a)–(h) applied to county court proceedings by CCR Ord 22, r 12.

12.44 Application for such an order should be to the district judge by summons or notice[1], supported by affidavit, which should explain the precise nature of the directions sought and the grounds. Where it is alleged that one party is frustrating a sale it may assist to have affidavit evidence from the estate agent detailing the complaints.

1 FPR 1991, r 10.9.

Directions for the settlement of instrument

12.45 Where the court makes an order for secured periodical payments or a property adjustment order, it may direct that the matter be referred to one of the conveyancing counsel of the court for him to settle a proper instrument to be executed by all necessary parties[1]. This is seldom used in practice. However, where there is a dispute as to the form of any document required to be executed in pursuance of an order for secured periodical payments or property adjustment, it may be used, although in practice it is only used in respect of complex documents. Where there is a dispute as to the wording of a more simple document, the usual practice is to refer the matter, under liberty to apply, to the judge who made the order for his decision.

1 MCA 1973, s 30(a).

Appointment of a receiver

12.46 Where a debtor has assets which cannot be reached by other methods of execution, the court may appoint a receiver to take them and apply them or the income produced by them in payment of the amount due under the order. The High Court may by order, whether final or interlocutory, appoint a receiver, in all cases where it is just and convenient to do so[1]. In the High Court, the application is to the district judge by summons[2]; in county courts, the application is on notice to the district judge[3]. In either case the application must be supported by affidavit verifying the amount due and showing how it is calculated[4]. Where interest is claimed the calculation should be included in the affidavit, and in county courts a copy of the calculation must be filed[5]. The appointment of a receiver is infrequently used in family cases but there are situations where it is helpful. Where a lump sum has been ordered and the only asset of the debtor is an interest under a trust for sale as tenant in common, if the other tenant refuses to join in a sale, then the court will order the appointment of a receiver by way of equitable execution coupled with liberty to the receiver to take proceedings to enforce a sale of the property[6].

1 Supreme Court Act 1981, s 39(1). This is followed in county courts, County Courts Act 1984, ss 38, 107.
2 RSC Ord 30, r 1; Ord 51, r 2.
3 FPR 1991, r 10.9.
4 Ibid, r 7(1).
5 CCR Ord 25, r 5A.
6 *Levermore v Levermore* [1980] 1 All ER 1, [1979] 1 WLR 1227, CA.

Registration in the magistrates' court

12.47 The payee of a High Court or county court maintenance order may apply to the court which made the order for registration of that order in a magistrates' court[1]. The term 'maintenance order' includes a lump sum[2]. An application for registration may be made and granted even though enforcement process is progressing in the original court[3]. If the enforcement process is not completed within 14 days then grant of the application becomes void[4]. However, a means of payment order[5] that has effect in respect of the original order, continues to have effect after registration[6]. An application to register a nominal order for maintenance will not be allowed, and except in special circumstances, leave to register will not be granted in respect of orders for maintenance pending suit or interim orders[7].

1 Maintenance Orders Act 1958.
2 See the Administration of Justice Act 1970, Sch 8.
3 Maintenance Orders Act 1958, s 1(1).
4 Maintenance Orders Act 1958, s 2(2).
5 Under the Maintenance Enforcement Act 1991.
6 Maintenance Orders Act 1958, s 2(6ZB).
7 *Practice Direction* [1980] 1 All ER 1007, [1980] 1 WLR 354.

12.48 The application for registration is by filing two copies of the application and a certified copy of the order. No supporting affidavit is required or necessary. If the application for leave to register is granted, the order is registered in the magistrates' court for the area where the payer lives[1]. The magistrates' court may not decline to register the order[2]. Any attachment of earnings order ceases to have effect on registration[3]. Unless a means of payment order is already in force, future payments must be made through the justices' clerk[4]. Once an order is registered, an application to vary the rate of payment under the order must be made to the magistrates' court where the order is registered[5], unless the payer is outside England and Wales or some other variation is sought, such as to the duration of the order[6]. Once registered all enforcement is through the magistrates' court[7].

1 FPR 1991, r 7.23(1).
2 Maintenance Orders Act 1958, s 2(5).
3 Attachment of Earnings Act 1971, s 11(1)(a).
4 Maintenance Orders Act 1958, s 2(6ZA)(b). See *Practice Direction* (22 May 1975, unreported) for the advantages of registration where the payee is in receipt of state benefits.
5 Maintenance Orders Act 1958, s 4.
6 Ibid.
7 Ibid, s 3.

Writ of ne exeat regno

12.49 The writ of *ne exeat regno* originated in about the thirteenth century as a prerogative writ used for the political purposes of the Crown, but by the nineteenth century had developed into an equitable counterpart to arrest on mesne process at law[1]. The writ takes the form of a command addressed to the tipstaff[2] that, if the respondent[3] should seek or attempt to leave the jurisdiction of the High Court[4] without having paid to the applicant[5] a specified sum, he shall arrest the respondent and bring him before a judge of the High Court forthwith or as soon as is reasonably practical, unless he provides security for the specified sum. When the respondent is brought before a judge, the writ may be left in force, discharged or varied and the judge may make such further or supplemental order as the circumstances dictate[6]. The court has a discretion[7] to grant leave to a party to issue a writ of *ne exeat regno* at any time before final judgment where the four conditions laid down in Debtors Act 1869, s 6, are satisfied[8]. These conditions are:

(a) the action is one in which the respondent would have been liable to arrest at law[9] prior to 1869;

(b) there is a good cause of action[10] for at least fifty pounds;

(c) there is probable cause for believing that the respondent is about to leave the jurisdiction unless apprehended; and

(d) the absence of the respondent from the jurisdiction will materially prejudice the applicant in the prosecution of the action[11].

An applicant for a writ of *ne exeat regno* must give an undertaking as to damages as the issue of a writ is a severe matter[12]. The standard of proof on the applicant is high[13], and the court must be convinced[14]. A writ of *ne exeat regno* may be issued, subject to the requirements of the Debtors Act 1869[15], in support of a Mareva injunction[16]. In the Family Division of the High Court the use of the writ is greatly limited by the requirements that a writ may only be issued before final judgment[17] and that it must be in respect of a debt that is due and payable[18]. The writ has been issued in the Family Division in *Thaha v Thaha*[19] in support of an application for a judgment summons[20]. Apart from the power of the High Court to issue a writ of *ne exeat regno* there is power under the inherent jurisdiction[21] for the High Court to grant an injunction restraining a party from leaving the jurisdiction and for delivery up of his passport[22].

1 For a full account of the history of the writ of *ne exeat regno* see *Felton v Callis* [1969] 1 QB 200, [1968] 3 All ER 673, Megarry J.
2 *Al Nahkel for Contracting and Trading Ltd v Lowe* [1986] QB 235, [1986] 1 All ER 729. The writ used to be addressed to the sheriff but should now be addressed to the tipstaff, his deputy, all constables and other peace officers.
3 The term 'respondent' is used to mean the party against whom the application is made, who may be petitioner or plaintiff, respondent or defendant in the action.
4 Ie England and Wales.
5 The term 'applicant' is used to mean the party who applied for the order.
6 *Al Nahkel for Contracting and Trading Ltd v Lowe*, above.
7 A writ of *ne exeat regno* is always at the discretion of the court; see *Felton v Callis*, above, following *Re Lehman, ex p Hasluck* (1890) 6 TLR 376. See also *Thaha v Thaha* [1987] Fam Law 234, Wood J.
8 *Hands v Hands* (1881) 43 LT 750, *Felton v Callis* [1969] 1 QB 200, [1968] 3 All ER 673.
9 The most obvious example is debt, see *Felton v Callis*, above at 215B-C and 682C-D. The debt must be due and payable, not a future debt; see *Colverson v Bloomfield* (1885) 29 Ch D 341, CA. This requirement will prevent the issue of writ of *ne exeat regno* where eg the claim is for a lump sum under the Matrimonial Causes Act 1973, s 23(1)(c) as such is a future debt.

10 The standard of proof is high: *Felton v Callis,* above.
11 The application in *Felton v Callis,* above was dismissed because there was no evidence that the defendant's absence from the jurisdiction would materially prejudice the plaintiff in the prosecution of the action. The defendant's presence was not necessary to obtain judgment against him.
12 *Felton v Callis,* above at 206G and 676G-H and see the authorities cited therein for the circumstances in which a defendant could claim under the undertaking.
13 *Felton v Callis,* above.
14 Ibid and see *Thaha v Thaha* [1987] 2 FLR 142, [1987] Fam Law 234. See also *Re Underwood* (1903) 51 WR 335 at 336.
15 Section 6.
16 *Al Nahkel for Contracting and Trading Ltd v Lowe* [1986] QB 235, [1986] 1 All ER 729.
17 Debtors Act 1869, s 6.
18 Ibid, and see *Colverson v Bloomfield* (1885) 29 Ch D 341, CA.
19 [1987] 2 FLR 142, [1987] Fam Law 234, Wood J.
20 Ie a summons under Debtors Act 1869, s 5 that the defendant appear and be examined on oath as to his means.
21 Supreme Court Act 1981, s 37.
22 *Bayer AG v Winter* [1986] 1 All ER 733, [1986] 1 WLR 497, CA where such orders were made in support of Mareva and Anton Piller orders; see also *Re I (a minor)* (1987) Times, 22 May.

Chapter Thirteen

Children

Judith Hughes

Residence Orders 465
Contact Orders 467
Prohibited Steps Order 468
Specific Issue Order 469
Family Assistance Order 470
Emergency Protection Orders 471
Care Orders 473
Orders in Wardship 475

RESIDENCE ORDERS

13.1 Residence orders are defined[1] as orders settling the arrangements to be made as to the person with whom a child is to live. Directions may be made as to how the order is to be carried into effect[2]. There is no principle that a court must order the return of a child who has been taken or kept even contrary to the terms of an existing residence order. The court must decide in each case what is in the best interests of the child[3].

1 CA 1989, s 8(1).
2 CA 1989, s 11(7).
3 *Re J (A Minor) (Interim Custody: Appeal)* [1989] 2 FLR 304. *Re B (A Minor) (Residence Order: Ex parte)* [1992] 2 FLR 1.

13.2 In cases where the court has made an order for residence the judge or district judge may, on the application of the person entitled to enforce the order, direct that the proper officer issue a copy of the order endorsed with or incorporating a penal notice, as to the consequences of disobedience, which should be served on the other party personally and before the expiration of the time in which he or she was required to hand over the child and no copy of the order shall be issued with any such notice endorsed or incorporated save in accordance with such a direction[1]. In the event thereafter the order is not complied with it is possible to commence committal proceedings in respect of the breaches which it is alleged have occurred in contravention of the terms of the order. However, it has been said on many occasions in the reported cases that committal for alleged breaches of residence and contact orders should be used as a last resort[2]. Moreover, this remedy cannot be used if the order is not injunctive but only declaratory of the rights of the respective parties.

1 FPR 1991, r 4.21A.
2 *Churchard v Churchard* [1984] FLR 635.

Committal proceedings

13.3 If it is decided to proceed by way of committal the matter must proceed by summons in the High Court and by notice in Form N78 in the county court. The procedure is the same for all alleged breaches of orders for residence, contact, or prohibited steps orders which it is decided to enforce by committal. A summons and a notice must each set out in detail the provisions of the injunction or undertaking which it is alleged have been disobeyed or broken and give full particulars of each and every breach. In either case there must be a full affidavit detailing the breaches. Clear particulars must be given as it is essential that a respondent to a committal application knows the case he has to meet[1]. At the hearing the judge must decide whether there has been a breach and, if he is satisfied that there has, what punishment to impose. He can make a committal order, a suspended committal order, fine or make no order[2].

1 CCR Ord 29, r 1(4A) which provides notice of the provision alleged to have been disobeyed or broken.
2 But see the comments of Bennett J in *Re H (Contact Enforcement)* [1996] 1 FLR 614 on the question of enforcement generally and fines in particular.

Enforcement other than by committal

13.4 If the matter is not to proceed by committal, in cases where a person is required by a residence order to give up a child to another person with whom thereafter it is intended that the child shall live and the court which made the order imposing the requirement is satisfied that the child has not been handed over in accordance with the order, the court may make an order authorising an officer of the court or a constable to take charge of the child and deliver him to the person in whose favour the order had been made[1]. An officer of the court or a constable has power to enter and search any premises where the person acting in pursuance of the order has reason to believe the child may be found and to give effect to the purpose of the order[2]. Such an application should be made to the court which made the order, High Court, county court or magistrates' court.

1 FLA 1986, s 34(1).
2 FLA 1986, s 34(2).

Procedure

13.5 There may be circumstances which justify the application being made ex parte in which case if the urgency is so great the applicant may simply present himself or herself at court and inform the court of the position and seek an immediate order. In all other circumstances the applicant should make the application in writing, support it with proposed statements of evidence and incorporate a request for directions as to serving statements and generally[1]. The application should be accompanied by a fee of £15 unless the applicant is exempt[2]. The applicant should then serve on the respondent the application, statement(s) in support, notice of hearing and any directions made. The respondent has of course the right to answer and file such evidence in support of his or her case as he wishes.

1 FPR 1991, r 4.4.
2 Family Proceedings Fees Order 1991, Sch I, Part I, para 5 except in the magistrates' court where there is no fee.

Enforcement in the magistrates' court

13.6 It is also possible to enforce a residence order made by a magistrates' court by seeking enforcement of the order in the magistrates' court[1] provided that it has been served on the other person[2]. In order to proceed it is necessary to issue a summons, reciting the disobedience of the order and requiring the defaulter to appear for the purpose of showing cause why an order that he be committed to prison should not be made. The summons should state details of the alleged breach with clarity and indicate date, time and place. The court must be satisfied that there has been deliberate and wilful disobedience before making any committal order[3].

1 CA 1989, s 14 and the Magistrates' Courts Act 1980, s 63(3).
2 CA 1989, s 14(2).
3 See *Stone's Justices Manual*, Vol 1, pp 211–212.

CONTACT ORDERS

13.7 A contact order is defined[1] as an order requiring the person with whom a child lives, or is to live, to allow the child to visit or stay with the person named in the order, or for that person and the child otherwise to have contact with each other. An order which directs a party to allow contact with another person at specified times can contain a penal notice[2] although this should not be included in interim orders[3]. Penal notices should not generally be included on orders but used where the person directed to allow contact has shown himself or herself to be a person unwilling to accept the rulings of the court[4].

1 CA 1989, s 8.
2 FPR 1991, r 4.21A.
3 *D v D* [1991] 2 FLR 34.
4 Ibid.

Committal proceedings

13.8 The court has exactly the same powers to enforce contact orders as it does in respect of residence orders[1]. Again committal should be used only as a matter of last resort but has been used where flagrant breaches of a contact order by a mother resulted in no contact between the child and her father which was contrary to the welfare of the child[2]. The procedure to be adopted in respect of committal applications has already been set out[3].

1 FLA 1986, s 34(1) and (2).
2 See *C v C (Access Order: Enforcement)* [1990] 1 FLR 462; *Re H (Contact: Enforcement)* [1996] 1 FLR 614.
3 See para 13.2.

Enforcement other than by committal

13.9 If committal is not considered appropriate, where a child who resides with one person but sees another for contact under an order is not returned after that contact, an application can be made to the court for the return of the child[1]. The application should be made to the court and the practice and procedure has already been set out[2]. It is also possible to enforce an order made in the magistrates court[3] and again it is necessary to show wilful disobedience rather than deliberate fault[4].

1 FLA 1986, s 34.
2 See paras 13.1 and 13.2.
3 Magistrates' Courts Act 1980, s 63(3).
4 Ibid, s 63(3) and see *P v W (Access Order: Breach)* [1984] Fam 32, [1984] 1 All ER 866.

PROHIBITED STEPS ORDER

13.10 A prohibited steps order is defined[1] as meaning an order that no step which could be taken by a parent in meeting his parental responsibility for a child, and which is of a kind specified in the order, shall be taken by any person without the consent of the court. It can be made on the application of a party to the proceedings or made by the court on its own motion[2]. It can be injunctive, provided it requires a person to do or not do a specific act, for example, a child being removed from the jurisdiction or from coming into contact with a particular person. An order can only be made to prohibit steps which could be taken in meeting parental responsibility. A prohibited steps order cannot be made to achieve a result which could be achieved by making a residence or contact order[3]. Prohibited steps orders cannot be made to make the child a ward of court, to give a local authority parental powers or to place a child in the care of, or under the supervision of, a local authority[4]. The wording of the definition would appear to include those other than parents who may be interfering in some way in the life of the person exercising parental responsibility to the detriment of the child and it may therefore go outside the normal principle that the court cannot grant an injunction against someone who is not a party to the proceedings. There has to be sufficient evidence of intention to do or not do something to justify the making of the order[5].

1 CA 1989, s 8(1).
2 CA 1989, s 10(1)(b).
3 CA 1989, s 9(5) and see *Nottinghamshire County Council v P* [1993] 2 FLR 134.
4 CA 1989, s 9(1) and (5)(b).
5 *Re E (Parental Responsibility: Blood Tests)* [1995] 1 FLR 392.

13.11 In *Croydon London Borough Council v A* [1992] 2 FLR 341 a prohibited steps order was made by justices forbidding parents of a boy of two having any contact with each other to ensure the bonding of the child and his younger sibling with their mother for their long-term benefit. On appeal Hollings J held, inter alia, that the justices were plainly wrong to make a prohibited steps order forbidding the parents from having any contact with each other since contact between adults was not a step which could be taken by a parent in meeting a parent's responsibility for a child and therefore fell outside their powers. In *Re H (Prohibited Steps Order)* [1995] 1 FLR 638 the Court of Appeal held that a judge had been wrong to make a prohibited steps order against a mother not to bring her children into contact with her cohabitee because the same result could have been reached by making a contact order and stating there should be no contact permitted by the mother to the cohabitant[1] and further that a prohibited steps order could be made against the cohabitant in this case but it was unnecessary to do so because the 'no contact' order would protect the position.

1 CA 1989, s 9(5).

Remedies for breach of a prohibited steps order

13.12 It is possible to have a penal notice attached to a prohibited steps order[1]. Thereafter the order must be personally served on the person against whom the prohibited steps are directed[2]. In the event that the order is not complied with committal proceedings may be taken using the procedure already set out herein[3]. The High Court has power to make an ouster order under its inherent jurisdiction where a prohibited steps order is not being complied with[4].

1 FPR 1991, r 4.12A.
2 CCR Ord 29, r 1.
3 See para 13.3.
4 CA 1989, s 4 and see *Re S (Minors) (Inherent Jurisdiction: Ouster)* [1994] 1 FLR 623.

SPECIFIC ISSUE ORDER

13.13 A specific issue order is an order giving directions for the purpose of determining a specific question which has arisen, or which may arise, in connection with any aspect of parental responsibility for a child[1]. An order should not be made if the same result could be reached by making a residence or contact order[2]. The remedy has been held to be quite inappropriate where a couple were unmarried but had two children and the mother made an application to return to the parental home and exclude the father therefrom[3]. The court may make this order of its own motion or on the application of one of the parties[4]. The court can deal with such matters as education and upbringing, medical treatment, removal permanently or temporarily from the jurisdiction and even change of surname by way of a specific issue order. In the event that the order was injunctive leave could be obtained for the insertion thereon of a penal notice[5] and the order could then be enforced by committal. It is respectfully suggested that it is more likely that the court would make a prohibited steps order to be enforced in this way if the circumstances so warranted it.

1 CA 1989, s 8.
2 Ibid, s 9(5).
3 See *Pearson v Franklin* [1994] 1 FLR 246.
4 CA 1989, s 10(1)(b).
5 FPR 1991, r 4.31A.

FAMILY ASSISTANCE ORDER

13.14 Where the court has power to make a residence or contact order, it may require a probation officer to be made available or a local authority to make an officer of that authority available to assist, advise and befriend any person named in the order. Such an order can only be made with the agreement of any person named in the order be it a parent or guardian, any person with whom the child lives and any person who has contact to the child. A family assistance order can only be made by the court if it believes that the circumstances of the case are exceptional. A family assistance order lasts for six months beginning on the day it is made unless the court orders it to last for a lesser period. If a probation officer is unable to carry out his duties or dies, another probation officer should be appointed[1]. Where a family assistance order and also a residence or contact order are in force, the officer concerned may refer to the court any question as to whether the order should be varied or discharged[2]. A family assistance order should not be made imposing obligations on the local authority unless the authority agrees or the child concerned lives in their area[3].

1 CA 1989, s 16.
2 Ibid, s 16(6).
3 Ibid, s 16(7).

Enforcement of a family assistance order

13.15 In the event that a local authority fails to provide any person to befriend, advise or assist a person named in the order or a probation officer is unavailable, the court could be asked to make further directions[1]. It may be that little will in practice be achieved thereby because of the time spent after the order is made when it becomes apparent that an officer will not be found and the time taken getting the case back to court may in fact take up the maximum time of six months that the order can exist. A possible direction which the court may have to consider when the matter is before it again is whether there should be an investigation to see whether it may be appropriate for there to be a care or supervision order made in respect of the child[2].

1 CA 1989, s 11(2)(b) although the court faced with such an application or an application by the local authority seeking to be released by reason of lack of resources to implement the order may make no order: *Re C* [1996] 1 FLR 424.
2 CA 1989, s 37.

EMERGENCY PROTECTION ORDERS

13.16 An emergency protection order[1] gives the applicant parental responsibility but only to the extent that it is reasonably required to safeguard or promote the welfare of the child for its duration, so for example for the applicant to authorise necessary medical treatment[2]; the child must be produced to the applicant[3]; the child can be removed or retained as appropriate but only if to do so is necessary to make the child safe and the applicant must return the child if it appears to him safe to return the child[4]; and the applicant must allow the child reasonable contact with his parents, any person who is not a parent of his but has parental responsibility for him, any person with whom he was living immediately before the making of the order; any person in whose favour a contact order is with respect to him and any person who has a section 34 contact order[5] and any person acting on behalf of those persons[6].

1 CA 1989, s 44.
2 CA 1989, s 44(4)(c) and (5).
3 Ibid, s 44(4)(a).
4 Ibid, s 44(10)–(12).
5 Ibid, s 34 (contact with children in care).
6 Ibid, s 44(13).

13.17 The court can give various directions to last while the emergency protection order is in force and it can indeed give directions at any time during the period it is in force even if these were not given initially[1]. For example, the court may direct that the applicant in exercising any powers which he has by virtue of the order, be accompanied by a registered medical practitioner, registered nurse or health visitor if he so chooses[2]. Where a direction has been made for the examination or assessment of a child, the child, if of sufficient age and understanding, may refuse to submit to it[3]. An application may be made[4] to vary an emergency protection order[5] although not until the order has been in existence for 72 hours[6]. No appeal may be made against the grant or refusal of an emergency protection order[7].

1 CA 1989, s 45 and Children (Allocation of Proceedings) Order 1991, art 4.
2 CA 1989, s 45(12).
3 Ibid, s 44(7). It is the duty of the guardian ad litem if appointed to advise the court as to the ability of the child to understand what has been ordered and make an informed decision: FPR 1991, r 4.11.

4 CA 1989, s 45(8): the child, any parent of his, any person who is not a parent but has parental responsibility for him and any person with whom he was living before the making of the order.
5 CA 1989, s 44(9)(b).
6 Ibid, s 45(9).
7 Ibid, s 45(10) and see *Essex County Council v F* [1993] 1 FLR 847.

Punishment for breach of an emergency protection order

13.18 It is an offence intentionally to obstruct any person exercising the power to remove or prevent the removal of a child[1]. A person guilty of such obstruction shall be liable on summary conviction to a fine, not exceeding level 3 on the standard scale[2].

1 CA 1989, s 44(15).
2 Ibid, s 44(16) and see the Criminal Justice Act 1982, s 37(2). At the present time £1,000.

Additional powers to support an emergency protection order

13.19 A warrant may be granted to support an emergency protection order if: (a) a person attempting to exercise powers has been prevented from doing so by being refused entry to the premises concerned or access to the child concerned; or (b) any such person is likely to be prevented from exercising any such powers[1].

1 CA 1989, s 48(9)(b).

13.20 The police have powers to protect children and to take them into police protection for up to 72 hours[1]. Where a constable[2] has reasonable cause to believe that a child would otherwise be likely to suffer significant harm[3] he may remove him to suitable accommodation and keep him there or take such steps as are reasonable to ensure that the child's removal from hospital or other place where he is accommodated is prevented. A child in respect of whom a constable has exercised his powers under this section is referred to as having been taken into police protection[4]. As soon as is reasonably practicable after taking a child into police protection the constable concerned shall inform the local authority of the steps which have been taken and the reasons for taking them and give full details to the authority of where the child is being accommodated and he should also inform the child if he appears capable of understanding the steps which have been taken in respect of him, the reasons therefore and the further steps which may be taken in respect of him[5]. The constable should take such steps as are reasonably practicable to discover the wishes and feelings of the child[6]. The constable must ensure that the case is investigated by the chief officer of the police area concerned and must ensure that the child is moved to accommodation which is either a refuge[7] or provided by a local authority. He must provide information to the child's parents, every person who is not a parent of his but who has parental responsibility for him and any other person with whom the child was living immediately before he went into police protection of the steps he has taken, the reasons for taking those steps and further steps that may be taken with respect to him under this section[8]. The child should be released from police custody after enquiries are completed unless the officer considers that there is still reasonable cause for believing that the child would be likely to suffer significant harm if released[9]. While a child is kept in police protection the designated officer may apply on behalf of the appropriate authority for an emergency protection order whether the authority are aware of it or not[10].

1 CA 1989, s 46(6).
2 Ibid, s 48(9). Any person holding the office of constable and not a member of a police force holding the rank of constable.
3 CA 1989, s 46(1).
4 CA 1989, s 46(2).
5 Ibid, s 46(3).
6 Ibid, s 46(3)(d).
7 Ibid, s 51.
8 Ibid, s 48(4).
9 Ibid, s 46(5).
10 Ibid, s 46(8).

CARE ORDERS

13.21 Where a care order is made with respect to a child it shall be the duty of the local authority designated by the order to receive the child into their care and to keep him in their care while the order remains in force[1]. Once the order is in force the local authority shall have parental responsibility for the child and shall have the power to determine to what extent a parent or guardian of his may meet his parental responsibility for him[2]. The local authority may not exercise the power giving a parent or guardian parental rights unless satisfied that it is necessary to do so to safeguard or promote the child's welfare[3]. Provisions exist[4] to enable the parents, any guardian of the child, any person with whom the child was living under a residence order immediately before the care order was made and any person who had care and control of him under a High Court order to have contact with the child in care and, if necessary, to apply for contact and, in addition to the people already mentioned who can apply, any other person who has obtained the leave of the court may apply.

1 CA 1989, s 33(1).
2 Ibid, s 33(3).
3 Ibid, s 33(4).
4 Ibid, s 34.

Abduction of children in care

13.22 A person shall be guilty of an offence if, knowingly and without lawful authority or reasonable excuse, he takes a child in care away from the responsible person[1] or keeps the child away from that person or induces, assists or incites the child to run away from that person. A person guilty of an offence under this section shall be liable on conviction to a term of imprisonment not exceeding six months or a fine not exceeding level five on the standard scale[2] or both[3].

1 CA 1989, s 49, the responsible person is defined as any person who for the time being has care of him by virtue of the care order, the emergency protection order or following their removal to police protection pursuant to ibid, s 46.
2 Presently £5,000.
3 CA 1989, s 49(3).

Recovery of abducted children

13.23 Where it appears to the court that there is reason to believe that a child in care, a child who is the subject of an emergency protection order or in police protection has been unlawfully taken away from the designated person[1], has run away or is staying away from that person or is missing the court may make a recovery order[2]. A recovery order operates as a direction to any person who is in a position to do so to produce the child on request to any authorised person[3]. The authorised person shall if asked to do so produce documentation to prove he is authorised[4]. It also authorises the removal of the child by any authorised person and requires anyone with information about the child to disclose that information if asked to do so by a constable or officer of the court and it authorises the constable to enter premises and search for the child using reasonable force if necessary[5]. However, premises may only be specified in the order if there are reasonable grounds for believing the child to be on them[6]. The court may make a recovery order only on the application of any person who has parental responsibility for the child by virtue of a care order or emergency protection order or by the designated officer[7] where the child is in police protection[8]. The recovery order shall name the child and any person who has parental responsibility for him by virtue of a care order or emergency protection order or the designated officer if the child is in police protection[9]. Where a child is looked after by the local authority any expenses reasonably incurred by an authorised person in giving effect to the order shall be recoverable from the authority[10].

1 'Designated person' is defined as the officer designated for police protection orders under CA 1989, s 46.
2 CA 1989, s 50.
3 'Authorised person' is defined in CA 1989, s 50(7) as any person specified by the court; any constable; any person who is authorised after the recovery order is made and by a person who has parental responsibility for a child by virtue of a care order or an emergency protection order to exercise any power under a recovery order.
4 CA 1989, s 50(8)(b).
5 Ibid, s 50(3).
6 Ibid, s 50(6).
7 See para 13.17.
8 CA 1989, s 50(4).
9 Ibid, s 50(5).
10 Ibid, s 50(12).

Punishments

13.24 A person shall be guilty of an offence if he intentionally obstructs an authorised person removing a child under a recovery order[1]. A person guilty of an offence under this section shall be liable on summary conviction to a fine not exceeding level three[2] on the standard scale. No person shall be excused from complying with any request to give information about the whereabouts of a child on the ground that complying with it might incriminate him or his spouse of an offence; but a statement or admission made in complying shall not be admissible in evidence against either of them in proceedings for an offence other than perjury[3].

1 CA 1989, s 50(9).
2 Presently £1,000 by virtue of the Criminal Justice Act 1982, s 37(1) as amended.
3 CA 1989, s 50(11).

ORDERS IN WARDSHIP

Abduction of a ward

13.25 The court has rights of custody of its ward in accordance with Article 5 of the Convention on the Civil Aspects of International Child Abduction of 1980, the Hague Convention. Proceedings can therefore be taken under the Convention as implemented by the Child Abduction and Custody Act 1985 in respect of a ward who has been abducted.

Enforcement by attachment or committal

13.26 The court may order that the person in whose de facto care the ward is should deliver him to the person entitled to its care and may enforce its order by provisions for attachment or committal or for intervention by an officer of the court[1]. The court may make a seek and find order directed to the tipstaff where a ward is missing from the person who has his care and control and this may be directed to the tipstaff to ascertain his whereabouts and secure his recovery. Failure to comply with an order for return or recovery is a contempt of court[2]. The power of the High Court to secure, through an officer attending upon the court, compliance with any direction relating to a ward of court may be exercised by an order addressed to the tipstaff[3]. A power of arrest cannot attach to an order in wardship[4].

1 The tipstaff is the proper officer to enforce wardship orders.
2 See *Re Witten* (1887) 57 LT 336 and *G v L* [1891] 3 Ch 126.
3 FPR 1991, r 5.2.
4 *Re G (Wardship) (Jurisdiction: Power of Arrest)* (1982) 4 FLR 538, CA; *Re S* [1989] FCR 765.

Chapter Fourteen

Injunctions

Robert Purdie

Committal to Prison 477
The Application to Commit 479
The Affidavit in Support 481
Service of the Application and Affidavit in Support 481
The Affidavit in Answer 482
The Hearing of the Application to Commit 483
Court Orders upon Proof of Breach 484
Orders for Committal 485
Suspended Committal Orders 487
Applications to Commit Non-Parties 488
Discharge from Prison of Person Committed for Contempt 489

COMMITTAL TO PRISON

14.1 Where the High Court or a county court has granted an applicant a prohibitory or mandatory injunction, or the respondent has given the court a formal undertaking[1] other than an undertaking to pay a sum or sums of money[2] which is recorded by the court, then the injunction or undertaking, if breached, may be enforced by applying to the court for an order that the party in breach of the injunction or undertaking be committed to prison or fined.

Orders that the respondent do not assault or molest the applicant or that a respondent do not return to the matrimonial home are examples of prohibitory injunctions. An order that the respondent do vacate the matrimonial home is an example of a mandatory injunction. However, before an injunction or undertaking can be enforced by committal, the applicant for the committal order must satisfy the court that the correct procedure has been followed. Committal to prison is a drastic order involving the liberty of the subject and as such the court will not make an order of committal unless the procedure as laid down by Rules of Court has been followed strictly[3]. It does not matter how disobedient the party against whom the order is directed may have been because unless the process of committal has been carried out strictly in accordance with the Rules he is entitled to his freedom. The Rules of Court have statutory force and where there are no express exceptions, the court has no power to dispense with their requirements[4]. The procedures are designed to ensure that:

(a) no alleged contemnor should be in any doubt as to the charges which are made against him;

(b) he has a proper opportunity of showing cause why he should not be held in contempt of court;

(c) if an order of committal is made, the accused (i) knows precisely in what respects he is found to have offended and (ii) is given a written record of those findings and the sentence passed upon him[5].

1 *Hipgrave v Hipgrave* [1962] P 91, [1962] 1 All ER 75, Scarman J. See also *Hussain v Hussain* [1986] Fam 134, [1986] 1 All ER 961, CA: 'Let it be stated in the clearest possible terms that an undertaking to the court is as solemn, binding and effective as an order of the court in the like terms and that the contrary has never been suggested' per Sir John Donaldson MR.
2 Debtors Act 1869, s 4.
3 *Gordon v Gordon* [1946] P 99, [1946] 1 All ER 247, per Lord Greene MR.
4 See eg *Husseyin v Husseyin* (1982) 12 Fam Law 154, CA.
5 *M v P (Contempt of Court: Committal Order), Butler v Butler* [1993] Fam 167 at 174, [1992] 4 All ER 833 at 839, CA per Lord Donaldson MR.

Injunctions

14.2 The court will not enforce an order by committal unless the order to be enforced has been endorsed with a penal notice[1]. The order, duly endorsed with the penal notice, must have been served personally upon the party against whom it is sought to enforce the order in the case of a mandatory injunction[2] but not necessarily in the case of a prohibitory injunction. Where a prohibitory injunction has not been served, it is necessary to prove knowledge of the injunction as where the party who is the respondent to the application for the order was in court at the time the order was pronounced[3].

The person who serves the order should swear an affidavit stating that he served the order personally[4]; the affidavit should explain how the server knew that he was delivering the order to the person named therein and should exhibit a copy of the order served. Notwithstanding these requirements for personal service, on an application to commit, the court may waive personal service in the following circumstances:

(a) Where pending service of a prohibitory order, the party against whom the order was made was present when the order was made by the court or had been notified of the order and of its terms by telephone, telegram or otherwise[5].

(b) Where, in the case of both prohibitory or mandatory orders it is just to do so[6].

Both the Rules of the Supreme Court and the County Court Rules are silent on the time at which the court should be invited to exercise its discretion to dispense with personal service. However, it may be appropriate to apply to the judge for dispensation at the time the injunction is granted.

Non-service of an order does not prevent the court from committing to prison a person arrested under a power of arrest attached to an order of the court[7].

1 RSC Ord 45, r 7(4); CCR Ord 29, r 1(3).
2 RSC Ord 45, r 7(2); CCR Ord 29, r 1(2).
3 *Husson v Husson* [1962] 3 All ER 1056, [1962] 1 WLR 1434.
4 RSC Ord 65, r 8; CCR Ord 7, r 2.
5 RSC Ord 45, r 7(6); CCR Ord 29, r 1(6).
6 RSC Ord 45, r7(7); CCR Ord 29, r 1(7); the power to waive personal service of a prohibitive order is only to be exercised in cases of deliberate evasion of service: *Hill Samuel & Co Ltd v Littaur (No 2)* [1985] LS Gaz R 2248, CA.
7 FPR 1991, r 3.9; CCR Ord 47, r 8(7).

Undertakings

14.3 An undertaking given by a party to the court is as solemn, binding and effective as an injunction[1]. An undertaking given by a party is recorded in a formal document[2] which explains the consequences of disobedience and is generally signed by the maker of the undertaking. The form of undertaking is served on the person making the undertaking[3]. There is no prescribed form in High Court proceedings, but in practice the county court form is used with the necessary modifications.

1 *Hussain v Hussain* [1986] Fam 134, [1986] 1 All ER 961, CA. See also *Hipgrave v Hipgrave* [1962] P 91, [1962] 1 All ER 75, Scarman J.
2 Following the decision in *Hussain v Hussain*, above, CCR Ord 29, r 1A was made, which requires an undertaking to be recorded in Form N117.
3 CCR Ord 29, r 1A.

THE APPLICATION TO COMMIT

14.4 In the High Court, where proceedings are under the Domestic Violence and Matrimonial Proceedings Act 1976 or the Matrimonial Homes Act 1983, the application to commit is made by summons supported by an affidavit[1]. Where the order it is sought to enforce was made by the High Court as an interlocutory order in a matrimonial cause, the application to commit is by summons supported by an affidavit[2].

In the county court where the order it is sought to enforce was made pursuant to the Domestic Violence and Matrimonial Proceedings Act 1976 or the Matrimonial Homes Act 1983, the proper officer on application of the applicant, issues a notice[3] to the respondent to attend the court to show cause why an order of committal should not be made against him. The notice should not be signed by the applicant's solicitors unless it is qualified by showing that the notice is issued on their application[4]. The Rules do not require that the application be supported by an affidavit although the universal practice is to support an application in the first instance with an affidavit which should be served on the respondent to an application to commit at the same time as the notice is sent to the respondent by the registrar. Where it is sought to enforce an order made by a divorce county court as interlocutory relief in a matrimonial cause, application to commit is made in exactly the same way as if it was sought to enforce by committal an order made pursuant to the 1976 Act.

1 RSC Ord 52, r 6(1) as applied by FPR 1991, r 7.2(1).
2 Ibid.
3 In Form N 78 – notice to show cause why order of committal should not be made: CCR Ord 29, r 1(4).
4 *Williams v Fawcett* [1986] QB 604, [1985] 1 All ER 787, CA.

Contents of the application

14.5 The application must state the grounds upon which it is sought to have the respondent committed to prison. Where an injunction or undertaking is in prohibitory terms, as for example that the respondent be restrained from assaulting, molesting or otherwise interfering with the applicant having recited the order, the application should state each and every act relied upon as a breach of the order and should give particulars of dates, times and places[1]. It is important and it must be emphasised that the application to commit should specify each and every breach relied upon as, in general, only the grounds specified in the application may be relied upon at the hearing[2].

In the case of a mandatory injunction or undertaking as for example an order or undertaking that the respondent do vacate the former matrimonial home, the application, having recited the terms of the injunction or undertaking, should state that the respondent has failed to carry out the terms of the order within the time specified for carrying out the same.

The specific and particular requirements of an application for committal are to enable the respondent to the application to know exactly what he is alleged to have done, which constitutes contempt of court, with sufficient particularity so that he can defend himself[3]. It is unclear whether it is sufficient for the alleged breaches to be particularised in the supporting affidavit[4]. Where the application fails to specify the breaches but the affidavit evidence does specify them a judge might well allow the application to proceed, dispensing with the requirements[5], on the ground that the respondent has not been prejudiced by the fact that the breaches are contained in an affidavit rather than in an application.

Where an application to commit has been dismissed by reason of the defects in the application a second application may be brought in respect of the same alleged contempt without offending the rule against double jeopardy[6].

1 RSC Ord 52, r 4(2); CCR Ord 29, r 1(4) and see *Woolley v Woolley* (1974) 124 NLJ 768 Bagnall J. See also *Williams v Fawcett* [1986] QB 604, [1985] 1 All ER 787, CA; *Chiltern District Council v Keane* [1985] 2 All ER 118, [1985] 1 WLR 619, CA.
2 RSC Ord 52, r 6(3). There is no corresponding provision in the CCR. The proper test for a notice initiating committal proceedings is whether it gives the alleged contemnor sufficient information to meet the charge: *Harmsworth v Harmsworth* [1987] 3 All ER

816 at 821, CA. The information may be given in a schedule to the application, but not it would seem in a wholly different document: *Harmsworth* and see *Latkin v Latkin* [1984] CA Transcript 488.
3 *Woolley v Woolley* (1974) 124 NLJ 768 per Bagnall J; *Williams v Fawcett* [1986] 1 QB 604, [1985] 1 All ER 787, CA; *Chiltern District Council v Keane* [1985] 2 All ER 118, [1985] 1 WLR 619, CA.
4 *Chanel Ltd v FGM Cosmetics Ltd* [1981] FSR 471, Whitford J states that the breaches must be made clear in the application not the affidavit; *Chakravorty v Braganza* (1983) Times, 12 October, Comyn J states that the application and supporting affidavit had to identify specifically the alleged breaches; *Chiltern District Council v Keane*, above does not deal with this conflict but refers to the notice of motion as having to state the breaches.
5 RSC Ord 52, rr 4(3), 6(3); CCR Ord 29, r 1(7).
6 *Jelson (Estates) Ltd v Harvey* [1984] 1 All ER 12, [1983] 1 WLR 1401, CA.

THE AFFIDAVIT IN SUPPORT

14.6 The affidavit in support of the application should set out in detail the circumstances of the breaches relied upon to support the application to commit. The purpose of this is so that the person whose committal is sought knows exactly what is being alleged against him[1]. Furthermore, it enables the court to decide, subject to oral evidence at the hearing, just how serious and wilful the alleged contempt is. It is good practice to ensure that the respondent to an application to commit is served with any affidavit in support well before the hearing so that an affidavit from the respondent in answer may be prepared and filed with the court prior to the hearing. Failure so to serve may result in an application by the respondent for an adjournment of the hearing in order to prepare evidence in answer which application is likely to be treated sympathetically by the court.

1 *Woolley v Woolley* (1974) 124 NLJ 768 and cases cited above.

SERVICE OF THE APPLICATION AND AFFIDAVIT IN SUPPORT

14.7 Applications to commit must be served personally[1] upon the respondent to such application together with affidavits in support. The court does, however, have a power to waive personal service if it thinks it just to do so[2].

The Family Division of the High Court has an inherent jurisdiction to make a committal order on an application ex parte[3] and may dispense with service of the notice of motion or summons[4] if it thinks it just to do so. The county court may hear an application to commit ex parte, by dispensing with service of the notice in Form 78[5]. For an order of committal to be made ex parte the circumstances must be exceptional[6]. A judge has a discretion to hear the application ex parte, and must balance the desirability of an immediate hearing and the urgency of the matter against the possibility that the evidence may not be complete[7].

There must, on an ex parte application, be a notice[8] although the judge may take account of breaches alleged to have been committed after the issue of the notice[9]. Personal service should only be waived where the matter is grave, the need for relief is urgent and the respondent has knowledge of the application[10]. Personal service will probably be waived where the applicant could show that the person whose committal was sought was deliberately evading service[11]. Where the hearing of an application to commit is adjourned, notice of the adjourned hearing must be served personally on the alleged contemnor[12], subject to the power to dispense with service[13].

An affidavit of service of these documents should be sworn and filed, in case the respondent does not attend at the hearing of the application for the committal order when the court would then need to be satisfied that the documents have been served[14]. The affidavit of service should include details of how the respondent was identified by the person serving the document; the circumstances in which the documents were served and exhibiting to the affidavit copies of all the documents that were served.

1 RSC Ord 52, r 4(2); CCR Ord 29, r 1(4). It should be noted that an application for committal for failure to give discovery of documents may be served on the respondent's solicitors; see RSC Ord 24, r 16(3); CCR Ord 14, r 10(3).
2 RSC Ord 52, r 4(3); CCR Ord 29, r 1(7).
3 *Hipgrave v Hipgrave* [1962] P 91, [1962] 1 All ER 75, Scarman J following *Gilbert v Gilbert* (1961) Times, 15 September, Plowman J; *Pearce v Pearce* (1959) Times, 30 January; *Deraux v Deraux* (1959) Times, 4 September; and *Moran v Moran* (1959) Times, 25 September. It must be emphasised that a committal order ex parte is a most exceptional remedy which will only be granted where delay by applying on notice might cause irreparable or serious mischief.
4 RSC Ord 52, r 4(3).
5 CCR Ord 29, r 1(7).
6 *Wright v Jess* [1987] 2 All ER 1067 [1987] 1 WLR 1076, CA. The very essence of a case being exceptional is that one is unlikely to find a precisely parallel set of facts in some other reported authority. *Harben v Harben* [1957] 1 All ER 379, [1957] 1 WLR 261, Sachs J, at p 381 and p 265.
7 *Lamb v Lamb* [1984] FLR 278, [1984] Fam Law 60, CA.
8 Specifying the alleged breaches; *Wright v Jess* above.
9 *Wright v Jess*, above.
10 *Spooner v Spooner* (1962) Times, 4 December.
11 Ibid.
12 *Chiltern District Council v Keane* [1985] 2 All ER 118, [1985] 1 WLR 619, CA. See also *Phonographic Performance Ltd v Tsang* [1985] LS Gaz R 2331, CA.
13 RSC Ord 52, r 4(3); CCR Ord 29, r 1(7).
14 Oral evidence of service may be given: *Savage v Savage* [1979] CA Transcript 537.

THE AFFIDAVIT IN ANSWER

14.8 Having been served with the application for committal, it is, of course, open to the respondent to file affidavit evidence in answer to the application. In his affidavit, the respondent should admit or deny whether or not he admits each and every alleged breach. If the breach or breaches are admitted, then any mitigating circumstances should be put forward in the affidavit no doubt coupled with a sincere apology to the court and a promise to abide by the order in the future. If the breaches are denied, then the affidavit will take the form of denying what is alleged in the applicant's affidavit and, indeed, the respondent may file affidavits sworn by such persons as can support his denial. An alleged contemnor cannot be compelled to give evidence against his will[1], although he may do so if he wishes[2]. The court may require a respondent to swear affidavit evidence in answer to the committal application, but the applicant may not make use of such evidence until it is deployed by the respondent[3].

1 *Comet Products UK Ltd v Hawkex Plastics Ltd* [1971] 2 QB 67, [1971] 1 All ER 1141, CA.
2 RSC Ord 52, r 6(4).
3 *Re B (Contempt: Evidence)* [1996] 1 FLR 239 per Wall J.

THE HEARING OF THE APPLICATION TO COMMIT

14.9 In the High Court, the application will, subject to certain exceptions, be heard in open court[1]. In any event, the order must be made in open court[2]. In the High Court an application for a committal order may not, without leave of the court, be made which relies on grounds other than those contained in the application for the committal order[3]. This practice is in general followed in the county court. It would seem that there is no power in the county court to hear the application except in open court.

All persons who have sworn affidavits either in support of or in opposition to the application for committal should attend the hearing so that they can be cross-examined upon their respective affidavits. In the High Court the alleged contemnor has a right to give evidence at the hearing if he so wishes[4]. This is generally followed in the county court.

During the course of the hearing, the applicant for an order for committal must prove:

(a) an injunction embodied in an order of the court endorsed with a penal notice, or that an undertaking has been given;

(b) that the order or undertaking mentioned in (a) above has been duly served personally upon the respondent or that such service has been dispensed with;

(c) that the respondent has wilfully disobeyed the order or that he has wilfully failed to obey the order[5];

(d) if the respondent does not attend the hearing of the application to commit, that service of the application to commit together with the affidavit in support has been effected upon the respondent or that such service has been dispensed with[6].

An application to commit is quite separate from any criminal proceedings which might arise from the same facts[7]. Therefore an application to commit should not be adjourned pending the outcome of a criminal trial[8]. It is important for committal proceedings to be dealt with swiftly and decisively[9].

However, the court retains a discretion to adjourn contempt proceedings if the same might prejudice the fairness of a subsequent criminal trial; there must be a serious risk or real prejudice which may lead to injustice[10]. Where there are concurrent proceedings and the committal application is the first to be heard, any punishment should be for the contempt and not for the offence[11]. The contemnor cannot plead autrefois convict on the hearing of the offence on the basis of any findings in respect of the contempt[12].

1 RSC Ord 52, r 6(1). For the purposes of this work the only really relevant exception is r 6(1)(a).
2 RSC Ord 52, r 6.
3 RSC Ord 52, r 6(5).
4 RSC Ord 52, r 6(4). Subject to complying with any requirement to swear affidavit evidence so that the applicant can prepare evidence in reply: *Re B (Contempt: Evidence)* [1996] 1 FLR 239, Wall J.
5 Proof of which must be beyond reasonable doubt: *Re Bramblevale* [1970] Ch 128, [1969] 3 All ER 1062, CA and see *Dean v Dean* [1987] 1 FLR 517, CA, overruling *West Oxfordshire District Council v Beratec Ltd* (1986) Times, 30 October. See also *Re B (Contempt: Evidence)* [1996] 1 FLR 239, Wall J; it is clearly established that the standard of proof is the higher criminal standard.
6 In general this will be by affidavit of service, though oral evidence of service is admissible – see *Savage v Savage*, above.
7 *Szczepanski v Szczepanski* [1985] FLR 468, [1985] Fam Law 120, CA, and see *Caprice v Boswell* (1985) 149 JP 703, [1986], Fam Law 52, CA. The question of double jeopardy was not considered.
8 Ibid, and see *Jefferson Ltd v Bhetcha* [1979] 2 All ER 1108, [1979] 1 WLR 898, CA, where it was held that a plaintiff in civil proceedings is not to be debarred from pursuing an action merely because to do so might result in the defendant, if he wished to defend, having to disclose his defence thereby giving an indication of his likely defence in contemporaneous criminal proceedings.
9 *Szczepanski v Szczepanski*, above, and *Caprice v Boswell*, above.
10 *H v C (Contempt and Criminal Proceedings)* [1993] 1 FLR 787, CA.
11 *Smith v Smith* [1991] 2 FLR 55, CA.
12 *R v Green* (1992) Times, 14 July, CA.

COURT ORDERS UPON PROOF OF BREACH

14.10 Breach of an injunction[1] or undertaking to the court[2] is a contempt of court. It follows that it is a matter for the court to decide whether or not imprisonment is the appropriate order to make upon the application to commit. The real purpose of bringing matters back to court on applications to commit, certainly in the context of orders made in family cases, is often not so much to punish disobedience of court orders as to secure compliance with the injunction in the future with the result that committal orders are and must be regarded as orders of the very last resort[3]. A judge has a very wide discretion as to whether or not to make a committal order where there has been a breach of an injunction[4]. Whilst the views of the applicant for the committal order are very relevant[5] it should be remembered by judges when exercising their discretion that orders to commit are potentially damaging to complainant spouses as to offending spouses particularly where children are concerned with the result that orders should be made very reluctantly and only when every other effort to bring the situation under control has failed or is almost certain to do so[6]. In particular, the power to order imprisonment is one which should be used very sparingly indeed in proceedings for contempt of custody and access orders[7].

Nevertheless and notwithstanding the foregoing, it must be remembered that unless the courts are prepared ultimately to exercise the power to commit in cases of breach, the purpose of making orders ousting parties from the matrimonial home and/or orders not to molest other spouses will be defeated. A short term of immediate imprisonment may be appropriate even where there has only been one breach of the order or undertaking if that breach is sufficiently serious and flagrant[8]. Where an application to commit has been adjourned generally, it is very similar to a deferment of sentence in criminal proceedings. Accordingly further breaches of the injunction or undertaking are likely to justify a custodial sentence[9]. Consecutive terms of imprisonment may be appropriate where there have been several different breaches[10]. It is fundamental that a contemnor cannot be sentenced twice for the same breach[11].

A committal order is not appropriate where there is a satisfactory alternative method of enforcing the order[12]. The High Court[13] and county courts[14] have power to punish contempt by a sentence of imprisonment of up to two years, or by an unlimited fine, or both. The sentence of imprisonment must be expressed as a fixed term[15].

The court has jurisdiction to enforce orders or binding undertakings made or given even where they are made or given after the decree has been made absolute[16]. Indeed, the court has jurisdiction to make an order even after the decree absolute has been pronounced[17]. An absurd situation would result if the court was able to make injunctions but unable to enforce them[18].

1 *Ansah v Ansah* [1977] Fam 138, [1977] 2 All ER 638, CA, per Ormrod LJ.
2 *Hipgrave v Hipgrave* [1962] P 91, [1962] 1 All ER 75.
3 *Ansah v Ansah*, above, at 144.
4 *McLean v Nugent* (1980) 1 FLR 26, CA, per Ormrod LJ. Committal should never be ordered in respect of a purely technical breach of an injunction or undertaking: see *Marshall v Marshall* (1966) 110 Sol Jo 112, CA. See also *Smith v Smith* [1988] 1 FLR 179, CA.
5 See *Boylan v Boylan* (1980) 11 Fam Law 76, CA.
6 *Ansah v Ansah*, above, at 144 and 643, per Ormrod LJ.
7 *R v R* (1979) 10 Fam Law 56, CA, per Orr LJ.
8 *Pickering v Pickering* [1980] CA Transcript 193, CA, and see *Re H* (1985) Times, 7 November, CA.
9 *George v George* [1986] 2 FLR 347, [1986] Fam Law 294, CA.
10 *Lee v Walker* [1985] QB 1191, [1985] 1 All ER 781, CA.
11 *B v B (Contempt: Committal)* [1991] 2 FLR 588; *Lamb v Lamb* [1984] FLR 278; *Kumari v Jalal* [1996] 4 All ER 65, CA.
12 *Danchevsky v Danchevsky* [1975] Fam 17, [1974] 3 All ER 934.
13 Contempt of Court Act 1981, s 14(1).
14 Ibid, s 14(4A), added by the County Courts (Penalties for Contempt) Act 1983 reversing the decision of *Whitter v Peters* [1982] 2 All ER 369; *Peart v Stewart* [1983] 2 AC 109, [1983] 1 All ER 859, HL.
15 *Westcott v Westcott* [1985] FLR 616, [1985] Fam Law 278, CA and see *Re C (a minor)* [1986] 1 FLR 578, [1986] Fam Law 187, CA.
16 *Stewart v Stewart* [1973] Fam 21, [1973] 1 All ER 31.
17 See para 11.4.
18 *Stewart v Stewart*, above.

ORDERS FOR COMMITTAL

14.11 If an order for committal is made by the court, the order as drawn up by the court staff must reflect exactly the order that is made by the judge[1]. In particular, any order which is drawn up by the court staff must reflect the period of imprisonment which has been imposed by the judge.

Where a committal order is made on an ex parte application the contemnor should be shown a copy of the order (whether or not he is shown the warrant) either before or shortly after his arrest[2]. An ex parte order should contain a proviso that the contemnor should apply for his release three days (a period necessary for practical purposes) after being taken into custody[3]. An ex parte committal order is not an interim order and if a judge on a later occasion hears evidence from the contemnor he may not increase the sentence[4] as a person may only be sentenced once for each contempt[5]. Where a contemnor applies for an order of committal, made in his absence, to be set aside the whole matter should be reheard[6]. The judge should not merely hear the contemnor's evidence[7]. However, it is important to distinguish between an application to set aside a committal order and an application for release, which is on the ground that the contemnor has purged, or is desirous of purging, his contempt[8].

The prescribed forms[9] must be drawn up accurately by the court staff. However defects in the formal parts of an order do not affect its validity[10]. If the court has exercised its powers to dispense with service of the injunction[11] or the application to commit[12] then the order must state the same[13]. An order of a county court must state the evidence that has been given[14].

An order of the High Court or a county court must state each and every contempt proved[15] although it would seem that where a breach is admitted by the contemnor it need not be particularised[16], nevertheless it is submitted that breaches should be specified in orders so that the court record is clear for the future.

Such a defect is not cured even where the judge has set out the contempts proved in his judgment[17]. The same requirements apply to suspended orders[18]. Unless justice otherwise requires an order for committal which does not specify the breaches will not be upheld[19]. While the court should not normally rectify a defective committal order[20], it is permissible to do so[21].

Where a period of imprisonment is ordered the term must be stated in the order[22], and imprisonment can only be for a fixed term[23]. The fact that the prescribed form in the High Court[24] seems to provide for an indefinite period of imprisonment does not alter the position[25].

A person can only be sentenced once for each contempt[26] therefore a judge may not increase a term of imprisonment imposed ex parte once he has heard from the contemnor[27] nor can a sentence be increased, once made, because of the effect of remission[28].

It would seem that an invalid order cannot be rectified by the court of first instance substituting a valid order[29]. However, on appeal, while an invalid order must be quashed[30], a valid order may be substituted[31]. If there has been a fair hearing without any material irregularity in the proceedings but merely an irregularity in drawing up the order there is no reason why the Court of Appeal may not substitute a just sentence[32], which could in an exceptional case be a longer one[33]. A court should hesitate long before increasing a sentence[34].

1 *Danchevsky v Danchevsky* [1975] Fam 17, [1974] 3 All ER 934. See also *Chiltern District Council v Keane* [1985] 2 All ER 118, CA; *Langley v Langley* [1994] 1 FLR 383; and *Clarke v Clarke* [1990] 2 FLR 115, CA.
2 *Egan v Egan* (1971) 115 Sol Jo 673, Lane J.
3 *Egan v Egan*, above.
4 *Lamb v Lamb* [1984] FLR 278, [1984] Fam Law 60, CA.
5 *Church's Trustee v Hibbard* [1902] 2 Ch 784, CA.
6 *Aslam v Singh* [1987] 1 FLR 122, [1986] Fam Law 362, CA.
7 *Aslam v Singh*, above.
8 RSC Ord 52, r 8(1); CCR Ord 29, 4 3(1).
9 RSC App A, Form 85, County Court (Forms) Rules 1982, Form 79.

10 *Palmer v Townsend* (1979) 123 Sol Jo 570; *Burrows v Iqbal* (No 2) [1985] Fam Law 188, CA.
11 RSC Ord 45, r 7(6) and (7); CCR Ord 29, r 1(7).
12 RSC Ord 52, r 4(3); CCR Ord 29, r 1(7).
13 *Nguyen v Phung* [1984] FLR 773, [1985] Fam Law 54, CA, and see *Williams v Fawcett* [1986] QB 604, [1985] 1 All ER 787, CA.
14 See County Court (Forms) Rules 1982, Form 79, and see *Cinderby v Cinderby, Pekesin v Pekesin (No 2)* (1978) 8 Fam Law 244, CA.
15 *McIlraith v Grady* [1968] 1 QB 468, [1967] 3 All ER 625, CA; *Chiltern District Council v Keane* [1985] 2 All ER 118, CA.
16 *Kavanagh v Kavanagh* (1978) 128 NLJ 1007, CA.
17 As in *Re M (minors) (Access: Contempt: Committal)* [1991] 1 FLR 355, CA and *Smith v Smith (Contempt: Committal)* [1992] 2 FLR 40.
18 *Re M (minors) (Access: Contempt: Committal)* [1991] 1 FLR 355, CA.
19 *C v Hackney London Borough Council* [1995] 2 FLR 681.
20 *Loseby v Newman* [1995] 2 FLR 754, CA.
21 *Abdi v Jama (Contempt: Committal)* [1996] 1 FLR 407, CA.
22 See the wording of the prescribed forms; RSC App A, Form 85, County Court (Forms) Rules 1982, Form 79.
23 Contempt of Court Act 1981, s 14 (11 *Halsbury's Statutes* (4th edn) 181 CONTEMPT OF COURT); *Linnett v Coles* [1987] QB 555, [1986] 3 All ER 652, CA.
24 RSC App A, Form 85.
25 In *Re C (a minor)* [1986] 1 FLR 578, [1986] Fam Law 187, CA. RSC Ord 1, r 9 is ultra vires the statute: Contempt of Court Act 1981, s 14, and the statute must prevail.
26 *Church's Trustee v Hibbard* [1902] 2 Ch 784.
27 *Aslam v Singh* [1987] 1 FLR 122, [1986] Fam Law 362, CA.
28 *Westcott v Westcott* [1985] FLR 616, [1985] Fam Law 278, CA.
29 *Hegarty v O'Sullivan* [1985] NLJ Rep 557, CA, but this decision must be read subject to *Linnett v Coles* [1987] QB 555, [1986] 3 All ER 652, CA.
30 *Linnett v Coles*, above.
31 *Linnett v Coles*, above, applying Administration of Justice Act 1960, s 13(3).
32 *Linnett v Coles*, above.
33 Ibid.
34 Ibid.

SUSPENDED COMMITTAL ORDERS

14.12 If the court is of the opinion that immediate imprisonment is not appropriate, it has power to make an order of committal suspended upon terms[1]. Care must be taken however when making a suspended committal order, to ensure that the terms upon which the committal is suspended do not have the effect of removing the respondents liberty from the judge's discretion and control[2]. In particular, orders which are expressed to take effect upon the filing of the document the veracity of which has been untested and without a further review by the court are bad orders.

In general, a suspended committal order is only appropriate where a mandatory injunction has been breached and the purpose of the committal order is to secure future compliance. It is often, for example, used where its purpose is to secure compliance with an order for discovery or for directions. If an affidavit is filed which states that the respondent has failed to vacate the matrimonial home, it is dealing with fact (and not with opinion) which will either be true of false. For that reason, it is frequently used to enforce such orders. Breaches of molestation orders are by their nature far from clear cut[3]. Molestation varies considerably in degree and what constitutes molestation in any given circumstances may well be in a grey area between fact and opinion.

Indeed, it would seem to be dangerous to commit a person to prison suspended on terms that he did not assault or molest the applicant and to provide that the suspension will be removed upon filing an affidavit that he had in fact assaulted or molested the applicant. In this context, it should be noted that under the power of arrest, a person can only be arrested if he is suspected of being in breach of non-molestation injunctions by reason of his use of violence[4]. Where terms are imposed on fulfilment of which a suspended committal order is to come into operation for breach of a non molestation order, the terms should be as particularly drafted as it is possible to do in the circumstances of the case. A suspended committal order must be for a specific time[5], and it seems cannot be made without specifying the terms and conditions of the suspension. It would seem that a suspended order cannot be made where the contemnor has already remedied the breach[6].

At the hearing of a committal application, if the application were not to be adjourned with liberty to restore, the court could attach powers of arrest to an injunction as this is in general an effective way of securing future compliance of a prohibitory injunction[7]. However, before the power of arrest can be attached, the statutory conditions must be fulfilled[8]. Where a power of arrest is imposed, control is maintained by the court in that the person arrested must be brought before the court within 24 hours[9].

1 RSC Ord 52, r 7 and see *Lee v Walker* [1985] QB 1191, [1985] 1 All ER 781, CA.
2 *Ansah v Ansah* [1977] Fam 138, [1977] 2 All ER 638, CA at 144C and 643g.
3 *Vaughan v Vaughan* [1973] 3 All ER 449, [1973] 1 WLR 1159, CA, and see paras 11.32 – 11.35 above.
4 Domestic Violence and Matrimonial Proceedings Act 1976, s 2(3).
5 *Pidduck v Molloy* [1992] 2 FLR 202, CA.
6 *Bluffield v Curtis* [1988] 1 FLR 170, CA.
7 *Ansah v Ansah*, above, per Ormrod LJ.
8 See *Lewis v Lewis* [1978] Fam 60, [1978] 1 All ER 729, CA, and paras 11.47 – 11.49, above.
9 Domestic Violence and Matrimonial Proceedings Act 1976, s 2, as amended by the Domestic Proceedings and Magistrates' Courts Act 1978, Sch 2.

APPLICATIONS TO COMMIT NON-PARTIES

14.13 Not only may an application be made to commit a party in breach of an injunction or his undertaking to the court, but application may also be made to commit to prison any person who with knowledge[1] of such injunction or undertaking to the court aids and abets a party to breach the injunction or undertaking[2]. A stranger to an action who is required, by an order in such action, to do or to refrain from doing something will be amenable to proceedings for contempt if he refuses to comply or obstructs compliance with the order[3]. This is so even if the stranger is not, in law, bound by the order[4].

The principle is indeed well established and is a power accepted and used by the court because it is not for the public benefit that the course of justice should be obstructed in a deliberate manner by strangers to the action. Indeed, if the court were not to take this power a very grave weakness in the battery of court powers would be revealed.

To enforce an order against a non-party, it is necessary to prove firstly knowledge[5] and secondly aiding or abetting a breach of the order by a party to the order.

The application to commit, however, must be served personally as required by the Rules[6] and should be made in the same manner and as if the application were to commit a party. The application should be supported by an affidavit to be served personally. In general, the order for breach of which it is proposed to apply to commit a stranger will have come to the stranger's notice one way or another at some stage prior to the application to commit being served since otherwise there would be little or no point in proceeding with the application. In general, it is submitted that a legal adviser when faced with breaches by a stranger should send an open letter to the stranger concerned enclosing a copy of the order by recorded delivery and inviting him to desist from breaching the order. Failure to comply with that letter when enclosing a copy of the order will be the most vital evidence to be exhibited to any affidavit in support of an application to commit a stranger.

1 See *Seaward v Paterson* [1897] 1 Ch 545.
2 *Thorne v Bunting (No 2)* [1972] 3 All ER 1084, CA, and see the cases cited therein.
3 *Bawden v Bawden (Note)* [1979] 1 QB 419n, [1978] 3 All ER 1216 at 420H–421B and at 1218d per Goff LJ obiter.
4 *Bawden v Bawden* above. It should be noted that an order which is good on its face remains in force and valid unless and until it is set aside by a court of competent jurisdiction on a proper application to do so: *McLean v Nugent* (1980) 1 FLR 26, CA.
5 Ibid. There may be a requirement that the order should have been served on the non-party where committal is sought: *Re L (a minor)* [1988] 1 FLR 255.
6 See above.

DISCHARGE FROM PRISON OF PERSON COMMITTED FOR CONTEMPT

14.14 A person committed to prison for contempt may apply to the court to be released from prison[1]. This application is normally made to the judge who made the committal order but may be made to any other judge of the court and in certain circumstances as set out in the Rules may be made to a district judge of the court. One of the functions of the Official Solicitor is to review the cases of persons committed for contempt[2]. Accordingly the Official Solicitor may bring an appeal against a sentence of contempt, in his discretion, irrespective of the wishes of the contemnor[3].

There is no requirement in the High Court that the application for release should be supported by an affidavit. In the county court, the application must be supported by an affidavit showing that the applicant has purged or is desirous of purging his contempt and it must be served with a copy of his application on the party who applied for his committal in the first place[4]. The general practice is to file such an affidavit in the High Court. Not only can the affidavit deal with the purging of the contempt, but furthermore it can deal fully with any change of circumstances since the order was made.

Where someone has been committed to prison for a fixed term, as it must be, it is perhaps difficult to argue (in the absence of a change of circumstances) that he should be released from prison because his contempt has been purged. Often, it is not the length of the imprisonment that is important but the fact of imprisonment itself. Certainly, no order should be made which prevents a person applying to the court for this purpose[5].

Once an application to discharge has been made, the question is one purely for the discretion of the judge to whom the application is made.

1 RSC Ord 52, r 8; CCR Ord 29, r 3; and FPR 1991, r 7.2(2).
2 This derives from a direction of the Lord Chancellor dated 29 May 1963, which is set out in Borrie & Lowe, *The Law of Contempt* (3rd edn) 1996, p 634.
3 *Churchman v Joint Shop Stewards' Committee* [1972] 3 All ER 603, [1974] 1 WLR 1094, CA.
4 CCR Ord, 29, r 3(1).
5 *Yager v Musa* [1961] 2 QB 214 at 219, [1961] 2 All ER 561 at 564, per Devlin. See also *Raymond v Honey* [1983] 1 AC 1, [1982] 1 All ER 756, HL.

Part VII

Legal Aid and Costs

Chapter Fifteen

Legal Aid and Costs

David Burrows

The Legal Aid Scheme 491
Conduct of Proceedings 498
Costs 500
Costs in Legal Aid Cases 502
The Legal Aid Statutory Charge 505

THE LEGAL AID SCHEME

Introduction

15.1 Availability of legal aid for an individual depends on three factors: the merits of his or her case (or of his defending a case against him); the means of the applicant; and the type of proceedings involved. This is subject to one major exception in respect of special Children Act proceedings, where legal aid is available regardless of an applicant's means or the merits of his or her case[1].

1 See para 15.9.

15.2 The legal aid scheme is governed by the Legal Aid Act 1988. This provides for the making by the Lord Chancellor of a number of sets of regulations which in their turn govern much of the operation of the scheme. Part II of the Act sets up the Legal Aid Board which operates the scheme and, amongst other things, publishes Notes for Guidance which define for practitioners and Board staff alike many of the detailed workings of the Scheme. The Act, the regulations and the Notes for Guidance are reproduced (without comment or annotation) in the *Legal Aid Handbook*[1] which is republished annually.

1 *The Legal Aid Handbook* (Sweet & Maxwell).

Legal aid for family and child law

15.3 Legal aid may be available for either civil or criminal proceedings. The civil legal aid scheme covers legal aid in family and children cases and is governed, for the most part, by the following sets of regulations:

(a) Legal Advice and Assistance (Scope) Regulations 1989 (LAA(S)R 1989) which define the extent of availability of advice and assistance: green form and advice by way of representation (ABWOR).

(b) Legal Advice and Assistance Regulations 1989 (LAAR 1989) which provide for operation of the green form scheme and ABWOR.

(c) Civil Legal Aid (General) Regulations 1989 (CLA(G)R 1989) which set out the operation of the civil legal aid scheme including the statutory charge, taxation of costs and the award of costs against assisted persons and against the Board.

(d) Civil Legal Aid (Assessment of Resources) Regulations 1989 (CLA(AR)R 1989) which deal with assessment of resources for civil legal aid.

(e) Legal Aid in Family Proceedings (Remuneration) Regulations 1991 (LAFP(R)R 1991) which provide for costs payable in certain family proceedings.

(f) Legal Aid in Civil Proceedings (Remuneration) Regulations 1994 (LACP(R)R 1994) which provide for costs payable in all civil proceedings which includes some forms of family proceedings, because of the narrow definition of 'family proceedings' in LAFP(R)R 1991.

Availability and eligibility

15.4 Legal aid is available as advice and assistance ('the green form scheme'), advice by way of representation (ABWOR) and assistance under a representation certificate (civil legal aid). Availability for the first two has been reduced substantially since 12 April 1993. Advice and assistance is available concerning the application of English law to a particular set of circumstances[1]; whilst representation is available for proceedings only in English courts[2].

1 LAA 1988, s 2(2)
2 'Representation' is defined by the LAA 1988, s 2(4) and consists of 'steps preliminary or incidental to any proceedings' and reaching a settlement such as 'to avoid or bring to an end proceedings'. LAA 1988, s 14(1) provides that 'proceedings' are those proceedings set out in Part I of Sch 2 for which see para 15.7.

Financial eligibility

GREEN FORM AND ABWOR

15.5 A simple form of assessment of resources applies to green form and ABWOR applications which is carried out by the solicitor using the eponymous green form[1]. An applicant who is receiving income support, family credit or disability working allowance is entitled automatically[2]. For others, their disposable income must be close to subsistence levels and their capital limited to a scale starting from £1,000 and graduated upwards according to the number of their dependents[3].

1 LAA 1988, s 9(1); LAAR 1989.
2 LAAR 1989, regs 9(4)(c) and 13(2).
3 Ibid, regs 9(4)(a) and (b) and 11(1).

CIVIL LEGAL AID

15.6 Assessment of resources is carried out from an extensive application form by the Legal Aid Assessment Office, attached to the Department of Social Security. Again assessment is according to an applicant's disposable income[1] and disposable capital[2]; but unlike green form assistance there is a band of means which enables the Board to accept a contribution as a condition of grant of legal aid[3]. On the basis of figures in operation from 8 April 1996[4] disposable means figures are as follows:

(a) *Disposable income.* An applicant with disposable income of £2,948 per annum or less is entitled to legal aid (subject to capital) on the basis of means; whilst a person with disposable income in excess of £7,403 is not eligible. In between these two figures a contribution of one thirty-sixth of the difference between £2,948 and actual disposable income is payable during the life of the certificate.

(b) *Disposable capital.* An applicant with disposable capital of £3,000 or less is eligible; but ineligible (subject to a residual discretion in the Area Director) if his or her disposable capital is above £6,750. In between he or she pays his or her capital as a contribution for legal aid.

1 LAA 1988, s 15(1); CLA(AR)R 1989, reg 4 and Sch 2.
2 LAA 1988, s 15(1); CLA(AR)R 1989, reg 4 and Sch 3.
3 CLA(AR)R 1989, reg 4(a) and (b).
4 These figures are reviewed annually. Recently the upper limits have not increased ensuring that, gradually, people with low savings slip out of the legal aid net.

Proceedings

15.7 The type of proceedings for which legal aid is sought defines whether or not it is available. (Green form assistance is not available for representation in any proceedings.) Civil legal aid or ABWOR will cover all the proceedings with which the family lawyer is concerned. These are provided for as follows:

(a) *Civil legal aid.* The list of proceedings for which civil legal aid is available is set out in the LAA 1988, Sch 2, Part I subject to the proceedings excluded by Part II, Sch 1. Part I[1] provides that proceedings before the the House of Lords (in its appellate capacity), before the Court of Appeal, the High Court and county courts are covered; as are certain proceedings in the magistrates' courts[2]. Part II then lists exceptions to the proceedings in Part I. Excluded proceedings which concern the family lawyer[3] are divorce and judicial separation proceedings (only) unless such proceedings are (i) defended; (ii) directed to be heard in open court; or (iii) the physical or mental incapacity makes representation necessary. Where the proceedings are interlocutory to the main suit legal aid is available for: (i) injunction proceedings; (ii) financial relief applications; (iii) children proceedings; and (iv) other proceedings which 'raise a substantial issue for determination by the court'. Tribunals (such as the child support appeal tribunals) are completely excluded from civil legal aid.

(b) *ABWOR.* The list of proceedings is set out in the LAA(S) R 1989, reg 9 and the Schedule to those regulations. The proceedings covered are in the magistrates' courts and include (amongst a relatively obscure list) the Domestic Proceedings and Magistrates' Courts Act 1978.

1 The list of proceedings here is taken from paras 1 and 2. Para 2 is not dealt with exhaustively; and there are other forms of proceedings referred to Part I which are not of immediate relevance to the family lawyer.
2 Proceedings under the Domestic Proceedings and Magistrates' Courts Act 1978, the CA 1989 and the Child Support Act 1991, ss 20 and 27 are included.
3 LAA 1988, Sch 2, Part II, para 5A.

Merits

15.8 Fundamental to the availability of most legal aid is that the application has merit, that is to say, it appears reasonable for the applicant to have legal aid. The exceptions to this rule are most green form assistance and specified Children Act proceedings[1].

(a) For green form assistance it seems only that it is necessary to show that a question of English law is involved. The merit of the application only arises when an extension on the cost limit is sought or a representative is applying for assistance for a person under a disability[2].

(b) For representation under ABWOR or a civil legal aid certificate the merit of the application is central to grant. The Board must consider whether it is reasonable that the applicant should have legal aid[3]; that is, has he shown that his case or his defence have a reasonable prospect of success? Further the Board may refuse if in the particular circumstances of the case they do not think the application reasonable[4].

1 See para 15.9.
2 LAAR 1989, regs 21(1) and 14(1).
3 LAA 1988, s 15(2) and LAAR 1989, reg 22(5). Notes for Guidance 6–08, and 6–11 consider these questions further.
4 LAA 1988, s 15(3)(a) and LAAR 1989, reg 22(6) considered further at Notes for Guidance 6–09.

Special Children Act proceedings

15.9 Certain specified public law proceedings under the CA 1989 give rise to special consideration as exceptions to the rules on financial eligibility and merits tests considered above. Known as 'special Children Act proceedings'[1] they comprise four categories.

(a) For a child, parent or person with parental responsibility involved in proceedings for a care or supervision order (s 31), for a child assessment order (s 43) or for an emergency protection order or for extension or discharge of such an order (ss 44 and 45) legal aid under a civil legal aid certificate is available regardless of the person's or child's means or the merits of their case[2].

(b) For the same category of persons legal aid is available for appeals against orders under s 31 regardless of the appellant's means but subject ony to the merits of the appeal[3].

(c) For anyone who applies to join or who is joined as a party to special Children Act proceedings legal aid is available regardless of the merit of their taking part in the proceedings but subject to asessment of their means[4].

(d) If a child brought before the court on an application for a secure accommodation order (s 25) wishes to be legally represented he must be granted legal aid regardless of his means or the merit of his defence of the application[5].

1 CLA(G)R 1989, reg 3(1).
2 LAA 1988, s 15(3C).
3 LAA 1988, s 15(3D).
4 Ibid, s 15(3E).
5 Ibid, s 15(3B).

Application for legal aid

15.10 Applications for legal aid in family proceedings are made on the following forms:

CLA 1   *Application – non-matrimonial*

Judicial review (eg CA 1989, Part III, education, etc); LPA s 30; assault proceedings between former partners.

CLA 2   *Application – matrimonial*

All forms of matrimonial proceedings; domestic violence (including where parties not married to one another); Children Act proceedings where other proceedings are pending (cf form CLA 5 below).

CLA 3   *Emergency legal aid application*

CLA 5   *Application – free-standing children applications*

Wardship, adoption and free-standing applications under the CA 1989 (other than special Children Act proceedings: see form CLA 5A below); and including applications by children[1].

1 Ie applications where FPR 1991, r 9.2A (see para 8.54) applies.

CLA 5A   *Application – special Children Act proceedings*

ABWOR 1   *Application for ABWOR*

In family cases: applies only in the magistrates' courts and not, for example, for special Children Act proceedings.

Notes

(1) Applications are made on forms CLA 2, CLA 5 and CLA 5A whether the proceedings are in the High Court, the county courts or the magistrates' courts (save where ABWOR applies in the magistrates' courts). Once granted, a civil legal aid certificate can be moved up and down if proceedings are transferred between courts.

(2) Statements of financial circumstances (all applications, save forms CLA 5A) must be accompanied by statements of means as follows:
   (a) form CLA 4A (with form L17 (employer's statement of income) or other evidence of income)
   (b) form CLA 4B (applicant on income support); or
   (c) form CLA 4F (child's statement of means).

CONDUCT OF PROCEEDINGS

Scope of the certificate

15.11   Essential to the conduct of all legally aided litigation is the scope of the certificate; for if the scope of the certificate does not cover the work to be done or if work is done outside the scope or without regard to a limitation on the certificate, then the solicitor will not be paid[1]. It is akin to a solicitor's retainer, this time by the Board on behalf of the assisted person. Nor can a certificate, or a limitation upon it, be amended retrospectively[2].

1 See eg *Littaur v Steggles Palmer* [1986] 1 All ER 780, [1986] 1 WLR 287, CA.
2 *Lacey v W Silk & Son Ltd* [1951] 2 All ER 128.

Duty to inform the Board

15.12   There are a number of duties which solicitors and counsel owe to the legal aid fund. For the most part these are set out in the CLA(G)R 1989, Part X. For example solicitors have a duty to report abuses of legal aid such as intentional failure to comply with regulations[1] or where an assisted person requires his case to be conducted unreasonably[2]; and there is a duty to report an assisted person's death or bankruptcy[3]. What is essential is to keep the Board informed if for any reason a solicitor, or counsel, think there is any doubt as to the way the case is proceeding[4].

1 CLA(G)R 1989, reg 67(1)(b) as, for example, where an assisted person deliberately fails to tell the Board of a change in financial circumstances.
2 CLA(G)R 1989, reg 67(1)(a).
3 Ibid, reg 71.
4 *Davy-Chiesman v Davy-Chiesman* [1984] Fam 48, CA; *Clarke v Clarke (No 2)* [1991] 1 FLR 179, Booth J in which Booth J also, at 187H and 192F, stressed the importance

of the 'duty of care to the legal aid fund' owed by solicitors. Both of these were cases where the legal representatives, counsel especially, proceeded with a case extravagantly and without regard to their duties to the fund.

15.13 Perhaps the most important duty of solicitors and counsel, is to provide the Area Director with information concerning the progress of a case if called upon to do under the CLA(G)R 1989, reg 70, as follows.

(a) The assited person's solicitor must report any reasonable offer of settlement to the Board, and any payment into court, whether reasonable or not[1]. Failure to do this, in extreme circumstances, might result in the solicitor losing costs, and even of payment of damages by him or her to the Board. For example if a *Calderbank* offer is made in ancillary relief proceedings by an unassisted respondent and he beats the offer, then he may seek costs against the Board[2]. If he is successful the Board may take the view that, had they known of the offer they would not have continued operation of the certificate, then they could claim their loss against the solicitor who failed to comply with reg 70(1)(a)[3].

(b) Regulation 70(2) further provides the Area Director with a machinery whereby he can call for a report on the reasonableness of the assisted person continuing to have a certificate. If a solicitor fails to respond within 21 days to such a request then there is the ultimate risk that the certificate may be discharged.

1 CLA(G)R 1989, reg 70(1)(a).
2 LAA 1988, s 18; *Gojkovic v Gojkovic (No 2)* [1992] Fam 40, [1991] 2 FLR 233, CA; and see para 15.22.
3 CLA(G)R 1989, reg 102 which enables the Board to defer payment of the solicitors' profit costs. If a loss is suffered then the Board can pursue its civil remedies (eg in negligence) against the solicitor.

Money on account

15.14 Money on account may consist of profit costs and of disbursements.

(a) Money on account of profit costs is available at certain stages of proceedings[1]. Further, it is worth noting that determination of a solicitor's retainer (as where the assisted person transfers to another solicitor) entitles him to seek a payment on account of profit costs[2].

(b) Money on account of disbursements is available from date of the grant of a certificate[3]; and as a matter of practice solicitors should always seek a payment on account unless there is very good reason why not[4]. However claims should only be made if they are genuine: the Board will investigate further where solicitors hold money on account without there being any likelihood of it being used for disbursements.

1 CLA(G)R 1989, reg 100.
2 CLA(G)R 1989, reg 100(6).

3 CLA(G)R 1989, reg 101(1)(a); LAAR 1989, reg 30A(1) (for ABWOR certificates). Both of these regulations state quite plainly that disbursements are those 'incurred or *about to be incurred*' (emphasis supplied).
4 Claims are made on forms CLA 28.

COSTS

Principles governing the award of costs

15.15 Costs are provided for by RSC Ord 62, Part II. This Part of Ord 62 is incorporated into the County Court Rules by CCR Ord 38, r 1(3). In the first instance costs are in the discretion of the court[1]; but if the court sees fit to award costs then costs should follow the event unless the court considers that some other order should be made[2]. In family proceedings the rule that costs follow the event does not apply strictly[3]. However it has been held that, whilst this may be so, there must be a 'starting point' for family judges which 'is that costs prima facie follow the event but [that it] may be displaced more easily than ... in other Divisions', for example in children cases[4].

1 Supreme Court Act 1981, s 51.
2 RSC Ord 62, r 3(3).
3 RSC Ord 62, r 3(5).
4 *Gojkovic v Gojkovic (No 2)* [1992] Fam 40, [1991] 2 FLR 233, CA per Butler-Sloss LJ; cited with approval in *Thompson v Thompson (Costs)* [1993] 2 FLR 464, CA.

Principles on which costs are awarded

15.16 In *Re Elgindata Ltd (No 2)* Nourse LJ set out the main principles on which orders for costs should be based[1]:

(a) costs are in the discretion of the court;

(b) they should follow the event, unless the court considers that in the circumstances of the case some other order should be made;

(c) these general rules do not cease to apply because a party raises issues on which he is not successful, though if, in raising those issues, he substantially lengthens the trial he may lose part or all of his costs;

(d) where a successful party raises issues or makes allegations improperly or unreasonably the court may deprive him of his costs and order him to pay the unsuccessful party's costs[2].

1 [1992] 1 WLR 1207, CA at 1214A – C.
2 RSC Ord 62, r 10(1).

What is the 'event'?

15.17 In those cases where the 'event' needs to be defined, for the purposes of RSC Ord 62, r 3(3), it is the main issue before the court whatever subsidiary issues may have been raised by a successful party[1]. Any award must then be subject to the 'well-established practice' (per Nourse LJ) of depriving a successful party of part or all of his costs if he prolongs the issue or behaves improperly or unreasonably[2].

1 *Re Elgindata (No 2)* [1992] 1 WLR 1207, CA.
2 See eg *Phillips v Pearce* [1996] 2 FCR 237, Johnson J where a mother who put her claim on behalf of her child under the Children Act 1989, Sch 1 too high was only granted two-thirds of her costs though her claim had otherwise been successful.

Calderbank letters

15.18 A *Calderbank* letter[1] sets out proposals for settlement of any issue in proceedings[2] and is expressed to be 'without prejudice save as to costs'. In considering discretion as to costs the court 'shall take into account' any *Calderbank* letters[3]; though where a party has delayed in responding to a *Calderbank* letter he may find himself penalised in costs[4]. Such offer shall not be communicated to the court until costs are to be considered[5]. In cases where there are one or more legally aided parties the Legal Aid Board should be contacted as follows:

(a) Where acting for unassisted party against legally aided person ensure any *Calderbank* offer is drawn to the attention of the Board, because, first, if the other party's certificate is discharged (though this is rarely likely) it may bring the case to an end or make it easier to settle; and, secondly, if later the unassisted party seeks costs against the Board under the Legal Aid Act 1988, s 18[6] the Board may allege it is not 'just and equitable' if a weakness in the assisted person's case has not been brought to their attention[7].

(b) Where acting for a legally assisted person ensure all reasonable offers of settlement are brought to the Board's attention if they are declined by the assisted person[8].

1 *Calderbank v Calderbank* [1976] Fam 93, [1975] 3 All ER 333, CA. As to appropriateness of when to write see *Family Court Practice*, note to Ord 62, r 14.
2 RSC Ord 22, r 14(1); CCR Ord 11, r 10.
3 RSC Ord 62, r 9(1)(d).
4 *A v A (Costs: Appeal)* [1996] 1 FLR 14, Singer J.
5 RSC Ord 22, r 14(2); FPR 1991, r 2.69.
6 See para 15.22.
7 *Re Spurling's Will Trusts, Philpot v Philpot* [1966] 1 WLR 920, CA; and see para 15.28.
8 CLA(G)R 1989, reg 70(1)(a).

Wasted costs orders

15.19 Wasted costs orders[1] apply to any costs incurred by any party either 'as a result of any improper, unreasonable or negligent act or omission' of a legal representative[2]; or which, if incurred after such act or omission, the court thinks it unreasonable to expect that party to pay[3]. These words should be given their ordinary meaning: 'the principles requiring gross misconduct laid down in the older authorities are [now no longer] applicable'[4].

1 Supreme Court Act 1981, s 51(6); RSC Ord 62, r 11; Matrimonial Causes (Costs) Rules 1988, r 15; CCR Ord 38, r 1. The meaning of 'wasted costs' was fully explained in *Ridehalgh v Horsefield* [1994] Ch 205, [1994] 2 FLR 194, CA.
2 The Supreme Court Act 1981, s 51(13) refers to 'legal or other representative' as being a person 'exercising a right of audience or right to conduct litigation'. Thus the rules apply also to members of the bar.
3 *Re a Barrister (Wasted Costs Order)(No 1 of 1991)* [1993] QB 293 where guidance was given by the Court of Appeal (Criminal Division) on wasted costs orders setting out principles which may be regarded as applicable in all jurisdictions; and see further *Family Court Practice* note to the Matrimonial Causes (Costs) Rules 1988, r 15.
4 *Sinclair-Jones v Kay* [1989] 1 WLR 114, CA per May LJ at 122A; and see *Gupta v Cromer* [1991] 1 QB 629, CA. For an explanation of the meaning of the words see *Ridehalgh v Horsefield* [1994] Ch 205, [1994] 2 FLR 194, CA.

COSTS IN LEGAL AID CASES

Costs against legally aided parties

15.20 The rights or liabilities of an assited person 'or the principles on which the discretion of any court ... is exercised' are not intended to be effected by the fact of their being legally aided[1]. Costs are a discretionary remedy[2]; and thus the court is entitled to consider an award of costs against a legally aided party. However that discretion in most legal aid cases is likely to be fettered considerably by the means of the assisted person, a fact reflected in the provisions of the Legal Aid Act 1988, s 17. The consequence of the Legal Aid Act 1988, ss 17 and 31(1)(b) is that assessment of costs against a legally aided person is a two-stage process: first, the court considers whether an order for costs would be made on ordinary principles in accordance with RSC Ord 62[3]; and, if so, the court then proceeds to assess the assisted person's ability to pay in accordance with s 17.

1 LAA 1988, s 31(1)(b).
2 RSC Ord 62, r 3; and see para 15.15.
3 RSC Ord 62; and see para 15.16.

Legal Aid Act 1988, s 17

15.21 The Legal Aid Act 1988, s 17(1) provides that the court cannot impose on an assisted person an order for costs which exceeds an amount 'which is a reasonable one for him to pay having regard to all the circumstances, including the financial resources of all the parties and their conduct in connection with the dispute'. Section 17(3) provides that in any such assessment the assisted person's house, clothes, furniture and the tools of his trade are ignored for the purposes of the court's assessment. Procedure under s 17 is governed by the CLA(G)R1989, Part XIII. In making its order the court can order no more than a reasonable amount[1]. The court takes acount of the resources of all the parties to the action: not only of the assisted person. Whilst s 17(3) leaves the assited person's home, clothing, furniture and so on out of assessment, any other assets including the subject matter of the dispute or any damages (subject to incidence of the statutory charge[2]) are available for assessment by the court[3]. The court also takes account of the conduct of 'all the parties' to the action in its assessment. Where an unassisted opponent has conducted the litigation particularly unreasonably this may be a basis for opposing a claim to costs under s 17.

1 In practice the court will often enquire whether or not the assisted person has been required to pay a contribution to his legal aid and this may be taken as an indication that he has some means to enable him to pay at least some of the costs.
2 See para 15.29 et seq.
3 But see *Chaggar v Chaggar* [1996] 1 FLR 450, Chadwick J where it is doubted that the LAA 1988, s 17(3) applies to the proceeds of sale of a dwelling house.

Costs against the Legal Aid Board

15.22 In certain circumstances an order for costs may be made in favour of an unassisted party against the Legal Aid Board[1]; but the conditions for such an order are governed strictly by the Legal Aid Act 1988, s 18 and the CLA(G)R 1989, Part XIV. Such an order can only be made against an unassisted party[2]. Before an order can be made the Board effectively becomes a party to the application and the assisted person ceases directly to be involved. To obtain an order it is important that the following questions be considered by the applicant and the courts.

(a) Is the applicant for costs an unassisted party; or is he unassisted for the period covered by the order?

(b) Were the proceedings finally decided in favour of the unassisted party?

(c) But for the existence of legal aid would an order for costs have been made against the assisted person?

(d) Has the assisted person any liability to pay under s 17?

(e) In the case of courts of first instance: (i) were the proceedings started by the assisted person; and (ii) will the unassisted party suffer severe financial hardship if no order is made against him?

(f) Is it just and equitable in all the circumstances for the unassisted party's costs to be paid out of the legal aid fund?

1 LAA 1988, s 18.
2 This term cannot include an assisted party: see definitions of 'legally assisted person' and 'unassisted party' in the LAA 1988, s 2(11); and this is so even though their costs will be statutorily charged on property recovered or preserved for them.

'Finally decided in favour of an unassisted party'[1]

15.23 Where the event is clear it will normally be plain in whose favour the case has been decided; but there will be cases where a number of issues are before the court and where therefore the dominant issue will decide what is the event[2]. Where a *Calderbank* letter is written in matrimonial financial relief proceedings (say, for a lump sum order) then the assisted party may have her application (ie 'the proceedings') decided in her favour; but because a *Calderbank* offer has not been beaten it is likely that the court will hold that, for the purposes of s 18(1), the proceedings have been decided in favour of the unassisted respondent[3]. A clear decision has to be made by the court on this question; for unless it is held that proceedings have been decided in favour of the unassisted party then there can be no further consideration under s 18. A decision is finally made once the time for appealling, or seeking leave to appeal, has passed or there is no appeal against the decision[4].

1 LAA 1988, s 18(1).
2 And see para 15.17 for a consideration of what is 'the event'.
3 *Kelly v London Transport Executive* [1982] 2 All ER 842, CA where the defendant paid into court £750 and offered £4,000. The court awarded £75. Though the plaintiff had succeeded on the claim the Court of Appeal held that the proceedings had been finally decided in favour of the defendant.
4 LAA 1988, s 18(7).

'An order for costs would be made'[1]

15.24 The court must clearly find that an order for costs 'would', not 'could', be made. Thus sympathy with an unassisted party in, say, a children case (where orders for costs are rarely made), is insufficient[2].

1 LAA 1988, s 18(4)(a).
2 *Keller v Keller and Legal Aid Board* [1995] 1 FLR 259, CA.

Section 17 ability to pay

15.25 Before proceeding further the court must 'consider' what order for costs should be made against the assisted person and if so what his liability should be under s 17[1].

1 See above para 15.21.

Proceedings instituted by an assisted party in 'a court of first instance'[1]

15.26 The restriction on unassisted parties obtaining costs after issuing proceedings in courts of first instance is to discourage relatively wealthy plaintiffs from issuing proceedings against poor defendants in the expectation that the Board will pay the costs if legally aided defendants lose. It will normally be clear what is a court of first instance; but it has been held that neither a judge hearing an appeal from the district judge (registrar as he then was) nor the Divisional Court hearing a judicial review application are courts of first instance[2] and so an unassisted party is able to seek costs against the Board.

1 LAA 1988, s 18(4)(b).
2 *Gayway Linings Ltd v Law Society* [1982] AC 81, [1981] 1 All ER 641; *R v Leeds County Court, ex p Morris* [1990] 1 QB 523, [1990] 1 All ER 550.

'Severe financial hardship'[1]

15.27 Since *Hanning v Maitland (No 2)*[2] the courts have been able to adopt an approach which is less stringent in assessment of hardship than the word 'severe' might suggest; but the hardship must still be 'financial', not, for example, resisting a hopeless case or expending time on, and suffering the inconvenience of, litigation. If the defendant could afford to pay part of the costs himself the court could only order the Board to pay so much of his costs as to save him from suffering hardship[3]. This test applies only in 'courts of first instance'[4]: no hardship test therefore applies in appellate courts.

1 LAA 1988, s 18(4)(b).
2 [1970] 1 QB 580, [1970] 1 All ER 812.
3 *Adams v Riley* [1988] QB 372, [1988] 1 All ER 89.
4 See para 15.26.

'Just and equitable in all the circumstances'[1]

15.28 Where an unassisted party is successful and the other conditions above apply, then the presumption must be that he is entitled to his costs. It will be for the Legal Aid Board to rebut that presumption, for example where the unassisted party brought the proceedings upon himself[2] or he was insured in respect of the costs[3]. A means whereby a practitioner could find his client deprived of costs is if he fails to inform the Board of a weakness in his opponent's case[4].

1 LAA 1988, s 18(4)(c).
2 *Hanning v Maitland (No 2)* [1979] 1 QB 580, [1970] 1 All ER 812.
3 *Lewis v Averay (No 2)* [1973] 1 WLR 510, CA.
4 *Re Spurling's Will Trusts, Philpot v Philpot* [1966] 1 All ER 745, [1966] 1 WLR 920. So for example, if a solicitor writes a *Calderbank* letter for his unassisted client and that letter is not subsequently beaten by the applicant, prima facie he is entitled to his costs. If all other s 18 conditions are satisfied, when the Board learn of the *Calderbank* offer they might take the view that had they known of it they would have discharged the applicant's certificate; and the court accepts this argument and rejects an application under s 18.

THE LEGAL AID STATUTORY CHARGE

Statutory charge

15.29 Once a case is concluded, whether or not proceedings have been issued and whether or not any application to the court was contested, then if money or property has been recovered or preserved, a legally aided person will have to pay their own costs from the money[1]; or, if there is no money, the costs will be charged against their property[2]. This is so even though those costs arose as a result of 'any compromise or settlement arived at to avoid the proceedings or bring them to an end'[3]. This is the legal aid 'statutory charge' which derives from the concept of the solicitor's lien, namely that he or she should have a charge for his costs on the proceeds of any litigation conducted by him or her on behalf of the assisted person, that is property recovered or preserved through his efforts on behalf of his client[4].

1 That is to say, any money above the statutory exemption (£2,500): CLA(G)R 1989, reg 94; and see para 15.31.
2 LAA 1988, s 16(6).

3 LAA 1988, s 16(7); and see *Van Hoorn v Law Society* [1985] QB 106, [1984] FLR 203, Balcombe J.
4 See eg the Solicitors Act 1974, s 73.

The statutory charge defined

15.30 The Legal Aid Act 1988, s 16(6) is written in mandatory terms and provides that costs over and above any contribution paid by the assisted person 'shall be a first charge[1] for the benefit of the Board on any property recovered or preserved for him in the proceedings'. Further, provided that the property has been recovered or preserved, it is 'immaterial what the nature of the property[2] is and where it is situated'[3]. As has already been mentioned, the charge also extends to property involved in a compromise or settlement of proceedings[4], even though the property which was actually recovered was not itself in issue in the proceedings[5].

1 Though stated to be a 'first charge' it can only be a first charge where there are no prior secured charges attaching to the property. Any chargees whose charges are not secured will take subject to the Board's charge.
2 For an indication of the types of property which can be charged see, eg the Charging Orders Act 1979, s 2 which defines and restricts the property over which a charge may be taken under that Act to land, trust funds, stock and other securities and funds in court. Bank and other such accounts can be garnisheed to similar effect, for more immediate payment out of funds.
3 LAA 1988, s 16(7).
4 Ibid, s 16(7)
5 *Van Hoorn v Law Society* [1985] QB 106, [1984] FLR 203, Balcombe J: property not in issue in proceedings accepted in settlement of proceedings about another property, charge applies to property accepted in settlement.

Creation of the charge

15.31 The statutory charge can only arise where property has been recovered or preserved and where that property was in issue in the proceedings. This brief analysis gives rise to four questions which should assist in defining whether or not the charge applies.

(a) *The proceedings*[1]. The proceedings are those proceedings for which the certificate was issued[2].

(b) *The property*. In most matrimonial proceedings it will be reasonably clear what the property is: broadly all matrimonial assets, that is property owned by both parties whether jointly or individually[3], will be property for this purpose.

(c) *Was the property in issue?* Whether or not the charge applies turns on whether or not the property was in issue in the proceedings[4]; for if it was not the question of the charge does not arise for there is no property to charge. To consider whether or not property was in issue it is necessary to look not only at any court order, but also at the affidavits or pleadings, even the correspondence between the parties[5]. The same principle would apply to the terms of any settlement deed or agreement; and in that case the background correspondence and terms of negotiations are likely to prove important in an assessment of what property was in issue.

(d) *Was the property 'recovered or preserved'?* If property is in reality in issue in proceedings then it will be said to have been 'recovered or preserved' and the charge applies unless any of the statutory exemptions apply[6]. Thus property is recovered if a person takes proceedings to convert it to his own use, for example a property adjustment order or a lump sum order; whilst property is preserved if a person successfully resists a claim to his property, for example an order for sale or a property adjustment order.

1 The term 'proceedings' in this context means proccedings which are settled and property recovered or preserved to avoid the issue of proceedings: LAA 1988, s 16(7).
2 *Hanlon v Law Society* [1981] AC 124, [1980] 2 All ER 199.
3 It should also be noted that there may be property which is brought into issue involved in the proceedings which belongs to neither party to the proceedings and cannot therefore be charged by the Legal Aid Board: eg an interest in expectancy in a trust fund, a spouse's pension fund, a spouse's cohabitant's solely owned freehold property, a relative's estate which a spouse is likely to inherit and so on.
4 For the definition of 'proceedings' in the context of a settlement or compromise see n 1 (above).
5 *Hanlon v Law Society* [1981] AC 124, [1980] 2 All ER 199.
6 Under the CLA(G)R 1989, reg 94 there are a number of exemptions form the charge which relate either to interim payments, maintenance and to the first £2,500 of lump sums paid in most forms of family proceedings (including eg the MCA 1973, the Inheritance (Provision for Family and Dependants) Act 1975 and the CA 1989, Sch 1) but not eg the LPA 1925, s 30 or for declarations as to property holding as between cohabitants.

Operation of the charge

15.32 The CLA(G)R 1989, Part XI and reg 85 set up the machinery for operation of the charge, its vesting in the Legal Aid Board and its enforcement and postponement. Any money arising in proceedings or a settlement thereof which is due to an assisted person must be paid to his or her solicitor or to the Board; for only they can give a good receipt[1]. The solicitor then pays that money to the Board (so far as it exceeds the £2,500 exemption in cases where that applies: that £2,500 is sent to the assisted person)[2]. Alternatively the solicitor can give an undertaking that his or her costs will not exceed a particular amount in which case that amount is sent to the Board and the balance sent to the assisted person[3]. Once costs are taxed the Board pays the balance to the assisted person[4]. As soon as the charge arises it vests in the Legal Aid Board[5] which may then enforce its charge by such means as are available to any chargee[6]; and it may only postpone enforcement of the charge where CLA (G)R 1989, regs 96 or 97 apply[7].

1 CLA(G)R 1989, reg 87.
2 Ibid, reg 90.
3 CLA(G)R 1989, reg 90(2).
4 Ibid, reg 92.

5 Ibid, reg 95(1).
6 Ibid, reg 95(2): such as foreclosure and power of sale and so on.
7 Ibid, reg 95(2).

Postponement of operation of the charge

15.33 The Legal Aid Board has power to postpone operation of the charge where the charge applies (a) to property in which the assisted person or her dependants[1] wish to live as a home[2] or (b) to money intended to be used to buy such a property[3]. For this power to be exercisable certain further conditions must also be met including:

(a) that the property was recovered 'in any proceedings'[4], but that the lump sum was ordered in certain family financial relief proceedings[5];

(b) whether it is property or money which is recovered or preserved:

  (i) by order of the court or the terms of the agreement between the parties the property is to be used as a home or the money to be used to buy property[6],

  (ii) the assisted person agrees in writing to execute a charge on the property purchased[7] and to pay interest on the charge[8],

  (iii) the Area Director is satisfied that the property will provide adequate security for the Board's charge[9],

  (iv) in the case of money intended to be used to buy property, which includes money arising from a sale of the former matrimonial home, the new property must have been bought within one year of the order or agreement[10].

If all the conditions above apply then, in addition, the assisted person can transfer the charge to another property in substitution to the original property[11]. The original charge will be released and the assisted person will then have to agree to execute another on the substituted property.

1 'Dependants' is defined by the CLA(G)R 1989, reg 3(1) as a person for whose maintenance the assisted person has assumed responsibility.
2 CLA(G)R 1989, reg 97.
3 Ibid, reg 96.
4 Ibid, reg 97(1): this condition has the effect of enabling the Board to postpone enforcement where property is recovered or preserved in proceedings of any nature, not solely proceedings taken under the statutes set out in reg 96(1).
5 CLA(G)R 1989, reg 96(1) lists the proceedings as follows: (a) MWPA 1882; (b) MCA 1973; (c) I(PFD)A 1975; (d) CA 1989, Sch 1; (e) MFPA 1984, Part III; and (f) LPA 1925, s 30.
6 CLA(G)R 1989, reg 96(1); and see *Practice Direction (Statutory Charge: Form of the Order of the Court)* [1991] 2 FLR 384, [1991] 3 All ER 896.
7 CLA(G)R 1989, reg 96(2)(b). There is no need for this condition where the assisted person already lives in the property recovered or preserved since the charge arises by statute.

8 CLA(G)R 1989, regs 96(3)(b) and 97(4). Interest is charged in accordance with reg 99(4).
9 CLA(G)R 1989, regs 96(2) and 97(3).
10 Ibid, reg 96(7).
11 Ibid, reg 98.

Attempts to defeat the statutory charge

15.34 To understand the concept of attempting to defeat the charge it is necessary to return to the solicitor's lien on property recovered or preserved in proceedings through his instrumentality. It works on a similar principle to the solicitor ensuring payment of his costs in privately funded proceedings: that is to say, were a solicitor to recover money for a client in such proceedings then, in nomal circumstances, he would ensure that his costs were paid before his client received his money; or that, at least, property was charged with payment of his costs. A solicitor for an assisted person owes a duty to protect the legal aid fund in much the same way as he would his own costs; and, in this respect, the solicitor acts more or less as an agent for the Board.

15.35 In *Manley v Law Society*[1] the Court of Appeal upheld the Law Society's[2] refusal to pay Dr Manley's legal representative's costs[3] in circumstances where Lord Denning MR held that they had tricked the legal aid fund: lawyers must not 'try and manipulate [money payable to an assisted person] so as to avoid the statutory charge'. Both he and Ormrod LJ spoke in terms of the solicitors' lien on property recovered or preserved in proceedings; for had Dr Manley not been legally aided there is no question but that his advisers would have ensured that their costs were provided for before settling on the terms they did[4].

1 [1981] 1 All ER 401, [1981] 1 WLR 335, CA.
2 Precursor to the Legal Aid Board.
3 Dr Manley was an inventor who agreed with Marconis that they would sponsor him. He incurred debts and when he attempted to rely on his alleged agreement with the firm they would not help him. He issued proceedings which, on the eve of a long trial, were settled on terms that nominees of Marconis acquired the debts leaving Dr Manley without liabilities and the legal aid fund with the bill for his costs. The Law Society refused to pay the costs.
4 In *Clark v Clark* [1989] 1 FLR 174 Booth J was highly critical of the legal representatives who took sequestration proceedings to recover a wife's financial relief at great expense to the fund and then accepted payment from the husband as arrears of periodical payments so that the charge would not apply.

15.36 In negotiating a settlement of matrimonial proceedings care must be taken not to evade the charge. Circumstances analogous to *Manley v Law Society* can easily arise in family proceedings. For example, where a husband agrees to clear a wife's debts in settlement of her claim against him for a lump sum, then insofar as those debts (if no other property is recovered or preserved) exceed £2,500 the wife's costs will have to come out of the money ear-marked for payment of the debts before the debts themselves are paid[1]. Further, where a lump sum is paid to children rather than to a spouse it must be shown that

Legal Aid and Costs

there is good reason for payment in that way; for such an arrangement has also been held to be designed to evade the charge[2].

1 LAA 1988, s 16(6): costs remaining to be paid are a 'first charge ... on any property recovered or preserved'; and see para 15.30.
2 *Draskovic v Draskovic* (1980) 11 Fam Law 87.

Appendix 1

Domestic Violence – the New Law

Appendix 1

Domestic Violence: the New Law

Robert Purdie

Introduction 511
Definitions 511
Parties to Applications 514
Occupation Orders 523
Non-Molestation Orders 541
Undertakings 543
Third Party Applications 544
Ex Parte Orders 544
Power of Arrest 546

INTRODUCTION

A.1 The Family Law Act 1996, Part IV introduces a comprehensive legislative code of remedies for applications relating to non-molestation and ouster injunctions. The previous provisions of the Domestic Violence and Matrimonial Proceedings Act 1976, the Domestic Proceedings and Magistrates' Courts Act 1978, and the Mental Health Act 1983 are all repealed. Throughout this Appendix all statutory references are to the Family Law Act 1996, unless otherwise stated. In *Richards v Richards*[1], Lord Scarman described the legislation as 'a hotchpotch of enactments of limited scope passed into law to meet specific situations or to strengthen the powers of specified courts'[2]. He called for the 'range, scope and effect of the powers to be rationalised into a coherent and comprehensive body of statute law'. Part IV seems to be such a statutory code, by providing a consistent series of remedies, and widening the scope of the previous law to cover former lacunae.

1 [1984] AC 174, [1983] 2 All ER 807, HL.
2 Ibid at 206 and 818.

DEFINITIONS

A.2 Part IV of the Family Law Act 1996 introduces new terminology including (a) cohabitants[1], (b) associated persons[2], and (c) relevant child[3]. In addition, ss 58 and 59 provide definitions and interpretation. Other terms such as matrimonial home rights[4], occupation orders[5] and non-molestation orders[6] will be considered in subsequent paragraphs. The Act imports several definitions from the CA 1989, such as 'harm' and 'significant harm'.

1 See paras A.3–A.8.
2 See paras A.9–A.27.
3 See paras A.28–A.29
4 Section 30, see para A.31.
5 Section 39, see paras A.30–A.67.
6 Section 42(1), see paras A.68–A.70.

PARTIES TO APPLICATIONS

Cohabitants and former cohabitants

Cohabitants

A.3 Section 58(1)(a) defines 'cohabitants' as a man and a woman who, although not married to each other, are living together as husband and wife. Section 62(1)(b) provides that 'former cohabitants' is to be read accordingly but does not include cohabitants who have subsequently married each other[1].

1 It is submitted that a void marriage would be ignored: *De Reneville (otherwise Sheridan) v De Reneville* [1948] P 100, [1948] 1 All ER 56, CA. See para A.11.

A.4 This represents a substantial change in the law from the provisions of the Domestic Violence and Matrimonial Proceedings Act 1976, s 2(2) by the introduction of former cohabitants. Previously, while an application could be brought after the termination of a relationship, it was limited to relief in respect of incidents that had occurred before such termination[1] and had to be brought promptly. The new law enables relief to be sought against acts of molestation long after the termination of a relationship.

1 *McLean v Burke* (1980) 3 FLR 70, CA.

A.5 Under the Domestic Violence and Matrimonial Proceedings Act 1976, s 2(2), the Act applied to 'a man and a woman who are living with each other in the same household as husband and wife'. The change from 'living with each other' to 'living together' is merely an alteration in drafting and does not affect the meaning. The abolition of the requirement of living in the same household may be of more significance. The word 'household' has been held[1] to have an abstract meaning rather than referring to something physical. While there could be two households under one roof, without physical division of the property[2]; in some cases a property could be so small that it was impossible to find two separate households rather than one unhappy household[3].

1 *Santos v Santos* [1972] Fam 247, [1972] 2 All ER 246, CA; a decision on the Divorce Reform Act 1969, ss 2(5) and 3(6), repealed and replaced by the MCA 1973, s 2(6).
2 *Hollens v Hollens* (1971) 115 Sol Jo 327.
3 *Adeoso v Adeoso* [1981] 1 All ER 107, [1980] 1 WLR 1535, CA.

A.6 The effect of this change is to remove the need for the applicant to show that there is only one household. There are, nonetheless, problems with proving that a couple are 'living with each other as husband and wife' or, in the case of former cohabitants, have lived with each other as husband and wife. These are problems of degree to be decided on the individual facts of each case, particularly where a relationship lasts for a short time.

A.7 The concept of 'living with each other as husband and wife' involves more than a man and a woman living in the same household as cohabitation can continue even though the parties are living apart[1]. Thus a couple who only physically live together at weekends may well be within the definition of 'cohabitants' where the intention to live together continues.

1 *Santos v Santos* [1972] Fam 247, [1972] 2 All ER 246, CA, and *Fuller v Fuller* [1973] 2 All ER 650, [1973] 1 WLR 730, CA. See also *Bradshaw v Bradshaw* [1897] P 24 at 26 per Sir Francis Jeune P.

Former cohabitants

A.8 Once cohabitants cease to live with each other as husband and wife they become 'former cohabitants'. The Act removes some of the difficulties in trying to identify precisely when a relationship has come to an end. Cohabitants who subsequently marry are not within the definition of 'former cohabitants'[1].

1 Section 62(1)(b). See para A.3.

Associated persons

A.9 Section 62(3) lists the categories of persons who are associated with another person for the purposes of the Act, the significance of which needs to be examined in some detail. Cohabitants and former cohabitants are associated persons[1], the meaning of these words has already been considered[2]. Spouses and former spouses, common householders, relatives, engaged couples, parents and those with parental responsibility, and parties to family proceedings are all associated persons, who have the right to bring applications against other persons with whom they are associated.

1 Section 62(3)(b).
2 See paras A.3–A.8

Spouses and former spouses

A.10 A person is associated with another person if they are or have been married to each other[1].

1 Section 62(3)(a).

SPOUSES

A.11 There must be a valid marriage which has not been dissolved, or voidable marriage that has not been annulled for there to be a subsisting marriage. A party to a void marriage is not a spouse as there never was a marriage[1], however such persons might well be cohabitants or former cohabitants for the purposes of the Act, common householders[2] or an engaged couple[3]. Parties to a valid polygamous marriage (whether actual or potential) are probably included[4]; the husband would be associated with each of the wives but the wives would not necessarily be associated with each other unless they were common householders[5]. Where there is doubt about the validity or subsistence of a marriage, the court may grant interim relief, pending a proper determination of the issue[6].

1 *De Reneville (otherwise Sheridan) v De Reneville* [1948] P 100, [1948] 1 All ER 56, CA.
2 See paras A.13–A.14
3 See paras A.18–A.22.
4 See *Re Sehota* [1978] 3 All ER 385, [1978] 1 WLR 1506, a case under the Inheritance (Provision for Family Dependants) Act 1975.
5 See paras A.13–A.14.
6 *Seray-Wurie v Seray-Wurie* [1987] Fam Law 124, CA.

FORMER SPOUSES

A.12 Parties to a marriage in respect of which a decree absolute of divorce has been pronounced and parties to a voidable marriage that has been annulled are former spouses. Parties to a void marriage that has been annulled are not former spouses because there never was a marriage and they were never spouses, the decree is merely declaratory[1].

1 *De Reneville (otherwise Sheridan) v De Reneville* [1948] P 100, [1948] 1 All ER 56, CA.

Common householders

A.13 A person is associated with another person if they live or have lived in the same household, otherwise than merely by reason of one of them being the other's employee, tenant, lodger or boarder. The Law Commission Report[2] indicated that this would include people who live or have lived in the same household other than on a purely commercial basis. Whether persons sharing a house or flat live in one household or several households is a question of fact and degree to be determined by considering such matters as how they share the outgoings, how they do their shopping, whether they take meals together, have the same living room and the degree to which they share the accommodation. 'Living in the same household' is an abstract concept[3] and it is submitted that 'household' has the same meaning as in matrimonial proceedings. The Law Commission recognised[4] that this might give rise to unfortunate distinctions such as where several friends shared a flat; if they are all joint tenants then they have remedies under the Act; if only one is the tenant who sub-lets to the others, then the Act would not apply between the tenant and the others, but would apply as between the sub-tenants.

1 Section 62(3)(c).
2 Law Com No 207, para 3.21.
3 *Santos v Santos* [1972] Fam 247, [1972] 2 All ER 246, CA.
4 Law Com No 207, para 3.22

A.14 This provision has the effect of providing that homosexual couples will be associated persons provided they share the same household[1]. The word 'merely' in s 62(3)(c) is very important. Thus, where parties to a homosexual relationship live or have lived in the same household, and one party is the tenant or owner and the other is a lodger, boarder or sub-tenant, it is submitted that the contractual relationship is not a purely commercial one and they would be associated persons for the purposes of the Act. The Law Commission Report proposed[2] that those who 'have or have had a sexual relationship with each other (whether or not including sexual intercourse)' should be a specific category of associated persons. This was rejected by the Government as presenting the courts with problems of definition and proof[3]. Such a provision would have included homosexual couples.

1 See the Proceedings on the Family Homes and Domestic Violence Bill in the Special Public Bill Committee, HL, Session 1994–95 No 55. Lord Chancellor, 9 March 1995 at p 6; and Hale J, 15 March 1995 at p 12.
2 Law Com No 207, para 3.24.
3 See the speech of the Lord Chancellor, on the Family Homes and Domestic Violence Bill HL, 23 Feb 1995, 2R col 1257.

Relatives

A.15 A person is associated with another person if they are relatives[1], which is further defined in s 63(1). The Table set out at para A.17 shows the relevant relationships. It is important to note that the provision is very wide and covers relatives of a person and of his spouse, former spouse, cohabitant or former cohabitant. This is a much needed extension of the law and enables direct protection to be given against molestation from within the family or the family of a partner. In addition, it enables direct protection to be given against molestation from the family of a partner or former partner. Previously it was necessary to bring a civil action for assault; or, where there was an injunction against the other partner, making an application to commit the third party for aiding and abetting a breach of the injunction[2].

1 Section 62(3)(d).
2 See *Seaward v Paterson* [1897] 1 Ch 545; *Thorne v Bunting (No 2)* [1972] 3 All ER 1084, CA; and *Bawden v Bawden (Note)* [1979] 1 QB 419n, [1978] 3 All ER 1216, CA, at 420H–421B and at 1218d, per Goff LJ obiter.

A.16 However, subsequent spouses or cohabitees of the former spouse or former cohabitee of a person are not within the definition of 'relatives'[1]. This may be an unfortunate lacuna as there are instances of (former) spouses or cohabitants molesting the current partner of the person with whom they had a previous relationship, particularly when the marriage or cohabitation is breaking down and one party is seeking to distance himself or herself from the current partner and form a relationship with a new partner. In such cases an indirect remedy may still be required. The courts have made orders in a matrimonial cause[2] on the application of a wife to exclude the husband's mistress from the matrimonial home; but not it would seem granted injunctions restraining molestation in such circumstances. Under the current law, in a matrimonial cause where such a person was a co-respondent or party cited he or she would be associated with the petitioner and respondent[3] and the remedy of a non-molestation injunction would be available. In marital proceedings[4] only the spouses are parties to the proceedings and so this remedy would not be available. Interlocutory relief is available in the tort of nuisance to restrain molestation[5].

1 See the Proceedings on the Family Homes and Domestic Violence Bill in the Special Public Bill Committee HL, Session 1994–95 No 55. Hale J, 15 March 1995 at p 22.
2 *Adams v Adams* (1965) 109 Sol Jo 899; *Jones v Jones* [1971] 2 All ER 737, [1971] 1 WLR 396, CA; and *Hense v Hense and Churchill* [1976] CA Transcript 403, CA.
3 By virtue of s 58(3)(g), see para 12.29.
4 By s 20(2) proceedings for divorce or separation orders are called 'marital proceedings' and the same are family proceedings by s 63(2)(a).
5 *Burris v Azadani* [1995] 4 All ER 802, [1995] 1 WLR 1372, CA. An injunction may include an exclusion zone to prevent the defendant going near the plaintiff's residence.

A.17 Table of relatives:

The following relatives are associated with a person[1]:

(a) the father, mother, stepfather, stepmother, son, daughter, stepson, stepdaughter, grandmother, grandfather, grandson, or granddaughter;

(b) the brother, sister, uncle, aunt, niece or nephew (whether of the full-blood or half-blood or by affinity);

(c) the father, mother, stepfather, stepmother, son, daughter, stepson, stepdaughter, grandmother, grandfather, grandson, or granddaughter of his or her spouse, former spouse, cohabitant or former cohabitant;

(d) the brother, sister, uncle, aunt, niece or nephew (whether of the full blood or half blood or by affinity) of his or her spouse, former spouse, cohabitant or former cohabitant.

1 Section 63(1).

Engaged couples

A.18 A person is associated with another person if they have agreed to marry, whether or not that agreement has been terminated[1]. This provision was recommended by the Law Commission[2] but initially rejected by the Government because of problems of definition and proof[3]. In the Special Public Bill Committee[4] on the Family Homes and Domestic Violence Bill the problem was considered in some detail. At the report stage what is now s 44 was added to overcome these problems and provides that the engagement must be evidenced in one of three ways[5].

1 Section 62(3)(e).
2 Law Com No 207, para 3.24.
3 See the speech of the Lord Chancellor on the Family Homes and Domestic Violence Bill, HL, 23 February 1995, 2R col 1257.

4 HL, Session 1994–95 Paper No 55.
5 See paras A.20–A.21.

A.19 It would seem that an agreement to marry need not be valid in order for the parties to be associated[1]; indeed the fact that an agreement to marry may be contrary to public policy could give rise to incidents requiring the intervention of the court. The law on this topic consists largely of cases on breach of promise[2] and different considerations may well apply under the Family Law Act 1996, Part IV. An agreement to marry by a person who is already married is void as being contrary to public policy, unless a decree nisi has been pronounced in respect of the subsisting marriage[3]. An agreement to marry on the death of an existing spouse is void as contrary to public policy[4]. Whether a person can enter into a valid agreement to marry with more than one person at the same time appears to be uncertain. It may be that a subsequent engagement would automatically terminate a prior engagement[5].

1 See *Shaw v Fitzgerald* [1992] 1 FLR 357, where it was held that there could be an engagement for the purposes of the LR(MP)A 1970, s 2 even where one party to the engagement was already married.
2 A cause of action abolished by the LR(MP)A 1970, s 1. The cause of action survives in Scotland; see Clive & Wilson, *The Law of Husband and Wife in Scotland* (2nd edn, 1982).
3 *Fender v St-John Mildmay* [1938] AC 1, [1937] 3 All ER 402, HL. With the abolition of decree nisi and decree absolute, the divorce order will be the relevant date.
4 *Wilson v Carnley* [1908] 1 KB 729, CA; *Robinson v Smith* [1915] 1 KB 711, CA.
5 Except where the parties had the capacity to enter into a valid actually polygamous marriage.

EVIDENCE IN WRITING

A.20 There must be evidence in writing of the agreement to marry[1]. This, it is submitted, would be fulfilled by an announcement in a newspaper, relevant correspondence between the parties to the agreement or invitations to an engagement party. More doubtful would be third party documents referring to the engagement, particularly where the fact of the engagement was denied.

1 Section 44(1).

OTHER EVIDENCE

A.21 Evidence in writing is not required where there is either (a) the gift of an engagement ring by one to the other in contemplation of their marriage[1], or (b) a ceremony entered into by the parties in the presence of at least one person assembled for the purpose of witnessing the ceremony[2]. The mere gift of an engagement ring does not necessarily constitute an agreement to marry[3]. The gift must evidence the agreement, which presupposes that the agreement must pre-date or be simultaneous with the gift. The provision relating to ceremonies, originally introduced in the House of Lords on the Family Homes and Domestic Violence Bill at the report stage[4] and amended on the Third Reading[5] of the same Bill, is intended to cover formal ceremonies of betrothal and those who have undergone a ceremony of marriage outside the requirements of English law. While it would cover certain void marriages, it is perhaps uncertain however whether a marriage that was void because either party was already lawfully married[6], or because the parties were not respectively male and female[7], would constitute evidence of an engagement as such persons could not lawfully marry and therefore could not validly agree to do so. Where a marriage is void under the provisions of the Marriage Acts 1949 to 1986 because of failure to observe certain requirements[8] or because it is an invalid polygamous marriage[9], the ceremony might well constitute sufficient to establish evidence of an agreement to marry.

1 Section 44(2)(a).
2 Section 44(2)(b).
3 Family Homes and Domestic Violence Bill, HL, 25 May 1995, Report col 1062.
4 Family Homes and Domestic Violence Bill, HL, 25 May 1995, Report col 1062.
5 Family Homes and Domestic Violence Bill, HL, 20 June 1995, 3R col 220.
6 MCA 1973, s 11(b); but see para A.19 and *Shaw v Fitzgerald* [1992] 1 FLR 357.
7 MCA 1973, s 11(c); see *Corbett v Corbett (Otherwise Ashley)* [1971] P 83, [1970] 2 All ER 33.
8 MCA 1973, s 11(a)(i)–(iii).
9 MCA 1973, s 11(d).

A.22 Where an agreement to marry is terminated no application can be made under s 33 (occupation order)[1] or s 42 (non-molestation order)[2] after three years from the date of termination of the agreement. This is consistent with the restriction on bringing proceedings under the Married Womens Property Act 1882[3] by formerly engaged couples.

1 Section 33(2).
2 Section 42(4).
3 As extended by the LR(MP)A 1970, s 2.

Parents or those with parental responsibility

A.23 A person is associated with another person if, in relation to any child, they are both persons who are parents or who have or have had parental responsibility[1]. The parents[2] of a child are the mother[3] and father[4]. Other natural persons who have parental responsibility are set out in the Table at para A.24. One consequence of this provision is that a man and a woman who have had a child without marriage, engagement or cohabitation would be associated for the purposes of the Act while their child was a minor[5].

1 Sections 62(3)(f) and 58(4). By s 63(1), parental responsibility has the same meaning as in the CA 1989, see s 3.
2 Family Law Reform Act 1987, s 1(1).
3 A mother always has parental responsibility: CA 1989, s 2; which can only be lost on the making of an adoption order; Adoption Act 1976, s 39(2).
4 A father has parental responsibility where he was married to the mother at the time of the birth of the child or acquires it subsequently.
5 This would enable a rape victim (who had given birth to a child conceived as a result) to obtain an injunction against the perpetrator in summary proceedings.

A.24 Table of parental responsibility.

Guardian:

(a) if appointed by the court when no one has parental responsibility, or a parent or guardian with a residence order[1] died while the order was in force[2];

(b) if appointed by a parent or guardian who died while they had a residence order in their favour[3];

(c) if he was appointed by a parent or guardian who died leaving no other parent or guardian with parental reponsibility[4].

Applicant for emergency protection order:[5] while the emergency protection order is in force:[6]

Applicant for adoption:

(a) on the making of an adoption order[7];

(b) on the making of an interim order[8];

(c) by order on an application for an overseas adoption[9].

Holder of a residence order: while the order is in force[10].

Holder of an order for custody or care and control: while the order is in force[11].

1 CA 1989, s 8(1).
2 Ibid, s 5(1).
3 Ibid, s 5(7)(b).
4 Ibid, s 5(7)(a).
5 Ibid, s 44.
6 Ibid, s 44(4)(c).
7 Adoption Act 1976, s 12.
8 Ibid, s 25(1).
9 Ibid, s 55(1).
10 CA 1989, s 12(2).
11 Ibid, Sch 14, para 7.

A.25 A local authority has parental responsibility if there is a care order or an interim care order in force[1]. An adoption agency has parental responsibility on the making of an order declaring the child free for adoption[2]. However, a body corporate and another person cannot be associated persons under s 62(3)(f) or (g)[3]. The purpose of this restriction is no doubt to prevent applications for non-molestation injunctions against local authorities and adoption agencies and other bodies corporate.

1 CA 1989, s 33(3).
2 Adoption Act 1976, s 18(5).
3 Section 62(6).

Parties to family proceedings

A.26 A person is associated with another person if they are parties to the same family proceedings[1] (other than under Part IV of the Act). The persons associated under this provision may also be associated under other provisions of s 58(3) but it will additionally cover co-respondents and parties cited in a matrimonial cause[2] and parties to applications under the Human Fertilisation and Embryology Act 1990[3], s 30.

1 Section 62(3)(g). Family proceedings are defined by s 63(1), (2) and follows the definitions in the CA 1989, s 8(4), and the CLSA 1990, s 58.
2 Until Part II of the Act is in force, after which only husband and wife can be parties to marital proceedings, see ss 6 and 20.
3 See FPR 1991, r 4A.3.

Additional provisions relating to adoption

A.27 Where a child has been adopted or has been freed for adoption under certain statutory provisions[1] two persons are associated for the purposes of the Act if one person is a natural parent or natural grandparent[2] and the other the child or an adoptive parent or an applicant for an adoption order[3] or a person with whom the child has at any time been placed for adoption[4]. The reason for this extension is that the natural parents cease to be parents once an adoption order is made[5]. Furthermore an adoption order is a final order and on the making of the order there would no longer be family proceedings between the natural and adoptive parents.

1 Those mentioned in the Adoption Act 1976, s 16; which are the Adoption Act 1976, s 18; the Adoption (Scotland) Act 1978, s 18; the Adoption (Northern Ireland) Order 1987, arts 17(1), 18(1).
2 Section 62(5)(a).
3 Section 62(5)(b)(i).
4 Section 62(5)(b)(ii).
5 Adoption Act 1976, ss 12, 39.

Relevant child

A.28 'Child' means a person under the age of 18 years[1]. A relevant child is one within any of the following three categories:

(a) any child who is living with or might reasonably be expected to live with either party to the proceedings[3],

(b) any child in relation to whom an order under the Adoption Act 1976 or the CA 1989 is in question in the proceedings[4], and

(c) any other child whose interests the court considers relevant[5].

1 Section 62(2).
2 Section 62(2).
3 Section 62(2)(a).
4 Section 62(2)(b).
5 Section 62(2)(c).

A.29 This definition is very much wider than the previous law. The Domestic Violence and Matrimonial Proceedings Act 1976 referred to 'a child living with the applicant[1]'. The Domestic Proceedings and Magistrates' Courts Act 1978 referred to 'a child of the family'[2]. The widest provision was in the Matrimonial Homes Act 1983 which referred to the 'needs of any children'[3] but did not define the term 'children'.

1 Section 1(1)(b).
2 Sections 16 and 88(1) defined child of the family in the same terms as in the MCA 1973, s 52(1).
3 Section 1(3).

OCCUPATION ORDERS

Introduction

A.30 Occupation orders replace ouster injunctions and orders regulating the occupation of a matrimonial home or cohabitants' home. Part IV of the Family Law Act 1996 gives to the courts a wide range of powers. The extent of the available powers depends in each case upon whether the applicant or the associated respondent (or neither) is entitled to occupy the dwelling house, whether they are spouses or former spouses, cohabitants or former cohabitants; and the status of the dwelling house as the home or intended home of the parties. The factors that the court must consider in determining an application are prescribed and these criteria depend upon the category of the applicant as an 'entitled applicant'[1], a 'non-entitled former spouse'[2], a 'non-entitled cohabitant or former cohabitant'[3], or a case where neither party is entitled[4]. The categories of applicants are set out in the flow chart in Appendix 3[5]. The duration of time for which an occupation order may be in force is also dependent upon the category under which applicant's case is brought. All these matters will now be considered in more detail.

1 Section 33.
2 Section 35.
3 Section 36.
4 Section 37 if spouses and s 38 if cohabitants.
5 See Table 1. The Tables referred to in this Appendix are to be found in Appendix 3.

Entitlement to apply

Entitled applicants and those with matrimonial home rights

A.31 Where a person (the entitled applicant) is entitled to occupy a dwelling house by virtue of a beneficial estate or interest or contract or by virtue of any enactment giving him the right to remain in occupation[1], or has matrimonial home rights in the dwelling house[2]; and the dwelling house is or has been at any time the home of the entitled person and of another person with whom he is associated[3] (the respondent)[4], or was at any time intended by the applicant and the respondent to be their home[5], then the applicant may apply to the court for orders under s 33(3), (4), (5) against the respondent[6]. Although parties to an agreement to marry which has been terminated are associated persons[7], no application may be made under s 33 by virtue of s 62(3)(e) more than three years after the agreement to marry has been terminated[8], unless the applicant and respondent are also associated under some other provision[9].

1 Section 33(1)(a)(i).
2 Section 33(1)(a)(ii). Thus a spouse is always an 'entitled applicant' because matrimonial home rights are given to a spouse without other rights, s 30.
3 For the meaning of 'associated', see paras A.9–A.27.
4 Section 33(1)(b)(i).
5 Section 33(1)(b)(ii).
6 Section 33(1).
7 Section 62(3)(e); see paras A.18–A.22.
8 Section 33(2).
9 For example, if they are former cohabitants.

Non-entitled former spouses

A.32 In order to apply under s 32, the applicant must be a former spouse[1]. A former spouse (the respondent) must be entitled to occupy a dwelling house by virtue of a beneficial estate or interest or contract or by virtue of any enactment giving him the right to remain in occupation[2] and the other former spouse has no such entitlement[3]. The dwelling house in question must have been, or have been intended by them to be their matrimonial home[4]. Where these conditions apply, the applicant may apply to the court for an order under s 35 against the respondent[5].

1 Section 35(1).
2 Section 35(1)(a).
3 Section 35(1)(b). The matrimonial home rights of a former spouse may continue after the dissolution of the marriage where the court has so ordered during the subsistence of the marriage, s 33(5), in which case an application should be brought under s 33.
4 Section 35(1)(c).
5 Section 35(2).

Non-entitled cohabitants or former cohabitants

A.33 In order to apply under s 36, the applicant must be a cohabitant or former cohabitant[1]. One cohabitant or former cohabitant (the respondent) must be entitled to occupy a dwelling house by virtue of a beneficial estate or interest or contract or by virtue of any enactment giving him the right to remain in occupation[2] and the other cohabitant or former cohabitant has no such entitlement[3]. The dwelling house in question must be or have been the home in which they lived together as husband and wife, or have been a home in which they intended so to live[4]. Where these conditions apply, the applicant may apply to the court for an order under s 36 against the respondent[5].

1 Section 36(1).
2 Section 36(1)(a).
3 Section 36(1)(b).
4 Section 36(1)(c).
5 Section 36(2).

Neither party entitled

A.34 The court may make occupation orders between spouses, former spouses, cohabitants or former cohabitants where neither party wished to establish a right to occupy the dwelling house or where one could not be established[1]. These provisions would apply where, for example, the parties were squatters or bare licensees. The Law Commission observed[1] that such cases, although probably rare, were covered by the terms of the Domestic Violence and Matrimonial Proceedings Act 1976 and the level of protection would be reduced if provision was not made for them.

1 Sections 37 and 38.
2 Law Com No 207, para 4.8.

NEITHER SPOUSE OR FORMER SPOUSE ENTITLED

A.35 Where one spouse or former spouse, and the other spouse or former spouse occupy a dwelling house which is or was their matrimonial home[1], but neither is entitled to occupy the dwelling house by virtue of a beneficial estate or interest or contract[2] or by virtue of any enactment giving him the right to remain in occupation[3], then either party may apply to the court for an order under s 37[4].

1 Section 37(1)(a).
2 Section 37(1)(b)(i).
3 Section 37(1)(b)(ii).
4 Section 37(2).

NEITHER COHABITANT OR FORMER COHABITANT ENTITLED

A.36 Where one cohabitant or former cohabitant and the other cohabitant or former cohabitant occupy a dwelling house which is the home in which they live or have lived together as husband and wife[1], but neither is entitled to occupy the dwelling house by virtue of a beneficial estate or interest or contract[2] or by virtue of any enactment giving him the right to remain in occupation[3], then either party may apply to the court for an order under section 38[4].

1 Section 38(1)(a).
2 Section 38(1)(b)(i).
3 Section 38(1)(b)(ii).
4 Section 38(2).

Range of orders available

A.37 The orders for which applicants may apply varies according to whether the applicant is an entitled applicant[1], a non-entitled former spouse, a non-entitled cohabitant or former cohabitant or whether neither party is entitled. The Table[2] shows the range of orders available in respect of each class of applicant. The range of orders is broadly similar to those previously available under the Domestic Violence and Matrimonial Proceedings Act 1976 and the Matrimonial Homes Act 1983; however, the Act goes further than the previous legislation and clarifies the extent of the powers of the courts.

1 This category includes spouses with matrimonial home rights, s 30.
2 Table 2.

Entitled applicants and those with matrimonial home rights

A.38 All orders in favour of entitled applicants are discretionary[1]. The following is a list of all the orders that may be made. An order may:

(a) enforce the applicant's entitlement to remain in occupation as against the respondent[2];

(b) require the respondent to permit the applicant to enter and remain in the dwelling house or part of the dwelling house[3];

(c) regulate the occupation of the dwelling house by either or both parties[4];

(d) where the respondent is entitled under s 33(1)(a)(i), prohibit, suspend or restrict the exercise by him of his rights to occupy the dwelling house[5];

(e) where the respondent has matrimonial home rights in relation to the dwelling house and the applicant is the other spouse, restrict or terminate those rights[6];

(f) require the respondent to leave the dwelling house or part of the dwelling house[7];

(g) exclude the respondent from a defined area in which the dwelling house is included[8].

An order may declare that the applicant is entitled under s 33(1)(a)(i), or has matrimonial home rights[9]. Where the applicant has matrimonial home rights and the respondent is the other spouse, an occupation order, made during the subsistence of the marriage, may provide that those rights are not brought to an end by the death of the other spouse or the termination (otherwise than by death) of the marriage[10].

1 Section 33(3) uses the word 'may'. See Table 2, col 1.
2 Section 33(3)(a).
3 Section 33(3)(b).
4 Section 33(3)(c).
5 Section 33(3)(d).
6 Section 33(3)(e).
7 Section 33(3)(f).
8 Section 33(3)(g).
9 Section 33(4).
10 Section 33(5).

Non-entitled former spouses

A.39 Where the court decides to make an order in favour of a non-entitled former spouse, the order will contain a mandatory provision and may contain further discretionary provisions.

MANDATORY PROVISIONS

A.40 If the applicant is in occupation, the order must contain a provision giving the applicant the right not to be evicted or excluded from the dwelling house or any part of it by the respondent for the period specified in the order[1] and prohibiting the respondent from evicting or excluding the applicant during that period². If the applicant is not in occupation, the order must contain a provision giving the applicant the right to enter into and occupy the dwelling house for the period specified in the order³ and requiring the respondent to permit the exercise of that right⁴.

1 Section 35(3)(a). See Table 2, col 2.
2 Section 35(3)(b).
3 Section 35(4)(a).
4 Section 35(4)(b).

DISCRETIONARY PROVISIONS

A.41 In addition, an order may:

(a) regulate the occupation of the dwelling house by either or both parties[1];
(b) prohibit, suspend or restrict the exercise by the respondent of his rights to occupy the dwelling house[2];
(c) require the respondent to leave the dwelling house or part of the dwelling house[3];
(d) exclude the respondent from a defined area in which the dwelling house is included[4].

1 Section 35(5)(a).
2 Section 35(5)(b).
3 Section 35(5)(c).
4 Section 35(5)(d).

Non-entitled cohabitants or former cohabitants

A.42 Where the court decides to make an order in favour of a non-entitled cohabitant or former cohabitant, the order will contain a mandatory provision and may contain further discretionary provisions.

MANDATORY PROVISIONS

A.43 If the applicant is in occupation, the order must contain a provision giving the applicant the right not to be evicted or excluded from the dwelling house or any part of it by the respondent for the period specified in the order¹ and prohibiting the respondent from evicting or excluding the applicant during that period². If the applicant is not in occupation, the order must contain a provision giving the applicant the right to enter into and occupy the dwelling house for the period specified in the order³ and requiring the respondent to permit the exercise of that right⁴.

1 Section 36(3)(a). See Table 2, col 3.
2 Section 36(3)(b).
3 Section 36(4)(a).
4 Section 36(4)(b).

DISCRETIONARY PROVISIONS

A.44 In addition, an order may:

(a) regulate the occupation of the dwelling house by either or both parties[1];

(b) prohibit, suspend or restrict the exercise by the respondent of his rights to occupy the dwelling house[2];

(c) require the respondent to leave the dwelling house or part of the dwelling house[3];

(d) exclude the respondent from a defined area in which the dwelling house is included[4];

1 Section 36(5)(a).
2 Section 36(5)(b).
3 Section 36(5)(c).
4 Section 36(5)(d).

Neither spouse or former spouse entitled

A.45 All orders where neither spouse or former spouse is entitled to occupy the dwelling house are discretionary[1]. An order may:

(a) require the respondent to permit the applicant to enter and remain in the dwelling house or part of the dwelling house[2];

(b) regulate the occupation of the dwelling house by either or both parties[3];

(c) require the respondent to leave the dwelling house or part of the dwelling house[4];

(d) exclude the respondent from a defined area in which the dwelling house is included[5].

1 Section 37(3). See Table 2, col 4.
2 Section 37(3)(a).
3 Section 37(3)(b).
4 Section 37(3)(c).
5 Section 37(3)(d).

Neither cohabitant or former cohabitant entitled

A.46 All orders where neither cohabitant or former cohabitant is entitled to occupy the dwelling house are discretionary[1]. An order may:

(a) require the respondent to permit the applicant to enter and remain in the dwelling house or part of the dwelling house[2];

(b) regulate the occupation of the dwelling house by either or both parties[3];

(c) require the respondent to leave the dwelling house or part of the dwelling house[4];

(d) exclude the respondent from a defined area in which the dwelling house is included[5].

1 Section 38(3). See Table 2, col 5.
2 Section 38(3)(a).
3 Section 38(3)(b).
4 Section 38(3)(c).
5 Section 38(3)(d).

Criteria for exercise of powers

A.47 The basis on which the courts should decide whether and if so in what manner to exercise their powers to make occupation orders was a matter of much debate in the Special Public Bill Committee[1]. The balance of harm test incorporates concepts from the CA 1989[2]. The question of conduct is specifically mentioned. The test under the Matrimonial Homes Act 1983[3] required the court to make such order as it thinks 'just and reasonable'; there is no such requirement under the Act. This may present difficulties to the courts if the application of the balance of harm test appears to produce an unjust result. The statutory factors must be considered by the court and vary according to whether the applicant is an entitled applicant, a non-entitled former spouse, a non-entitled cohabitant or former cohabitant, whether neither spouse or former spouse is entitled, or whether neither cohabitant or former cohabitant is entitled[4].

1 Family Homes and Domestic Violence Bill, HL, Session 1994–94 No 55. Conservative backbenchers in the House of Commons indicated considerable opposition to the provisions that did not differentiate between cohabitants and spouses, as a result of which the Bill was dropped.
2 Section 31(2).
3 Section 1(3).
4 See Table 3.

Entitled applicants and those with matrimonial home rights

A.48 In deciding whether, and if so in what manner, to exercise its powers under s 33(3) the court shall have regard to all the circumstances[1] including:

(a) the respective housing needs and housing resources of the parties and any relevant child[2];

(b) the financial resources of the parties[3];

(c) the likely effect of any order, or of any decision by the court not to exercise its powers, on the health, safety or well-being of the parties and of any relevant child[4]; and

(d) the conduct of the parties in relation to each other and otherwise[5].

The court must also apply the balance of harm test[6]. As the statute does not provide that any one factor is to be given more weight in the decision-making process than another, it is for the judge determining the application to give such weight to each factor as seems appropriate on the facts of each individual case[7]. If it appears to the court that the applicant or any relevant child is likely to suffer significant harm[8] attributable to the conduct of the respondent if an order containing one or more of the provisions in sub-section (3) is not made, the court shall make an order unless it appears to the court[9] that:

(i) the respondent and any relevant child is likely to suffer significant harm if the order is made[10], and

(ii) the harm likely to be suffered by the respondent or child in that event is as great as or greater than the harm attributable to the conduct of the respondent which is likely to be suffered by the applicant or child if the order is not made[11].

1 Section 33(6). See Table 3, col 1.
2 Section 33(6)(a).
3 Section 33(6)(b). 'Health' includes physical or mental health, s 63(1).
4 Section 33(6)(c).
5 Section 33(6)(d).
6 Section 33(7).
7 *Richards v Richards* [1984] AC 174 at 222, [1983] 2 All ER 807 at 830, HL per Lord Brandon.
8 See para A.56.
9 Section 33(7).
10 Section 33(7)(a).
11 Section 33(7)(b).

Non-entitled former spouses

MANDATORY ORDERS

A.49 In deciding whether, and if so in what manner, to exercise its powers to make a mandatory order under s 35(3) or (4) the court shall have regard to all the circumstances[1] including:

(a) the respective housing needs and housing resources of the parties and any relevant child[2];

(b) the respective financial resources of the parties[3];

(c) the likely effect of any order, or of any decision by the court not to exercise its powers, on the health, safety or well-being of the parties and of any relevant child[4];

(d) the conduct of the parties in relation to each other and otherwise[5];

(e) the length of time that has elapsed since the parties ceased to live together[6];

(f) the length of time that has elapsed since the marriage was dissolved or annulled[7];

(g) the existence of any pending proceedings between the parties for an order under MCA 1973[8], for an order under the CA 1989, Sch 1, para 1(2)(d) or (e)[9] or relating to the legal or beneficial ownership of the dwelling house[10].

1 Section 35(6). See Table 3, col 2.
2 Section 35(6)(a).
3 Section 35(6)(b). 'Health' includes physical or mental health, s 63(1).
4 Section 35(6)(c).
5 Section 35(6)(d).
6 Section 35(6)(e).

7 Section 35(6)(f).
8 Property adjustment orders in connection with divorce, judicial separation or nullity: s 35(6)(g)(i).
9 Orders for financial relief against parents: s 35(6)(g)(ii).
10 Such would probably include an application for transfer of tenancy under Sch 7: s 35(6)(g)(iii).

DISCRETIONARY ORDERS

A.50 The next stage involves the court considering whether to exercise its power to make discretionary orders under sub-section (5), and if so, in what manner; this involves repeating the part of the previous process. In deciding whether, and if so in what manner, to exercise its discretionary powers under s 35(5) the court shall have regard to all the circumstances[1] including:

(a) the respective housing needs and housing resources of the parties and any relevant child[2];

(b) the respective financial resources of the parties[3];

(c) the likely effect of any order, or of any decision by the court not to exercise its powers, on the health, safety or well-being of the parties and of any relevant child[4];

(d) the conduct of the parties in relation to each other and otherwise[5]; and,

(e) the length of time that has elapsed since the marriage was dissolved or annulled[6].

The court must also apply the balance of harm test[7]. As the statute does not provide that any one factor is to be given more weight in the decision-making process than another, it is for the judge determining the application to give such weight to each factor as seems appropriate on the facts of each individual case[8]. Where the court decides to make an order under s 32 and it appears to the court that, if the order does not include one of the provisions in sub-section (5)[9], the applicant or any relevant child is likely to suffer significant harm attributable to the conduct of the respondent[10], the court shall include the provision under sub-section (5) in the order unless it appears to the court[11] that:

(i) the respondent and any relevant child is likely to suffer significant harm if the provision is included in the order[12], and

(ii) the harm likely to be suffered by the respondent or child in that event is as great as or greater than the harm attributable to the conduct of the respondent which is likely to be suffered by the applicant or child if the order is not made[13].

1 Section 35(7). See Table 3, col 2.
2 Section 35(7) and (6)(a).
3 Section 35(7) and (6)(b). 'Health' includes physical or mental health, s 63(1).
4 Section 35(7) and (6)(c).
5 Section 35(7) and (6)(d).
6 Section 35(7) and (6)(e).
7 Section 35(8).

8 *Richards v Richards* [1984] AC 174 at 222, [1983] 2 All ER 807 at 830, HL per Lord Brandon.
9 Set out in para A.47 and see Table 2, col 2.
10 Section 35(8) and see para A.56.
11 Ibid.
12 Section 35(8)(a).
13 Section 35(8)(b).

Non-entitled cohabitants or former cohabitants

MANDATORY ORDERS

A.51 In deciding whether, and if so in what manner, to exercise its powers to make a mandatory order under s 36(3) or (4) the court shall have regard to all the circumstances[1] including:

(a) the respective housing needs and housing resources of the parties and any relevant child[2];

(b) the respective financial resources of the parties[3];

(c) the likely effect of any order, or of any decision by the court not to exercise its powers, on the health, safety or well-being of the parties and of any relevant child[4];

(d) the conduct of the parties in relation to each other and otherwise[5];

(e) the nature of the parties relationship[6];

(f) the length of time during which they have lived together as husband and wife[7];

(g) whether there are or have been children who are children of both parties or for whom both parties have or have had parental responsibility[8];

(h) the length of time that has elapsed since the parties ceased to live together[9];

(i) the existence of any pending proceedings between the parties[10] for an order under the CA 1989, Sch 1, para 1(2)(d) or (e)[11], or relating to the legal or beneficial ownership of the dwelling house[12].

In considering the nature of the parties' relationship[13], the court must have regard to the fact that they have not given each other the commitment involved in marriage[14].

1 Section 36(6). See Table 3, col 3.
2 Section 36(6)(a).
3 Section 36(6)(b).
4 Section 36(6)(c). 'Health' includes physical or mental health, s 63(1).
5 Section 36(6)(d).
6 Section 36(6)(e), subject to s 41.
7 Section 36(6)(f).
8 Section 36(6)(g).
9 Section 36(6)(h).
10 Section 36(6)(j).
11 Orders for financial relief against parents: s 36(6)(j)(i).

12 Such would probably include an application for transfer of tenancy under Sch 7: s 36(6)(j)(ii).
13 Under s 36(6)(e).
14 Section 41.

DISCRETIONARY ORDERS

A.52 The next stage involves the court considering whether to exercise its power to make discretionary orders under sub-section (5), and if so, in what manner; this involves repeating the part of the previous process. In deciding whether, and if so in what manner, to exercise its discretionary powers under s 36(5) the court shall have regard to all the circumstances[1] including:

(a) the respective housing needs and housing resources of the parties and any relevant child[2];

(b) the respective financial resources of the parties[3];

(c) the likely effect of any order, or of any decision by the court not to exercise its powers, on the health, safety or well-being of the parties and of any relevant child[4];

(d) the conduct of the parties in relation to each other and otherwise[5]; and

(e) the nature of the parties' relationship[6].

The court must also consider the questions mentioned in sub-section (8)[7]. As the statute does not provide that any one factor is to be given more weight in the decision-making process than another, it is for the judge determining the application to give such weight to each factor as seems appropriate on the facts of each individual case[8].

The court must consider:

(i) whether the applicant or any relevant child is likely to suffer significant harm attributable to the conduct of the respondent if a provision under sub-section (5) is not included in the order[9]; and

(ii) whether the harm likely to be suffered by the respondent or child if the provision is included is as great or greater than the harm attributable to the conduct of the respondent which is likely to be suffered by the applicant or child if the provision is not included[10].

This is a significant difference in wording from the provisions of ss 33 and 35 in that under those provisions the court must make an order on the basis of greater harm to the applicant or relevant child if an order is not made. In considering the nature of the parties' relationship[11], the court must have regard to the fact that they have not given each other the commitment involved in marriage[12].

1 Section 36(7). See Table 3, col 3.
2 Section 36(7)(a) and (6)(a).
3 Section 36(7)(a) and (6)(b).
4 Section 36(7)(a) and (6)(c). 'Health' includes physical or mental health, s 63(1).
5 Section 36(7)(a) and (6)(d).

6 Section 36(7)(a) and (6)(e).
7 Section 36(7)(b).
8 *Richards v Richards* [1984] AC 174 at 222, [1983] 2 All ER 807 at 830, HL per Lord Brandon.
9 Section 36(8)(a).
10 Section 36(8)(b).
11 Under s 36(6)(e).
12 Section 41.

Neither spouse entitled

A.53 In deciding whether, and if so in what manner, to exercise its powers under s 37(5) the court shall have regard to all the circumstances[1] including:

(a) the respective housing needs and housing resources of the parties and any relevant child[2];

(b) the financial resources of the parties[3];

(c) the likely effect of any order, or of any decision by the court not to exercise its powers, on the health, safety or well-being of the parties and of any relevant child[4]; and

(d) the conduct of the parties in relation to each other and otherwise[5].

The court must also apply the balance of harm test[6]. As the statute does not provide that any one factor is to be given more weight in the decision-making process than another, it is for the judge determining the application to give such weight to each factor as seems appropriate on the facts of each individual case[7]. If it appears to the court that the applicant or any relevant child is likely to suffer significant harm[8] attributable to the conduct of the respondent if an order containing one or more of the provisions in sub-section (3) is not made, the court shall make an order unless it appears to the court[9] that:

(i) the respondent and any relevant child is likely to suffer significant harm if the order is made[10], and

(ii) the harm likely to be suffered by the respondent or child in that event is as great as or greater than the harm attributable to the conduct of the respondent which is likely to be suffered by the applicant or child if the order is not made[11].

1 Section 37(4), 33(6). See Table 3, col 4.
2 Section 37(4), 33(6)(a).
3 Section 37(4), 33(6)(b).
4 Section 37(4), 33(6)(c). 'Health' includes physical or mental health, s 63(1).
5 Section 37(4), 33(6)(d).
6 Section 37(4), 33(6).
7 *Richards v Richards* [1984] AC 174 at 222, [1983] 2 All ER 807 at 830, HL per Lord Brandon.
8 See para A.56.
9 Section 33(7).
10 Section 33(7)(a).
11 Section 33(7)(b).

Neither cohabitant or former cohabitant entitled

A.54 In deciding whether to exercise its powers under s 38(3) the court shall have regard to all the circumstances of the case[1], including:

(a) the respective housing needs and housing resources of the parties and any relevant child[2];

(b) the financial resources of the parties[3];

(c) the likely effect of any order, or of any decision by the court not to exercise its powers, on the health, safety or well-being of the parties and of any relevant child[4];

(d) the conduct of the parties in relation to each other and otherwise[5];

(e) the questions mentioned in sub-section (5)[6], which are:

   (i) whether the applicant or any relevant child is likely to suffer significant harm attributable to the conduct of the respondent if a provision under sub-section (5) is not included in the order[7]; and,

   (ii) whether the harm likely to be suffered by the respondent or child if the provision is included is as great or greater than the harm attributable to the conduct of the respondent which is likely to be suffered by the applicant or child if the provision is not included[8].

As the statute does not provide that any one factor is to be given more weight in the decision-making process than another, it is for the judge determining the application to give such weight to each factor as seems appropriate on the facts of each individual case[9].

1 Section 38(4). See Table 3, col 5.
2 Section 38(4)(a).
3 Section 38(4)(b).
4 Section 38(4)(c). 'Health' includes physical or mental health, s 63(1).
5 Section 38(4)(d).
6 Section 38(4)(e).
7 Section 38(5)(a). See para A.56.
8 Section 38(5)(b).
9 *Richards v Richards* [1984] AC 174 at 222, [1983] 2 All ER 807 at 830, HL per Lord Brandon.

Harm and related definitions

A.55 The concepts of 'harm' and 'significant harm' were introduced by the CA 1989[1]. Part IV of the Family Law Act 1996 develops these concepts. In relation to an adult, 'harm' means 'ill-treatment or the impairment of health'[2]. In relation to a child, 'harm' means ill-treatment or the impairment of health or development[3]. In relation to a child, 'ill-treatment' includes sexual abuse and forms of ill-treatment which are not physical[4]. In relation to an adult, ill-treatment is not defined but it is submitted would include violence, threats of violence and forms of ill-treatment which are not physical. It is probably impossible to define 'ill-treatment' but it is relatively simple to say whether specific conduct is or is not 'ill-treatment'[5]. 'Health' includes physical or mental health[6]. 'Development' means physical, intellectual, emotional, social or behavioural development[7].

1 See the CA 1989, ss 31(9), (10) and 105(1).
2 Section 63(1).
3 Ibid.
4 Ibid.
5 Similarly 'molestation' is almost impossible to define; see further para A.68.
6 Section 63(1).
7 Ibid.

Likely to suffer significant harm

A.56 Where the question of whether harm suffered by a child is significant turns on the child's health or development, his health or development shall be compared with that which could reasonably be expected of a similar child[1]. Thus the test is objective. The Act uses the words 'is likely to suffer' significant harm, thus decisions on the threshold conditions[2] in care proceedings may assist in interpretation[3]. The word 'likely' has caused some difficulties of interpretation in other contexts[4]. In care proceedings the word 'likely' in the CA 1989, s 32(1)(a) is being used in the sense of a real possibility, a possibility that cannot be ignored having regard to the nature and gravity of the feared harm in any particular case[5]. Clearly, the court must evaluate both the chance of harm occurring and the magnitude of the harm if it does in fact occur. It is submitted that Parliament intended these words in the Family Law Act 1996 to have the same meaning as in the CA 1989. Thus once a judge has made findings of fact as to the conduct of the parties and the other matters to which the court must have regard, it is then possible to evaluate the future risks to the applicant or child of significant harm attributable to the conduct of the respondent[6].

1 Section 63(3), which is in identical terms to the CA 1989, s 31(10).
2 See *Re M (A Minor)(Care Orders: Threshold Conditions)* [1994] 2 AC 424, [1994] 3 All ER 298, HL.
3 See paras A.64–A.65.
4 It has been construed as meaning 'a reasonable prospect' of something happening, see *Dunning v United Liverpool Hospital's Board of Governors* [1973] 2 All ER 454 at 460, [1973] 1 WLR 586 at 594 per James LJ; overruled on another point by *McIvor v Southern Health and Social Services Board* [1978] 2 All ER 625, [1978] 1 WLR 757, HL. Equally it has been said that the word 'likely' is imprecise: it is capable of covering a whole range of possibilities from 'it is on the cards' to 'it is more probable than not', see *R v Sheppard* [1981] AC 394, [1980] 3 All ER 899, HL per Lord Diplock.
5 *Re H (Minors)(Sexual Abuse: Standard of Proof)* [1996] AC 563, [1996] 1 All ER 1, HL.
6 Sections 33(7), 35(8), 36(8), 37(4), 38(5).

Balancing the risk of significant harm

A.57 On applications by entitled applicants[1], a non-entitled former spouse[2], and cases where neither spouse or former spouse is entitled[3], the court is obliged to make an occupation order where without an order the applicant or any relevant child would be likely to suffer significant harm attributable to the conduct of the respondent, unless it appears that the respondent or any relevant child would be likely to suffer significant harm *and* that harm is likely to be as great or greater than the harm attributable to the conduct of the respondent which is likely to be suffered by the applicant or child if the order is not made[4]. It is of note that in this exercise, the significant harm to the applicant or child likely to be suffered if an order is not made must be attributable to the conduct of the respondent. However, the significant harm likely to be suffered by the respondent or child if an order is made, may arise from any source. Where a respondent establishes a likelihood of equal or greater harm, it is submitted that the court may nonetheless make an occupation order in the exercise of its discretion in accordance with the statutory criteria, where for example the harm likely to be suffered by the applicant or child arises from unsatisfactory temporary accommodation.

1 Section 33, including spouses with matrimonial home rights.
2 Section 35.
3 Section 37.
4 Sections 33(7), 35(8), 37(4). See Table 3, cols 1, 2 and 3.

Orders

A.58 Where the court decides to make an occupation order, the type of order may range from regulating the occupation of the dwelling house to ousting the respondent. In deciding the measure of protection to be afforded to the applicant by an occupation order, the court will apply the statutory criteria to the individual facts of each particular case. It is submitted that an ouster order will continue to be regarded as a drastic measure and only to be made where no lesser measure will adequately protect the applicant or child[1].

1 *Burke v Burke* [1987] 2 FLR 71, CA; *Bassett v Bassett* [1975] Fam 76, [1975] 1 All ER 513, CA.

Procedure

A.59 An application for an occupation order may be made in other family proceedings[1] or in a free standing application under the Family Law Act 1996, Part IV[2]. Where an application for an occupation order is made under s 33, 35, 36, 37 or 38 and the court considers that it has no power to make an order under the section concerned, but that it has power to make an order under one of the other sections, the court make may an order under that other section[3]. The fact that a person has applied for an occupation order under ss 35 to 38, or that an order has been made under one of those sections, does not affect the right of any person to claim a legal or equitable interest in any property in subsequent proceedings, including subsequent proceedings under Part IV of the Act[4]. The jurisdiction to make occupation orders may be exercised by the High Court, a county court or a magistrates' court[5]. The Lord Chancellor may by order specify that certain proceedings or in particular circumstances may only be commenced at a particular level of court or class of court and for transfer of proceedings between levels or classes of court[6].

1 Section 39(2). Family proceedings are defined by s 63(1), (2). See para A.27.
2 Section 39(2), rules of court will be made to prescribe that free standing applications may be made under the Act. See para A.73 for applications made under s 60 by 'a representative'.
3 Section 39(3).
4 Section 39(4).
5 Section 57; rules of court may specify that certain applications may only be commenced at a particular level and may specify provisions for transfer between levels.
6 Section 57. Such order may be broadly similar to the C(AP)O 1991.

Duration of orders

A.60 The maximum duration of occupation orders is specifically addressed in the Act. Previously, courts were required to consider a time limit[1]. Where no other proceedings were instituted to resolve long-term housing problems, an order without limitation of time could operate as a summary transfer of property order[2].

1 *Practice Note* [1978] 2 All ER 1056, sub nom *Practice Direction* [1978] 1 WLR 1123, which suggested that in most cases a period of three months would be sufficient.
2 *Hopper v Hopper* [1979] 1 All ER 181, [1978] 1 WLR 1342n, CA.

Orders under section 33

A.61 These orders[1] may be (a) for a specified period, (b) until the occurrence of a specified event[2], or (c) until further order[3]. The court should always specifically consider the appropriate duration of the order. Where an order is limited in time, an application may be made to extend the operation of the order.

1 Section 33(10); see Table 4, col 1.
2 Such as the hearing of an application for ancillary relief or transfer of tenancy.
3 Where a non-property owning party has been excluded it may be appropriate for the order to be expressed 'until further order': *Spencer v Camacho* (1983) 4 FLR 662, 13 Fam Law 114, CA.

Orders under sections 35 and 37

A.62 These orders must be for a specified period not exceeding six months[1], but may be extended (on one or more occasions) for a further specified period not exceeding six months[2]. The effect of this is that a respondent excluded under s 35 could be deprived of the enjoyment of property rights indefinitely, by repeated extensions of an occupation order. On an application to extend an occupation order under ss 35 or 37 it is submitted that the court should have regard to any changes in circumstances since the order was made and apply the statutory criteria to those changed circumstances so far as possible, particularly as to the existence or progress of any application for ancillary relief[3]. It may also be relevant to consider the extent to which the parties have complied with any financial or consequential orders under s 37. Under s 34 where neither spouse has the right to occupy, financial issues are likely to be of some relevance, save that the question of property adjustment in respect of the matrimonial home will probably not arise.

1 Sections 35(10), 37(5); see Table 4, cols 2 and 4.
2 Ibid.
3 Section 35(6)(g)(i).

Orders under section 36 and 38

A.63 These orders must be for a specified period not exceeding six months[1], but may be extended on one occasion for a further specified period not exceeding six months[2]. On an application to extend an order under s 36, the existence of an application for transfer of tenancy or under the CA 1989, Sch 1 will be relevant. Financial matters will be less relevant on applications under s 38.

1 Sections 36(10), 38(6); see Table 4, cols 3 and 5.
2 Ibid.

Variation and discharge

A.64 An occupation order may be varied or discharged by the court on the application on notice of the respondent[1] or the person on whose application the order was made[2]. Where a spouse's matrimonial home rights are a charge on the estate or interest of the other spouse or of the trustees for the other spouse[3] an order under s 33 against the other spouse may be varied or discharged by the court on the application of any person deriving title under the other spouse or under the trustees and affected by the charge[4]. There are no factors prescribed for the court to consider on an application to vary or discharge an occupation order. It is submitted that the court should consider any changes in circumstances since the order was made and apply the statutory criteria to those changed circumstances, so far as possible. It may also be relevant to consider the extent to which the parties have complied with any financial or consequential orders under s 40.

1 Section 49(1)(a).
2 Section 49(1)(b).
3 See s 32.
4 Section 49(3).

Financial and consequential orders

A.65 Under the Matrimonial Homes Act 1983, the court had limited power to make financial or consequential orders[1]. Part IV of the Act provides that on making an occupation order under s 33,[2] 35[3] or 36[4] or at any time thereafter while the occupation order remains in force[5] the court may make financial and consequential orders. These orders are:

(a) imposing on either party obligations as to the repair and maintenance of the dwelling house or as to the discharge of rent, mortgage payments[6] or other outgoings affecting the dwelling house[7];

(b) ordering a party[8] occupying the dwelling house or any part of it to make periodical payments to the other party in respect of the accommodation, where the other party would (but for the order) be entitled to occupy the dwelling house by virtue of a beneficial estate or interest or contract or by virtue of any enactment giving him the right to remain in occupation[9];

(c) granting either party possession or use of furniture or other contents of the dwelling house[10];

(d) ordering either party to take reasonable care of any furniture or other contents of the dwelling house[11];

(e) ordering either party to take reasonable steps to keep the dwelling house and any furniture or other contents secure[12].

1 MHA 1983, s 1(3). The court could order a spouse occupying the whole or part of a dwelling house by virtue of a right of occupation to make periodical payments to the other spouse in respect of that occupation, or impose on either spouse obligations as to the repair and maintenance of, or the discharge of liabilities in respect of, the dwelling house. Such orders were comparatively rare because, between spouses, such matters were usually dealt with by way of an application for maintenance pending suit or interim periodical payments.
2 Entitled applicants, including those with matrimonial home rights.
3 Non-entitled former spouse.
4 Non-entitled cohabitant or former cohabitant.
5 Section 40(3).
6 By s 63(1) 'mortgage payments' includes any payments which the mortgagor is required to make under the mortgage, and so could accordingly include endowment premiums and building insurance depending upon the terms of the deed.
7 Section 40(1)(a)(i), (ii).
8 Including one who is entitled to occupy by virtue of a beneficial estate or interest or contract or by virtue of any enactment giving him the right to remain in occupation: s 40(1)(b).
9 Section 40(1)(b).
10 Section 40(1)(c).
11 Section 40(1)(d).
12 Section 40(1)(e).

A.66 Where a party is excluded the question of consequential orders should always be considered. While 'outgoings' would cover buildings and contents insurance, water rates, council tax, gas, electricity and telephone, it is uncertain whether hire purchase commitments would be included. The Act does not provide any specific provision for enforcement of such orders. Orders in the nature of an injunction would be enforceable by committal, subject to the procedural requirements[1]. Enforcing orders for the payment of money, particularly to third parties is more difficult[2]. Section 37 orders cannot be included in an occupation order under ss 37 or 38[3]. While this is understandable in respect of outgoings and periodical payments, issues as to furniture and contents may be nonetheless important.

1 See chapter 14.
2 See chapter 12.
3 Cases where neither party is entitled, s 37 relates to spouses or former spouses and s 38 to cohabitants or former cohabitants.

A.67 In deciding whether and, if so, how to exercise its powers under s 40, the court shall have regard to all the circumstances of the case[1] including:

(a) the financial needs and other resources of the parties[2], and

(b) the financial obligations which they have or are likely to have in the foreseeable future, including obligations to each other and to any relevant child[3].

The Act does not contain any specific provision for the variation or discharge of financial and consequential orders, save that such an order ceases to have effect when the occupation order to which it relates ceases to have effect[4]. It would appear that the provisions of s 46 would not enable the court to vary or discharge and order under s 37 because such an order is not an occupation order[5].

1 Section 40(2). Where the parties have not been married, factors such as the nature and duration of the relationship, and whether or not there are children of the parties should be relevant.
2 Section 40(1)(a).
3 Section 40(1)(b). This would include an assessment under the Child Support Act 1991. It must be very difficult for a court to take into account such an obligation where the method of calculation is so complex.
4 Section 40(3).
5 Section 39(1) defines 'occupation order' as an order under s 33, 35, 36, 37, or 38. The marginal note to s 40 refers to additional provisions that may be included in certain occupation orders, but this conflicts with s 40(3) which seems to suppose that a s 40 order is not an occupation order.

NON-MOLESTATION ORDERS

Meaning of 'molestation'

A.68 It is, as was recognised by the Law Commission[1], difficult to define molestation. In *Vaughan v Vaughan*[2] the meaning of 'molestation' was considered and in the absence of authority[3], the court considered the definitions in the *Concise Oxford Dictionary*[4] and approved the definition in the *Shorter Oxford Dictionary*[5] which is in the following terms: 'to cause trouble; to vex; to annoy; to put to inconvenience'. Molestation includes acts and threats of violence[6] and 'a multitude of other things'[7]. It could include attempted sexual intercourse without consent[8] and includes vexatious communications by telephone or post[9] especially where they contain threats, although not necessarily threats of violence. Oral harassment, which cannot be strictly classed as a threat, is actionable if it causes physical or psychiatric illness to the victim[10]; where there is a risk that the cumulative effect of such harassment might cause such illness, a quia timet injunction may be granted[11]. The jurisdiction of the court is not limited to the restrain of conduct that is in itself tortious or otherwise unlawful[12].

1 Law Com No 207, para 3.1.
2 [1973] 3 All ER 449, [1973] 1 WLR 1159, CA.

3 Apart from one indirect authority, *Phillips v Phillips* (1905) Times, 19 December.
4 5th edn, 'meddle hostilely or injuriously with (person)'.
5 3rd edn.
6 *Davis v Johnson* [1979] AC 264 at 341A, [1978] 1 All ER 1132 at 1150d, per Lord Salmon. It is an assault for one person to threaten another with violence if the person making the threat is immediately able to carry out the threat and either intends to do so or the person threatened actually fears violence; see 45 *Halsbury's Laws* (4th edn) 1384, and *R v Savage* [1992] 1 AC 699, [1991] 4 All ER 698, HL.
7 *Davis v Johnson* [1979] AC 264 at 341A, [1978] 1 All ER 1132 at 1150d, per Lord Salmon.
8 *Paton v British Pregnancy Advisory Service Trustees* [1979] QB 276 at 280E–F, [1978] 2 All ER 987 at 990h, per Baker J.
9 *Horner v Horner* [1982] Fam 90, [1982] 2 All ER 495, CA. See also *R v Ireland* [1996] 3 WLR 650, CA.
10 *Khorasandjian v Bush* [1993] QB 727, [1993] 3 All ER 669, CA.
11 Ibid.
12 *Burris v Azadani* [1995] 4 All ER 802, [1995] 1 WLR 1372, CA.

Scope of powers and statutory criteria

A.69 A non-molestation order means an order which contains a provision (a) prohibiting the respondent from molesting a person with whom he is associated[1], (b) prohibiting the respondent from molesting a relevant child[2,] or (c) both[3]. The order may be expressed so as to refer to molestation in general, to particular acts of molestation, or both[4]. Where the applicant and the respondent are associated by virtue of having been engaged[5], no application may be made under s 39(2)(a) more than three years after the agreement to marry is terminated[6]. An application for a non-molestation order may be made in other family proceedings[7] or in free standing proceedings under Part IV[8]. The court may make a non-molestation order of its own motion in any family proceedings to which the respondent is a party, if the court considers that such order should be made for the benefit of any other party or any relevant child[9]. In deciding whether to make a non-molestation order and, if so, in what manner, the court must have regard to all the circumstances of the case[10] including the need to secure the health, safety and well-being of (a) the applicant[11], (b) in a case within s 42(2)(b), the person for whose benefit the order would be made[12], and (c) and relevant child[13]. The jurisdiction to make non-molestation orders may be exercised by the High Court, a county court or a magistrates' court[14].

1 Section 42(1)(a). For the meaning of 'associated persons' see paras A.9–A.27
2 Section 42(1)(b). For the meaning of 'relevant child' see paras A.28–A.29.
3 Section 42(1).
4 Section 42(6).
5 Section 62(3)(e), see paras A.18–A.22.
6 Section 42(4). The parties may be associated under some other provision of section 62(3).
7 Section 42(2)(a). Family proceedings are defined by s 63(1), (2). Section 42(3) provides that family proceedings include proceedings in which the court has made an emergency protection order under the CA 1989, s 44, if an exclusion requirement has been included under ibid, s 44A(3).
8 Section 42(2)(a).
9 Section 42(2)(b).
10 Section 42(5).

11 Section 42(5)(a).
12 Ibid.
13 Section 42(5)(b).
14 Section 57; rules of court may specify that certain applications may only be commenced at a particular level and may specify provisions for transfer between levels. See para A.59.

Duration, variation and discharge

A.70 A non-molestation order may be made for a specified period or until further order[1]. A court granting a non-molestation order should always give consideration as to the length of time for which an order should remain in force. A non-molestation order made in other family proceedings ceases to have effect if those proceedings are withdrawn or dismissed[2]. A non-molestation order may be varied or discharged by the court on an application by the respondent[3] or by the person on whose application the order was made[4]. Where a non-molestation order has been made by the court of its own motion[5] the order may be varied or discharged by the court of its own motion[6].

1 Section 42(7).
2 Section 42(8).
3 Section 49(1)(a).
4 Section 49(1)(b).
5 Section 42(2)(b).
6 Section 49(2); the respondent can nonetheless apply under s 49(1)(a) to vary or discharge an order.

UNDERTAKINGS

A.71 Under the previous law, undertakings were frequently offered to narrow the issues in dispute and to save time and money. The offer of an undertaking would not involve the person giving the same in making any admission as to past conduct. Where the court has power to make an occupation order or a non-molestation order, it may accept an undertaking from any party to the proceedings[1]. An undertaking so given to the court is enforceable as if it were an order of the court[2]. A power of arrest cannot be attached to an undertaking[3], and the court shall not accept an undertaking where a power of arrest would otherwise be attached to the order[4].

1 Section 46(1). The words 'any party' make it clear that cross-undertakings may be given.
2 Section 46(4). This merely confirms the existing law; see eg *Hipgrave v Hipgrave* [1962] P 91, [1962] 1 All ER 75, Scarman J. See also *Hussain v Hussain* [1986] Fam 134, [1986] 1 All ER 961, CA: 'Let it be stated in the clearest possible terms that an undertaking to the court is as solemn, binding and effective as an order of the court in the like terms and that the contrary has never been suggested' per Sir John Donaldson MR.
3 Section 46(2). This follows the previous law under the Domestic Violence and Matrimonial Proceedings Act 1976, s 2 and see *Carpenter v Carpenter* [1988] 1 FLR 121, CA.
4 Section 46(3). For the circumstances where a power of arrest is attached to an order, see paras A.76–A.79.

A.72 No doubt undertakings will continue to be offered as a means of trying to resolve applications. It seems that an undertaking will be at least as effective as previously because an undertaking given to the court is enforceable as if it were an order of the court[1]. For the purposes of arrest for breach of an order[2], an occupation order or a non-molestaion order is a 'relevant order'[3]. Where a relevant order has been made without a power of arrest, an applicant, who considers the respondent to be in breach of the order, may apply to the relevant judicial authority[4] for the issue of a warrant for the arrest of the respondent[5]. Accordingly it seems that the combination of ss 46(4) and 47(8) enable a warrant to be issued for the arrest of a party who has breached an undertaking. Thus the offer of an undertaking will be one of the circumstances to consider under s 47(2) as to whether the applicant will be adequately protected without a power of arrest.

1 Section 46(4).
2 Under s 47.
3 Section 47(1).
4 See s 63(1).
5 Section 47(8).

THIRD PARTY APPLICATIONS

A.73 The Law Commission proposed[1] that the police should have power to apply for a civil remedy on behalf of the victim where they had been involved in an incident of molestation or actual or threatened violence or its aftermath. The police would have been obliged to consult the victim, whose views would have been taken into account by the court. A 'representative' may act on behalf of another in proceedings under Part IV[2], and may make an application on behalf of another for an occupation order or a non-molestation order[3]. These provisions will be amplified by extensive rules of court which will prescribe the persons or categories of persons who may be representatives[4], the conditions to be satisfied before a representative brings an application[5], and matters to be considered by the court on such an application[6].

1 Law Comm No 207, para 5.18–5.23 and 7.26–7.27. This was rejected by the Government in its Reply to the Third Report from the Home Affairs Select Committee.
2 Section 60(1).
3 Section 60(2).
4 Section 60(1). Section 60 was introduced as an Opposition amendment at the Report Stage in the House of Commons.
5 Section 60(3(a).
6 Section 60(3)(b).

EX PARTE ORDERS

A.74 Under the previous law an ex parte application should only be made or granted where there was a real immediate danger of serious injury or irreparable damage[1]. On an ex parte application the court may not be able to reach a rational and balanced decision[2] by virtue of hearing only one side of the facts.

In any case where it considers that it is just and convenient to do so, the court may make an occupation order or a non-molestation order even though the respondent has not been given the notice to which he would otherwise be entitled under the rules[3]. In determining whether or not to make an order ex parte, the court must have regard to all the circumstances of the case[4], including:

(a) any risk of significant harm to the applicant or a relevant child, attributable to the conduct of the respondent, if the order is not made immediately[5];

(b) whether it is likely that the applicant will be deterred or prevented from pursing the application if the order is not made immediately[6]; and

(c) whether there is reason to believe that the respondent is aware of the proceedings but is deliberately evading service and that the applicant or a relevant child will be seriously prejudiced by the delay involved[7] in effecting service[8] or in effecting substituted service[9].

An alternative to granting ex parte relief is to abridge the time for serving notice on the respondent. This is quite often done where the circumstances are urgent but do not justify the extreme step of granting relief ex parte. It is submitted that an ex parte order to exclude a respondent from his home would continue to be a very exceptional order[10].

1 *Practice Note: Matrimonial Cause: Injunction* [1978] 2 All ER 919, [1978] 1 WLR 925.
2 *Rennick v Rennick* [1978] 1 All ER 817, [1977] 1 WLR 1455, CA.
3 Section 45(1).
4 Section 45(2).
5 Section 45(2)(a).
6 Section 45(2)(b). See *Ansah v Ansah* [1977] Fam 138, [1977] 2 All ER 638, CA where the fear of a violent response to the service of proceedings was held to justify an ex parte order.
7 Section 45(2)(c).
8 Section 45(2)(c)(i), where the court is a magistrates' court.
9 Section 45(2)(c)(ii), where the court is the High Court or a county court.
10 See *Masich v Masich* (1977) 7 Fam Law 245, CA.

A.75 Where the court makes an ex parte order it must afford the respondent an opportunity of making representations relating to the order as soon as just and convenient at a full hearing[1]. An occupation order made ex parte, is referred to as an 'initial order'[2]. Where at a full hearing the court makes an occupation order[3] then for the purpose of calculating the maximum period for which the full order may be made to have effect, the relevant section[4] applies as if the period for which the full order will have effect began on the date on which the initial order first had effect[5]. Where the initial order regulates the occupation of the dwelling house or requires the respondent to leave part of it, but the full order ousts him from the dwelling house altogether, it is unclear whether the time limit on the full order runs from the date of the initial order because the orders are in different terms. The policy of the legislation appears to be to limit the duration of orders and so it is submitted that the time would run from the date of the initial order. Where at a full hearing, the court makes an occupation order, the provisions of ss 33(10) and 35(6) as to the extension of orders apply as if the full order and the initial order were a single order[6], thus time runs from the date of the initial order.

1 Section 45(4). A full hearing is one in respect of which notice has been given to all parties in accordance with the rules, s 42(5). In *Ansah v Ansah* [1977] Fam 138, [1977] 2 All ER 638, CA it was said that a return date should take place as soon as possible after the ex parte hearing.
2 Section 45(5).
3 'The full order'.
4 Sections 33(10), 35(10), 36(10), 37(5), or 38(6): s 45(5).
5 Section 45(4)(a).
6 Section 45(4)(b).

POWER OF ARREST

A.76 Where the court makes an occupation order or a non-molestation order[1] and it appears to the court that the respondent has used or threatened violence against the applicant it shall attach a power of arrest to the one or more provisions of the order unless it is satisfied that in all the circumstances the applicant or child will be adequately protected without a power of arrest[2]. Previously a power of arrest could only be attached to an injunction where the respondent had caused actual bodily harm[3] to or physically injured[4] the applicant or child and was likely to do so again[5]. A power of arrest was not a routine remedy[6], the change in the law by Part IV of the Act means that a power of arrest is to be attached far more readily than before, but it is submitted that in considering adequate protection for the applicant and any child, the court should also have regard to the serious consequences that may follow from the imposition of a power of arrest.

1 An occupation order or a non-molestation order is a 'relevant order' for the purposes of s 47, s 47(1).
2 Section 47.
3 Domestic Violence and Matrimonial Proceedings Act 1976, s 2(3). Actual bodily harm included any hurt or injury calculated to interfere with the health or comfort of the victim; see OAPA 1861, s 47; an injury to a person's mind for the time being was within the definition of actual bodily harm: *R v Miller* [1954] 2 QB 282 at 292, [1954] 2 All ER 529 at 534c, per Lynsky J. See also *R v Chan-Fook* [1994] 2 All ER 552, [1994] 1 WLR 689 and *R v Ireland* [1996] 3 WLR 650, CA.
4 Domestic Proceedings and Magistrates' Courts Act 1978, s 18(2).
5 Domestic Violence and Matrimonial Proceedings Act 1976, s 2(1) and Domestic Proceedings and Magistrates' Courts Act 1978, s 18(2).
6 *Lewis v Lewis* [1978] Fam 60 at 63 and 64, [1978] 1 All ER 729 at 731, 732, CA and *McLean v Nugent* (1980) 1 FLR 26, CA.

A.77 Where a relevant order is made following an ex parte application[1], the provisions of s 47(2)[2] do not apply but the court may attach a power of arrest to a relevant order where the respondent has used or threatened violence to the applicant or a relevant child[3] and there is a risk of significant harm to the applicant or child attributable to the conduct of the respondent if the power of arrest is not attached immediately[4]. Where a power of arrest is attached to a relevant order on an ex parte application, it may have effect for a shorter period than the ex parte order[5] but may be extended on one or more occasions on any application to vary or discharge the initial order[6]. In any event, the question of a power of arrest must be reconsidered at the full hearing when the court will be applying the test under s 44(2) and will be able to make findings of fact having heard evidence from both sides.

1 Ie one under s 45(1).
2 Automatic attachment where the use or threat of violence is proved.
3 Section 47(3)(a).
4 Section 47(3)(b).
5 Section 47(4).
6 Section 47(5).

A.78 Rules of court will be made to prescribe the procedure on grant of a power of arrest and these will probably contain provisions similar to those which provided for the order and also for any order varying or discharging the power of arrest to be sent by the court to the local police station[1].

1 FPR 1991, rr 3.9(6) and (7), 3.10.

A.79 Where a power of arrest has been attached to a relevant order, a constable[1] may arrest without warrant a person whom he has reasonable cause for suspecting to be in breach of the provisions of the order to which a power of arrest has been attached[2]. This is a significant change from the previous law in respect of non-molestation orders; under the old law[3] an arrest could only be made in respect of a violent breach of a non-molestation order. Now it would seem that an arrest could be made for any breach, however trivial or technical. Nevertheless, a constable has a discretion whether or not to effect an arrest.

1 'Constable' means any person holding the office of constable (as to which see 36 Halsbury's Laws (4th edn) 201 ff), not a member of a police force holding the rank of constable. As to the attestation of constables see the Police Act 1964, s 18, Sch 2, and as to their jurisdiction, ibid, s 19.
2 Section 47(6).
3 Domestic Violence and Matrimonial Proceedings Act 1976, s 2(3) and Domestic Proceedings and Magistrates' Courts Act 1978, s 18(2).

A.80 Apart from statute, the police have common law powers. Where a victim of domestic violence has invited police into premises, the police have an implied licence to enter the home and remain there long enough to take reasonable steps to inquire as to the whereabouts and safety of the complainant and any children, and to be satisfied that there is no reasonable fear of a breach of the peace[1]. The complainant's partner is not able unilaterally to revoke the licence to enter, so as to make the police officers trespassers from the moment that they are told to leave, or as soon thereafter as they could reasonably be expected to leave[2].

1 *R v Thornley* (1980) 72 Cr App Rep 302.
2 Ibid.

Warrant for arrest

A.81 Where the court has made a relevant order[1] but has not attached a power of arrest[2], then if the applicant considers that the respondent has failed to comply with the order, he may apply to the relevant judicial authority for a warrant for the arrest of the respondent[3]. An undertaking[4] is enforceable as if it were an order of the court[5]. Accordingly it would seem that a warrant for arrest can be issued in respect of an alleged breach of an undertaking. A warrant may only be issued where the application is substantiated on oath[6], and the court has reasonable grounds for believing that the respondent has failed to comply with the order[7].

1 An occupation order or a non-molestation order: s 47(1), (8).
2 Or has only attached the power to certain provisions.
3 Section 47(8).
4 Given under s 46(1).
5 Section 46(4).
6 Section 47(9)(a). In the High Court and county courts, it is probable that rules of court will provide that an application for a warrant is made ex parte on affidavit; in magistrates' courts an application will probably be made on the oral evidence of the applicant.
7 Section 47(9)(b).

Procedure subsequent to arrest

A.82 Where a respondent is arrested under a power of arrest for a suspected breach of an order, he must be brought before the relevant judicial authority[1] within 24 hours[2]. If the matter is not disposed of when the respondent first appears before the relevant judicial authority[3], he may be remanded[4], either in custody[5] or on bail[6]. There may be further periods of remand[7]. A person arrested on a warrant may be remanded by the court[8].

1 Relevant judicial authority is defined by s 63(1).
2 Section 47(7)(a); no account is taken of Christmas Day, Good Friday or any Sunday: s 47(7).
3 On such appearance the court should begin to enquire into whether a breach is admitted or proved and if so, decide in what manner to deal with the contempt. See s 58.
4 Section 47(7)(b). The power to remand is new. Previously, the court could adjourn the proceedings for evidence to be adduced: *Roberts v Roberts* [1991] 1 FLR 294. There was no power to detain a contemnor between the finding of contempt and passing sentence at a subsequent date: *Delaney v Delaney* [1996] 1 FLR 458, CA.
5 Sch 5, para 2(1)(a) in the case of the High Court or county courts; Magistrates' Courts Act 1980, s 128 in the case of magistrates' courts.
6 Sch 5, para 2(1)(b); Magistrates' Courts Act 1980, s 128.
7 Sch 5, paras 2(2), 3; Magistrates' Courts Act 1980, s 129.
8 Section 47(10).

A.83 A contemnor may be remanded for the purpose of a medical examination and obtaining a medical report[1]. A remand for such purpose may be on bail for up to four weeks[2] or in custody for up to three weeks[3]. Where the court[4] has reason to suspect that the contemnor is suffering from mental illness or severe mental impairment, the court has the same power to make an order under the Mental Health Act 1983, s 35 as the Crown Court[5].

1 Section 48.
2 Section 48(2).
3 Section 48(3).
4 The relevant judicial authority.
5 Section 48(4).

Committal

A.84 An order for committal is one of last resort[1]. Breach of an order does not automatically lead to committal[2], and the views of the victim are very relevant[3]. A short term of imprisonment may be appropriate even where there has only been one breach if that is sufficiently serious and flagrant[4]. Blatant and aggravated contempt will justify immediate imprisonment, particularly where the contemnor has been given judicial warnings about his behaviour[5].

1 *Ansah v Ansah* [1977] Fam 138, [1977] 2 All ER 638, CA.
2 *Smith v Smith* [1988] 1 FLR 179.
3 *Boylan v Boylan* (1980) 11 Fam Law 76, CA.
4 *Pickering v Pickering* [1980] CA Transcript 193, CA.
5 *Jones v Jones* [1993] 2 FCR 82, CA.

Powers of courts

A.85 The High Court and county courts may imprison for up to two years[1], and/or impose an unlimited fine[2]. An order for committal may be suspended and consecutive terms may be imposed for different breaches[3]. A magistrates' court may commit a contemnor to prison for up to two months[4], and may make a suspended order[5]. A fine may be imposed of £50 for every day of default up to a maximum of £5,000[6].

1 County Courts Act 1984, s 14(1), (4A).
2 *Phonographic Performance Ltd v Amusement Caterers (Peckham) Ltd* [1964] Ch 195, [1963] 2 All ER 493.
3 *Lee v Walker* [1985] QB 1191, [1985] 1 All ER 781, CA.
4 Magistrates' Court Act 1980, s 63(3)(b).
5 Section 50(1).
6 Magistrates' Court Act 1980, s 63(3)(a). This is difficult to apply in family cases as the section emphasises the duration not the gravity of the breach.

Appendix 2

Intestacy

Table 1   Table of Distribution on Intestacy   553
Table 2   Table of Intestate Succession   556
Table 3   Interest on the Fixed Net Sum   557

Table 1

Table of Distribution on Intestacy

Distribution on death after 1952. Where a person dies intestate on or after 1st January 1953 his estate is to be distributed or held on trusts as follows:

A. The surviving spouse takes the personal chattels[1] absolutely[2].

B. The surviving spouse takes the fixed net sum[3] absolutely[4].

C. Subject to the above, the estate is distributed or held on trust as follows (note that if there are relatives of any class there is no need to proceed to a subsequent class) (see overleaf):

Appendix 2: Intestacy

	Relatives Surviving	Distribution of Estate		Notes
		Where Surviving Spouse	Where no Surviving Spouse	
1	Issue.	One-half to surviving spouse for life and then to issue on statutory trusts[5]: other half to issue on statutory trusts[6].	All to issue on on statutory trusts[7].	If the trusts for the issue fail in lifetime of surviving spouse, the residuary estate devolves as if the intestate had died without leaving issue[8].
2	Parent(s).	One-half to surviving spouse absolutely[9]; other half to parent (or parents equally) absolutely[10].	All to parent (or parents equally) absolutely[11].	The parents do not take on the statutory trusts.
3	Brother(s) and/or sister(s) of whole blood (including issue of deceased ones, ie nephews and nieces).	One-half to surviving spouse absolutely[12]; other half to brother(s) and/or sister(s) on statutory trusts[13].	All to brother(s) and/or sister(s) on statutory trusts[14].	Nephews or nieces take deceased parent's share. If all brothers and sisters are dead, nephews and nieces take per stirpes[15].
4	Brother(s) and/or sister(s) of half-blood (including issue of deceased ones).	All to surviving spouse absolutely[16].	All to brother(s) and/or sister(s) on statutory trusts[17].	
5	Grandparent(s).	All to surviving spouse absolutely[18].	All to grandparent (or grandparents equally) absolutely[19].	Grandparents do not take on statutory trusts.
6	Uncle(s) and/or aunt(s) of the whole blood (including issue of deceased ones).	All to surviving spouse absolutely[20].	All to uncle(s) and/or aunt(s) on statutory trusts[21].	Cousins take deceased parent's share. If all uncles and aunts are dead the cousins take per stirpes.
7	Uncle(s) and/or aunt(s) of the whole blood (including issue of deceased ones).	All to surviving spouse absolutely[22].	All to uncle(s) and/or aunt(s) on statutory trusts[23].	
8	No relative of above classes.	All to surviving spouse absolutely[24].	All to Crown Duchy of Lancaster or Duke of Cornwall[25].	Second or more remote cousins have no rights.

Notes

1 For the definition of 'Personal Chattels' see Administration of Estates Act 1925, s 55(1)(x).
2 AEA 1925, s 46(1)(i), Table, paras (2), (3).
3 The fixed net sum is currently £125,000 where there is issue and £200,000 where there is no issue in respect of deaths after 1 December 1993. See SI 1993/2906. For previous amounts of the fixed net sum see separate table.
4 AEA 1925, s 46(1)(i), Table, paras (2), (3),
5 AEA 1925, s 46(1)(i), Table, para (2)(a). The terms of the statutory trusts are set out in AEA 1925, s 47 as amended.
6 AEA 1925, s 46(1)(i), Table, para (2)(b).
7 AEA 1925, s 46(1)(ii).
8 AEA 1925, s 47(2)(a).
9 AEA 1925, s 46(1)(i), Table, para (3)(a).
10 AEA 1925, s 46(1)(i), Table, para (3)(b)(ii).
11 AEA 1925, s 46(1)(iii), (iv).
12 AEA 1925, s 46(1)(i), Table, para (3)(a).
13 AEA 1925, s 46(1)(i), Table, para (3)(b)(ii).
14 AEA 1925, s 46(1)(v), first head.
15 Taking 'per stirpes' means taking according to stock. Ie, the nephews and nieces take the share of their deceased parent equally.
16 AEA 1925, s 46(1)(i), Table, para (1).
17 AEA 1925, s 46(1)(v), second head.
18 AEA 1925, s 46(1)(i), Table, para (1).
19 AEA 1925, s 46(1)(v), third head.
20 AEA 1925, s 46(1)(i), Table, para (1).
21 AEA 1925, s 46(1)(v), fourth head.
22 AEA 1925, s 46(1)(i), Table, para (1).
23 AEA 1925, s 46(1)(v), fifth head.
24 AEA 1925, s 46(1)(i), Table, para (1).
25 AEA 1925, s 46(1)(vi).

Table 2

Intestate Succession

The Fixed Net Sum (the Statutory Legacy) Administration of Estates Act 1925, s 46

Death on or after	Issue £	No Issue £	
1 Jan 26	1,000	1,000	S 46 AEA 1925
1 Jan 53	5,000	20,000	S 1 IEA 1952
1 Jan 67	8,750	30,000	S 1 FPA 1966
1 July 72	15,000	40,000	SI 1972/916
15 March 77	25,000	55,000	SI 1977/415
1 March 81	40,000	80,000	SI 1981/255
1 June 87	75,000	125,000	SI 1987/799
1 Dec 93	125,000	200,000	SI 1993/2906

Table 3

Interest on the Fixed Net Sum

*Death on
or after*

1 Jan 25	5%	S 46(1)(i) AEA 1925
1 Jan 53	4%	S 46(1)(i) AEA 1925 and S 1 IEA 1952
		Administration of Justice Act 1977, s 28, in force 15 September 1977 (SI 1977/1490)
15 Sep 77	7%	SI 1977/1491
1 Oct 83	6%	SI 1983/1374

Appendix 3

Occupation Orders

Table 1   Entitlement to Apply   561
Table 2   Range of Orders Available   562
Table 3   Criteria for Exercise of Powers   564
Table 4   Duration   567

Table 1: Entitlement to Apply 561

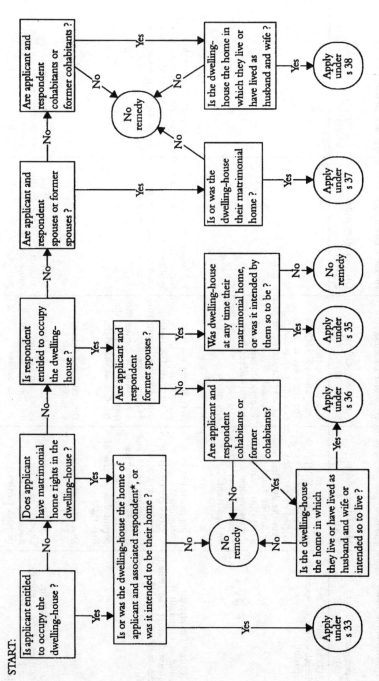

* Where the applicant and respondent are associated persons only by virtue of having agreed to marry one another (s 62(3)(e)), no application for an occupation order may be made more than three years after the date on which the agreement to marry was terminated (s 33(2))

Appendix 3: Occupation Orders

Section 33 applicants Entitled applicants and those with matrimonial home rights	Section 35 applicants Non-entitled former spouse	Section 36 applicants Non-entitled cohabitant or former cohabitant	Section 37 applicants Neither spouse nor former spouse entitled	Section 38 applicants Neither cohabitant nor former cohabitant entitled
Discretionary orders: S 33(3)	Mandatory orders: S 35(3), (4)	Mandatory orders: S 36(3), (4)	Discretionary orders: S 37(3)	Discretionary orders: S 38(3)
S 33(3)(a): Enforce the applicant's right to remain in occupation.	If applicant in occupation: S 35(3)(a): The right not to be evicted or excluded from the dwelling-house or part of it and S 35(3)(b): Prohibiting the respondent from excluding or evicting the applicant, or If applicant not in occupation: S 35(4)(a): The right to enter into and occupy the dwelling-house, and S 35(4)(b): Requiring the respondent to permit the exercise of that right. Discretionary orders: S 35(5)	If applicant in occupation: S 36(3)(a): The right not to be evicted or excluded from the dwelling-house or part of it and S 36(3)(b): Prohibiting the respondent from excluding or evicting the applicant, or If applicant not in occupation: S 36(4)(a): The right to enter into and occupy the dwelling-house, and S 36(4)(b): Requiring the respondent to permit the exercise of that right. Discretionary orders: S 36(5)		
S 33(3)(b): Require the respondent to permit the applicant to enter and remain in the dwelling-house or part of it.			S 37(3)(a): Require the respondent to permit the applicant to enter and remain in the dwelling-house or part of it.	S 38(3)(a): Require the respondent to permit the applicant to enter and remain in the dwelling-house or part of it.
S 33(3)(c): Regulate the occupation of the dwelling-house by either or both parties.	S 35(5)(a): Regulate the occupation of the dwelling-house by either or both parties.	S 36(5)(a): Regulate the occupation of the dwelling-house by either or both parties.	S 37(3)(b): Regulate the occupation of the dwelling-house by either or both parties.	S 38(3)(b): Regulate the occupation of the dwelling-house by either or both parties.

Table 2: Range of Orders Available

S 33	S 35	S 36	S 37	S 38
S 33(3)(d): If the respondent is entitled under s 33(1)(a)(i), prohibit, suspend or restrict the exercise of his right to occupy the dwelling-house.	S 35(5)(b): Prohibit, suspend or restrict the exercise by the respondent of his right to occupy the dwelling-house.	S 36(5)(b): Prohibit, suspend or restrict the exercise by the respondent of his right to occupy the dwelling-house.		
S 33(3)(e): If the respondent has matrimonial home rights and the applicant is the other spouse, terminate those rights.				
S 33(3)(f): Require the respondent to leave the dwelling-house or part of it.	S 35(5)(c): Require the respondent to leave the dwelling-house or part of it.	S 36(5)(c): Require the respondent to leave the dwelling-house or part of it.	S 37(3)(c): Require the respondent to leave the dwelling-house or part of it.	S 38(3)(c): Require the respondent to leave the dwelling-house or part of it.
S 33(3)(g): Exclude the respondent from a defined area in which the dwelling-house is included.	S 35(5)(d): Exclude the respondent from a defined area in which the dwelling-house is included.	S 36(5)(d): Exclude the respondent from a defined area in which the dwelling-house is included.	S 37(3)(d): Exclude the respondent from a defined area in which the dwelling-house is included.	S 38(3)(d): Exclude the respondent from a defined area in which the dwelling-house is included.
S 33(4): Declare the applicant is entitled under s 33(1)(a)(i), or has matrimonial rights.				
S 33(5): During the subsistence of the marriage: If the applicant has matrimonial home rights and the respondent is the other spouse, order that the rights shall not be brought to an end by (a) the death of the other spouse, or (b) the termination (otherwise than by death) of the marriage.				

Section 33 applicants Entitled applicants and those with matrimonial home rights	*Section 35 applicants* Non-entitled former spouse	*Section 36 applicants* Non-entitled cohabitant or former cohabitant	*Section 37 applicants* Neither spouse nor former spouse entitled	*Section 38 applicants* Neither cohabitant nor former cohabitant entitled
In deciding whether, and (if so) in what manner, to exercise its powers under sub-s (3) the court SHALL have regard to—	In deciding whether applicants and those with matrimonial home, and (if so) in what manner, to make an order of the kind mentioned in sub-ss (3) or (4) the court SHALL have regard to—	In deciding whether, and (if so) in what manner, to make an order of the kind mentioned in sub-ss (3) or (4) the court SHALL have regard to—	In deciding whether, and (if so) in what manner, to exercise its powers under sub-s (3) the court SHALL have regard to—	In deciding whether, and (if so) in what manner, to exercise its powers under sub-s (3) the court SHALL have regard to—
S 33(6) All the circumstances including— (a) the respective housing needs and housing resources of the parties and any relevant child; (b) the respective financial resources of the parties; (c) the likely effect of any order or decision not to exercise its powers under sub-s (3) on the health, safety or well-being of the parties and any relevant child; (d) the conduct of the parties in relation to each other and otherwise.	S 35(6) All the circumstances including— (a) the respective housing needs and housing resources of the parties and any relevant child; (b) the respective financial resources of the parties; (c) the likely effect of any order or decision not to exercise its powers under sub-ss (3) or (4) on the health, safety or well-being of the parties and any relevant child; (d) the conduct of the parties in relation to each other and otherwise; (e) the length of time that has elapsed since the parties ceased to live together; (f) the length of time that has elapsed since the marriage was dissolved or annulled;	S 36(6) All the circumstances including— (a) the respective housing needs and housing resources of the parties and any relevant child; (b) the respective financial resources of the parties; (c) the likely effect of any order or decision not to exercise its powers under sub-ss (3) or (4) on the health, safety or well-being of the parties and any relevant child; (d) the conduct of the parties in relation to each other and otherwise; (e) the nature of the parties' relationship; (f) the length of time during which they have lived together as husband and wife; (g) whether there are or have been any children who are children of both parties or for whom the parties have or have had parental responsibility;	S 33(6) All the circumstances including— (a) the respective housing needs and housing resources of the parties and any relevant child; (b) the respective financial resources of the parties; (c) the likely effect of any order or decision not to exercise its powers under sub-s (3) on the health, safety or well-being of the parties and any relevant child; (d) the conduct of the parties in relation to each other and otherwise.	S 38(4) All the circumstances including— (a) the respective housing needs and housing resources of the parties and any relevant child; (b) the respective financial resources of the parties; (c) the likely effect of any order or decision not to exercise its powers under sub-s (3) on the health, safety or well-being of the parties and any relevant child; (d) the conduct of the parties in relation to each other and otherwise; and (e) the questions mentioned in sub-s (5) (see below).

Table 3: Criteria for Exercise of Powers

S 33(7) If it appears that the applicant or any relevant child is likely to suffer significant harm attributable to conduct of the respondent if an order is not made, the court SHALL make an order containing a sub-s (3) provision unless it appears that—
 	
 (a) the respondent or any relevant child is likely to suffer significant harm if the order is made, and
	(g) the existence of any pending proceedings between them
	  (i) for an order under MCA 1973, ss 23A or 24, or
	  (ii) for an order under CA 1989, Sch 1, para 1(2)(d) or (e),
	
	 (h) the length of time that has elapsed since the parties ceased to live together;
	
	 (j) the existence of any pending proceedings between them
	  (i) for an order under CA 1989, Sch 1, para 1(2)(d) or (e), or
	  (ii) relating to the legal or beneficial ownership of the dwelling-house.
		S 35(7) In deciding whether and (if so) in what manner to exercise its power to include a sub-s (5) provision, the court SHALL have regard to all the circumstances including the matters in sub-s (6)(a) to (e).
		
		 S 35(8) If the court decides to make an order and it appears that, if the order does not include a sub-s (5) provision, the applicant or any relevant child is likely to suffer significant harm attributable to conduct of the respondent, the court SHALL include a sub-s (5) provision unless it appears that—
			S 36(7) In deciding whether and (if so) in what manner to exercise its power to include a sub-s (5) provision, the court SHALL have regard to all the circumstances including—
			
			 (a) the matters in sub-s (6)(a) to (d), and
			 (b) the questions mentioned in sub-s (8).
			
			 S 36(8) The questions are—
			 (a) whether the applicant or any relevant child is likely to suffer significant harm attributable to conduct of the respondent if a sub-s (5) provision is not included; and
			 (b) whether the harm likely to be suffered by the respondent or child is as great as or greater than the harm attributable to conduct of the respondent which is likely to be suffered by the applicant or child if the provision is not included.
				S 33(7) If it appears that the applicant or any relevant child is likely to suffer significant harm attributable to conduct of the respondent, if an order is not made, the court SHALL make an order containing a sub-s (3) provision unless it appears that—
				
				 (a) the respondent or any relevant child is likely to suffer significant harm if the order is made, and
					S 38(5) The questions are—
					
					 (a) whether the applicant or any relevant child is likely to suffer significant harm attributable to conduct of the respondent if a sub-s (5) provision is not included; and
					 (b) whether the harm likely to be suffered by the respondent or child in that event is as great as or greater than the harm attributable to conduct of the respondent which is likely to be suffered by the applicant or child if the provision is not included.

(b) the harm likely to be suffered by the respondent or child in that event is as great as, or greater than, the harm attributable to conduct of the respondent which is likely to be suffered by the applicant or child if the order is not made.	(a) the respondent or any relevant child is likely to suffer significant harm if the provision is included, and (b) the harm likely to be suffered by the respondent or child in that event is as great as or greater than the harm attributable to conduct of the respondent which is likely to be suffered by the applicant or child if the provision is not included. S 41(1), (2) Where the parties are cohabitants or former cohabitants, and the court is required to consider the nature of the parties' relationship, it is to have regard to the fact that the parties have not given each other the commitment involved in marriage.	(b) the harm likely to be suffered by the respondent or child in that event is as great as, or greater than, the harm attributable to conduct of the respondent which is likely to be suffered by the applicant or child if the order is not made.

Table 4: Duration

Section 33 orders	Section 35 orders	Section 36 orders	Section 37 orders	Section 38 orders
Entitled applicants and those with matrimonial home rights	Non-entitled former spouse	Non-entitled cohabitant or former cohabitant	Neither spouse nor former spouse entitled	Neither cohabitant nor former cohabitant entitled
S 33 (10)— MAY be (a) for a specified period, (b) until the occurrence of a specified event or (c) until further order.	S 35(10)— MUST be limited for a specified period not exceeding six months, MAY be extended (on one or more occasions) for a further specified period exceeding six months.	S 36(10)— MUST be limited for a specified period not exceeding six months, MAY be extended on one occasion for a further specified period not exceeding six months.	S 37(5)— MUST be limited for a specified period not exceeding six months, MAY be extended (on one or more occasions) for a further specified period not exceeding six months.	S 38(6)— MUST be limited for a specified period not exceeding six months, MAY be extended on one occasion for a further specified period not exceeding six months.
S 33(9)(b)— Unless order under s 33(5)(a), orders cease to have effect on the death of either party.	S 35(9)(b)— Orders cease to have effect on the death of either party.	S 36(9)(b)— Orders cease to have effect on the death of either party.		

S 49(1): An occupation order MAY be varied or discharged by the court on the application of (a) the respondent or (b) the person on whose application the order was made.

S 49(3): If a spouse's matrimonial home rights are a charge on the estate or interest of the other spouse or the trustees for the other spouse, an order under s 33 against the other spouse MAY also be varied or discharged by the court on application by any person deriving title under the other spouse or under the trustees and affected by the charge.

Index

Abduction of child
  child in care
    generally 13.22
    recovery of 13.23
      punishment for intentional obstruction 13.24
  ward 13.25
Abortion
  see also UNBORN CHILD
  injunction to prevent 7.20
Adoption
  abroad see overseas adoption below
  agency see ADOPTION AGENCY
  application for 7.65-7.67
    child to live with adopters 7.68
    father, by 7.67
    following prior refusal 7.69
    legal aid 15.10
    more than one person, by 7.66
    mother, by 7.67
    payment prohibited 7.70
    single person, by 7.65
    uncontested 2.19
  citizenship, and 7.58
  Convention adoption 7.77, 7.95
  effect of 7.57, 7.58
  freeing order
    adoption agency action post-freeing 7.89
    contact order, cross-application for 7.88, 8.31
    effects of 7.86
    generally 7.86
    pre-conditions 7.87
    procedure on application 7.92
    revocation of 7.90
  generally 7.56
  inheritance, and 6.9
  international see overseas adoption below
  legitimacy, and 7.50, 7.57
  money, for 7.70
  more than one person, by 7.66
  name, change of 7.58
  non-agency placements
    generally 7.62
    investigation of 7.64

Adoption—*contd*
  non-agency placements—*contd*
    notice of 7.64
  order 7.85
    terms and conditions 7.85
  overseas
    Convention adoption 7.77, 7.95
    generally 7.62
    international adoptions 7.97, 7.98-7.99
    notice to Home Office 7.71
    procedure 7.94
    recognition at common law 7.96
  parental agreement
    child abandoned or neglected, where 7.82
    consent 7.77
    definition of 'parent' 7.77
    dispensing with 7.78-7.84
    generally 7.76
    ill-treatment, where 7.83, 7.84
    oral agreement 7.77
    parent cannot be found, where 7.79
    parent incapable of giving agreement, where 7.79
    persistent failure to discharge parental responsibility, where 7.81
    persistent ill-treatment, where 7.83
    serious ill-treatment, where 7.84
    timing of 7.77
    withdrawal of 7.77
    withholding unreasonably 7.80
    written agreement 7.77
  parental responsibility of adoptive parents 7.03, 7.57, 7.86
  placement for 7.61
  placement stage, getting to 7.63
  post-placement protection 8.135
  procedure
    in county court 7.91
    freeing applications 7.92
    in High Court 7.91
    in magistrates' court 7.93
  prohibited degrees of relationship 7.58
  recording of 7.58
  single person, by 7.63

Adoption—contd
  surrogacy arrangement, and 7.62
  trans-racial 8.134
  ward of court, placing for 7.63
  welfare of the child 8.134
  who may apply to adopt 7.65-7.67
  who may be adopted 7.71-7.75
Adoption agency
  Adoption Panel
    appointment of members 7.60
    establishment of 7.60
    referral to 7.74
      subsequent procedure 7.75
  approval of 7.60
  child, duties to 7.72
  decision of, informing prospective
    adopter 7.75
  duties of 7.72, 7.73
  establishment of 7.59
  freeing order, and 7.89
  guardian, duties to 7.72
  local authorities, duties of 7.59, 7.60
  notice of non-agency placement 7.64
  notification to parents 7.75
  parents, duties to 7.72
  placement for adoption 7.61
  prospective adopters, duties in respect of
    7.73
  record-keeping 7.60
  regulation of 7.60
Age
  acquisition of independent rights 7.20
  blood test, consent for 7.53
  consent, of 7.21, 7.22
  contact, refusal of 8.27
  contact order, application for 7.21
  Gillick competence 7.24-7.26
  majority, of 7.18
  medical treatment, consent to 7.21, 7.22,
    7.24-7.26
  residence order, and 8.21
  16 year olds, rights of 7.21
  17 year olds, rights of 7.23
  welfare of child, and 8.08
Agreements between the parties
  deeds of separation, and 4.165-4.171
  Edgar principle, and 4.166, 4.170,
    4.170n
  full application for financial relief 4.168
  mediation, reached in 4.169
  orders, relationship with 4.166
    see also CONSENT ORDER
    application for notice to show cause
      why agreement should not be made
      into order 4.167
  recited in minutes of order 4.171
  status of 4.165
  to oust jurisdiction of court 4.141, 4.170
Annulment of marriage *see* NULLITY
Ante-nuptial settlement *see* NUPTIAL
  SETTLEMENTS

Anton Piller order
  see also INJUNCTIONS
  application for 4.187, 4.189
    acting for parties to
      applicant 4.191
      respondent 4.192
      third party 4.193
    documentation required 4.190
  character of 4.188
  generally 4.173, 4.188
  grounds for seeking 4.187
  in personam operation of 4.186
  jurisdiction for making 4.186
    inherent 4.186n
  procedural requirements 4.187
Appeals
  application to set aside order 2.66, 2.69,
    2.72
  basis for allowing 2.68
  child support commissioners, from 10.82
  child support commissioners, to 10.78-
    10.79
  child support tribunals, to
    generally 10.74-10.75
    procedure 10.76
    successful appeals 10.77
  children proceedings
    case law concerning 8.125
    generally 8.122
    principles governing 8.123
    time for 8.124
  county court, from 2.2
  Court of Appeal, to 2.2, 2.75
  deduction from earnings order, against
    10.91
  disposal of 2.73-2.75
  district judge, from 2.74
  education
    appeals against decisions 9.17
    special needs 9.21
  emergency protection order 8.118
  family proceedings courts, from 2.2, 2.75
  generally 2.66
  High Court 2.2
  House of Lords, to 2.2
  leave to appeal out of time 2.66, 2.70
  magistrates' court, from 2.2, 2.75
  procedure 2.71
  rehearing, order for 2.69
  routes to 2.67
Application to set aside order
  generally 2.66, 2.69
  procedure 2.72
Artificial insemination
  see also SURROGACY AND EMBRYOLOGY
  legitimacy, and 7.47
Attachment of earnings
  county courts, in 12.19-12.20
  enforcement by 12.17-12.23
  generally 12.17-12.18
  High Court, in 12.19-12.20

Attachment of earnings—*contd*
  magistrates' court, in 12.21
  the order 12.23
  powers of all courts 12.22
Bank accounts
  division of moneys 5.32
Bankruptcy
  after acquired property, and 4.273
  effect of 4.250
  family breakdown, and 4.249-4.281
  household items, and 4.271-4.272
  lump sum order, and 4.277-4.281
  maintenance, and 4.274-4.276
  matrimonial home, and
    case law guidance 4.254-4.255
    equity of exoneration 4.262
    establishing a beneficial interest 4.256-4.257
      significance of 4.258
    generally 4.251
    jointly owned, where 4.259-4.261
    reviewable transactions
      case law 4.265
      generally 4.263
      transactions at an undervalue 4.264
      transactions defrauding creditors 4.268-4.269
      voidable preferences 4.266-4.267
    soley owned 4.252-4.253
Barry directions 4.7
Bigamy
  see also NULLITY
  marriage void for 3.8
Blood tests
  consents 7.53
  DNA testing 10.66
  failure to comply with directions for 7.54-7.55
  HIV testing 8.40
  inferences drawn from refusal of 7.54, 7.55
  power to order 7.52
Burden of proof *see* EVIDENCE

Calderbank **letters** *see under* COSTS
Capital gains tax
  maintenance, and
    generally 4.244
    indemnities 4.247
    matrimonial home 4.245
    principal private residence exemption 4.246
    stamp duty 4.248
Care order
  abduction of children in care 13.22
    recovery order 13.23
      punishment for intentional obstruction 13.24
  application for 2.17

Care order—*contd*
  care and criminal proceedings 8.75
  care plan 8.68, 8.69
  conditions 8.68
  directions 8.68
  effect of 8.63, 13.21
  enforcement 13.21-13.24
  fact finding 8.67
  interim order
    duration of 8.95
    grounds for making 8.94
    judicial guidance on 8.97
    medical or psychiatric examination 8.96
  local authorities, and 8.63
  orders by consent 8.70
  orphans 8.74
  parental responsibility conferred by 8.63
  residence order as alternative 8.78
  restrictions on making of 8.62
  section 37 reports 8.98, 8.99
  supervision order
    distinguished 8.77
    made on application for 8.65
  threshold criteria 8.60-8.61, 8.66
  undertakings in 4.146n
  variation and discharge of 8.100
  withdrawal of application 8.71
Care proceedings
  commencement of 2.3
  criminal proceedings, and 8.75
  undertakings in 4.146n
Charging order
  enforcement by 12.30-12.33
Child
  adopted *see* ADOPTION
  age of *see* AGE
  blood tests, consent for 7.53
    see also BLOOD TESTS
  in care *see* CHILD IN CARE
  contact order *see* CONTACT ORDER
  defining
    see also AGE
    acquisition of independent rights 7.20
    Adoption Act 1976, under 7.19
    age of majority 7.18
    child in need 9.2-9.3
    Children Act 1989, under 5.51, 7.19
    for education purposes 9.16n
    emergency treatment 7.25
    Family Law Reform Act 1969, under 7.22
    Gillick competence 7.24-7.26
    limitations on proceedings for older children 7.23
    'minor' 7.19
    16 year olds 7.21
  education 9.16
    see also EDUCATION
  embryology *see* SURROGACY AND EMBRYOLOGY

Child—*contd*
  emergency treatment *see* medical
    treatment *below*
  of the family, definition 5.52, 10.01
  financial support of *see* CHILD MAINTENANCE
    ORDERS; CHILD SUPPORT ACT 1991; CHILD
    SUPPORT AGENCY
  foetus *see* UNBORN CHILD
  Gillick competence 7.24-7.26
  guardianship of *see* GUARDIAN
  illegitimacy *see* ILLEGITIMACY
  independent rights, acquisition of 7.20
  inheritance 6.17, 6.25
    intestate succession
      adopted children 6.9
      children of void marriage 6.9
      entitlement 6.10
      Human Fertilisation and
        Embryology Act 1990, and 6.9
      illegitimate children 6.9
      legitimate children 6.9
      legitimated children 6.9
      qualification 6.9
      step-children 6.18
    step-children 6.18, 6.26
  judicial review, and *see* JUDICIAL REVIEW
  legitimacy *see* LEGITIMACY
  maintenance of *see* CHILD MAINTENANCE
    ORDERS; CHILD SUPPORT ACT 1991; CHILD
    SUPPORT AGENCY
  majority, age of 7.18
  medical examination
    consent to 8.106
    making of interim care or supervision
      order, on 8.96
  medical treatment
    consent to 7.21, 7.22
    emergency treatment 7.25
    Gillick competence 7.24-7.26
  parental responsibility for *see* PARENTAL
    RESPONSIBILITY
  paternity *see* PATERNITY
  physical examination 2.61
  pre-birth injuries 7.20
  proceedings involving *see* CHILDREN
    PROCEEDINGS
  prohibited steps order *see* PROHIBITED STEPS
    ORDER
  protection of, duty to investigate 8.102-
    8.103
  residence order *see* RESIDENCE ORDER
  section 8 orders *see* SECTION 8 ORDERS
  16 year old, rights of 7.21
  17 year olds 7.23
  specific issue order *see* SPECIFIC ISSUE ORDER
  step-child, inheritance, and 6.18, 6.26
  support *see* CHILD MAINTENANCE ORDER; CHILD
    SUPPORT ACT 1991; CHILD SUPPORT AGENCY
  surrogacy *see* SURROGACY AND EMBRYOLOGY
  unborn *see* UNBORN CHILD

Child—*contd*
  void marriage, of, inheritance, and 6.9
  wardship *see* WARDSHIP
  welfare of *see* WELFARE OF THE CHILD
Child assessment order
  application for, treated as emergency
    protection order 8.105-8.106
  compliance with 8.106
  grounds for making 8.104
  purpose of 8.104
Child in care
  arrangements for child to live abroad
    8.79
  contact with
    application for leave 8.91
    case law on court orders 8.88-8.89
    contact defined 8.86
    discharge of 8.92
    general requirement for reasonable
      contact 8.85
    limitations on reasonable contact 8.86
    orders for contact by parent, *etc* 8.87
    variation of 8.92
    when order may be made 8.90
  emigration of 8.80, 8.81
  order permitting refusal 8.86
  withholding 8.86
Child of the family
  definition 5.52, 10.01
Child maintenance orders
  see also CHILD SUPPORT ACT 1991; CHILD
    SUPPORT AGENCY
  appeals 5.61
  child, definition 5.51
  child of the family, definition 5.52,
    10.01
  Child Support Act 1991, effects of 5.46
  Children Act 1989, under 5.44
    Schedule 1 Orders 5.47
  county court, orders in 5.48
  factors taken into account by court 5.53
  High Court, orders in 5.48
  joinder with other applications 5.45
  liability of person not father or mother
    5.54
  lump sums 5.55
  magistrates' court, in 5.49, 12.47
  parent, definition 5.50
  persons over 18 5.57
  procedure 5.60
  registration in magistrates' court 12.47-
    12.48
  retrospective and continuing powers 5.59
  tenancy, where 5.56
  variation and discharge 5.58
Child in need
  definition 9.2-9.3
Child Support Act 1991
  see also CHILD SUPPORT AGENCY
  duty to maintain 10.04

Index 573

Child Support Act 1991—*contd*
effects of 5.46
essential terminology
'absent parent' 10.07
'child support maintenance' 10.07
'day-to-day care' 10.07
'effective date' 10.07
'parent with care' 10.07
'person with care' 10.07
'qualifying child' 10.07
'relevant week' 10.07
generally 10.03
law prior to 10.01-10.02
situations falling outside 10.05-10.06
welfare of the child 3.39, 7.22, 8.02-8.12, 10.08
Child Support Agency (CSA)
see also CHILD MAINTENANCE ORDERS; CHILD SUPPORT ACT 1991
appeals
child support commissioners, from 10.82
child support commissioners, to
generally 10.78-10.79
procedure 10.80-10.81
child support tribunals, to
generally 10.74-10.75
procedure 10.76
successful appeals 10.77
Court of Appeal, to 10.83
generally 10.84
arrears of maintenance 10.98
interest on 10.99-10.100
assessable income 10.14
additional element in case of higher income families 10.23-10.24
nil and no assessable income 10.22
protected income 10.25
special cases
both parents absent 10.27-10.28
persons treated as absent parents 10.29-10.30
care provided in part by local authority 10.36
cases where child support maintenance is not to be payable 10.37
child in boarding school or hospital, where 10.38
generally 10.26
multiple applications involving one absent parent 10.32-10.33
one parent absent and other treated as absent 10.31
parent with whom child is placed by local authority 10.39
person caring for children of more than one absent parent 10.34
persons with part-time care 10.35
Chief Child Support Officer 10.09

Child Support Agency—*contd*
child maintenance bonus 10.59
collection 10.86-10.88
deduction from earnings order *see under* enforcement *below*
'the departure direction' 10.52-10.54
regular payment condition 10.55-10.58
enforcement
committal to prison, by 10.97
deduction from earnings order 10.90
appeal against 10.91
penalties for non-compliance 10.92
generally 10.89
liability orders, by
enforcement by distress 10.95
enforcement in county courts 10.96
generally 10.93-10.94
exempt income
excessive housing costs 10.16
housing costs 10.15
pre-April 1993 transfers 10.18-10.19
travel costs 10.17
generally 10.09
inspectors
appointment of 10.60
entry powers 10.60
role of 10.60
judicial findings 2.33
judicial review of decisions 10.85
jurisdiction of 10.05
consent order attempting to exclude 4.163
liability orders *see under* enforcement *above*
maintenance application form 10.10
maintenance assessment
aim of 10.10
appeals *see* appeals *above*
application for
authorisation for recovery of child support maintenance 10.43
fees 10.45
maintenance application form (MAF) 10.44
procedure 10.41-10.45
who may apply 10.41-10.42
discretionary termination 10.63
final assessment 10.50
the formula 10.11
general rule 10.20
generally 10.10, 10.46
interim assessments 10.48
cancellation of 10.49
categories of 10.48
maintenance enquiry form 10.10, 10.46
maintenance periods 10.47
mandatory termination 10.62
review of *see* reviews *below*
maintenance pending suit, and 4.128

574 *Index*

Child Support Agency—*contd*
  maintenance periods 10.47
  maintenance requirement 10.12-10.13
  paternity
    disputes as to 10.64-10.65
    DNA testing 10.66
    proof of 2.33
  reduced benefit direction 10.51
  regular payment condition 10.55-10.58
  reviews
    change of circumstances, for 10.61
    child support officer's decision, of 10.73
    effective date of fresh maintenance assessments 10.70
    form of review 10.68
    fresh application 10.69
    generally 10.67
    procedure on 10.71-10.72
  staff of 10.09
  tax relief on payments 10.40
Children proceedings
  see also FAMILY PROCEEDINGS
  allocation of 2.24
  appeals
    case law concerning 8.125
    generally 8.122
    principles governing 8.123
    time for an appeal 8.124
  applications without leave
    prohibition against further 8.121
    section 8 orders 8.46
  avoidance of delay 2.17
  care order *see* CARE ORDER
  Children Act 1989, under 2.17
  contact order *see* CONTACT ORDER
  delay, avoidance of 8.03
  disposal of applications 8.77-8.81
  evidence and procedure
    see also EVIDENCE
    disclosure
      of expert reports 8.72
      local authorities, by 2.48
      nature of duty of 2.41
    excessive assessment or examination, protection from 2.56
    expert evidence 2.56, 8.132
      disclosure of expert reports 8.72
    hearsay 2.29
    inter-agency disclosure 8.73
    issue estoppel 8.76
    judicial findings 2.33
    judicial notice 2.31
    orphans 8.74
  examination of children 2.17, 2.61
    excessive, avoidance of 2.56
  generally 8.01
  guardians ad litem *see* GUARDIAN AD LITEM
  hearsay evidence 2.29
  issue estoppel 8.76

Children proceedings—*contd*
  practice and procedure
    allocation of proceedings 8.129
    avoidance of delay 2.17, 2.24
    case management 8.130
    Children Act 1989 proceedings 2.17
    experts 8.132
    Family Proceedings Courts (Children Act 1989) Rules 1991 8.128
    Family Proceedings Rules 1991 8.127
    generally 8.126
    justices' reasons 8.133
    leave to commence 2.17
    post-placement protection 8.135
    prescribed from of application 2.17
    procedural rules 2.17
    time estimates 8.131
    timetable 2.17
    welfare of the child 8.134
  prohibited steps order *see* PROHIBITED STEPS ORDER
  residence order *see* RESIDENCE ORDER
  section 37 reports 8.98-8.99
  section 8 orders *see* SECTION 8 ORDERS
  specific issue order *see* SPECIFIC ISSUE ORDER
  supervision order *see* SUPERVISION ORDER
  transfer of cases 2.24
  welfare of the child *see* WELFARE OF THE CHILD
  welfare and social work reports
    confidentiality and 8.17
    welfare officers
      attendance of 8.16
      conciliation, and 8.18
      recommendations of 8.15
    welfare reports 8.13
    who should report 8.14
    written or oral 8.13
Children's home
  local authority 9.10
Citizenship
  adoption, effects of 7.58
Clean break
  Duxbury sums
    element of risk in 4.42
    factors for consideration by parties 4.42
    generally 4.41
    suitable cases for 4.43
    taxable in another jurisdiction 4.243
  effective date 4.234
  financial provision orders, and 4.39
Cohabitants
  agreements between 3.3
  breakdown of relationship 3.3
  children of
    see also ILLEGITIMACY
    parental responsibility for 3.3, 5.06
  definition 5.05
  domestic violence, rights to protection 3.3, 5.05, 11.8-11.9

Cohabitants—*contd*
  financial support 3.3
  inheritance, and 6.16, 6.24, 6.27
  rights of 3.3
  sharing of property 3.3
  unmarried parents, parental
    responsibility, and 3.3, 5.06, 7.04-
    7.06, 7.45
Cohabitation agreements
  generally 3.3
Consent order
  agreements between the parties,
    relationship with 4.166
  see also AGREEMENTS BETWEEN THE PARTIES
  application for notice to show cause
    why agreement should not be made
    into order 4.167
  arbitration by third party 4.94
  Child Support Agency, attempting to
    exclude 4.163
  documents to be filed at court when
    applying 4.150, 4.151
  draft order
    agreements in 4.148, 4.149
    filing of 4.151
    recitals 4.144
    statement endorsing 4.151
      filing of 4.151
    subject matter of orders 4.145
    undertakings in 4.146, 4.147, 4.149
      to oust jurisdiction 4.149
  drafting of 4.142
    pitfalls in 4.147
  enforcement of 4.145
  Forms M11 and M13 4.152, 4.161
  generally 4.141
  neglect to maintain, where 4.200
  statement of information
    completion of 4.153
    contents of 4.155-4.162
      accommodation arrangements 4.158
      ages of parties/children 4.156
      capital resources and net income
        4.157
      duration of marriage 4.156
      orders relating to pension 4.160
      other significant matters 4.162
      remarriage/cohabitation, intentions
        regarding 4.159
      transfer of property 4.161
    drafting of 4.154
    erroneous completion of 4.164
    form of statement in variation/interim
      periodical payments application
      4.163
    reason for 4.154
  statutory authority for making 4.143
  third party, arbitration by 4.94
Consummation of marriage
  inability to consummate 3.8

Consummation of marriage—*contd*
  wilful refusal 3.8
Contact order
  see also SECTION 8 ORDERS
  adoption order, cross-application for
    7.88, 8.31
  age of child, and 7.21
  application without leave 8.46
  cessation of 8.24
  checklist, and 8.34
  definition 8.19, 13.7
  direct contact 8.24
  enforcement
    committal proceedings 13.8
    generally 13.7
    other than by committal 13.9
  forms of 8.24
  implacable hostility, where 8.26
  importance of contact 8.25
  indirect contact 8.24, 8.29
  infrequent contact 8.29
  interim contact 8.32
  local authorities, and 8.35, 8.63
  no knowledge of father, where 8.28
  other relatives 8.30
  paper dismissal 8.33
  refusal of contact, examples 8.27
  sexual abuse, where 8.27
  statutory restriction on making 8.43
  supervised contact 8.24
  transsexual parent, where 8.27
Costs
  Calderbank letters 15.18
  legal aid cases, in
    costs against the Legal Aid Board
      15.22-15.28
    costs against legally aided parties
      15.20-15.21
    statutory charge
      attempts to defeat 15.34-15.36
      creation of 15.31
      defined 15.30
      generally 15.29
      operation of 15.32
      postponement of 15.33
  principles governing award of 15.15,
    15.16
  'event' 15.17
  wasted costs order 15.19
County courts
  adoption procedure 7.91
    freeing application 7.92
  appeals from 2.2
  application for financial provision out of
    deceased's estate 6.31
  child, financial provision orders for 5.48,
    5.60
  declaration of trust, procedure for 5.41-
    5.42
  equitable jurisdiction 5.41

County courts—contd
  family proceedings in 2.2, 2.15
    see also FAMILY PROCEEDINGS
  financial relief proceedings 2.24
  injunctions
    domestic violence, where
      ex parte applications 11.2, 11.10-11.13
      inter partes applications 11.23-11.25
      generally 11.1
  liability orders, enforcement of 10.96
  Married Women's Property Act, jurisdiction under 5.34, 5.41
  witness summons 2.52, 2.53
Court of Appeal see APPEALS
Court welfare officers
  opinion evidence 2.65
  recommendations of 2.65
  report of 2.65
  role of 2.65

Death
  presumption of, dissolution of marriage 3.9
Disclosure
  see also DISCOVERY
  absolute duty to disclose 2.41
  children proceedings, in 2.41, 2.48, 8.72, 8.73
  definition 2.40
  discretion to order 2.43-2.47, 2.49
  documents tending to criminate 2.47
  excessive 2.42
  expert reports, of 8.72
  financial circumstances, of 3.28
  full and frank disclosure 1.8, 2.42
  full relevant disclosure 1.8, 2.42
  generally 2.39
  immunity from 2.44-2.47
  inter-agency 8.73
  legal professional privilege 2.45
  list, by 2.44
  local authorities, by 2.48
  medical report, of 8.72
  nature of duty 2.41
  parties, by 2.48
  pension, of 4.101
  privilege see PRIVILEGE
  public interest immunity 2.46
  relevant 2.42
  social workers, by 2.48
  'without prejudice' correspondence 2.46
Discovery
  see also DISCLOSURE
  compelling, as between parties 2.49-2.51
  definition 2.40
  documents tending to criminate 2.47
  evidence from third parties 2.52-2.54
  financial relief proceedings 2.18

Discovery—contd
  generally 2.39
  interrogatories 2.50
  particular documents, of 2.49
  production appointment 2.53
  rule 2.63 questionnaire 2.50n, 2.51
  specific discovery by third parties 2.54
  subpoena 2.52
  subpoena duces tecum 2.53
  video evidence 2.54
  witness summons 2.52, 2.53
Divorce
  assistance to attempting reconciliation 3.16
  children of the family 3.11
  decree absolute 2.19, 3.11
  decree nisi 2.19, 3.11
  Family Law Act 1996, under 3.19
    application for 3.31-3.32
    arrangements for the future 3.27
    children of the family 3.29
    financial arrangements 3.27
      court order 3.27
      declaration of no significant assets 3.27
      declaration as to 3.27
      exemption from 3.27
      negotiated agreement 3.27
    generally 3.19
    information meeting 3.22
    irretrievable breakdown 3.33-3.35
    jurisdiction 3.20
    legal advice 3.23
    orders preventing divorce 3.30
    period for reflection and consideration 3.25-3.26
    statement of marital breakdown 3.24
    steps to obtaining 3.21-3.35
  financial hardship bars 3.6, 3.17, 3.30
  financial provision orders see LUMP SUM ORDER; PERIODICAL PAYMENTS ORDER; PROPERTY ADJUSTMENT ORDER; SECURED PERIODICAL PAYMENTS ORDER
  framework of existing law 3.2
  inheritance, effect on 6.4
  irretrievable breakdown 3.1, 3.4, 3.6
    proof of 2.9, 3.1, 3.4
    five facts 3.4, 3.6
  jurisdiction 3.12-3.14, 3.20
    domicile 3.13, 3.20
      see also DOMICILE
    habitual residence 3.14, 3.20
  mediation 1.3, 3.1, 3.35
  new law 3.1
  old law 3.1
  order for, Family Law Act 1996 3.18
  orders preventing 3.30
  overseas, financial relief after 4.10
  pension rights, effect on see PENSIONS

Divorce—*contd*
  petition
    contents of 2.9
    defended 2.9
    pleadings in civil court 2.9
  procedure 3.10-3.11
  time bars 3.15
  wills, effect on 6.4
DNA testing
  disputes as to parentage 10.66
Documents
  discovery *see* DISCOVERY
  primary evidence, as 2.28
  tending to criminate 2.47
Domestic violence
  cohabitants, rights of 3.3, 5.05, 11.8-11.9
  generally 1.3, 3.2
  injunctions
    Children Act 1989 11.13, 11.17
    cohabitants, rights of 11.8-11.9
    Domestic Violence and Matrimonial Proceedings Act 1976 11.2-11.3, 11.10, 11.14, 11.23, 11.26
    ex parte applications
      county court, to 11.2, 11.10-11.13
      High Court, to 11.3, 11.14-11.18
      power of arrest 11.22
      principles applicable to determination of 11.20
      procedure upon the hearing 11.19
      time limits 11.21
      wardship proceedings, in 11.18
    exclusion injunctions
      Domestic Violence and Matrimonial Proceedings Act 1976 11.40
      financial consequences of exclusion 11.45
      generally 11.36
      house other than matrimonial home 11.44
      interlocutory relief in a matrimonial cause 11.41
      Matrimonial Homes Act 1983 11.38-11.39
      re-entry into matrimonial home 11.46
      rights of occupation 11.37
      third party, exclusion of 11.43
      Wardship and Children Act 1989 11.42
    inter partes applications
      adjournments 11.31
      county court, to 11.23-11.25
      High Court, to 11.26-11.29
      urgent applications procedure at the Royal Courts of Justice 11.30
      wardship proceedings, in 11.29
    interlocutory relief in a matrimonial cause 11.4, 11.11, 11.15, 11.24, 11.27, 11.41

Domestic violence—*contd*
  injunctions—*contd*
    Matrimonial Homes Act 1983 11.5-11.6, 11.12, 11.16, 11.25, 11.28, 11.38-11.39
    molestation, restraint of
      generally 11.4
      jurisdiction 11.32
      meaning of molestation 11.33
      principles on which the court acts 11.34
      undertakings 11.35
    ouster order 11.4
    power of arrest
      arrest for breach 11.48
      attachment of 11.47
      committal for breach 11.49
    wardship proceedings, in 11.6-11.7, 11.18, 11.29
  legal aid application 15.10
  occupation order *see* OCCUPATION ORDER
  unmarried couples, rights of 3.3, 5.05, 11.8-11.9
  wardship proceedings, application in 11.6-11.7, 11.18, 11.29
Domicile
  of choice 3.13
  of dependence 3.13
  divorce jurisdiction, and 3.13, 3.20
  establishing change of 3.13
  of origin 3.13

Education
  appeals against decisions 9.17
  local authorities, duties of 9.16
  parents
    duties of 9.16
    wishes of 9.16
  special needs 9.17, 9.18-9.19
    appeals against 9.21
    statement of 9.20
Education supervision order
  generally 8.93
Embryology *see* SURROGACY AND EMBRYOLOGY
Emergency protection order
  additional directions with 8.112-8.113
  additional powers to support 13.19-13.20
  appeals 8.118
  application for child assessment order treated as 8.105-8.106
  contact, and 8.113
  discharge of 8.117
  discovery of child 8.119
  duration of 8.115
  effect of 8.111, 13.16
  enforcement 13.16-13.20
  generally 13.16-13.17
  grounds for application 8.107-8.110
  local authority application 8.109
  procedure for 8.116
  punishment for breach 13.18

578 *Index*

Emergency protection order—*contd*
  return of the child 8.114
  significant harm, evidence of 8.108
Emigration
  child in care, of 8.80
  child looked after by local authority, of 8.81
Enforcement of financial orders
  appointment of receiver 12.46
  arrears complaint 12.14-12.16
  arrears over 12 months old 12.9
  attachment of earnings
    county courts, in 12.19-12.20
    generally 12.17-12.18
    High Court, in 12.19-12.20
    magistrates' court, in 12.21
    the order 12.23
    power of all courts 12.22
  charging order 12.30-12.33
  choosing the best method 12.5
  execution of instrument 12.34-12.35
  garnishee proceedings
    defences by the garnishee 12.26
    generally 12.24
    order absolute 12.27
    order nisi 12.25
  generally 12.1
  judgment summons 12.10-12.13
  means of payment order
    generally 12.28
    the order 12.29
  methods of 12.4
  oral examination 12.6-12.8
  order for possession 12.36-12.38
  order for sale 12.41-12.42
    directions as to manner of carrying out 12.43-12.44
  orders to be enforced 12.2-12.3
  receiver, appointment of 12.46
  registration in magistrates' court 12.47-12.48
  settlement of instrument, directions for 12.45
  writ of ne exeat regno 12.49
  writ of sequestration 12.39-12.40
  writ or warrant of possession 12.36-12.38
Engaged couples
  engagement, definition of 5.04
  financial disputes 5.08
  matrimonial home, improvements to 5.12
  termination of 5.08
Estoppel
  issue, children proceedings, in 8.76
  proprietary 5.25
Evidence
  admissibility 2.36-2.38
    cogency distinguished 2.38
    hearsay evidence 2.38

Evidence—*contd*
  admissibility—*contd*
    relevancy 2.37
    report of guardian ad litem 2.64
  admissions 2.34
  affidavits 2.10, 2.11
    as primary evidence 2.28
  burden of proof 2.26, 2.35
  demeanour 2.28
  disclosure *see* DISCLOSURE
  discovery *see* DISCOVERY
  documents 2.28
  dynamic nature of family cases, and 2.25
  exhibits 2.28
  expert *see* EXPERT EVIDENCE
  facts not needing proof 2.31-2.34
  financial relief proceedings 2.18
  forms of 2.28-2.30
  function of 2.1
  generally 2.25
  hearsay 2.28, 2.29
    admissibility of 2.38
  issue estoppel 2.32
  issues in the case
    cogency 2.38
    defining 2.36
    generally 2.36
    relevance 2.37
  judicial findings 2.33
  judicial notice 2.31
  magistrates' court, in 2.21
  means of proof 2.27-2.34
  opinion *see* EXPERT EVIDENCE
  oral 2.28
  presumptions 2.35
    rebuttable 2.35
  primary 2.28
  'real' 2.28
  res judicata 2.32
  rules of 2.25
  secondary 2.29
  standard of proof 2.26
  statements 2.11, 2.28
  tertiary 2.30
  text books 2.30
    see also EXPERT EVIDENCE
  third parties, from 2.52-2.54
  weight of 2.38
Execution of instrument
  enforcement by 12.34-12.35
Expert evidence
  acknowledged qualifications 2.59
  before the court 2.61
  characteristics of 2.58-2.59
  children proceedings, in 2.56, 8.132
    disclosure of expert reports 8.72
  cogency 2.60
  confidential documents 2.61
  court welfare officers 2.65
  credibility 2.59

Expert evidence—*contd*
evidence on the issue 2.60
examination of children 2.61
generally 2.25, 2.55
guardian ad litem 2.64
impartiality 2.58
limits of expertise 2.59
meeting of experts 2.57
mutuality of evidence 2.56
object of 2.55
Official Solicitor 2.63
opinions from known sources 2.59
partiality, avoidance of 2.59
personal prejudices and obsessions, avoidance of 2.59
primary evidence 2.29
secondary evidence 2.29
sources, reliance on 2.59
tertiary evidence 2.30
'without prejudice' meeting of experts 2.57

Family assistance order
discharge of 13.14
duration of 8.59, 13.14
enforcement 13.15
generally 8.59
person named in 8.59
purpose of 8.59
variation of 13.14

Family Law Act 1996
clean break, effective date of 4.234
divorce order *see* marital orders *below*
financial provision orders
after divorce/separation orders 4.223
capital orders on variation application 4.233
different orders on different occasions 4.221
generally 4.217
interim orders 4.219
occasions for 4.220
lump sum order 4.212, 4.213, 4.219, 4.222, 4.229
nullity cases, in 4.224-4.225
pension splitting orders 4.214, 4.231
periodical payments order 4.219, 4.229
property adjustment orders 4.212, 4.213, 4.224-4.225, 4.226-4.228, 4.230
secured periodical payments order 4.229
timing of 4.218
variations etc following reconciliation 4.230
financial relief
amendments to existing law 4.210-4.214
generally 4.209
nullity 4.211

Family Law Act 1996—*contd*
financial relief—*contd*
Part I, and 4.215
pensions 4.214
s 15 and Sch 2, and 4.216
timing of orders 4.212
variation/discharge of capital orders 4.213
generally 1.10, 3.18
marital orders 3.19
application for 3.31-3.32
arrangements for the future 3.27
children of the family 3.29
financial arrangements 3.27, 4.209
see also financial provision order; financial relief *above*
court order 3.27
declaration of no significant assets 3.27
declaration as to 3.27
exemption from 3.27
negotiated agreement 3.27
generally 3.21
information meeting 3.22
irretrievable breakdown 3.33-3.35
jurisdiction 3.20
legal advice 3.23
orders preventing divorce 3.30
period for reflection and consideration 3.25-3.26
statement of marital breakdown 3.24
steps to obtaining 3.21-3.35
nullity cases, effects on 4.211, 4.224-4.225
pension splitting orders 4.214, 4.231
separation order *see* marital orders *above*

Family proceedings
affidavit evidence 2.10, 2.11
allocation of proceedings 2.23-2.24
appeals *see* APPEALS
application to set aside order 2.66, 2.69
case management 2.22
children proceedings *see* CHILDREN PROCEEDINGS
defining 2.4
disclosure *see* DISCLOSURE
discovery *see* DISCOVERY
evidence *see* EVIDENCE
family courts 2.2, 2.15
see also COUNTY COURTS; FAMILY PROCEEDINGS COURTS; HIGH COURT; MAGISTRATES' COURT
family proceedings *see* FAMILY PROCEEDINGS COURTS
financial relief proceedings *see* FINANCIAL RELIEF PROCEEDINGS
generally 2.1, 2.14
interrogatories *see* INTERROGATORIES
judicial review in 9.32
see also JUDICIAL REVIEW
magistrates' court process 2.21

Family proceedings—*contd*
matrimonial causes 2.19
meaning of 2.1
originating summons 2.10, 2.20
procedural rules 2.16-2.21
see also CHILDREN PROCEEDINGS; FINANCIAL RELIEF PROCEEDINGS; MATRIMONIAL CAUSES; ORIGINATING SUMMONS
generally 2.16
procedure, generally 2.14-2.24
rehearing, order for 2.69
skeleton arguments, filing of 2.11n
statements 2.11, 2.28
transfer of cases 2.24

Family proceedings courts
see also PROCEDURE
appeals from 2.2, 2.75
children applications 2.8
financial relief applications 2.8
jurisdiction 2.2, 2.15
pleadings contrasted with applications in family proceedings 2.8-2.9
procedure 2.1, 2.2-2.3, 2.15
rules for family process 2.5-2.6

Father
see also MOTHER; PARENTAL RESPONSIBILITY; PATERNITY
acquisition of parental responsibility 5.06, 7.04-7.06
adoption, application for 7.67
Human Fertilisation and Embryology Act 1990, and 6.9

Financial disputes
engaged couples 5.08
Married Women's Property Act 1882 5.10
Matrimonial Causes (Property and Maintenance) Act 1958 5.11
matrimonial home, improvements to 5.12
see also MATRIMONIAL HOME
people who have married 5.07
trust *see* TRUST

Financial hardship bars
matrimonial causes 3.6, 3.17, 3.30

Financial orders
enforcement of *see* ENFORCEMENT OF FINANCIAL ORDERS

Financial provision orders *see* LUMP SUM ORDER; PERIODICAL PAYMENTS ORDER; PROPERTY ADJUSTMENT ORDER; SECURED PERIODICAL PAYMENTS ORDER

Financial relief *see* MAINTENANCE

Financial relief proceedings
see also FAMILY PROCEEDINGS
affidavit evidence 2.18
allocation of 2.24
discovery 2.18
evidence 2.18
interrogatories 2.18, 2.50

Financial relief proceedings—*contd*
originating summons procedure 2.10, 2.18
procedural rules 2.18

Foetus *see* UNBORN CHILD

Foster parents
local authority 9.8
placement with 9.8
residence orders, application for 9.9

Gamete donors *see* SURROGACY AND EMBRYOLOGY

Garnishee proceedings
defences by the garnishee 12.26
enforcement by 12.24-12.27
generally 12.24
order absolute 12.27
order nisi 12.25

Gillick **competence**
generally 7.24-7.26

Guardian
appointment of 7.08
  by court 7.09
    procedure 7.10
  by parent 7.11
  by previous guardian 7.12
effect of 7.13
revocation of 7.15, 7.17
taking effect of 7.14
court revocation of guardianship 7.17
disclaimer of guardianship 7.16
parental responsibility, and 7.02, 7.03

Guardian ad litem
appointment of 2.64
  specified proceedings, in 8.52, 8.101
case law guidance 8.101
confidentiality 8.101
duties of 2.64
generally 8.101
Official Solicitor as 2.63, 8.56
opinion evidence 2.64
records, right to examine 8.101
report of 2.64
role of 2.64

Habitual residence
divorce jurisdiction, and 3.14
meaning 3.14

High Court
adoption procedure 7.91
  freeing application 7.92
appeals from 2.2
appeals to, from family proceedings court 2.2
application for financial provision out of deceased's estate 6.30
attachment of earnings order 12.17-12.20
child, financial provision orders for 5.48, 5.60

High Court—*contd*
  declaration of trust, procedure for 5.43
  family proceedings, in 2.2, 2.15
    see also FAMILY PROCEEDINGS
    section 8 orders 2.3
  financial relief proceedings 2.24
  injunctions
    domestic violence, where
      ex parte applications 11.3, 11.14-11.18
      inter partes applications 11.26-11.29
    generally 11.1
  Married Women's Property Act, jurisdiction under 5.34
  oral examination of debtor in 12.7-12.8
  subpoena 2.52
  wardship
    defendants to 7.36
    inherent jurisdiction
      basis of 7.28
      generally 7.27
      limitations on 7.29, 7.30, 7.33
      procedure under 7.37
      uses of 7.31, 7.34
    proceedings 7.35
HIV testing
  order permitting 8.40
Homosexual parent
  residence order, and 8.21
House of Lords
  appeals to 2.2

Illegitimacy
  see also COHABITANTS; LEGITIMACY
  birth, beginning of 7.45
  concept of 7.45
  declaration of 7.51
  inheritance, and 6.9
  legitimation 6.9, 7.48, 7.51
  parental responsibility, and 3.3, 5.06, 7.04-7.06, 7.45
  subsequent marriage, and 7.48
In vitro **fertilisation** *see* SURROGACY AND EMBRYOLOGY
Incest *see* PROHIBITED DEGREES OF RELATIONSHIP
Income tax
  maintenance, and
    generally 4.236
    increases in maintenance 4.240
    new rules
      election for 4.242
      payments 4.241
    old rules 4.237
    payee 4.239
    tax paid in another jurisdiction 4.243
    tax relief 4.238
Independent visitor *see under* LOCAL AUTHORITIES
Inheritance
  divorce, effect of 6.4

Inheritance—*contd*
  family provision
    children 6.17, 6.25
      step-children 6.18, 6.26
    classes of applicants 6.13-6.19
    cohabitants 6.16, 6.24, 6.27
    former spouse 6.15, 6.23
    generally 6.12
    net estate
      contracts 6.36
      defined 6.32-6.36
      donationes mortis causa 6.32
      inter vivos dispositions 6.35
      joint tenancies 6.33
      nominations 6.32
      powers of appointment 6.32
    other dependants 6.19, 6.27
    procedure 6.29
      county courts 6.31
      High Court 6.30
    spouse 6.14, 6.22
    statutory criteria 6.21-6.27
    threshold conditions 6.20
    time limits 6.28
    types of order 6.37
  intestate succession
    generally 6.6
    issue
      adopted 6.9
      entitlement 6.10
      Human Fertilisation and Embryology Act 1990, and 6.9
      illegitimate 6.9
      legitimate 6.9
      legitimated 6.9
      qualification 6.9
      of void marriage 6.9
    partial intestacy 6.6
    relatives 6.11
    spouse
      entitlement 6.8
      fixed net sum 6.8
      life interest 6.8
      marriage 6.7
      matrimonial home 6.8
      personal chattels 6.8
      survival 6.7
  judicial separation, effect on 6.5
  marriage
    effect of 6.2
    wills in expectation of 6.3
  matrimonial home 6.8
  nullity, effect of 6.4
  partial intestacy 6.6
  pension rights 4.110
  personal chattels 6.8
  polygamy, and 6.14
  step-children 6.18, 6.26
  succession, intestate 6.6
  wills
    divorce, effect of 6.4

Inheritance—contd
  wills—contd
    in expectation of marriage 6.3
    marriage, effect of 6.2
    nullity, effect of 6.4
Injunctions
  abortion, prevention of 7.20
  breach, court orders upon proof of 14.10
  domestic violence, and *see under* DOMESTIC VIOLENCE
  effect of 11.1
  enforcement
    committal to prison 14.1, 14.2
      application to commit
        affidavit in answer 14.8
        affidavit in support 14.7
          service of 14.7
        contents of 14.5
        generally 14.4
        hearing of 14.9
        non-parties 14.13
        service of 14.7
      discharge from prison of person committed for contempt 14.14
      order for committal 14.11
      suspended committal orders 14.12
    court orders upon proof of breach 14.10
  exclusion injunctions *see under* DOMESTIC VIOLENCE
  financial relief, and
    acting for parties to applications
      applicant 4.191
      respondent 4.192
      third party 4.193
    Anton Piller order *see* ANTON PILLER ORDER
    avoidance of transactions intended to prevent or reduce 4.175
    costs 4.184
    disposition
      intended to defeat claims of wife 4.177, 4.178
      meaning of 4.179
      reviewable *see* reviewable disposition *below*
      setting aside 4.177
    financial relief
      defeating a person's claim for 4.176
      definition of 4.176
    generally 4.172
    Mareva injunction *see* MAREVA INJUNCTION
    obtaining undertakings rather than orders 4.174
    order freezing money in bank account 4.177
      see also MAREVA INJUNCTION
    orders which can be made 4.177
    procedure
      affidavit 4.181
      application 4.180

Injunctions—contd
  financial relief, and—contd
    procedure—contd
      directions 4.182
      interveners 4.183
      reasons for application 4.172
      reviewable disposition
        making of 4.177
        meaning of 4.178
      types of order available 4.173
  jurisdiction to grant 11.1
  Married Women's Property Act 1882, under 5.38
Interrogatories
  discovery, and 2.50
  discretion of the court, and 2.50
  financial provision for children 2.50
  financial relief proceedings 2.18, 2.50
  purpose of 2.50
Issue estoppel *see under* ESTOPPEL

Judgment summons
  application for committal by way of 12.10-12.13
Judicial findings
  see also EVIDENCE
  generally 2.33
Judicial notice
  see also EVIDENCE
  generally 2.31
Judicial review
  certiorari 9.30
  Child Support Agency (CSA), decision of 10.85
  declarations 9.30
  discharge of leave 9.26
  family proceedings, in 9.32
  grant of leave 9.27
  injunctions 9.30
  interim order 9.28
  legal aid 15.10
  mandamus 9.30
  meaning 9.22
  oral evidence 2.28n
  persons whom proceedings may be brought against 9.25
  private law cases 9.34
  procedure 9.23
  prohibition 9.30
  public law cases, examples 9.33
  purpose of 9.22
  refusal of 9.37
  remedies 9.30
  representation of children, and, under Children Act 1989 9.38
  scope of 9.30
  steps to be taken by respondent 9.29
  substantive application for 9.27
  time limit 9.31
  wardship, and 9.35-9.36

Index 583

Judicial review—*contd*
who may apply 9.24
Judicial separation
see also MATRIMONIAL CAUSES
effect of decree 3.7
financial provision orders *see* LUMP SUM ORDER; PERIODICAL PAYMENTS ORDER; PROPERTY ADJUSTMENT ORDER; SECURED PERIODICAL PAYMENTS ORDER
generally 3.7
grounds for 3.7
inheritance, effect on 6.5
mediation 3.1
no time bar 3.15
pension rights, effect on 4.105
see also PENSIONS
procedure 3.10
wills, effect on 6.5

Legal aid
ABWOR application 15.5, 15.7, 15.8, 15.10
adoption application 15.10
application for 15.10
availability 15.1, 15.4
civil proceedings 15.3
conduct of proceedings
 duty to inform Board 15.12-15.13
 money on account 15.14
 scope of certificate 15.11
costs
 against the Legal Aid Board 15.22-15.28
 against legally aided parties 15.20-15.21
 statutory charge *see* statutory charge *below*
criminal proceedings 15.3
eligibility
 ABWOR applications 15.5, 15.7, 15.8
 civil legal aid 15.6-15.8
 disposable capital 15.6
 disposable income 15.6
 financial 15.5-15.6
 green form applications 15.5, 15.8
 merits 15.8
 proceedings 15.7
emergency application 15.10
family and child law, for 15.3
forms 15.10
free-standing children application 15.10
generally 1.9, 15.1-15.2
green form applications 15.4, 15.5, 15.8
judicial review 15.10
matrimonial application 15.10
non-matrimonial application 15.10
special Children Act proceedings 15.9
statutory charge
 attempts to defeat 15.34-15.36
 creation of 15.31
 defined 15.30

Legal aid—*contd*
statutory charge—*contd*
 generally 15.29
 operation of 15.32
  postponement of 15.33
wardship application 15.10
Legal professional privilege *see* PRIVILEGE
Legitimacy
see also ILLEGITIMACY
adoption, and 7.50, 7.57
artificial insemination, and 7.47
birth, beginning of 7.45
common law, at 7.46
declaration of 7.51
generally 7.45
inheritance, and 6.9
 legitimated children 6.9
legitimation 6.9, 7.48, 7.51
parental responsibility, and 7.45
presumption of 7.46
statute, by 7.47
void marriages, and 7.49
voidable marriages, and 7.49
Local authorities
adoption services 7.59
appeals 9.17
child assessment orders 8.104-8.106
child in care of *see* CHILD IN CARE
child in need defined 9.2-9.3
children's homes 9.10
contact orders, and 8.35, 8.63
disclosure, children proceedings, in 2.48
duties of, generally 9.1
duty to investigate 8.102-8.103
education 9.16
 appeals against decisions 9.17
 parents' wishes 9.16
 special needs *see* special needs *below*
emergency protection order, application for 8.109
foster parents 9.8
independent visitor
 appointment of 9.11
 role of 9.11
placement of children 9.8
protection of children, duty to investigate 8.102-8.103
Register of Disability 9.3
representations 9.15
reviews 9.13
 child in secure accommodation 9.14
section 37 reports 9.98-9.99
secure accommodation 9.12
 detention period 9.12
 reasons for 9.12
 review of cases 9.14
services which must be provided
 children living with their families, for 9.4-9.5

Local authorities—*contd*
 services which must be provided—*contd*
  children looked after by local
   authorities, for 9.6-9.7
  special needs
   see also education *above*
   children having 9.18-9.19
   parents' appeal against assessment 8.21
   statement of 9.20
  wardship, application for 7.30
Lump sum order
 appropriation directions 4.55-4.56
  assurances and undertakings 4.56
 bankruptcy, and 4.277-4.281
 child, financial provision for 5.55
 clean break, and 4.39
 discharge of 4.11, 4.134, 4.137, 4.213
 enforcement *see* ENFORCEMENT OF FINANCIAL
  ORDERS
 Family Law Act 1996, effect of 4.212,
  4.213, 4.219, 4.222, 4.229
 generally 4.3, 4.53
 interest on 4.59
 neglect to maintain, where 4.197
 one lump sum order 4.54
 order for sale of property *see* SALE OF
  PROPERTY, ORDER FOR
 payment by instalments 4.57, 4.135,
  5.55
 pensions 4.57, 4.115
 person over 18, for 5.57
 punitive 4.233
 securing 4.58
 specified lump sum 4.54
 time for payment of 4.60
 timing of 4.212
 unspecified further amount 4.54
 variation of 4.135, 4.213
  application for
   factors to be taken into account
    4.139
   limitation on orders that may be
    made in 4.136
   procedure 4.140
  following reconciliation 4.229
  powers of the court 4.11, 4.134

Magistrates' court
 see also FAMILY PROCEEDINGS; FAMILY
  PROCEEDINGS COURTS
 adoption procedure 7.93
 appeals from 5.61
 application to 2.21
 attachment of earnings order 12.21
 care proceedings 2.3
 child, financial provision orders for 5.49,
  5.60
  appeals against 5.61
 emergency protection order, application
  for 8.116

Magistrates' court—*contd*
 evidence in 2.21
 maintenance order, registration of 12.47
 process 2.21
 residence order, enforcement of 13.6
Maintenance
 alteration of agreements by court during
  lives of parties 4.9
 bankruptcy, and 4.274-4.276
  see also BANKRUPTCY
 Barry directions 4.7
 capital gains tax, and *see* CAPITAL GAINS
  TAX
 child, of *see* CHILD MAINTENANCE ORDERS; CHILD
  SUPPORT ACT 1991; CHILD SUPPORT AGENCY
 clean break *see* CLEAN BREAK
 consent orders and agreements *see* CONSENT
  ORDERS AND AGREEMENTS
 discharge of orders 4.11, 4.134, 4.137
 Domestic Proceedings and Magistrates'
  Courts Act 1978 4.8
 Family Law Act 1996, and *see under*
  FAMILY LAW ACT 1996
 financial provision orders
  divorce, nullity, judicial separation, in
   see LUMP SUM ORDER; PERIODICAL PAYMENT;
   PERIODICAL PAYMENTS ORDER; PROPERTY
   ADJUSTMENT ORDER; SECURED PERIODICAL
   PAYMENTS ORDER
  neglect to maintain, where *see* neglect
   to maintain *below*
 generally 4.1
 income tax, and *see* INCOME TAX
 injunctions and financial relief *see under*
  INJUNCTIONS
 interim order for
  see also MAINTENANCE PENDING SUIT
  Family Law Act 1996, and 4.219,
   4.220
  occasions for 4.220
  variation of 4.135
   application for
    factors to be taken into account
     4.139
    limitation on orders that may be
     made in 4.136
    procedure 4.140
   powers of the court 4.11, 4.134
 lump sum order *see* LUMP SUM ORDER
 Matrimonial and Family Proceedings Act
  1984, Part III
  avoidance of transactions intended to
   defeat applications for financial
   relief 4.208
  filter of leave 4.204
  generally 4.201
  jurisdiction race 4.202
  leave to make application for financial
   relief
   procedure 4.205

Maintenance—*contd*
Matrimonial and Family Proceedings Act 1984, Part III—*contd*
leave to make application for financial relief
progress following grant of 4.206
no financial relief in overseas proceedings 4.203
substantive orders under 4.207
uses of 4.202-4.203
neglect to maintain, financial relief application
considerations in determining 4.196
generally 4.6, 4.194, 4.197
jurisdiction 4.195
precedent matters 4.200
procedure 4.198
service on respondent 4.199
types of orders 4.197
pending suit *see* MAINTENANCE PENDING SUIT
pensions *see* PENSIONS
periodical payments order *see* PERIODICAL PAYMENTS ORDER
property adjustment order *see* PROPERTY ADJUSTMENT ORDER
sale of property, order for *see* SALE OF PROPERTY, ORDER FOR
section 25 factors
age of each party 4.24
capital 4.21
children of the family 4.13, 4.30-4.31
duration of marriage 4.25-4.29
earning capacity, and 4.18
exercise of powers under 4.14-4.29
financial obligations and responsibilities 4.22-4.23
generally 4.12
income 4.17, 4.20
needs and resources 4.15-4.16
property and other financial resources 4.19
terminating each party's financial obligations 4.32
tax considerations *see* CAPITAL GAINS TAX; INCOME TAX
variations *see* VARIATIONS
Maintenance pending suit
application
affidavit in reply 4.132
affidavit in support 4.131
procedure for making 4.130
time for making 4.129
Child Support Act implications 4.128
corresponding orders 4.133
discharge of 4.11, 4.134, 4.137
enforcement *see* ENFORCEMENT OF FINANCIAL ORDERS
Family Law Act 1996, and 4.219
generally 4.5, 4.125
meaning 4.125

Maintenance pending suit—*contd*
no existing regime of maintenance, when 4.127
retention of status quo 4.126
variation of 4.135
application for
factors to be taken into account 4.139
limitation on orders that may be made in 4.136
procedure 4.140
powers of the court 4.11, 4.134
Mareva injunction
see also INJUNCTIONS
application for 4.187
acting for parties to
applicant 4.191
respondent 4.192
third party 4.193
documentation required 4.190
effects of 4.185
generally 4.173, 4.185
grounds for seeking 4.187
in personam operation of 4.186
jurisdiction for making 4.186
inherent 4.186n
procedural requirements 4.187
Marriage
age of consent 7.21
consummation of
inability to consummate 3.8
wilful refusal of 3.8
definition 5.03
nullity of *see* NULLITY
remarriage, effects of 4.33, 4.37
wills
effect on 6.2
in expectation of 6.3
Married women
financial disputes 5.10
personal property 5.30
Martin **order** *see under* PROPERTY ADJUSTMENT ORDERS
Matrimonial causes
assistance to attempting reconciliation 3.16
divorce *see* DIVORCE
Family Law Act 1996 *see* FAMILY LAW ACT 1996
financial hardship bars 3.6, 3.17, 3.30
generally 3.5
improvements to 5.24
judicial separation *see* JUDICIAL SEPARATION
jurisdiction
domicile 3.13, 3.20
see also DOMICILE
generally 3.12, 3.20
habitual residence 3.14, 3.20
meaning 3.5
nullity *see* NULLITY

586 *Index*

Matrimonial causes—*contd*
  presumption of death and dissolution 3.9
  procedure 3.10-3.11
    procedural rules 2.19
    undefended cause, where 2.19
  time bars 3.15
  trust, law of, and *see* TRUST
Matrimonial home
  bankruptcy, and
    case law guidance 4.254-4.255
    equity of exoneration 4.262
    establishing a beneficial interest 4.256-4.257
      significance of 4.258
    generally 4.251
    jointly owned, where 4.259-4.261
    reviewable transactions
      case law 4.265
      generally 4.263
      transactions at an undervalue 4.264
      transactions defrauding creditors 4.268-4.269
      voidable preferences 4.266-4.267
    soley owned, where 4.252-4.253
  capital gains tax 4.245
  contributions to purchase price other than through mortgage 5.19
  disputes as to 5.12
    see also TRUST
  documents of title 5.16
  equity of exoneration, and 4.262, 5.26
  exclusion injunctions *see under* DOMESTIC VIOLENCE
  formerly engaged couples, and 5.12
  improvements to 5.12
  inferred common intention 5.18
  intestate succession, and 6.8
  mortgages
    contributions to payments 5.20, 5.22
    liability as contribution 5.20, 5.21
  occupation, rights of 11.37
  orders relating to 4.145
  re-entry into 11.46
  sale of 5.29
  settlement of property 4.69
Means of payment order
  enforcement by 12.28-12.29
  generally 12.28
  the order 12.29
Medical examination
  consent to 8.106
  making of interim care or supervision order, on 8.96
Medical report
  disclosure of 8.72
Medical treatment
  consent to 7.21, 7.22
  emergency treatment 7.25
  Gillick competence 7.24-7.26
  sterilisation of minor 8.40

Mesher order *see under* PROPERTY ADJUSTMENT ORDERS
Mother
  see also FATHER; PARENTAL RESPONSIBILITY; SURROGACY AND EMBRYOLOGY
  adoption, application for 7.67
  definition, Human Fertilisation and Embryology Act 1990 6.9, 7.41

Neglect to maintain *see under* MAINTENANCE
Next friend
  Official Solicitor as 2.63, 8.56
'Non-adversarial' procedures
  generally 1.7
Nullity
  see also MATRIMONIAL CAUSES
  financial provision orders
    see also LUMP SUM ORDER; PERIODICAL PAYMENTS ORDER; PROPERTY ADJUSTMENT ORDER; SECURED PERIODICAL PAYMENTS ORDER
    Family Law Act 1996, effect of 4.211, 4.224-4.225
    generally 3.1, 3.8
    inheritance, effect on 6.4
  jurisdiction 3.12
  no time bar 3.15
  void marriage *see* VOID MARRIAGE
  voidable marriage *see* VOIDABLE MARRIAGE
  wills, effect on 6.4
Nuptial settlements
  see also PROPERTY ADJUSTMENT ORDERS
  Brooks 4.79, 4.108n
  definition of 4.78-4.79
  pensions, and 4.108
  settlements which are not 4.80-4.81
  variation of 4.77

Official Solicitor
  guardian ad litem, as 2.63, 8.56
  next friend, as 2.63, 8.56
  opinion evidence 2.62, 2.63
Oral examination
  enforcement of financial orders by 12.6-12.8
Order for possession
  enforcement by 12.36-12.38
Order for sale of property *see* SALE OF PROPERTY, ORDER FOR
Originating summons procedure
  see also PLEADINGS; PROCEDURE
  affidavit evidence 2.28
  financial relief proceedings 2.18
  generally 2.10, 2.20
Orphan
  care order 8.74

Overseas adoption
  Convention adoption 7.77, 7.95
  generally 7.62
  international adoptions 7.97, 7.98-7.99
  notice to Home Office 7.71
  recognition at common law 7.96
Overseas divorce
  financial relief after 4.10, 4.203

Parent
  definition of 5.50
    see also FATHER; MOTHER
  homosexual 8.21
  transsexual 8.27
Parentage
  declaration of 7.51
Parental orders
  see also SURROGACY AND EMBRYOLOGY
  application procedure 7.43
  conditions to be satisfied 7.42
Parental responsibility
  acquisition by father 5.06, 7.04-7.06
  adoptive parents 7.03, 7.57, 7.86
  care order conferring 8.63
  cohabitants 3.3, 5.06
  definition 7.02-7.03
  generally 5.06
  guardian, and 7.02, 7.03
    see also GUARDIAN
  illegitimacy, and 7.45
    see also unmarried parents *below*
  legitimacy, and 7.45
  local authorities, and 7.03
  more than one person having 7.03
  parental responsibility agreement 7.05
  parental responsibility order 7.06
  persons having 5.06, 7.03
  residence order, where 7.03
  rights conferred by 7.02
  termination of 7.07
  unmarried parents 3.3, 5.06, 7.04-7.06, 7.45
Paternity, proof of
  blood tests *see* BLOOD TESTS
  Child Support Agency, and *see under* CHILD SUPPORT AGENCY
Pensions
  application of the law 4.102-4.104
  attachment of pension order 4.113
  capital locked up in pension schemes 4.104
  commutation of benefit 4.114
  dealing with 4.107
  disclosure of 4.101
  duty to consider making an order relating to pension 4.116
  ear-marking 3.30, 4.111
  Family Law Act 1996, and 4.214
  generally 1.3, 4.100

Pensions—*contd*
  information by and to pension schemes, provision of 4.121
  Inheritance Act claims 4.110
  loss of pension rights 4.105-4.106
  lump sum order 4.57, 4.115
  new provisions, commencement of 4.122
  nuptial settlements, and 4.108
  occupational pension schemes 4.101
  orders and undertakings relating to
    undertaking to make nomination 4.109
    variation of settlement 4.108, 4.163
  pension scheme, definition of 4.123
  pension-splitting 3.30, 4.111, 4.214, 4.231
  Pensions Act 1995, s 166 4.111-4.124
    amendments under 4.112
    regulations under 4.120
  personal pension policies, interest under 4.101
  self-administered pension scheme, interest under 4.101
  self-employed retirement annuity contracts 4.101
  source of periodic payments, as 4.103
  trustees
    determining discretion of 4.118-4.119
    notices to
      application for consent order, where 4.160
      change of circumstances, where 4.121
    orders directed at 4.117
  unapproved schemes and arrangements 4.101
  undertaking to make nomination 4.109
  variation of pension orders 4.124, 4.163
  variation of settlement 4.108
Periodical payments order
  clean break, and 4.39
    Duxbury sums
      element of risk in 4.42
      factors for consideration by parties 4.42
      generally 4.41
      suitable cases for 4.43
  death of payee 4.33
  death of payer 4.33
  discharge of 4.11, 4.134, 4.137, 4.233, 5.58
  dismissal of 4.44-4.45
  duration of 4.36
  enforcement *see* ENFORCEMENT OF FINANCIAL ORDERS
  Family Law Act 1996, and 4.219, 4.229
  further duty of the court 4.40
  generally 4.3, 4.9
  maintenance pending suit 4.125
  neglect to maintain, where 4.197

Periodical payments order—*contd*
non-extendable term orders and dismissals 4.35
order without term 4.33
payment of periodical payments 4.38
pensions as source of periodical payments 4.103
period of 4.229
persons over 18, relief for 5.57
remarriage, effect of 4.33, 4.37
secured *see* SECURED PERIODICAL PAYMENTS ORDER
term order 4.33
term order and dismissals 4.34
variation of 4.48, 4.135, 4.163, 4.233, 5.58
  application for
    factors to be taken into account 4.139
    limitation on orders that may be made in 4.136
    procedure 4.140
  powers of the court 4.11, 4.134

Personal property
bank accounts 5.32
county court jurisdiction 5.41
express agreement, arrangement or understanding as to ownership 5.32
generally 5.32
Law of Property Act 1925, under 5.31
  procedure 5.40
Married Women's Property Act 1882, under
  form of application 5.35
  generally 5.30
  injunction, grant of 5.38
  jurisdiction 5.34
  particulars of property and mortgage 5.37
  procedure 5.33-5.39
  respondent 5.37
ownership of chattels used in part-exchange 5.32
source of money used to buy 5.32
trust, declarations of 5.41
  procedure
    in county court 5.42
    in High Court 5.43

Pleadings
affidavits, contrasted with 2.11, 2.36
applications in family proceedings, contrasted with 2.8-2.9
contents of 2.36
crystallisation of issues 2.13
divorce petitions 2.9
evolving issues 2.12
function of 2.1
generally 2.7
originating summons procedure 2.10
quasi-pleadings 2.11n
statements, contrasted with 2.11, 2.36

Police
protection of children by 8.120
Polygamy
see also NULLITY
inheritance, and 6.14
marriage void for 3.8
Post-nuptial settlement *see* NUPTIAL SETTLEMENTS
Pre-birth injuries
suing for 7.20
Presumptions
death and dissolution, of 3.9
generally 2.35
legitimacy, of 7.46
rebuttable 2.35, 3.9
Private agreements between the parties *see* AGREEMENTS BETWEEN THE PARTIES
Privilege
see also DISCLOSURE
documents tending to criminate 2.47
generally 2.41
legal professional 2.45, 8.72
public interest immunity 2.46
'without prejudice' correspondence 2.46
Prohibited degrees of relationship
adoption, effect of 7.58
marriage void for 3.8
Prohibited steps order
see also SECTION 8 ORDERS
age of child, and 7.21
definition 8.19, 13.10
enforcement 13.10-13.11
generally 8.36
jurisdiction, removal from 8.37, 8.38
non-party, against 8.39
penal notice attached to 13.12
remedies for breach 13.12
restrictions on local authority 8.44
restrictions on use 8.36
statutory restriction on making 8.43
Property adjustment orders
ante-nuptial settlement *see* nuptial settlements *below*
charge
  in favour of a party 4.71
  fixed sum 4.72
  proportion of equity/sale proceeds 4.72
  redemption before determining event 4.76
  terms of 4.73
clean break, and 4.39
discharge of 4.11, 4.134, 4.137, 4.213
Family Law Act 1996, and 4.212, 4.213, 4.224-4.225, 4.226-4.228, 4.230
generally 4.3, 4.61
jurisdiction of court to make one or more orders under s 24 4.64
Martin orders 4.70
Mesher orders 4.70
nullity cases, in 4.224-4.225

Property adjustment orders—*contd*
  nuptial settlements
    Brooks 4.79, 4.108n
    definition of 4.78-4.79
    settlements which are not 4.80-4.81
    variation of 4.77
  order for sale of property *see* SALE OF PROPERTY, ORDER FOR
  post-nuptial settlement *see* nuptial settlements *above*
  precautionary measures 4.62
  procedure on applications
    affidavit 4.83
    Form M11/M13 4.84
    generally 4.82
  property held in name of third party on behalf of one of parties to marriage 4.67
  punitive 4.233
  remarriage, effect of 4.37
  service on third parties 4.85
  settlement of property 4.68
    former matrimonial home 4.69
    variation of 4.135
  substitute property, purchase of 4.74
  third parties
    affidavit in answer by 4.86
    service on 4.85
  timing of 4.63, 4.212, 4.227-4.228
  transfer of property 4.65
    practicality of 4.66
  trust
    purchase of substitute property 4.74
    responsibility for outgoings 4.75
    terms of 4.73
  types of 4.61
  variation of 4.11, 4.134, 4.137, 4.213
    application for
      factors to be taken into account 4.139
      limitation on orders that may be made in 4.136
      procedure 4.140
    following reconciliation 4.230
    powers of the court 4.11, 4.134
Proprietary estoppel *see* ESTOPPEL
Psychiatric examination
  consent to 8.106
  making of interim care or supervision order, on 8.96
Public interest immunity
  see also DISCLOSURE; PRIVILEGE
  generally 2.46

Receiver
  appointment of 12.46
Recovery order *see* ABDUCTION
Relationships *see* COHABITEES; ENGAGED COUPLES; MARRIAGE
Remarriage
  effects of 4.33, 4.37

Residence *see* HABITUAL RESIDENCE
Residence order
  see also SECTION 8 ORDERS
  age of child, and 7.21, 8.21
  alternative to care order, as 8.78
  ancillary relief 8.21
  application for
    after wardship order 8.22
    foster parents, by 9.9
    without leave 8.46
  case law 8.21
  children together 8.21
  definition 8.19, 13.1
  effects of 8.20
  enforcement
    committal proceedings 13.3
    generally 13.1-13.2
    magistrates' court, in 13.6
    other than by committal 13.4
    procedure 13.5
  ex parte order 8.23
  family arrangements unsettled, where 8.21
  generally 8.20
  homosexual parent, and 8.21
  parental preference, and 8.21
  religion, and 8.21
  shared 8.57
  siblings 8.21
  status quo, maintenance of 8.21
  statutory restriction on making 8.43

Sale of property, order for
  clean break, and 4.39
  directions as to manner of carrying out 12.43-12.44
  discharge of 4.11, 4.134, 4.137
  enforcement by 12.41-12.42
  examples of 4.88
  generally 4.4, 4.87, 4.99
  procedure 4.97
  termination of 4.98
  terms of
    arbitration clauses 4.94
    conduct of sale 4.93
    estate agents 4.92
    generally 4.89
    sale price 4.91
    supplemental provisions 4.95
    timing of sale 4.90
  third parties, involving 4.96
  variation of 4.135
    application for
      factors to be taken into account 4.139
      limitation on orders that may be made in 4.136
      procedure 4.140
    powers of the court 4.11, 4.134
School *see* EDUCATION

Section 8 orders
applicants for
applications without leave 8.46
aunt 8.48
children 2.3, 8.49
grant of leave to 8.50
elder brother 8.48
foster parents 8.48
generally 8.47
grandparents 8.48
natural parent after freeing order 8.48
natural parents of adopted children 8.48
burden of proof 8.67
conditions, with 8.58
contact order *see* CONTACT ORDER
defined 8.19
discharge of 8.46
family assistance order *see* FAMILY ASSISTANCE ORDER
power of court to make 8.45
prohibited steps order *see* PROHIBITED STEPS ORDER
representation of the child
child without next friend/guardian 8.54
in non-specified proceedings 8.53
Official Solicitor, role of 8.56
residence order *see* RESIDENCE ORDER
restrictions on local authority 8.44
specific issue order *see* SPECIFIC ISSUE ORDER
standard of proof 8.67
statutory restriction on 8.42-8.45
threshold criteria 8.60-8.66
variation of 8.46
withdrawal of application 8.71
Secure accommodation for children *see under* LOCAL AUTHORITIES
Secured periodical payments order
see also PERIODICAL PAYMENTS
bank accounts 4.49
clean break, and 4.39
see also CLEAN BREAK
death of payee, effect of 4.98
discharge of 4.11, 4.134, 4.137, 4.233, 5.58
dismissal of 4.44
drafting of security documentation 4.51
effective date 4.52
enforcement *see* ENFORCEMENT OF FINANCIAL ORDERS
Family Law Act 1996, and 4.229
generally 4.3, 4.46
neglect to maintain, where 4.197
order for sale of property *see* SALE OF PROPERTY, ORDER FOR
period of 4.229
real property 4.49
remarriage of payee, effect of 4.98
the security 4.49
security after payer's death 4.50

Secured periodical payments order—
contd
termination of 4.98
variation of 4.48, 4.135, 4.138, 4.233, 5.58
application for
factors to be taken into account 4.139
limitation on orders that may be made in 4.136
procedure 4.140
powers of the court 4.11, 4.134
where appropriate 4.47-4.48
Separation deeds *see* AGREEMENTS BETWEEN THE PARTIES
Settlement of property
enforcement *see* ENFORCEMENT OF FINANCIAL ORDERS
matrimonial home 4.69
property adjustment order 4.68
variation of 4.135
application for
factors to be taken into account 4.139, 4.139
limitation on orders that may be made in 4.136
procedure 4.140
powers of the court 4.11, 4.134
Special needs *see under* EDUCATION
Specific issue order
see also SECTION 8 ORDERS
age of child, and 7.21
change of surname 8.40
definition 8.19, 13.13
enforcement 13.13
generally 8.40
HIV testing 8.40
leave to interview children in respect of alleged criminal activity 8.40
limitations on 8.41
removal of child from jurisdiction 8.40
statutory restriction on making 8.43
sterilisation of minor 8.40
Stamp duty *see* CAPITAL GAINS TAX
Standard of proof *see* EVIDENCE
Step-children
inheritance, and 6.18, 6.26
Step-parent
definition of 5.50
Succession *see* INHERITANCE
Supervision order
application for 2.17
care order
distinguished 8.77
made on application for 8.65
conditions attached to 8.84
duration of 8.83
duties of supervisor 8.82
education supervision order 8.93
effect of 8.82

Supervision order—contd
 fact finding 8.67
 interim order
  duration of 8.95
  grounds for making 8.94
  judicial guidance on 8.97
  medical or psychiatric examination 8.96
 restrictions on making of 8.62
 section 37 reports 8.98, 8.99
 threshold criteria 8.60-8.61, 8.66
 variation and discharge of 8.100
Surname
 change of
  on adoption 7.58
  application for 8.40
Surrogacy and embryology
 adoption, and 7.62
 artificial insemination 7.47
 egg donation 7.41
 gamete donors 7.42
 generally 7.38
 in vitro fertilisation 7.41
 mother, definition of 6.9, 7.41
 parental order 7.42-7.44
  application procedure 7.43
  conditions to be satisfied 7.42
 sperm donation 7.41
 surrogacy arrangements
  Act 1985 7.39
  commercial arrangements 7.40
  generally 7.39
  mother, definition of 7.41
  offences 7.40
  unenforceability of 7.40
 Warnock Report 7.38
 whose child? 7.41

Tax considerations in financial relief
 see CAPITAL GAINS TAX; INCOME TAX
Tenancy
 financial provision for child, and 5.56
Transsexual parent
 contact, and 8.27
Trust
 bringing outstanding claims together 5.14
 constructive 5.15, 5.25
 contributions to purchase price other than through mortgage 5.19
 date for quantification of shares 5.28
 declaration of 5.41
  procedure
   in county court 5.42
   in High Court 5.43
 documents of title 5.16
 equity of exoneration 5.26
 express agreement, arrangements or understandings 5.17
 generally 5.09, 5.13
 improvements to property 5.24
 inferred common intention 5.18-5.23

Trust—contd
 mortgages
  contributions to payments 5.20, 5.22
  liability approach 5.20, 5.21
 proprietary estoppel 5.25
 resulting 5.15
 sale of property 5.29
 shares, date for quantification of 5.28
 size of share claimed 5.27
 statutory provisions 5.15

Unborn child
 see also SURROGACY AND EMBRYOLOGY
 abortion 7.20
 pre-birth injuries 7.20
 rights of 7.20, 7.29
 wardship, and 7.29
Undertaking to the court
 court order upon proof of breach 14.10
 enforcement of 14.3
Unmarried couples
 see also COHABITANTS
 rights of, domestic violence, and 3.3, 5.05, 11.8-11.9
Unmarried parents
 parental responsibility, and 3.3, 5.06, 7.04-7.06, 7.45

Void marriage
 see also NULLITY
 child of, inheritance, and 6.9
 generally 5.03
 grounds for annulment 3.8
 legitimacy, and 7.49
 prohibited degrees of relationship 3.8
Voidable marriage
 see also NULLITY
 bars to application 3.8
 generally 5.03
 grounds for annulment 3.8
 legitimacy, and 7.49

Wardship
 abduction of ward 13.25
 adoption, placement for, and 7.63
 age of child 7.29
 defendants to 7.36
 domestic violence, injunctions preventing 11.6-11.7, 11.18, 11.29
 effects of 7.28
 generally 7.27
 inherent jurisdiction of High Court 7.27
  basis of 7.28
  limitations on 7.29, 7.30, 7.32
  procedure under 7.37
  uses of 7.31-7.33
 judicial review, and 9.35-9.36
 legal aid application 15.10
 limitations due to age and presence of child 7.29

Wardship—*contd*
  local authorities, application by 7.30,
    7.33
  orders in
    enforcement by attachment or
      committal 13.26
    residence order following 8.23
  presence of child 7.29
  proceedings 7.35
  unborn child, and 7.29
  uses of 7.34
Wasted costs order *see* COSTS
Welfare of the child
  adoption, and 8.134
  age of the child 8.08
  capability 8.10
  change of circumstances 8.07
  Child Support Act 1991 3.39, 7.22, 8.02-
    8.12, 10.08
  delay 8.03
  disclosure of expert reports 8.72
  harm 8.09

Welfare of the child—*contd*
  needs of the child 8.06
  no order 8.12
  paramountcy of 3.29, 7.22, 8.02, 11.35
  range of powers 8.11
  welfare checklist 8.04
    contact, and 8.34
  wishes and feelings of the child 8.05
Wills
  see also INHERITANCE
  Divorce, effect of 6.4
  in expectation of marriage 6.3
  marriage, effect of 6.2
  nullity, effect of 6.4
Writ of ne exeat regno
  enforcement by 12.49
    see also ENFORCEMENT OF FINANCIAL ORDERS
  generally 4.173
Writ of sequestration
  enforcement by 12.39-12.40
Writ or warrant of possession
  enforcement by 12.36-12.38